M000281761

Richmond Must Fall

CIVIL WAR SOLDIERS AND STRATEGIES

Brian S. Wills, series editor

Richmond Must Fall: The Richmond-Petersburg Campaign, October 1864

HAMPTON NEWSOME

Richmond Must Fall

The Richmond-Petersburg Campaign,

October 1864

Hampton Newsome

The Kent State University Press
Kent, Ohio

© 2013 by The Kent State University Press, Kent, Ohio 44242
All rights reserved
Library of Congress Catalog Card Number 2012039124
ISBN 978-1-60635-132-1
Manufactured in the United States of America

Library of Congress Cataloging-in-Publication Data
Newsome, Hampton.
  Richmond must fall : the Richmond-Petersburg Campaign, October 1864 / Hampton
Newsome.
    pages cm — (Civil War soldiers and strategies)
  Includes bibliographical references and index.
  ISBN 978-1-60635-132-1 (hardcover) ∞
  1. Petersburg (Va.)—History—Siege, 1864–1865. 2. Richmond (Va.)—History—Siege,
1864–1865. 3. Boydton Plank Road, Battle of, Va., 1864. I. Title.
  E476.93.N49 2012
  973.7'37—dc23
                            2012039124

17 16 15 14 13   5 4 3 2 1

Contents

Preface

≈

From June 1864 to April 1865, Union and Confederate forces endured a gruel-ing campaign outside Richmond and Petersburg. During these eleven months, Ulysses S. Grant sought repeatedly to overwhelm Robert E. Lee's defenses and end the Civil War. But Union success on the Richmond-Petersburg front was slow in coming, and events elsewhere dominated headlines during much of the war's final year. Eventually, on April 2, 1865, Grant's forces swept over the Confederate trenches southwest of Petersburg, and the next day, both Petersburg and Rich-mond fell. Over the course of the campaign, Grant conducted no less than nine separate operations to sever vital supply lines or capture these cities outright. This book covers one of the lesser-known periods of the campaign, the military opera-tions of October 1864.

In the fall of 1864, the impending election loomed over Lincoln's presidency and promised to dictate the war's ultimate outcome. A Lincoln victory would ensure a continued vigorous Union war effort. Defeat would put George B. McClellan in charge and yield uncertainty by weakening Union resolve and boosting Confed-erate morale. As the November election approached, cautious optimism buoyed the president's supporters. Union commanders had achieved notable victories at Atlanta in August and in the Shenandoah Valley in September. But the war was far from over, and little had changed in the crucial military contest at the gates of Richmond and Petersburg.

In the weeks before the election, Grant and Lee did not wait patiently for events elsewhere. On October 7, Lee launched one of his last major offensives of the war. At the Darbytown and New Market Roads east of Richmond, he sought to drive Union forces out of their positions and away from the rebel capital. Lee recognized the brittle nature of Confederate hopes and sought dramatic results in this opera-tion. More than two weeks later, Grant replied with a forty-thousand-man attack-ing column aimed at seizing the South Side Railroad, the last direct Confederate rail link into Petersburg. In launching this offensive, Grant gambled, thrusting tremendous manpower into harm's way a mere two weeks before the presidential election. The operation, Grant's sixth offensive of the campaign, would culminate in battles at Burgess Mill south of Petersburg and at the Williamsburg Road east of Richmond. Though the designs conjured by Lee and Grant in October did not yield decisive results, the battles provided important insights into the decision making of these two pivotal leaders. The events also laid the groundwork for operations that would end the war several months later.

Acknowledgments

~

This project began over a decade ago as a vague notion and would not have progressed beyond mere aspiration without the generous help of many people. Bryce Suderow, a veteran researcher and writer, helped initiate this effort by sharing sources from his vast collection of material and urging me to dive into the work. At the end of the process, he provided recommendations on the finished product. Lynn Kristianson, of the Arlington Public Library, fielded an endless chain of interlibrary loan requests, locating rare and obscure sources. Linda Miller, archivist at Roanoke College, prepared the index. Others who helped with various research questions and other issues include Richard Sauers, Christopher Calkins, John Anderson, Sandra Burgess and Robert Diehl (descendants of Mary Burgess), Robert Trout, Robert E. L. Krick, Matthew Brown, Louis Manarin, Lance Herdergen, Charles Bowery, Alan Bilger, Michael Gorman, David Mowery, John Horn, John Selby, Roger Skalbeck, Phil Phalen, Walter Veirs, D.J. Peterson, Henry Persons, Gary Laine, James Blankenship, and Robert Rogers. I also would like to thank several individuals who reviewed drafts of the manuscript and provided much-needed contributions. A. Wilson Greene, executive director of Pamplin Historical Park and author of two excellent books related to Civil War Petersburg, prepared extensive comments on an early version of the manuscript, furnishing broad suggestions and identifying specific changes. Robert E. L. Krick, a historian at the Richmond National Battlefield Park, provided feedback grounded in his extensive knowledge of the Henrico battlefields. David Lowe, also a historian with the Park Service as well as editor of Colonel Theodore Lyman's invaluable notebooks, eyed a draft and offered helpful insights about the fortifications around Petersburg. Author William Marvel shared his vast knowledge of the war and his well-grounded skepticism of postwar recollections, born from his work on many thoughtful, original books on the conflict. Freelance writer Michael Snyder provided many welcome editorial changes, identified slips in military terminology, and shared observations about Union strategy in 1864. Of course, any errors are my own. Finally, I would like to thank Margot, Jake, and Silas for their endless patience and constant encouragement.

Confederate Autumn

~

On August 25, 1864, Confederate forces attacked the Union Second Corps at Reams Station, a remote rail stop in southern Virginia. The federal troops, led by General Winfield Hancock, had been engaged in destroying a section of the Weldon Railroad, a key supply line to the Confederate stronghold of Petersburg. Over the summer, the Second Corps had suffered several embarrassing defeats but remained the most respected formation in the Union Army of the Potomac. To halt the Second Corps' progress, Confederate infantry and cavalry slipped from their trenches and camps and converged on Reams Station. After several unsuccessful efforts, a late afternoon assault punctured Hancock's position. As men in blue panicked and bolted for the rear, Hancock's entire command began to collapse. The general bellowed into the stampede thundering past him. "Come on!" he cried. "We can beat them yet. Don't leave me, for God's sake!" His exhortations produced little effect. He approached a staff officer manning a nearby battery. With his hand on the man's shoulder, Hancock shouted, "Colonel, I do not care to die, but I pray God I may never leave this field!" But soon the Confederate wave swept over his disintegrating line. Through the chaos, his officers managed to mend the broken ranks and avoid disaster. But the Confederate victory shamed Hancock and his demoralized command.[1]

Several days before the misfortune at Reams Station, President Abraham Lincoln in Washington received a status report from his campaign manager, Henry J. Raymond, that painted a grim picture. Correspondents from all points predicted a sound defeat at the polls in November. Raymond reported that the president's prospects were sagging under Union military failures and the administration's focus on emancipation. Raymond's prescription was drastic. He urged Lincoln to consider peace negotiations with Confederate president Jefferson Davis.

The discouraging portrait did not shock Lincoln. Criticism had been building all summer. The sources of discontent were many. Foremost, the absence of military gains severely burdened the president's reelection campaign. To the delight of Democratic opponents, he had also instituted an unpopular draft to address the severe manpower shortage facing the Union armies. Adding to the woes, pro-war Democrats had wavered in their support of the Republican president, their enthusiasm diluted by Lincoln's open embrace of a war for abolition. By expanding the war effort beyond a struggle for union to include a crusade against slavery, Lincoln directly addressed the fundamental cause behind decades of sectional conflict and the lever that initiated the brutal war. For many Democrats, though, he had overreached, diluting their enthusiasm for the fight. At the same time, some abolitionist Republicans, the so-called radicals, harbored doubts about his commitment to these issues. They were considering alternative candidates, searching for a more passionate advocate of their policies.[2] In short, Lincoln's support was crumbling on all sides.

Amid these challenges, the last days of August marked some of the lowest of Lincoln's tenure. He began to consider desperate measures. He drafted a response to Raymond's plea for negotiations, authorizing the pursuit of peace talks with Confederate president Jefferson Davis. He scribbled out another letter, to a War Democrat, suggesting that his administration might abandon emancipation as a peace condition. In the end, however, the letters remained in his desk, unsent. He did not initiate a pre-election peace conference. He did not discard his commitment to freedom to placate the South. As was his common practice, he prepared the two missives to aid his own deliberations and then quietly filed them away. Lincoln held fast to his convictions. He concluded that efforts to bargain with Davis would be more detrimental to the country than his own defeat at the polls.[3] He also maintained his firm support for emancipation. To him, it had become an essential war aim, a powerful tool against the rebellion. He resolved to hold the course he had set to undermine the Confederacy. He explained, "There have been men who have proposed to me to return to slavery the black warriors of Port Hudson & Olustee. . . . I should be damned in time & eternity for doing so. The world shall know that I will keep faith to friends & enemies, come what will."[4]

George McClellan, once the commander of the Army of the Potomac, opposed Lincoln in the political contest. The Democrats had nominated the "Young Napoleon" at their Chicago convention in late August and promptly fastened the former general to a platform of peace that called for negotiations and the dissolution of the war effort. While the platform echoed the sentiments of some, it went too far for many, especially those unwilling to ignore the great costs already incurred for the cause. McClellan's own views on the fundamental issue of war and peace were enigmatic. Though he sought to distance himself from the stated goals of his own party and publicly opposed capitulation to the secessionists, his views mostly generated confusion. He failed to cement a clear understanding of his planned course in the public's mind. Some expected that a President McClellan would prosecute the war aggressively to the end.[5] Others suspected that he had a softer side that would lead to peace without Northern victory and to an independent Confederacy.[6]

George McClellan, however, may not have offered the answer Confederates sought.[7] Given his support for the war, some questioned whether a McClellan presidency would provide any benefit to the Confederate cause.[8] Others, Vice

President Alexander Stephens among them, viewed McClellan with optimism, believing he would suspend hostilities and negotiate for peace. Many Confederate soldiers in the field may have felt the same way. In early October a rebel deserter reported "that the people of the South regard the election of McClellan . . . as the only hope for the success of the Confederate cause."[9] The Confederate president was less enthusiastic.[10] Jefferson Davis, who believed Confederate military victories offered the best means to influence Northern opinion, worried that a McClellan triumph might breed Confederate complacency and lure some states back into the union.[11] One rebel leader took a more pragmatic view. At a dinner party in Petersburg that autumn, Lee's Third Corps commander, A. P. Hill, expressed his hope for a McClellan victory explaining that, if forced to surrender, he preferred "to do so to McClellan."[12]

Amid the political predictions and posturing, the fate of the election rested more than anything else on battlefield events. The Union military campaign in 1864 had begun with great promise. Lincoln had designated Ulysses S. Grant as the single architect of the nation's war effort. He lifted Grant to the rank of lieutenant general in the regular army, a position not previously held by anyone since George Washington. The president hoped this understated midwesterner would develop a coherent military strategy to destroy the Confederate government and restore the Union. Over the previous three years, Grant had forged spectacular successes in the west. In 1862, he threw open the Tennessee and Cumberland Rivers, important water routes into the Confederate heartland, by capturing Forts Henry and Donelson. Then he gained a hard-won victory at Shiloh. The next year, he seized Vicksburg, bringing the entire Mississippi River under Union control, and orchestrated the capture of Chattanooga, unlocking the direct route to Atlanta. Grant had achieved all of this through calm, patient leadership. He maintained his focus on important goals and managed to avoid unnecessary distractions. "The art of war is simple enough," he explained. "Find out where your enemy is. Get at him as soon as you can. Strike him as hard as you can, and keep moving on."[13]

In his strategic and operational planning, Grant was willing to consider indirect approaches that cut enemy supply lines and avoided costly direct assaults. In anticipation of the 1864 campaign, he, along with his military collaborator William T. Sherman, had proposed a large-scale raiding strategy to break up Confederate communications. Grant planned to unleash whole armies into the Southern interior to destroy railroad lines and draw Confederate forces away from strong positions. He and Sherman gave life to this approach during the Meridian campaign in February, when Sherman broke up Confederate rail lines while operating in Mississippi without a firm supply connection.

For the 1864 campaign in Virginia, Grant initially proposed to transport a sixty-thousand-man column to Suffolk, in southeastern Virginia near Norfolk, and march it into the rebel interior toward Raleigh, North Carolina, destroying the

Weldon Railroad along the way.[14] This strategy required no direct attacks against Lee's army or risky attempts to capture Richmond. The raiding army would draw supplies from New Bern, the Carolina port town captured by Ambrose Burnside in 1862. For Grant, the plan held many charms. It would flush Confederate troops out of Virginia away from their chosen defensive positions, goad North Carolina troops to desert their posts elsewhere to protect their homes, remove slaves from their Confederate masters, and block the port of Wilmington.[15]

But Grant's idea failed to gain traction in Washington. The proposed operations in North Carolina would leave fewer troops between Lee and the Northern capital. Leaders in Washington found this unacceptable. Accordingly, in early 1864, Grant redrew his plans for the eastern theatre and opted for a more direct line south, one that pitted the Army of the Potomac against Lee's veterans north of Richmond. Overall, he developed a multipronged strategy to hit the Confederates at multiple points, concentrating all possible force against the Confederate armies in the field.[16] The plan launched Union columns at several targets: the Red River in the deep south, the key strategic rail center of Atlanta, the Shenandoah Valley, the James River near Richmond, and Lee's army in central Virginia. Once implemented in the spring of 1864, this strategy of "simultaneous advances" achieved steady yet unspectacular progress.[17] At all points, Union forces failed to defeat the forces before them. In addition, Atlanta and Richmond remained firmly in Confederate hands.

In fact, August marked a high point for Confederate hopes. The failure of Grant's strategy to achieve decisive victories during the summer of 1864 lifted rebel spirits. Many Confederates hoped that the Northern populace would tire of the war and vote to abandon it. During the summer, Northern fatigue indeed rose. The enduring conflict eroded Union will by minimizing Northern military successes and maximizing casualties. The rebels could achieve such results without battles of annihilation, brilliant tactical victories, or territorial gains.[18] Confederate armies could simply stand their ground and frustrate the offensive plans of Lincoln, Grant, and Sherman. Secessionists understood that success against Union forces in 1864 could affect the election and help achieve their ultimate goal of an independent slave-based country. Robert E. Lee, writing to his son in February 1863, explained that only a "revolution" among the Northern electorate would arrest the administration's war effort.[19] To his wife later that year, he predicted that military success would trigger "a great change in public opinion at the North," destroy the Republicans, and usher "the friends of peace" into office.[20] As the summer of 1864 ended, the rebels had reason for optimism. Their hopes fed on Northern opposition to the draft and concerns over Lincoln's emancipation efforts. At the same time, many Confederates realized that the political contest would ultimately turn on the performance of U.S. forces outside Richmond and

Atlanta. The *Richmond Examiner* predicted in August 31, 1864, "If Atlanta were to fall, or Petersburg, or if Sheridan should drive Early back to Lynchburg—or if any one of these events should befall, then all the Peace principles and peace presidents of Chicago would be at the election next November where last year's snow is, and last night's moonshine."[21] Overwhelming Union military victories would melt those other concerns away. But in August such events had not occurred. The main Union armies remained bogged down, and the war's end seemed distant.

"Unbounded Exultation"

In early September, everything changed. On the fourth, Lincoln received a telegram from Sherman that read, "So Atlanta is ours, and fairly won."[22] The announcement spread jubilation throughout the North. Both sides recognized the event for what it was, a critical turning point in the war. The *New York Times* joyously proclaimed that victory was "so great in itself, of such wide scope, such far-reaching result" that the country would receive the news with "unbounded exultation." The Republican paper did not waste the opportunity to malign Lincoln's opponents: "What infamy it is that at such an hour croakers should be croaking, and Copperheads hissing, and men actually contemplating a disgraceful surrender to this thrice-accursed rebellion."[23] Many white Southerners made no attempt to sugarcoat the news. Decades of political brinksmanship had preserved slavery in the United States, and then several years of war had maintained Confederate hopes for independence. Atlanta's loss appeared to deal a mortal blow to those hopes. The *Richmond Examiner* acknowledged that Sherman's conquest had saved Lincoln's party and knew it would "diffuse gloom over the South."[24] The Union victory at Atlanta began the steady decline of Southern popular will that would contribute greatly to the Confederacy's demise early the next year. Distraught Southern diarist Mary Chesnut captured the sentiment of many, predicting, "We are going to be wiped off the face of the earth."[25]

Despite the importance of Atlanta's fall, two months remained before the election, and the war itself was far from over. Grant's 1864 offensive had produced its share of bitter failures, particularly in Virginia. Lincoln's critics continued to hammer away, questioning the president's accomplishments and criticizing Grant's military operations.[26] And, though the U.S. triumphs instilled guarded optimism in the president's supporters, success was not certain. An election during wartime held no guarantees for anyone. A military disaster in Virginia could dampen Lincoln's chances and possibly reverse the impact of victories elsewhere. By late September, though, such a catastrophe seemed remote. With Atlanta taken, the military focus shifted to Richmond. Lee's army remained firmly ensconced in the earthworks outside Petersburg and Richmond. Overwhelming Union victory there not only would ensure a win for Lincoln but could also bring the war to a close. But would Grant risk another offensive so close to the election?

"Virginia has indeed been enriched with
some of the best blood of our land"

The Union Army of the Potomac had traveled a difficult road to the gates of Petersburg and Richmond. Grant began the 1864 campaign west of Fredericksburg by driving Union troops into Robert E. Lee's Army of Northern Virginia. Brutal fighting ensued and stretched into a month-long series of battles known as the Overland campaign. At the Wilderness, Spotsylvania, North Anna, and Cold Harbor, the armies lurched southeast, locked in a struggle of sustained violence previously unseen on the American continent. As Grant arrived at Cold Harbor outside Richmond, the combat spilled into June, and, after disastrous Union attacks against heavy rebel fortifications there, the armies reached an awkward stalemate. To replace the tremendous Union losses, a steady stream of inexperienced reinforcements flowed south from the garrisons ringing Washington.

For Robert E. Lee, Grant's arrival introduced a new element to the battlefields of Virginia: a determined Union commander willing to press forward even in the face of tactical defeats. In the three years of war before Grant's arrival, the Army of the Potomac had followed a familiar pattern. After a loss in battle, Union commanders would withdraw to allow their troops to rest and recover; in the wake of the occasional victory, the army would fail to pursue the enemy aggressively. All that changed when Grant came to Virginia. After two days of fierce fighting in the Wilderness, he pressed the offensive without hesitation. Lee found himself on the defense constantly, unable to gain the initiative. He continued to seek opportunities to hit back hard, but such chances were scarce. He was no longer the only general who sought to dictate the terms of the fight. This was an unwelcome development for the Confederates.

The Overland Campaign also brought surprises for Grant. He arrived in Virginia unperturbed by Lee's reputation. At the Wilderness, according to one postwar account, he chastised Union officers for exaggerating Lee's abilities: "Oh, I am heartily tired of hearing about what Lee is going to do. Some of you seem to think he is suddenly going to turn a double somersault, and land in our rear and on both our flanks at the same time. Go back to your command, and try to think what we are going to do ourselves, instead of what Lee is going to do."[27] But by the time the smoke cleared at the Cold Harbor front, he had gained a healthy appreciation for Lee's generalship and the endurance and high morale of the Virginian's army. He would eventually describe his adversary as a "man of much dignity" who had fought long and valiantly. But his respect for Lee had its limits. He had little regard for Lee's cause, later describing it as "one of the worst for which a people ever fought, and one for which there was the least excuse."[28] Grant considered slavery "a stain on the union," later explaining that "as soon as slavery fired upon the flag it was felt, we all felt, even those who did not object to slaves, that slavery must be destroyed."[29]

Grant's failure at Cold Harbor highlighted a particular concern for the Union high command. During the campaign, Union units shattered themselves with alarming frequency against the formidable works constructed by Lee's veterans. These costly assaults fostered a heightened sense of caution in the commanders and the soldiers. The campaign taught regimental officers that veteran troops would not press their attacks against well-manned field works. The generals came to understand this. Reluctant to sacrifice men in fruitless attacks, Grant sought to avoid such bloodletting.

"a mere question of time"

With the lull in fighting at Cold Harbor in early June, the two armies crouched in their trenches east of Richmond. In some places, only a hundred yards separated the lines. Lee chose this time to detach his battle-scarred Second Corps under Jubal Early to counter the Union threat to the Shenandoah Valley and Lynchburg. But shortly before Early's departure, Grant moved again. Seeing that the Army of the Potomac could gain nothing at Cold Harbor while crammed into miles of intricate fortifications with little room to maneuver, Grant chose to cross the Chickahominy River and head south for the James River.

Lee detected Grant's movement but was baffled by its design. Concerned foremost with Richmond's safety, the Virginian shifted his forces into the old fortifications east of the capital. There his men waited in vain. Instead of attacking Richmond, the blue columns kept marching south, away from rebel eyes and ears, many crossing the James River on a long pontoon bridge, a marvel of engineering. By June 15, several Union corps stood at the gates of lightly defended Petersburg. With Grant's decisive move, the swift capture of Petersburg would spell doom for Richmond. But General P. G. T. Beauregard scraped together the limited available Confederate units and shuffled men along the trenches to hold Petersburg until the arrival of Lee's veterans. After the initial Union assaults failed, Grant halted. Beauregard's sound decisions had bought the Confederacy more time.

Though Petersburg did not fall, Grant's efforts provided Union forces a secure base. At the beginning of the Overland campaign, he had relied on Virginia's railroads for his army's supply. However, railroads running through hostile country offered an imperfect system. William T. Sherman had explained earlier in the war, "Though our armies pass across and through the land, the war closes in behind and leaves the same enemy behind."[30] As the Overland campaign progressed and Union forces approached Richmond, Grant and Meade kept the army close to Virginia's waterways, ensuring ideal, uninterrupted supply lines. At Petersburg, the James River provided a means to continue that approach. However, this supply line ended at a place called City Point, a small port on the James River northeast of Petersburg. Beyond there, Grant had to rely on roads and rail lines once again. To cut off Richmond and Petersburg, and ultimately defeat Lee, he would have to extend his lines through hostile territory. The farther he stretched his lines beyond the City Point base, the more troops he needed to guard his supply connections.

As Grant established his position outside Petersburg, the Federals transformed City Point into a gigantic depot that received arms, ammunition, food, and other supplies by water from the North. Union naval superiority ensured that ships could pass undisturbed on their way to the Chesapeake Bay and the North. Grant could thank Major General Benjamin F. Butler in part for the new position. Early in the campaign, Butler had threatened Richmond through the James using a small force. Though he bungled much of this operation in May, he did manage to seize City Point and Bermuda Hundred, a peninsula at the confluence of the James and Appomattox Rivers. The Massachusetts politician turned general recognized the importance of this triangular swatch of land and recommended its seizure to Grant in May.[31] Union forces took full advantage of the foothold and settled down to take Richmond and Petersburg.

Lee understood the challenge he faced early in the 1864 campaign. "We must destroy this army of Grant's before he gets to the James River," he reportedly said. "If he gets there, it will become a siege, and then it will be a mere question of time."[32] From a strict military perspective, this was certainly true. Not only did the James River provide the invading force with a clear, safe supply line, but the Union bases along its banks yielded ideal springboards for offensives against Petersburg, Richmond, and points in between. Back in June, Grant had acknowledged as much to officials in Washington when he wrote, "My idea from the start has been to beat Lee's army if possible north of Richmond; then after destroying his lines of communication North of the James, to transfer the army to the south side and besiege Lee in Richmond, or follow him South should he retreat."[33]

From June to September, Grant gradually hemmed Lee into the Richmond and Petersburg defenses. During this period, Grant's forces did not remain idle. Frequent Union operations kept Lee occupied and prevented the transfer of rebel troops to the deep South. Grant arranged the Union lines so as to ensure that, in many places, his troops maintained continuous contact with enemy forces, maintaining a "close embrace" of his opponent.[34] He had employed this approach during the Overland campaign and continued its use at Petersburg. Wherever Lee halted, Grant pushed his men as close as possible to the Confederate forces. At Petersburg, only a few yards separated opposing pickets in many locations along the lines. The proximity posed a continual threat to the defenders, forcing them to constantly occupy the trenches. Lee yearned to attack, but with so many troops tied down on defense, he had precious few units to conduct any offensive operations of his own.[35]

In pressing close to the enemy, Grant sought to methodically choke Petersburg. Like spokes in a wheel, roads and rails connected the city to the balance of the South. After the initial assaults against Petersburg failed in mid-June, Grant began to extend around the city to sever these lines one by one, beginning with the Jerusalem Plank Road in late June and then the Weldon Railroad and Halifax

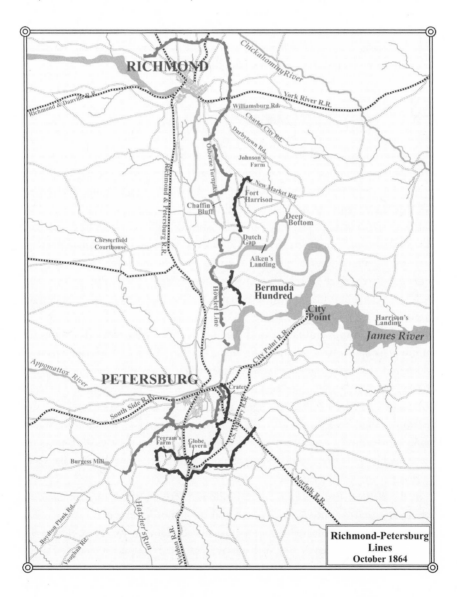

Richmond-Petersburg
Lines
October 1864

Road in August. None of these indirect movements yielded a decisive victory and the one attempt at a direct assault, the Crater battle in July, failed miserably.

In addition to these operations at Petersburg, Union forces gained a lodgment on the north bank of the James in Henrico County just southeast of Richmond. In an effort to distract Lee from an assault at Petersburg in July, Union forces seized the Deep Bottom landing on the north bank of the James. Although the toehold there yielded little success over the summer, it forced Lee to dedicate scarce troops to cover the direct approaches to Richmond. As Lee explained in a September 2 dispatch to Jefferson Davis, "The enemy's position enables him to move his troops to the right or left without our knowledge, until he has reached the point at which he aims, and we are then compelled to hurry our men to meet him, incurring the risk of being too late to check his progress and the additional risk of the advantage he may derive from their absence."[36]

"once my troops are there"

As Northern troops made slow progress at Petersburg, events continued to unfold in the Shenandoah Valley. Throughout the war, Confederate leaders had used the region to occupy Union troops that would otherwise operate against Richmond. Confederate pressure in the Valley also threatened Washington. With limited re-sources Early had achieved much over the summer, including an extensive raid north that brought his men to the ramparts of the capital. But in late Septem-ber, General Philip Sheridan turned the tide, with victories against Early in the Shenandoah Valley at Winchester on September 19 and Fisher's Hill on the 22nd. Early, weakened but unvanquished, remained in the Valley to threaten Sheridan's command.

Over the summer and fall of 1864, Lee performed a dangerous balancing act, shuttling troops between Early's command in the Valley and his own army at Richmond. The effort faltered in September when he recalled Joseph Kershaw's division from the Valley just when it was needed to help blunt Sheridan's strike at Winchester on the 19th and then again at Fisher's Hill three days later. Kershaw's division rushed back to Early's support but failed to arrive in time. Kershaw's limbo represented a significant miscalculation for Lee and Early. With precious few available units, the Confederates could not afford to leave troops idle, espe-cially the seasoned veterans with Early.

In the wake of Fisher's Hill, Grant prodded Sheridan to advance on Charlot-tesville and destroy the railroads there and the James River canal nearby.[37] But Sheridan demonstrated a reluctance to push ahead, claiming that he could not ad-equately supply his men during such a move. Instead, his command seeped south through the Valley, torching farms along the way. After October 10, his force set-

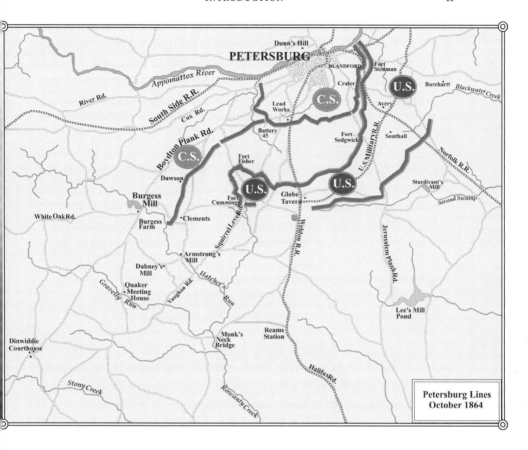

Petersburg Lines
October 1864

tled into an extended bivouac near a meandering stream known as Cedar Creek, just south of Winchester. Despite Grant's urging, Sheridan declined to finish Early off or push south toward Charlottesville. On October 14, 1864, Grant again telegraphed Sheridan, directing him "to threaten the Virginia Central Railroad and canal in the manner your judgment tells you is best, holding yourself ready to advance, if the enemy draw off their forces."[38] Sheridan's inactivity created two problems. It threatened to deprive Grant of much needed reinforcements on the Richmond-Petersburg front, and it delayed final Union victory in the Valley.

Back at Petersburg, the South Side Railroad was the only rail line connecting the city to the rest of the South. Its loss would perfect the Union chokehold on Petersburg and would leave Richmond with a single supply line to the south, the Danville Railroad. Petersburg's fall would likely bring Richmond's collapse, for it was difficult, perhaps even impossible, for the rebels to defend one city without controlling the other.

In an effort to protect both locations, the Confederate trenches formed an awkward thirty-mile front that straddled both the James and Appomattox Rivers.

These works split into three sections: the fortifications outside of Richmond, the Bermuda Hundred (or "Howlett" line) defenses, and the lines stretching around Petersburg. Despite the difficulty, Lee planned to defend Richmond even after Petersburg's fall. In October correspondence with the commander of the James River squadron, J. K. Mitchell, he discussed the consequences of a possible Union lodgment on the right bank of the James north of Bermuda Hundred and the subsequent loss of Petersburg:

> I should regard this as a great disaster and as seriously endangering the safety of the city. We should not only lose a large section of country, from which our position around Petersburg enables us to draw supplies, but the enemy would be brought nearer to the only remaining line of railway communication between Richmond and the south, upon which the whole army, as well as the population of the city would have to depend mainly for support. It would make the tenure of the city depend upon our ability to hold this long line of communication against the largely superior forces of the enemy, and I think would greatly diminish our prospects of successful defense.[39]

As Lee's discussion illustrates, Petersburg formed the lynchpin to Northern victory in Virginia. Over the summer, Grant severed all lifelines to the city except for the Boydton Plank Road and the South Side Railroad. In August, Union troops cut the Weldon Railroad. But instead of abandoning the line altogether, the Confederates offloaded supplies from the railroad miles below Petersburg at Stony Creek Station. Wagon trains then transported them along the Boydton Plank Road west around the Union fortifications. The South Side Railroad, farther to the west, was even more important than the Plank Road. It provided Lee with an uninterrupted connection to other Southern states. This fact was not lost on Grant. According to one of his aides, the lieutenant general had recognized the rail line's importance earlier in the spring. During a discussion of plans for the upcoming campaign, Grant had stood over a map and pointed to the South Side Railroad, saying, "When once my troops are there . . . Lee must surrender or leave Richmond."[40]

Though Richmond's fall may have seemed imminent as a matter of military engineering, the year's limited gains and bitter setbacks demonstrated that victory would take time. Grant appreciated that the arithmetic of beans, bullets, and manpower favored him. However, he also understood that lack of progress and military failures could degrade Union will and destabilize Lincoln's support. Excessive delay, or worse yet, disaster to Northern forces in Virginia, could damage Lincoln at the polls and ultimately disrupt the calculus of Richmond's demise. The absence of progress proved an inviting target for Lincoln's opponents. The *New York World*, a reliable critic of the administration, proclaimed that Grant had achieved "absolutely nothing" in his recent operations. It criticized him for a host of mistakes, including the failures to concentrate his army, close off rebel supply lines, and shut down Confederate operations in the Valley.[41] Though Grant probably paid little attention to the harping, it was clear that more progress could be made on the Richmond-Petersburg front.

"difficult for us to maintain ourselves"

Lee faced other problems. His army was bleeding men.[42] In August, he wrote to the Confederate secretary of war, James Seddon, "I regret to state that the desertions are increasing in some of the regiments of this army. General Hill reports, on the 12th instant, the desertion of a lieutenant and twenty-four men from the Ninth Alabama Regiment. . . . Unless this practice be checked, our army will be seriously weakened."[43] Federal soldiers would no doubt have agreed with Lee's assessment. Each day, they witnessed hungry, exhausted Confederates slipping through the picket lines seeking food, clothing, and, most important, an end to their Confederate service. In early September, a Maine volunteer observed that rebel "deserters are so plentiful that we are often at our wits' end to know what to do with them or how to care for them. It is not uncommon for them to arrive in squads of twenty or thirty."[44] Official Union correspondence dutifully recorded the arrival of deserters from the enemy lines during September and October, especially when those men brought news of Confederate dispositions and activities. The daily dispatches of the Union provost-marshal-general's office and the diaries of ordinary soldiers attest to the steady stream of voluntary attrition from Lee's ranks. A New Hampshire officer noted that almost "every morning there is held a 'Deserters' Powow' so called, at our garrison camp-fire, where all deserters from the Confederates are welcomed, warmed and fed."[45] Whether due to lack of pay, the shortage of food, homesickness, or general fatigue, Confederate desertion showed no signs of slackening.

But desertion represented only part of the problem. For Robert E. Lee and the Army of Northern Virginia, the fall of 1864 was a time of increasing anxiety and frustration. Though Union troops had achieved much elsewhere, Lee had managed to limit gains in central Virginia. Richmond's defense was essential. Its fall would demoralize the Confederate populace, cause great material loss, and drastically shrink the rapidly disappearing Confederacy. It would also severely hamper any further Confederate operations in the Valley. Efforts to defend the capital were becoming increasingly vexing. His deployment of Jubal Early to the Valley had yielded political and military benefits in the summer and eased pressure on the capital. Early's losses in September, however, signaled the beginning of the end to that diversion, an end that would allow Grant to concentrate his forces. Lee's options to counter such a move were few.

Throughout the war, Lee had exhibited a highly aggressive, even audacious, approach to operational and tactical decision making. His affinity for offensive warfare, especially in the form of large-scale flank attacks, had not wavered, even in 1864, when he was forced onto the tactical defensive. During the Overland campaign, in which Grant hurled one offensive after another, Lee and his commanders continued to launch significant, often corps-sized assaults wherever they could. At the Wilderness, Harris Farm near Spotsylvania, Jericho Ford on the North Anna, Bethesda Church along the Totopotomoy, and Cold Harbor, Lee struck out at the Army of the Potomac. In most of these battles, the rebels sought to damage isolated Union troops. More often than not, though, such forays yielded little benefit and left Confederates with more casualties than they could afford.

Lee's approach during the Petersburg campaign had been no different. There, he continued to apply the offensive-defensive approach that had served him throughout the war. As Grant inched around Petersburg during the summer, Lee and his subordinates pounced on the advancing columns at every turn and enjoyed much tactical success. But despite such rebel tenacity, Grant and Meade achieved steady gains. And, as the campaign wore on, Lee's ability to take the initiative against Grant or even to blunt Union advances dwindled.

To take the fight to Grant, Lee simply needed more men. Confederate forces at Richmond and Petersburg contained several veteran formations that had served throughout the war, along with many less-renowned regiments and brigades and some militia units pulled from Richmond's factories and government offices. October inspection returns placed Lee's strength at more than fifty thousand men. Charles Field's and Robert Hoke's divisions, numbering about eight thousand, all told, manned the lines in Henrico County north of the James. In that sector, these veterans were joined by three thousand men of Richard Ewell's Department of Richmond and a cavalry brigade under Martin Gary. Another three thousand reserve and militia from Richmond could occupy the trenches there in a pinch. At the rebel center between Richmond and Petersburg, the six thousand or so members of George Pickett's division held the relatively quiet Howlett line west of Bermuda Hundred. At Petersburg, Bushrod Johnson's seven thousand men crouched in the trenches directly east of the city. The balance of the Petersburg fortifications housed the three veteran divisions of A. P. Hill's Third Corps, numbering close to fifteen thousand in all, and another five thousand artillerymen assigned to various commands also manned the lines.[46] Finally, protecting the vital right flank to the south and west of Petersburg, Wade Hampton's six thousand cavalrymen picketed the roads and bridges stretching south for miles.[47] These commanders and their men had reaped resounding victories for Lee earlier in the war. Now, however, they hunkered down in their ditches, awaiting the enemy's next move.

Other challenges also afflicted Lee. The length of the front prevented him from taking personal command in many instances. Dozens of miles separated key sectors. He could not be everywhere at once, and his army in late 1864 lacked the inspired quality leadership to compensate. Though Lee's aggressiveness had served him well, it fueled an astounding attrition rate among his commanders. Earlier campaigns claimed corps commanders such as Thomas "Stonewall" Jackson, mortally wounded at Chancellorsville, and James Longstreet, seriously injured in the Wilderness. Lee also lost dozens of other officers at the division and brigade levels. Although his army still contained capable officers, the enormous loss of experienced combat leaders degraded the quality of the thousands of decisions made in the army every day, whether on the battlefield or in camp.

Lee also struggled with his own failing health, which stemmed from heart problems that would eventually claim his life after the war. Walter Taylor, a member of Lee's small headquarters staff, described the general's condition during that year as "somewhat impaired."[48] On September 18, Lee himself acknowledged his ill health to his wife, explaining, "I am sensible . . . of my failing strength & approaching infirmities & am as careful to shield myself from exciting causes as I can be. But what care can a man give to himself in a time of war?"[49] His condition increased the need for reliable subordinates who could execute his plans.

Without more soldiers to man the defenses, Lee expected disaster in Virginia. In September, he wrote President Davis describing, at some length, the problems caused by the lack of manpower. He offered three suggestions. First, he urged the Confederate government to substitute black men for "all able bodied white men" then employed as teamsters, cooks, mechanics, and laborers. "It seems to me that we must choose between employing negroes ourselves, and having them employed against us," he argued. He also recommended an immediate review of the army's muster rolls to bring exempt and detailed men back to duty at the front. Finally, he asked Davis to consider bringing reserve units to the lines. He reasoned that such troops could man the trenches, freeing his regular veterans for mobile defensive and offensive operations in front of Richmond.[50] Later that month, he warned officials in Richmond that the "most serious consequences must result" if the disparity in numbers remained unchecked.[51]

On October 4, 1864, Lee raised the same issues in a dispatch to the secretary of war, James Seddon. He explained that it would be "very difficult for us to maintain ourselves" without increasing the army's size. The "enemy's numerical superiority enables him to hold his lines with an adequate force, and extend on each flank with numbers so much greater than ours that we can only meet his corps, increased by recent recruits, with a division, reduced by long and arduous service." Without more men from Virginia and North Carolina, Lee predicted the result would be "calamitous."[52] He also wrote to Zebulon Vance, governor of North Carolina, pleading for that state's units, including the 68th N.C. Regiment, which, to Lee's mind, would better serve the Confederacy in lines outside Richmond than in the Old North State.[53] President Davis shared Lee's concerns. In a public speech

delivered in Macon, Georgia, he appealed to Confederate citizens to boost numbers in the army. The speech, widely reported in the press, was met with derision
in the North as a clear indication of rebel desperation.[54]

While Confederate leaders strained to expand muster rolls, Lee sought military
victories. Consulting with General Wade Hampton in September, he explored ways
to attack the Union rear south of Petersburg. Though no direct assault ensued, the
discussions spawned Hampton's daring cattle raid, which plucked thousands of
pounds of beef "on the hoof" from the Union corrals south of City Point, right under the noses of Yankee pickets.[55] Weeks later, Lee's thirst for an offensive persisted.
On October 4, he informed Hampton, "I have written to General Hill as regards his
operations against the enemy, and have suggested, should he attempt to break the
enemy's center, that you should operate against his flank or rear."[56] Lee's imagination remained unconstrained, but the means to accomplish his plans were lacking.

With the November election rapidly approaching, both Grant and Lee schemed.
The latter searched for ways to reverse the tide, while the former sought to land
the deathblow. The two commanders had no intention of waiting passively at Richmond and Petersburg as events unfolded elsewhere. October would not pass quietly.

Part I

The Darbytown Road Battles

In early October, the countryside east of Richmond became a focal point for military activities in Virginia. On the 7th, along the Darbytown Road, Robert E. Lee would seek to reverse the Union gains of September by launching one of his last large-scale offensives of the war. While Lee strove for advantage, the Union army remained active. Benjamin Butler, commander of federal forces in this sector, conducted operations of his own a week later, generating additional fighting in the same area. The October battles near the Darbytown Road demonstrated Lee's thirst for the initiative, as well as the tough nature of the politician-general Butler. The operations also sparked a prisoner controversy that touched on the issues of slavery and race underlying the conflict.

CHAPTER 1

Johnson's Farm

⁓

"present for duty"

Two federal armies loomed outside Richmond. George G. Meade's Army of the Potomac manned the lines to the south at Petersburg, and Benjamin F. Butler's Army of the James stood poised east of Richmond in Henrico County. Both forces brought their own strengths, liabilities, and reputations to the gates of the Confederate capital. By October, both had experienced their share of hard fighting, and both had failed to achieve a decisive victory.

The Army of the Potomac, the largest Union force in the East, shouldered a heavy burden throughout the war, fighting in the major campaigns in Virginia, Maryland, and Pennsylvania. Despite low points, the army enjoyed some successes. Notably, it had checked Robert E. Lee's forays into the North at Antietam in 1862 and Gettysburg the following year. But, too often, it felt the sting of Robert E. Lee's operational and tactical excellence, while suffering under its own series of uneven commanders. George Meade had taken charge in late June 1863, however, and furnished the army with steady, albeit unremarkable, leadership. In the spring of 1864, Meade continued in command but operated under the watchful direction of Grant, who remained in the field.

The grueling campaign of 1864 generated few accolades for Meade's men while exacting a staggering toll. More than 100,000 strong at the outset of the Overland campaign in May, the army suffered more than 50,000 casualties before reaching the outskirts of Petersburg in late June.[1] Summer and fall operations outside Petersburg and Richmond added thousands to a tally that outpaced the steady stream of replacements from the north. By September, casualties, scheduled discharges, and deployments elsewhere had reduced the army to slightly more than 50,000 men, according to September inspection reports.[2] During this time, the army contained three infantry corps: the Second, led by Major General Winfield Hancock; the Fifth, commanded by Major General Gouverneur K. Warren; and the Ninth, headed by Major General John G. Parke. The army also contained one cavalry division under Brigadier General David M. Gregg. By October, battlefield losses, the expiration of terms of service, and the arrival of replacement troops of an indifferent quality had dramatically altered the army's three infantry corps. As a result, the reliability of troops eroded noticeably.[3] In engagements throughout the summer, Union forces reeled back under pressure they might have withstood earlier in the year.

Benjamin Butler's Army of the James served as Grant's other weapon outside Richmond. September returns tallied this force at 30,000 men and officers present for duty.[4] Most of the troops were concentrated in two infantry corps, the Tenth and the Eighteenth, each with about 12,000 men. The Tenth Corps, led by Major General David B. Birney had served in operations along the South Carolina and Florida coast before arriving in Virginia and had endured hard-fought actions at Olustee, Morris Island, Battery Wagner, and Secessionville. These soldiers acquired a familiarity with siege warfare and the dangerous business of assaulting fortifications that went along with it.[5] Butler's other corps, the Eighteenth, commanded by Brevet Major General Godfrey Weitzel, contained a motley collection of units with little collective experience. Many of the units had served only on garrison and outpost duty. Though some of the men had fought in Virginia and eastern North Carolina in 1862, most had seen little combat before their arrival on Virginia soil in 1864.[6]

"enemy must be weak enough"

Though Meade and Butler managed the day-to-day operations of their respective commands, Grant exercised overall control, determining when and where to strike the enemy. At Richmond and Petersburg, the lieutenant general had poked and prodded the Confederate defenses throughout the campaign, pursuing different approaches with each attempt. But nothing had brought success. Grant failed to create an overwhelming, decisive breakthrough against Lee's fortifications or otherwise cut rebel supply lines and flush the Virginian out of his defenses.

In late September, Grant launched his fifth offensive of the campaign, seeking to cut Petersburg's last remaining supply line and, if possible, storm Richmond directly.[7] He had hoped to begin this operation in early October. But Sheridan's victories in the Valley at Winchester and Fisher's Hill altered this timetable. To prevent Lee from reinforcing Confederates in the Valley and to test those rebel troops left in Richmond's defense, Grant advanced his schedule a week, setting the operation for September 29.[8] He planned first to have Butler's men hit the Confederate defenses north of the James, while Meade's army poised to take advantage of opportunities at Petersburg.

Over the summer, Grant had employed variations of this two-pronged approach. In July, he sent Hancock's Second Corps to attack Confederate positions north of the James River at Deep Bottom while Union engineers at Petersburg detonated a deadly mine underneath the main Confederate trench. The blast triggered the unsuccessful Crater attack. Several weeks later, Grant followed the failed mine assault in August by, once again, dispatching Hancock's Second Corps, this time to Deep Bottom, and unleashing Warren's Fifth Corps against the Weldon Railroad. Although Warren ably secured a lodgment on that line, the summer offensive did not generate a dramatic breakthrough to drive Lee from the Confederate capital.

In planning his fifth offensive in September, Grant followed the same recipe. North of the James, Butler struck the Confederate lines outside of Richmond while Meade poised to attack the Boydton Plank Road and the South Side Railroad at Petersburg should Butler make gains. By giving Meade contingent orders, Grant remained flexible and waited to respond to events as they unfolded.

During the attacks on September 29, Butler's troops achieved surprising success. His assault washed over portions of the ditches and fortifications that formed Richmond's defenses. Early in the morning, the outermost defensive layer fell when African American troops (i.e., the United States Colored Troops [USCT]) from Butler's Tenth Corps swept over New Market Heights.[9] The second layer, the "exterior" line, lay closer to Richmond and ran north from Chaffin's Bluff on the James River to the south bank of the Chickahominy River east of the city.[10] While the USCT captured New Market Heights, Butler's Eighteenth Corps, with Major General Edward Ord leading, stormed Fort Harrison, a strongpoint at the junction of the Confederate exterior and intermediate lines. Before Confederate officers could reinforce the fort, Ord's men vaulted over the parapet and captured the prize.

Fort Harrison's loss tore a hole in the Confederate defenses and posed an immediate threat to Richmond. In response, Lee cobbled together his forces to patch the trench line. However, the seizure of Fort Harrison rendered large portions of the exterior trenches useless to him. To make matters worse, Butler's forces sought further gains to the north at Fort Gilmer, but Confederate reinforcements thwarted these efforts. Butler and his generals soon resigned themselves to fortifying their new positions and preparing for Confederate counterattacks, while rebel commanders and engineers scrambled to rearrange the tattered defenses.

Fort Harrison's capture also created federal opportunities at Petersburg by drawing Lee's forces north of the James to aid a counterattack against the fort. Because this transfer catered to Grant's plan, he wrote to Meade, "It seems to me the enemy must be weak enough at one or the other place to let us in."[11] Meade responded and, with the Fifth and Ninth Corps, totaling approximately 25,000, rolled over the rebel trenches along the Squirrel Level Road southwest of Petersburg and overran Confederate positions at Peebles' Farm there.[12] As the U.S. forces surged beyond the captured line, they inched closer to the works along the Boydton Plank Road. These partially built defenses formed the last barrier between Meade's troops and the vital South Side Railroad. However, the Confederates cut the advance short of this last ditch with a sharp counterattack at Pegram's Farm.

Though Union forces consolidated their new holdings and dug in, the fighting generated by Grant's offensive was not over. On the 30th, Lee, with several brigades stripped from the Petersburg sector, attempted to retake Fort Harrison, but Butler's men beat off the desperate, poorly coordinated Confederate assaults at great loss to the rebels. Likewise, at Petersburg on October 1, Confederate division commander Major General Henry Heth led four brigades against the new Union position at Peebles' Farm, only to find fresh earthworks blocking the way. Gouverneur Warren, the Union Fifth Corps commander, had anticipated the Confederate attack and ordered his men to fortify the position overnight. His decision blunted any chance of a dramatic Confederate counterattack. Overall, though, the Union offensive had failed to sever any of Petersburg's remaining arteries. On October 2nd, Meade sought more ground and ordered further advances toward the Boydton Plank Road.[13] But these movements achieved nothing. Union troops pulled back to fortify their new positions in the vicinity of Pegram's Farm.

With Grant's fifth offensive over, the generals on both sides assessed the results and the implications for the future. Meade concluded that Lee had been "cautious" in not attacking the weakened federal center. He predicted that the rebel leader would only act defensively and not take chances to attack.[14] However, Confederate artillery commander Brigadier General E. Porter Alexander judged that it was Grant who had missed an opportunity in balancing the weight of his double-pronged attack. Alexander believed that Union forces would have taken Richmond immediately had Grant "put his whole strength into" Butler's attack. With the diluted strength of the double attack, neither "blow was heavy enough to accomplish any important result."[15]

Alexander's observation highlighted the puzzle the Confederate defenses posed for Grant. Throughout the campaign, he had focused on multiple simultaneous attacks to prevent Lee from reinforcing a threatened sector. However, through the end of September, this approach had yielded only incremental results. As Alexander's observation illustrated, the Union forces had yet to concentrate enough striking power in a single sector to create a decisive breakthrough that would sever crucial supply lines or capture Richmond or Petersburg outright.

For Lee, the Union gains underscored the vulnerability of his position. As Meade had recognized, Lee had limited capacity to gain the initiative against the Federals. He did not possess enough men to protect the miles of earthworks fronting Petersburg and Richmond, and he could not easily march them out to threaten Union positions. Following Grant's offensive, the Confederates managed to salvage the lower segment of these exterior trenches. Engineers quickly traced a new line near Fort Harrison, neatly connecting Forts Hoke and Maury at Chaffin's Farm to Forts Johnson, Gregg, and Gilmer north of the captured work. Farther north, the Confederate trenches now ran along the Osborne Turnpike toward the capital for more than two miles, eventually connecting with the "inner" or "intermediate" line. This third layer of trenches arced westward around Richmond, connecting with the banks of the James upstream from the city. Finally, inside the intermediate line, Richmond's fourth and final defense layer consisted of a series of unconnected, star-shaped forts placed directly at the city's outskirts. These various layers continued to stand in Grant's way.

"like the breaking of a hard winter"

Following Grant's September offensive, General Butler's Army of the James quickly consolidated its gains, particularly the ground around the newly captured Fort Harrison. As Butler established his new positions, Grant, concerned that the captured ground was too large and vulnerable to flank attacks, suggested that Butler choose a compact line that could be defended by one corps. Butler pondered this advice but concluded to occupy the position his men had taken in their attacks.[16] In the first days of October, Butler, in consultation with Grant's chief engineer, J. G. Barnard, established new works stretching from Signal Hill on the James north to the New Market Road and Fort Harrison at the center of this position.[17] At the line's southern terminus, the Union engineers and soldiers constructed a large redoubt, subsequently named Fort Brady.[18] In the northern sector, Tenth Corps troops quickly occupied and reversed the rebel exterior trench line running from Fort Harrison to the New Market Road near the "Clyne" house.[19] Following Butler's suggestion, the Tenth Corps commander, David Birney, bent the line back along the New Market Road to guard the right flank.[20]

Benjamin Butler, the man overseeing these activities, was a complicated person. Obnoxious, arrogant, and, in some eyes, militarily incompetent, he was also clever, creative, aggressive, and unafraid to make controversial decisions. A native New Englander, Butler had a keen mind, which fueled a successful career as a trial lawyer and Democratic politician before the war. In the courtroom, he was a brilliant, persuasive advocate who thought well on his feet and exhibited a knack for unorthodox arguments that won cases. His photos reveal a squat, trollish, stringy-haired figure. Writer and humorist Mark Twain noted that the "forward part of his bald skull, looks raised, like a water blister . . . [he] is dismally & drearily homely, & when he smiles it is like the breaking of a hard winter."[21]

A pro-war Democrat, Butler proved a popular commodity for the Republican administration. In 1861, he commanded forces at Fort Monroe in eastern Virginia but stumbled early at the battle of Big Bethel. Despite this setback, he gained notoriety by classifying escaped slaves as "contraband of war," a wry turn of phrase that helped forge a legal basis for protecting the newly freed men, women, and children.

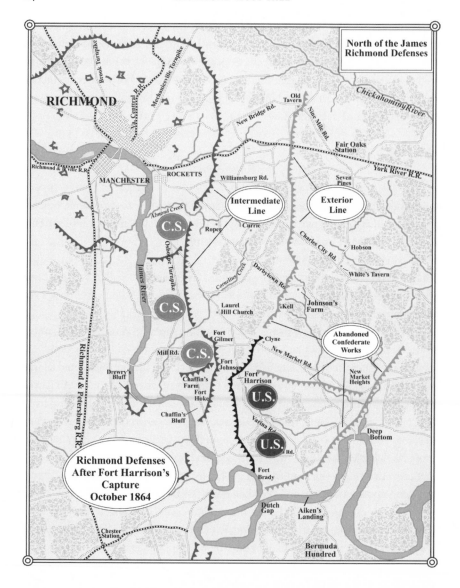

North of the James
Richmond Defenses

RICHMOND

MANCHESTER   ROCKETTS

Intermediate
Line

Exterior
Line

C.S.

C.S.

C.S.

Abandoned
Confederate
Works

U.S.

U.S.

Richmond Defenses
After Fort Harrison's
Capture
October 1864

Brook Turnpike
Va. Central R.R.
Mechanicsville Turnpike
Chickahominy River
Old Tavern
New Bridge Rd.
Nine Mile Rd.
Fair Oaks Station
York River R.R.
Richmond & Y'ville R.R.
Williamsburg Rd.
Seven Pines
Almond Creek
Roper
Currie
Charles City Rd.
Hobson
White's Tavern
Osborne Turnpike
James River
Cornelius Creek
Darbytown Rd.
Laurel Hill Church
Kell
Johnson's Farm
Fort Gilmer
Clyne
New Market Rd.
Mill Rd.
Fort Johnson
New Market Heights
Drewry's Bluff
Chaffin's Farm
Fort Hoke
Fort Harrison
Chaffin's Bluff
Varina Rd.
Deep Bottom
Richmond & Petersburg R.R.
Rd.
Fort Brady
Chester Station
Dutch Gap
Aiken's Landing
Bermuda Hundred

Many white Southerners hated him for his abrupt, unpolished style and un-apologetic support for African Americans and the Union cause. During his tenure as military governor of captured New Orleans, he insulted the city's women by equating them with prostitutes in an official order intended to halt their harass-ment of his soldiers. Confederate General P. G. T. Beauregard afterward dubbed Butler "the Beast," and the sobriquet stuck.

Butler lacked the military pedigree enjoyed by most of his peers in the regular army. He had not graduated from West Point, nor had he served in the Mexican War. His membership in the Massachusetts State militia in the antebellum years held little cachet with regular army officers.[22] He did not excel as a combat leader, a fact that attracted criticism from within and without the army. In June, when his abrasive comments irritated subordinates, private murmurs suggested that he lacked the willingness or perhaps the capability to lead in the field. Some saw him as the archetypical political general, incompetent on and off the battlefield.[23]

Butler also had a reputation for unorthodox thinking. He could conjure up plans that were unusual or even bizarre. During a visit to Butler's sector north of the James, a member of Meade's staff gathered examples of several hare-brained schemes, including "a fire engine to squirt down their [the enemy's] earthworks; a petard to blow up their abattis; an iron net, thrown by mortars, to net them; and finally an auger, 5 feet in diameter, to bore under ground to Richmond."[24] According to Meade's aide, Colonel Theodore Lyman, Butler poked fun at himself, explaining that "when they made him a lawyer they spoiled a good mechanic; when they made him a general they spoiled a good lawyer!"[25] Though Butler rarely led from the front and occasionally implemented some strange ideas, he did not completely lack tactical or strategic acumen. He could draft sound, detailed battle plans and had the organizational skills to implement them.

Though often maligned, Butler had his supporters. According to one officer under his command, the general's "nervous temperament and long habits of study and forensic practice unfit him, perhaps, for a great general, but the power and vigor of his mind, his legal knowledge, his political influence, his insight into human nature, place him among the first men of the country."[26] He pushed to have African Americans armed and did not hesitate to use those soldiers in all aspects of his operations. In discussing the infusion of black troops into the Richmond lines, he remarked to Secretary of War Stanton, "I told you they would do well in my department. . . . Their praises are in the mouth of every officer in this army. Treated fairly and disciplined, they have fought most heroically."[27]

Grant tolerated Butler, whose strong political connections insulated his position to a degree, especially so close to the election. But Grant did not think highly of the lawyer's military abilities. In a July 1, 1864, note to Halleck, Grant explained, "Whilst I have no difficulty with General Butler, finding him always clear in his conception of orders and prompt to obey, yet there is a want of knowledge how to execute and particularly a prejudice against him as a commander that operates against his usefulness." Grant recognized Butler's superior talents as an administrative officer, however, and believed that he would be an ideal pick to command a department "where there are no great battles to be fought, but a dissatisfied element to control."[28] Grant worked with and even encouraged the former lawyer despite his missteps and difficult personality. Together, the two presented an odd pair. During a hospital inspection in October, an observer noted their striking differences. While Grant, plainly dressed, had all the appearances of a civilian except for the stars on his shoulder, there was no mistaking Butler's identity, for he wore a sword, belt, jackboots, and a gold-embroidered military cap. Grant, slim, straight, and quiet, walked with his officers, listening to their remarks. Butler stayed in front of his staff "with the air and mien of one who is accustomed to command."[29]

As Butler tended his lines outside Richmond in early October, he remained mindful of the offensive possibilities created by his recent success. The geography east of Richmond favored him, for Henrico County's road network furnished several convenient approaches to the rebel capital. North of Fort Harrison, five substantial roads, spaced at two-mile intervals, fanned across the exterior rebel line running east to west. Butler's new trench line touched the New Market Road, the first of these routes. Two miles north ran the Darbytown Road, named after the collection of houses nearby. Farther on, the Charles City, Williamsburg, and Nine Mile roads offered more paths to Richmond, all of which coursed through a mostly flat countryside of farms and scattered forests, interrupted here and there by swampy streams.[30]

Butler did not wait long to test these approaches. On Saturday, October 1, a Tenth Corps division spilled onto the Darbytown Road, led by New Hampshire and Connecticut infantrymen from Colonel Joseph C. Abbott's brigade. The reconnaissance crossed the Roper Farm and Almond Creek and headed toward the Confederate intermediate line. A cavalry brigade also advanced along the Charles City Road to the north. The Union column reached within three miles of Richmond and well north of rebel concentrations at Fort Gilmer and the Chaffin Farm. A breakthrough west of the Roper Farm would isolate rebel units to the south, including the veterans of Field's and Hoke's divisions. At the tip of the Union advance, Abbott's brigade stirred up defenders but did not launch a substantial attack. The fight at Roper's Farm ended with a Union withdrawal back to the trenches.[31] In response to the Union incursion, Robert E. Lee ordered Richard Anderson, commander of the First Corps, to shift men to the threatened point. Anderson in turn dispatched two brigades from Charles Field's division to meet the danger, but the rebels arrived only to find that the enemy had withdrawn without attacking.[32] Butler's reconnaissance ended there.

Following Saturday's foray, Butler met with his two corps commanders, David Birney and Godfrey Weitzel, to discuss further operations. The three agreed that a full advance by the Tenth and the Eighteenth Corps along the Darbytown and Charles City Roads would break open the enemy's intermediate line. In Butler's estimation, the Confederate works in this sector held nothing but militia scraped together from Confederate government employees. In addition, a deserter had identified gaps in the rebel line used by pickets that would aid an attacking force. In a Sunday morning dispatch to Grant, Butler proposed that Meade release a corps from Petersburg to defend Fort Harrison while he launched a full offensive the next morning.[33]

Grant, however, had no enthusiasm for Butler's plans. In his view, further offensive operations could not occur without additional men. In fact, he had scheduled a trip to Washington on Tuesday, October 4, to discuss the need for more troops at the Richmond-Petersburg front. He also predicted that forty thousand additional men would arrive from the Valley in less than two weeks.[34] Grant delayed his trip but eventually departed on Wednesday, the 5th, leaving Butler and Meade to handle things at the front.[35]

"gravel by the cart-load"

As their commanders discussed future operations, the soldiers of the Tenth and Eighteenth Corps tried to settle into their new surroundings. However, the extensive network of fortifications around Fort Harrison occupied by the federals drew unwelcome attention from the rebels. "We have been almost constantly under mortar shelling," wrote a Vermont officer in the Eighteenth Corps, "the most villainous kind, as they come straight down from the sky and its no use trying to get behind anything for protection as you do for other shells."[36] The captured fort soon became a zone of misery. Sharpshooters peppered the lines. One hidden Confederate rifleman maintained a continuous fire throughout the daylight hours. "Not a man can exhibit himself along almost the whole division," noted a Northern reporter.[37] A Richmond newspaper claimed that a single rebel marksman killed eleven unlucky Yankees in a single day. The Union men also endured nightly shelling from the Confederate gunboats in the James, less than a mile away, and fire from the land batteries across the river during the daytime.[38] The gunboats presented a serious threat, hurling eleven- and thirteen-inch shells into the Union trenches.[39] Watchmen announced incoming rounds to Union working parties, giving them just enough time to find cover.[40] The "shells plow deep," wrote a Union diarist, "and spread gravel by the cart-load."[41] The editors of the *Richmond Whig* crowed, "From what we learn, the occupancy of Fort Harrison will prove a barren success."[42]

Amid the trials of the living, the dead left by earlier fights dappled the ground. From the parapet at Fort Gilmer, one Southern observer counted the bodies of thirty black soldiers sprawled out where they had fallen in a determined assault on September 29. "Those fellows fought well sir," remarked a nearby Confederate, who explained that the Union men rushed forward and leapt into the fort's ditch as hand grenades rained down on them. That "fellow you see lying just there," the witness recounted, "was bending over one of them in order to pick it up and throw it back to us, when it exploded the top of his head off." The observer walked farther down the works and found more sickening sights. The "space of

over a thousand yards," he wrote, "is burdened . . . with the slaughtered Yankees."[43] But the Union dead were not alone. Lee's desperate attempt to retake Fort
Harrison had also produced great losses. "We have buried inside our picket line
over 275 of dead Confederates of Hoke and Wilcox Divisions," wrote Vermonter
Edward Ripley, "and they lie just as thickly outside, where neither they nor we
can touch them."[44] The foul odor of decay so bothered a New York officer that he
approached the enemy pickets waving a newspaper and arranged a truce. Men in
blue and gray shouldered their spades, stepped forward, and buried hundreds of
Confederate corpses. One New Hampshire soldier remarked that many bodies
rested in dense brush and could be found only by their stench.[45]

On October 4, the *Richmond Dispatch* informed readers that Butler's men
were strengthening Fort Harrison. The paper also reported that, farther north,
the Unionists had fortified a place on the Darbytown Road, owned by Jacob S.
Atlee, five miles from Richmond.[46] Because Atlee's son-in-law, Dr. Jesse L. Johnson, lived at the farmhouse, Union commanders and reporters often referred to
the property as Johnson's Farm.[47] The newspaper report was correct. Butler had
stationed a small division of cavalry at the farm under the leadership of Brigadier
General August V. Kautz. The position at the Johnson Farm offered an access
point to various roads into Richmond. From there, the Darbytown, Charles City
and Williamsburg roads all lay within easy reach of Butler's camps. His forces
could swing north toward, or even over, the Chickahominy River and attack Richmond from the east or northeast.

"We will try to be even yet"

The Confederates chafed at Fort Harrison's loss. Its capture greatly complicated
Richmond's defense and demoralized troops and civilians. According to Confederate Porter Alexander, Lee "was more worried at this failure than I have ever seen
him under similar circumstances."[48] The defeat offered a grim reminder of the capital's vulnerability and spread gloom throughout Richmond. "We live now among
perpetual firing of cannon," recorded one resident. "The loss of Fort Harrison is,
I fear, a very serious loss to us."[49] The failure to regain the position added to the
discouragement. "Our effort to retake it was not an energetic nor systematic one,"
lamented Lee's adjutant, Walter Taylor.[50] Alexander concluded that Lee's troops
"have fought so long behind breastworks that they have lost all spirit in attacking."[51]
Indeed, the counterattack accumulated casualties without producing any benefit.

Lee sought to mitigate the loss and even reverse the result. He recognized the
threat posed by Butler's new works on the New Market Road and the federal cavalry at Johnson's Farm. During October's first days, Confederate engineers, soldiers, and slaves managed to patch together a formidable line to cover the gap cre-

ated by Fort Harrison's capture. But weakness lay at the flanks, especially the left, where the mostly unmanned trenches extended for great distances. In addition, Lee gained limited satisfaction from blunting further Union progress. Instead, he yearned to drive Butler's units out of their new positions and, if possible, recapture Fort Harrison altogether and seize back what had been lost. "We will try to be even yet," wrote Taylor.[52]

Lieutenant General Richard H. Anderson commanded the two largest infantry divisions in the Richmond sector. He had achieved success as a division commander earlier in the war and took the helm of the First Corps after General James Longstreet's grievous wound at the Wilderness in May. However, he failed to demonstrate the aggressiveness and drive that marked Lee's favored subordinates. On the other hand, he managed to avoid tremendous mistakes and exhibited a cautious reliability. In October, only two divisions fell under his immediate operational leadership. Major General Charles W. Field's division, seasoned First Corps veterans, contained brigades from Texas, Georgia, Alabama, and South Carolina. The other division, led by Major General Robert F. Hoke, consisted of men from North Carolina, Georgia, and South Carolina who had arrived to fight in Virginia earlier in the year. Hoke's division was temporarily attached to the First Corps.[53] In addition to these two divisions, the six thousand Virginians of Major General George Pickett's division, also part of the First Corps, manned the relatively peaceful trenches of the Howlett line at Bermuda Hundred, south of the James between Richmond and Petersburg.

In addition to these veterans, Lee relied on an odd mix of regular, reserve, and militia units for the defenses outside Richmond. He tapped Lieutenant General Richard Ewell to organize and command these troops. Ewell, a rising star under Stonewall Jackson in 1862, had ascended to lead Lee's Second Corps in 1863. However, the grueling stress of the 1864 Overland campaign exacted a toll on his mental faculties, and he became acutely ill in late May. Lee took the opportunity to quietly hand the Second Corps to Jubal Early. But the autumn found Ewell in command of the Department of Richmond, which included Brigadier General Martin Gary's cavalry brigade, a Tennessee infantry brigade, the Virginia Reserves, a collection of local defense forces, and several heavy artillery units.[54] Ewell managed these responsibilities competently. In fact, at Fort Harrison, his cool leadership helped stitch together the torn Confederate lines and avoid total collapse.[55]

With these forces at his disposal, Lee decided to strike back at Butler. On Thursday, October 6, he convened a war council at Chaffin Farm, a collection of houses and outbuildings behind the new Confederate lines near the James. From headquarters there, his staff could glimpse Richmond's church spires north on the horizon.[56] To the south and east, not much more than a mile away, loomed the new federal trenches. The meeting gathered the key combat commanders in the Richmond sector, including Richard Anderson, Robert Hoke, Charles Field, and cavalry commander Martin Gary. In addition to these officers, Confederate president Jefferson Davis made the short ride down the Osborne Turnpike from Richmond to join the discussion.

Lee knew too well the dangers of attacking entrenchments and, no doubt, sought a way to lure the enemy onto open ground. Though the commanders discussed several plans during the meeting, Martin Gary improvised a promising scheme to exploit the weakness of Butler's dispositions and turn the Union troops out of their new line.[57] He understood that the Union line ended abruptly at the New Market Road with no significant earthworks or natural obstacles to anchor the flank. Only August Kautz's weak cavalry force north at Johnson's Farm, well detached from Butler's main line, screened this vulnerable flank. Under Gary's plan, Field's and Hoke's veteran divisions would withdraw from the trenches that evening and concentrate at the Darbytown and Charles City roads west of Johnson's Farm. Early the next morning, they would advance down the Darbytown Road against Kautz's position, while Gary's horsemen, along with one of Field's brigades, would swing along the Charles City Road.[58] The force would sweep over Kautz's outpost and then drive south into Butler's right flank at the New Market Road, penetrating deep behind Fort Harrison and the balance of the Union line.

With this plan, the Confederates sought to overwhelm Butler's right flank and turn the Union Tenth Corps out of its trenches north of Fort Harrison. If successful, the operation would catch Union infantry unprotected and unprepared and regain the ground lost a week before. The scheme was ambitious, the kind of large-scale offensive that had become all too rare for the Confederates. No mere probe or reconnaissance, it had the potential to strike a crushing blow and reap substantial gains for Lee. Fort Harrison's recapture would threaten the entire Union position and send the Army of the James tumbling back to its bridgehead at Deep Bottom.

Although Fort Harrison was the operation's tangible military goal, those at the meeting may have sought much broader impacts. Fort Harrison's loss, while demoralizing, had been hardly disastrous for Lee and his fellow rebels. Confederate engineers managed to repair the defense line and maintain an adequate barrier to Richmond. In addition to the practical benefits of Fort Harrison's recapture, however, a smashing rebel victory outside Richmond could temper Northern enthusiasm for the recent gains in the Valley and possibly influence some votes in a tight election. Such political considerations occupied the minds of many attending the meeting, no doubt. President Davis's participation suggests that the operation drew interest from the highest level of the Confederate government. Throughout the year, Davis had stressed the importance of Confederate military victories to the minds of Northern voters. He hoped that vigorous Confederate action would cool Northern desire to prosecute the war. In a speech in Montgomery, Alabama, only a few days before the war council at Chaffin's Farm, Davis had proclaimed, "Victory in the field is the surest element of strength to a peace party. Let us win battles and we shall have overtures soon enough."[59] The war council at Chaffin's Farm also addressed more than the next day's assault and its potential impacts. Lee also spoke with President Davis about the need to increase the army's ranks. "I hope he [Davis] will get us some *men*," Taylor wrote. "We want *men* badly." But Taylor focused on the next day's attack. "We will in all probability be at them again tomorrow," he reported to his sweetheart, "but unless you hear of an attack thro another source, say nothing of this."[60]

With the plan hatched, the operation commenced almost immediately. At 10 P.M., Hoke and Field pulled their divisions from the trenches and marched north into bivouac at the Currie house between the New Market and Darbytown roads. Richmond's militia units filled the vacant works in place of the veterans.[61] That evening, two artillery battalions joined the infantry near the Currie house. Just to the north, on the Charles City Road, the Alabama infantry brigade from Field's division, led by Colonel Pinckney Bowles, joined Gary's cavalry, gathering outside the interior defense line.[62] Like other units, the 7th South Carolina Cavalry Regiment, one of Gary's units, had received orders in the afternoon to head down the Charles City Road and halt there. In the evening, each man drew forty rounds of ammunition and two days' cooked rations. "It was understood that there was hot work ahead of us," noted one of his men.[63]

"a very dangerous position"

The 1864 campaign had been difficult for Benjamin Butler's cavalry commander, August Valentine Kautz. A graduate of West Point, Kautz served in the regular army before the war.[64] One observer described him as "a short, thick-set soldier of the rough-and-ready type, with a bullet head and black beetling eyebrows."[65] Assigned to Butler's army at the beginning of 1864, Kautz, with help from others, had bungled an attack against lightly defended Petersburg on June 9. That day, he dawdled at the Jerusalem Plank Road in front of a ragged collection of "old men and young boys" sifted from the town's citizenry. In the following years, Petersburg citizens would mark the day for celebration and remembrance, but for Kautz and his comrades, it stood as another failure in a long list of setbacks. Kautz also conducted several ineffective raids against Lee's supply lines over the summer, and his command failed to arrest Wade Hampton's cattle raid in September. Despite these disappointments, Kautz retained Butler's support, however, and continued to serve as chief of the army's cavalry.

After Fort Harrison's capture, Kautz held the extreme end of the new Union line at Johnson's Farm, more than a mile north of the infantry on the New Market Road. His position was less than ideal. The Johnson house sat on a broad field bordered in part by the forks of Four Mile Creek, a swampy stream that meandered southeast through Henrico County. A narrow, muddy path, which cut through a brambly forest, served as the only lifeline to Butler's force. The path did not comfort Kautz.[66] He recognized that a hasty withdrawal from his position could turn ugly. To make matters worse, his men had no entrenching tools. It was "a very dangerous position," he would recall. When he explained his predicament to the army commander, Butler replied that all available picks and shovels were already in the hands of busy infantrymen fortifying the new line southward. Surely exasperated by this response, Kautz pleaded for guidance. Butler replied curtly that "cavalry had legs and could run away."[67]

Two brigades of horsemen and two artillery units fell under Kautz's immediate command, about seventeen hundred men. He stretched his picket line for miles in a wide arc that curved first north along the exterior line to White's Tavern on the Charles City Road, then back east, screening the Union far right and rear.[68] With his vedettes spread across the countryside, he concentrated the balance of his force at the Johnson Farm. There, his men reversed portions of the rebels' abandoned exterior trenches west of the farmhouse. His second brigade manned the right, north of the Darbytown Road. Colonel Samuel Spear led this unit, which contained the 11th Pennsylvania and a few members of the 1st D.C. Cavalry. On the left, Colonel Robert West's brigade, with the 3rd New York and 5th Pennsylvania, covered the western edge of the Johnson fields. Despite the paucity of tools, Kautz's command managed to construct new works for the guns of the 4th Wisconsin Light Battery and Battery B of the 1st U.S. Artillery (Robert Hall's battery). Lieutenant Dorman L. Noggle of the 4th Wisconsin Battery placed his four guns within yards of the old exterior line. One section sat just to the south of the Darbytown Road, while the other deployed to the north and slightly farther to the rear.[69] For its part, Hall's battery unlimbered well back of the exterior line, to the rear of the Wisconsin gunners covering the center and right of Kautz's division.[70]

Far to Kautz's left, the 1st New York Mounted Rifles, operating independently of Kautz's command, posted a picket line along the exterior works.[71] The New Yorkers' line passed the deserted Kell house, which sat on a small rise halfway between the New Market and Darbytown roads. The officer in charge of the pickets, Major David Edward Cronin, had appropriated the dwelling as his headquarters.[72] Despite Cronin's presence, Kautz's troops still dangled largely unsupported at Johnson's Farm.

"we have positive information"

At about 10 P.M. on Thursday, October 6, several refugees and four deserters stumbled into Kautz's camp. Members of the group reported that "a [Confederate] force, consisting of Law's, Benning's, and Gregg's brigades, passed Thorne's [that] evening, going north, toward the York River road." Kautz, now wise to Lee's plans, began to prepare and promptly shuttled the refugees and deserters south to Butler's head-quarters.[73] With trouble brewing, Kautz's thoughts veered to the narrow, muddy path that formed his vital connection to the Army of the James. Late on Thursday, he directed a staff officer from the 1st New York Mounted Rifles to repair the road, but his order arrived too late. Resigned to the conditions in his rear, Kautz focused on his sector and ordered his men to prepare for an attack early the next morning.[74]

Along the main Union lines Thursday evening, commanders received the alarming news. Butler ordered his generals to be prepared.[75] At army headquar-ters, *New York Herald* reporter Thomas M. Cook observed Butler quietly read-ing a newspaper while dispatches arrived. At midnight, the journalist wrote, "We have positive information that [the Confederates] are putting into operation their desperate and foolhardy enterprise of flanking us." According to Cook, Butler knew the enemy column's composition, strength, and route of march. "Every de-viation is reported with as much accuracy as if they were a column of our own troops whose couriers were sent to the commanding general at every step and turn." To Cook, the receipt of these recent reports underscored Butler's "most wonderful talent" for gathering intelligence about the enemy, "whatever he may be as a field officer."[76] As the general apprised his commanders of the growing threat, the rank and file slept through the chilly night.

"mad enough to bite nails"

A few miles to the west, the two hundred or so members of the 7th South Carolina from Gary's cavalry brigade slept under the open sky. At about 2 A.M., the troop-ers emerged from their slumber. No bugles sounded. The men fed their horses. Within two hours, they climbed into their saddles. Their commander, Alexander Haskell, delivered a short speech explaining that Lee "expected much that day from Gary's brigade" and that the unit's failure would doom the entire offensive.[77] He warned that a pistol fired "before the enemy was routed was a death offence." He assured the men that the officers would lead and that the men were expected to follow. Fortified by these words, the regiment trotted down the Charles City Road with Haskell at the front and soon joined the Hampton Legion and the 24th Virginia Regiment, also of Gary's brigade.[78]

Other Confederates moved, as well. Robert E. Lee planned to join the attacking column in person that morning. The preceding afternoon, he set the departure time from the Chaffin's Farm at 2 A.M. But he arose just after midnight Friday morning convinced that the scheduled hour was 1 A.M. Perhaps anxious about the upcoming offensive or worn by recent events, his usual reserve escaped him, and he lashed out at his staff with a string of impatient directives. In the cool darkness, his staff attempted to correct the misunderstanding, but Lee ignored their efforts. The general mounted his horse, Traveller, and headed off without much breakfast and without any escort. A small entourage of officers and couriers hurried to catch up.[79]

Lee's mood soured further, exhibiting a severe temper that occasionally broke through his self-restraint and visited misery on those working under him. Like many in the rank and file, his small staff maintained an ample reverence for the general. His reputation as a gentleman stood rooted in his professional, even-handed, sober treatment of those around him. At the same time, the young officers at headquarters did not always cherish their proximity to the Confederate icon. Sometimes, he could be an ill-tempered and exacting boss and would tease his staff in a way that may have been amusing to him but was not always appreciated by the targets of his humor.[80] Despite their deep respect for "the Chief," his aides occasionally noted his irascible tendencies in letters and memoirs. Walter Taylor, who served with Lee for most of the war, had written in August that the general was "so unreasonable and provoking at times."[81] In an earlier letter, Taylor referred to Lee as "the cruel, old Chief."[82] Charles Venable, another staffer, wrote, "I am too high-tempered to stand a high-tempered man and consequently I become stubborn, sullen, useless and disagreeable."[83] Lee was not consistently testy, but under the strain and fatigue of active campaigning, his calm demeanor could slip his grasp.

Ahead through the darkness, Porter Alexander gazed into his campfire at the Dunn property, about a hundred yards west of the Osborne Turnpike. The young, enterprising commander of the First Corps artillery had worked closely with General Lee during the campaign. In late October, he would tell his wife that Lee "is always very kind to me + I feel as much at home in his presence as in yours."[84] In the early morning of October 7, Alexander expected to join Lee's party, but, like his peers at headquarters, he understood the time of departure to be 2 A.M. About 1:30 A.M., Charles Venable arrived at Alexander's camp on horseback. "Aleck, Come On!" he urged. "The Old Man is out here waiting for you & mad enough to bite nails." The young artillerist mounted his horse and rode out to Lee on the Osborne Pike. There he sought to explain matters "as good naturedly & blandly as" he could. "One o'clock, Sir, was the hour!" Lee abruptly replied. The pronouncement quickly ended the discussion. Lee then asked Alexander whether a guide had been procured for the trip. This request, like the new departure time, took the young man by surprise, and his ignorance brought more invective from the general. The quick-thinking Alexander then suggested that the party follow the tracks worn by the infantry divisions that afternoon. Still unhappy, Lee ordered Venable to guide the group, but Venable missed the instruction, for he was busy talking with another staff member. Lee turned to one of his couriers and said, "Evans, I will have to ask you to act upon my staff today for my officers are all disappointing me."[85] Venable soon discovered his error and became "deeply mortified."

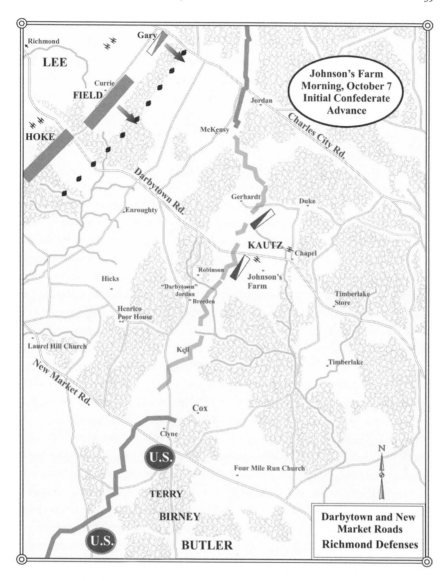

Thus arranged, the group rode along a pine-draped path east of the Osborne Pike and across a section of interior line. Along the way, Lee roused a civilian and forced the man to lead the group. But this did not last long, and the man was allowed to return to his sleep. Lee's entourage eventually traversed the New Market Road, then, using a crossroad, arrived at the Darbytown Road, where Hoke and Field's infantry gathered.[86]

Once Lee reached the combat troops, the Confederate commander arranged his attack force into two wings. On the right, Robert Hoke's and Charles Field's divisions formed along the Darbytown Road, with the Johnson Farm a mile or two ahead in their front. On the left to the north, Lee formed his flanking force on the Charles City Road, with Gary's cavalry regiments and the Alabama infantry brigade (detached from Field's division and led by Pinckney Bowles), along with an artillery battalion.[87] Members of the Texas brigade marched forward at dawn, the Lone Star soldiers passing Lee who waited at the side of the road. Apparently, his foul mood had faded away.[88]

"badly located"

August Kautz and his men knew difficult work lay ahead that morning. Before dawn, Kautz deployed two wings along the remnants of the Confederate exterior line west of the Johnson house. South of the Darbytown Road, on the left wing, Colonel Robert West formed his five hundred men along "badly located" trenches.[89] On the right, Kautz's second brigade, under Colonel Samuel Spear, manned a weak trench dug the day before with the few tools available. This unimpressive position stretched "about 100 yards long and 18 inches high, incomplete and easily flanked and enfiladed."[90] According to Kautz's report, it formed only an "unfinished rifle pit."[91] The precise location of Spear's trench is unclear, but it was most likely at the remnants of the old rebel works several hundred yards north of the Darbytown Road, just east of the Gerhardt house,[92] which stood near a wide band of farmland between the Darbytown and Charles City roads.[93] Although Spear's command contained over five hundred men, mostly from the 11th Pennsylvania, with a handful from the 1st D.C., many fewer joined the ranks on the field that morning. One hundred of Spear's men filled Kautz's protracted picket line near the Charles City Road and elsewhere. Others held the horses in the rear of the line. Taking into account these detachments and orderlies, Spear's position on the right just north of the Darbytown Road held only about two hundred men.[94] Spear also pushed skirmishers out in front through a "long growth of scrub pine" that fronted his position west of the Gerhardt house. Two woodpaths spilled out of these trees, one leading from the Charles City Road and another farther to the right, connecting north to White's Tavern.[95]

Finally, the two artillery units supported Kautz and his position. On the left, behind West's line, the 4th Wisconsin Battery deployed in two sections on either side of the Darbytown Road.[96] Robert Hall's battery anchored the center of Kautz's position. His guns rested in two earthworks "in a very commanding position" several hundred yards behind Kautz's main line north of the Darbytown Road and near a small Baptist chapel. Hall's field of fire covered the approaches to the exterior line and the Johnson Farm fields. In his immediate front, a wide, shallow ravine ran forward toward Spear's position.[97] With his small force in place,

Kautz waited for the attack promised by the deserters the night before. The Confederates did not disappoint.

"We went in like a hurricane"

The early dawn brought a crisp and clear October day. Kautz's picket posts, well west of the Johnson Farm, looked out for the enemy. Enoch Stahler, a first lieutenant in the 3rd New York, commanded vedettes north of the Darbytown Road, stationed in "an open field beyond a rail fence, a few rods from a piece of woods." More trees stood to their front and right. Stahler was on edge, having spent a sleepless night anticipating unpleasant work.[98] At daybreak, the sun peeked from behind his back revealing shapes creeping through the tangled branches and thickets ahead. The Confederates had arrived. It was about 6:30 A.M. "'Ping, Ping,' came their bullets, and 'Crack, crack,' went our reply," recalled Stahler. His comrades slapped their horses rearward. A bullet pierced Stahler's light-colored sorrel ensuring he would spend the rest of the morning on foot.[99] As the rebels pressed, couriers from other posts reported the enemy approaching along the Darbytown Road. Confederate troops also appeared on the right along the path that emptied into the open field near the Gerhardt house.[100]

Off to the Union right, Haskell's 7th South Carolina pushed down the Charles City Road. At sunrise, Haskell heard gunfire from the point of advance. Sergeant W. DuBose Snowden soon arrived on a wounded horse to report enemy contact. Armed with the news, Haskell took personal command of two companies, about forty-five men in all, and surged forward. They brought their mounts to a trot, drew sabres, sped to a gallop, and responded wholeheartedly to Haskell's cry of "Charge!" The group thundered ahead, four riders abreast. A small group of Union cavalrymen appeared in front as Haskell's detachment hurtled forward with overwhelming speed and momentum. It was no contest. "We went in like a hurricane," recalled Haskell years later, "and in a flash it was all over; the enemy routed and we pursuing up a gentle ascent."[101]

In the face of Haskell's advance, Colonel Spear hurried additional men forward to reinforce the pickets. The Confederate cavalrymen engaged the thickening federal screen and drove Colonel Spear's detachment back toward its main position. Haskell continued to pursue his prey.[102] The stubborn resistance by the Union pickets forced Haskell to halt his men and wait for the rest of the regiment to arrive. With everyone at hand, he dismounted three-fourths of his command, "leaving the sabres hanging to the saddles." Haskell himself changed horses. His mount, named Jeb Stuart, a new acquisition, had turned out to be "nervous and blundering in the charge." The Confederates formed a line of battle and pushed farther. This time, the

Unionists withdrew to Kautz's main trenches behind the Gerhardt house.[103] In the action, Haskell's new horse received a disabling wound, and the colonel climbed aboard his third of the morning, "a compact brown about 15 hands high."[104]

As the Confederates sparred with the skirmishers near the Gerhardt house, Union captain Colin Richardson positioned a squad on the south shoulder of the Darbytown Road, and Captain George F. Dern led about thirty to the north of the road.[105] Gray-clad infantrymen from Charles Field's division bore down on the small pockets of blue. One Confederate described the Union screen as "a strong line . . . protected by the trees and undergrowth of an almost impenetrable thicket."[106] The 5th South Carolina from Brig. Gen. John Bratton's brigade charged through the trees with a yell. Richardson and Dern pulled their men back, while some in Dern's group climbed into a small isolated redoubt at the edge of woods, a work left by McClellan's forces in 1862, according to one account.[107]

The Union skirmishers had slowed the Confederates for more than an hour.[108] All the while, Captain Hall lobbed percussion shells into the rebel-filled woods twelve hundred yards to the front. The pickets completed their withdrawal. Stahler's group withdrew from the old redoubt at the woods' edge and traced back a quarter mile to a ditch, most likely a portion of the exterior line north of the Darbytown Road.[109] Dern's small party manned the old exterior line just across the road on the Union right. Captain Richardson's pickets joined West's brigade in the trenches on the left, south of the road.

With the woods clear of Federals, Field's men gained a clear view of Kautz's main position. To the attackers, the Union line looked anything but weak. One rebel observer wrote that there was a "formidable redoubt and strong chain of works crossing the road at right angles." Obstructions crowded the front, the timber and brush forming "an almost impassable abatis, swept by artillery and musketry."[110] But these looks deceived. Kautz's fortifications may have appeared strong in a few sections, but the force defending them was decidedly weak. In any case, Field took no chances. He surveyed the ground ahead and soon ordered G.T. Anderson's and John Bratton's brigades to deploy in battle line and prepare to attack.[111]

Over on the Confederate left, Gary's rebel cavalry emerged into the field at the Gerhardt house and Alexander Haskell deployed a battery at the woods' edge. The crew loaded their guns and launched shells toward the Union cannon in the distance.[112] A "lively" duel ensued.[113] As projectiles filled the air, the Confederate attack began to take shape. Colonel Thomas Logan's Hampton Legion and Colonel William T. Robin's 24th Virginia Cavalry Regiment deployed along with the Alabama infantry brigade. The Alabamians, under Colonel Pinckney Bowles, connected their right with Bratton's brigade to the south.[114] With the units forming for the fight, Haskell met with Martin Gary, in overall command of the Confederate left wing. Haskell placed half of his regiment into the battle line

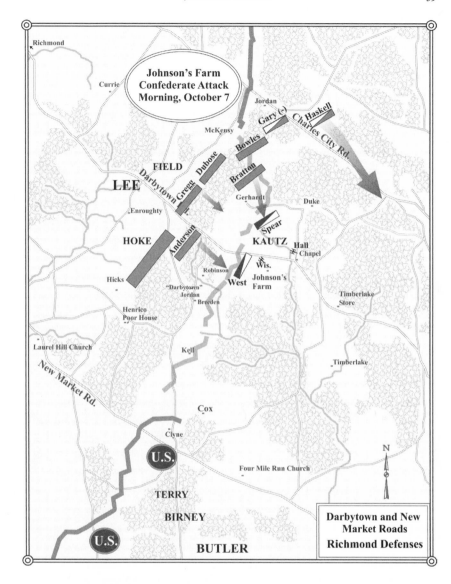

Johnson's Farm
Confederate Attack
Morning, October 7

Richmond

Currie

Jordan

Gary (-)

Haskell

Charles City Rd.

McKensy

Bowles

FIELD

Dubose

Darbytown

Gregg

Bratton

LEE

Gerhardt

Duke

Enroughty

Spear

Anderson

HOKE

KAUTZ

Hall

Chapel

Hicks

Robinson

Wis.

"Darbytown"

West

Johnson's
Farm

Jordan

Breeden

Timberlake
Store

Henrico
Poor House

Laurel Hill Church

Kell

Timberlake

New Market Rd.

Cox

Clyne

N

U.S.

Four Mile Run Church

TERRY

BIRNEY

Darbytown and New
Market Roads
Richmond Defenses

U.S.

BUTLER

and held the other portion, about a hundred men, in reserve.[115] The Confederates advanced against the main Union position. As the rebel attack began flooding out of the woods, Kautz ordered the horses rearward, along with men to hold them, thus reducing his already diminutive force.[116] Gary's cavalry and the Alabama infantrymen lunged forward toward the Gerhardt house but were easily repulsed.[117] On the rebel right, at the Darbytown Road (in Field's front), one regiment, most likely Georgians from Anderson's brigade, also moved forward, only to reel back under fire from West's brigade.[118]

"charging with great spirit"

The early Confederate probes had generated little success. Peering out beyond his lines, Kautz wondered whether the enemy operation had run its course.[119] To his right, officers and men from Colonel Samuel Spear's command congratulated themselves on the easy victory. But the celebration was premature. Rebel commanders realized their initial advance had been too narrow. Colonel Haskell ordered a wider flanking movement. Directing one of his officers to take command of half of the 7th South Carolina, Haskell gathered the other half to conduct a strike far around the Union right.[120]

As Haskell schemed, Charles Field, to the south, prepared his infantry division for a determined assault. G. T. Anderson's Georgians formed south of the Darbytown Road, and John Bratton's South Carolinians deployed to the north.[121] Bratton pushed Colonel Asbury Coward's 5th South Carolina Regiment out as skirmishers and placed his other regiments (the 1st, 2nd, and 6th South Carolina, as well as the Palmetto Sharpshooters) into line with the right touching the Darbytown Road.[122] Farther to the north, Bowles's Alabamians proceeded along with Gary's cavalrymen.

At about 8 A.M., the full attack began. Field's "two brigades moved in beautiful style across the brush and felled timber, in the face of a most galling fire," recounted one witness soon after the fight.[123] Bratton's brigade and the Alabama regiments stepped out of the scrub pines and headed directly for the weak Union right flank with their battle flags waving.[124] The South Carolinians "advanced to storm the redoubt on the enemy's extreme right."[125] Hapless members of the 11th Pennsylvania Cavalry in Colonel Spear's sector readied for the oncoming wave.[126] But no desperate combat occurred along the ill-formed parapet.[127] Opting against futile heroics, Spear's troopers fled from their shallow trench. Many headed south across the Darbytown Road, and some passed farther to the rear across Hall's battery. Hall shouted to the fugitives, begging "them to stay and support the guns, but the appeal was useless."[128] With little ceremony, Kautz's right wing began to give way.[129]

As the right collapsed, pressure on the entire Union position mounted. Kautz's left wing, manned by the two regiments of Robert West's brigade, continued to hold back G. T. Anderson's Georgians. But just north, across the road, Captain George F. Dern's little picket force of thirty men was in trouble. As the Confederates flushed Spear's brigade from the right flank, a separate line of rebels headed for Dern's squad.[130] Enoch Stahler, in these works with Dern and the other New Yorkers, emptied his revolver into the mass of Confederates until he received a ball in his left elbow.[131] Like Spear's men minutes earlier, Dern's tiny force abandoned its position.[132] Using "sinuosities of the line" for cover, the rebels edged along the trench south toward Kautz's only remaining brigade.[133] The wounded Stahler managed to escape and stagger onto the Johnson field. There he dropped to the ground to examine his wound and felt the sickening crunch of broken bones in his arm. On the verge of unconsciousness, he heeded an officer who warned him to withdraw as quick as possible to avoid capture.[134]

The Confederate attack now enclosed West's brigade from two sides, with Anderson's Georgians pushing from the west and Bratton's men sweeping from the north. Bratton's brigade formed three lines, wheeled toward the Darbytown Road, and traversed a shallow depression. The force headed directly toward a section of the Wisconsin battery dug in on the road's northern shoulder.[135] As John Bratton explained, his South Carolinian force "turned upon the flank and rear of those in Anderson's front but was checked by a work at the enemy flank."[136] Robert West, largely ignoring the Georgians to his front, ordered his men to cover their right flank. One of his regiments, the 5th Pennsylvania, led by Lieutenant Colonel Christopher Kleinz, rushed rearward under heavy fire and formed in a ditch facing north along the Darbytown Road.[137] According to one account, a collapsed stone wall provided some nominal cover there.[138] Two squadrons of Ferris Jacobs's 3rd New York, also dismounted and piled into the ditch near a section of the Wisconsin guns.[139]

The pressure on Kautz's position at the Johnson Farm reached a bursting point. The final Union collapse began with the Wisconsin gunners. The gun crews, led by a sergeant, limbered up and withdrew across the Johnson field.[140] According to one of the battery members, "We moved back four times, constantly working our guns, our men falling in every direction and to check to the rebels who were within 15 or 20 rods of us when we were ordered to retreat."[141] Deprived of their direct artillery support, the blue cavalrymen crouched in the ditch and braced for the attack. The Confederates swept through low ground north of the road, drawing case shot from Hall's guns, still in action off to the east. The fire broke and scattered the rebel column into a "disordered mass," in Hall's estimation.[142]

While the Union cavalrymen along the Darbytown Road stared out at the Confederate advance, a curious thing occurred. About two hundred of the secessionists emerged from the shallow ravine and "ran forward, throwing down their guns, with loud cries of 'Deserters!'"[143] A second line of Confederates fired at the backs of the would-be fugitives, prompting them to pick up their weapons and resume the fight.[144]

As the unusual incident unfolded, Ferris Jacobs piled his New Yorkers into the redoubt to confront the Confederates who advanced from the north across the ravine immediately in front of Hall's battery.[145] This force probably contained the South Carolinians of Bratton's brigade. After crushing the Union right flank, General Field directed Colonel James R. Hagood, who commanded the 1st South Carolina, "to change front to the right, and attack in the flank . . . a redoubt further to the right which was defying the efforts of Anderson's entire brigade."[146] "I executed this order," recalled Hagood, "the men charging with great spirit and driving from the work a body of the enemy."[147] Hagood halted his regiment, along with the 2nd South Carolina, about eight hundred men in all, a few times to ensure their alignment. Within two hundred yards of the redoubt, the line lurched forward at the double-quick, tearing away the abatis.[148]

Men from Ferris Jacobs's 3rd New York continued their stand along the ditch and in the redoubt and, by Hagood's recollection, "fired so wildly" that their bullets fell too short or too long.[149] Jacobs finally lost hope and promptly withdrew his troopers past the Johnson house toward the woods and swamps beyond.[150] Along the ditch, men from the 5th Pennsylvania did the same. Out of ammunition, they recognized that further resistance would yield no benefit.[151]

Kautz's line toppled, and Bratton's wave poured over the Darbytown Road, rendering the main defensive line useless. Anderson's Georgians, stymied throughout the attack, arrived in the wake of the fleeing cavalrymen, rushing into the captured redoubt "cheering like fools," according to Hagood. Much to his annoyance, the Georgians planted their flags in the parapet before the South Carolinians.[152]

The Union positions at Johnson's Farm had fallen easily. First, Spear's line on the far right collapsed. Then Dern's little party fled from its works just north of the Darbytown Road. Finally, West's brigade melted away. The weight of the Confederate attack simply overwhelmed the slight and poorly manned union line. As suggested by Butler, it was time for the cavalrymen to use their legs and leave as Anderson's Georgians, Bratton's South Carolinians, and Bowles's Alabamians spread into the fields around the Johnson house. "The men went yelling, running and driving right through horses, wagons, cannon and camp, troopers fleeing in every direction," recalled R. T. Coles of the 4th Alabama.[153]

Though the cavalrymen had given up, Robert Hall fought on joined by Colonel Spear and a few dismounted men. From his spot in the rear, his battery continued to deliver a "rapid fire and showed no disposition to run away."[154] When the rebels edged closer, Hall's cannon sprayed canister through their ranks. The Confederates "received a sweeping fire from the right section, which commanded it," Hall recalled after the fight, "and met a withering fire from the left section as they reached the [Johnson House]."[155] According to Hall, his fire caused "so much confusion at this time on my left and front that a small infantry force on the flanks would easily have driven them back." But no such force appeared. Kautz's cavalrymen and the Wisconsin artillerymen rushed for the rear and the safety of the New Market Road. Hall's unsupported guns stood fast for at least a "full ten minutes," tossing shells into the approaching Confederates.[156]

Though a slight ridge concealed the guns themselves from view, the Union battery's effectiveness did not escape General Bratton's attention.[157] Its impact was unmistakable, for it "embarrassed [the] attack." Bratton ordered James Hagood's force (the 1st and 2nd South Carolina) forward to clear out the annoying cannon "posted on the further edge."[158] The South Carolinians swerved east on the double and soon received canister from Hall's crews.[159] With the enemy only thirty yards away, Hall finally limbered up his guns and made his escape.[160] In addition to thirty-one rounds of canister, lethal at close range, his crews fired off three hundred rounds of shell and fifty-four of case shot over the course of the engagement.[161] The brave stand bought time for Kautz's retreat. A Confederate staff officer later suggested that Hall had remained too long but acknowledged the battery's deadly effectiveness.[162] With his work done, Hall and his gun teams trotted toward the woods in the wake of Kautz's command.

"with loud yells"

At his picket post on the Kell property, Captain David Cronin of the 1st New York Mounted Rifles could hear the battle unfold on the Johnson Farm to the north. As the din grew, he edged toward the fight on horseback and encountered a group of pickets from West's brigade, who had become isolated from Kautz's command and were galloping south. A lieutenant with the squad reported a large enemy force crossing the Darbytown Road. Cronin deployed the group as skirmishers and dispatched messengers to the New Market Road. In the meantime, the trees to the north became a "roaring rebel den," causing Cronin and his men to ease back south. About halfway to the Kell house, Cronin reached high ground, which offered a view of the Johnson Farm and Kautz's men. Years later, he recorded his vivid recollection of the fight: "I saw the dismounted cavalrymen rise from their pits and ascend the slope at a walk. Scores of them fell in a few minutes. Some turned and fired a few times and then dropped, but the majority were out of ammunition. Not one of them ran. I saw the rebels pouring over the breastworks with loud yells and taking many prisoners."[163] Enemy fire halted Cronin's observations, and he withdrew to the Kell house. From his perspective, Kautz's initial withdrawal exhibited an admirable orderliness, given the difficult conditions.[164]

But at the Johnson Farm, the calm did not last long. As the cavalrymen fled, an unfortunate incident completely changed the nature of the retreat. Lieutenant Dorman Noggle, commanding the Wisconsin battery, had suffered through a challenging morning. As the rebels pressed against Kautz's line, Noggle's entire battery fled the field altogether. Though the fighting at Johnson's Farm would bring no laurels for his command, the retreat would saddle it with ignominy that would taint Kautz's entire division.[165] During their flight, the Wisconsin gun teams raced along the improvised path that connected Kautz's position to the New Market Road. According to Kautz's recollection, this narrow road, the same poorly engineered path he had sought to repair the night before, crossed Four Mile Creek southeast of the Johnson field.[166] Disaster struck when the guns reached a boggy section of the road. The wheels of Noggle's first limber sank into the mud and

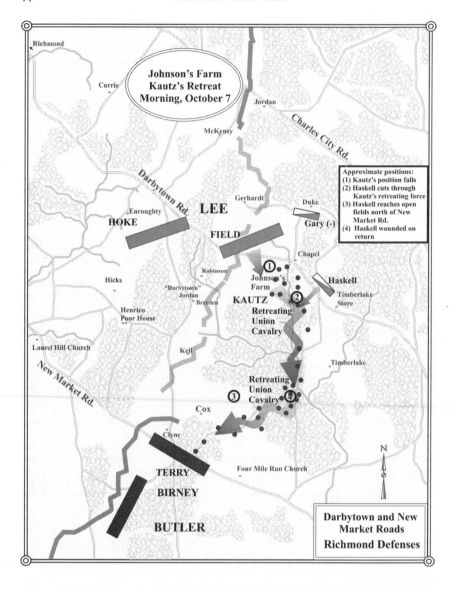

ceased to turn. The horses, caisson, and gun descended into the ooze and became completely stuck. The stalled team blocked the cramped, swampy road and all the cavalrymen and gunners fleeing from the Johnson Farm.[167] Noggle's mishap created a fatal bottleneck. Christopher Kleinz, commander of the 5th Pennsylvania, found the retreat path blocked.[168] Ferris Jacobs, of the 3rd New York, also arrived and turned his men to face the enemy threat. Noggle's crew struggled to extract the equipment, but it was no use. The frozen guns, along with the dozens, if not hundreds, of led horses, rapidly formed a tangled jam at the crossing. Soon, Robert Hall's guns and caissons appeared fresh from their dramatic stand, with the enemy "close and in hot pursuit." Like the cavalrymen before him, Hall found his only path blocked by the Wisconsin battery.[169]

"break any standing body"

As the Union forces piled up along the muddy path, an unwelcome sight appeared in the fields to the east. Colonel Alexander Haskell's small force of one hundred Confederate horsemen from the 7th South Carolina had completed its circuit around the Union right flank. Haskell's band had galloped down the Charles City Road well behind the Johnson Farm and over to the Darbytown Road. Over the fields in his front, he spied a stream, a "boggy sink," some scrubby "black-jack" woods, and a road in the distance. As the South Carolinians crossed over the field, Union cavalrymen opened fire from the trees. Haskell had found Kautz's retreating column helplessly stuck in the mud of Four Mile Creek. As Haskell would later recount, the "command, 'Charge,' was given instantly, and with the Colonel and a few officers and well mounted men leading in fours, the little column dashed into the point where the entrance of the road made a slight gap in the woods." Haskell rode straight to the guns, slashing at men in his way, and drove into the disorganized cavalry beyond. "We shot right through them," he remembered, "and they filled the road with routed fugitives."[170]

The Union withdrawal quickly deteriorated from a dignified retreat into a disastrous rout. The Confederates killed artillery horses in their traces and eliminated any hope of freeing the guns.[171] Noggle received an order to abandon the pieces in the swamp, though the Wisconsin men managed to save a few horses. But they left the four guns and the equipment at the creek blocking the road.[172] As Haskell approached, Christopher Kleinz could not form the remnants of the 5th Pennsylvania in defense and ordered them to withdraw, a difficult task in the midst of the crowded road and wooded swamp.[173] To his regret, Hall also ordered his men to spike his four guns and head rearward with all "the material and horses that could be brought away."[174] The gunners, who had stood so bravely at the Darbytown Road, fled through the woods, leaving their cannon behind. With the Confederates within twenty yards, Hall escaped by crashing through the trees and entering the nearly impassable swamp.[175] Gunners and cavalrymen alike did whatever they could to get away. As Haskell's men cut their way through the ranks, Kautz's command simply fell apart.

The tiny rebel column surged forward with Haskell at the head armed with a straight Austrian saber, a five-shot revolver, and a nine-shot French revolver. He pressed south along the wood road, and his small force smashed through the remnants of Kautz's division. "As long as the head of the column lives, it can drive on and in and break any standing body," he explained later.[176] Haskell's charge harkened back to the war's early days and the swashbuckling, cavalier tactics of Jeb Stuart's dragoons. His action also demonstrated a basic principle of small-unit tactics—that a small compact, organized force, applied at the appropriate point and in the correct manner, can wreak havoc on a larger opponent. The woods concealed the Confederates' numerical weakness.[177]

Kautz's panicked and exhausted men sought to rally again and again. One agonized officer managed to form "a little half circle across the road, but in a flash it went to the winds."[178] Haskell rushed through the Union column. Some vanquished Union soldiers became prisoners. Others spilled off the road to try their luck in the tangled swamp. Haskell, his saber "red to the hilt," emptied all the rounds from his pistols into the enemy and split the side of one federal's head with his saber.[179] "I saw Col. Haskell shoot and cut down a number of men. I don't like to mention the number," wrote one of Haskell's comrades, William Hinson, in his diary. Another witness put the toll at thirteen.[180]

Haskell's force swept south for about half a mile and finally halted at the edge of the timber, "near some big old gnarled and knotted oaks."[181] The colonel paused to let the horses rest and designated the field in front as his regiment's rallying point. Less than a mile ahead, over the fields of the Cox Farm, lay the New Market Road. His column had slashed through much of Kautz's force. He ordered Private W. H. Welch back to General Gary to request "a force of infantry to take charge of the prisoners" now scattered along the road to the rear.[182]

Haskell scanned the ground ahead and climbed a nearby hill to examine the Union infantry to the south. On the rise, he found the "showy" headquarters wagon of the 1st New York Mounted Rifles. The wagon carried a lone driver, an Irishman who refused to surrender until the colonel threatened to drive his sword into the teamster. "Now drive down this hill like a good fellow, and when you get to those big trees you will find my men," directed Haskell. The prisoner complied.[183]

With this capture complete, Haskell took out his field glasses and observed the Union infantry forming south across the fields. The Confederate attack "had evidently created great consternation, and there was disorder in the ranks," he recalled. Haskell had pushed far from the Johnson Farm and far ahead of Lee's infantry columns.[184] Just to the west, New Yorker David Cronin surveyed the same scene from a "slight eminence overlooking the entire field north of the New Market Road." Hearing "yelling and shrieking" from the right rear, Cronin was "startled to behold hundreds of the rebel cavalry emerging from the woods" pursuing the remnants of Kautz's division.[185] Back across the field, Haskell continued to examine the conditions to the south. And, after a brief duel with a lone Union cavalryman, he trotted down the hill and headed back to the towering trees where he had left his officers. There, he met Sergeant DuBose Snowden, and the two proceeded north into the woods, toward the main Confederate force, to report conditions at the front.[186]

"this little private battle"

As Haskell and Snowden reached a curve in the narrow, tree-lined road, they encountered Private Welch returning from his appointed task. They also caught up to the Irishman's wagon making its way toward the Johnson Farm and captivity. While Welch halted to speak with Haskell, a Union "squadron with a General and Staff" appeared on the path ahead.[187] Haskell, true to form, ordered his men to charge and cut through the enemy riders. The two sides closed quickly. The Union general was none other than August Kautz, who had been "floundering through the swamp" on his wounded horse before finding the road. Well behind the rest of his men, accompanied by only a dozen fellow riders, Kautz sought to return to the New Market Road as best he could. He called upon Haskell's group to surrender.[188] But, as the foes converged, Haskell fired his pistol, hitting a soldier on his right and then another on his left. The South Carolinian poised to dispatch a third, but the horseman lifted a carbine to his shoulder and fired at Haskell's face.[189] The bullet entered his left eye and exited behind his left ear.[190] Another ball knocked Sergeant Snowden out of his saddle. Welch, whose sword was in its scabbard and his rifle slung across his back, nearly became the next casualty as a Union trooper waved his saber at him. A Union officer stepped in, however, and knocked away the weapon, sparing Welch's life. The Unionists had won "this little private battle." They ordered Welch, now disarmed and dismounted, to place the stricken Snowden into the wagon. Snowden, who lay there with a "small bullet hole in his jacket," was seriously wounded. Welch then looked at Haskell "lying in the road, and saw [the Colonel's] face covered with blood." He assumed his colonel was dead.[191]

Kautz did not wait to investigate and rode south toward the New Market Road. He soon encountered a captured Union soldier who expressed astonishment to find him there and explained that rebel cavalry had deployed in the open field beyond. Kautz guided his horse off to the east and into the woods.[192] To north, some federal soldiers remained next to Haskell's body, taking a watch, a ring, and some papers from the stricken colonel. They considered moving him, but one of them, perhaps a surgeon, said, "No. He is dying. If you move him he will die instantly. You can't do anything for him." The Union men left Haskell alone with his horrid wound.[193]

When Kautz arrived in the infantry line later, one of his men overtook him and reported that the injured officer back in the woods had three stars on his collar. Kautz explained that such markings were worn by colonels in the Confederate army. "Well then, I have killed a rebel colonel, and here are some things I found on him," the soldier explained. The effects included Haskell's gold watch and a bundle of papers containing orders General Gary had issued the previous night for the day's operation.[194]

"General Lee himself"

As Haskell struggled for life, Confederate infantry regrouped at the Johnson Farm. Though the morning's victory had extracted a toll in officers and men, Lee's force had swept away Kautz's division swiftly and decisively.[195] Now Field's infantry gathered around the Johnson house and prepared to march south toward the Union infantry position on the New Market Road. To the west, across the old exterior line, Major General Robert Hoke's division, unscathed by the morning's events, also readied itself to advance. With some luck, these two veteran divisions would smash Butler's flank and gain the vulnerable areas behind the new Union trenches. Such a move would outflank Fort Harrison and threaten the entire federal position north of the James.

Back at the high ground around the Kell house, New Yorkers David Cronin and Colonel Edwin Sumner could see the Johnson Farm and the Darbytown Road in the distance. They observed the Confederates forming near the Johnson house. The rebels cheered as a group of mounted officers rode down the Darbytown Road. Through field glasses, Cronin "could distinctly see the faces of this group and the details of their uniforms. One of them, as we learned afterward, was General Lee himself, in the midst of his staff."[196] Cronin continued to watch as the Confederates formed into three lines. He noted that Lee's veterans showed "no pervading tint of uniform along the lines. The poor fellows looked dingy and mottled enough."[197]

Martin Gary's plan, adjusted by Haskell on the field, had worked. Kautz's troopers had no chance. Unable to fortify the position properly, they also lacked a force of sufficient size. But, in the end, the narrow, muddy woods road, the defective escape route, turned a bad situation worse.[198] The appearance of Haskell and his small, spirited squad of cavalrymen ensured the loss of most of Kautz's artillery. But for the veterans in gray and butternut, the rout of a couple of poorly prepared cavalry brigades hardly ranked as a sparkling victory. There was much more work ahead if they wished to achieve a significant success.

CHAPTER 2

The New Market Road

~

"be ready to meet the enemy"

For Benjamin Butler's infantry, the rumors and reports of Lee's movement the previous night warned of more combat Friday morning. At daylight, federal units prepared for a fight. But when the dawn passed and nothing happened, relief filtered through the ranks and "many a joke cracked over the last needless scare."[1] However, about an hour after sunrise, the sounds of battle drifted from Johnson's Farm and floated into the infantry camps south of the New Market Road. The thud of far-away cannon and the crackle of rifles offered little novelty to veteran ears. But "between 6 and 7 o'clock we heard heavy firing on our extreme right," recalled one soldier,[2] and it became clear that the distant thunder signaled more than mere skirmishing. Any uncertainty ended when the long roll sounded, and the infantrymen shouldered their weapons.[3]

Alfred Terry's division from the Tenth Corps took position at the New Market Road. In the Union army, each corps bore its own distinctive badge, a system initiated by General Joseph Hooker in 1863. The Tenth Corps badge featured a four-bastioned fort, a fitting symbol, as Terry's men had spent the last few days plunging spades into the captured Confederate works and refacing them west. The remodeled parapet stretched north from Fort Harrison and covered Butler's right flank. Not everyone was happy with the new defense line, though. In particular, Butler's acting chief engineer, Peter Michie, had misgivings. He wrote that the "portion occupied by the Tenth Army Corps is very weak and not well laid out. It is simply the old rebel line reversed. I have urged a new line, with appropriate works, to protect our right flank and make it secure, but an unwillingness has been manifested to have this carried out for the present."[4] The underlying problem was obvious. The terminus of the works at the New Market Road bent back for only a short stretch. The Union flank there had no anchor. It was completely "in the air." And the Confederates, after their victory at Johnson's Farm on Friday morning, headed straight for this vulnerable spot.

Though the fortifications may have been subpar, the Union commanders assigned to this sector were not. The Tenth Corps chief, Major General David Birney, was an able combat leader. Born in Alabama in 1825 to the son of an antislavery leader, he had practiced law in Philadelphia before the war and, during the conflict, had participated in numerous campaigns. Despite a tendency to clash with superiors, his solid leadership helped to ensure a deserved rise through the command ranks.[5] He proved to be a tough fighter and excellent division commander in Winfield Hancock's Second Corps during the Overland campaign. However, he crossed Meade by siding against him in intra-army squabbling over events at Gettysburg.[6] Nevertheless, the army "had few officers who could command 10,000 men as well as he," in the view of Colonel Theodore Lyman.[7] After joining the Army of the James, Birney achieved mixed results while leading the Tenth Corps at Deep Bottom in August and in the late September fighting. Now, on this bright clear Friday, Birney held the point of danger against an attack that threatened the safety of Butler's entire position. Unfortunately, Birney was grievously ill, suffering from a "malarious fever" that had plagued him for some time. Nevertheless, ignoring his physician's advice to remain in his tent, "he was up and in his saddle" when the alarm sounded that morning.[8]

At army headquarters, Benjamin Butler also prepared for battle. With Grant in Washington, Butler enjoyed unfettered control over the decisions on the field. But the pudgy lawyer was no steely pugilist. Few occasions found him at the front, under fire, barking out orders. Indeed, he generally left battlefield decisions to his subordinates. However, he possessed a decent tactical sense and, as news from the Johnson Farm arrived, he clearly understood the threat to his open right flank. Throughout the morning, he peppered David Birney with urgent directives. At 8:20 A.M., Birney received a note requesting that he "be ready to send assistance to Kautz when he needs it." At 8:55 A.M., Butler admonished, "Let your right fall back and be ready to meet the enemy, who are advancing." About ten minutes later, his third dispatch cautioned, "Take good care that the enemy do not get between your right and Deep Bottom."[9] Butler expressed most concern about the depth of the Confederate strike. "I am inclined to think that the enemy, if they are in earnest on the right, will make the attack pretty far down toward New Market [Road], so as to turn us if possible."[10] The previous Sunday, he had urged Birney to bend the line's right flank sharply back at the New Market Road.[11] Now, with the collapse of Kautz's position, these earlier instructions were proving prescient.

Birney quickly shifted his command northward to greet the oncoming rebels. The open ground running parallel to the New Market Road presented the most vulnerable point. This "post of honor" went to the three brigades of Major General Alfred Terry's division, men who had participated in the capture of New Market Heights the week before and the excursion to Roper's Farm on October 1.[12] General Terry was a tall, attractive man "with fair complexion, light hair and blue eyes."[13] Serving at First Bull Run and along the southeastern coast later, he developed a solid reputation as a soldier and commander.[14] In one reporter's estimation, he was "affable, intelligent, and polished."[15] He also enjoyed the affection and confidence of his men.

Terry deployed his three brigades in a crescent-shaped line nearly parallel to the New Market Road, with Colonel Francis B. Pond's command on the left near the Clyne house, Colonel Joseph C. Abbott at the center facing out toward the Cox farm, and Colonel Harris M. Plaisted on the far right.[16] To support Terry, Birney pulled Colonel Martin Curtis's brigade from the Corps' second division. Terry found his position partially fortified. On the left, Pond's men occupied the short extension of the trenches Butler had ordered earlier in the week. "The left stretched across an open field and occupied strong works that had been constructed previous to this affair," wrote a reporter on the scene.[17] Recently cut trees littered the field to the front "forming ugly obstacles to a quick advance."[18] Farther to the right, well-formed ditches and parapets offered protection.[19] However, as Terry stretched his battle line east, parallel to the New Market Road, the works trailed off. Abbott, whose brigade occupied the center of Terry's position, reported that he had "advanced in line of battle through the woods, until my line was a prolongation of that in the entrenchments, with the right somewhat refused."[20]

While Abbott's men deployed in the center, Plaisted's brigade covered the right, several hundred yards north of the New Market Road,[21] where it found thick woods sewed with half-formed rifle pits.[22] Facing north, with their backs to the New Market Road, the 11th Maine and 24th Massachusetts formed the left of Plaisted's line. The Maine regiment looked toward the fields and toward trees beyond. The 24th Massachusetts set up before a pine thicket and bent its right flank back toward the New Market Road. Some seventy-five yards to the rear of the Massachusetts men, the 10th Connecticut and 100th New York formed the far right of the Union position and deployed in echelon along "a commanding ridge of ground, with open pine wood in front for about 100 yards."[23]

As the foot soldiers hurried into position, Lieutenant Colonel Richard Jackson, chief of artillery, wheeled four batteries, twenty-four cannon in all, into the gun emplacements on the left of the line. "From this position a clear view could be had of the fields over which the rebels must pass to reach the woods on the right, in which the right of the line posted," wrote a reporter for the *New York Herald,* "which fields were literally swept by these guns."[24]

In the midst of these preparations, Kautz's routed cavalrymen tumbled back from Johnson's Farm. A New Hampshire lieutenant in the center of Birney's line watched on as "the cavalry came breaking out of these woods as though the devil was after them; there was no organization, every man for himself and all making straight for Deep Bottom. Riderless horses with empty saddles under their bellies galloped about in great confusion."[25] On the right flank, at Plaisted's position, many horsemen scrambled through hatless, along with several horses, all coming "on in one stream of wild confusion."[26] Some of the infantrymen looked on with contempt at their disheveled brethren. One cavalryman, hatless and flustered, allegedly cried, "The Rebs are coming, I seen a lot of them and one of the bloody cusses shot right at me!"[27] But, to be sure, though, some bore the evidence of a hard fight. Colonel Samuel Spear, who had commanded Kautz's right wing and then supported Hall's guns to the bitter end, arrived with torn clothes, missing buttons, and sore ribs from a bullet that had glanced off some "obstacle" on his person.[28] He also lost three horses during the engagement, by one account.[29] Hall also made it back but was "so completely covered with mud that his most familiar acquaintances could hardly have recognized him."[30]

Near the Kell house, one cavalry unit remained intact. The 1st New York Mounted Rifles, posted south of the Johnson Farm, held together as Kautz's units flew rearward. But Colonel Sumner and Captain Cronin, who had observed the events from the small rise at the Kell house, found their own regiment in trouble. "It was soon discovered that the enemy's cavalry [Haskell's squad] had passed to my right and rear," wrote Sumner, "and they appeared in some force at Cox's house."[31] Sumner immediately sent word to Birney and quickly withdrew his men, reforming them in front of Terry's new infantry line as enemy fire filled the air.[32] The New York cavalrymen, armed with breech-loading repeating carbines, dismounted under the heavy fire and hopped into rifle pits scattered among stumps and recently felled trees on a low hill crest. Cronin cautioned his men to conserve their ammunition, believing his "chief duty was to prevent our men from exhausting their ammunition, the temptation of continually firing an easy breech-loading rifle being almost irresistible."[33]

"ready for an assault"

For Robert E. Lee, the morning's victory at Johnson's Farm was encouraging but not particularly remarkable. His troops had forged a promising start to his first real offensive in months. The attack had overwhelmed the first Union obstacle, but the ground along the Darbytown Road offered little value and, without tangible gains, the morning's success would ring hollow. Fort Harrison, the object of his plan, remained firmly in Union possession. In fact, many men and more than two miles of ground continued to separate Lee's strike force from this target.

The Confederates gathered for a new advance south. The two infantry divisions formed with Field on the left and Hoke on the right. Gary's cavalry brigade looked out for the extreme left, east of Field's line.[34] Though time was limited, the formation did not take shape immediately. South Carolinian James R. Hagood later puzzled over the reason for the pause.[35] It is possible the topography contributed. An anonymous correspondent to a Richmond paper wrote, "Immediately in the direct line of march lay an impassable bog and swamp, and on either side dense, rough, hilly woodland, so that considerable time elapsed before the division could pass these obstructions and get into position beyond ready for an assault."[36] To Hagood, the ground resembled the Wilderness west of Fredericksburg, crammed with small scrubby oaks, "so densely placed you could not see ten paces."[37] Regardless of its cause, the delay burned through precious minutes.[38]

Field's men prepared to pass through the same soggy ground Kautz had encountered in his embarrassing flight. Hoke's division gathered west of this topographical mess and faced over largely open, dry ground. Hoke would advance and attack simultaneously with Field's brigades.[39] At least that was what Field and his officers expected. In preparation for the movement, Field formed his men shoulder to shoulder, with Gregg's Texans on the far right, joined by Anderson's Georgians, then Bratton's South Carolinians, and finally Bowles's Alabamians on the left. Benning's brigade, under temporary command of Colonel Dudley DuBose, formed the division's reserve. Thus arrayed, Field's command proceeded toward Alfred Terry's Union line, pushing blue skirmishers back through the woods and across the swampy ground.[40] Hoke's division also began inching forward.

"like swarms of bees above our heads"

As the enemy crawled forward, Richard Jackson brought his Union batteries into action along the New Market Road. The guns of Battery D from the 1st U.S. Artillery poked through the embrasures and opened fire. Annoyed by this shelling, some of Field's men shifted east and descended into the trees and swamps in their path.[41] An hour after Jackson's guns opened, the Confederates finally picked their way through the boggy undergrowth and leaked out of the timber onto the Cox Farm. In front of the rebels, members of the 1st New York Mounted Rifles, screening the main federal line, peered from their rifle pits at the rebels. Captain Cronin, who shared one of the holes with Major Edgar A. Hamilton, pleaded with his men to fire deliberately and conserve their ammunition for the fight ahead. But their cartridge boxes lightened as the skirmishers "kept the whole front of the rebel army at bay."[42] As Cronin recalled, "The bullets came like swarms of bees above our heads. The enemy fired in regular discharges and noting the pauses between their firing, the major and I would spring up and shout to the men not to fire so fast, and the instant we saw the white puffs of smoke at the edge of the woods, we dropped in our pit and the hissing storm of lead would burst over us, chipping the earth from the top and sides of our shallow shelter and spinning away with a hum."[43]

Cronin's companion, Hamilton, was a tall man, and when he dodged and rolled into the rifle pit, the awkward maneuver injected some humor into an otherwise uncomfortable situation. The mirth did not last long. Through the din of battle, Cronin could hear the anguished cries of several comrades as rebel bullets hit home. Soon the New Yorkers received an order to retire. Taking advantage of a brief lull, they quickly sprinted away, soon reaching below the brow of the hill and safely out of the enemy's line of sight.[44]

The New York cavalrymen were not the only soldiers on the skirmish line. To the right, Lieutenant Colonel James Randlett had deployed about seventy-five members of the 3rd New Hampshire, one of Abbott's regiments.[45] Next to these men crouched two companies of the 11th Maine of Plaisted's brigade.[46] Randlett had arrived on the skirmish line with orders to hold back the enemy as long as possible. But his men found the Confederates determined to advance. "I discovered from the bristling bayonets of the enemy and his quiet yet exposed deportment that he was determined to advance," recalled Randlett.[47] He also found that the New Yorkers to his left had retired, leaving a gap, which he struggled to fill. Soon, the rapid fire of his men's carbines depleted their cartridges, and he sent word back for more ammunition. Abbott, his brigade commander, had no rounds to spare and instead sent seventy-five men from the 7th Connecticut to help. This infusion improved matters, but the Confederates, determined to push back the Union skirmish line, fixed bayonets and charged in two lines of battle. The gray mass overwhelmed the skirmishers, and Randlett's small force trickled back to the main line. Some Federals on the left, where the cavalry had been stationed, continued to engage the enemy at fifteen yards. Recognizing their plight, many destroyed their carbines and surrendered. Thirteen fell into enemy hands. Others, however, hid on their bellies under logs and hoped for the best.

Sumner, Randlett, and the others on the skirmish line had bought precious time for Birney's entire division. The New York cavalrymen, in particular, drew praise from a reporter, who noted they "displayed their valor and the efficiency of that particular arm of the service by manoeuvring before the enemy long enough for Gen. Birney to form his corps and get ready to meet the rebels, and then retired in good order."[48] The strong effort also made an impression on the Confederates. One rebel officer recalled that the skirmishers' heavy fire "shook up our advancing line of battle, which dropped men here & there all along." However, the rebel force "gathered itself & with fresh cheers & fresh impetus threw itself forward."[49]

The approach of the rebels sparked panic behind the main Union line. A jumbled collection of men and material choked the roads leading to the rear. Ambulances, baggage wagons, cooks with their pots and kettles, invalids, sutlers and their wares, and the usual shirkers all struggled rearward in anticipation of the assault.[50] To add to the confusion, the quartermaster and ammunition trains stood within range of the rebel artillery fire. "Teamsters lashed their mules and swore as only army teamsters can swear and the whole outfit made for the rear," recalled a New Hampshire soldier, "some even reaching Deep Bottom before they were checked."[51]

The flight helped clear the road but also had the unfortunate effect of dragging the Tenth Corps' ammunition train away from where it was most needed. The panic did not last, though, as Union officers stepped up and quickly quelled the stampede.[52]

"fairly rained iron on both sides"

In addition to the Confederate infantry preparing to storm across the Cox fields, a new threat emerged on the Union left. Confederate artillery, under the steady hand of Porter Alexander, arrived. With two battalions under his control, Alexander ventured south from the Darbytown Road, skirting the Richmond side of the old Confederate breastworks to the west of Field's line. The open country there allowed him to use a maneuver identified in the manuals as "fire advancing by half battery." In essence, he leapfrogged his guns across the open plain, with half of a battery standing and firing while the other advanced a short distance. The technique allowed the guns to maintain a constant fire on the Union positions while stepping forward all the while.[53] By about 9 A.M., the Confederate guns opened on Pond's brigade on the Union left. The rebels brought six 12-pounders and six rifled guns to bear against his batteries, according to one Union observer.[54]

The Union gunners replied. Cannon from two units, Battery C of the 3rd Rhode Island Artillery and Battery E of the 3rd U.S. Artillery, belched out from the trenches near the New Market Road. In addition to conventional cannon, Tenth Corps artillery chief Richard Jackson employed a pair of unusual weapons, two "Requa" guns commanded by Lieutenant Silas J. Truax of the 16th New York Artillery.[55] The Requa gun, manufactured by the Billinghurst Company beginning in 1861, had twenty-five .58 caliber barrels mounted in a row on top of a platform. The cartridge clips loaded the twenty-five rounds at the same time, and a percussion cap fired all barrels simultaneously. The gun, crewed by three men, could fire seven volleys per minute at a range of thirteen hundred yards. Despite these impressive specifications, the Requa gun did not see wide use during the war, perhaps because of its tendency to malfunction under wet conditions. It is not clear whether the gunners of the Army of the James held the weapon in high regard. Nevertheless, three years into the war, two of the guns were on hand at the fight along the New Market Road.[56]

The Union fire, "delivered slowly and efficiently," checked the Confederate progress and swept the ground to the Darbytown Road.[57] But Alexander rolled forward and eventually halted his batteries several hundred yards from the Union line on high ground at the Kell house.[58] For Union commanders, this would not do. Jackson scrambled to drive the enemy guns from the Kell house knoll, going as far as deploying one section of Battery D, 1st U.S. Artillery, out two hundred yards into a cornfield beyond the earthworks. Isolated and exposed, the section was roughly handled. Nevertheless, the guns continued to fire for some time. Eventually, though, the crews withdrew into the works, rolling one cannon by hand, pushing and pulling past the carcasses of battery horses scattered amid the corn.[59]

Amid the fray, Union combat artist William Waud rendered the scene from behind Jackson's guns. His sketch captured four cannon firing from their embrasures over abatis tangled in front of the works and several enemy guns returning fire in the distance near a small house. To the rear of the Union works, battery limbers, with full horse teams attached, backed up to the guns. To the right, Waud penciled infantrymen stooped behind the parapet waiting for the rebel attack.[60]

Waud's sketch did not capture everything, though. The concentration of so many guns fired at such close range yielded extraordinary violence. Lieutenant John Myrick's Battery E, 3rd U.S. Artillery, suffered heavily, losing three men killed and eight wounded, along with seventeen horses. One shell blew apart a limber from Myrick's battery, raising "a general hurrah along our line," recalled Alexander years later.[61] Myrick sent what was left of the gun and its equipment out of the fight and distributed the newly idle gunners to the other crews.[62] The Confederate shells killed or wounded about thirty horses. A *New York Times* reporter wrote that "it fairly rained iron on both sides." The intense fire forced General Birney's staff to move his headquarters.[63]

With the Confederate infantry attack imminent, Jackson sought to destroy Alexander's exposed guns or at least drive them away from the Kell house. He pulled three cannon of the 5th New Jersey battery out of works near the center and repositioned them closer to the left. The added weight swelled Jackson's force to the better part of four batteries, about twenty-four pieces.[64] His cannonade may have proved to be the tipping point. The Union crews peppered the rebel batteries, injuring so many horses that gunners had to drag some pieces away by hand.[65] "I am happy to say that his artillery fire was soon silenced," wrote Jackson in his official report the next day, "and that all the guns that could be brought to bear on his infantry were used with good effect."[66] Jackson now focused on the Confederate infantry headed for Terry's line. Years later, Porter Alexander would remember things differently. "I largely silenced the enemy's fire," he recalled. Perhaps his memory failed him, or perhaps he simply misread Jackson's efforts to greet the rebel infantry as a sign of Union defeat. Whatever the case, Alexander believed the Confederates were about to "smash" the enemy.[67]

"at double-quick and with a yell"

The Confederates had cause for optimism. To the left of Alexander's guns, Charles Field's infantry division pushed back the Union skirmishers and now bore down on Birney's hastily formed line along the New Market Road. Field, a native of

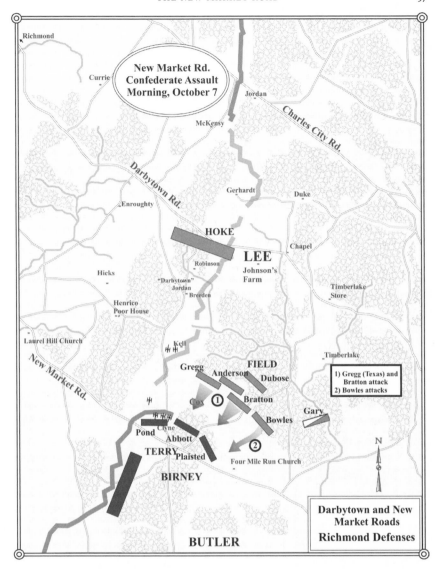

New Market Rd.
Confederate Assault
Morning, October 7

1) Gregg (Texas) and
   Bratton attack
2) Bowles attacks

Darbytown and New
Market Roads
Richmond Defenses

Kentucky and a graduate of West Point, had served throughout the war and had received a severe wound at Second Manassas. After becoming a major general in early 1864, he provided steady leadership throughout the Overland and Richmond campaigns.[68] Somewhere off to Field's right sat Robert F. Hoke's division, which had marched south across largely open fields. Hoke, a North Carolinian, had excelled early in the war. Generally considered modest, he possessed enough ambition to propel himself to major general and division command. The Tar Heel garnered praise for his victory at Plymouth, North Carolina, in April 1864. But once he rose to division command, his luster faded. At Cold Harbor, in June at

Petersburg, and during the fighting at Fort Harrison in late September, he played a conspicuous role in failed offensives. Several of these reverses involved joint operations with Charles Field, his fellow division commander, and, in the wake of one bungled attack, ill feelings simmered between the two.[69] On the morning of October 7, Hoke advanced his men under the fire of Jackson's guns. Field expected his fellow division commander would join him in the attack

Field's units had shouldered the lion's share of the attack against Kautz's outpost on Johnson's Farm. Many, no doubt, expected that Hoke's men would pitch in at the New Market Road. Field recalled that, "[Hoke,] I understood, was to assault simultaneously with me."[70] Counting on Hoke's support, Field ordered his men forward.[71] A Southerner described the scene:

> Gregg was at the head of his brigade. Anderson was in the midst of his troops gallantly cheering them on. Bratton, with his cool, sturdy nerve, was inspiring his South Carolinians with increased confidence by his own intrepid example. Colonel Bowls [sic] was bravely leading the Alabama brigade, and the intrepid Gary was at the head of his troopers. Regimental and line officers were at their posts, and those sturdy veterans of more than a score of battle fields were moving steadily forward, confident of success, if supported as promised. The roll of musketry, the booming of artillery and the screaming of shells were deafening.[72]

The Confederate attack approached the Union center about 9:30 A.M.[73] The bulk of Field's assault steered toward Abbott's brigade, which contained two Connecticut regiments, two New Hampshire regiments, and seven companies of the 16th New York Heavy Artillery (fighting as infantry).[74] This unit, a "fighting brigade," according to one description, crouched hidden behind a slight rise covered with recently cut trees."[75] Field's line also headed for a portion of Plaisted's brigade, farther on the Union right. A member of the 11th Maine recalled that the rebel assault rolled through the thick trees. The federals held their fire until the skirmishers could clear the way to open up on "the shrieking, dingy lines of the enemy within short file range."[76] The Confederates lunged forward "at double-quick and with a yell," not bothering to deploy skirmishers.[77] Without a screen in their front, they stumbled well within reach of the federal rifles before any shots were fired. The Union men remained patient. The entire line stayed low and waited until the Confederates approached within fifty yards.[78]

"grave work of butchery"

The trap sprang. From short range, only a few dozen yards in some places, the U.S. troops rose with a shout and unleashed a staggering volley.[79] In the middle of Abbott's line, the 16th New York Heavy Artillery opened on Bratton's brigade after "laying quiet in the dark woods." The gray coats absorbed the first fusillade and closed within thirty yards.[80] According to one New Yorker, the Confederates reached "within fifteen yards, when a rebel captain, planting his colors in the ground, shouted, 'Now, you d—d Yankees, there is our flag; we will fight for it.'" The captain fell immediately with a bullet in his eye.[81] The Union fire brought Bratton's brigade to a sudden halt. Every man hit the ground, seeking cover from the "leaden storm which roared through the woods."[82]

With the initial Union volley, the promise of rebel success flickered. Heavy fire rocked the Confederates back and revealed a problem in Field's battle line. Though the division attacked on a four-brigade front, the units did not share the burden equally. According to some accounts, Anderson's Georgia brigade, nestled between Bratton and Gregg, did not shoulder its load. Bratton recalled that the Georgians "did not come up, and the enemy in its front poured its fire into me."[83] To the Texans on the far right, Anderson's failure was conspicuous. The Georgians "failed to advance and . . . disgraced themselves," wrote Joe Joskins of the 5th Texas.[84] In addition, the Alabama brigade on the left drifted south of the federal flank and missed the initial attack altogether. Accordingly, only two of Field's five brigades, Bratton's South Carolinians and Gregg's Texans, carried the weight of the first assault. Contemporary inspection reports indicate that Field's division mustered about 4,000 men in early October. But it appears only half this number engaged the Union line. Bratton's South Carolinians probably numbered about 1,300 or perhaps fewer. A September inspection report for the Texas brigade showed 609 men present for duty. These figures suggest that Charles Field's attack brought fewer than 2,000 muskets to bear.[85] By contrast, Alfred Terry's Union division faced Field's attacking force with more than 3,000 men.[86]

Those Confederates who made it to the firing line did not hold back. At the center, fewer than one hundred yards separated the foes.[87] "The woods were filled with a continuous roar of musketry and the grave work of butchery was going on with marked rapidity," wrote reporter Thomas Cook.[88] The combat resembled the war's earlier battles, in which the participants faced across open ground and loaded and fired until one side broke. By late 1864, such duels were unusual. During the Virginia campaign that year, soldiers had dug trenches without prompting. As a result, when fighting broke out, at least one side usually fired from cover. Along the New Market Road on October 7, however, the men had little protection along many parts of the line. Abbott's men and, in all likelihood, most of Plaisted's force had no time to dig adequate trenches. The relatively flat ground, covered in places by trees, offered no obvious advantage to either side. Along the battle line, where comparable numbers faced off, it looked to be a fair fight except for one important factor, the Spencer rifle.

The Spencer predated the war. Its introduction to combat, however, had been a slow one. Issued in both a rifle and a carbine model, the weapon carried seven rounds housed in a tube embedded in its base. A lever expelled used cartridges and loaded fresh rounds into the magazine. Compared to the muzzle-loading rifles carried by most Confederates and many Union infantrymen, the Spencer performed better in most respects. Alfred Pleasonton, who analyzed the rifle early in the war, concluded that the Spencer was "simple and compact in construction and less liable to get out of order than any other breech-loading arm now in use."[89] Soldiers experienced with the Spencer could fire a round every three to four seconds.[90] Most of Abbott's regiments carried these weapons, including the 7th Connecticut, 7th New Hampshire, 6th Connecticut, and 3rd New Hampshire regiments.[91]

The gunfire from the Union battle line at the New Market Road overwhelmed the Confederates. On Field's left, Bratton's South Carolina brigade hit the Union formation near its right flank, where it bent back slightly to the rear. This brought some Carolinians closer to the enemy rifles than others.[92] One Union veteran recalled that fire from the seven-shooters split the air. "Seven volleys in one," he wrote, "Flesh and blood could not stand such a cyclone of lead; and the rebels stopped broke and fell back to cover, leaving the woods piled with their dead and dying."[93] From behind Terry's formation, David Cronin of the 1st New York Mounted Rifles noted that the repeaters went off "with a noise like appalling peals of thunder."[94]

Much of this Union storm hit the Texas brigade at the right of Field's line. As a unit, the Texans did not stand out for their good discipline. One inspector explained, "The discipline as it has been enforced in the Texas Brigade, so far as keeping the command together in camp and on the march, preventing the destruction of public and private property, maneuvering in face of the enemy, and under fire and engaging enemy, are concerned has seemed to meet with necessities of the service. But not withstanding that much good, there is neglect of specialities and precision."[95]

Though the brigade may not have been the choice for a parade competition, it generally fought with unsurpassed intensity. In approaching the New Market Road, the Texans traversed difficult ground crowded with felled trees whose branches poked at their "eyes, faces, bodies, and clothing."[96] As the men navigated the obstacles, bullets smacked into the logs and stumps. Some men reached within thirty paces of the enemy only to be "pinned down and either captured or shot." Still others became "hopelessly tangled in the abatis," exposed to the federal sharpshooters and artillery. The balance of the brigade simply withdrew toward the woods. Some sought cover in a low spot about three hundred yards in front of the Union line.[97] A few hundred of the Lone Star soldiers remained standing, and, according to the recollection of one Unionist, many "threw up their caps and handkerchiefs, as if offering to surrender."[98] However, not all did so; many continued their fire, erasing any hope for a peaceful end to the ordeal.

The commander of the Texas brigade, Brigadier General John Gregg, accompanied his men in the attack. An Alabama native who had adopted Texas as his home, Gregg strongly advocated secession before the war and did not shirk from the clash he helped bring about.[99] He may have sensed rough work for Friday. The night before, he drafted careful directions for the management of his affairs, in case of his absence.[100] During the attack at the New Market Road, he advanced with his command and led it into the battle.[101] In the thick of the fight, a Union bullet found his neck, knocking him to the ground and killing him instantly. His "body lay sprawled in a pool of blood" about one hundred yards from the Union line.[102] When the Texans withdrew, they left their leader's lifeless form. Brigade command devolved to Colonel Frederick Bass. Captain John Kerr, from Gregg's staff, calmly walked along the line and informed the head of the 4th Texas, Colonel Clinton Winkler, of Gregg's fate. A moment later, Kerr returned and reported, "Bass is wounded; you must take command." Winkler pulled the brigade back and ordered his men to reform in a shallow depression to the rear.[103] Another member of Gregg's staff, Lieutenant John I. Shotwell, received permission to retrieve the general's body lying between the opposing forces.[104] Shotwell, with three other men, crawled forward, rolled Gregg's body in a blanket, and carried it safely to the rear.[105]

To the left of the Texans, Bratton's South Carolinians confronted their own trial. Added to the Spencers, Bratton faced fire from the 16th New York Heavy Artillery at the middle of Abbott's line. These New Yorkers held Enfield rifles, a reliable but conventional muzzle loader which lacked the Spencer's impressive firing rate.[106] According to one account, the rebels carefully surveyed the line and chose the 16th as the point of attack.[107] Whether that was true or not, the Confederates appeared before the New York regiment in force.[108] Union major Frederick W. Prince calmly cheered on his New Yorkers as they stood firm in line, even as many dropped, wounded or killed.[109] On either side, Union regiments armed with Spencers easily held their own and added their power to Prince's rifles. South Carolinian John Bratton noted the reduced Union strength in the middle of the line. "The fire was not near so heavy as on the right," he wrote, but "the storm of lead" poured from other sections of the Union line. The bullets continued to fly, but most shots ranged high, and Bratton's loss was "less than [he] feared it would be."[110] The Confederates persisted for half an hour. According to a New Hampshire soldier, the Confederates in front of the Enfield-wielding New Yorkers fell back once they began receiving enfilade fire from the Spencers.[111]

The Confederate attack also engaged Plaisted's brigade on the Union right. Here, other regiments in Bratton's formation also proceeded without skirmishers and eventually neared the 11th Maine and the 24th Massachusetts. One Massachusetts soldier recalled, "We opened at less than 75 yards, and down went the Johnies in rows, back they kited perfectly panic stricken leaving the dead and numbers of the wounded in our possession."[112] The rebel line did not stand for long; it reeled back under the convincing bark of the Spencer rifles.[113] "The repulse was complete and severe," concluded Plaisted.[114] On the right, tucked back near the New Market Road, the members of the 10th Connecticut could hear the roar of the fight in the Union center. The noise from Plaisted's brigade "was beyond anything I ever heard," recalled a Connecticut soldier. The rate of fire was tremendous. "We knew that," he continued, "as always, nine shots out of ten must be wasted. Yet, as it afterward proved, that tenth shot did fearful execution."[115]

Though the Spencers dominated the firing line, the marvelous weapon's best attribute also proved to be its Achilles' heel. If handled improperly, the rifle simply consumed too much ammunition. The Confederates' push forced Abbott's regiments to fire many rounds. The Spencer had performed perhaps too well. While the rapid fire was impressive, an empty weapon could not halt Confederate attacks. To avoid catastrophe, Ferd Davis of the 7th New Hampshire sought to hurry more cartridges forward. He came across General Terry, who was already keenly aware of the shortage. "Not more than five minutes could have elapsed," wrote Davis, "before I saw men running to the front with boxes of much needed ammunition." Davis believed that an additional line of the enemy would have driven the Union men from their position.[116] But no such support appeared.

The weight of metal from the new cartridges crushed the South Carolinians and Texans. The federal soldiers "cooly continued the work of destruction upon the shattered and retreating rebels, literally covering the ground with dead and wounded," wrote a New York Times correspondent.[117] The Confederates eventually retreated in confusion and with heavy loss.[118] In front of Abbott's brigade at the Union center, the Confederates broke "into complete disorder," fleeing "wildly back" under the continuous Union fire. The main attack sputtered to a halt. The Texans and South Carolinians were spent. One diarist reported that the Texas brigade "was pretty well used up."[119] The center of Field's line shrunk back.

But there was still hope for the rebels on the left. There the Alabama brigade and parts of Bratton's command continued to work around the woods on the Union right, in the direction of Four Mile Run Church. The Alabamians escaped Bratton's notice, however, for, after the fight, he reported that "the brigade on my left fell back and entirely out of the contest."[120] But accounts suggest the Alabamians did press the attack. Union scouts reported to Plaisted that the enemy "was forming in the field" out on the extreme right, five hundred yards in front of Plaisted's regiments, waiting patiently on the very end of Birney's line.[121] Alarmed, Plaisted pulled forty men from the 11th Maine and placed them to the right of the 100th New York at the extreme end. The soldiers from Maine and New York spread into dense woods that framed a narrow path leading from Four Mile Run Church toward the Cox plantation.[122]

The Alabama brigade edged through the pines in front of the 10th Connecticut and 100th New York on the Union right. "A rattling volley in our own front showed that the skirmishers were engaged," wrote Major Henry Ward Camp of the 10th Connecticut.[123] Camp and his men held their fire as skirmishers scampered back from their forward positions. The Confederates nipped at the skirmishers' heels.

"One poor fellow staggered toward where I stood, the blood pouring down his face from a wound just received," witnessed Camp. Peering into the trees, Camp discerned the rebel feet beneath low foliage. Soon, Confederate bullets zipped from the woods. With a few of their own pickets still hurrying back to the line, the Federals could wait no longer and pulled their triggers. At least one wounded federal skirmisher did not clear the ground and became the first victim of the volley.[124] The Confederates returned the fire, and the combat began in earnest. The tiny 10th Connecticut, with only one hundred men in line, resembled a company more than a regiment. Nevertheless, these men did not budge. A Maine veteran who stood nearby recalled, "I can see the 10th now as it stood on our immediate right, every man of it fighting with impetuous vigor to protect our flank."[125] "Each man stood fast," he added. "Where a comrade fell they gave him room to lie, no more. There was no random firing in the air, but rapid loading, cool aim, and shots that told."[126] Farther to the right, however, conditions were different.

The 100th New York protected the crucial Union right flank on the New Market Road. This sector's collapse would open the door to Birney's rear and possibly unhinge the entire position. Though veterans, the New Yorkers had nearly completed their service. Many of these short-timers manned the picket line, and, when the rebel attackers bore down, they tumbled back, causing "disorder."[127] According to the regiment's commander, the flight caused "some confusion," but the officers "instantly rallied" the fugitives, and the danger abated.[128] But other observers saw it differently. Colonel John Otis of the 10th Connecticut reported that the "skirmishers in our front came in on the run without making the least resistance, and the regiment on our right, following the example, broke and ran in confusion—not an officer or man remaining on the field."[129]

While the 100th New York wavered and exposed the vital right flank, the tiny 10th Connecticut remained steadfast in the face of the panic. The Connecticut men gave a loud cheer "just to show the enemy they had no thought of giving ground, then turn[ed] steadily to their work."[130] Brigade commander Plaisted noted that the 10th Connecticut stood in line like a "wall of granite."[131] The Confederates, Bowles's Alabamians and Bratton's South Carolinians, also continued to fight. At one point, the rebels broke, but officers urged them back into line. In the end, though, the attack could not last. The Confederates crumbled into confusion and fell back for the last time, leaving their dead and wounded.[132] The Union right had held.

The Confederates tested Alfred Terry's line elsewhere after the initial assault failed. A portion of Field's division, perhaps members of the Texas brigade, probed the Union left near the Clyne house, where Jackson's artillery and Pond's brigade waited behind the earthworks. The Confederates "were driven back, much cut up, though a few of them succeeded in getting inside the breastworks, never to return," according to a Northern reporter.[133] Back at the center, Field's brigade commanders had seen enough. In the midst of the combat, a bullet or shell fragment hit Bratton's left shoulder. His men brought him off the field. He would convalesce for over a month.[134] With Bratton and Gregg down and the attack clearly faltering, Charles Field ordered Dudley DuBose's Georgia brigade up from its reserve position. "Amidst the smoke of battle, the whiz of minnies and the crash of shells, [DuBose's] tall form was seen in double quick, moving to the assault." But the attack had already failed before he came near the crest.[135] Field's troops pulled away from the Union battle line. "Falling back under protection of the hill, the division was rallied and the line re-formed. After a lapse of a few hours, the division was quietly withdrawn to the Darbytown Road."[136] Field's attack ended with his division reduced to tatters. On the right, Robert Hoke's division did not advance. On the battlefield, Robert E. Lee could only observe as his offensive yielded to the surprising effectiveness of the Union Army of the James.

"I am Shot Through Both Arms, General"

As the fighting at the New Market Road wound down, a teenager stumbled back from the maelstrom in Field's front, his gray uniform stained with blood and his arms hanging uselessly by his sides. The youngster looked up to see Robert E. Lee standing with First Corps chief Richard Anderson and several staff officers. The soldier pleaded, "General! If you don't send some more men down there our boys will get hurt sure." When Lee asked the young man about the nature of his wounds, the reply was "I am shot through both arms, General; but I don't mind that General! I want you to send some more men down there to help our boys." Lee asked a staffer to help the wounded man but declined to feed more troops into the failed operation.[137]

The Confederate brigades withdrew north toward the Darbytown Road, leaving the battle's wreckage in their wake. As some members of Field's division limped back north, Union pickets, who had secreted themselves under the logs and branches during the initial assault, emerged from their hiding places and gobbled the exhausted rebels. New Hampshire riflemen from Abbott's brigade captured thirty-one unlucky souls.[138] Private Philip Francis, of the 3rd New Hampshire, crawled out from cover, brandished his carbine, and captured three men single-handedly.[139]

Along the New Market Road, Union reinforcements arrived, including two New York regiments (the 112th and 142nd) to protect the right flank.[140] "Just as our victory was assured," reflected a Maine veteran, "reenforcements came up on the road on the double-quick to protect our extreme right. Panting and exhausted as they were by their efforts to reach us in time to be of service, they had breath enough left to give hearty cheers for our stand-up victory."[141] The New Yorkers deployed on the right flank, but, instead of fighting more, they attended to the grim business of burial. The chaplain of the 10th Connecticut, Henry Clay Trumbull, oversaw the interment of the unit's fallen.[142] Only an hour before, the "fighting chaplain," revolver in hand, had helped to hold the regimental line.[143] But now he attended to his spiritual duties and "the sound of prayer mingled with the echoes of artillery and musketry and the crash of falling pines for hastily constructed breast-works."[144] In the center, the Enfield-bearing New Yorkers of the 16th Heavy Artillery used cups, plates, and bayonets to improve their defenses and bury their dead.[145]

The Unionists suffered substantial losses. Abbott's brigade counted 136 casualties, the largest share coming from the 16th New York Heavies.[146] On the flanks, the damage was less severe. Plaisted tallied 5 killed and 35 wounded on the right, and Pond suffered 32 casualties on the left.[147] Confederate losses offered a different story. The rebel bodies lay scattered along the ground in front of Plaisted and Abbott's brigade. On the Union right after the battle, federal skirmishers found the dead and dying from the Alabama and South Carolina brigades.[148] Bratton's South Carolinians alone lost 190 in killed and wounded, a relatively large sum considering 1,459 officers and men were present for duty at a recent inspection.[149] One report counted 90 casualties for the Palmetto Sharpshooters alone.[150] Another recorded the loss for Anderson's Georgia brigade at 71.[151] The results from the Texas brigade were also harsh. One member of the unit estimated a loss of at least 200 out of the 450 men that entered the fight. Another source pegged the number at 119.[152] Only 411 Texans attended the monthly inspection several weeks later, significantly down from the 609 men and officers present for duty in an earlier report.[153]

Estimates for Lee's total loss for the day vary. With no official tally available, one newspaper reported 350 killed, wounded, or captured.[154] Another source suggested 500 casualties.[155] Benjamin Butler, in a note to Meade, put the number at 1,000 Confederate casualties and 150 prisoners and deserters.[156] The "missing" soldiers might have included demoralized rebels who had taken advantage of the tangled terrain and battle confusion to end their service in Lee's army. Some Confederates captured after the battle said the woods were full of their comrades hoping to surrender but fearing retaliation from the USCT.[157]

"After all was quiet"

By 11:15 A.M., David Birney reported to Butler that the repulse had been achieved "with great slaughter" and that the rebels appeared to be entrenching along the Darbytown Road.[158] He also suggested that Pickett's division had joined Field in the attack. Butler suspected that Lee was not finished and warned of a possible assault near Fort Harrison. But nothing developed in that sector except for some vigorous Confederate shelling.[159] Butler, hoping to do more than absorb the enemy's blows, sought to take the fight to the Confederates. "They may be on the move to get to our right," he wrote Birney, "if so, I think we may send two divisions after them and get between them and their base."[160] Less than an hour later, he asked Birney to consider a strike around the enemy's flank beyond the Darbytown Road. Birney replied that he would "try them at once."[161]

Thus, by Friday evening, Terry's division, along with Colonel Martin Curtis's brigade from the second division, had pressed north and reoccupied Johnson's Farm and other ground along the Darbytown Road. Curtis's men took the point of the advance. "After all was quiet, Gen. Terry thought, I suppose, as we didn't belong to his division we might as well do the hard work," wrote one perturbed New Yorker, "so he advanced our Brigade in front of his line and moved us forward through woods and fields, where the enemy were supposed to be, without protecting either flank."[162] But Abbott's brigade, which had received the brunt of the rebel attack in the morning, supported Curtis. Abbott sent ahead the 6th and 7th Connecticut to the Darbytown Road but found no sign of the enemy.

The Confederates had recoiled with no further fighting. Birney spread Terry's division across the Darbytown Road and pushed out a strong skirmish line.[163] Field's and Hoke's divisions, along with Alexander's artillery, withdrew to the west of Cornelius Creek, and Gary's cavalry brigade guarded the Charles City Road.[164] In short, the Confederates returned to their starting point. Butler and his officers had erased all of Lee's gains.

Saturday's daylight revealed the battle's bloody work. Parties of Union soldiers scoured the woods searching for wounded and the dead. David Cronin, from the 1st New York Mounted Rifles, found the "ground in front of our lines" strewn with the enemy corpses. In a grove of shattered pines, he discovered a soldier resting on his knees with both hands on his musket. A closer inspection revealed a "ragged bullet hole" in his skull and a slight touch sent the dead man rolling onto the ground. Elsewhere, Cronin found numerous shallow rifle pits etched out by the Confederates, "often composed of only a few rails with a little heap of dirt thrown around them, barely sufficient to protect men lying down." At the Kell house, where he had lounged the previous morning before the attack, he found that the rebel artillery crews had dug individual holes "to protect the gunners during intervals of firing." "In our army it was quite otherwise," he observed, "reckless exposure was the rule." Continuing to the Johnson house, he viewed "numbers of Union dead stripped of their clothing, except their blue pantaloons, and laid out by the enemy, in rows."[165]

In Washington, Grant followed developments by telegraph. To keep the enemy occupied at Petersburg, he ordered Meade to make demonstrations on the left the next morning to distract the Confederates and prevent "any concentration north of the James River."[166] Like Butler, Grant suspected that Lee had further plans for the north side. In response to Grant's directive, Meade's probes on Saturday, the 8th, south of Petersburg generated sporadic fighting along a wide front. Troops from two Union corps, the Ninth and the Fifth, clashed with A. P. Hill's Third Corps divisions. Ninth Corps troops drove a rebel working party from an un-completed work on the Church Road and dislodged rebel sharpshooters from the Hawks and Smith houses west of the Union lines. To the north, Fifth Corps units ventured forward and destroyed the buildings on the W. W. Davis farm, which had served as nests for rebel sharpshooters. The fighting yielded no dramatic re-sults. However, a Ninth Corps diarist noted that the movement helped to establish a "new and advanced picket line."[167] On Sunday, General Grant returned from Washington to find relative quiet north and south of Petersburg.[168]

"choice clusters of flowers"

Back on the north side of the James, the Union defenders expressed pride at re-pulsing such a large enemy force on the New Market Road.[169] "We won it without the protecting works so necessary to break the headlong impetus of an assaulting force," recalled a veteran of the 11th Maine.[170] The men who endured the engage-ments at Johnson's Farm and the New Market Road also noted the battle's feroc-ity.[171] An Alabama soldier wrote home to suggest that First Manassas ranked as a mere skirmish by comparison. Earlier in the war, he said, men would spend months analyzing a particular battle; by October 1864, however, soldiers would discuss a fight around the campfire that night and perhaps read accounts in the papers, but no more would be said of the event after that.[172]

For Tenth Corps commander David Bell Birney, the affair qualified as a re-sounding success. Under Butler's urging, he had acted quickly and decisively to deploy Terry's division at the point of danger. He had remained with his troops for most of the day. For almost an hour during the morning, he rode up and down the line under fire with his full staff, four riders abreast, only stopping once or twice to rest beneath a brush shelter.[173] By afternoon, though, his illness had worsened, and he became entirely exhausted. Unable to remain in the saddle, he climbed into an ambulance.[174] By the evening, his fever had increased. Ignoring the pleas of his friends and the advice of his doctors, he refused to apply for leave while his corps faced the prospect of battle.[175] Over the next two days, his condition continued to decline, and, on October 9, Butler ordered him home without further delay.[176] In one of his last acts with the army, Birney urged August Kautz to construct "a good strong corduroy road, wide and ample, from Doctor Johnson's house to my right flank."[177] That evening, Birney transferred command of the Tenth Corps to Alfred Terry and on Monday morning boarded a fast steamer to Baltimore, reaching his house in Philadelphia the next day.[178] But home brought no improvement. Despite his condition, he managed to vote in the state elections that week.[179] On the 15th, Birney's aide-de-camp reported to Butler that the General's malarious fever was "at its height and is accompanied by bad dysentery which completely prostrates and weakens him."[180] On October 18, David Birney's life slipped away. The funeral services were held at his house on Race Street three days later where his body, displayed for mourners, "presented a most natural and lifelike appearance . . . clad in full uniform, and surrounded by choice clusters of flowers."[181] Many fellow soldiers, including generals Daniel Sickles and George Cadwalader, gathered around his coffin to bid farewell to their friend and comrade.[182]

"a great deal of humiliation"

While the declining Birney reaped praise, August Kautz drew criticism. Although the collapse of his command at Johnson's Farm was regretttable, the conspicuous rout of his troopers, racing broken and disorganized through the infantrymen along the New Market Road, was mortifying. Thomas Cook of the *New York Herald* took the lead, writing that the "rout and stampede of Kautz's cavalry was a disgraceful affair" and had threatened the safety of the entire Union position.[183] The well-sourced *Army and Navy Journal* piled on, informing its readers that Kautz and his officers had not prepared for the attack and could not halt the "utter stampede" of their troops, who "broke in a perfect rout, streaming over the country to the rear with little organization." The *Journal* suggested the size of the attacking force furnished "some excuse" for the cavalry's behavior, but the rapidity of the collapse and the disorganization of the retreat ranked with the other cavalry defeats that summer.[184]

Predictably, the criticism displeased Kautz. In his mind, the affair unraveled as it did through a lack of entrenching tools and Benjamin Butler's inflexible directive to hold a weak position against a superior enemy. "We received no credit for hanging on until the last moment," he complained, noting that his men "had to stand a great deal of humiliation" for about a week after the battle.[185] Some defended Kautz. The *Army and Navy Journal,* which also served as forum for intra-army squabbling, carried a letter from "T." seeking to "correct many errors made by those who were not eyewitnesses of the affair."[186] The correspondent complained that observers had been unreasonable to expect a small, poorly entrenched force of cavalry to hold against eight or nine enemy infantry brigades.[187] A correspondent for the *New York Times* also reported that the cavalry "fought bravely, standing up to their work for more than an hour, until they found that the enemy not only was in front of them and at the right, but also had got a strong force in their rear."[188]

Benjamin Butler appeared relatively unconcerned with the affair. After the fight, Kautz reminded him of the problems predicted with the Johnson Farm position, particularly the swampy line of retreat. When Kautz fretted about the loss of the cannon under his command, Butler snapped back, "What's a gun? You gentlemen of the regular service attach altogether too much importance to the loss of a gun. The money value of a gun is about $3,000. The value of a soldier, with all the Government and local bounties, is about $1,500, and a gun is therefore only equal to two soldiers. Now if you lose two soldiers killed, you may or may not mention it, but if you lose a gun you are brokenhearted."[189] Later, Butler teased Kautz about his performance. Sensing the anger in his subordinate, he extended a dinner invitation and devoted "several hours to smoothing the fur he had rubbed the wrong way."[190] At the meal, he announced that he had recommended Kautz for a brevet promotion. In later years, Kautz speculated that Butler made the gesture on the spot to mollify the ill feeling generated earlier that day.[191] In reality, though, Butler had forwarded his recommendation to Washington on October 6, the day before Kautz's performance at the Darbytown Road.[192]

"the spoils of this brilliant fighting"

Lee injected a positive tone about the failed offensive in his reports to Richmond. He declined to provide much detail other than to note that Confederate forces had driven the enemy to the New Market Road. He emphasized the capture of arms, equipment, and men and only briefly mentioned the cost of the venture, saying simply, "Our loss is said to be small." In another note the next day, he provided more specifics about the Confederate gains, pointing to the capture of "9 guns, 10 caissons, 2 stand of colors, about 100 horses, over 100 prisoners, a large number of entrenching tools, and a quantity of forage." But he omitted any mention of the dear price paid for this limited benefit.[193] Some members of the Southern press shared his rose-colored interpretation. The *Richmond Enquirer* described the results this way: "Having secured the spoils of this brilliant fighting maneuvre our new lines were modeled to command the position which necessitated the withdrawal of our troops to within a mile and a half of our original lines."[194]

While some Confederates looked for silver linings, others acknowledged the defeat. In South Carolina, editors at the *Columbia Daily* suggested that Lee's failures occurred because the men had fought behind breastworks for too long, and too many Confederate commanders had died or become incapacitated.[195] However, with Lee directly supervising and the likes of Gregg and Bratton present at the Darbytown Road battle, lack of leadership seems an unlikely culprit. And, though a certain rational timidity may have contributed, the performance of Union troops had more to do with the results than Confederate missteps. Combining technological innovation with sound tactical decision making, the Union commanders, including Birney, Terry, Plaisted, and Abbott, simply stopped the Confederate advance. The Spencer repeating rifle demonstrated its worth, giving the U.S. troops a rate of fire several times greater than that of their rebel counterparts. In the end, the Union commanders' only real concern was whether their ammunition would last.

"approved for his caution"

The October 7 battle also generated discord between two of Lee's key commanders. Long after the fight, Field remained bitter that Hoke did not participate in the attack at the New Market Road, and he continued to grumble beyond the war's end.[196] Years later, Martin Gary noted the ill feeling among Field's subordinates who complained that Hoke had been "derelict" at the Darbytown Road.[197] Colonel James R. Hagood, who led the 1st South Carolina Regiment in Bratton's brigade, confirmed this opinion in his postwar memoirs.[198] Field himself raised the issue after the war, writing that "Hoke, for some unexplained cause, did not move forward. The consequence was that the whole fire was concentrated on my fellows."[199] A particularly inflammatory account of Hoke's conduct appeared in North Carolina papers soon after the fight. The *Raleigh Confederate* printed an allegation that Hoke had actually refused to carry out the attack. According to the anonymous source, Hoke had said to gunner Porter Alexander that "he would fight no more."[200] The serious charge made its way into other publications. In response, a source friendly to the general fired back in the same paper several days later explaining, "Gen. Hoke had orders to have his division in position and form a portion of the attacking force at the hour named. He did so; but the other force which was to have acted with him, had anticipated the time . . . had gone in and suffered repulse. To have put his division in under the circumstances, would not have been in obedience to orders, and would have subjected it to a like fate. We have reason to believe that Gen. Hoke was approved for his caution."[201]

This writer not only sought to exonerate Hoke but also managed to cast blame on Field for moving too early. Another account supports the counterclaim. According to one veteran, a brigade in Field's division mistook an order to advance for an order to attack and precipitated an ill-timed charge for the entire division while Hoke waited for the appointed time.[202] In any case, questions about Hoke's performance persisted well after the battle. Porter Alexander speculated that Hoke may not have pressed forward because the ground in his front was "more exposed & wider than Field's."[203] Similarly, Richard Jackson, the Union artillery commander, specifically claimed to have kept "Hoke's division . . . from moving forward to assist the assault of the enemy."[204] Perhaps the heavy artillery fire belching from the works at the New Market Road prevented Hoke from getting underway. The official diary of the Confederate First Corps mentions obliquely, "Hoke cannot get at the enemy out of his trenches and does not move."[205]

Considering these bits of information, it seems likely that Hoke operated under Lee's direction or at least with his consent. In fact, several accounts place Lee directly on the field. Richard Anderson, the First Corps commander, reported that Lee "had in person conducted the attack."[206] After the war, Johnson Hagood recalled that Lee stayed "with the reserve during most of the day, and just before and during the last assault he was with" Hoke's division.[207] The accounts suggest that Lee may have directly ordered Hoke to hold off his advance. Johnson Hagood speculated that Lee wanted to guard the approaches to Richmond and that Hoke's division was the only substantial Confederate force between Butler's army and the capital. The commitment of Hoke's division to the attack would have left that avenue open and vulnerable.[208]

In conducting military operations, Lee typically employed a decentralized command style and avoided detailed, written orders. He did not maintain an extensive professional staff to communicate important directives and ensure their implementation, at least for matters on the battlefield.[209] In contrast, Union General George Meade, used his chief of staff, Andrew Humphreys, and senior engineers extensively to plan operations in detail. Lee worked differently. He tended to prefer broad brushes and trust his subordinates to implement his general plans.[210] His personal staff was small, generally consisting of a few junior officers, who mostly focused on administrative work at his headquarters. Though Lee gradually formed a small general staff that attended to supply, ordnance, and similar matters, he never developed a cadre of officers dedicated to operational planning and battlefield coordination.[211]

The confusion and bitterness generated by the October 7 action suggests that, perhaps, Lee's approach to command did not help matters that day. Even after the battle, key participants remained ignorant of the operation's details. Porter Alexander, who commanded the artillery during battle, noted long after the war that "Hoke's line on his right never moved. I never knew why."[212] Field, as discussed before, remained baffled and embittered by Hoke's inaction. An anonymous correspondent to the *Richmond Enquirer* wrote, "For some reason, Gen. Hoke never attacked. I do not speak this in censure of him; because I do not know the reasons of his failure. I allude to it as a misfortune and disappointment to the division that did attack. Had he assaulted vigorously, as was expected, the works, in all probability, would have been carried, and the enemy forced to abandon Fort Harrison."[213] These accounts suggest that little or no communication occurred even after the battle. Field's lingering confusion suggests that the officers on the field may have not shared a common understanding. Perhaps parts of the plan—Hoke's role, for example—changed during the fight. If so, such information, whether from Lee or from his staffers, did not reach Field either during or after the operation. In the end, most participants may have just moved on to the next challenge, seeing no need to dwell on the offensive's failure and dissect its causes. Nevertheless, key commanders simply never knew what had happened on the battlefield that day.

"The gallant deceased"

The offensive had begun with such promise for Lee. He had managed to maneuver two veteran divisions onto the enemy's exposed flank, creating a chance to meet the enemy in the open. He constantly looked for opportunities to free his forces from their trenches and strike the enemy. On October 7, he managed to do just that. However, the poor results underscored his difficulties in achieving positive results under even seemingly favorable conditions. It is unclear whether he could have done more. After the war, Johnson Hagood suggested that Hoke could have shifted into Field's position, freeing Field to move farther around Birney's right flank and into the Union rear.[214] However, the deeper Lee drove beyond the Union right, the weaker the Confederate center became. In the days following Fort Harrison's capture, Butler had demonstrated a fervent desire to push the offensive. With only one division directly confronting Lee's attack, he had many other units available for a devastating counterattack to cut Hoke and Field off from Richmond. Accordingly, even though Lee had managed to confront Union forces on relatively open ground along the New Market Road, the Union numbers generated slim odds for Lee and his offensive. He was willing to take risks even where the possibility of success was remote.

According to a rumor recorded in the diary of a Confederate official, Lee complained to his staffer Colonel Robert Chilton afterward that, without additional men, "all that is left for us is to make peace on the best terms we can."[215] Whether or not he actually uttered these words, the New Market Road fight must have been deeply discouraging to him. Whatever the "could have beens," the results brought him no closer to reversing the losses of Grant's fifth offensive. Fort Harrison remained firmly in Union hands. The open battlefields of 1862 had become a distant memory. Lee's shock troops had lost their punch, and the unsung soldiers in Butler's army had achieved more success. For Robert E. Lee, the battle would mark one of his last attempts to launch a substantial offensive aimed at achieving significant gains.[216] For the Confederate army, the battle yielded another loss in a long string of exhausting engagements that further depleted its thin ranks. In fact, Lee had no realistic path to success in Virginia absent a favorable result from the presidential election.

But the election was weeks away, and, in Richmond, many were focused on more immediate concerns. On Saturday, the 8th, Confederate Postmaster General John H. Reagan escorted the body of his personal friend John Gregg into Richmond.[217] There, an undertaker placed Gregg's remains in a metallic burial case and dressed his body "in the uniform in which the gallant deceased fell, and the outlines of the face retained the characteristicks [sic] that distinguished the deceased among men."[218] That afternoon, Gregg's casket rested in the Capitol's rotunda next to George Washington's statue. Flowers, Confederate flags, Texas banners, and the general's exposed face greeted the mourners as they passed by.[219] On Sunday, soldiers of the Texas brigade accompanied the funeral procession to Hollywood Cemetery. Pallbearers placed the general's body in a private vault. The Texans left their commander on the bluffs of the James and trudged back to the trenches east of Richmond.[220]

CHAPTER 3

Union Reconnaissance on the

Darbytown Road (October 13)

∾

In the wake of Lee's failure at the New Market Road on October 7 and the sporadic fighting outside Petersburg the next day, the appetite for combat diminished on all sides. Though Butler still hoped for further operations, Grant showed little interest. Thus, the Army of the James went to work bolstering its positions. The Tenth Corps troops strengthened their trenches along the New Market Road, the same front they had ably defended on Friday.[1] Union engineers constructed a redoubt near the Clyne House just to the north of New Market Road.[2] Federal soldiers also bolstered trenches and added bombproofs in and around Fort Harrison, renamed Fort Burnham after a Union officer killed in the September assault.[3] Across the lines, Confederates also improved defenses, activity that would soon precipitate yet more combat near the Darbytown Road.

"scattered shorter lines in many places"

For the Confederates, recent battles had reshaped the defensive front. In early October, First Corps artillery chief, Porter Alexander, tried to make sense of the new position by studying the trenches in Henrico County. What he found was not encouraging. Vague and inaccurate Confederate military maps offered little help to commanders trying to deploy their men. On the ground, the fortifications themselves were "more or less scattered shorter lines in many places," lacking the continuity necessary for adequate defense. On Sunday, the 9th, Alexander inspected the works. That afternoon, he returned to Richmond and consulted with chief of the Confederate Engineer Bureau Jeremy Gilmer. The two pored over maps, with Alexander penciling in forts and ditches.

After reviewing the maze of trenches and roads east of Richmond, Alexander identified an opportunity. Though Fort Harrison's loss handed the enemy large portions of the old exterior line, the artillerist believed he could neatly suture the tear by constructing a new line connecting the works at Fort Gilmer north to the old exterior line near the Darbytown and Charles City roads. He brought this plan to Lee, who approved it immediately. On Sunday evening, directions went out to the rebel engineers, and work began the next day.[4]

The rebel infantrymen pitched in. After the October 7 debacle, Hoke and Field had pulled their divisions behind Cornelius Creek, a small stream running northeast from Fort Gilmer. On Monday the 10th, the infantry commanders brought their men forward to help construct Alexander's new line.[5] On that chilly morning, Confederate spades broke through the frost-covered grass and into the soil.[6] By Wednesday the 12th, the engineers had traced the full extent of the new defenses stretching from Fort Gilmer, northeasterly to the Charles City Road.[7] This new creation eventually included redans for gun platforms, cleared fields of fire several hundred yards in front of the works, and V-shaped pits for pickets beyond the main line.[8]

Confederate soldiers were not the only men wielding the spades and picks on the new trenches. Following Fort Harrison's capture, rebel authorities had scoured Richmond for civilians to fill existing works and to build new ones. Confederate provost officials seized men off the street and sent them to the front. Officials also mobilized clerks and other workers from Richmond's militia units. John B. Jones, a well-known antebellum writer serving as a clerk in the War Department, reported that the unpopular dragnet sent many of "the most ultra and uncompromising secessionists" into hiding.[9]

Though many unhappy clerks manned the trenches, much of the manpower for the new fortifications probably came from slaves. Over the course of the conflict, the Confederate government tapped liberally into this labor force to erect defenses. Earlier in the war, the Confederate Congress began to allow authorities to impress slaves into duty as military laborers, much to the irritation of some slave owners.[10] The government used these men to construct trenches at Richmond, Petersburg, and elsewhere. In the fall of 1864, Robert E. Lee asked officials in Richmond for slaves to help his army.[11] With the crisis at Fort Harrison, he requested additional slave labor. In the wake of his request, provost officials seized blacks from the Richmond streets even before such measures had been officially sanctioned.[12]

"A practice justified by no rule of war"

Along with rebel soldiers, office clerks, and slaves, another group of men toiled away at Alexander's project. On Wednesday the 12th, some unpleasant news made its way to Benjamin Butler's headquarters. Enemy deserters reported that black U.S. prisoners-of-war were working on the ditches and parapets east of Richmond. Butler immediately gathered sworn affidavits from the deserters. Samuel Miller, a member of the 18th Virginia Artillery Battalion, declared to have seen seventy-five to eighty African Americans clad in U.S. uniforms, digging fortifications between

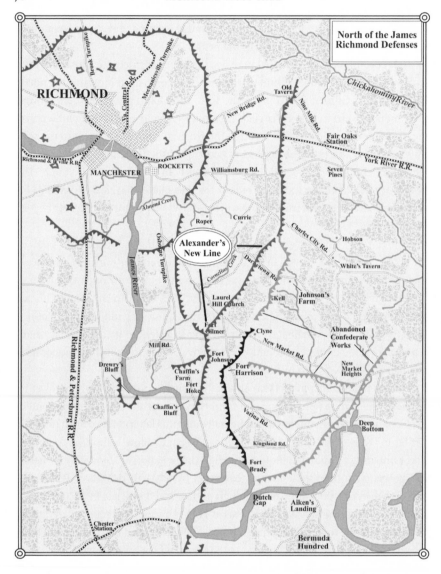

North of the James
Richmond Defenses

the Charles City and Darbytown roads. He added that the prisoners traded "their clothes and shoes with Confederate soldiers for food, owing to an insufficiency being furnished them."[13] Two members of the 38th North Carolina also swore that about a hundred captured USCTs had been working in the trenches near Fort Gilmer in recent days. Like Miller, one of these Tar Heels mentioned that the prisoners had swapped their personal effects for rations. James Knight, from the 59th Virginia, had a similar story. He reported that authorities had pulled eighty-two black soldiers from Libby Prison and forced them to work between the New Market and Darbytown roads over the previous few days.[14]

To Benjamin Butler, the deserters' stories had the ring of truth, given earlier Confederate policies and actions. Throughout the war, Confederate officials had struggled with their policy toward captured black soldiers. In 1862, Secretary of War James Seddon had informed Confederate commanders that slaves "in flagrant rebellion are subject to death by the laws of every slave-holding State" and that "summary execution must therefore be inflicted on those taken."[15] As a practical matter, Confederate officials generally did not follow this policy, and Confederate commanders did not follow a consistent approach on the ground. However, in notable cases, such as Fort Pillow at Tennessee in April and the Crater battle at Petersburg in July, Confederate soldiers had simply killed captured black prisoners.[16] Less than two weeks before Butler gathered the recent news, Lee had balked at exchanging prisoners who were proven to be former slaves, arguing that "deserters from our service and negroes belonging to our citizens are not considered subjects of exchange."[17] Although Confederate policy and practice toward captured free black U.S. soldiers was often vague, by 1864 Confederate officials generally treated them as they would white soldiers.[18]

Whatever the evolving official Confederate policy, the forced labor extracted from captured black soldiers of the Army of the James served as a tipping point for General Butler. As Grant's designated liaison to Confederate authorities on prisoner issues, he was accustomed to dealing with Confederate officials. Shortly after hearing the disturbing news, he fired off a dispatch to his rebel counterpart, Robert Ould, the Confederate Commissioner of Exchange. Summarizing the deserters' statements and attaching their signed affidavits, he asserted that the labor extracted from U.S. prisoners was "a practice justified by no rule of war or claim heretofore made by the Confederate authorities."[19]

Butler did more than complain. At 11:15 on Wednesday morning (the 12th), he directed Marsena Patrick, the provost marshal general, to place 150 Confederate prisoners at Dutch Gap along the James River, where Butler's men had been digging a huge canal. Here the prisoners became vulnerable to their own battery fire hurled at the Union canal diggers. Butler informed Richmond authorities of his action and promised to add more prisoners to the canal until the Confederates ceased using captured black U.S. troops to build rebel fortifications.[20] Though his decision would increase his unpopularity among white Southerners, he had little concern for his reputation in those circles. Genuinely outraged by this recent news, he was willing to escalate matters to protect Union soldiers. Grant stood behind Butler and approved the retaliatory action.[21]

On Wednesday afternoon, Butler sent his inspector general, Lieutenant Colonel George Kensel, beyond the Union works near Fort Harrison with a flag of truce. Kensel carried Butler's letter and the deserters' affidavits, along with additional papers related to other matters.[22] After arriving at the picket line, he handed the packet to rebel vedettes with directions to deliver the letters to General Ewell. Kensel

waited for a reply that never arrived. Under the rules governing such matters, neither side could conduct military actions when a flag of truce was out along the line.
Until Kensel's flag returned, Butler was duty bound to observe the truce he had set
in motion. On most days, such a delay would have had little practical impact. On
Wednesday the 12th, the prolonged truce affected Butler's military efforts.[23]

"make a reconnaissance"

Following the reports of prisoner misuse, more news had arrived from the front
on Wednesday morning. August Kautz's pickets had discovered the Confederates
constructing a battery beside the Darbytown Road less than half a mile from the
old Confederate trenches west of Johnson's Farm. Porter Alexander's project was
no longer a secret. The newly found rebel fort formed part of his new trench system, which stretched northeast from Fort Gilmer.[24]

Butler, perhaps sensitive to Grant's desire to avoid further operations, merely
forwarded Kautz's report to the lieutenant general with no recommendation or
proposal. Grant, however, did not want to allow the Confederates to fortify the
Darbytown Road unmolested. He immediately wired back and suggested "a strong
reconnaissance of infantry and cavalry to drive the enemy from the work they are
doing." At the same time, he sought to limit the effort's scope, warning that such "a
reconnaissance should not go far enough to endanger their being cut off."[25]

Given his desire to pressure the Confederates in the wake of the late September
offensive, Butler no doubt looked forward to hitting the enemy again. By early
afternoon, he had drafted orders to initiate operations. Alfred Terry, commanding the Tenth Corps in David Birney's absence, received Butler's directive to take
two divisions and "make a reconnaissance in force and drive away, if practicable,
the enemy from the works they are now building on the Darbytown (or Central)
road." Butler added Kautz's cavalry to the mission but held back Weitzel's Eighteenth Corps to support the probe, should any problem arise. In Butler's assessment, six thousand veterans from two Confederate divisions manned the front.
Mindful of Grant's instructions, he cautioned Terry to push no farther than the
enemy's old fortifications unless "indications of giving way will justify it."[26]

In reply to Butler's order, Alfred Terry slated two of his three divisions for
the mission. His first division would move forward along the north side of the
Darbytown Road. This command, now led by Adelbert Ames, following Terry's
recent promotion, contained the three brigades that had repelled the Confederate
assaults at the New Market Road the week before. The second division, wholly
formed from USCT units and led by William Birney (David Birney's brother),
would advance on the left toward the Kell house. Kautz's cavalry would cover
Terry's right between the Darbytown and Charles City roads. Taking into account

men absent on detail and picket duty, Terry estimated that the first division would bring 3,100 men and the second division would have 1,600.[27] In his diary that day, August Kautz confessed: "I do not like the proposed movement as it is not made in sufficient force and may prove disastrous."[28] By 4:30 P.M., Connecticut men from Plaisted's brigade snaked through the sally port cut into the works along the New Market Road. As the column filed north onto the Cox Farm fields, some officers looked on from the front porch of the house there. The soldiers halted outside the works and waited as officers milled around in small groups. An autumn rain began to fall, but the "men lolled on the wet grass, talking and laughing as merrily as though they had no wish for better quarters."[29]

Everything seemed in order for another fight. But Butler's reconnaissance hit a snag before it had even launched. Near Fort Harrison, Lieutenant Colonel Kensel's flag of truce was still missing. Until it returned, Terry could do little more than shuffle his units around the Cox plantation. Throughout the afternoon, Butler wired updates to Grant at City Point. In each transmission, he reported that the flag of truce had not returned from beyond the picket line. As the afternoon closed, it had become too late for Butler's advance.[30] The movement would have to wait until next morning. Grant concurred with the decision to postpone the reconnaissance. Terry's men filtered through the sally port and back into their camps.[31] One member of the 16th New York Heavy Artillery recalled that the afternoon's efforts succeeded only to display "our forces to the enemy." The rain continued and thoroughly soaked the men as they funneled back to their camps and dry tents.[32]

Though unwelcome, the delay provided Terry further time to plan. That evening, he received additional intelligence from the provost marshal's office noting that Field's and Hoke's divisions manned the Confederate works to the west. The report also incorrectly suggested that four regiments from Pickett's command, about six hundred men, waited in reserve. The signal corps also gathered information. Climbing into a high tree along the Tenth Corps position, Paul Brodie caught a glimpse of the new rebel works on the New Market Road. He identified "three field fortifications immediately in front of the station, mounting in all four guns—two on the work to the right, one on the center work, and one on the left-hand work; all Parrott guns, of either 20-pounder or 30-pounder caliber."[33] Brodie's high-altitude observation provided a comprehensive view, confirming what Kautz's pickets had seen. With Monday and Tuesday's labor under their belts, the Confederate soldiers, slaves, and impressed laborers had almost completed formidable works only several hundred yards in front of the Tenth Corps pickets. Porter Alexander's brainstorm from a few days before had led to a new fresh line of dirt stretching several miles across the Henrico countryside.

That night, Terry and Butler refined their scheme. They continued to anchor their designs on the assumption that the new enemy forces did not stretch all the

way to the Charles City Road but instead ended somewhere north of the Darbytown Road. Butler contributed to this understanding, explaining that Kautz
would be available to turn the enemy's left, and thus implying that there was such
an endpoint to turn. That night, Terry ordered his first division under Ames to
form in the open ground near the Darbytown Road. Under the plan, the column would move forward with the road on its left and "attack the enemy and endeavor to find and turn the left of their intrenchments."[34] One brigade of William
Birney's USCT division would gather on the other side of the road and keep pace
with Ames's command. Still farther south at the Kell house, the position occupied by Confederate artillery the previous Friday, Colonel Martin Curtis's brigade
would anchor the expedition's left flank and connect to the main Union position
near the New Market Road. For his part, August Kautz would venture along the
Charles City Road, gain the rear of the enemy position, and take the rebels in
reverse. Before he could launch any bold flanking maneuver, though, he drew the
task of escorting the Tenth Corps batteries north to the Darbytown Road.[35]

Alfred Terry fixed 4 A.M. as the departure time for his troops. He and his staff
would congregate at the Johnson house to direct operations.[36] His overall plan
promised to uncover valuable information about rebel dispositions and perhaps,
in the bargain, turn the Confederates out of their works. But the plan seemed to
assume the unlikely probability of significant cooperation from the Confederates.

"marching out to lose several hundred"

The Unionists prepared for the next day. Brigadier General Joseph Hawley, back
from leave and now in command of Joseph Abbott's brigade in Terry's first division, arrived at camp on that rainy Wednesday evening to find his unit preparing
for the next morning's probe. He ordered coffee for 3:30 A.M.[37] Over at Plaisted's
brigade, veterans of the 10th Connecticut enjoyed a night of relative rest, thank-
ful to have avoided the "fatigue and exposure" of the Cox fields.[38] The men wrote
letters home and conversed well past midnight, leaving precious little time for
sleep. At 3 A.M., they awoke, and, an hour later, shouldered their rifles and passed
outside the works onto the Cox Farm once again. The column continued north
through the swampy ravine formed by Four Mile Creek and emerged onto the
open ground of Johnson's Farm. One member of Plaisted's brigade found that
Kautz's "improved" road compared unfavorably with those back home in New
England, complaining that tree stumps had been "left standing some two feet
high."[39] At the Darbytown Road, the column halted and formed, ready to probe
westward.[40] To the south, William Birney's two USCT brigades filed into position
and prepared to support Terry's advance. Curtis's brigade from the second division covered Birney's left flank.[41]

The Confederates just west across the fields had devoted the last three days to their new earthworks. However, they had only begun to dig the line north of the Darbytown Road the day before. On Wednesday, Charles Field recognized that the line had no anchor, natural or manmade. There "was nothing easier than for the enemy to come up the Darbytown Road and get on my flank and rear," he wrote later.[42] Facing this clear danger, he urged his corps commander, General Richard Anderson, to shift troops into the breach. When nothing came of his request, Field took matters into his own hands late on Wednesday. He withdrew the Texas brigade from its place in the line and shoved it into the vulnerable sector.[43] As the rain fell on Wednesday night, the Texans trudged north and immediately began improving the works there in the darkness.[44] In front of the Kell house, south of the Darbytown Road, the sounds of creaking wheels and axes reached the ears of Union pickets and were reported to Union division commander Adelbert Ames.[45]

No longer burdened by the flag of truce, Ames's division pushed north of the Darbytown Road at sunrise on Thursday, scattering rebel pickets before it. The morning air bore a chill and frost covered the ground.[46] Hawley's brigade, including the Spencer-wielding regiments so crucial to the previous week's fight, hugged the north shoulder of the road on the left. Plaisted's brigade took the center, its ranks facing the Gerhardt house. Francis Pond's brigade, which had seen little action on the previous Friday, deployed on the far right of the division's line. But, with the infantry ready, no sign of August Kautz's horsemen appeared at the Charles City Road, a delay significant enough to warrant mention in Terry's official report.[47] Afterward, Kautz wrote that the movement commenced with "the feeling on the part of nearly every officer and soldier in the command that we were simply marching out to lose several hundred men and be repulsed." He was also "unusually depressed during the movement" due to the onset of a malarial fever.[48]

When Kautz finally arrived on the right flank, Ames's division stepped off, at 6:35 A.M.[49] Deploying north of the Darbytown Road, Ames threw about a third of his entire division into the skirmish line.[50] On the left, Hawley sent the 7th Connecticut ahead and put two other regiments in the battle line and two more in reserve. The brigade crept forward over the abandoned exterior lines, across a field, and then into a "thick and troublesome young wood."[51] In the center, Plaisted's brigade, with four companies of the seasoned 10th Connecticut leading, crossed the Gerhardt Farm and entered the stand of thick scrub oaks.[52] Pond's brigade formed on the right, with the 62nd Ohio and a portion of the 39th Illinois out ahead. His brigade also entered the woods.[53]

The Unionists forged ahead through the trees and undergrowth several hundred yards beyond the Gerhardt home, encountering sporadic shots from enemy pickets. But around 8 A.M., a sharp fire sprayed through the timber, halting the entire division. In some places, shouts from unseen Confederate commanders penetrated the thickets. An abatis of cut branches, still green with foliage, loomed

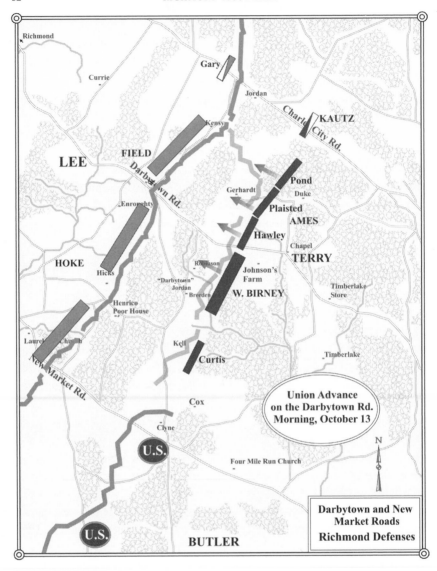

Richmond

Gary

Currie

Jordan

Kensy

Charl[es] City Rd.   KAUTZ

LEE   FIELD

Darbytown Rd.

Pond

Gerhardt   Duke

Enroughty   Plaisted

AMES

Hawley

Chapel

Robinson   TERRY

HOKE   Johnson's

Hicks   Farm

"Darbytown"   Timberlake
Jordan   Store

Breeden   W. BIRNEY

Henrico
Poor House

Laurel   Church   Timberlake

Kell

New Market Rd.   Curtis

Cox

Clyne

U.S.

Union Advance
on the Darbytown Rd.
Morning, October 13

N

Four Mile Run Church

U.S.   Darbytown and New
Market Roads
BUTLER   Richmond Defenses

as high as ten feet. In Hawley's front, the 7th Connecticut rocked back in the face of a severe volley, its skirmishers diving for cover. A captain climbed a tree and could see cut limbs littering the ground ahead, 100 to 150 yards wide in some places. Behind the tangled mass lay a "strong breast-work well lined with rebels, and at an angle thereof were at least two guns in position, which at various times during the day fired shot, spherical case, and canister."[54]

Across the Darbytown Road to the south, William Birney's USCT division found much of the same. Birney possessed a keen intellect, having studied at four colleges, written numerous journal articles on the arts, and conducted a successful law practice. An indefatigable advocate of union and abolition, his political views fit well in Butler's army. Though he did not possess much in the way of military acumen,[55] the morning's operation presented him with a straightforward task. His two brigades had pushed forward to find the Confederates. The 7th and 9th USCTs of Colonel Alvin Voris's brigade formed with their right on the Darbytown Road. Birney's other brigade, under Colonel Ulysses Doubleday, deployed farther to the left, with skirmishers from the 8th USCT regiment plunging into thick woods beyond the old exterior works.

Early in the morning, Charles Field's rebel pickets had tumbled back in the face of the Union advance.[56] Colonel Doubleday's men herded the Confederate pickets away from a fence line and into the main trenches about one hundred yards to the rear. Doubleday's men could see a Confederate battery unlimbered beyond a barn. One Confederate battle flag waved over the works nearby, and another poked out from the trenches to the right.[57] All along the line, the pattern continued. At every point, the probing Union line found infantry parapets, redoubts, and artillery emplacements crowning a low ridge a mile and a half west of the Johnson house.[58]

To Colonel Harris Plaisted, north of the Darbytown Road, the scene formed "altogether an ugly looking chance for a charge."[59] As Confederate artillery shells screamed in from several directions, case shot crashed into his brigade's position. In the crowded trees, the rebel shells dislodged heavy limbs, dropping them onto vulnerable troops below.[60] Many men hugged the ground, but few, if any, broke and ran.[61] A member of the 10th Connecticut recalled that, as a small group of officers sat chatting with each other, an occasional "flying bullet or shell fragment would cause a passing remark, or, perhaps, raise a laugh. No one expected to be hit himself, for he had escaped so many times before." As the men endured the shelling, lunch arrived at the battle line and was consumed under fire. Major Henry Ward Camp, a favorite young officer in the 10th Connecticut, stretched out on the ground and fell asleep amid the din.[62]

By 10:30 A.M., Terry reported the results of the reconnaissance to Butler. The Tenth Corps had found strong rebel works everywhere. He expressed doubt about further progress. "I think we cannot pierce their works except by massing on some point and attacking in column," he advised Butler. "I hesitate to do this without further instructions from you."[63] Despite his hesitance, Terry sought more information about the extent and strength of the Confederate trenches. North at the Charles City Road, Kautz's horsemen, meeting resistance, had failed to divine the strength of the rebel works in that sector. Terry directed Kautz to look further, asking him to "ascertain how far the enemy's intrenchments extend to our right, and whether or not they are on the Charles City road."[64] Kautz took up the task. Back on the left toward the New Market Road, soldiers from the 45th USCT also reconnoitered forward.[65]

As the Tenth Corps continued to gather information, Butler forwarded Terry's news to Grant at City Point, who furnished a clear response. "I would not attack the enemy in his intrenchments. The reconnaissance now serves to locate them for any future operation. To attack now we would lose more than the enemy and only gain ground which we are not prepared to hold."[66] The day's operation had run its course, or so it appeared. Terry's two divisions had fixed the new Confederate position astride the Darbytown Road and found the rebel works formidable and well manned. Nothing more could be done.

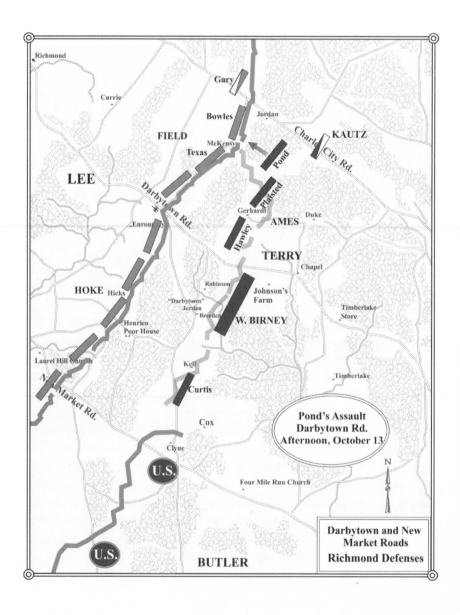

Pond's Assault
Darbytown Rd.
Afternoon, October 13

Darbytown and New
Market Roads
Richmond Defenses

But along the front, continued searching bore fruit. Around 2 P.M., Kautz provided some promising news. As Terry later explained, for about half a mile south of the Charles City Road, "there appeared to be no works of consequence and that the enemy was still intrenching."[67] Ames conducted a personal examination and reported to corps headquarters that there "was nothing in his front, or if there were works, that no obstacles covered them."[68] Satisfied by the new information, Terry ordered an attack. Not yet privy to Grant's most recent instructions to Butler, he directed Ames to extend his right flank and try "to break in" to the Confederate line.[69] But shortly after he had directed the new movement, he received a disturbing note from Butler: "I would not attack the enemy in their intrenchments. Having carefully reconnoitered the enemy, found their position, and looked out all the roads, retire at leisure."[70] The note must have given Terry an uneasy feeling. In command of the Tenth Corps for only four days, he had committed his troops to an attack that contradicted the judgment of his superiors. By the time Butler's dispatch arrived, it was too late to halt the operation. He wrote to Butler explaining the sequence of events and promised to keep the general apprised of developments.[71] He could do nothing but wait for news from the battle line.

As the Union commanders planned, Charles Field managed his defenses. Throughout the morning, the Texas brigade, stationed in the new trenches north of the Darbytown Road, performed well, blunting the initial advance of Ames's skirmish line. The Confederate artillery contributed, too. The guns of Haskell's battalion launched shells into the oncoming federals.[72] As the fighting intensified, Robert E. Lee arrived.[73] Another welcome sight also appeared. General James Longstreet rode up, dressed in civilian clothes, his arm hanging in a sling. Still recovering from his Wilderness wounds, he was not quite ready for field command, but, by one estimate, the "well known sour face and bulky form of the famous old fighting chieftain of the 1st Corps was, in itself, equal to a considerable reinforcement."[74]

Though Longstreet's presence gave moral support, adequate troop strength at the point of danger was the necessary ingredient for success that afternoon. Field's weak left held few men. Lee directed Field to reinforce the Texans' line. In response, Field shifted three brigades farther north along Alexander's trench line past the Texans,[75] including the Alabama brigade under Pinckney Bowles, which filed into the line just south of the Charles City Road. Bowles directed his men to begin digging and to hack down bushes and trees. The men spread the limbs in front.[76]

"a chill ran over many an old soldier's frame"

On the Union line along Ames's front, Colonel Francis Pond's brigade prepared to conduct the attack hatched by Kautz's probing, Ames's observations, and Terry's orders. Pond's command contained four regiments, the 39th Illinois, 85th

Pennsylvania, and two Ohio units, the 62nd and 67th. To augment the assault, Ames attached about seventy men of the 10th Connecticut of Plaisted's brigade and included the 3rd New Hampshire from Hawley's command. With this strike force, Pond formed his column about a half mile south of the Charles City Road, with "each regiment in double column on the center, at half-distance."[77] The arrangement placed each regiment together in a tightly packed formation. The 62nd Ohio, 39th Illinois, and then the 67th Ohio formed from left to right. The 3rd New Hampshire and the 85th Pennsylvania remained in reserve, deployed thirty yards behind the other regiments.[78] Pond placed the Connecticut veterans and their colonel, John Otis, the senior regimental commander, in Pond's force at the right front of the attack formation. By Pond's reckoning, the entire force contained 570 men.[79]

As Pond's men gathered, "a chill ran over many an old soldier's frame," recalled a member of the 10th Connecticut. The men and officers feared that the well-entrenched Confederates waited a few hundred yards in front. Even a quick glance revealed that the path ahead was covered by a "dense thicket of scrub-oaks, and laurels, and tangled vines." They understood that they would have to charge, not by a spirited dash, but by a slow, agonizing crawl through the twisted limbs. "There was a disturbed look on the face of every officer, and outspoken protests were heard from many."[80] But young Henry Ward Camp of the 10th Connecticut kept his chin up, murmuring to a friend, "I don't like this blue talking. The men see it, and it affects them. If we must go, we must; and the true way is to make the best of it."[81] General Hawley later informed his wife that "every officer protested against being ordered up."[82] The men and officers of the 39th Illinois also sensed futility. All "the officers of the brigade were opposed to the charge, and reported so to the General commandeering the corps; but it made no difference," recalled one Illinois soldier. As George W. Yates, a color sergeant with the 39th, waited for the orders to step off, he "took out all of his letters from his pocket, read them over, and then tore them to pieces and scattered them to the winds." He then confided to his fellow color guard members that he did not expect to survive the charge.[83]

Through the brush and slashing, the Alabama troops caught wind of the assault. Shouts of the Union officers penetrated the leaves and branches, and soon the unmistakable order to advance reached Confederate ears. The Alabamians "resolved to stand to the last and give them the bayonet in the event they came near enough," remembered William McClendon of the 15th Alabama. As he examined his comrades, he realized "there was no thought of surrendering or retreating."[84] "The situation was critical," wrote a soldier in Field's division a few weeks afterward. "Stretched out in one thin rank and without breastworks, with a heavy force confronting, any but stout hearts would have quailed at the prospect." The Confederates continued in earnest to improve the trench line and found enough time to form decent cover.[85]

At about 2:30,[86] Pond's force pushed ahead with a loud cheer delivered in "a tone that indicated rather a willingness to obey than a hope of success."[87] The tightly packed regiments struggled through the thicket. Years later, Sergeant D. H. Slagle, of the 39th Illinois, told his fellow veterans, "You all recall that terrific yell, as we made the assault through the brush, the air seeming filled with whizzing bullets, the scream of solid shot and shell, the rattle and sweep of grape and canister through our ranks."[88] Three hundred yards to the rear, several Union surgeons took cover behind the corncrib in the Gerhardt house yard as the brigade advanced. Before their eyes, a rain of shell and grapeshot hit the crib, "scattering splinters and debris in all directions."[89] Pond had stirred up a hornet's nest.

The fatal flaw in the earlier Union reconnaissance became clear. What had appeared as a gap in the rebel line was no gap at all. The "apparent absence of works arose from the fact that the line was refused at a point just west of the attack," later reported Terry matter-of-factly.[90] In other words, the Confederate works angled sharply rearward for a stretch at the weak point alleged by Kautz and Ames. The shape of the Confederate trench formed a trap for the advancing blue regiments. For Pond's men, the negligent reconnaissance proved disastrous. The unlucky regiments exposed their left flank to this angle in the enemy earthworks. Hours before, the trenches here may not have been formidable. But the Alabama brigade, rushed to the spot by generals Lee and Field, had managed to dig out "a substantial rifle-pit . . . covered by a difficult abatis of scrub oak, and . . . amply manned."[91] The Confederate rifles tore into Pond's force.

Portions of Pond's line advanced through the "crashing sweep of grape and canister, and the fatal hiss and hum of flying bullets."[92] "O it was awful," wrote a Connecticut soldier.[93] Clay Trumbull, the chaplain of the 10th Connecticut, attended to the wounded and dying dropping along the way. Some attackers eventually emerged into an open space just a few rods in front of the Confederate earthworks. Henry Ward Camp, the young, level-headed Connecticut major, paused and waited for his line to reform amid the heavy fire, yelling, "Come on, boys, come on!" As he turned to his men emerging from the woods behind him, a bullet ripped into his chest. He collapsed on his side and "was pierced yet again and again by the thickcoming shot."[94] The Connecticut men paused before the works. George Yates, the color sergeant of the 39th Illinois, who had destroyed his letters minutes before, had been correct in his morbid prediction. Within sight of the rebel works, a rebel volley riddled his body with four bullets.[95]

The attack lost what little momentum it had, and further effort would gain nothing. The fruitless charge stopped. Colonel John Otis pulled back the "little band" of Connecticut men, now numbering fewer than fifty.[96] They left the body of their friend and comrade Henry Camp lying where he fell. Yates's comrades tore the colors out of his hands and made their way to the rear.[97] The colors of the Illinois regiment "were completely riddled, and the color-guard all killed or wounded with the exception of three."[98]

The Confederates did not sit and observe the withdrawal but leapt over the works in pursuit. On the Charles City Road, Martin Gary's cavalry pursued Kautz's men. Elsewhere along the works, other rebels, perhaps from DuBose's and Anderson's brigades, hopped out of their trenches and ventured forward but did not achieve much.[99] The day's heavy fighting had run its course, and the sporadic, apparently spontaneous, rebel pursuit was weak.[100]

The Union attack failed. The disorganized remnants of Pond's regiments streamed to the rear. The surgeons at the Gerhardt house withdrew to the old exterior works, where they could dress the wounded in comparative safety and send them along to the corps hospital.[101] General Terry simply reported, "I regret to say that in this movement we met with considerable loss."[102] Out of the 570 that Pond estimated in the attack, his force suffered more than 220 casualties. The 10th Connecticut lost over half of the seventy members engaged, whittling down the already threadbare regiment. The two reserve units, the 85th Pennsylvania and the 3rd New Hampshire, made it through largely unscathed, losing eleven men between them.[103] According to one Confederate account, the Alabamans found "one stand of colors, many wounded, and forty or fifty dead, including two Majors," one of them the brave Henry Camp.[104] The number of Union men killed in the attack, about fifteen, was surprisingly small relative to the total casualties. Pond attributed this to the low trajectory of the enemy's fire.[105] The Confederates loss was "small," not more than fifty men, by one estimate.[106] The *Richmond Dispatch* reported the official Confederate loss at thirty.[107] By nightfall, the Union troops had returned to their works south of the New Market Road.[108]

Charles Field and Robert E. Lee had made all the difference in the battle. Without Field's thought and initiative, the Texas brigade would have remained south of the Darbytown Road on Wednesday night. Ames's battle line would have pressed on the next morning into open ground, vacant but for scattered cavalry. As the two Union divisions advanced, Field and Lee ensured that defenders plugged the vulnerable spots, particularly the weak left flank filled by the Alabama troops. Once the butternut troops took their new position and began to dig, the engagement's conclusion was practically foregone. The Confederates needed only to load their rifles and empty them into the brush. Robert E. Lee provided a brief description of the action, stating that the "enemy had been repulsed in every attempt" and withdrew "leaving many dead."[109] That afternoon, Lee ordered Anderson to hold Field's division in its present position and connect with Gary's cavalry. Hoke would stretch his right south to touch the New Market road with Colquitt's brigade. Lee noted that the enemy had retired after pushing a brigade towards the Henrico Poor House, an effort beaten back by Hoke's skirmishers.[110]

The affair pleased the Southern press. One account described it as a "complete little battle and victory."[111] The *Richmond Whig* labeled the fight a "great victory," one much more significant than General Lee's dispatch suggested. In South Carolina, the *Columbia Daily* sensed exaggeration from the Richmond papers but nevertheless concluded that the Confederates had completely foiled the Northerners.[112] This was a fair assessment.

The battle demonstrated the wisdom behind Porter Alexander's plan to mend the Richmond defenses. The new works not only proved their strength but also significantly eased the Confederate efforts to meet future attacks against Richmond. The retrenchment created breathing room for the defenders and a single, contiguous line to facilitate troop movement.

The reconnaissance at the Darbytown Road also met Union objectives. Butler and his generals gained a clear understanding of the new Confederate defenses. They found works complete with redans, connected by curtains of trenches, slashing, and abatis. Union commanders now understood that the rebel line stretched more than three miles from Fort Gilmer over the Darbytown Road and north toward the Charles City Road. "The discovery of this line of works was important to us," recorded John Spear of the 24th Massachusetts, "as we had on two occasions moved over this very ground, while our cavalry, until last Friday had picketed this entire region."[113] One Northern journalist noted that the rapid construction of the line highlighted "the energy, skill and perseverance of the soldier brought into existence by this war."[114] This sector would offer no easy passage into Richmond.

Though Union commanders may have gained valuable information, they also recognized that cost of Pond's attack had been much too high. The finger-pointing began, particularly from the regimental officers of commands assigned to Pond's attack. Lieutenant Colonel James Randlett, from the 3rd New Hampshire in Hawley's brigade, penned a harsh assessment in an unusually candid official report: "I cannot refrain from comment on this charge. . . . I do not think the position could have been carried with the force of our command . . . the ground was not thoroughly skirmished before the charge was made."[115] Colonel John Otis of the 10th Connecticut echoed these sentiments, explaining, "I have not seen a more hopeless task undertaken since I entered the [service]." Otis, who led his veterans at the tip of assault, declined to apologize for the failure of his men, explaining that his unit "in more than forty battles and skirmishes, never before fell back under fire."[116] The 10th's chaplain, Clay Trumbull, described the devastation in a letter to the *Hartford Daily Courant* two days later, opening his account by announcing that the "Old Tenth has finally been checked."[117] General Hawley, in a letter home, noted that, in fact, Terry "felt badly at losing so many for nothing."[118]

It is clear that at least three commanders shared the blame for the poor results. Kautz's faulty reconnaissance initiated the blunder. Adelbert Ames contributed by confirming Kautz's assessment after a personal examination of the ground. Alfred Terry, in turn, sanctioned the attack despite his discussions with Butler the night before about the limited nature of the operation. Not everyone had been thrilled about the plan, though. Francis Pond, whose brigade fell in the enemy's

crosshairs, had expressed concern about the order.[119] A Connecticut soldier reported that "Col. Pond . . . opposed it as did all the other officers."[120] According to one account, "Col. Pond was reluctant to order his command to make the
charge . . . and only did what he was ordered to do when he found it could not be
avoided."[121] After the battle, Ames claimed that Pond had been sluggish and stubborn throughout the day.[122] But this may have been a clumsy attempt to deflect
blame.[123] In fact, Pond's apparent indifference may have been a demonstration
of his reluctance to sacrifice his men needlessly. Right or wrong, Pond lost command of the brigade within a week.[124]

Benjamin Butler quickly moved beyond the day's events. By 8:00 P.M., he was
exchanging messages with Grant about the adequacy of artillery assets along the
Bermuda Hundred lines. Years later, he did not even mention the October 13 fight
in his war reminiscences.[125] For his commanders, the reconnaissance graphically
illustrated the futility of unsupported attacks against strong defenses. By this time
in the war, engineers on both sides had perfected the design and rapid construction
of effective fortifications. Alexander's new works reflected this trend. As illustrated
repeatedly in official reports, the wide bands of slashing, the bushes and limbs covering the ground, formed a nearly impassable obstacle. The defenses slowed the
progress of skirmishers, broke up battle lines, and, most important, trapped slow-
moving formations in the killing zone. Caught in this web, the attacking troops
offered easy targets. Given time, the Confederates would add more features to the
line, including more abatis, chevaux de frise (racks of sharpened logs), ditches and
moats in front of the works, and head logs along the top of parapets to allow men to
fire on attackers while minimizing their own exposure. The Union high command
usually avoided grinding their troops against such obstacles by this time in the war.
In fact, Grant had warned Butler against this practice. The debacle at the Darbytown Road on October 13 underscored the wisdom of such counsel.

As was usually the case, the rank and file suffered for these poor choices. For
the members of the 10th Connecticut, the mistakes were particularly sad and
costly. The death of the beloved Henry Ward Camp dealt a heavy blow. Camp had
collapsed just yards from rebel defenders. Some of the Confederates inspected
the corpse and, in a practice all too common, stripped the lifeless young man
of his sword, pistol, watch, regatta ring, money, papers, and even outer clothes.
On Friday morning, Clay Trumbull, the Connecticut regiment's chaplain, along
with several others, carried a flag of truce up the Darbytown Road and requested
Camp's remains. A Confederate captain explained that his men had already buried the young officer but would disinter the body. Soon, the rebels bore the corpse
forward. Camp had been shot seven times. The Confederate captain "expressed
his sincere regret" about the missing clothes and personal effects. Trumbull, a
close friend of Camp, asked for the young man's diary. The missing volume was
soon located and returned through the lines.[126]

"regardless of color or nationality"

With his reconnaissance complete, General Butler returned his attention to the reported Confederate abuses of black prisoners. Several days before, he had lectured captured Confederate officials about the need to exchange Union and Confederate prisoners "man for man" regardless of race. "I owe it to these colored men who are fighting in our armies, in fulfillment of the pledges I made them in behalf of my Government at the beginning of the war, and by heaven, sirs, those pledges shall be fulfilled," he explained.[127] Now that his captured soldiers were digging rebel trenches, Butler had no intention to let the matter rest.

He continued to gather information. On the 13th, the U.S. Provost Marshal's Office reported that captured Union cavalrymen in Richmond had witnessed white civilians examining 125 captured black soldiers at Libby Prison. The Confederates seized custody of any men recognized as former slaves.[128] To add to these reports, Butler relied on the curious misadventures of two officials from the Confederate War Department. The pair, Messrs. McCrae and Henly, had been snared by the Confederate dragnet following Fort Harrison's capture. Placed on picket duty, the two lost their way and accidentally stumbled into Union control. Their garb caught the attention of a *New York Times* reporter. McCrae, a former major, "wore his cast off regiments, and stood with bent head, and features almost obscured by the peak of his little gray cap, which rested upon his grizzled mustache." Henly sported a "thread-bare, swallow-tail coat and stovepipe hat, and his shoulders swathed in a dingy white blanket."[129] As Henly and McCrae stood over a Yankee campfire, they exchanged polite apologies for their collective mishap.

Once in Butler's hands, the two enjoyed the dubious privilege of joining other Confederate prisoners at Dutch Gap who were placed under the fire of their own guns. Butler singled out McCrae, however, and permitted him to return to Richmond "to learn whether the Federal prisoners were really required" to work on the rebel trenches. According to Confederate War Department clerk John B. Jones, no strings were attached to McCrae's visit, no parole or other restrictions. After his stay in the capital, McCrae returned to Butler.[130] Reports conflict as to the content of McCrae's findings. However, clerk Jones's own diary admitted, "We had Federal prisoners at work."[131] Jones described Butler's gesture to McCrae as a "generous action" and noted that it had escaped mention in the Southern newspapers.[132]

While Butler continued to build his case, Robert E. Lee also reacted to the prisoner dispute. In response to Butler's action at Dutch Gap, the Virginian ordered Porter Alexander to place one hundred Union prisoners in a corral near the rebel batteries shelling Dutch Gap.[133] Writing home to his wife, Alexander explained that he planned to put the prisoners "in a pen fifteen yards square—just room to bury them—where they would all have been killed the first day."[134] However, it appears the project was never completed. In addition, it is not clear whether

Union commanders knew of Lee's designs, but on the 18th, Butler ordered an additional fifty prisoners to Dutch Gap because so many of the original rebels placed there had taken the oath of allegiance to the United States.[135]

The next day, after consulting with the secretary of war, Lee wrote Grant to describe his government's position on the matter of black prisoners and to furnish details about the U.S. soldiers who had been digging the Confederate fortifications. According to Lee, Confederate policy dictated that all captured black Union prisoners "not identified as the property of [Confederate] citizens" would be treated as prisoners of war. He explained that no labor was extracted from such prisoners. On the other hand, those federal prisoners identified as escaped slaves faced a different fate. "It has been uniformly held that the capture or abduction of a slave does not impair the right of the owner to such slave," he explained, "but that the right attaches to him immediately upon recapture."[136]

As for the black prisoners forced to work outside Richmond, Lee wrote that fifty-nine recently captured soldiers were identified as slaves and sent to work on the Richmond lines. Once Lee became aware of the situation, he ordered the men moved into the interior because he did not wish "to employ them" in constructing the defenses. However, a "misapprehension of the engineer officer in charge" sent the same men to work on the Petersburg lines. Once Lee gained knowledge of this action, he again ordered officials to send the men into the interior. Lee also explained that, "If any negroes were included among the number who were not identified as the slaves of citizens or residents of some of the Confederate States they were so included without the knowledge or authority of the War Department, as already explained, and the mistake when discovered would have been corrected." In other words, if free (i.e., non-slave) black Union soldiers were digging the Confederate lines, the matter had been a misunderstanding or just an honest mistake.[137] In any case, Lee argued that the Confederates, in contrast to General Butler, were not forcing these prisoners into harm's way.

Internal Confederate documents gathered by the U.S. War Department in later years confirmed some of the details of the practices mentioned by Lee. However, these communications also indicate that Confederate officials had forced free black prisoners, not just former slaves, to construct Richmond's fortifications. An October 5, 1864, note from Provost Marshal I. H. Carrington directed Major Thomas Turner, the head of the Confederate military prisons at Richmond, to deliver "all negroes on hand not employed about the [Libby] prison" over to Brigadier General Barton for work on the fortifications. In describing his actions more than a week later, Turner reported delivering eighty-two black prisoners dressed in uniform for work on the fortifications around Richmond and an additional sixty-eight USCTs, captured at the Crater battle in July and imprisoned at Castle Thunder.[138] Turner's postscript to his note reads, "I learn from Castle Thunder, which is not under my charge, that sixty-eight negro soldiers were sent to the works on the 2d instant. These negroes were captured at Petersburg July 30, 1864. Eleven of them are free; the rest are slaves."[139] These dispatches, drafted by and distributed among a variety of Confederate officials, give no hint of the policy Lee described in his letter to Grant. However, by October 19, such a policy was certainly in place, as noted in John B. Jones's diary, which explained, "Gen. Lee writes to-day that negroes taken from the enemy, penitentiary convicts, and recaptured deserters ought not to be sent . . . to work on the fortifications."[140]

Grant refused to engage Lee in the debate about Confederate slave policy. In his reply, he simply explained to Lee, "I have nothing to do with the discussion of the slavery question, therefore decline answering the arguments adduced to show the right to return to former owners such negroes as are captured from our Army."[141] Grant wrote that it was his "duty to protect all persons received into the Army of the United States, regardless of color or nationality." For the time being, however, he was satisfied that Lee had withdrawn the men from the trenches around Fort Gilmer, and he ordered Butler to cease the retaliatory actions at Dutch Gap. He did not directly address the fact that Lee had sent Union soldiers back into slavery. He did warn, however, that when "acknowledged soldiers of the Government are captured they must be treated as prisoners of war, or such treatment as they receive inflicted upon an equal number of prisoners held by us."[142] The "Dutch Gap affair" ended there.[143]

As Lee prepared his brief defending Confederate slave laws and policies, a *New York Tribune* reporter gathered more accounts of the rebel treatment of black prisoners. According to him, two deserters from a Virginia regiment claimed that the Confederates required captured black prisoners to work on the trenches for eleven hours a day. The deserters, who swam the James River to reach Union territory, reported that black prisoners "experience various indignities, and are subject to cruel and harsh treatment" and that a man named Moody, "an overseer or boss," had whipped and beat them. The deserters further attested that Moody had killed one of the prisoners. According to the same article, a former Confederate gunboat crew member claimed that rebel soldiers, standing on the banks of the James, had fired repeatedly into a towed barge full of wounded Union prisoners on its way to Richmond in late September. The bullets from shore killed at least three of the men. In addition to the deserters' stories, Lieutenant John B. Viers of the 5th USCT, who had been captured during the September 29 fight at Fort Gilmer, reported that all the wounded black soldiers at the battle "who were unable to move away were bayoneted or shot where they lay by the soldiers of the 15th Georgia Regiment."[144] As Confederates executed the wounded black troops, they "cursed and threatened" the injured Viers, asking him if he was "not ashamed to command" such men. Viers's captors neglected his wounds until the next day. Unexpectedly, Confederate authorities paroled him less than two weeks after the fight, an event the lieutenant attributed to an administrative mistake. When Viers returned to Butler's army, he shared his story.[145]

Given the deaths of black prisoners at Fort Gilmer in September and the Crater in July, as well as the evolving Confederate policy on these issues, there was little to suggest that Confederates would exercise great care to ensure fair and just treatment of black prisoners. Similarly, it is unclear whether Confederate officials would carefully distinguish slaves from free men among the captured USCTs lucky enough to survive the battlefield.[146] In this context, Lee's assurances to Grant, though not in themselves particularly comforting, probably held little meaning to the average black soldier in the field. Stories from deserters and comrades suggested that many black U.S. troops could expect death or at least abuse in rebel hands. And, despite official statements to the contrary, the evidence suggests that some Confederate authorities sent blacks to work on the rebel trenches with no distinction regarding their status as slave or free.

The captured soldiers had an able advocate in Benjamin Butler, who had moved decisively to address their plight. Though Butler's retaliation at Dutch Gap may have horrified secessionist leaders in Richmond, admirers in the Northern press showered him with praise. "Butler is a man of action as well as words," sung the editors of the *Philadelphia Inquirer* several days later. "His decision of character, and prompt, business-like method, are unlike the red-tape tardiness which thwarts expeditious movements among many of our officers."[147] In commenting on Butler's handling of the crisis, the article concluded that "by such means only is it possible to infuse proper ideas of humanity, and of their duties to prisoners, into Confederate minds."[148] Similarly, Butler enjoyed support from the ranks. Connecticut soldier Silas Mead approved Butler's retaliation—"that is what I believe. If the government uses negroes for soldiers it is right they should protect them."[149]

As the prisoner controversy played out, soldiers on the front continued to endure the trenches outside Richmond. During the previous months, military operations had transformed the countryside into a curious tapestry. On a beautiful day in late October, a *New York Tribune* correspondent walked through Benjamin Butler's camps north of the James. His subsequent dispatch, wired on October 21, painted a picture of the Henrico County front. Near the James, the journalist found "peaceful cornfields" that gave little hint of the thousands of men crowded in fortifications and camps nearby. To the rear, unharvested grain remained in the fields, trampled into the soil. "Dismantled and demolished houses" layscattered about. The Union camps sprawled everywhere, their white tents dotting the landscape. He also witnessed the arrival of Southern refugees "with their starving, half-clad families, asking for protection and food." The fields, "scarified by shot and shell," bore the carcasses of horses and mules rotting in the sun. The same ground also held the graves of the fallen, "sprinkled thicker than the harvest sheaves." At the front, deep "gashes furrow the face of the country, where the red earth has been piled in long lines of traversing intrenchments, edged with slashing and abatis, or heaped in fortifications bristling with threatening cannon."[150]

Under these conditions, Benjamin Butler and the Army of the James had settled into a period of relative quiet outside of Richmond. On the 16th, Butler received a welcome note from his wife, Sarah, announcing her arrival at Fortress Monroe from their hometown of Lowell, Massachusetts. Butler soon left camp to meet her. Before his departure, though, he ordered young Godfrey Weitzel, now commander of the Eighteenth Corps, to take charge of the entire army. This assignment rankled Alfred Terry, the Tenth Corps chief, who believed he deserved the honor, based on seniority. Weitzel agreed and appealed to Grant for clarification. When the lieutenant general confirmed Butler's decision, Weitzel reluctantly took charge.[151]

As Butler visited Fortress Monroe, the Confederates continued to improve their fortifications. On Monday, the 17th, Union signal officers reported that about two hundred black laborers worked all day on the breastworks running from Fort Gilmer to New Market Road.[152] The lookouts made a similar observation the next day. The Army of the James made some improvements of its own.

By Tuesday, the 18th, when Butler returned to the front with his wife, he received some good news from Adjutant General Lorenzo Thomas, who reported that six regiments of African American troops (totaling 5,500) were en route from Baltimore.[153] Thomas had begun organizing the units from Kentucky in July. "Physically they are the best I have organized," he wrote, "and I only regret they have not had more time for drill. I am satisfied they will do the work assigned them." The first of these units, the 115th USCT, arrived at Deep Bottom that week.[154] Two days later Butler saw his beloved Sarah off to Fortress Monroe. "Goodnight love," she wrote that evening. "I hope you will sleep well in your tent tonight (no one to crowd you, no one to pet you, no one to tease you)." Butler replied that night. "I got your note tonight," he penned, "I was very lonely indeed after you went away."[155]

"much less than his reward"

As more troops arrived to bolster the Army of the James, Union soldiers stationed along the Darbytown Road stood guard over the private houses of civilians who had taken an oath of allegiance to the United States. One of these was Dr. Johnson, whose house stood in the thick of the recent fighting. Nearly a week after the heavy Union reconnaissance along the Darbytown Road, many women and children, along with a few men, including Dr. Johnson, continued to live in the middle of the war zone. On October 8, August Kautz reported to his diary that "Dr. Johnson is with us and does not seem disposed to leave us."[156] The civilians' presence had become a significant problem for Union troops. By the third week in October, five federals assigned to safeguard these dwellings had been shot by Southern "bushwhackers." This was too much for Butler, and he ordered his men to depopulate the hamlet of Darbytown, a collection of homes south of the road bearing the same name. Union authorities announced the civilians would receive passage north, should they choose to go. If not, officials would transport them beyond the U.S. lines southeast to Suffolk. On or about Wednesday, October 19, Darbytown's residents received two days' notice, and, at the deadline, more than forty women and children rode in wagons south across the New Market Road to General Butler's headquarters. Near Aiken's Landing, they boarded the steamer *Greyhound.* One observer was less than impressed by their appearance and said many were dressed "nearly in rags." "Some little boys . . . had on Uncle Sam's pants, made up, of course, to fit," according to the witness. Dr. Johnson, who had apparently taken the oath of allegiance to the United States, escaped to Richmond and did not accompany the others. "This double traitor has received much less than his reward," wrote J. McDuff in the *Philadelphia Inquirer*, "but should the fortune of war ever throw him in General Butler's lines again, he will undoubtedly lose his neck, as well as his property."[157]

Part II

Grant's Sixth Offensive

In the wake of the battles along the Darbytown Road in Henrico County, attention drifted back south to Petersburg. Over the following weeks, Grant would plan and execute his sixth major offensive of the campaign. In doing so, he sought to complete his stranglehold on Petersburg and hasten Richmond's fall. The operation would bring much maneuvering and intense fighting southwest of Petersburg and, also, east of Richmond. Once again, Union forces would test Confederate defenses. And, once again, Lee would scramble to plug gaps and hold on, with the fate of the war in the east at stake.

CHAPTER 4

The Petersburg Front

~

Over the summer and fall, the Union and Confederate armies had transformed the landscape around Petersburg into a dizzying array of trenches, rifle pits, fortifications, and military roads. George F. Williams, a *New York Times* reporter who had covered much of the campaign, provided readers in October with a vivid account of the earthworks ringing the city, describing the maze of forts, trenches, lunettes, covered ways, saps, and ravelins that festooned the countryside.[1] Every hill along the line hosted a fort, a strong point linked by long trenches called "curtains," which formed interlocking fields of fire into all approaches. The trenches stretched over rises and through hollows "like a huge serpent." In front of the works lay chevaux de frise, rows of sharpened stakes planted in eighteen-foot sections. Evidence of the war was difficult to avoid.

The opposing lines began at Appomattox River east of town and stretched south on a tight parallel. In this sector, high ground along the Union line offered a clear view of the city's steeples and rooftops. The combatants had settled into these opposing works after the initial failed Union assaults in June. The earthworks exhibited a haphazard quality, dug by men under fire often where they found themselves at the end of combat. At the Jerusalem Plank Road, the opposing lines swerved west. The Confederate trenches hugged Petersburg's outskirts, while the Union works pulled away to the south, eventually reaching across the Weldon Railroad. Union troops had planted these fortifications through a series of methodical advances conducted from June through October. In late June, they seized the Jerusalem Plank Road. In August, they severed the Weldon Railroad farther to the west, an important supply artery into Petersburg. In late September, they ventured out and stormed Confederate positions along the Squirrel Level Road near Poplar Spring Church. After each advance, the federal troops extended their trench lines, siting forts at key locations and connecting their new positions to their base at City Point through a network of roads and rails. By October, nearly fifteen miles of continuous parapets and ditches stretched from the south bank of the Appomattox River almost halfway around Petersburg.

West of the Jerusalem Plank Road, the soldiers did not labor under the same, claustrophobic conditions that existed east of the city. To Williams, the *New York Times* reporter, the works in the west sector had a "pretension to beauty and symmetry." In this area, timber dotted the wide expanse of no-man's-land. In many places, Union soldiers had felled trees to create a "teasing and torturing abattis," which dispensed with the need for chevaux de frise. Felled trees also lined the parapets to form revetments, which increased the strength and durability of the works. Williams noted numerous bombproofs, logged frame structures sunk into the ground. Opposing pickets in this sector looked out across a wide space. With this breathing room, the regimental camps nestled closer to the front lines. Still farther back stood the headquarters of the brigade, division, and corps commanders. Behind the wagon and ambulance parks, miles and miles of corduroy roads connected this vast network, constructed with long straight pine trunks called sleepers, and shorter, cross-ways logs, all covered by dirt and pine tops.[2]

The configuration of the Union lines around Petersburg granted Meade and his army a significant advantage. The lines, pressed close against the Confederate works east of Petersburg, forced the soldiers in gray to man their posts night and day to prevent a sudden assault. Grant had employed this strategy of maintaining continuous contact with the enemy throughout the fighting in 1864, beginning with the Overland campaign. West of the Jerusalem Plank Road, however, the substantial buffer between the opposing trenches allowed the Federals to form their mobile columns free from the prying eyes of Confederate pickets. At Petersburg and Richmond, this arrangement afforded Union commanders the flexibility to plan their offensives, while severely limiting Lee's ability to conduct his own operations.

Outside Petersburg, a Union military railroad augmented the web of dirt roads and facilitated troop and supply movement. By October, these rails reached from the Union base at City Point all the way to the Weldon Railroad near the Globe Tavern (also known as the "Yellow House"). In some areas, Union soldiers erected earthworks to protect the rail line from rebel fire.[3] The railroad was uneven, constructed under the exigencies of war with no proper bed. Engineers and laborers included fills and cuts only where absolutely necessary; along many stretches, the rails rested directly on the earth. As a result, the cars bobbed and wobbled noticeably along the route. According to one of Grant's staffers, the railroad's "undulations were so marked that a train moving along it looked in the distance like a fly crawling over a corrugated washboard."[4]

Forts, camps, roads, and railroads were not the only notable features of the war torn landscape outside Petersburg. The countryside also bore witness to the human cost of the heavy combat that summer and fall. Williams wrote,

> No matter where you go, the graves of the heroic dead meet your eye. In the vicinity of the hospitals, behind camps, in the covered ways leading to some

important or exposed post, in the fields in front of our works, beneath some wide-spreading tree, and by the dusty roadside. On every side, and at the most unexpected times, you come across these mute and melancholy testimonials to the awful loss of life that this accursed rebellion has brought upon the country. Generally a rude railing is erected round these graves, and sometimes a loving hand plants a shrub, or scatters a heap of cedar boughs over the last resting place of some mourned comrade. Virginia has indeed been enriched with some of the best blood of our land, but they have died in behalf of their country, and a grateful people will forever more hold their memory sacred.[5]

As a journalist, Williams could describe the landscape at Petersburg during his visit, but the soldiers who endured the conditions there day in and day out had the best understanding of the war zone. At the front, they navigated the ditches and covered ways, avoided deadly spots exposed to enemy sharpshooters, and endured the hazards of picket duty at posts sited only yards from the enemy. Danger was everywhere. Pickets would blaze away at any object that met their eye, "animate or inanimate," using up as many as sixty rounds a day.[6] Along the front, incoming fire would erupt at the slightest provocation. Sporadic gunshots would often build to a continuous "roll and reverberation of hundreds of heavy guns."[7] When not on the picket line, many of the men pulled fatigue duty, building breastworks, excavating pits, and throwing up redoubts for field artillery. Much of this work occurred at night and was subject to frequent halts when the fire was hottest.[8]

Some weapons added particular misery to the grim conditions. Mortars of various sizes threw high-trajectory shells that could drop over the highest parapet and bring sudden death. On October 11, two Maine volunteers died instantly from gruesome head wounds as they gazed skyward toward the screech of an incoming mortar shell that landed directly on top of them.[9] The mortar fire spurred the soldiers on both sides to dig small "gopher" holes and larger bombproofs.[10] Men piled as much as eight feet of dirt atop the more substantial structures.[11] The protective caves were not invulnerable, though, and certain shells, like those thrown by Whitworth rifled gun and some of the large mortar projectiles, could cause damage even to the thick bunkers. Over the course of the campaign, the men learned to distinguish incoming rounds by their distinctive whines and took actions necessary to spare life and limb.[12] Perhaps the most unusual airborne object was the occasional ramrod, which through design or accident would fly over the lines, emitting an odd whirring sound. Soldiers listened for these with more than a casual interest, for they could be deadly.[13]

Given the harrowing conditions of the front lines, soldiers and officers looked for diversions wherever they could. Many Union officers relieved the stress of the campaign through horse racing. During October, one stretch of the Halifax Road adjacent to the Weldon Railroad served as a popular spot for such equine contests.[14]

In the camps, sutlers roamed about selling pies and other stuffs not generally available from daily rations. Writing home in October, a Vermont soldier, fortunate enough to camp near some butchers from the Second Corps, reported, "We are altogether in a fair way to live & get fat."[15] Another soldier from the 117th New York wrote in late October that they had "all we want to eat we have fresh meat and soft meat hard tack fresh . . . coffee and shooger."[16]

Despite the tremendous length of Union lines, the federal army controlled limited ground around Petersburg. Near the Peebles' Farm at the western end of the Union lines, the trenches swerved south and, after more than a mile, bent back eastward in a series of curtain segments and forts facing south. Thus, the Union lines had two sides: one that faced Petersburg and the Confederate works, and a second, a mile or two to the south, that doubled back and protected the army's rear. In essence, the engineers had constructed a protected corridor housing an armed camp that reached around much of Petersburg. Confederate scouts and cavalry patrols infested the country beyond this enclave.

In September, Wade Hampton, Lee's cavalry chief, vividly illustrated the limitations of Union control around Petersburg when he launched the "beefsteak" raid. One of Hampton's scouts had penetrated the picket line near the federal base at City Point and gathered detailed information about Union dispositions. This intelligence allowed Hampton's men to conduct a prodigious raid, nabbing several thousand cattle grazing near Coggins Point on the James River. The raiders escorted the beeves to the banks of Hatcher's Run southwest of Petersburg, yielding an ample beef supply for hungry rebels in October.[17]

While Confederates roamed freely, Union scouting parties emerged from the federal fortifications at their peril. Out in the countryside, blue horsemen found tight-lipped civilians, roads blocked with debris, and combative enemy cavalry pickets. A Union reconnaissance to Stony Creek on October 12 failed after federal cavalrymen could not push aside a small infantry detachment. Interviews conducted during the operation with citizens and slaves produced little useful information.[18] In some cases, though, such forays brought positive results. Two days after the Stony Creek mission, twenty Pennsylvania troopers ventured down the Weldon Railroad toward Reams Station, where they encountered a few enemy scouts and captured two wagons and their "contraband" drivers. The expedition netted seventy bushels of oats, several barrels of salt, and a rebel conscription agent thrown in for good measure.[19] Rebel guerrillas also wrought havoc on federal communications. In mid-October, Union officials found themselves forced to detach an entire regiment to patrol a section of telegraph line along the James River.[20]

"The men suffer for it"

While conditions remained difficult for the Union army at Petersburg, Confederate soldiers and Petersburg's civilians endured worse. Life in the trenches brought lean times for the defenders. Low stocks, poor organization, and inefficient distribution hampered Confederate supply efforts, making even the basic necessities hard to come by. "The water here is very bad," wrote one soldier, "we have little wells dug along the ditches, but the water is muddy and full of frogs. The men suffer for it, of course, and are very sickly along here."[21] With limited manpower, Confederate commanders posted their units in the trenches for long periods. In the squalor of the front lines east of the city, soldiers found it hard to bathe or even wash. Simple movements were difficult under the gaze of the enemy sharpshooters. Men yearned for the brief respites that would bring their regiments off the line to the rear, even if only for a few days.

In town, there was also little comfort. Petersburg's citizens had endured a harsh introduction to the military campaign. Beginning in June, Union artillery batteries began hurling shells directly into the city streets. The cruel fire had little tactical purpose but succeeded in terrorizing Petersburg's residents. Within a month, the intermittent shelling had flushed much of the population out of the town, leaving vacant houses in their wake, some of which then filled with refugees from elsewhere. Though the Union artillery fire slackened by the end of July, other issues, such as severe food shortages, continued to plague those who remained.[22]

Civilians in the rural areas faced their own problems. With many men off in the army, the families remaining on the farms and homesteads struggled to produce food for their tables. For one Dinwiddie County resident, Mary Curtis Burgess, the conflict brought special challenges. In 1854, she had moved from Herkimer County, New York, to Dinwiddie with her new husband, William Burgess. The couple took up residence at a farm jointly owned by her husband and father-in-law. The property lay astride the Boydton Plank Road about eight miles southwest of Petersburg. In the war's first years, the family's northern roots had bred suspicion among the natives. But these concerns subsided when three of the Burgess men joined the ranks of the Confederate army. As the war raged elsewhere in Virginia, life on the farm continued amid the columns of Confederate soldiers that occasionally marched past the farmhouse along the Plank Road. Rebel soldiers would call constantly, eating at the Burgess table almost every day. Some would steal chickens from the coops or vegetables from the garden and then ask Mary Burgess for her own kettle to stew them in. Others would raid the grapevines in the family vineyard. To save the plantation's honey supply, the family brought one hive into the house and placed it in an open window. Despite the deprivations, Burgess and her family survived on flour hidden in the granary, corn meal from the fields, and fish from the mill pond. Some of the visiting soldiers sought out more than food. Far away from their own families, they would spend time with the Burgess family to escape their harsh life in the army. Such visits would often bring tears to the eyes of these homesick men. One young Confederate apologized for his despondency and explained that he had a "wife and babes at home."[23]

The summer of 1864 brought the Union and Confederate armies to Dinwiddie County and increased military activity close to the Burgess Farm. Though the farm was many miles from the initial battles along the Dimmock line and the Jerusalem Plank Road, the distance was not as great as Mary Burgess may have wished. Early on the morning of July 30, a heavy jolt shook her home. Mrs. Burgess toppled from her bed "nearly paralyzed with fear."[24] More than nine miles away, the Army of the Potomac had detonated a mine under the Confederate trenches east of Petersburg, and the Crater battle had begun. Her husband raced into town to witness the fight, only to become so sickened by the scene that he "fell prostrate" at the home of a friend.[25]

The summer also brought more immediate danger. One day, two Confederate soldiers, aware of the family's northern origin, came looking for trouble. The pair approached the farmhouse from the west along the White Oak Road, armed to the teeth and hurling epithets. Mrs. Burgess's husband, William, picked up his double-barreled shotgun and a long meat knife. When the soldiers burst into the home and threatened to kill him, Mary Burgess rushed to his side, wrapping her arms around him, holding tight despite his efforts to break her loose. Two of their children did the same. Stymied by her tactics, the Confederates backed off, promising to return and finish their work. The malcontents reappeared twenty minutes later, hoping to find an easier time against the elder Burgess, Mary's father-in-law. "The old man is at the pond and we will go for him," they boasted. With Mary Burgess and the children hidden in the garden, the younger Mr. Burgess once again grabbed his gun and raced to his father's house across the White Oak Road. He sprinted through the orchard to the icehouse overlooking the pond. The soldiers had also reached the banks and were busy heaving sticks and rocks at the elderly man, who was just then stepping out of his boat onto shore. A brick hit home, knocking him to the ground. From the icehouse, the younger Burgess raised his rifle and fired, piercing one of the renegades at the shoulder. The unwounded soldier dumped his comrade into a cart and beat a hasty retreat. After tending to his father, Burgess mounted his horse and rode down the Plank Road to the Dinwiddie courthouse to turn himself in for his transgression. But when he stated his case, the authorities "told him he did wrong in not shooting in the first place."[26] Burgess climbed back on his horse and returned to the farm and his family.

"if we can't get the men"

As civilians endured the war zone, politicians and soldiers focused on broader matters in anticipation of November's presidential election. Recent events brought heartening news for Lincoln. In late September, general Philip Sheridan's victories at Winchester and Fisher's Hill in the Shenandoah Valley had boosted his prospects. Sheridan had commanded infantry under Grant in the west and led the Army of the Potomac's cavalry during the Overland campaign. Now, he directed the forces in the Valley. His hard-hitting, cocksure style may have annoyed many, but it yielded tangible results in a theater that had seen few clear Union victories. As the diminutive fighter whipped the rebels, Confederate hopes elsewhere continued to slip. The rebels yearned for battlefield victories, but the means to bring about such results were meager. They needed spectacular gains, and, without them, Robert E. Lee's anxiety and despondency grew. His personal correspondence revealed his concerns of imminent collapse. In October, he warned his wife that her residence in Richmond was "very hazardous in the present uncertainty of events."[27]

The general had good reason to fret. His army's position left him few options. The Richmond-Petersburg front tied down his troops into an awkward string of ditches, blotting any opportunity for maneuver, a necessity for offensive operations. According to postwar interviews with his staff officers, Lee believed that the Richmond lines were ultimately indefensible, and searched for ways to withdraw his men west and away from the navigable rivers that formed ideal Union supply lines. For instance, the Staunton River to the west may have offered Lee a good defensive line.[28] Grant also recognized this possibility and, after the war, confessed anxiety at the prospect of abandoning his City Point supply base to pursue Lee into the interior.[29]

According to historical convention, the stalemate at Petersburg spelled doom for Lee by binding his forces to trenches and preventing fights on open ground. But defusing his offensive capabilities would not necessarily yield Union victory. Rather than hastening the war's end, the complex earthworks covering Richmond and Petersburg may have actually prolonged the life of the Confederacy and offered its best chances for victory. The strong defenses blunted Union advances and spared rebel strength. The lack of Union success increased Northern war weariness and boosted the electoral chances of a Democratic candidate.[30]

Whatever the Petersburg campaign's ultimate impact on Confederate fortunes, in the fall of 1864, Lee continued to display a stubborn resolve to attack Grant.[31] He consistently sought opportunities to punish Union forces despite his smaller numbers. He believed that the Confederate path to victory lay in aggressive operations, not in passive defense. As early as June, he directed his commanders to seize offensive opportunities whenever possible. In a dispatch to Third Corps commander A. P. Hill, he wrote, "The time has arrived, in my opinion, when something more is necessary than adhering to lines and defensive positions. We shall be obliged to go out and prevent the enemy from selecting such positions as he chooses." Although Lee lacked the manpower to launch large-scale offensives, he explained to Hill, "You must be prepared to fight him in the field, to prevent him taking positions such as he desires, and I expect the co-operation of all the corps commanders in the course which necessity now will oblige us to pursue."[32] Lee did not waiver from this course. He sought to punch and counterpunch wherever he could. In August, he asked the secretary of war for a few thousand men to occupy strong portions of the line and allow the use of veteran troops to "good effect" elsewhere. Without more men, he explained, "I cannot see how we are to escape the natural military consequences of the enemy's numerical superiority."[33] Again, in early September, he requested additional reserves to free the regular troops "for any opportunity to strike at the enemy."[34] He needed more men.

"Fight him in the Field"

In the midst of declining hopes, Lee arrayed his troops to block further Union progress. Immediately east of Petersburg, he stationed the four brigades of Bushrod Johnson's division. These men drew the unenviable task of manning the lines from the Appomattox River south past the Crater, where opposing picket posts crouched, uncomfortably close to each other.[35] While Johnson's men endured the misery of the trenches, much of the campaign's fighting and marching had fallen on the shoulders of the Third Corps, led by Major General Ambrose Powell Hill and his three division commanders, William Mahone, Henry Heth, and Cadmus Wilcox. Faulted for his earlier performance at engagements such as Bristoe Station, Jericho Ford, and the Wilderness, A. P. Hill had served reliably throughout the fighting at Petersburg, avoiding grave mistakes and ably checking a string of Union offensives.

Little is known of A. P. Hill's personal actions during the campaign. He did not survive the war, and few of his battle reports from the Petersburg campaign remain. Much of his personal correspondence is lost, as well. Despite this dearth of source material, the efforts of his command speak loudly enough. In a postwar sketch of the general, William E. Cameron, Mahone's assistant adjutant and in-spector general, wrote that Hill was a familiar sight to the soldiers at Petersburg, "constantly on the lines" and rarely attended except for an occasional staff offi-cer or courier. "Of ordinary height, his figure was slight but athletic, his carriage erect, and his dress plainly neat."[36] A chaplain, who spotted Hill at a troop review in October, described the general as "a small man, can be scarcely more than 5 ft. 8 in. high, nor weigh more than 125 or 130 lbs; . . . he wears a heavy, long sandy beard; he looks rather weather-beaten; he was dressed very plainly, rode a splen-did grey horse and seemed to have perfect control of himself & of his horse in the saddle; he seemed to be very lively and talkative."[37]

Ongoing illness during the Petersburg campaign often removed Hill from the battlefield and forced him to rely on his division commanders.[38] Such reliance yielded a great windfall for Robert E. Lee and the Confederacy. At Petersburg, William Mahone, who had failed to stand out in previous campaigns, demonstrated a keen tactical acumen and a winning aggressiveness. Throughout the summer, he met a series of Union advances with devastating attacks. A railroad man before the war and a native of southeastern Virginia, Mahone knew the terrain around Petersburg, having personally surveyed much of it. He used this knowledge to maneuver against Union forces. Other commanders also performed well. Henry Heth and Cadmus Wilcox contributed their share. In addition, the cavalry, under command of South Carolinian Wade Hampton, continued to match a foe that was sometimes larger and always better armed and equipped. Hampton's two divisions at Petersburg, under Rooney Lee and Matthew Butler, had provided invaluable service picketing roads, snuffing out federal raids, and doing some hard fighting.

Indeed, the Confederate generals managed to achieve significant tactical success. Whenever Union forces sought to gain ground south of Petersburg, the Confederate Third Corps attacked any opening they could find in the Union column. Hill followed Lee's directive to fight the enemy "in the field." This approach contributed to successes at the Jerusalem Plank Road in June, the Crater in July, and the Weldon Railroad and Reams Station in August. In each of these battles, Confederate columns met Union advances at and around Petersburg with devastating counterattacks, usually in the form of assaults against vulnerable Union flanks.

At Reams Station in August 1864, Hill's and Hampton's men overran a poorly placed Union position on the Weldon Railroad and dealt a devastating blow to Winfield Hancock's Second Corps. The victory may have hinted to some a return to the former glory of Lee's veterans, but, in reality, the successes produced little benefit. Union forces continued to occupy other sections of the Weldon Railroad. In fact, the results at Reams Station illuminated a disturbing pattern for the Confederates. Despite the temporary gains and captured prisoners from these tactical victories, the rebel operations did little to loosen the Union grip tightening around Petersburg. Robert E. Lee recognized that Petersburg was slipping away. He understood that the end was near unless drastic changes occurred. With each new Union offensive, the rebel defenders stretched their lines farther and farther to fill the extended ditches; the needed men were simply not available. In the wake of Grant's late September offensive, Bushrod Johnson's division became the sole occupant of lines immediately east of Petersburg, trenches previously manned by two full divisions and a few extra brigades. The balance of the Petersburg lines held the infantry brigades of Heth, Mahone, and Wilcox and some of the cavalry units of Hampton's command.

"The enemy must be defeated"

Lee's efforts earlier in October had led nowhere. His attack at the Johnson Farm and the New Market Road on October 7 ended in utter failure and provided Benjamin Butler and his generals with fair warning of similar moves in the future. South of the James, Lee yearned for decisive action against Meade. At the beginning of the month, he urged A. P. Hill to find a way to "break the enemy's center," a surprising suggestion given the formidable rows of ditches, parapets, abatis, and chevaux de frise such an effort would have to overcome.[39] With the forts and trenches on the backside of the Union line, even one of Lee's audacious flanking marches would simply bring the attacking column into the face of more fortifications. Lee eventually declined to attempt such desperate measures. Perhaps he could not find the right circumstances, or had abandoned hope for a military miracle at Petersburg. By October 10, he began to focus on the army's defensive preparations. He was convinced that Grant planned another offensive between October 10 and 15. In warning Hill of such an operation, he predicted Grant would hit the Confederate left near the Chickahominy River and would also seek to sever the South Side Railroad at Petersburg. He urged Hill to draw as many men as possible into the trenches.[40]

With his offensive plans at Richmond fading away, Lee sought to wring benefits from the Shenandoah Valley. Throughout the war, the Confederates had relied on that region to tie down Union troops and threaten Washington. The Valley provided a convenient thoroughfare into Maryland, which the rebels used on the march to Gettysburg, and during Jubal Early's recent raid on Washington.[41] Into the fall, Lee looked for results from Early even after the defeats at Winchester and Fisher's Hill. "The enemy must be defeated, and I rely upon you to do it," he wrote on September 27. Urging Early to gather his forces and hold the "enemy in check until you can strike him with all your strength," he predicted that "one victory will put all things right." He also gently chastised Early for committing his troops piecemeal in recent battles.[42]

Lee had high hopes for the Valley. Unfortunately, he also had a poor grasp of the situation there. From his headquarters outside Richmond, he informed Early that Sheridan's troops "cannot be so greatly superior to yours. His effective infantry, I do not think, exceeds 12,000 men." Lee's assessment was incorrect. Contemporaneous Union reports placed 32,000 U.S. soldiers under Sheridan's active command, while Early only mustered about 15,000.[43] Armed with this faulty information, Lee continued to funnel troops to Early. He dispatched Rosser's cavalry brigade with the expectation that the extra men would help to land a crushing blow. As the weeks went by, his misperception endured. On October 12, he wrote to Early, reminding him of the sacrifices made to send precious manpower to the Valley. Yet again, Lee downplayed Sheridan's strength, and he urged Early to strive for "success" and to "proceed on the principle of not retaining with you more troops than you can use to advantage in any position the enemy may take and send the rest to me."[44]

Lee's misunderstanding created a serious problem. Sheridan had badly mauled Early's tiny force at Winchester and Fisher's Hill in September. As Lee lectured Early about concentrating his force and striking a blow, Early actually faced odds greater than two to one. Whether due to faulty intelligence or unreasonable optimism, Lee simply did not understand conditions in the Valley. As a result, he had committed a number of his best commanders and thousands of battle-hardened veterans to a dubious, potentially disastrous enterprise. He urged his subordinate to seek a decisive victory. However, with better information, he might have directed Early to harass Sheridan while the Confederate forces sought to gain traction against Grant outside Richmond. Instead, he goaded Early into offensive operations against a much larger opponent. With such guidance from Richmond, conditions would lead to a dramatic result but perhaps not the outcome Lee had in mind.

The Valley was only once piece of the puzzle. The chessboard in the eastern theater also included Wilmington, North Carolina, the last remaining eastern rebel gateway to the sea and European markets. As early as August, Lee had warned Confederate officials of a possible attack on the North Carolina port.[45] His concern was well placed. Indeed, throughout September and October, the Union navy had pleaded with Grant to support an operation against Fort Fisher, the sprawling rebel installation guarding Wilmington's approaches. Grant, in turn, raised this possibility with Sherman through correspondence and a personal trip by his aide, Horace Porter. The lieutenant general proposed to detach ten thousand men for a Wilmington attack while the Army of the Potomac simultaneously attempted to sever the South Side Railroad at Petersburg. The navy began preparations, but Grant soon grew cool to the enterprise. Concerned about diluting his strength at Richmond, he backed off from the Wilmington venture, at least for the time being. Nevertheless, the Confederates noticed the naval activity, and by October the U.S. plans had become something of an open secret and were known to General W. H. C. Whiting, then commanding Wilmington's defenders.[46]

"growing stronger every day"

While Lee struggled to gain some control over events elsewhere, early October brought good news to the Richmond-Petersburg front. His repeated pleas for additional men had begun to yield results from the Confederate government. Concerns that he voiced after Fort Harrison's fall had caused "grave anxiety" in the mind of War Secretary James Seddon, who intended to "strain the powers and

means of the Department to accomplish efficient recruitment."[47] The War Department struggled to bring more men into the battle lines, increase the use of
slave labor in the armies, and deliver more horses for Lee's men.[48] On October 5,
Adjutant and Inspector General Samuel Cooper issued General Orders No. 76,
which revoked all details in the army with the exception of men involved with
munitions, other supplies, and "work indispensable to military operations." The
directive also called for a review of all exemptions related to physical disability.[49]
Two days later, Lee ordered A. P. Hill to place "all extra duty men in all the depart-
ments—wagoners, cooks, clerks, couriers, &c." into the ranks and put reserves
and militia at Petersburg into the trenches.[50]

These efforts to combat the manpower crisis yielded tangible results. John H.
Claiborne, in charge of Petersburg's military hospitals, observed, "The army here is
filling rapidly—and the conscripts and detailed men [are] coming in by squads."[51]
Similarly, a surgeon with the 13th South Carolina Infantry reported that about
twelve thousand men arrived at the front from Richmond, including men working for the Confederate government and "gentlemen of leisure." Provost dragnets
combed the capital's streets, rounding up men with little apparent regard to their
current occupation and organizing them into battalions. According to the surgeon,
the veterans in the lines relished these developments.[52] Artillery commanders sent
"half the drivers of each battery and all the surplus men to the trenches," according
to one gunner who predicted the directive would reap two to three thousand.[53]
The army's efforts also emptied the hospitals of the walking wounded. Another soldier observed that some of the infirm looked "as though they should be in bed."[54]
The practice appalled one Carolinian, who suggested that the responsible authorities had "neither hearts nor consciences."[55]

At Petersburg, rebel deserters shared the news of the increases with their Union
captives. General Winfield Hancock reported that the Confederates had piled detailed men into the trenches.[56] Additional reports suggested that slaves were taking
the place of teamsters and other detailed men, just as Lee had urged.[57] North of the
James, the story was similar. A soldier correspondent from Field's division noted
that, "Our ranks had been handsomely recruited, by the revocation of details and
the return of convalescent soldiers." Several field officers also rejoined their commands, sufficiently recovered from wounds suffered in earlier battles.[58] "Detailed
men are flocking to Richmond; crowded trains come in daily, and the fast gathering
hosts at Camp Lee promise soon to make our army as strong, if not stronger, than
ever before," wrote one Southerner.[59] Some veterans derisively referred to these new
arrivals as "bomb-proof" men.[60] On the 19th, Porter Alexander explained to his wife
that detailed men and reserves were "arriving in Richmond at the rate of about a
thousand a day." He also noted that the army was receiving a "great many negroes to
relieve soldiers who are teamsters," adding that the "engineers have a force of over a
thousand of them working constantly on our fortifications."[61]

The press, north and south, also took note of the measures. Editors of the *New York Tribune* viewed the Confederate efforts as a sign of desperation, explaining that every man, "of whatever age, condition, occupation or position, is hurried to the defenses and put on duty."[62] Southern papers implored men to fill the ranks.[63] The *Daily Confederate,* published in Raleigh, noted the increase in Lee's army and reported that the corps, divisions, brigades, and regiments were "assuming their former proportions." According to the same story, an unnamed Virginia regiment turned out eleven hundred muskets at a Sunday dress parade in October.[64] One Richmond paper, describing the young recruits on the capital's streets, sought to put a good face on things, remarking that these young soldiers "are extremely well grown for their age." But the *Philadelphia Inquirer* replied, "If such be the infants of Old Virginia, what are the grown people like?"[65]

The October inspection reports confirmed what soldiers and reporters had observed. The army had grown considerably, according to the inspector general of Lee's army, Lieutenant Colonel H. E. Peyton. Hill's Third Corps alone swelled by five thousand men. Pickett's division of the First Corps, manning the lines at Bermuda Hundred, had also increased, particularly in the Virginia and North Carolina units. Peyton cited several causes for the new tallies but singled out the efforts of Lee and the War Department. He also noted the gradual return of wounded men and the "abatement of ague and fever—a disease which had greatly depleted some commands" and declared that the returning soldiers were the "best in the army and the country."[66] Lee's cavalry commander, Wade Hampton, reported, "My command is growing stronger every day, and it is in good condition for a fight."[67]

There was a limit to such growth, though. There were only so many men recovering from wounds or absent on other duties. In addition, the Confederacy's already limited pool of new recruits and draftees was nearly bone dry. And while there may have been men under arms in other parts of the Confederacy, politics and poor military organization rendered them unavailable to Lee.[68] Under these conditions, a growing chorus called for the Confederate government to arm slaves, a suggestion that had only been mentioned in whispers and sporadic public statements before. In October, the public debate about slave soldiers gathered steam. As Longstreet's aide, Thomas Goree, put it, "We must have more men, and the places of detailed men will have to be supplied by negroes—and, if needs be, I say put the negroes in the ranks and make soldiers of them—fight negro with negro."[69] With the manpower concerns looming in Confederate minds, several newspapers, led by the *Richmond Enquirer,* publicly urged the rebel government to send enslaved men to fight for their owners.[70]

Other Southern newspapers opposed the idea.[71] However, coincident with these reports, Lee embraced the proposal in a letter to Confederate congressman William Porcher Miles.[72] By early 1865, the Confederate government would eventually enact a limited program to arm blacks, which came too late to have an impact on the battlefield. In October 1864, though, as Lee and Davis strained to increase the army defending Richmond, that debate simmered in its early stages and retained an academic quality with no clear resolution in sight.[73]

"my men made it all for me"

With thousands of soldiers arriving at the front line, there was one particularly notable return. On October 7, General James Longstreet, steadily recovering from the wounds he had suffered in the Wilderness, wrote to Lee's staff seeking assignment to "any service that I may be able to discharge," including a post in the western theater.[74] Lee had no desire to send his "Old War Horse" to the west. On the 13th Longstreet reported to the First Corps but did not officially resume command until six days later.[75] Throughout the war, Longstreet had been a reliable, steady force in a constellation of dim lit stars. Unshakable and persistent, he had excelled at defensive tactics and led his share of devastating attacks. Upon returning, he took charge of Hoke's and Field's divisions north of the James, Pickett's division at Bermuda Hundred, Martin Gary's cavalry brigade, and the other mixed units of Richard Ewell's department.[76] In response to a passerby's compliment on the way to report for duty, Longstreet replied, "I have some little reputation, but my men made it all for me."[77] When he resumed his duties, his right arm remained paralyzed from his wound, and doctors predicted full recovery would take a year or more. On Saturday, the 15th, he visited the lines with Richard Anderson, the officer who had sought to fill his shoes for the past six months.[78] As Longstreet made his appearance along the trenches, the soldiers of the First Corps "mounted the breastworks and . . . made the welkin ring with cheers for the 'old bull of the woods.'"[79] "They felt that the old pilot had returned to his ship," noted one soldier at the time, "and would guide it safely through the storm breakers."[80]

CHAPTER 5

Petersburg Becomes the Key

~

"Politics absorb more and more of the time and thoughts of officers and men," wrote one federal artillery commander on October 16.[1] In the Union trenches and regimental camps, the upcoming election was on everyone's mind. While opinions varied, Lincoln appeared to enjoy an advantage among the rank and file. As Union general Joshua Chamberlain explained later, McClellan's "personal popularity in the army was something marvelous," but the soldiers "were unwilling that their long fight should be set down as a failure, even though thus far it seemed so."[2] Similar views filled the diaries and letters of the soldiers.[3] One New Yorker wrote that McClellan "ambitiously thrusts his private interests in advance of the interests of the country and lays himself open to the accusation of being a demagogue."[4] An anonymous correspondent to the *New York Tribune* summed up the pro-Lincoln sentiment in the army: "Do you think it possible for soldiers to labor as we have labored, to march as we have marched, to fight as we have fought, and when on the point of reaping the benefit of our labors and sufferings, vote for a party which would give up everything for which we have labored and fought?"[5] Others were more direct. A letter from a Wisconsin soldier, reprinted in the Appleton paper, explained that the "intelligent soldiery will be unanimous in support of the government—for old Abe and Union, and against McClellan and treason."[6]

Held in the midst of war, the election offered a testament to the country's resilience. For the first time in U.S. history, many soldiers would cast their votes in the field. Not all fighting men, however, had this option. Those hailing from New Jersey, for example, a Democratic-leaning state, could vote only if they received permission to return home to cast their ballots. This produced discord. The "feeling of indignation among the New Jersey troops was great," recalled a veteran historian of the 11th New Jersey.[7] The voting rules did not deter the regiment from expressing its views. In the absence of formal voting, the members simply conducted their own polling and forwarded the results as "an expression of its choice."[8] Robert McAllister, a New Jersey native and brigade commander in Hancock's Second Corps, regretted his inability to vote for Lincoln. Back home, his wife sought to offset his missing ballot by sponsoring meetings for the president.[9]

Lincoln's support in the army was by no means unanimous. Marsena Patrick, Meade's provost marshal general, planned to vote for McClellan because "it would most surely, bring to us peace."[10] Others were more belligerent. A sharpshooter in the Second Corps forwarded photos of Grant and Meade to his mother and followed up with the comment: "They are very good portraits of our commanding *murderers!*" He also warned an acquaintance back home that "if he does not want this Lincoln power to always reign to do all in his power to free the country from such a viper & cast an over whelming vote for Little Mac."[11]

As the soldiers discussed the election, events at home continued to shape the future. In mid-October, three states (Pennsylvania, Ohio, and Indiana) held elections for state and local offices. These contests served as a bellwether for the upcoming presidential contest.[12] The results brought good news for Lincoln and his supporters. Republican candidates won significant victories. To the *Philadelphia Inquirer,* the Ohio tallies foreshadowed November's presidential election "in unmistakable figures."[13] The *Richmond Dispatch* echoed that assessment, predicting that "the returns from the North leave no doubt to the re-election of Lincoln."[14] Soldiers in the trenches also recognized the importance of the mid-October state elections. When the election news arrived at Petersburg, rebels could hear cheers from across the lines.[15] A clerk at the Fifth Corps headquarters outside Petersburg believed in mid-October that there was "no reason to doubt of success next month."[16]

Despite these high hopes and warm predictions for Lincoln, the presidential campaign was not over. Some Democrats found a silver lining in the October results, suggesting that the close numbers and the potential for McClellan support in the army still bode well for their candidate. A close advisor to McClellan predicted that his man would win by more than thirty electoral votes. Lincoln, however, maintained cautious optimism. After reviewing the October results, he formed his own prediction for November, projecting a six-vote electoral victory for his ticket.[17] Nothing was sure, though, and, beyond Washington, events on the battlefield still had the potential to affect the election's outcome.

"I shan't have time to smoke my cigar"

Outside Petersburg on Sunday morning, October 16, General Meade's breakfast halted abruptly when news arrived that Lincoln's secretary of war, Edwin Stanton, would soon drop by for a visit. Meade's aides scrambled to prepare the camp. The general simply growled, "The devil! I shan't have time to smoke my cigar." Colonel Theodore Lyman, Meade's friend and aide, quickly donned his coat, sash, and white gloves. Lyman had met Meade before the war while researching marine starfish in Florida, and, though lacking in military experience, he had joined Meade's staff in late 1863. He was an astute and literate observer of camp interactions, and his letters and diaries provide rich descriptions of many personalities in the Union army.[18]

As Lyman and other members of Meade's staff rushed to prepare, messages raced to the corps commanders.[19] In the end, though, Stanton's arrival took time. Eventually, a posse of dignitaries rode up, with General Grant in the lead. Meade escorted the group on a short tour of the lines in the vicinity of Fort Wadsworth, a large enclosed work within yards of the Weldon Railroad. Secretary Stanton peered out over the picket line with interest, but, upon hearing of his proximity to the rebel position, he checked his watch and suggested that he really should be "going back." Thereafter, the gaggle made its way to City Point and then later to Hancock's headquarters for supper.[20]

Stanton's tour covered several Union positions outside Richmond and Petersburg. Fifth Corps artillery chief, Charles Wainwright, sarcastically quipped that Stanton "came to these headquarters in a wagon, drove to one or two works not in sight of our enemy, and returned, no doubt fully informed as to the state of matters down here."[21] The previous day, Stanton had enjoyed a boat excursion with Butler and Grant on the James. The outing appeared to agree with the secretary. Away from his desk in Washington, he said he felt "like a boy out of school."[22] He also spoke highly of Lincoln, with a "manifested personal affection," which came as a surprise to his listeners, given some press reports to the contrary. Stanton also confided to the boat passengers that the upcoming election had caused him much anxiety.[23]

Stanton's visit, just a few weeks before the crucial presidential election, marked more than just another dog and pony show for the army's high command, however. There was much substance to discuss, including events on the Richmond-Petersburg front and the Union war effort throughout the South. During their talks, Grant and Stanton both commended Sheridan's effort. The lieutenant general reportedly commented that the cavalry commander was "an improvement upon some of his predecessors" in the Valley of Virginia.[24] Grant and Stanton no doubt discussed not only matters in Virginia but also Sherman's efforts in Georgia. On Stanton's last day, the two held further discussions, and then the secretary boarded his steamer back to Washington.[25]

"the whole problem"

Back at City Point, Grant continued to manage affairs in other theaters. Though Atlanta had fallen, Sherman sought to make more progress in Georgia. Grant endorsed Sherman's proposal to cut loose from his supply base and conduct a massive raid across that state, a move that would crush Confederate morale and bring Sherman's forces to the Atlantic Coast and its unfettered supply line north. In the Shenandoah Valley, Sheridan spent much of early October destroying farms and other property in the "breadbasket of the Confederacy." Jubal Early appeared to have little appetite for fighting after Sheridan's devastating blows at Winchester and Fisher's Hill and the stinging defeat of rebel cavalry at Tom's Brook in early October.[26] But Sheridan's force gained little advantage in its current location, and the transfer of his troops would increase options for Grant at Richmond and Petersburg. Upon his return to Washington, Stanton recalled Sheridan for consultation with Chief of Staff Henry Halleck.[27] During the conference, the men agreed that Sheridan should leave a small force in the Shenandoah and send the bulk of his men directly to Grant. Under the plan, Sheridan would not venture south to damage the Virginia Central Railroad or the James River Canal, as Grant had suggested earlier.

At Petersburg, Grant agreed it was time for a change. He wired Halleck on the 18th directing Sheridan either to use all his force in the Valley or to "send his surplus here." Grant wanted Sheridan's veteran Sixth Corps, which had served in the Army of the Potomac for most of the war, and some of his cavalry. With these reinforcements, Grant would have an ample force to move against Lee, advancing Union lines to the banks of the Appomattox River west of Petersburg and severing the Danville railroad.[28] For months, Grant had used the Army of the Potomac and the Army of the James to bind Confederate forces in central Virginia. This strategy had prevented Lee from sending troops to aid in Atlanta's defense and complicated the transfer of Confederate units to the Valley. The Union military effort in Georgia, the Valley, and elsewhere continued to chip away at the territory controlled by the rebel government. In essence, the Confederacy was shrinking.

In the swirl of these events, Grant pondered his next steps. He could launch another offensive before the election or simply wait until Lincoln had won a second term before initiating further military operations. A preelection offensive at Petersburg and Richmond held risks. A devastating Union defeat just weeks before the election could affect that contest. Delay offered the safe choice, but a successful offensive promised enticing benefits. Richmond's fall would trigger an accelerated, if not imminent, end to the conflict.

Despite abundant reasons for caution, Grant explored further operations at Richmond and Petersburg. North of the James, Butler's capture of Fort Harrison had pierced Lee's intermediate line and created a fulcrum for flank movements against the Confederate left. At Petersburg, the Union lines lay only a few miles from the Boydton Plank Road and the South Side Railroad just beyond. Petersburg's survival hung on the railroad. By October, Grant had not lost sight of this vital goal, but he still needed the manpower for an effective attack column. Late in the month, with Sherman firmly in control of Atlanta and Early well in hand in the Shenandoah, Grant poised for decisive action.

After arriving at Petersburg in June, Grant had launched five separate offensives.[29] These operations achieved some success by eliminating Lee's mobility and cutting off several important lifelines to the region. But the lens of popular opinion focused on the army's failure in Virginia to destroy Lee and capture the Confederate capital. Over the summer months and into the fall, the campaign's operations had already generated an extensive list of engagements: the initial assaults on Petersburg, the Jerusalem Plank Road, First Deep Bottom, the Crater, Second Deep Bottom, the Weldon Railroad, Reams Station, Fort Harrison, Poplar Spring Church, Johnson's Farm, the New Market Road, and the Darbytown Road. Though these names represented large-scale clashes in most cases, they did not sit on the tips of Northern tongues. The notable victories occurred elsewhere, under the leadership of Sherman and Sheridan. Many people had come to anticipate bad or indifferent news from the battlefields outside Petersburg and Richmond.[30]

In each offensive, Grant demonstrated patience in waiting for the right conditions as well as flexibility in trying new approaches. The extraordinary length of the Confederate front allowed him to vary the location, strength, and intensity of his advances. In June, the initial direct assaults almost overwhelmed the thinly guarded lines. Several days later, Union forces edged south and west around the Confederate left, successfully reaching the Jerusalem Plank Road. In late July, Grant's third offensive coupled a direct assault at the Union mine dug under the Confederate works east of Petersburg with a feint north of the James at Deep Bottom. The next plan, unleashed in August, involved another diversion on the right at Deep Bottom, followed several days later by a massive movement on the left toward the Weldon Railroad, an important supply route that ran directly south into Petersburg. During Grant's fifth offensive, at the end of September, Butler attacked the enemy north of the James, and Meade followed closely with a push on the left, west of the Weldon Railroad below Petersburg. During this string of operations, Grant tried different combinations of movements and strengths, multipronged and single attacks, diversions, lunges at different locations along the rebel line, and different force sizes. However, he had yet to conjure a successful plan that would bring Richmond's fall.

In mid-October, Grant began to consider further operations. He directed his chief engineer, John G. Barnard, to study the various means to hasten Richmond's collapse. The gray-haired Barnard, described by Colonel Lyman as "an ungainly, studious looking man, with a stoop in his shoulders,"[31] devoted careful thought to "the whole problem" set out by Grant. The engineer's assessment did not inspire optimism. In an October 15 memorandum to Grant, Barnard declined to suggest any particular approach "save that of waiting for an increase of the army, until we can get a marching column of 40,000 men." Without a force of this size, Barnard could not recommend further operations at Petersburg. He also ruled out operations against the Howlett line at Bermuda Hundred,[32] an idea apparently suggested by Grant and explored by engineering officers.[33] However, he offered this broad observation: "In the present state of military and political affairs it is better to do nothing until our forces are much more adequate than they are now to effect decisive results. At present everything is well enough, and Richmond must ultimately fall, unless the course of things is changed by a disaster which would strengthen the hands of the peace and 'cessation' party."[34]

Grant's request to Barnard and his search for additional troops demonstrate that he sought to attack Lee before the November election. Horace Porter, one of the general's aides, confirmed as much in a postwar account.[35] But Grant doubted whether Meade's and Butler's commands had the strength to execute a successful offensive. Accordingly, he continued to prod Sheridan either to do more in the Valley or send his unneeded troops to Petersburg. Grant did not know whether Meade could assemble the forty-thousand-man marching column recommended by Barnard's memo. And, without troops from the Valley, he would strain to bring off his next move. However, with those troops, the Union forces at Richmond and Petersburg could coil themselves for an overwhelming attack against Lee's extended lines.[36]

"this business in the Valley"

Unfortunately for Union strategists, Jubal Early did not stand idly by as they schemed. Instead, he concocted his own plans for Sheridan's force. Prodded by Lee's continued calls for action, he marched his small army north along the Valley and, at dawn on October 19, launched a surprise assault against Sheridan's unwary force, which was camped along a shallow stream called Cedar Creek, south of Winchester. Early's audacious attack reaped dramatic results, routing much of the Union force within the first few hours. But the fight did not end there. The Union men, led by the Sixth Corps, rallied and prepared to sweep Early's force from the field. In the meantime, Sheridan returned from his meeting in Washington and, in one of the war's storied moments, galloped along the lines, urging his men on. The ensuing assault demolished Early's force, handing a stunning reversal to the Confederates. They withdrew in tatters, leaving many guns behind. Early's war mostly ended there, and so did Confederate fortunes in the Valley.

At City Point the next afternoon, Grant received the Cedar Creek news via telegraph. He solemnly approached his staff and began to read Sheridan's dispatch. Without breaking stride, he delivered the first half of the message describing the morning's reverses. "That's pretty bad, isn't it?" he remarked. He then reported the engagement's ultimate result, and a celebration ensued. Grant ordered a one-hundred-gun salute to honor the victors of Cedar Creek.[37] Across the picket lines, Confederate observers acknowledged the disaster. A South Carolina surgeon at Petersburg, who believed Early had won little and lost much in the Valley, concluded that it was "time for a new commander there."[38] Confederate Ordnance Chief Josiah Gorgas agreed. He hoped for Early's retirement, explaining, "It is really ludicrous this business in the Valley."[39] One of Longstreet's staff hoped Lee would replace Early with someone who "can take care of troops and artillery."[40]

For Lee, Cedar Creek brought an end to the strategic benefits delivered by the region. He no longer wielded an effective force there to threaten Washington or occupy large numbers of Union troops. The balance he had maintained throughout the summer in Virginia had faded and then disappeared altogether. For Grant and his troops, the result in the valley brought reason for cheer. In the camps, regimental bands played late into the night on the 20th.[41] Amid the celebration, the lieutenant general continued to consider the opportunities at Petersburg.

"rumors of a move"

With the Cedar Creek news fresh in his mind, Grant asked Meade to ride out and inspect the lines west of the Weldon Railroad early on Friday, October 21. Grant boarded a train at City Point and headed for Meade's headquarters near the Aiken house, west of the Jerusalem Plank Road.[42] The pair rode to the new Ninth Corps trench lines, where the army had quickly incorporated the ground gained in late September into its network of earthworks. The men there had built a series of enclosed forts connected by curtains of dirt and otherwise "fencing in" the new property.[43] John G. Parke's Ninth Corps spent much of the month, as one officer put it, "strengthening our lines, working on redoubts, constructing abatis, and slashing timber."[44] The new works, studded with forts, variously named Fisher, Welch, Gregg, and Cummings, formed a blunt end to the Union lines reaching around Petersburg. Fort Fisher, a large, four-pointed work, stood near the Peebles' farm at the northwest corner of the sector and stretched 120 feet wide and 100 feet deep. Ninth Corps troops had installed seven guns, added rows of sharpened abatis, and slashed the remaining timber in front.[45]

As Grant and Meade inspected these positions on Friday, they undoubtedly gazed west over the parapet into the Dinwiddie countryside and toward the enemy. They knew the Confederates were busy stretching their defenses and piling dirt on their existing lines. A successful assault here would be difficult. However, to the southwest, the rural landscape rolled out to Hatcher's Run and to thick wooded tracts beyond. Along Hatcher's Run, squads of Confederate cavalry picketed the roads, bridges, and fords. This sector to the southwest offered the most promising avenue of attack. Conducted properly, an advance there would place Union columns beyond the reach of the rebel trench line along the Boydton Plank Road and toward the South Side Railroad.

Grant's visit to Meade was more than a sightseeing tour. He had made a decision. During his outing with Meade, or perhaps even beforehand, he concluded to move against the South Side Railroad.[46] Its capture would cut to the heart of the rebellion by severing Petersburg's last life line and clearing a path to Richmond's last remaining rail connection south, the Danville road. A lodgment on the South

Side line would also allow Meade's units to cross that river to the west and close off the city completely. Such a move would take the Howlett line at Bermuda Hundred in reverse, allowing federal troops to approach Richmond from the south. A move by Sheridan from the west would complete Richmond's encirclement and doom any rebel troops remaining there.

The election was two weeks away. Broadly speaking, many factors pointed to a Lincoln victory: the seizure of Atlanta, Mobile Bay's capture, the mid-October state elections, and Sheridan's success in the Valley. The president's reelection would

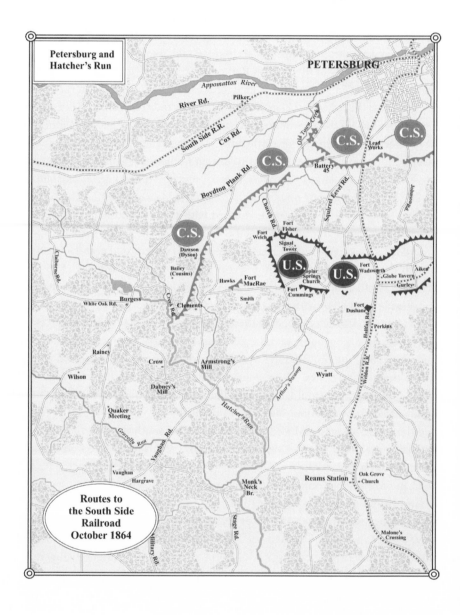

eliminate the political urgency weighing on Grant's military efforts. Four more years of a Lincoln presidency would furnish Grant sufficient time and resources to stamp out the rebellion. Even as the pressing need for military success waned, the Cedar Creek victory may have inspired Grant to consider a strike against Lee despite ample reasons for caution. Election or no, he would not hold back.

In deciding to move against the South Side Railroad, Grant did not embrace the safe, cautious choice. A sharp military setback at Richmond and Petersburg could tip the balance of the election in key states. Grant understood this risk. Later, in recounting Sheridan's successes in the Valley, he recalled that he had had "reason to believe that the administration was a little afraid to have a decisive battle fought at that time, for fear it might go against us and have a bad effect on the November elections."[47] Despite the need for caution, several good reasons supported a pre-election strike. First, the victory at Cedar Creek increased the possibility that remnants of Jubal Early's command would soon join Lee at Richmond, adding strength there and complicating Grant's efforts. In addition, the cold, rain, and occasional snow of winter would soon arrive in southern Virginia and might prevent another tug at Lee. Finally, the triumph at Cedar Creek may have, in a sense, created some insurance for Lincoln and Grant, opening the door for another offensive. Whether he considered these factors or not, Grant pushed aside caution and prepared to press matters against Lee and end the war in Virginia.

When Grant and Meade returned from their ride, staff officers learned of the plans. James Biddle, a member of Meade's staff, wrote to his wife later that day, "Everything is very quiet here. There is nothing going on, but I do not think this quietness will last a great while longer. I trust the next movement will meet with success, and enable me to return to you."[48] Colonel Lyman, at Meade's headquarters, confided in his journal that Grant and Meade had "rode round the lines, with an object doubtless, for [artillery chief] Hunt has orders to put the redoubts in condition, as to artillery, and we have rumors of a move."[49] The soldiers in the trenches sensed something, too. A Vermont infantryman observed the generals riding along the trenches and concluded that their presence suggested a new offensive was not far behind.[50] At City Point on Friday afternoon, Grant dispatched fresh instructions to Sheridan, urging a move against the Virginia Central Railroad, a critical supply link to the Shenandoah Valley. The message conveyed an unprecedented urgency. Grant acknowledged the difficult task but urged Sheridan to make the effort even if it required his troops to subsist on half rations. Success from Sheridan would sever Lee's army from western Virginia.[51]

"this precious dust"

In ordering the attack at Richmond and Petersburg, Grant may have also considered information gleaned by his Bureau of Military Information. U.S. planners
relied on a robust system to gather data about enemy positions, troop movements,
and other activities. In addition to daily reports spilling from the mouths of Confederate deserters, the Union command relied on signal stations dotting the Union
trench system. Using manmade towers and tall trees, federal observers kept their
telescopes trained on the rebel works and road networks to the rear.[52] Union intelligence officers also tapped into the expertise of telegraphers who managed to
break into the enemy circuits and gather information on enemy operations.[53]

Union officers sorted through information to form a coherent picture of enemy
forces. In these endeavors, General Benjamin Butler stood out. He expended great
energy tracking the identity, strength, and organization of the enemy forces in his
front. From deserter reports and other sources, he maintained an "Organization
Book," which listed the Confederate "regiments arranged in their brigades, divisions,
and corps; the commanders of each; and notes as to the effective strength of each."
This data came "by cross-questioning successively the members of each regiment
represented in a batch of prisoners, who meanwhile are not allowed to communicate
with each other." Butler used the book to determine which Confederate reinforcements had been sent to a particular sector or to track the movements of Lee's army.[54]

Butler's information also came from sources behind enemy lines. In one of
his more significant achievements, he helped the Bureau of Military Information
foster the development of the Richmond underground, a spy ring nested right under Jefferson Davis's nose that arguably became the war's most successful covert
network. Elizabeth Van Lew, a wealthy Richmond native who harbored a hatred
of slavery and maintained a steadfast loyalty to the United States, served as the
network's most notable operative. From her mansion on Church Hill, she coordinated activities of covert Unionists, aided federal soldiers locked in Richmond's
military prisons, and funneled valuable information through the lines to Butler's
hands. During the autumn of 1864, Van Lew and her comrades shunted a steady
stream of reports to Union intelligence officers.

Butler first opened communications with Van Lew in January 1864 using invis-
ible ink. With acid and heat, she unlocked its hidden invitation "to aid the Union
cause by furnishing [Butler] with information." The dispatch's bearer, Union agent
H. S. Howard, instructed Van Lew how to use a cipher, a chart of letters and numbers, to encrypt her future communications.[55] Throughout 1864, Van Lew and her
network furnished reports to Union officials about the movement of Union prisoners and the disposition of Confederate troops. They also did more than gather
information. After an ill-fated Union raid on Richmond in late February, Van
Lew and her colleagues managed to exhume the body of slain Union colonel Uric

Dahlgren from Richmond's Oakwood Cemetery and rebury the remains at a farm outside the city. The Richmond underground reveled in this act of defiance. Every "true Union heart, who knew of this day's work, felt happier for having charge of this precious dust," wrote Van Lew.[56]

During October, Van Lew's network continued to harvest Confederate information and deliver it to the Union provost marshal general's office. On October 14, Richmond agents reported the arrival of rebel soldiers from the Valley, including members of Jubal Early's artillery units who had lost their guns in the recent battles there. These men joined the local defense forces in the trenches outside Richmond. The same dispatch reported Lee's headquarters "at James Taylor's farm, near and northwest from Chaffin's Bluff."[57]

On Thursday, October 20, the day before Grant discussed plans for the offensive with Meade, John McEntee, an assistant to Grant's chief intelligence officer, General George Henry Sharpe, passed along more information from the Richmond agents. The report contained a series of bits and pieces about rebel activities: the Confederates were planting land mines, or "torpedoes," on the roads leading to Richmond; Lee was still determined to retake Fort Harrison and was looking for a weak point; the fortifications from the James River near Chaffin's to the Darbytown Road were very strong; an "iron-clad railroad battery" rested on the York River railroad near the exterior line east of Richmond; and a newspaper was advocating the arming of slaves. The following note also appeared amid this stream of information: "Informant estimates the force in and about Richmond (north of the James) at about 20,000 men, and states that many of them will not fight."[58] The next day McEntee reported that the local defense forces, workers from Richmond's key industries, were manning the trenches. He listed these city battalions by name, "Tredegar, Department, Navy, Arsenal, Armory, City, and Hensley's," and said all contained about 250 men each. Confederate authorities had filled these men's position back in Richmond with blacks. For example, the Tredegar Rolling-Mills had impressed 300 black workers.[59]

The impact of this information on Grant's decision-making is unclear. Circumstantial evidence, however, suggests a connection between it and the lieutenant general's decision to launch a pre-election offensive. The *Army and Navy Journal*, which enjoyed access to many sources within the army, later wrote on November 5 that Grant's plan for the offensive "may doubtless be specifically traced," to information Butler had gathered about the enemy's strength. "General Butler's spy-system, perfected by assiduous labor, enables him not only to compute with considerable accuracy the total force now in the Richmond trenches, but to draw inferences, also, as to the strength of particular portions of the lines." The paper concluded the Confederates, with only about half of the Union numbers, could not "check us everywhere." Whatever the motivations behind Grant's decision, Meade and Butler began the work necessary to plan and organize the expedition.

"the number of men and guns"

Despite Grant's decision to act, Meade's ability to scrape together a sufficient striking force remained an open question. Engineer John Barnard had recommended
forty thousand men for an offensive. At Petersburg, September returns showed
the Army of the Potomac with an effective strength of nearly 51,000.[60] Most of
this strength lay in three infantry corps: Hancock's Second Corps, with more than
sixteen thousand men; Gouverneur Warren's Fifth Corps, with twelve thousand;
and the Ninth Corps, now commanded by John Parke, with fifteen thousand.
Meade's cavalry division, led by David Gregg, numbered about five thousand.
Over the course of October, these numbers generally increased.[61] In fact, the
monthly inspection reports behind these numbers only provided a snapshot of
the army's strength. Combat casualties, sickness, replacement troops, and reas-
signment continually changed the effective strength of the various commands.
Even the men in charge of tabulating force strength had difficulty tracking the
numbers.[62] The regular tallies furnished Meade with a general idea of his army's
size and whether enough men were available. However, in addition to soldiers
for the strike force, he needed men to protect the trenches during the offensive.
When he returned from his ride with Grant on Friday, he wrote to Second Corps
chief General Hancock, "The lieutenant-general commanding desires a formidable movement made to our left with a view of seizing and holding the South Side
Railroad."[63] Meade wanted to know how many men Hancock required to protect
his sector, as well as the force Hancock could free for the operation.

The next day, October 22, Meade relayed the latest news in a letter to his wife.
He expected Sheridan would move to destroy portions of the Virginia Central
and greatly aid Grant's efforts at Petersburg. He also explained that Richmond's
evacuation would not occur without the destruction of the Central Railroad "even
if we succeed in seizing or breaking the Southside and Danville Roads." He concluded by saying, "I suppose, in a short time, a movement will be made to get on
the Southside Road and complete the investment of Petersburg, from the Appomattox, below to above the town."[64] That morning, he asked Warren and Parke
the same question he had posed to Hancock the night before: "I would like to
know the number of men and guns it will require to hold the line of redoubts and
inclosed batteries now held by your corps."[65]

In response to Meade's inquiry, his three corps leaders submitted encouraging reports. After several notes back and forth with Meade's chief of staff, Andrew Humphreys, Hancock reported that he could leave his first division, under
Brigadier General Nelson Miles, to protect the trenches stretching from the Appomattox River to Fort Howard, about a mile west of the Jerusalem Plank Road.[66]
Hancock planned to maintain his pickets during the movement to hide the true
strength of the force left behind.[67] The subtraction of Miles's force would pro-

vide Hancock, in his estimation, with a mobile force of approximately twelve thousand.[68] Unlike Hancock's sector, General Warren's line, stretching from Fort Howard across the Weldon Railroad to Fort Fisher, enjoyed a wide buffer separating the Union troops from the enemy. Warren reported that he could cover this sector with the rifles of Henry Baxter's brigade, leaving his Fifth Corps with approximately thirteen thousand men for the attacking column.[69] John Parke's Ninth Corps sector formed the end of the Union defenses west of the Weldon Railroad. Parke's picket line ran from his right at Fort Fisher in the vicinity of the J. C. Boswell farm and swung west and south, terminating at Fort Cummings. Parke estimated that the picket line and the works themselves, about 2,300 yards in length, could manage with fifteen hundred men. This left the Ninth Corps with over eleven thousand troops for the operation, including the nearly five thousand men from the USCTs of Edward Ferrero's Third Division.[70]

The numbers began to add up for Meade. About thirty-six thousand available infantry, coupled with the five thousand men of General David Gregg's cavalry division, formed the requisite force for an operation against the South Side Railroad. According to a postwar account by Grant's staffer, Adam Badeau, Meade reported that forty thousand men were available for the operation.[71] Grant now had gathered the sum Barnard had called for in the October 15 memorandum. Meade would leave a small force crouching in the Union trenches around Petersburg to provide a frail tether for the attacking column. The rest would attack the rebels.

"History was not based on newspapers"

The operation's details fell to George Meade and his staff. From the outset of the Overland campaign in May, Meade had watched his control and authority evaporate as Grant gradually took charge of operational decision making. Grant served as the main planner, while Meade implemented his designs. The latter complained to his wife that the newspapers had counted him out "entirely" in favor of recognizing Grant. Meade wrote in May that if there were "any honorable way of retiring from my present false position, I should undoubtedly adopt it, but there is none and all I can do is patiently submit and bear with resignation the humiliation."[72]

At Gettysburg, Meade had gained a signal victory which boosted Northern morale. Unfortunately, his tremendous performance soon became a distant memory to officials in Washington. For Lincoln and his advisors, Meade did not pursue Lee following the battle with adequate vigor. His performance during the following months failed to improve his reputation. Indeed, officials viewed him as too methodical and cautious to take the war to Robert E. Lee.[73]

In late November of 1863, Meade launched his first large-scale offensive since the Gettysburg campaign. Known as the Mine Run campaign, the operation shed more light on his generalship. He developed a clear plan but ultimately failed to catch Lee's men out in the open. When he arranged his troops for a massive assault, Gouverneur Warren, then commanding the Second Corps, declined at the last minute to move against the strong enemy position. Meade endorsed Warren's action and called off other assaults along the line, subsequently withdrawing his men from the field. Though Meade's action prevented a costly defeat and many unnecessary deaths, the campaign achieved little. Bad luck, excessive caution, and bumbling subordinates helped reach this result. However, in the final analysis, Meade had failed to achieve additional Union victories. No doubt anticipating more criticism, he concluded his official report with the following statement: "Considering how sacred is the trust of the lives of the brave men under my command, but willing as I am to shed their blood and my own where duty requires, and my judgment dictates that the sacrifice will not be in vain, I cannot be a party to a wanton slaughter of my troops for any mere personal end."[74]

Grant's arrival in Virginia in 1864 altered Meade's independent control and the opportunities and burdens such control entailed. From the start, their relations were cordial, but the pair presented a study in contrasts. Calm, persistent, and certain commitment marked Grant's decision-making. The high-strung Meade was cautious and perhaps too attentive to the various contingencies inherent in any military operation.[75] Charles Mills, a member of Hancock's staff, wrote about Meade on October 8, saying, "We don't think much of that respectable nonentity here. He does well enough for a subordinate under Grant, except that his little feelings are too much for him sometimes."[76] While his generalship may have been conservative, Meade also exhibited a fiery temper, and invective often filled his exchanges with unfortunate subordinates. Though such tirades may have damaged his image with other officers, Grant nevertheless respected his abilities and saw no need to alter this command structure. At the same time, he recognized the embarrassment that the arrangement caused the Pennsylvanian.

By mid-October, although the two had formed an effective team and Meade had survived the subordination, he was still acutely aware of how far his star had fallen since Gettysburg. In an October 13 letter to his wife, he expressed satisfaction that he had retained his command despite the efforts of "influential men, politicians and generals, to destroy me."[77] A few days later, he wrote again saying, "I am astonished I have been able to hold on as I have done—and wonder I have not long since been cast aside."[78]

In the midst of planning for the upcoming offensive, he learned of a personal attack against him printed in Henry Ward Beecher's paper, the *Independent*. The article painted Meade as one who "hangs upon the neck of General Grant like an old man of the sea, whom he longs to be rid of, and whom he retains solely in deference to the weak complaisance of his constitutional commander-in-chief."[79] His staff had kept this unpleasant depiction from Meade's eyes, but, somehow, during a visit to Grant's headquarters, the matter became known to him. That day, Meade wrote his wife about the unkind words and concluded, "After all, it is probably not worthwhile to notice it."[80] The next day, however, the issue had firmly lodged under his skin, and he forwarded an extract of the article to Grant. He asked the lieutenant general to provide "such evidence as will place it in my power to correct the extraordinary misapprehension." Grant replied the same day, explaining, "I have felt as much pained as you at the constant stabs made at you by a portion of the public press." He offered to furnish copies of every dispatch involving Meade that had been sent to Washington.[81]

Meade declined to review the dispatches but asked Grant to provide some sort of public statement to clear his name. His bitterness persisted. He wrote Grant, "In all successful operations I was ignored, and the moment anything went wrong I was held wholly responsible, and rather than continue in this way, I would prefer retiring."[82] He understood, however, that such controversies did not perturb Grant, and this controversy, like those before it, faded away. Back at army headquarters, he discussed the matter with Colonel Lyman, who "told him not to mind, that he had Grant and Stanton on his side and a good record, and history was not based on newspapers."[83] This comment produced a laugh from Meade, who returned to planning the upcoming offensive.

"It is known he is preparing to move"

At Confederate headquarters, Robert E. Lee expected Grant to move but could only guess the location and time. Others agreed. Wade Hampton predicted that Grant, concerned about the tight October election results, would make a desperate effort in the next few days to gain success.[84] On October 20, Longstreet wrote that Grant would launch an attack north of the James within the week or attempt to gain a lodgment behind Pickett's lines at Bermuda Hundred. Coincidently, this was the same scheme considered by Grant's engineers only a day earlier.[85] Confederate guesswork was not confined to the high command. On October 7, an Alabama captain, writing to his wife, predicted that Grant would rest on his laurels and not risk an attack before the election.[86] The next day, a South Carolina major wrote that it seemed "pretty certain" the Federals would attempt to take the South Side Railroad, "where and in what force it is impossible to say."[87] The journal of a Mississippi rifleman indicated that "those in the know" expect another battle soon.[88] Others were not so sure. "I doubt now whether there will be a fight before the election," wrote Confederate medical officer John Claiborne in October. He reasoned that, with an electoral victory imminent, there was no reason for the Northern commanders to risk a battle at Richmond.[89]

The Southern press also weighed in. The *Daily Confederate* in Raleigh proclaimed that Grant would not let the October days slip by without seeking "another holocaust like that which attended the explosion of the famous mine at Petersburg." The man painted by the Carolina newspaper was irrational and bloodthirsty, the "butcher" of popular lore. They predicted that Grant would launch the attack, "cost what it may in hireling blood."[90] On the 17th, the *Richmond Dispatch* puzzled over Grant's delay in launching another attack, even though "it is known he is preparing to move on our position." The paper speculated that he would wait for Butler to complete the Dutch Gap canal and allow greater cooperation with the navy. The *Dispatch* also noted Grant's need for more troops.[91] As the election neared, however, the *Dispatch* expected that Grant would lean on Sheridan's victories and not "run the risk of spoiling the game by an unsuccessful move on the Richmond lines."[92] Of course, these were all just guesses. Those who could end this speculation were hard at work planning the Confederacy's demise.

CHAPTER 6

Plans for the Sixth Offensive

~

On Sunday evening, October 23, Grant met with Meade and Butler separately
to discuss the upcoming operation.[1] The next day, he issued official orders for
Meade to launch an offensive to seize, hold, and fortify the South Side Railroad
on Thursday, October 27. Following its secondary role in the late September offensive, Meade's army would lead the upcoming operation and Butler's Army of the
James would support. Once Meade gained the railroad, Grant wanted the army to
construct fortifications extending back to the Ninth Corps lines at Peebles' Farm.
Such an effort would form continuous, connected Union works around much of
Petersburg.[2] Grant did not seek an assault. Instead, he wanted to seize ground
and force Lee to react. And, like his previous efforts, Grant's new plan had a second prong. On Monday, he discussed the upcoming offensive with General Butler
and, in a subsequent dispatch, ordered him "to demonstrate against the enemy
in your front, substantially as we talked the matter over last evening and as you
proposed" and "feel out to the right beyond the front, and, if you can, turn it."[3]

As in recent operations, Grant planned to send two columns against the Confederate defenses, one south of Petersburg and another far to the north against
the Richmond defenses. In September, the primary blow landed in the Richmond
sector, with a secondary push later at Petersburg contingent on the results of the
first. Now Grant would try something different. His attacking columns would hit
Lee's defenses simultaneously. In addition, the weight of the column in the Petersburg sector would be much greater than those before.

Meade, his staff, and his corps commanders had hard work ahead.[4] In earlier
operations, the Army of the Potomac had often moved around, instead of through,
the rebel lines. Now, in late October, Meade did not stray from this formula. He
sought to bypass the new rebel fortifications barring the way to the railroad. These
works began at the southwest corner of the Dimmock line, near Petersburg's Lead
Works, and stretched southwest along the Boydton Plank Road toward Hatcher's
Run. Meade did not know the length and strength of these rebel trenches, however.
Without complete knowledge of what lay ahead, the necessary routes, marching

distances, and force strengths remained unknowable. Accordingly, Meade's success would rely on the quality of Union intelligence.

"we are completing heavy works"

The Confederates had begun constructing the Boydton Plank Road trenches as early as September 16.[5] In its nascent stages, the works stretched approximately four miles southwest from Battery 45 on the Dimmock line to the Harman Road near the Dabney house. They ran parallel to and east of the Plank Road and consisted of long sections of ditches and parapets interrupted occasionally by small redans.

This new rebel line was built for mobile defense. Its proximity to the Boydton Plank Road allowed Confederates to shuttle their limited forces to threatened points. The open redans adorning the line facilitated the rapid deployment of artillery arriving from distant points along the trenches or from rear areas. The Confederate works contrasted with their Union counterparts. Over the past several months, Union engineers had concentrated their efforts on constructing enclosed forts along their lines. Such forts, carefully sited to ensure deadly, interlocking fields of fire, could not be manned as rapidly as the open Confederate works. However, their inherent strength allowed the Unionists to limit the force manning the fortifications and to free large numbers for mobile operations.[6]

The Confederates had traced the Boydton Plank trench line down to Hatcher's Run, a meandering stream girded by banks crammed with impenetrable vegetation, which provided a logical endpoint. The stream flowed southeast and then south, eventually joining Gravelly Run to form Rowanty Creek. This stream network offered the Confederates a natural obstacle of formidable strength, a deep ditch that yielded few crossings

Wade Hampton's cavalry occupied the defense line south of the Dabney house. In October, his command consisted of two divisions, one under South Carolinian Matthew Butler and the other led by Virginian William "Rooney" Lee, the army commander's son, as well as James Dearing's unassigned brigade, horse artillery under Major Preston Chew, and several hundred dismounted men. Matthew Butler's division at Petersburg contained two brigades led by Hugh K. Aiken's South Carolinians and Georgians commanded by Pierce Young. Rooney Lee's division also contained two brigades, Richard Beale's Virginians and Rufus Barringer's North Carolinians.[7]

Throughout October, Hampton's men guarded the fords and bridges along Hatcher's Run and farther south along Rowanty Creek. The cavalrymen spent much of their time picketing roads and scouting Union positions to the west. "It is a curious mode of life, ours—living all the time in the open air, never going into a tent except at night or when it rains," wrote Hampton. "This makes us care very little for either sun or wind, though it does not improve the complection."[8] Hampton understood the need for strong works north of Hatcher's Run to guard the Plank Road and the railroad beyond. On October 11, he explained to Robert E. Lee, "I have made a line from the right of the infantry works to Hatcher's Run, in front of and below Cousins' house, and I can hold the line from Dyson's house near Dabney's to the creek."[9] Hampton expected the Unionists to attack near Dabney's and recommended that Lee strengthen the works there and post infantry permanently in that sector. "All his dismounted men are on the lines, as well as a part of Butler's," he wrote. "If the line we have constructed can be held till supports come up, there will be no fear of the enemy's reaching the plank road."[10]

Hampton's cavalry and A. P. Hill's infantrymen toiled on the new line. Some work fell to the dismounted men in Hampton's corps. Due to a shortage of horses, Hampton had collected more than 600 men to serve on foot, a force deployed on the far right of the Boydton Plank Road trench line.[11] Captain A. B. Mulligan and his men, a battalion of 120 of these dismounted troopers, helped to construct these breastworks. On many days, they began at 8 A.M. and labored well into the afternoon. As with Alexander's line outside Richmond, Confederate soldiers did not labor on the lines alone. On October 11, Norfolk artilleryman John Walters, stationed in the Petersburg trenches, witnessed guards in Petersburg arresting many black men, both free and slave. "During the day they gathered up from fifteen hundred to two thousand," Walters wrote. "They were wanted to throw up some batteries to the right of our line and the usual method of obtaining them is too slow for emergencies."[12] Commanders understood the urgent need for these defenses and prepared to stretch them as far as necessary. "We are completing heavy works on this front," wrote one South Carolinian, "and have a line laid out running between the Weldon and South Side roads which the engineers say we will continue to the North Carolina line if that be necessary in order to prevent the enemy from gaining any ground west of where they are now."[13]

"seize a commanding position"

As the Confederates dug, the Army of the Potomac's intelligence system sought to gauge their progress. Throughout October, Captain John C. Babcock of the Bureau of Military Information tracked rebel troop locations and other activity along the new trenches. Almost every day, he summarized new information gained from deserters and other sources to help Union officials paint a hazy picture of rebel positions. On October 7, a Confederate runaway explained that Heth's division and three brigades of Wilcox's division manned the Petersburg lines west of the Weldon Railroad and were busy throwing up works.[14] Daily reports from Union signal stations noted the enemy's frequent movements along the Boydton Plank Road.[15] The

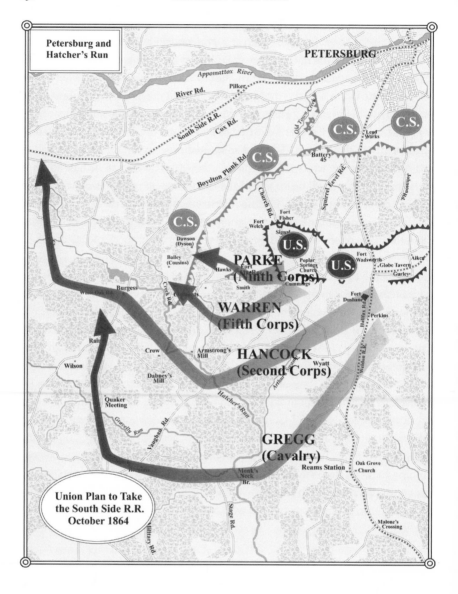

PETERSBURG

Appomattox River

River Rd.   Pilker

South Side R.R.   *Cox Rd.*   *Old Town Creek*

C.S.   *Lead
Works*   C.S.

Boydton Plank Rd.   C.S.   *Battery
45*

Squirrel Level Rd.

Church Rd.   *Fort
Fisher*

C.S.   *Fort
Welch*   *Signal*

*Dawson
(Dyson)*   U.S.

*Bailey
(Cousins)*   **PARKE**   *Poplar
Springs
Church*   *Fort
Wadsworth*   *Aiken*

Hawks   *Fort   (Fifth Corps)*   U.S.   *Globe Tavern*

Burgess   *Creek Rd.*   *Smith*   *Cummings*   *Gurley's*

Wine Oak Rd.   *Clements*   *Fort
Dushane*   *Perkins*

**WARREN
(Fifth Corps)**

Rai...   *Crow*   *Armstrong's
Mill*   **HANCOCK**   *Wyatt*

Wilson   *Dabney's
Mill*   **(Second Corps)**   *Arthur...*

*Quaker
Meeting*   *Hatcher's Run*

Gravelly Run   *Vaughan Rd.*   **GREGG
(Cavalry)**

Reams Station   *Oak Grove
Church*

*Monk's
Neck
Br.*

Stage Rd.   *Malone's
Crossing*

Military Rd.

elevated observers also reported the appearance of new enemy camps behind the
trenches.[16] On October 18, Andrew Humphreys, on Meade's staff, asked Babcock to
update a map used at headquarters to track Confederate positions.[17]

On October 24, Babcock appended a sketch of Confederate positions to his
daily report. According to this drawing, the Confederate line, held by Heth's division, stretched southwest to the vicinity of the Dabney property. Babcock reported
ongoing construction at least a mile south of Dabney's. At one spot, Confederate
working parties, including dismounted cavalry, tore down a house to clear a field

of fire. According to Babcock's sketch, the rebel line bent westward intersecting the Plank Road where that route crossed Hatcher's Run at Burgess Mill.[18] The October 24 report also suggested that the rebel trench line was incomplete, especially from the Dabney Farm south to Hatcher's Run.

Armed with these reports, Meade and his staff prepared their plans for the upcoming offensive, and considered the available avenues of advance. The most direct approach would send troops west from Fort Cummings to the Clements house and then along the Creek Road toward the Boydton Plank Road. If the lines were, in fact, incomplete between Hatcher's Run and Dabney's house, as Babcock's report suggested, Union troops could hit the Plank Road directly and, if successful there, march straight to the South Side Railroad. However, if the new works were fully formed and occupied, even lightly, the column would make little progress.[19] The more promising routes lay to the south on a series of roads that crossed Hatcher's Run and opened into the Confederate rear. Hampton's men picketed these crossings, which included Armstrong's Mill south of the Clements house, Cumming's Ford along the Vaughan Road, Monk's Neck bridge at the Stage Road, and Malone's Crossing farther south. Once across the run, the most direct route to the railroad ran through the Burgess Farm at the Boydton Plank Road on the south bank of the run. From there, the White Oak Road stretched west and, after a mile and a half, joined the Claiborne Road, just beyond that lay the South Side Railroad.

With these various routes to consider, Meade chose to send three columns to attack the rebel defenses. On Tuesday, the 25th, he issued orders to his corps commanders detailing the scheme of the operation. The first column, made up of Parke's Ninth Corps, would head directly west to the Plank Road, fixing any defenders in place there. By a "secret and sudden" movement in the early morning, Parke would surprise the enemy and "carry their half-formed works." If successful, he was to "follow up the enemy closely, turning toward the right." Meade's orders identified Parke's target as the rebel trenches from Hatcher's Run to the vicinity of the Dabney house. In the earlier dispatch to Meade, Grant had cautioned against attacking an entrenched enemy line, but, did not discourage an advance should the opportunity present itself.[20]

The second, and most complicated, task went to Gouverneur Warren's Fifth Corps column. Warren would "move simultaneously with the Ninth Corps, and proceed to the crossing of Hatcher's Run, below the plank road bridge, from which point he will support the Ninth Corps, and if the attack is successful, follow up the enemy, moving on the left of the Ninth Corps." If Parke failed to break the enemy's line, Warren would cross Hatcher's Run, move up the south bank, and turn the enemy's "right by recrossing at the first practicable point above the Boydton plank road." Once back across the run, Warren would proceed back down the stream along the north bank to the Plank Road and seize the bridge at Burgess Mill. This plan assigned Warren a dual-pronged support role with a host of contingencies.[21]

The third column, Hancock's Second Corps, would swing well south around the enemy's right flank, cross Hatcher's Run, and strike out westward toward the South Side Railroad. Meade's orders specified the route: "Move by the Vaughan road, cross Hatcher's Run, pass by Dabney's Mill and Wilson and Arnold's steam saw-mill on the Boydton plank road; cross the open country to Claiborne's road near its intersection with the White Oak road, and, recrossing Hatcher's Run near the Claiborne road bridge." From the Claiborne Road, the column would march northwest to the railroad and "seize a commanding position" there.[22] The plan put Hancock's men on a twelve-mile tramp into the Confederate rear, avoiding the main defense line north of Hatcher's Run.[23] David Gregg's cavalry division would also join the expedition, traveling farther south to guard Hancock's flank.

Meade's orders also touched on the operation's logistical details. Each man would carry sixty rounds of ammunition and full rations for four days. Supply wagons would transport another forty rounds per man. Each artillery battery would stuff its limber chests and caissons with shells. Caissons from the cannon remaining in the works would join the expedition, bringing another fifty rounds per gun. Ambulance wagons, equipped with stretchers, would accompany the operation, along with a medicine wagon and a hospital wagon for each brigade. Meade specifically instructed his commanders to bring entrenching tools. These shovels and picks would allow soldiers to implement Grant's plan to fortify the new ground occupied during the march. And, if matters went awry, the shovels would throw up hasty defenses at any location. All superfluous wagons would proceed to City Point the day before the operation, Wednesday, the 26th. Finally, Meade planned to transfer his headquarters on Wednesday from the Aiken house west to Poplar Springs Church, positioned in a clearing west of the Weldon Railroad within the fortifications recently dug by the Ninth Corps.[24]

Meade's plan, if implemented successfully, would apply overwhelming pressure. Its tiered design relied on more than a single attack at a fixed point. Instead, the multiple prongs increased the chances that at least one Union attacking column would find success and unhinge the Confederate defense line. If Parke's initial movement prevailed, the Ninth and Fifth Corps would break through the rebel works, pour over the Boydton Plank Road, and march directly toward the railroad beyond. If this direct approach failed, the twenty thousand men of the Fifth and Ninth Corps column would draw Confederate strength to the lines and free Hancock's advance. If Hancock's column did not breach the Hatcher's Run line or managed to become tangled in terrain to the south, Warren's secondary instructions provided yet a third option to skirt past Burgess Mill and get in the Confederate rear.

Meade's plan kept the marching columns in contact with each other and, most important, in contact with the Union fortifications and the supply base at City Point. Consistent with Grant's previous movements at Petersburg, it did not call for a large, army-sized raid that would free the attacking column from its supply base to operate in the Virginia interior. Grant and Sherman had already devised and even launched such offensive operations elsewhere. In fact, only weeks before, Sherman had proposed a grand-scale raid across Georgia to the Atlantic Coast. Sherman had argued, "I could cut a swath through to the sea, divide the Confederacy in two, and come up on the rear of Lee."[25] His scheme matched Grant's directive earlier in the year to "get into the interior of the enemy's country as far as you can, inflicting all the damage against their war resources."[26]

With the election looming, Grant and Meade chose not to pursue such a raiding strategy for the upcoming offensive. In the following months, Sherman would follow through on his plans by marching toward the Atlantic Coast, a safe supply source. However, at Petersburg, any Union column marching away from City Point would have no such luxury, for the hostile country west of Richmond offered no waterway or safe rail line. Thus, Grant and Meade devised a conservative plan for the pre-election offensive. It did not involve a single freewheeling strike force to occupy the South Side Railroad against all counterattacks regardless of supply lines. Instead, if all went as planned, its multiple columns would remain within supporting distance of each other, ensuring a connection to the existing Union fortifications.

"half-formed works"

Though Meade's plan appeared sound on paper, it had several problems. First, it did not call for the application of one overwhelming blow at a single point. The flanking column, Hancock's Second Corps, was relatively small, mustering only twenty thousand men, a force similar in size to Meade's attacking column during the fifth offensive several weeks earlier. It was unclear whether such an arrangement would provide sufficient force to pierce the Confederate lines.

In addition, the plan presented Warren with vague and complicated instructions surrounded by contingencies. For instance, if Parke's movement stalled, the plan directed Warren to cross Hatcher's Run at an unspecified location in a remote region, poorly mapped and reconnoitered. It then instructed him to recross the stream west of the Plank Road at a different, unstated point. Unfortunately, a large pond stretched west from Burgess Mill, preventing any crossing for almost a mile west of the Plank Road. In fact, the Claiborne Road itself, the object of Hancock's long flank march, offered the nearest available crossing at Hatcher's Run west of the Burgess Farm. Union planners did not seem to understand such details.

Finally and perhaps most important, the Union plan relied on two critical assumptions about the enemy's location and strength along the Boydton Plank Road. First, it supposed that the new rebel trench line was incomplete. Meade's orders specifically stated, "It is probable that the enemy's line of intrenchments is incomplete at [the point of the Ninth Corps advance], and the commanding general expects, by a secret and sudden movement, to surprise them and carry their half-formed works."[27] Unfortunately for Union planners, this assumption was incorrect. Indeed, by the 24th, the Confederates had finished the works. On October 21, a diarist in Davis's Mississippi brigade reported that "the breast works in our front are good fronted with palisades & abatiss the enemy in our front is about 1½ mile in front."[28] Every day, rebel cavalryman A. B. Mulligan observed cavalry commanders, including Hampton, Rooney Lee, Matthew Butler, and James Dearing, inspecting the line's progress. On Sunday, October 23, he noted that Hampton was anxious to finish the works down to Hatcher's Run. He predicted that the Confederates would have the line completed by the next day.[29] In addition, Hampton himself reported that the defenses would be ready for occupation on Sunday, the 23rd.[30] The next day, Monday, he wrote Lee again to announce that the "work is now finished."[31]

Second, the Union planners incorrectly assumed that the enemy earthworks terminated where the Plank Road crossed Hatcher's Run at Burgess Mill. Captain Babcock's map from the 24th might have contributed to this understanding, for it showed a westward bend in the line converging with the Plank Road at Hatcher's Run.[32] This also was incorrect. The new trenches did not end there.[33] Instead, they halted at a spot nearly a mile downstream. Thus, the Confederate right wing, the target of Parke's advance, lay about a mile closer to the Union advance than expected by Meade and his staff. To further complicate matters, the landscape on the south bank of Hatcher's Run was a perfect wilderness. Unionists would soon find the terrain there choked in "tangled, thick undergrowth that almost stops the passage of a man."[34] During the planning, however, Union officers did not appreciate the challenges this ground would pose.

In essence, Union planners misjudged these crucial aspects of the operation. However, with limited information, such mistakes were understandable. Hostile pickets and cavalry patrols closed off much of the territory to Union eyes, frustrating efforts to gather information. The incorrect assumptions, however, did not bode well for Meade's operation. The plan promised to send thousands of soldiers bumbling into a web of poorly mapped roads and streams. Though the many facets of Meade's plan offered flexibility, this ignorance of the conditions on the ground threatened the operation's success before it even began.

Oddly, a curious piece of correspondence in the *Official Records* suggests that a more accurate assessment of the enemy position may have been available to Meade and his staffers before the offensive. On Tuesday, the 25th, the same day Meade circulated orders for the operation, Babcock's daily intelligence report summarized information brought in by deserters: "The works are not of an extensive character but are all constructed with slashings or abatis. In McGowan's front they are fully completed, and informant thinks the whole line must be nearly finished by this time."[35]

On its face, the new information contradicted a key assumption buttressing the plan. Perhaps Babcock's note arrived after Meade's orders had been distributed; or maybe Meade understood Babcock's report to mean that the rebel trenches were "incomplete" and "half-formed," as described in his orders. Or maybe he and his staff did not credit the report or simply overlooked it amid the blizzard of preparations. In any event, the impact of the communication on the high command's planning is unclear.

"the prize is large"

North of the James, Butler also prepared. Grant hoped the Massachusetts lawyer's efforts would prevent Lee from sending reinforcements to the Petersburg sector. In his directive, he urged Butler to turn the Confederate left. However, he also emphasized the need to avoid unnecessary assaults: "Let it be distinctly understood by corps commanders that there is to be no attack made against defended, intrenched positions." Grant expected that the Army of the James would travel lightly, with few wagons and ambulances, three days' rations in the troops' haversacks, and sixty rounds of ammunition per man. All wagons not necessary for the operation would head south of the James. He also warned of possible counterattacks against the left flank and rear of Butler's position.[36]

By Tuesday, the 25th, Butler had passed the word to his corps commanders. Eighteenth Corps officers would withdraw their troops from the vicinity of Fort Harrison on the 26th and mass them in the rear.[37] On Wednesday, Butler circulated detailed orders to govern his army's movements.[38] His subordinates had seen his long-winded directives before. His orders brimmed with detailed instructions, minor and major tangents, encouraging words, and useful enemy intelligence. He crammed his written work with broad themes and mind-numbing minutiae. His directives were nothing if not comprehensive. The orders for Thursday's offensive presented no exception.

Butler's plan was relatively straightforward. The Tenth Corps would fix the Confederates in their works on the Darbytown Road. Alfred Terry, still in command of that corps, would "feel along the enemy's lines" north of the Darbytown Road. Butler proclaimed that the Confederate works extended only a short distance north of that road and "certainly" did not reach beyond the Charles City Road, a bizarre pronouncement in light of lessons learned from Pond's attack the previous Thursday. As the Tenth Corps prodded the rebel lines in front, Godfrey Weitzel's Eighteenth Corps would probe north and seek to turn the enemy's exterior defenses, thus forcing the Confederates either back toward Richmond or into an open fight. A force of approximately twenty-five hundred would remain in the trenches around Fort Harrison, yielding a balance of seventy-five hundred to Weitzel's attacking force. Butler expected the Eighteenth Corps to march north and then drive toward Richmond on the Williamsburg Road or, if possible, the

Charles City Road. Colonel Robert M. West, now leading the cavalry in place of the ailing August Kautz, would screen the Eighteenth Corps column.

According to Butler's vision, Weitzel would push through an undefended exterior line at the Williamsburg Road and quickly gain the interior line. "There will be found artillery, with a small guard, in the redoubts of that line, and if we wait long enough it will be defended," he warned. Weitzel had the green light to assault these works and enter Richmond if he found, in Butler's words, "a reasonable prospect of possible success." Butler did not limit his thinking. "The prize is large, and if we are that near the attempt to seize it will justify loss, specially if successful." He emphasized "celerity and promptitude," directing that a "strong and vigilant" provost guard follow the columns to prevent straggling. In the event of a Confederate counterattack on the Union left, he directed Terry to push forward, passing "beyond the enemy's line," and "attack his flank." Butler estimated enemy strength north of the James at seven thousand "good troops and about as many more conscripts and reserves," a remarkably accurate figure when compared to contemporary Confederate returns.[39]

The strength of Butler's plan lay in the fact that Confederates could not cover every location. After confronting Terry's divisions at the Darbytown Road, Lee would have little to spare to meet Weitzel's column. More important, the plan allowed Union commanders to choose the time and location of the flanking column's advance. No matter what happened, Butler would meet Grant's expectations by simply showing up with his troops outside the rebel lines on the morning of October 27.

In the midst of their verbosity, Butler's instructions contained a remarkable omission in that they failed to discourage attacks against entrenched, manned positions. In essence, his orders clearly outpaced and ignored his commander's paramount concern. In his note to Butler, Grant had devoted two of his thirteen sentences to this consideration. Butler, in his thirteen-hundred-word blueprint for the October 27 operation, could not bring himself to address the subject at all, at least not directly. His orders addressed the question obliquely, urging his commanders to push ahead where no opposition lay and to demonstrate in front of manned trenches. Nowhere, though, did he clearly pass along Grant's admonition that "there is to be no attack made against defended, intrenched positions." In fact, when summarizing the operation's purpose, he declared, "Let it be understood that this is to be a movement to try to meet the enemy outside of his works, and the sooner he comes out the better." His aggressiveness shines through the document. Grant's low expectations failed to constrain Butler's ambitions.[40] Nevertheless, Grant seemed unbothered, informing Butler that the orders "meet the case in hand exactly."[41]

Butler's orders trickled down through the chain of command. Weitzel's headquarters forwarded the plan to the division commanders along with a note setting the next morning's departure time for 5 A.M.[42] The news may not have surprised many in the rank and file. Rumors had swirled through the camps about pending operations, but no one could seize upon any details. In any case, the men packed their gear on Wednesday night in preparation for the next day's operation.[43]

As Meade and Butler prepared on Wednesday, the 26th, Grant received disappointing news from the Valley. Despite a string of firm suggestions from City Point, Sheridan reported that he could not strike the Virginia Central Railroad due to supply and forage difficulties. He had examined the various approaches and concluded that they were all "impracticable" or premature.[44] Grant wanted Sheridan to remain aggressive. Inactivity there presented the least desired outcome. An idle Sheridan would dampen chances for ultimate success at Richmond. Even if Meade managed to sever the South Side Railroad, Richmond's other lifelines would remain open if unmolested by Sheridan. For the immediate future, however, Sheridan's news meant little. With forty thousand men staging to march west into the Dinwiddie countryside, Grant set his sights on Petersburg.

"we will give them a warm reception"

Earlier in the month, Wade Hampton had predicted that the federals would attack the new Boydton Plank Road line at the Dabney house. He was ready. "My men here think that they can whip anybody now, and they are in the finest possible spirits," he wrote. "If a great battle comes off I think that they will make their mark."[45] The men in the trenches shared the sentiment. Spencer Welch, a surgeon in McGowan's South Carolina brigade, reported to his wife, "Our troops seem as happy and lively as men could be, although they have nothing to eat now but bread and meat."[46] As the Confederate defenses neared completion, Hampton described his dispositions to A. P. Hill. He planned to hold about seven hundred dismounted men permanently in the trenches, primed to repel a Union assault. The left end of his line connected to the North Carolinians from Cooke's infantry brigade near the Dabney house.[47] Hampton also stationed James Dearing's cavalry brigade near Burgess Mill with orders to fill the trenches east of the Boydton Plank Road should the enemy attack.

Hampton could pour between sixteen hundred and eighteen hundred men into the new defenses.[48] But he could stretch his men only so far. Matthew Butler's division guarded the crossings from Armstrong's Mill down to Monk Neck's bridge, and, farther south, squads from Rooney Lee's division served as the tripwire to the Confederate rear. Hampton's men could cover the trenches for about a mile north of Hatcher's Run to where a ravine cut through Cousin's field. But this was the limit. Hampton urged General Hill to shift some infantry down the line to allow more cavalrymen to protect the Hatcher's Run and Rowanty Creek crossings.[49] To the south, he had also built five separate dams at various locations along Hatcher's Run and Rowanty Creek.

On Tuesday, the 25th, Hampton and Hill rode together along the new works. Hampton urged his counterpart to insert an additional thousand infantrymen in the trenches to allow the cavalry to concentrate its four thousand troopers behind Hatcher's Run. If a Union column attacked the new Confederate trenches, Hampton would throw these men across one of his dams and into the enemy's flanks while looking out for Union cavalry to the south. He was confident he could repel such a Union attempt. After examining the front with Hill on Tuesday, he wrote to Lee about the plan and asked for additional men at Petersburg for the defenses north of Hatcher's Run.[50]

Hampton's men formed a loose net draped across the landscape southwest of Petersburg. As troops shuffled along the fresh trenches and stream crossings, they watched and waited for developments to the east. The 9th Virginia, stationed at Malone's Crossing, spent the days with drilling and picket duty.[51] William Stokes of the 4th South Carolina cavalry had written from his camp at Armstrong's Mill on October 18 that Hatcher's Run was "very well fortified, and if the Yanks undertake to advance on the South Side R.R., we will give them a warm reception."[52] On Tuesday, Stokes's regiment shifted about a mile closer to the Boydton Plank Road, most likely in the vicinity of Dabney's Saw Mill. Other elements of the South Carolina brigade camped on the Quaker Road south of Burgess Mill.[53]

CHAPTER 7

The Union Army Prepares for Battle

~

"you will soon hear of it"

In the camps of Meade's army, the rumor mill turned. On Monday, the 24th, a member of the 12th New York wrote that from "all indications something of importance is going to happen soon."[1] As preparations commenced, some soldiers correctly predicted the object of the upcoming operation. A Pennsylvanian in the Fifth Corps noted that the orders were "quickly interpreted to mean a determined effort to reach and hold, or destroy, the South Side Railroad."[2] On the 24th, Meade's army began to move. Winfield Hancock's Second Corps stirred first. His men would have the longest march on Thursday, the 27th, the day of the operation. To reach its staging point well before the offensive, the Second Corps began its movement on the 24th. The two divisions assigned to the operation (Hancock's second and third) vacated the lines east of Petersburg late Monday and crept rearward, away from prying enemy eyes. In their place, General Nelson Miles's first division, with more than 6,000 muskets, filled the vacated works.

After withdrawing from the front, Hancock's second division, commanded by Brigadier General Thomas Egan, halted in an open space just west of Fort Bross.[3] Egan's movement was not flawless. Early on the 25th, one of his brigades had sauntered across an open plain in "full view of the enemy," much to Hancock's displeasure.[4] Despite the imperfections, Egan's division eventually gathered behind Fort Bross. On the 25th, the gun crews of the 10th Massachusetts Battery and their six three-inch Parrott rifled guns joined the infantrymen. The Bay State gunners lay about, "hearing and circulating" rumors of the upcoming move.[5] But despite a lot of talk, no one budged that afternoon.

Through the woods to the west, Major General Gershom Mott's third division occupied the forest-lined field on the Southall Farm late on Monday, the 24th.[6] Though some commanders remained ignorant of the details, they guessed an important movement was in the offing.[7] The men woke to a fine, cool morning on the 25th and prepared to march again. According to a Maine volunteer, the troops waited all day as wagons rolled through the Southall property laden with rations and ammunition. Artillery crews steered their teams to the southwest, further fueling rumors that the infantrymen would soon follow.[8] Finally, an order arrived from Second Corps headquarters directing the men to fold tents at noon the next day (the 26th).[9] Another directive called on each man to take four days' rations and directed the quartermasters to bring an additional three days' rations of beef "on the hoof." Despite the hints, most members of the Second Corps turned in Tuesday night still unsure of the timing and nature of the upcoming operation.[10]

On Wednesday morning, the 26th, the division commanders received word to depart at two o'clock and head for the Weldon Railroad. The appointed route ran "from the Southall house, through the wood by the Widow Smith's, Williams', and Gurley's houses, and Fort Dushane," a redoubt guarding the Halifax Road and Weldon Railroad. That evening, the corps would camp outside the Union earthworks near the Vaughan house. Hancock's orders confined the men to their bivouacs, prohibited bugle calls, and allowed only small fires.[11]

"We are still here but we will move in an hour. We don't know where, yet it is a very important move and you will soon hear of it," wrote Colonel Robert McAllister on Wednesday.[12] About thirty-six hours had passed since the fields at Fort Bross and the Southall house had filled with Hancock's soldiers. At two o'clock Wednesday afternoon, the men finally stepped off toward the Vaughan Road on what would be a long, tiring march. For Nelson Armstrong, a fever-stricken member of the 8th New York Heavy Artillery, Wednesday's march was weary and painful. "We hurried along the narrow roads, hastily cut through the timber by the pioneers," he wrote. Night found Armstrong and the rest of the marching column in a dark forest, where they finally reached a clearing.[13] With no fires to warm the night air, Hancock's men flopped down to sleep.[14]

As the Second Corps' foot soldiers marched westward on Wednesday, the army's mounted arm also prepared. David M. Gregg, Meade's cavalry commander, was a solid, dependable, and well-liked veteran who had performed ably so far during the Petersburg campaign. On Thursday, he and his men would cover the roads to the south and protect Hancock's left flank. This arrangement probably pleased Hancock, who had expressed great confidence in Gregg.[15] Gregg would bring his entire command on Thursday's march. At the beginning of October, it had contained two brigades, the first led by Henry Davies, and the second by Charles Smith. But Gregg reshuffled his command on the 18th, adding a third brigade headed by Smith, and assigning Colonel Michael Kerwin to lead the second brigade.[16]

The Northern troopers had battled Wade Hampton's men throughout the summer and into the autumn. During Grant's fifth offensive, in September, Gregg's aggressive probes along the Vaughan Road and elsewhere sparked a series of sharp skirmishes. But October brought relative calm. Gregg's men split their time between picket duty, camp, and the occasional reconnaissance.[17] During the lull, several units upgraded their firepower. Members of the 1st Maine, from Smith's newly formed brigade, turned in their Sharps and Burnside carbines for a mix of Spencer seven-shooters and Henry sixteen-shooters.[18] The 16th Pennsylvania, in Kerwin's brigade, also received Spencers. "We have a great time issuing them by night—Our men pleased we realize increased power and efficiency," recorded one diarist.[19]

Meade's orders for the offensive brought an end to the horsemen's comparative inactivity. On Wednesday afternoon, Gregg's brigades broke camp and trotted south along the Jerusalem Plank Road and then turned west along the trenches, past the Gurley Farm and on to the Perkins house on the Weldon Railroad. There, they dismounted and camped, with orders to rise at 2 A.M.[20]

"confront and threaten"

Gouverneur Warren's Fifth Corps also carried out preparations for Thursday's movement. Warren's men manned the Union lines from the Jerusalem Plank Road to Fort Conahey, west of the Weldon Railroad. Given its proximity to the Confederate lines along the Boydton Plank Road, Warren's corps had no need to leave on Wednesday and thus prepared to embark early the next morning.[21] The first division, commanded by Brigadier General Charles Griffin, would serve as the vanguard.[22] Nearly 60 percent of the division's men (2,803 out of 4,707) had never fired a musket.[23] Warren's two other divisions, led by Brigadier Generals Romeyn Ayres and Samuel Crawford, would follow Griffin. To guard the Fifth Corps lines, Warren planned to leave a single brigade, Henry Baxter's command from Crawford's division.[24]

On Wednesday evening, Andrew Humphreys, writing from the army's temporary headquarters at Poplar Springs Church, sent the details for the next day's march to the corps commanders. Both Warren and Parke would leave from Fort Cummings, the work at the southwestern tip of the Union trench lines. Parke received instructions to cut two openings in the parapet to allow the two corps to exit simultaneously and minimize delays and confusion. The task of digging down the parapet fell to the 43rd USCT Regiment of Ferrero's Ninth Corps division. The black troops scraped down the breastwork and filled the outside ditch. As the regiment completed its assignment, General Meade and his staff appeared. The soldiers formed to salute the general. Meade admired the new gap, looked over the men with approval, and remarked to their commanding officer, "Well done, Lieutenant, well done."[25] At eight o'clock, Parke officially reported to army headquarters that the camp wall had been cut and the abatis cleared outside of Fort Cummings.[26]

That evening, Humphreys informed Warren that Fort Cummings was ready for the next day's expedition. Warren's assigned path traced southwest on a narrow, wooded road that emerged onto the Westmoreland property about a mile away. From there, the Fifth Corps would travel over a network of narrow roads past small farms to the Duncan Road and Hatcher's Run.[27] Though the guidance was a bit vague, one of Warren's aides, future bridge builder Washington Roebling, knew the roads mentioned in the headquarters' dispatch.[28] Upon Warren's direction, he had "reconnoitered everywhere in that direction" but did not venture beyond the Union cavalry pickets, who were stationed, by Warren's later estimation, "but a short distance out."[29] On Wednesday evening, Meade altered Warren's departure time to 4 A.M., more than an hour earlier than previously planned.

John G. Parke's Ninth Corps, stationed west of the Weldon Railroad, would travel a shorter distance than their Fifth Corps counterparts. These men, many of whom were new draftees,[30] had spent the last few weeks building their new trenches and forts. On Wednesday, they gathered rations, beef cattle, ammunition, entrenching tools, wagons, and ambulances and prepared to leave behind the recent fruits of their labor.[31] Brigades and artillery batteries readied for the 3 A.M. departure. As Parke prepared, Meade wrote to stress the need for coordination with Warren. Meade hoped the Ninth Corps would surprise the enemy. However, consistent with Grant's earlier instructions, he discouraged attacks against strong and well-manned works. Instead, he urged Parke to "confront and threaten" the enemy in his lines.[32]

"it is almost certain to storm"

As the Fifth and Ninth Corps prepared on Wednesday, Hancock reported at 6:30 P.M. that his men had gone into bivouac near the Lewis and Perkins houses, just off the Weldon Railroad and Halifax Road.[33] Hancock's third division, led by Brevet Major General Gershom Mott, followed the appointed route earlier in the day passing the Gurley house, filing through the Union breastworks, and tramping southwest across open country until reaching the Lewis house at 5 P.M., near the Halifax Road.[34] The 17th Maine, a regiment in Mott's division, camped near the 1st Maine Cavalry Regiment, from Gregg's command. The horse soldiers visited their comrades and discussed their faraway homes and the prospects ahead. One infantryman scribbled in his journal that the cavalrymen "have orders to be in the saddle at daylight, but it looks very much like rain might interfere with the arrangements. Whenever this army plans a movement, it is almost certain to storm. Our orders are a good barometer."[35] Wednesday had furnished a pleasant, cool autumn day for the army's operations. Toward dark, however, the sky suggested a turn in the weather.

Hancock initially set the start time at 2 A.M. His column, led by Thomas Egan's second division, would march on the Vaughan Road, across Hatcher's Run and onto the Boydton Plank Road. As Hancock advanced, Gregg's cavalry would swing well to the south, covering the left flank of Hancock's column. Gregg would move by Rowanty Post Office to the Vaughan Road, "communicating with the infantry column whenever practicable."[36] However, later, Hancock changed his plans slightly. According to reports from rebel deserters, tree limbs blocked portions of the Vaughan Road, including the crossing at Hatcher's Run. In response, Hancock questioned the early start time. A difficult night march through rebel obstructions would gain little and could exhaust and disorganize his men. He suggested a later time to allow his men to "make the same distance in better order."[37] Meade and Humphreys agreed. The Second Corps would depart at 3:30 the next morning.[38]

That night, Hancock's troops cleared the camps. They loaded sick men, extra baggage, and commissary stores into wagons and sent them to the supply base at City Point, under the protection of defenses there and gunboats in the river.[39] The camp sutlers, a ubiquitous presence under normal conditions, also headed back to City Point.[40] The garrison there had improved the existing defenses. The position's capture would spell doom for Meade's army, which would be exposed on its march to the South Side Railroad. H. W. Benham, the officer in charge at City Point, deployed over fifteen hundred armed engineers and infantry and twenty-four guns in the series of redoubts that protected the vital position. On Tuesday, two days before the offensive, he assured Grant, "The place will never be surrendered by me."[41]

"an army in better spirits"

North of the James, Butler's army prepared for its supporting role. The troops had done little since the bloody reconnaissance at the Darbytown Road on October 13. However, a violent engagement between Union batteries and several Confederate gunboats had broken the relative tranquility in recent days. Early on Saturday morning, the 22nd, two Union batteries, including seven heavy Parrott guns in a new work along Signal Hill, opened fire on the Confederate James River Squadron resting within easy range. Placed during the night, the guns surprised the crews of the thin-skinned gunboats, which steamed out of danger, tucking under the river bank at Chaffin's Bluff. The rebel ironclads also sought cover and, for a time, hid under the bank downstream from the Union guns. The shelling blew a hole in the *Fredericksburg*'s smokestack, which protruded from the river bank's cover. The wood splinters from a shattered grating wounded five men aboard. The ironclads eventually escaped upstream, out of range. Across the river, Confederate shore batteries joined in, but the engagement soon ended.[42]

As talk of this naval engagement receded, federal troops turned their attention to the new offensive. Just south of the New Market Road, the camps of Alfred Terry's Tenth Corps divisions bustled. "All is activity," wrote Joseph Hawley to his wife, "we move sometime tonight—whither I don't think a soul in the Corps knows save Gen. Terry."[43] Godfrey Weitzel's Eighteenth Corps withdrew from the works near Fort Harrison and gathered at the Henry Cox house, which sat on a wide field bordered mostly by woods and the winding branches of Three Mile Creek. The Cox house had served as the venue for court martial hearings earlier that month,[44] but on Wednesday evening, the homestead was transformed into an immense camp. Weitzel's men stacked their rifles and set up tents. Commissary details cooked three days rations.[45] Each soldier drew sixty rounds of ammunition, and another hundred rounds per man found their way into wagons. The commanders received word to begin the march at 5 A.M. Weitzel's force consisted of his first division, commanded by Brigadier General Gilman Marston; two brigades from the second division under Brigadier General Charles Heckman; and the two USCT brigades of the third division, led by Colonel John Holman.[46] Some units had traveled from positions at Bermuda Hundred across the James to join the balance of the corps.[47] To cover the vacated Union earthworks, Weitzel left behind two brigades stretched paper thin.[48]

At the Cox Farm, hope rose from the bustling camp. Thomas Chester, an African American correspondent for a Philadelphia newspaper, noted, "Never was an army in better spirits, or more confident of a victory."[49] Brigade commander Colonel Edward Ripley dreamt of entering Richmond. "What consists of our bill of fare at the Spottswood House, will be the subject of a letter I hope ere long, unless General Lee out-generals us," he told relatives back home in Vermont.[50] Around the fires of the third division's black regiments, strong voices rose into the October night, filling the air with "John Brown," "Rally Around the Flag," "Colored Volunteer," and other standards.[51] A different kind of enthusiasm coursed through some white first division soldiers, members of Lieutenant Colonel John Raulston's brigade, thanks to whiskey distributed by negligent commissaries or opportunistic sutlers. While their singing may have been heartfelt, the drunken soldiers drew more attention for several fights and the general disturbance they caused.[52]

"The Ball will open tomorrow"

At City Point, General Grant considered the next day's operation. The pieces were in place. Parke, Warren, Hancock, and Gregg stood poised to launch their columns into the Dinwiddie countryside and stretch for the South Side Railroad. Butler prepared for his demonstration north of the James. As the gears of his military machine turned, Grant wrote his wife, "To-morrow a great battle will probably be fought. At all events, I have made all the arrangement for one and unless I conclude through the day to change my programme it will take place. I do not like to predict results therefore will say nothing about what I expect to accomplish."[53] Despite the cautious words, he hoped to accomplish much. The capture of the

South Side Railroad would bring Petersburg to its knees and perhaps flush Lee's army out of Richmond altogether. Grant's aide, John Rawlins, had "little doubt" the operation would "bring on a great battle."[54] In a nearby office, Marsena Patrick also opened his diary, his nightly habit, and recorded, "Genl. Meade moved his Head Quarters, this morning, to Poplar Springs Church, beyond the Weldon Railroad and the Ball will open tomorrow."[55]

The Confederates learned of these preparations. North of the James, James Longstreet received reports Tuesday of Union troop movements across the James into Henrico County. He put Charles Field's division on alert and ordered a regiment to cover the Charles City Road and place obstructions there.[56] In addition, Confederate cavalry stacked felled trees and other obstacles at road crossings to the White Oak Swamp, north of the Charles City Road.[57] South of Petersburg, the upcoming Union offensive had not remained a secret, either. On Wednesday morning, Confederate pickets in front of Union Fort Fisher asked their counterparts why no attack had occurred the night before. Apparently, an indiscreet member of the 35th Massachusetts had broadcast the upcoming movement to anyone willing to listen. In addition, Confederate pickets assured their counterparts that they "had a line of battle ready to receive [Union soldiers] and give [them] a warm reception," according to one federal diarist.[58] On Wednesday evening, from the siege lines east of Petersburg, Confederates in Archibald Gracie's brigade noted that the sound of Union wagon movements were more pronounced than usual.[59] But the Confederates knew no details.

CHAPTER 8

The Williamsburg Road

~

The Army of the James rose on Thursday, the 27th, for its move against Richmond. At dawn, the Tenth Corps commander, Alfred Terry, ill from a recurrent malarial fever, climbed into a buggy and headed north.[1] After reaching the Darbytown Road, he established headquarters at the Johnson house and waited for his three divisions to arrive.[2] Terry's mission was simple and largely free of the uncertainty and contingencies of other operations. The plan called for a demonstration to develop the Confederate defenses but did not necessarily require any determined attacks. Benjamin Butler hoped the mere presence of the Tenth Corps in the Darbytown Road sector would prevent rebel commanders from shifting their forces to meet threats elsewhere. For Terry and his division commanders, the ground ahead presented no mystery. The reconnaissance of the 13th had fully uncovered the true nature of the rebel works, a continuous, well-planned, and well-constructed trench line, complete with redans for artillery and extensive obstacles in front.

At about 7 A.M., Terry's second division, led by Brigadier General Robert Foster, filed past the Johnson house and deployed at the center of the Tenth Corps' line, just south of the Darbytown Road. Foster dispatched skirmishers from Colonel Martin Curtis's brigade to cover the front. Colonel Louis Bell's brigade formed in reserve, and Colonel Galusha Pennypacker's brigade came up, as well.[3] Fifteen minutes after their arrival at the Johnson Farm, the blue-clad soldiers began drawing fire from rebel pickets just beyond remnants of the old exterior line, the eroded works Kautz had occupied unsuccessfully several weeks before.[4] "Immediately in front of the Johnson house the ground is level and clear for a considerable distance," described a reporter at the scene. "The rebel pickets, just in the edge of the wood and around two or three houses, were plainly seen with the naked eye from headquarters."[5] Concerned with enfilade fire from the old trench line just north of the Darbytown Road, Foster covered his right flank with skirmishers from Pennypacker's brigade, men from the 76th Pennsylvania and one company of the 97th Pennsylvania. The Pennsylvanians flushed the enemy pickets from the abandoned trenches and edged toward several barns and sheds beyond, most likely the outbuildings of the Gerhardt Farm.[6]

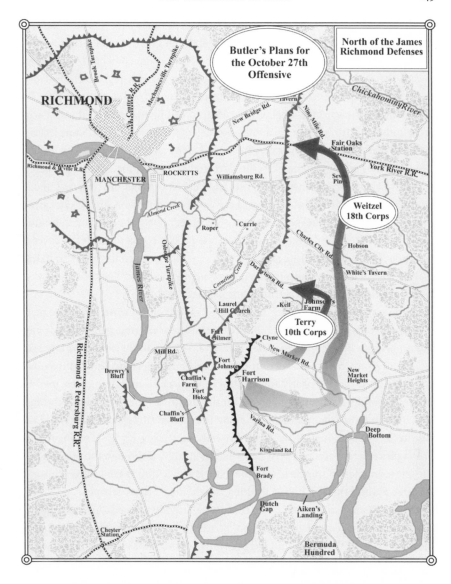

On the right, the first division, led by Brigadier General Adelbert Ames, formed next to Foster and fanned out north of the Darbytown Road. Ames's soldiers found themselves on familiar ground, the same farms, fields, and timber they had struggled through during the October 13 reconnaissance. In Foster's wake, Ames's brigades passed the Johnson house, and then faced west toward the enemy works.

On the left flank to the south, Terry's third division, USCTs under Brigadier General Joseph Hawley (who had commanded a brigade earlier in the month), gathered at the Kell house, a landmark from the October 7 fight. The slight rise there had served as the Confederate artillery position during Charles Field's attack on the New

Market Road.[7] Unlike many of the other Tenth Corps units, Hawley's men had seen little action since their assault on Fort Gilmer at the end of September. The division's two brigades spread out through the dense woods west of the Kell house and inched toward the rebel picket line. The 29th Connecticut (a black regiment) formed in front of the division as skirmishers and advanced toward well-built rebel pits. The troops sprinted toward the rebel pickets, who, according to Captain Edward Bacon of the 29th, quickly ran away, apparently terrified of the black soldiers. Some fell captive and "made haste onto their very knees and really craved for mercy and for life." "Now the master begs favors from the slave and gets them too," observed Bacon.[8] The skirmishers overran the picket posts and pushed through the "meanest undergrowth" until they arrived at the edge of the woods. Before them stretched a narrow strip of slashing, a cornfield, and a chain of rebel redoubts connected by substantial breastworks. Bacon and his men could see the pickets flying to reach the cover of the works, their forms offering excellent targets as they climbed the fresh dirt to leap over the parapet. "We took delight in hitting them," Bacon recalled. With no orders to advance farther, Hawley's skirmish line halted there.[9]

In these initial advances, the Tenth Corps maintained a slow, deliberate pace. With the strong works ahead and little expectation of tangible gains, Terry's men had no need to hurry or press. After Foster's first push to the old exterior works, activity all along the Tenth Corps front noticeably declined and Terry's three divisions stretched out for nearly three miles in the face of trench line designed by Porter Alexander. In the center, Foster's units continued to edge forward through trees and underbrush, eventually reaching the enemy rifle pits.[10] They could see little in the thick undergrowth. A captain in the 117th New York, searching for the Union picket line, became a prisoner when he stumbled through the thickets and into the Confederate trenches.[11] To the left, Hawley's USCTs trod slowly through the trees beyond the Kell house, flushing the enemy from its rifle pits.

On the Tenth Corps' right, north of the Darbytown Road, Ames's brigades extended to the Charles City Road and filtered through the woods, pushing back enemy pickets.[12] The 67th Ohio from Colonel Alvin Voris's brigade managed to snare a section of enemy rifle pits, along with five unlucky gray coats.[13] But the dense strip of woods stretching across their path hampered further progress. Many in the 7th New Hampshire from Colonel Joseph Abbott's brigade completely lost their bearings and became separated from their command. Ferdinand Davis, a New Hampshire officer acting on Abbott's staff, ventured into the tangled undergrowth to find his wayward companions. Through bullets flying "about in a most callous manner," he finally located the regiment's line near the Charles City Road. From there he returned to Abbott by a safer route.[14]

The lead Union elements found no opening in the formidable rebel line. Even on the far right, along the Charles City Road, cavalry reported a rebel battery planted in the middle of the road.[15] To the men, the lack of forward progress probably came as no surprise, but the low body count may have been unexpected.

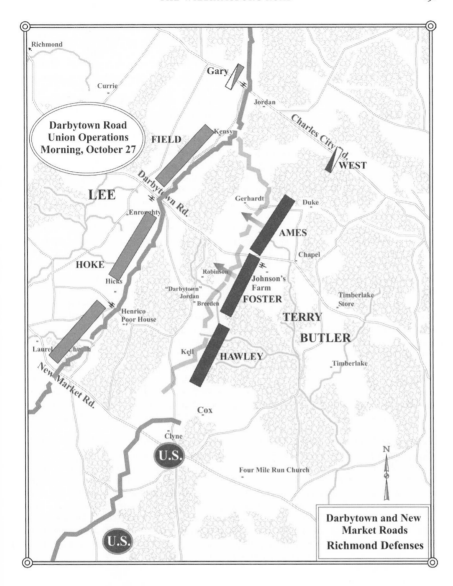

"We had moved out so frequently on armed reconnaissance," recalled a New York veteran later, "that the boys would simply say, 'Now for a little more butchery, a little more slaughter.'"[16] To the soldiers' relief, however, few casualties accompanied the tentative advance.

As the Tenth Corps tested the rebel line, General Butler arrived at Dr. Johnson's house with his staff and mounted escort. By 11 A.M., rain began to fall. Butler's entourage included William Waud, an English-born architect and *Harper's Weekly* illustrator who had witnessed the bombardment of Fort Sumter three years before while working for *Leslie's Illustrated*. Waud, along with his older brother, Alfred, had tracked Union operations throughout the 1864 Virginia campaign. The two had penciled a large cache of eyewitness sketches depicting combat operations and troop movements. From Virginia's battlefields, they shipped their hastily drawn work back north to the *Harper's Weekly* offices, where staff redrew the sketches and prepared them for publication. While the final, printed illustrations of these first-person impressions of the war received a wide distribution, the combat artists' original sketches better conveyed the chaos of battle than the more sterile versions rendered by the engraver's chisel.[17]

Late that morning, Waud's pencil captured Butler and a cluster of officers inside Dr. Johnson's house, peering out at the battlefield. The resulting sketch depicts at least eighteen men wearing their cloak coats, hats, and heavy boots, crowded along a row of three windows. The room is bare, with no sign of furnishings, and the floor appears strewn with leaves or other debris. Waud also peered out the windows himself as the mounted gun crews of Captain James Clinton's 1st Connecticut Light Battery pounded past and unlimbered four rifled pieces on the southern shoulder of the Darbytown Road. The balance of the Tenth Corps batteries remained parked to the rear.[18] Looking out from the second floor, Waud captured these scenes. On the left side of his sketch paper, he penciled in Clinton's four rifled guns firing shells northwest across the Darbytown Road. The limbers and accompanying horse teams stood thirty or forty yards to the rear of the guns, nestled in a depression in the Johnson fields. Clinton's weapons hurled their shells beyond the Gerhardt house and, apparently, at the house itself, seeking to flush the rebel skirmishers who had sought cover there.

Waud also traced groups of soldiers huddled behind two redoubts along the road to the right of Clinton's battery, most likely the works Kautz's cavalry had defended unsuccessfully on October 7. The sketch depicted horsemen returning to the house along the same depression that hid Clinton's limber. Waud identified the mounted group as "Butler, staff & body guard." Beyond the Darbytown Road, he drew the Union battle line, containing the men from Ames's division crouched behind the abandoned exterior works facing the Gerhardt house and the woods beyond. Farther away, battle smoke rises thick from distant trees. The artist included other details such as the infantry and cavalry provost guards posted at intervals in the Johnson yard and ambulances waiting near the Johnson house and moving up the Darbytown Road toward the action. A *New York Times* reporter, who accompanied Waud and the others at the Johnson house, described the scene:

> From the upper windows of Dr. Johnson's house, a very fair view of the skirmish line could be had. Our pickets were lying behind a small breastwork, about one hundred yards from the edge of trees, and all day long a desultory firing was kept up. There was nothing very exciting in all this. One becomes even tired of watching the little puffs of blue smoke that invariably follows the sudden rising of one of the crouching black specks whom we know to be men lying down along the distant parapet, as well as of noting the little clouds of gray dust that

are thrown up by the rebel bullets which strike the ground in front of our boys, who are snug under shelter of the ridge of earth.[19]

As boredom afflicted some safely ensconced in the Johnson house, the men in the ranks faced the danger out on the battlefield. Though the fighting at the Darbytown Road that morning did not have the makings of decisive battle, the exposure to enemy fire and the cold, wet conditions were notable enough to the rank and file. "A more cheerless, comfortless day is rarely seen even in October," recalled one veteran.[20]

As matters reached a standstill, Benjamin Butler sought to maintain contact with Grant south of the James. At 9:30 A.M., he reported, "Terry has advanced to Darby Road, driving in the enemy's pickets. Weitzel's column was on Darby Road at 8 o'clock, where it joins Drill-Room road, in time, and where he ought to be. All going on well."[21] Though his army was not cast in the starring role, Butler had high hopes his men would find a way into Richmond. As of late morning, however, all doors remained firmly closed.

"Some other was the point of danger"

While Butler aspired, an air of anxiety hung over the Confederate commanders. Major General Robert Hoke had caught wind of the Union preparations the night before. Years later he recalled, "We heard the rumbling of artillery and all other noises which showed that General Butler was on the move, and I soon arrived at the conclusion that he was going to attack that part of the works immediately across the Newmarket road." The Confederates massed infantry units at the point of danger and wheeled the guns of Robert Hardaway's and A.W. Stark's battalions "with shell and canister shot arranged for close work."[22] Hoke's prediction bore out as the Union Tenth Corps spread before the Confederate works on either side of the Darbytown Road. In Field's front, some units were not as prepared. A South Carolinian in Bratton's brigade recalled that the attack commenced while men were still in their quarters. But the rebels rushed to the trenches, unleashed a few volleys, and brought the Union advance to a halt.[23]

News of the Union offensive spread alarm through the Confederate high command. At Lee's headquarters on the Chaffin Farm, Walter Taylor, Lee's adjutant, sifted through reports streaming across his desk. Lee and his staff sought to make sense of the news arriving from different sectors along the attenuated line. From Petersburg, A. P. Hill reported a general enemy advance threatening the South Side Railroad. From the lines east of Richmond, the news also indicated activity on Butler's front. Taylor, who helped manage the mountains of paperwork that crowded Lee in his headquarters each day, was a busy man that morning. As the reports poured in and Grant's legions pressed right and left, he found time to scribble a note to his sweetheart, Bettie Saunders, back in Richmond. "There are indications of a general movement," he wrote. "The enemy is in motion at all points. We may have to move any moment."[24]

The news from Petersburg and from the Richmond lines left no doubt that Grant had launched a new attack on the rebel positions. With cannon booming in the distance, Lee mounted his horse and rode away alone from camp to inspect the front. In September, Grant's main thrust had fallen on the lines protecting Richmond. Now it was too early to divine where the primary blow would land.[25] The Virginian found Hoke at the trenches and, as Hoke recalled many years later, asked, "What will they do, General Hoke?" In the North Carolinian's estimation, Lee "simply did not know where Butler intended to strike."[26] The Confederate chieftain understood that Grant's easiest route to Richmond passed through the Confederate left flank in Henrico County. The Charles City Road, the Williamsburg Road, and the Nine Mile Road all offered avenues that pierced through the formidable but undermanned earthworks. According to Longstreet, Lee assumed that "sooner or later" Grant would attempt to seize Richmond by applying "great force" on the north side of the James. With this concern in mind, Lee rode toward the trenches at the New Market and Darbytown roads.[27] Back at headquarters, Taylor, pressed by military matters, ended his letter by asking, "Wouldn't it be nice to receive a telegram from Petersburg stating that we had beaten the enemy . . . Ha! You see how I am catching at straws."[28]

Hints of the attack also reached Hoke's fellow division commander Charles Field, who had ridden along the trenches preparing his units to greet the attack. "I never saw his troops in finer trim and with more enthusiasm," wrote one member of his command.[29] As the Union line inched forward, Field doubled his skirmishers.[30] The rebels could see the men of the Union Tenth Corps tramping over the Johnson Farm with the national banner flapping in the breeze. The advance halted, however, in the face of Field's "strong skirmish line and a few well aimed shells" from the Confederate cannon rapidly wheeled into the new rebel field works. The defenders witnessed several half-hearted advances by the federal troops, but the attackers "were driven back by the skirmishers and Major Stark's battalion of artillery."[31]

The approach of the Union Tenth Corps along the Darbytown Road furnished James Longstreet with his first dose of combat since his return to active duty. Lee's "Old War Horse" watched as Field's sharpshooters, nestled in the fresh earthworks, peppered away at Union skirmishers. He observed that the Union troops kept to the outer edge of the abatis, showing no inclination to venture further. Pondering the enemy's apparent timidity, he concluded that "some other was the point of danger" and became convinced that the commotion was nothing more than a feint. He believed that another Union column was marching well behind the Johnson Farm, seeking to cross the White Oak Swamp and assail the Confederate line far to the left. According to Longstreet's later recollection, Lee was not so sure. The commanding general had no word from Martin Gary's cavalry pickets in that vulnerable sector. Any movement across the swamp or along the Williamsburg Road by a sizable enemy force could not easily escape detection by the rebel videttes.[32] But Lee did not quarrel with his lieutenant, and soon Longstreet ordered General Field to "pull his division out of the works and march for the Williamsburg Road," which was about two miles to the north, leaving only his skirmish line intact.[33]

To fill the vacated works, Longstreet directed Hoke to extend his force toward the Charles City Road and to double the sharpshooters on his skirmish line.[34] Union eyes beyond the abatis spied the shifting troops and noted the arrival of Hoke's men in the early afternoon. The news soon found its way to Union headquarters. Though the movement convinced some Union pickets that the rebel line had been strengthened,[35] Confederate Brigadier General Johnson Hagood, commanding one of Hoke's brigades, later wrote that the works were "defended by a single rank deployed at intervals of three to six feet, with no reserves." The rebels shifted along the trenches, "now closing up to repel an assault, now deploying to fill a gap, and sometimes leaving long stretches undefended except by field guns in battery."[36] Longstreet was correct. Somewhere in the distance, the Union column he feared was headed for the Confederate left. Godfrey Weitzel and the U.S. Eighteenth Corps marched for Richmond. With Longstreet's urging, Charles Field's infantrymen began a race to prevent disaster.

"I think you are over-rating me"

Their packs stuffed with three days of rations, Weitzel's men formed their columns on Thursday morning and marched west from the Cox Farm along the Kingsland Road. Weitzel's force contained his entire first division (three brigades under Brigadier General Gilman Marston), a portion of the second (two brigades under Brigadier General Charles Heckman), and part of the third (two brigades under Colonel Alonzo Draper). The 13th New Hampshire led the procession. Near Deep Bottom, the route veered north, intersecting the New Market Road, where the column jogged west a short distance and then passed the vacant, useless enemy trenches along New Market Heights, the same works Alonzo Draper's USCTs helped capture several weeks before. At the Drill Room, a building next to the New Market Road, the column shifted north once again and steered toward the Darbytown Road. To the front, Colonel Samuel Spear's cavalry regiments fanned ahead, clearing roads and fields of enemy scouts and pickets.[37]

Along the way, some noncombatants lent support to the column. Reporter Thomas Chester, who accompanied the infantry, noted that women emerged from their dwellings and readily identified the distances and names of roads to the passing soldiers.[38] According to another journalist, the march itself was admirable, producing few stragglers.[39] Not everything remained with the ranks, though. Chester noted "several muskets and accoutrements, which were heaped together, and no one to claim them" along the roadside.[40]

Through the march, General Weitzel maintained a steady stream of correspondence to Butler. After reaching the Darbytown Road at 8 A.M., he reported some skirmishing in his front, which was, he surmised, the result efforts to clear the way.[41] An hour and fifty minutes later, he wrote again, fixing his location at White's Tavern on the Charles City Road, not much more than a mile beyond his position an hour before.[42] His frequent missives betrayed a gnawing anxiety. Though his wartime photographs present a stern, heavily bearded visage, this forceful appearance masked a heap of cautiousness and self-doubt, and this morning he was particularly concerned.

The son of German immigrants, Weitzel demonstrated a gift for mathematics and an interest in military matters as a youth in Cincinnati. In 1850, he gained an appointment to West Point, where he excelled at engineering, graduating second out of a class of forty-three. Before the outbreak of war, he had served as an army engineer, designing fortifications at New Orleans, under P. G. T. Beauregard's command. He also taught at West Point shortly before the secession crisis boiled over.[43] After stints at Fort Pickens in Florida and in his hometown Cincinnati in the war's first year, he returned to Louisiana in 1862 and served as Butler's chief engineer; his knowledge of the locale greatly aided the Union capture of New Orleans. At the Crescent City, the young Weitzel impressed Butler, and, when the Massachusetts lawyer took charge of the Army of the James in 1864, he tapped Weitzel as his chief engineer and as commander of the second division of the Eighteenth Corps.[44] During the Richmond campaign, Weitzel continued to demonstrate his considerable engineering abilities, overseeing the construction of defenses at Bermuda Hundred and bridging over the James and Appomattox rivers. His performance as a combat commander, however, was undistinguished.

The young Weitzel possessed the ingredients necessary for success. He was intelligent and managed to avoid ruffling the feathers of his commanders and colleagues. When Butler needed someone to replace Edward Ord at the helm of the Eighteenth Corps in late September, Weitzel offered a reasonable choice, on paper at least. However, in reality, he had not acquired the necessary confidence for corps command, for, in his own mind, he was not quite prepared. In an extraordinarily candid letter to Butler, he wrote, "I often (I tell you frankly) mistrust my own abilities. I think you are over-rating me. . . . I do not wish to be shoved ahead too fast." [45]

Weitzel's mission, as set out in Butler's orders, was ill suited for one with such doubts. The directive required him to make several key decisions amid the fog of imperfect information. The burden of decision fell on Weitzel's shoulders first at White's Tavern on the Charles City Road. Butler had suggested the Charles City Road might provide a good avenue for Weitzel's advance but left the choice to him, depending "on the state of things existing on arrival there."[46] When the Eighteenth Corps reached White's Tavern shortly before 10 A.M., Weitzel received a report from Colonel Robert West, who led the army's cavalry on October 27 in the absence of the ailing Kautz, that the enemy works ahead were "formidable

and heavily manned." Weitzel also learned that the Tenth Corps battle line did
not extend fully to that road, news he conveyed to Butler.[47] At the time, the Eighteenth Corps stood fewer than two miles away from Butler and Terry at Dr. Johnson's house. According to West's report, an attack by the Eighteenth Corps on the
Charles City Road did not hold much promise. With this avenue blocked, Butler's
orders directed Weitzel to continue to the Williamsburg Road in the vicinity of
Fair Oaks several miles to the north. Despite the clear instructions, Weitzel's next
dispatch betrayed uncertainty. "I suppose that . . . you desire me to take the road
. . . to the Williamsburg road, and I shall move on that supposition," he wrote.
"Please send me orders what you wish me to do now."[48]

With the Charles City Road shut off, the Eighteenth Corps tracked back half a
mile and turned onto a narrow, wooded path leading north. Within a few hundred
yards, the men splashed across White Oak Swamp, shallow from lack of rain.[49]
Weitzel's men climbed the opposite bank, past the orchards and buildings of Mrs.
Hobson's property pushing back rebel cavalry pickets.[50] Continuing north along a
partially wooded road, the column waded over another small tributary and passed
through the remnants of Union earthworks dug in 1862 during the Peninsula campaign. Stepping through the eroded trenches, Weitzel's command emerged onto
the old Fair Oaks (or Seven Pines) battlefield. Because no one at the head of the
column, including Weitzel, knew the ground, a veteran of the previous fights from
the 2nd New Hampshire was called to the front. He immediately confirmed, "This
is the Williamsburg road. These are Hooker's old intrenchments . . . you will find
the rebel works just beyond the woods."[51] A *New York World* reporter accompanying Weitzel's men described the scene: "A little to the front once stood the celebrated Seven Pines. They have, however ceased to be a landmark to the veteran
who may in future years visit this celebrated field of his exploits. A few rods farther
and we were on the battlefield proper. How eagerly, and with what an animated
countenance, the old veterans pointed out each familiar object, even to a strange
clump of undergrowth."[52] Graves from McClellan's campaign also met the eyes
of the troops, a grim reminder of the war's bloody toll.[53] A Union chaplain, who
walked the ground the following spring, noted spots of lush green grass here and
there, "where the richer than wonted luxuriance of Southern vegetation showed
that the fertile soil of Virginia was further enriched with Northern patriot blood."[54]

Out ahead of Weitzel's column, cavalrymen from the 11th Pennsylvania encountered rebel pickets at the Williamsburg Road and drove them back.[55] "The sharp
cracking of the cavalry rifles in front drowned at times by the occasional roar of the
rebel artillery announced as plainly as words could," wrote a reporter, "no left flank
here, plenty of rebels though."[56] As Weitzel's infantry poured onto the Williamsburg
Road, a squad of Pennsylvanians under Captain Stephen Tripp challenged Confederate cavalrymen "formed in the ridge of a thin skirt of pines, and drove them
into their fortifications."[57] With their opponents brushed aside, the Union cavalry
deployed to picket the flanks.

The Eighteenth Corps had made contact with the enemy. The head of the infantry column reached the Williamsburg Road near Fair Oaks at about 1 P.M.[58]
It was time for the Unionists to test the works and determine whether this door
to Richmond would budge. Separated from the Tenth Corps by several miles as
well as the White Oak Swamp, Weitzel felt "entirely lost from Terry," a point he
emphasized to Butler at the time.[59] As he passed the Fair Oaks battlefield, he rode
through a large open area where the abatis and slashing from the federal works
had stood two years before. Beyond the cleared ground, the strip of pine woods
that had housed the rebel cavalry stood across his approach. The stand was a half
mile thick and very dense, an "almost impassable jungle," in places.[60]

Brigadier General Gilman Marston's division, heading the column all morning, formed the corps' spearhead and traversed the old battlefield and into
the pines ahead. The ground bore the landmarks of the 1862 battles, including
French's Farm (which sat several hundred yards south of the Williamsburg Road),
King's School House, and Oak Grove (north of the Williamsburg Road).[61] Marston ordered skirmishers, from the division's sharpshooter corps and the 118th
New York into the pines, where they found little opposition.[62] The skirmish line
straddled the Williamsburg Road, with a portion of the 118th stretching south
about two hundred yards. Though no foe was there, the skulls and bones of men
lost in earlier fighting littered the skirmishers' path.[63] In support, New York and
New Hampshire men of Marston's first brigade, led by John B. Raulston, deployed
across the center of the road at about 1:15 P.M. The skirmishers, all carrying Spencer rifles, broke through the trees and emerged into an open field.[64]

About eight hundred yards in their front, the enemy's main line loomed. In the
intervening space, two shallow depressions or gullies stretched across the field on
either side of the road, topographical features a casual observer might have missed.
Sensing an opportunity, the skirmishers "made a rush upon" the enemy's trenches,
for they appeared to be "only slightly manned." But the "heavy and formidable"
works proved "wholly unassailable by the feeble skirmishing force," wrote one
New Yorker later.[65] The skirmishers, led by Major Levi Dominy, found cover as fire
erupted from the Confederate works.[66] Some crept to within one hundred yards
of the enemy but eventually lay on the ground.[67] In addition to the small arms fire
peppering the advance, one piece of artillery belched from the rebel position.[68]

Marston and his officers halted the skirmish line and reconnoitered the enemy
defenses. Under orders from Weitzel, Marston brought up his second brigade and
rested his left on the Williamsburg Road. The division's third brigade, Lieutenant
Colonel Joab Patterson's regiments, formed in a "column of divisions and [was]
held in reserve about 100 yards in rear" of the line's center.[69] As Marston positioned the second division north of the Williamsburg Road, Brigadier General
Charles Heckman shepherded his division's two brigades into the woods on the
left. Heckman, a "thin, small, nervous, wiry" man, was extraordinarily coura-

geous and cool under fire. In one veteran's opinion, he was "the best fighter of the Army of the James."[70] Heckman connected his right with Marston's line across the road to the north.[71] In addition, a USCT brigade from the third division under Colonel Alonzo Draper arrived in support. "In a few minutes we were assigned our position and immediately filed to the left into a thick forest. We were to lie concealed and await orders," wrote Joseph Scruggs of the 5th USCT. "We lay quiet, listening to the musical overture of battle and the sweet patter of rain on the autumn foliage."[72] To the rear, Draper's other brigade, under Colonel John Holman, was still on the march.

Weitzel had arrived at his appointed destination. His vanguard had knocked the enemy pickets back into their works. He had formed a four-brigade front across the Williamsburg Road at the edge of the woods, ready to advance. More brigades continued to come up in support. It was time for more decision making. Once the Williamsburg Road had been reached, Butler's orders simply stated, "A vigorous push there may secure the second line before the enemy can reach it."[73] Weitzel met with Heckman and Marston. The three picked their way forward to observe the enemy position. As one reporter explained, "All agreed in the opinion that dismounted cavalry only was holding the works in our front, and that an attempt to carry the position was possible."[74] It is unclear whether everyone shared his view, though. Marston appears to have seen things differently. According to him, Major Dominy, the New Yorker in charge of the skirmish line, "reported to me that there appeared to be a considerable force in his front, and that reenforcements were arriving, which facts I reported to the brevet major-general commanding the corps."[75] In his own report, Weitzel gave no mention of Marston's views but simply stated that the enemy's breastworks were "defended by only three pieces of artillery and a small body of dismounted cavalry." He emphasized that this was his sincere belief at the time.[76]

Weitzel chose to attack. His reasoning, according to one observer, was thus: "If their works are held only by dismounted cavalry I shall be able to carry them with a small force, and a great advantage will have been gained. If on the contrary they are held by a heavier force than I anticipate, two brigades will be all I care to subject to the enemy's fire."[77] Weitzel may have been filled with doubt. In fact, he admitted several days later that the situation made him "uneasy and nervous."[78] But his state of mind did not produce timidity. Instead, he ordered his troops ahead.[79]

Weitzel called on two brigades to conduct the assault, each from a different division. He initially asked Lieutenant Colonel Joab Patterson of the third brigade, first division, to volunteer to attack. Patterson declined but said he would attack if ordered.[80] Instead, Colonel Edgar Cullen stepped up to volunteer his brigade.[81] On the right, Cullen's five regiments, men from New York, New Hampshire, and Maryland, would advance. The twenty-one year old Cullen, one of the youngest colonels in the Union army, had an eagerness to achieve military glory but had become embarrassed, pale, and flustered during his first combat, at Cold Harbor in May.[82] He worked to cope with his condition and eventually became a regular on the firing line.[83] In late September, he received a citation for "gallant bearing" during the Fort Harrison fight.[84]

With Cullen's command on the right, the seven hundred men of Colonel Harrison Fairchild's brigade from Heckman's second division took up the left wing. Fairchild's unit formed on the south side of the Williamsburg Road. His regiments included the 89th and 148th New York, the 19th Wisconsin, and one company of the 2nd Pennsylvania Heavy Artillery.[85] To support the attack, Battery A of the 1st Pennsylvania Light Artillery (Captain William Stitt's battery) clattered through the pines and unlimbered at the woods' edge primed with "instructions to fire as quickly as possible." The gunners immediately drew enemy artillery and musket fire.[86] As the projectiles flew, Cullen's and Fairchild's brigades stepped out to cross the open ground in front of the Confederate trenches. Weitzel hoped the works would hold little more than thinly spaced cavalrymen. He was deeply concerned.[87] His worry was well founded.

"as if he had command of a regiment"

Earlier that Thursday morning, Confederate general Charles Field met with two scouts from the 1st Texas Regiment, J. W. Trowbridge and Sam Watson. The general asked the pair to investigate the gunfire drifting in from the east. During the brief interview, he handed over two Whitworth rifles recently sent to headquarters "to be tested for accuracy," and suggested that the Texans might find an opportunity to try them out. The Whitworth, invented by a British engineer, weighed less than ten pounds and featured a hexagonal barrel. Though it had a tendency to foul easily and often became difficult to load after use, it could kill at a thousand yards and served as a wicked tool in the hands of a competent marksman.[88] The Texans shouldered their newfound arms and stepped out toward the muffled sounds of battle in the distance.[89]

Along the Charles City Road that morning, Martin Gary's cavalry witnessed the Union push firsthand. North of the road, the Confederates had strengthened the parapets and ditches of the original exterior works, which ran due north, toward the Williamsburg Road. At key points along the earthen curtains, engineers and laborers had cut redans for artillery pieces at intervals sufficient to ensure coverage of the ground in front. The small work on the Charles City Road bore the moniker "Battery Longstreet," according to Confederate maps. From this position, a few artillery pieces threw shells at Weitzel's advance earlier that morning. Beyond the main ditch, rifle pits cluttered the plain in front. Still farther east, a double line of strong abatis buffered the trenches.[90]

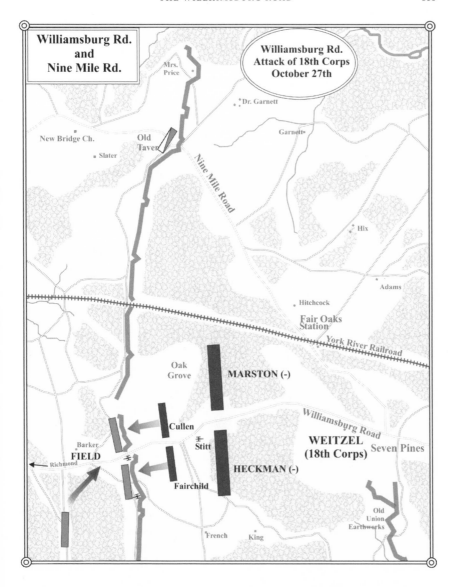

To the north, near Fair Oaks, the line looked much the same. Beside the Williamsburg Road stood a redan named "Battery Gracie," and several hundred yards farther south, another one labeled "Battery Cowherd" (perhaps named for South Carolina colonel Asbury Coward) fit into the line.[91] At the Williamsburg Road itself, the trenches formed a narrow gap or sally port, and the line boasted several artillery embrasures nearby. The parapet there stared out at nearly eight hundred yards of open space, which ended at a thick belt of trees astride the Williamsburg Road. Cut by a shallow gully for a brief stretch, the line resumed and formed a continuous parapet north across the York River Railroad and the Chickahominy

River. According to one account, poor construction marred the trenches there, and no obstructions covered the front.[92]

On the afternoon of the 27th, only a thin rebel force manned the defenses across the Williamsburg Road. But Field's troops—including Trowbridge and Watson, the Whitworth-wielding Texas scouts—raced to bolster the position. To their astonishment, they arrived to find a single lieutenant and twenty members of the Virginia Home Guard clinging to the defenses for a two-hundred-yard stretch and holding off a "strong skirmish line of Yankees." "The lieutenant had deployed his men behind the works," Trowbridge recalled, "and while they were keeping up a brisk fire, he was running up and down the works, shouting at the top of his voice, giving orders as if he had command of a regiment of men." Watson and Trowbridge hurried to the parapet and joined this little band, using their "long-range guns at short range."[93]

"The Column Almost Vanished"

Weitzel's initial assessment had been correct. When he reached the Williamsburg Road, only a sprinkling of cavalry and militia protected the line. But, as a chilly rain fell, rebel strength rapidly grew. "There seemed to be but few men in our front at first," a New Yorker recalled years later, "but soon the Johnnies began to arrive." The Confederates transported men to the front on horseback, riders carrying "an extra man (and sometimes two) on their horses." The passengers sprung off and the riders wheeled about to retrieve more.[94] As a result of Longstreet's canny decision, a stream of troops arrived from the Darbytown and Charles City roads.[95] But such troop movements took time, and, for the Confederates, time was running out.

At about 3:30 P.M., orders rang along the Union front calling on the men to advance. North of the Williamsburg Road, Cullen's brigade formed in a single battle line and surged forward. Less than a month before, these men had defended the newly captured Fort Harrison against desperate rebel counterattacks. Now they would play a much different role. Just across the road to the Union left, members of Fairchild's brigade also stepped ahead, making their way "over the prostrate forms of the men of the Second Brigade" toward the enemy's line.[96] Emerging from the trees, they burst onto a ploughed field, "deploying on both sides of the road in solid ranks."[97] With the crack of scattered rifle fire ahead, Fairchild ordered his command "to charge on the double-quick."[98] Both brigades sprang ahead under a light artillery fire.[99]

Trowbridge, with his Whitworth in hand, prepared to greet the Union attack along with his comrades. Nearby, the militia lieutenant strolled behind the works to gain a better view. He returned and reported a solid Union battle line "extending right and left as far as he could see." "Boys, I am afraid there are too many for us," he said according to Trowbridge's recollection, "but if you will stick to me we'll die right here, for it won't do for them to get these works."[100] But the officer's concern soon vanished. "Just then we heard the old familiar yell," Trowbridge recalled, "and, looking to our right, we saw the old Texas Brigade coming down the works at a double-quick." The lieutenant tossed his hat in the air and exclaimed: "'Glory to God, we are saved!'"[101] Field's men had arrived and the Texans spread down the trench to cover the works. The small brigade "stood in single line, about eight feet apart." Field's two Georgia brigades followed closely behind.[102]

The Union attackers moved forward rapidly "until they reached a rise of ground about 400 yards" from the enemy's works.[103] The two brigades stalled at the first depression in the field, and there the new Confederate strength revealed itself. The fortifications erupted with a sheet of flame, and the federals met a withering fire from the front, left, and right. The volley "staggered the men for a moment, but being enthusiastically cheered on by the officers of the command, they rallied with a yell and rushed forward," to within 150 yards of the rebel line.[104] But they would reach no farther.

Weitzel's gamble had failed. Instead of a weakly manned line, his brigades had marched into a steel trap. "The opinion that nothing but a cavalry skirmish line held the works was most fatally exploded," wrote a reporter of the *New York World*.[105] Another journalist explained that the rebel "artillery opened from two or three different points, pouring into our ranks a cross fire of shell, spherical case, grape and cannister with very destructive effect." Augmenting the heavy guns, rebel riflemen opened on the advancing federals.[106]

The appearance of so many Confederate infantrymen surprised the attackers. Edward Ripley, with his Vermont brigade back in the woods, looked on in astonishment. "But you cannot appreciate my sensations when the column charged and the enemy developed their unexpected strength by a most infernal Artillery and Infantry fire, and the column almost vanished under it."[107] Rebel cavalrymen in the trenches north of the Williamsburg Road held their fire until they could read the letters "U.S." on the belts of their foes.[108] To Ripley, it was the most "magnificent musketry firing" he had ever witnessed.[109] The attackers "were at once in fair canister range," reported General Longstreet, "and soon under the terrific fire of a solid line of infantry,—infantry so experienced that they were not likely to throw as much as one bullet without well directed aim."[110] One South Carolinian recalled, "We poured volley after volley into them."[111] The attacking column reached the second depression, about one to two hundred yards in front of the rebel works. But the advance lost all momentum and stopped. Men fell on their hands and knees seeking whatever protection the ground afforded.[112] Cullen's and Fairchild's brigades were spent.

On the left, Fairchild's command received enfilade and direct fire from the enemy's muskets, as well as shell from six artillery pieces.[113] "Just imagine," wrote a Wisconsin survivor from Fairchild's brigade the next day, "600 in the field, exhausted from 12 miles march, the last three quarters of a mile on the run, led against 1500 rebels, well covered by breastworks fronted by deep ditches, and protected by abattis."[114] The 19th Wisconsin, fresh from a two-month furlough, had participated in the attack at the left of Fairchild's line. Though many members had served three years, the regiment had not gained extensive combat experience. In addition, some members had questioned their officers' bravery in the past. But the charge at the Williamsburg Road dispelled much of that concern. In the midst of the fight, Captain William H. Spain,[115] who led two of the regiment's companies, stood in front and yelled, "Now boasters run and leave your officers, here we stand between you and your enemy." Elsewhere along the Wisconsin line, Captain Patrick Bennett fell as he waved his hat and shouted, "Give it to them, boys."[116]

The rest of Fairchild's battle line also crumbled. On the right, the 89th New York Regiment could not reform after the initial blows. Once again, Captain William Spain raced before the 19th Wisconsin, and ordered the handful of survivors to form and shift right "till we show our neighbors from New York how to form a line under [enemy fire]."[117] With fifteen privates and five sergeants, Spain and the remains of the 19th stumbled ahead. Fairchild's line reformed, numbering an effective strength of only eighty men, by one estimate.[118] There was a limit to such heroics, though, and, after the "very air seemed to be turned from its course by rebel bullets," the Wisconsin soldiers, along with the entire Union attacking fine, stopped "and hugged the earth close" in the swale.[119]

The advance had been shockingly difficult. But the soldiers soon found that the retreat would be just as dangerous. With the Confederate rifles sighted over every inch of open ground, the men could not conduct a standing withdrawal. Many of them lacked the cover to load their rifles, even while prone. Some soldiers attempted to fetch the wounded and carry them rearward, a nearly impossible task amid the bullets tearing through the air.[120] James R. Hagood, leading the 1st South Carolina Infantry Regiment, recalled an Irish color bearer seated in the field, his mangled leg under him, urging his comrades to continue the fight with no success. Disgusted at the lack of resolve, the Irishman waved the flag in defiance against "a thousand rifles" that were "flashing their deadly contents at the spot on which he sat."[121]

Weitzel's charge had become a spectacular failure, yielding significant casualties and trapping Fairchild's and Cullen's brigades within two hundred yards of hostile rifles with no clear escape. Though much blame fell to Weitzel, excellent Confederate decisions added to the outcome. In rushing brigades to the Williamsburg Road, Longstreet and Field had taken full advantage of their interior lines. Little more than two miles separated the earthworks at the Darbytown Road from those on the Williamsburg Road, a considerably shorter distance than that marched by Weitzel that morning. When the alarm sounded, Field's men reached the threatened sector easily and shut down Weitzel's efforts.

Time, distance, and the sound thinking of Confederate commanders had all combined to frustrate Benjamin Butler's design. In the open fields astride the Williamsburg Road, the Union infantrymen stuck between the lines suffered for it. Those who could raise their heads would have glimpsed yet more Confederates arriving, some by horses freighting up to three riders.[122] Back at the edge of the pines, Brigadier General Gilman Marston had watched the unproductive attack unfold. He reported the results to Weitzel, who immediately ordered a withdrawal. Captain Elder of Marston's staff volunteered to carry the directive into the killing zone. Casting aside his equipment, Elder crawled through the woods on the right and passed the word along to the men huddled in front of the Confederate works.[123]

To suppress the deadly Confederate fire, Marston also directed John Raulston to throw out a strong skirmish line from his brigade on the right, "with instructions to keep up a sharp fire."[124] Another member of Marston's staff, a Lieutenant Cook, sought to find Colonel Cullen and order that young officer's brigade off the field. This was easier said than done. Cook edged to the brigade's right, where the ground offered more cover and a safer route back to the pine trees. Cook relayed the withdrawal orders to nearly "the whole line," but he could not find Colonel Cullen anywhere. Nearer the Williamsburg Road lay more of Cullen's men, but they were out of reach "across a plain in full view of the enemy's line."[125] According to one account, Cullen did receive the order to retreat and, standing erect amid the storm of bullets, walked calmly to the rear.[126]

At about 5 P.M., Colonel Fairchild, on the left, ordered his command to fall back and seek better cover, but, as with portions of Cullen's line, escape from the shallow ditches and folds was simply infeasible. Some men rose to obey, only to fall dead or wounded.[127] Others crept back by "twos and threes," reforming along a cart path, which may have offered some modest protection.[128] A color bearer in the 89th New York, Sergeant Edward Smith, buried his flag in anticipation of an enemy advance, but then managed to crawl rearward, dragging the muddy standard behind him. On the field, a comrade heard him remark that the enemy "could kill him or take him prisoner, but they could not have the colors."[129]

William Stitt's gunners did what they could to cover the retreat, hurling shells at the rebel infantry and artillery. One projectile struck a rebel caisson, blowing it up and sending several Texans scrambling outside the earthworks for safety. In the Texas brigade, now led by Colonel Clinton Winkler in place of the deceased John Gregg, two men from each company received instructions to concentrate their fire on the Union guns and kill all the battery horses.[130] Stitt's crews remained on the field "without any protection from the missiles that were rained thickly around." They stuck to their work for a while. But in the face of the Texans' fire, they eventually hitched up their cannon and galloped to the rear, having lost seven men.[131]

The battle reached an awkward stalemate. Confederate commanders and their soldiers had endured the engagement with relative ease. Along the earthworks, the rebels looked out at the dead and wounded attackers. All across the field, pockets of Union men huddled in the washes and gullies. Beyond this meager protection, small groups of federals navigated their way to the rear.[132] But many simply pressed their noses to the ground.

Field's line included John Bratton's South Carolina regiments—the same units that were in the thick of the New Market Road fight three weeks before—though Bratton had not returned from the shoulder wound received in that October 7 battle. At the Williamsburg Road, the South Carolinians added their firepower to the devastating repulse. But, with the Union soldiers trapped before them, the late October afternoon was slipping away. Then something extraordinary happened. As the Unionists huddled in front, Joseph Banks Lyle, a captain serving on Bratton's staff as acting inspector, stepped forward.[133] Recognizing that darkness would soon envelop the stranded federals and blanket their escape, Lyle sought permission to advance outside the works with skirmishers and capture the enemy troops. Superiors denied his request, and the standoff continued.

But Captain Lyle possessed an unusual determination.[134] At five feet, nine inches, with blue eyes and light hair,[135] he "was highly endowed with what are called 'battle instincts,'" according to General Bratton. Relying "implicitly on his intuitions of the conditions of the enemy, he acted on them whenever he had authority to so."[136] As a member of the 5th South Carolina, he had received nine wounds.[137] James Hagood described him as "one of those reckless characters who are never so happy as when on some daredevil's expedition."[138] On this Thursday, Lyle, who was about to take leave and get married, would have the opportunity for a little more recklessness before heading home.

Orders or not, Lyle took matters into his own hands, for he was convinced the Confederates could capture the stricken federals easily. Unable to find volunteers for his unauthorized mission, he ventured forward alone and eased his way toward the enemy. The solitary figure in gray aroused suspicions of desertion and triggered a friendly fire "so heavy that the dust stirred by the bullets falling around him almost concealed him from view."[139] But, eventually, Bratton's men managed to pass the word to halt the fusillade. Still standing, Lyle approached the first gully and began to round up the bluecoats pinned there.

Somehow Lyle managed to gobble up most of the Union infantrymen in Field's front. Though the story hardly seems credible, multiple sources, including contemporary accounts, corroborate the event.[140] For his part, Lyle wrote in his diary, "I get three stands of colors & a large number of prisoners before I can prevail on a single one of the skirmishers to follow me—six Captains surrender to me alone."[141] During this feat, he approached the wounded Irish color bearer, who handed his flag over with tears in his eyes, saying, "Captain, I'll give to ye now, for our men have got no more fight in them."[142] In the midst of the massive capture, a federal officer berated his men for surrendering and urged them to kill or seize

Lyle. Tossing aside the captured swords and flags, Lyle bent down and picked up a rifle and headed straight for the officer, "presenting the carbine and threatening to blow his brains out if he did not surrender."[143] The officer obeyed. Only later did Lyle realize the weapon was empty. Eventually, more Confederates came to help. His comrades, in Lyle's words, finally managed to throw "forward a line of skirmishers, & capture more than 500, 8 stands of colors, & many small arms." He figured his take alone was "at least 400—a low cowardly, demoralized crowd of wretches."[144] With the capture complete, Confederates mounted their works and roared "with exclamations of admiration." After the fight, members of Anderson's Georgia brigade took credit for the captured swords and colors, but that injustice was later rectified. General Bratton recommended Lyle for promotion, a gesture endorsed by Charles Field. Unfortunately for Lyle, the recommendation was never acted upon.[145]

The Union prisoners filed over the parapet. As they did so, one wounded captive asked a young Confederate cavalryman whether he was an officer. When the Southerner replied no, the injured man exclaimed, "Well Sir, I'll surrender my sword to you then!" At that, Lieutenant Colonel Rollin M. Strong, commander of the 19th Wisconsin, handed over his blade. During the fight a bullet had passed through his knee, and he had sat helplessly as his own men rushed past him, disinclined to retard their efforts to reach safety.[146] After his surrender, he was sent to a Richmond prison, where surgeons would amputate his leg.[147]

Weitzel's effort at the Williamsburg Road near Fair Oaks, called the battle of "Second Fair Oaks" by some veterans, was over. The engagement crushed the two federal brigades involved. Cullen lost 10 killed, more than 70 wounded, and nearly 260 missing (presumed captured), for a total of 344 casualties, according to official returns.[148] Fairchild suffered 27 killed, more than 75 injured, and 263 captured or missing. The 19th Wisconsin alone tallied 141 casualties out of approximately 180 men who went into battle, with missing soldiers accounting for more than 90 percent of the loss.[149] The regiment lost its color guard and its colors in the attack. The 148th New York also lost its entire color guard, along with the national flag, but regiment members managed to save the state colors.[150]

Across the trenches, the rebels had survived the battle relatively unscathed, with Field's entire division losing only 45 (8 killed, 32 wounded, and 5 missing) during the day.[151] Longstreet and his subordinates had shuffled their men to the right place at the right moment. In contrast, Weitzel's timing could not have been worse, and his effort at Williamsburg Road ground to a dead halt. Though his operation tied up Confederate troops and prevented Lee and Longstreet from sending troops south to Petersburg, he could have accomplished that without losing a single man, as Grant had hoped. Butler's orders coupled with Weitzel's decisions had brought a different result and triggered a debacle.

CHAPTER 9

Nine Mile Road

~

The severe repulse at the Williamsburg Road did not exhaust Godfrey Weitzel's opportunities east of Richmond. As his initial efforts faltered, he received a message
from Butler directing a probe of the York River Railroad, which was farther to the
north.[1] Such a reconnaissance would stretch the Confederate left even more, not
only prohibiting Confederate commanders from sending troops to Petersburg but
also possibly opening opportunities for Union troops elsewhere in Butler's sector. In
response to the order, Weitzel detached the three USCT regiments of Colonel John
Holman's brigade from the third division. Holman's men had reached Fair Oaks
around 3 P.M., after the commencement of the fighting there, and taken a position in
reserve. With the claps and booms of combat penetrating the pine woods, Weitzel
directed Holman to advance along the York River Railroad until he arrived "within
sight of the enemy's line, and then to halt and report to corps headquarters."[2]

"an equal grave when he falls"

John Holman's brigade represented one of several African American units serving
in Benjamin Butler's army in the autumn of 1864. Among Union commanders,
Butler stood out as a steadfast supporter of the black soldiers, the United States
Colored Troops.[3] During October, his army counted six USCT brigades.[4] He took
pains to seek competent officers to lead these units and backed equal pay for the
black troops. "The colored man fills an equal space in the ranks while he lives,"
he explained, "and an equal grave when he falls."[5] He did not relegate the black
troops to secondary roles. They participated in assaults and manned the front
lines, just as the white troops did. Butler took an interest in more than their fighting abilities, as well, devoting time and resources to educate the hundreds, if not
thousands, of former slaves in his army. He also ensured the availability of excellent medical care for these men.[6]

With orders in hand, Holman led his troops northwest along the Nine Mile Road with the 22nd USCT in the van. The route led from Seven Pines, across the York River Railroad at Fair Oaks, and eventually to the New Bridge Road at a spot identified on period maps as "Old Tavern," probably nothing more than a chimney or perhaps a few bricks by October 1864.[7] The rebel trenches passed through this spot on their way north to a bluff at Mrs. Price's farm overlooking the Chickahominy River.[8] Beyond the Old Tavern junction, the roads coursed west to Richmond.

In 1862, General George McClellan had identified the high ground at Old Tavern as the lynchpin to Richmond's fall. He reasoned that heavy artillery, concentrated on this rise four miles from the city, would pummel the inner defenses and help bring the capital to its knees. But his efforts to seize this ground failed.[9] By 1864, the Old Tavern position no longer held the same luster for Union commanders. No mention of it appears in Union battle reports for October 27. At Petersburg and Richmond, Grant had not seriously pursued siege tactics during the campaign. The Old Tavern site had become just one position of many along the dizzying chain of ditches comprising the Confederate lines.

As the USCTs neared the Old Tavern site, five officers from Holman's staff and three orderlies, including an unarmed surgeon, encountered a squad of enemy cavalry across their path. The Union men drew their sabers and spurred forward. The Confederates emptied their weapons and then "fled in great disorder."[10] Ahead, more Confederate cavalry appeared near the Confederate defenses. In the distance, a small Confederate fortification known as Battery Ewell blocked the Nine Mile Road.[11] Between this small battery and Holman's advancing regiments lay a patch of woods south of the road. Beyond this timber the Confederates had cleared the ground, and to the north stretched more open land, crossed by a narrow stream.

Concerned about the obstacles and men in his front, Holman prepared for a fight and formed his regiments into battle line with the 1st and 22nd USCT on the left, south of the Nine Mile Road, and the 37th USCT on the right. The three regiments presented a mix of backgrounds. The 1st USCT, filled with District of Columbia residents, had been the first federally authorized black regiment. The 22nd USCT formed at Camp William Penn, a training facility outside Philadelphia. Beginning in 1863, Camp Penn produced a series of black regiments that significantly aided the Union war effort. Holman's third regiment, the 37th USCT, contained men recruited from the Union-controlled counties of eastern North Carolina.[12]

These units pressed forward. Lieutenant Colonel Abial Chamberlain, in charge of the 37th USCT, estimated that fifteen hundred to two thousand rebels protected the works ahead. In 1862, Chamberlain had received a serious head wound at the battle of Oak Grove, the very fight in which McClellan sought to take the high ground at Old Tavern. Now he had returned.[13] However, his estimate of enemy strength was surely inflated. Gary's entire Confederate cavalry brigade, strung out over miles of defenses, numbered no more than 1,300.[14] In fact, only a few members

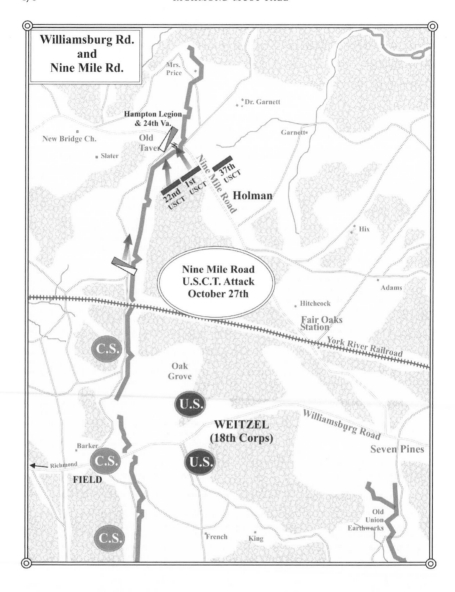

of the 24th Virginia Cavalry manned the works there. They had raced back and forth along the defenses throughout the day seeking to cover weak points and make a show of force.[15] Nevertheless, Holman apparently found Chamberlain's estimate plausible and took immediate defensive measures. A superior force, bearing down on his isolated regiments, would swallow his entire command. On his right, he formed the 37th USCT into a hollow square, a vintage formation more at home on the Napoleonic battlefield. On his left, the 1st and 22nd regiments remained in the woods and waited for the enemy to advance. But the feared attack never materialized.

Indeed, the Confederate defenders facing Holman's force had endured a busy day. Members of the Hampton Legion, including young Stephen E. Welch, had left the Charles City Road at noon and trotted north to the Williamsburg Road. There they found the 24th Virginia Cavalry preparing to slow Weitzel's advance.[16] They then rode farther north toward the Nine Mile Road but found no sign of the enemy and returned south in time to witness the end of the Union debacle at the Williamsburg Road. With little more to do, Welch and his friends lay in the rain and gazed at artillery shells streaking overhead. Soon, however, word arrived of a new threat on the Nine Mile Road.[17] And, once again, the Hampton Legion mounted their horses and raced north to aid their comrades there.

In the rebel trenches at Old Tavern, about forty men from Colonel William Robins's 24th Virginia Cavalry joined the two guns of Colonel John Haskell's battalion and looked out to the east.[18] The Confederates wheeled two cannon from Haskell's unit into Battery Ewell and opened on the black troops in front.[19] To Holman, the rebel shells were more than annoying. Instead of pulling back, he chose to attack and ordered the 1st and the 22nd USCT regiments to charge.[20] On the left, Colonel Joseph B. Kiddoo's 22nd regiment filtered through the trees. Kiddoo, a native of Allegheny County, Pennsylvania, had enlisted as a private in late 1861 and rose to regimental command by 1864.[21] His regiment contained many green recruits who "had never had any drill of any account."[22] Their inexperience became apparent from the first moments of the charge. In the ranks, the order to advance "by the left flank" was misapprehended, unheeded, or simply unheard. Whole companies milled together, and the entire regiment dissolved into confusion.[23]

Ahead, the Confederates could hear the shouts of federal officers from the trees in front.[24] Soon, the 22nd USCT battle line emerged about 150 yards from the Confederates in a "seriously deranged" condition, confused and "in no condition for an assault."[25] But Kiddoo resigned himself to this imperfection and proceeded. Dispensing with formalities, he ordered Captain Albert Janes, commanding the company on the far right end of the line, to "turn to the left and go on."[26] Kiddoo hurried to the head of the jumbled mass and shouted, "Forward!" A few companies remained intact and surged across the field toward the rebel works.[27] The enemy fire increased. Kiddoo, pressing ahead with "utter disregard for his own personal safety," fell with a serious wound within fifty yards of the Confederate works.[28] With the colonel down, Lieutenant Colonel Ira Terry took command and urged the men forward.[29] On the right, some companies managed to reach within ten yards of the parapet. But a "severe fire" halted further progress.[30] The men came close enough to realize the works were poorly manned,[31] but, even so, their weak force could not breach this last obstacle, and those who could fell back three hundred yards, with Captain Janes and his company covering the withdrawal.[32]

While the 22nd regiment faltered, the 1st USCT achieved better results, pushing forward over less cluttered ground with its right flank hugging the Nine Mile

Road.[33] Journalist T. M. Chester described the 1st as "a fighting regiment" and noted, "When Col. Holman urges them forward they have never been known to fail or falter."[34] The District of Columbia men, with bayonets fixed, charged over several hundred yards "exposed to a severe fire of musketry, grape, and canister."[35] Enemy case shot opened holes in their formation,[36] and within two hundred yards of the enemy, Colonel Holman himself fell wounded.[37] But his men pushed on.

To the south, rebel cavalrymen from the Hampton Legion, rushing to bolster the handful of defenders, raced to beat the black regiment to the point of danger. In the works, the rebel guns fired a steady cadence, but their tempo was too slow. The USCTs "came on with a yell, at full charge."[38] "Our brave little band cut many down," wrote one Virginian, "but on they came like an avalanche until they reached our works and planted their 'old gridiron' upon the ramparts, and not until then did a single man falter."[39] The Confederate reinforcements, including Stephen Welch and his comrades, had reached the battery, but the black troops arrived soon after and in greater force.[40] No clash of arms occurred. The Confederates fled. The African American soldiers scrambled over the parapet and captured the guns, along with the crews straining to remove them from the work.[41]

The 1st USCT regiment had achieved what other units had not. It had pierced the Confederates' exterior line, gaining a lodgment a mere four miles from Richmond. As a result, Union commanders had the breakthrough they wanted, and the Confederates had a serious problem on their hands. The Confederates had tried to cover miles of earthworks. They stood firm against the Union Tenth Corps at the Darbytown Road and the Eighteenth Corps at the Williamsburg Road. In fact, as the black troops gained success at the Nine Mile Road, Confederate commanders at the Williamsburg Road were scheming to hit Weitzel's flank with portions of Gary's brigade.[42] But Holman's advance put an end to such plans. If Union commanders could reinforce their initial success, the fissure at Old Tavern on the Nine Mile Road would expand into a gaping hole. At the Williamsburg Road, General Gary shouted, "Mount, men, mount," and the rebel cavalrymen rushed north.[43]

Back at Old Tavern, the 1st USCT held on to the captured battery and sought to strengthen the foothold. Lieutenant Colonel Giles Rich, leading in Holman's place, prepared "to charge down the enemy's line to the left," which still contained rebel cavalrymen.[44] But Rich had no support and received heavy fire from beyond the fortifications. In addition, more of Gary's cavalry hurried along the trench line seeking to seal the breach.[45] They halted near the fort and dismounted.[46] From the fortifications, Welch recalled, "Just at this time the 24th Va. & 7th S.C. came tearing up, yelling like demons & the portion of the Legion that retired returned."[47] The gray coats skirted along the outside of the parapet seeking to cut off the Union soldiers at the captured redan. The USCTs searched the woods behind them for reinforcements.

It was a "bluff game" and the federals lost.[48] Lieutenant Colonel Rich abandoned hope and directed his men to withdraw. Their triumph had lasted about ten minutes. Most of these momentary victors retraced their steps east and reached the safety of their sister regiments. Captain Henry Ward and a dozen others, however, remained at the redan, straining to roll the captured guns away with them. With time running out, they spiked the pieces, rendering them useless. But they had no time for escape and found themselves prisoners.[49] According to one South Carolina veteran, Gary's men gave no quarter to the black troops captured in the counterattack. "They were actually clubbed to death," wrote the cavalryman. "One or more of our company were court martialed for this cruelty. I could give full details but will pass it by."[50] However, another South Carolinian explained that more prisoners were not murdered because "few among even the roughest of our soldiers can be found who, much as they may approve and justify the act [of killing black prisoners] in theory, have hearts sufficiently hardened to enable them, in cold blood, to shoot down a defenseless man."[51]

As the 1st and 22nd regiments stumbled back, the 37th USCT dispatched squads to cover the withdrawal.[52] The hope of Union victory at the Nine Mile Road receded. Colonel Chamberlain, now commanding the brigade, received orders from Weitzel to return to the Williamsburg Road.[53] According to a correspondent with the *New York World*, Weitzel concluded that, given the repulse at Williamsburg Road, it "would be unsafe for Holman to attempt any movement so far from any support."[54] In reporting the events to Butler, Weitzel simply said, "Colonel Holman reports that he finds the enemy with intrenchments on the York River road."[55] Several hours later, Weitzel would write that he learned of Holman's success only after he had already ordered the withdrawal. He brushed aside the issue, concluding that it was too late to gain any advantage from the capture of the rebel battery.[56]

The brief success at the Nine Mile Road exacted a dear price on the black troops. Holman's brigade lost 15 men killed, 142 wounded, 1 officer captured, and 16 men missing.[57] Confederate casualties were surprisingly low.[58] According to official Confederate returns, Gary's brigade lost only 2 killed, 3 wounded, and 3 missing over the course of the entire day.[59] Despite the light losses, the breakthrough at the Nine Mile Road illustrated the precarious nature of Confederate fortunes. But for the lack of troops, Union forces could have flooded the exterior line. Longstreet recognized the close call and would later blame Gary for failing to watch the approaches to the Nine Mile Road more carefully.[60]

"press the enemy's lines vigorously"

At the Darbytown Road, the rainy afternoon brought more fighting. The strong Confederate defenses and the rebel troops manning them offered little chance for Union success there. Nevertheless, Butler and his subordinates bungled their way into another bloodbath. Though eager for some tangible gain that afternoon, Butler did not want to push matters without consulting Grant. "Field's right rested this morning near the Darbytown road," he wrote. "He has extended, therefore, four miles. Shall I make a trial on this outstretched line?"[61] Between the Darbytown and Charles City roads, Tenth Corps brigade commanders reported, "The enemy's line is quite strong and with considerable force behind them."[62] On the left, however, skirmishers from Joseph Hawley's third division west of the Kell house could see Confederate troops, bearing knapsacks, shifting to the right.[63] Butler saw promise in Hawley's news and determined to test the enemy works along the Darbytown Road once again. Without waiting for a reply from City Point, he directed Alfred Terry to try his hand. In turn, Terry directed Hawley to "push in" if "you think they have stripped the works in front of you of troops."[64]

North of the Darbytown Road, Adelbert Ames, commander of the first division, also ordered his brigades to "press the enemy's lines vigorously." At the head of Joseph Abbott's brigade, the directive trickled down to skirmishers led by James Randlett, who inched forward gingerly for about a hundred yards and found "less infantry fire from the enemy than in the earlier part of the day, but heavy artillery fire from their redoubts."[65] Randlett shifted his men to the right across the Charles City Road, flushing the Confederate pickets and flanking the enemy rifle pits in his front.[66] His maneuver cleaned out the rifle pits and pushed the enemy into its main works, gaining a "fine view of the Charles City road and the line of works generally." Good tactics rather than raw force accomplished the mission and avoided the slaughter produced by earlier probes in that sector. In doing so, his total loss reached seven killed and eight wounded.[67]

The directive to advance also reached Brigadier General Robert Foster, whose division rested south of the Darbytown Road. Here the story was different. Terry desired a strong demonstration, and hoped Foster's division would gain the enemy rifle pits and perhaps even the main works. Foster immediately sent forward two brigades. On the left, Colonel Martin Curtis's men led the way, burrowing "through an almost impenetrable underbrush." The Confederates pulled their skirmishers back into the trenches and generated "a terrific shower of case shot and grape and cannister spiced with balls of musketry." Amid the chaos, Union soldiers stumbled ahead, blindly firing into the trees.[68] They reached within eight rods of the main enemy works but could go no farther. "Volleys of musketry greeted the advance of our line, while a heavy enfilading fire was poured into it from artillery on either flank," wrote a *Philadelphia Inquirer* reporter.[69]

"Great suffering" and "heavy losses" resulted. Spent bullets knocked Curtis down four times, but he continued to lead the brigade, his overcoat nearly "torn to tatters by the storm of missiles."[70] Many other officers on the skirmish line lost their way in the undergrowth or received wounds.[71] The brigade absorbed artillery fire from the guns of Stark's and Hardaway's battalions.[72] Two of Stark's pieces sat across the Darbytown Road, and a pair of Hardaway's guns commanded the ground to the left near the Henrico Poor House.[73] Hermon Clarke, a member of the 117th New York in Curtis's command, later recalled that the Confederates "gave us grape, shrapnel, and minie balls at an awful rate."[74] At the Henrico Poor House on the rebel right, Hardaway engaged the Union artillery of the Third Company Howitzers (Smith's battery) and one gun of Dance's (Powhatan) battery.[75] Members of Curtis's brigade remained on the ground "for a half an hour listening to the shrieking and howling of missiles overhead."[76] They could not possibly advance farther.[77]

On Curtis's right, Colonel Louis Bell's brigade also stepped forward and deployed just north of the Darbytown Road.[78] In the ranks, the order to move was most unwelcome. According to a New Yorker, the advance "was useless and against the judgment of our officers."[79] Nevertheless, Bell's movement made some progress, carrying two lines of rifle pits. Eventually, though, the men broke under the severe artillery and musketry fire. Foster saw little reason to push his division farther. He pulled Bell's and Curtis's men out of range and brought forward Colonel Galusha Pennypacker's brigade from its reserve position.[80] The withdrawing troops carried their dead and wounded with them.[81] Around five o'clock, corps headquarters ordered Foster to cease further demonstrations. He withdrew his division to Johnson's Farm and threw out a strong line of pickets.

The useless demonstration carried an astounding cost. Foster's three brigades lost 28 killed, 267 wounded, and 19 missing.[82] The 117th New York, Hermon Clarke's unit, lost 52.[83] As with Butler's reconnaissance two weeks before, the operation provided no tangible gain and generated a similar toll. Though records do not furnish a Confederate tally, the rebels, fighting from cover, probably suffered comparatively light losses. Butler and his commanders were familiar with the ground, the enemy defenses, and the Confederates protecting them. They should have known that any probe was likely to produce much slaughter and minimal gain. They had little excuse for their actions.

Blue and gray soldiers were not the only casualties along the Darbytown Road that afternoon. During the engagement, surgeons from the Tenth Corps heard the signs of "great consternation and excitement" in the Gerhardt house, a dwelling that straddled the war zone. The structure shielded Confederate pickets in the morning and became a target of Union artillery fire. By the afternoon, however, rebel fire peppered the place. Despite the combat over the past few weeks, the Gerhardt family had not abandoned in their home. Over the course of the day, Union officers begged them to leave, but they refused.[84] During the Union advance that morning, the family placed "barrels and sacks of potatoes and furniture" along the walls and huddled together.[85] As the noise of combat increased, the mother and one of her children took cover under a feather bed. A Confederate shell exploded over the house, spraying shrapnel into the room, "scattering feathers in all directions," and piercing the mother's leg. In the afternoon, Union soldiers pulled the family out and escorted them to the rear.[86] Members of the 117th New York, from Colonel Curtis's brigade, observed the mother pass by their unit, laid out on a stretcher, with three "half-naked" and "half-starved" children walking by her side. "It was touching to see these wet and shivering little ones hovering over the faded embers," recalled James Mowris, "and to see their tearful care-worn faces as they begged for the meanest crumbs in a soldier's haversack." The New Yorkers furnished the children a "substantial supper of meat and bread" before the ambulance conveyed the family to the rear.[87] At the Tenth Corps hospital, M. S. Kittinger, surgeon for the 100th New York Volunteers, amputated Mrs. Gerhardt's leg, with, according to one source, the aid of Clara Barton,[88] who was serving in the Tenth Corps hospitals at the time.[89]

In the afternoon, Butler finally received the requested guidance from Grant. The lieutenant general wrote that it was "too late to direct an attack," and advised Butler to "hold on where you are for the present."[90] There was little more for Butler to do. As the dreary afternoon dissolved into evening, the prospects for continued operations dimmed. But the next morning held promise, and Butler requested further orders. Grant responded with no specific instructions other than to hold close to the enemy and prepare to repulse any attacks. He also advised, "You need not make any further advance, however, unless it be in following up a repulse of the enemy."[91] With that, Butler's operations north of the James drew to a merciful close. Alfred Terry's Tenth Corps abandoned any further effort against the Confederate works in the Darbytown sector. For the hundreds of damaged men on his front, the directive was maddeningly late. Across the rifle pits and abatis, the Confederates hunkered down all along the Alexander line. To the south, Hawley's black regiments backed through the woods and halted behind the old rebel works near the Kell house. Northward, Foster and Ames settled their divisions along the same Confederate works straddling the Darbytown Road.[92] Nevertheless, skirmishing continued along this line until the afternoon of the next day.[93]

At the Williamsburg Road, General Godfrey Weitzel's day ended, also. Isolated from the balance of the Army of the James by the White Oak Swamp, the young engineer brought his troops off the battlefield. The Eighteenth Corps withdrew around seven o'clock, as the rain began to pour in earnest. The men, "slipping, and jostling, and cursing," retraced their steps south through Seven Pines and the old Union trenches, past Mrs. Hobson's house, and over the White Oak Swamp.[94] Weitzel pulled Marston's brigade off the field first. The return south, to Weitzel, "had an awful effect on the organization" of the corps.[95] The miserable night pulsed with a heavy rain that made communications along the Union lines nearly impossible.[96] Weitzel halted the column at the Charles City Road for the evening. Not all of his men made it off the field, though. Sloppy staff work stranded the 38th USCT and four companies of the 36th USCT near the Williamsburg Road.[97]

The operations in Henrico County on Thursday the 27th drew to an end. His command had successfully occupied the Confederate forces outside Richmond. Lee and Longstreet barely managed to cover the lines north of the James; they could hardly think of sending troops to Petersburg. In accomplishing this, however, Butler's efforts produced hundreds of unnecessary casualties. He sought too much for himself and his troops outside Richmond and, in doing so, stretched beyond Grant's instructions. His men paid the price. With these results outside Richmond, the success of Grant's offensive would depend on Meade's efforts to gain the South Side Railroad in the Dinwiddie countryside southwest of Petersburg.

CHAPTER 10

The Fifth and Ninth Corps Advance

～

South of Petersburg, soldiers of the Union Ninth Corps broke camp at 3 A.M. Thursday, quickly washed down hard tack with coffee, and marched out into the darkness.[1] The badges on their caps bore a cannon tube crossed over an anchor, in recognition of their successful operations along coastal North Carolina in 1862. Through much of the 1864 campaign, though, the Ninth Corps had served under the under the affable, unlucky, and underappreciated Ambrose Burnside. In July, they had suffered the ignominy of the Crater assault. After the high command nudged Burnside out of his job, corps leadership devolved on John G. Parke, "a very pleasant-looking man and liked apparently by everyone."[2] He was no stranger to the Ninth Corps, having served under Burnside for much of the war. Colonel Lyman, Meade's opinionated staffer, wondered if Parke was "stern & rough enough to bring" the loose ends of the Ninth Corps into shape.[3] For Parke and his three infantry divisions, the day's mission offered the hope of immediate success. If his column could punch through the nascent Confederate defenses along the Boydton Plank Road, he would open a path to the South Side Railroad.

"push ahead more rapidly"

Parke's first division, commanded by Brigadier General Orlando Willcox, led the way. The procession stepped through the parapet at Fort Cummings and tramped due west along Hawks' Road.[4] Beyond Fort Cummings to the west, the road gradually ascended into woods and over more open ground dotted by small farms and houses. On the left stood the Smith house, several hundred yards to the south and just down the road off to the right, sat the Hawks house. Farther west, Confederate pickets crouched and beyond, somewhere in the darkness, loomed the new rebel trenches. The federal commanders could only guess at the strength of the works and the number of troops manning them.

The Ninth Corps' start seemed smooth enough. The soldiers massed behind the lines on high ground and exited Fort Cummings. But, as noted by Corporal

George Allen of the 4th Rhode Island, a potential problem arose: "Now, it seemed to our 'unofficial' minds, that if a surprise movement on the left was to be attempted, there was a big blunder right on the start, in massing us on this hill near headquarters. It was in plain view of the rebel lines, and as soon as it became light enough to see us they crowded on the top of their works and watched to see which way we were going to move."[5]

Detected or not, the column did not go far. The troops soon halted for some reason and sat down beyond the slashing near the outer picket posts.[6] Parke's command did not resume its advance until daybreak, about 5:30 A.M. Once on the move, the column encountered its first obstacle, a small rebel redoubt known as Fort MacRae. The earthen work sat athwart Parke's advance on a slight rise between the road and the Hawks house. It formed the southwest terminus of the old Confederate Squirrel Level line, trenches captured by Union forces during Grant's September offensive. Beyond the grasp of the new Union lines, the small fort continued to provide Confederates with a fortified picket post. If given the chance, the handful of secessionists at Fort MacRae would quickly spread the alarm to Hampton's and Heth's men sleeping in their camps to the rear.

General Willcox and his three brigades sought to neutralize this trip wire. The general ordered Colonel Napoleon McLaughlen, commanding his division's third brigade, to penetrate the right and rear of the fort and capture anyone posted there.[7] McLaughlen, in turn, assigned the task to Major James Doherty of the 57th Massachusetts. As the cloudy sky brightened, Doherty and forty others crept through a patch of woods adjacent to the Hawks yard and then rushed the rebel picket post. Success appeared certain. However, before the position fell, a musket went off, shattering the dawn's stillness.[8] With their presence betrayed, the Union soldiers hurried forward, killing one Confederate. But three others escaped to spread the news.

McLaughlen pushed the balance of his brigade to the redoubt.[9] The troops immediately began to reverse and extend the captured works.[10] As Fort MacRae fell, men from Colonel Byron Cutcheon's brigade deployed a few hundred yards to the south and swept across the Smith farm with the 60th Ohio on the left, the 1st Michigan Sharpshooters on the right, and the 2nd Michigan out in front on the skirmish line. Once at the house, the colonel realigned his regiments. From a strip of trees to the west came the sharp crack of rifles, signaling that the Union advance had stirred up more rebel pickets.[11] In addition, looking west down the Hawks Road, the Ninth Corps' skirmishers glimpsed a curious sight. A large column of about a thousand men crossed the road directly in front of them, heading south.[12] Cutcheon's skirmishers traded a few shots, but these rebels continued on their way.

Parke's force rolled on. Cutcheon's skirmishers glided west past the Smith farm, outpacing McLaughlen's brigade, then halting near the Hawks house. Cutcheon's right edged across the Hawks Road, where one of his Michigan regiments, led by

Lieutenant Colonel Edwin March, lost time crossing swampy ground. In the resulting confusion, the skirmish line veered north, delaying the advance for half an hour.[13] Eventually, the line straightened out, and Cutcheon ordered his command ahead, followed by Willcox's first brigade, under Brigadier General John Hartranft. The division's other brigade, McLaughlen's, remained back at Fort MacRae for the time being.[14]

Though Parke's force made slow, steady progress, the morning wasted away. In fact, as skirmishers probed the woods beyond the Smith house, some of Parke's men had yet to leave the Union works. At 7:30 A.M., Meade's headquarters complained that Edward Ferrero's USCT division was still filing out of Fort Cummings. The note admonished Parke to "push ahead more rapidly and get into position."[15] It was now well after sunrise, and his men had not even arrived at the works they were supposed to attack.

Cutcheon's brigade forced the Confederate pickets west through a thin skirt of trees and emerged at its next landmark, the Watkins Farm, located on a large field several hundred yards due west of the Smith place. There rebel resistance stiffened somewhat.[16] A chaplain with Cutcheon's 1st Michigan Sharpshooters recalled that the men passed "over open fields and through the woods, up hill and down hill, on the level and on ground that was rough and rolling."[17] When the skirmishers reached the Watkins clearing, Willcox formed a two-brigade front, with Hartranft's brigade on the left and Cutcheon on the right.[18] The force entered another band of trees and crossed Rocky Branch, a stream running south toward Hatcher's Run. Though the movement triggered heavy gunfire, the resulting casualties did not match the ammunition expended.[19] Cutcheon's and Hartranft's men easily pushed forward.

Beyond the Watkins Farm, Cutcheon's skirmishers passed over the Duncan Road and emerged into the yard of the Clements house at about 9 A.M.[20] Parke had slipped well behind schedule. He had burned through the better part of three hours jousting with dismounted rebel cavalry over a few farms and two strips of woods. A quarter-mile past the Clements house, however, the crawling advance came to an abrupt halt. The skirmishers scraped through the dense foliage and stumbled into a maze of abatis and felled timber. Just beyond, a wall of fresh dirt covered the entire front. Parke had found the Boydton Plank Road trench line.

The Ninth Corps had reached its appointed location. The two brigades formed for attack, with Cutcheon on the right and Hartranft on the left. Parke's lead division made contact with the Confederate line just south of the Dabney house, the spot Wade Hampton had predicted for a Union advance. Against a weakly manned rebel line, Parke's lead division had the ability to blow a gaping hole, roll up the line toward Petersburg, and open the way to the Boydton Plank Road and the South Side Railroad. However, if the works were filled with gray coats, such success would be unlikely.

"necessarily slow"

The Union Fifth Corps had enjoyed an early Thursday morning of comparative leisure, casting off at 4 A.M., at least an hour after their Ninth Corps counterparts. The Maltese cross, the badge of the Fifth Corps, adorned the sleeves and kepis of these troops as they trudged out of their camps. Their chief, Major General Gouverneur K. Warren, had planned to head out at 5:30 A.M., but Meade countermanded him, dictating an earlier start. An intelligent, skilled engineer, Warren was a hero of Gettysburg and an officer of great promise. However, beginning with the Overland campaign in 1864, his reputation began a slow, ragged descent. He showed signs of excessive caution and strain.[21] He demonstrated a tendency to question orders or, as one observer put it, a persistent inclination "to set up his own judgement against that of his superiors."[22] Meade complained that Warren exercised discretion even when none was given.[23]

Soured by Warren's performance, Grant developed a decidedly negative opinion of the young general. In postwar memoirs, he criticized Warren for a preoccupation with operations outside his authority and for micromanaging his individual divisions to the detriment of his entire command.[24] Grant acknowledged Warren as a man of ability, intelligence, and courage but concluded that his talents were best applied to "a small command," presumably smaller than the corps entrusted to him at Petersburg. Grant also viewed Warren's caution as a hindrance: "He could see every danger at a glance before he had encountered it. He would not only make preparations to meet the danger which might occur, but he would inform his commanding officer what others should do while he was executing his move."[25] As these opinions gelled in the minds of his superiors, Warren's reputation plummeted. "Warren is not up to a corps command," for his supervision led to "partial and ill-concerted and dilatory movements," wrote Theodore Lyman after overhearing a late-night conversation between Meade and Grant at Spotsylvania in May.[26]

Despite the criticism, the Fifth Corps chief was not without talents. He had managed to gain some significant battlefield successes. At Bristoe Station in October 1863, he commanded the tail of Meade's withdrawing army and, by the keen disposition of his command along a railroad bed, beat back Confederate attacks by A. P. Hill's corps. At Jericho Mills on the North Anna River in late May 1864, he held a bridgehead against determined attacks, again from Hill's troops. At Petersburg in August, he gained a permanent hold on the vital Weldon Railroad despite several rebel counterattacks. And, a month later, his men spread the Union lines westward, seizing Peebles' Farm and fortifying the position to beat off Confederate attempts to retake it. In all these cases, he found success by gaining objectives and blunting enemy assaults.

However, the plan for Thursday, October 27, assigned Warren an intricate role. The orders directed him to advance on the Ninth Corps left toward the point

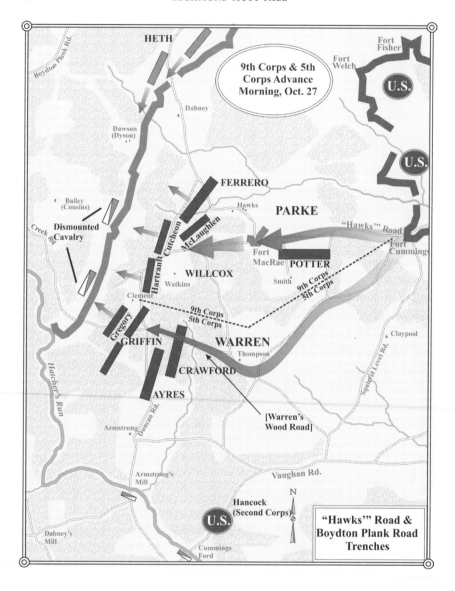

9th Corps & 5th
Corps Advance
Morning, Oct. 27

"Hawks'" Road &
Boydton Plank Road
Trenches

where the Boydton Plank Road crossed Hatcher's Run. Should Parke's movement against the Confederate line there prove unsuccessful, Warren was to cross
Hatcher's Run, proceed along its south bank, and then recross it somewhere in the
rebel rear. This directive, vague on geography and full of contingencies, provided
Warren with many opportunities to question, complain, and interpret.

But such concerns lay ahead, and, on Thursday morning, Warren faced more
immediate problems. The predawn blackness had frustrated his command's progress. In his view, the start time dictated by headquarters was too early, and, with
little tact, he criticized the decision in his report:

It commenced to rain lightly about 4.45 A.M., and it was very dark from the clouded state of the sky. Parts of the command soon got mixed up, and connections between parts of brigades were lost everywhere in the command, on account of the darkness, soon after starting. I think it quite impracticable, from this and previous experience, to move troops in the dark over any but the broadest and plainest roads, unless they are previously familiar with the route. It was light enough to see at 5.30 A.M., and we began to move the head of the column about this time into the woods beyond our intrenchments.[27]

Under cloudy skies and "some rain," the Fifth Corps wound out of Fort Cummings and followed a narrow path southwestward.[28] Brigadier General Charles Griffin's division marched in the lead, ahead of generals Romeyn Ayres and Samuel Crawford. An interesting sight greeted the column as it passed through Fort Cummings. There sat General Grant on a log, drawing a cigar to his mouth, with General Meade nearby.[29]

Once his corps was outside of the Union lines, Warren's difficulties began. The map provided by Meade's headquarters was inaccurate. Because Union topographers lacked detailed knowledge of the roads and streams southwest of Petersburg, only an outdated map of Dinwiddie County guided the march.[30] Accordingly, Warren's column headed southwest into largely unknown ground framed by the Hawks Road to the north and the Squirrel Level Road to the south. The path wound through tree-covered ground and over a small stream. It passed the Westmoreland house and arrived at the Thompson Farm about a mile and a half from Fort Cummings. Along the way, obstructions, placed by Confederates, blocked the route. One veteran later recalled, "The morning was dark and rainy, and the progress of the troops through the woods, which covered a large portion of the country was necessarily slow."[31] As his column headed southwest, Warren sought to maintain contact with the Ninth Corps troops to his right. Henry Didcock, a thirty-six-year-old member of the 187th New York, noted that the farms along the route showed signs of neglect if not abandonment, suggesting that many locals had determined the war was far too close. Across the "rebel ground," Didcock observed, "Corn was not cut nor the Chinese Sugar Cane. Sweet Potatoes was not dug. Rail fences left as the farmer left them."[32]

At the Thompson house, Warren worried that his column was drifting too far south. As he understood his orders, the assigned route would lead into the Duncan Road, from which he "was to hunt up a road" west. But no such connection materialized. With no easy solution available, he improvised, ordering a road cut straight through the woods west of the Thompson Farm.[33] This effort opened the desired route, but the resulting path was less than perfect. Robert Tilney, a clerk at Warren's headquarters, observed that it "ran through a dense wood, the road only wide enough to take two men abreast, so horsemen were strained to travel through the wood." Tilney, on horseback, struggled through tight spaces that threatened to crush his knees between bark and saddle.[34]

Despite the path's defects, it put the Fifth Corps on the right track. After a half mile, the trail emerged at the Duncan Road, only a few hundred yards south of the Clements house, the same spot reached by Parke's Ninth Corps. Once on the Duncan Road, the Fifth Corps ventured west. From the Clements house, skirmishers in Charles Griffin's division crept along another wooded road. By 9 A.M., they began trading fire with the enemy. As the bullets zipped through the air, Colonel Edgar Gregory's brigade formed "and advanced through the woods, driving the enemy into a line of breastworks."[35] Both Warren and Parke had reached the Boydton Plank line.

"checking the enemy's advance"

To the west, the Confederate alarm sounded. Wade Hampton's dismounted men rushed to fill the new breastworks along the Boydton Plank Road. West of the Clements house, eighty South Carolinians under J. M. Hough guarded a trench section stretching from the Cousins house south toward Hatcher's Run. On the morning of October 27, Hough's troopers roused from their camp downstream from Burgess Mill after orders arrived at dawn "to double quick down [the] Run" to the new trenches. Reaching the fortifications, Hough found that the pickets and scouts had been driven in from their posts. He "hurriedly covered the works—men five spaces apart" and braced for what was to come.[36]

On October 27, Hough's cavalry squad fell under the temporary command of Major General Henry Heth, who, in fact, controlled not only his own infantry division but also Lane's and McGowan's brigades of Cadmus Wilcox's division, Dearing's cavalry (normally under Hampton's command), and about seven hundred of Hampton's dismounted men. Heth's own division had been in the thick of the action throughout the Petersburg campaign. It tangled with Hancock's Corps at Reams Station in August and helped check the Union incursion at the Peebles Farm in late September. On Thursday, October 27, Heth's command totaled between fifteen and eighteen thousand men.[37]

Born in Chesterfield County just south of Richmond, the thirty-nine-year-old Heth had distinguished himself at West Point by graduating at the bottom of the 1847 class. Before the war, he served in Mexico and on the western frontier. In 1861, he sided with the secessionists and resigned his U.S. commission. He led the 45th Virginia Infantry through early campaigning in West Virginia. Although often remembered for piling his brigades into John Buford's cavalry on the first day at Gettysburg, Heth endured other low points during the war.[38] The setbacks blotting his record included defeats at Lewisburg, West Virginia, in 1862; at Falling Waters and Bristoe Station the next year; and in the Wilderness in 1864.[39] A Heth biographer concluded that he "had a persistent tendency to act on impulse before evaluating his own and the enemy's capabilities" and an "inability to foresee with any degree of accuracy what the enemy would do to counteract his moves."[40] Factors outside his control, such as poor decisions by others and plain bad luck, contributed to his disappointing results. Despite his uneven record, he remained a solid, competent division chief.[41] A. P. Hill and Robert E. Lee trusted him with the right flank of the Petersburg lines, perhaps the most sensitive sector south of the James. During the campaign, he had performed solidly. On October 27, Grant's sixth offensive would test his abilities once again.

News of the Union advance most likely reached Heth at his headquarters in the Pickeral house, about 150 yards behind the Confederate trenches near the Boydton Plank Road.[42] In the first hours of Thursday morning, he knew Confederate fortunes rested on the dismounted cavalry standing in the newly dug works. Heth's infantry division filled the trenches north of the Cousins house, and when news arrived of the enemy movement on his right, Heth directed Joseph Davis's brigade to rush down the breastworks and reinforce the dismounted men south near the Creek Road and Hatcher's Run.[43] More of Heth's brigades followed. The safety of the Confederate line and, for that matter, the South Side Railroad lay in their hands.

"with reasonable prospect of success"

With the morning hours slipping away, the Ninth Corps sought the dramatic breakthrough along the Boydton Plank Road envisioned by Union planners. Parke had arrived at the Confederate trench lines and his men ventured forward to test them. Cutcheon's brigade led the advance with the 2nd Michigan regiment, headed by Lieutenant Colonel Edwin March, at the tip of the spear. After 9 A.M., skirmishers picked their way through the thick woods west of the Clements house and found completed earthworks "well filled with men." In this sector, four pieces of rebel artillery, including at least one rifled weapon, poked out of the works.[44] Colonel March pressed his line to the slashing, and his left edged into the tangled branches. But he found "the position too strong to attack" and halted."[45] With no chance of progress, Cutcheon's brigade stopped and began to etch rifle pits into the dirt.

The pattern continued elsewhere along the Ninth Corps' front. John Hartranft's brigade to the left, also from Willcox's division, encountered the rebel trenches several hundred yards west and north of the Clements house. Skirmishers from the 51st Pennsylvania reached within one hundred yards of the works and found that "the enemy was moving about considerably, but mostly to [their] right."[46] Hartranft deployed all his regiments behind the skirmishers and stopped.[47]

There was nowhere to go. The Ninth Corps advance halted. In Hartranft's front, "every point of the enemy's line [was] carefully felt and examined for a weak point; none such, however, was found."[48] The enemy trenches lay a mere hundred yards in front, but they might as well have been several miles away. Whether from Fort MacRae's survivors or another source, the warning had reached Confederate commanders and the defenders had manned the works in time. Willcox and his subordinates recognized the strength of the Confederate trenches and tempered their advance accordingly. Despite the caution, the lead units did not get through the morning unscathed. Cutcheon's and Hartranft's brigades suffered thirty casualties each. Nearly half of those losses came from the two leading regiments, the 2nd Michigan from Cutcheon's brigade and the 51st Pennsylvania from Hartranft's.[49] A Pennsylvanian marveled that the force "did not lose more for the enemy gave us a hard shelling."[50]

Disappointed with the lack of progress, Parke ordered a careful reconnaissance to find "some weak point" to "attack with reasonable prospect of success."[51] His men searched for an opening. But rafts of abatis and piles of timber appeared everywhere.[52] On the right, at Cutcheon's position, "almost impervious slashing" barred the way.[53] On the left, Hartranft's skirmishers reported a heavy enemy presence.[54] Willcox brought up McLaughlen's brigade in support and concluded little more could be done.[55]

General Parke pulled forward his other divisions to aid Willcox and connect with the Fifth Corps to the south. On the right, he ordered his third division, commanded by Brigadier General Edward Ferrero, to connect with "the First Division, and to push forward and see what was in their front."[56] Ferrero commanded the only black troops in the Army of the Potomac. At the Crater in July, his men had suffered heavily from the poor decisions of their superiors and the savage counterattacks of Confederate troops. Throughout the campaign, Ferrero's men had received little opportunity to fight in battle. As the division surged forward across the Dinwiddie countryside on Thursday morning, they expected difficult work. Sergeant John C. Brock, in the 43rd USCT, recalled that many "a man lay there with an anxious heart." Some shook each other's hands and bid farewell. One corporal handed Brock a letter home, along with his money and watch. Others approached the sergeant with similar requests.[57] Company B of the 43rd spread out as skirmishers and pushed ahead. Before Ferrero's men encountered any sign of the enemy, one recruit suggested that the "Johnnies are all gone," but "an older and wiser soldier" said that they would hear from the rebels "soon enough."[58]

Ferrero's division passed through pines and then entered timber "sprinkled with the white oak" due west of the Hawks house. On the left, his first brigade, led by Colonel Delevan Bates, inched forward, and, to the right, his second brigade, under Colonel Charles Russell, joined in.[59] According to Ferrero, "nothing unusual occurred until we arrived at a point opposite the Clements house," where his command joined Willcox's division on the left.[60] As Ferrero's troops stepped through the felled timber and tangled abatis, a hail of lead greeted them from one hundred yards away.[61] The units in front suffered heavily from the brief encounter. By Sergeant's Brock's estimation, the 43rd USCT of Bates's brigade, alone lost "one officer and several killed, twelve to fourteen wounded."[62] Official sources placed the regiment's loss at twenty-eight killed, wounded, and missing. Ferrero's entire division tallied eighty casualties, almost all from Bates's brigade.[63] The praise received by the unit may have helped soothed sting of these losses. According to Brock, "our behavior in this battle, it is spoken of as being very good."[64] A *New York Herald* reporter who witnessed the advance also commented, "All the colored troops engaged during the day, behaved in a most satisfactory manner."[65]

With Ferrero's and Willcox's divisions probing the defenses, Parke held his remaining division, commanded by Robert Potter, in reserve.[66] At the same time, the Ninth Corps' artillery commander, Colonel John Tidball, searched for suitable locations to place his guns. Only two batteries accompanied Parke that day, the 19th and 34th New York Light, commanded by Edward Rogers and Jacob Roemer, respectively.[67] The artillery commanders searched but could find no adequate location to post their guns in the heavily wooded countryside.[68] Tidball eventually ordered one of the New York batteries into the old enemy works north of the Hawks house and the others to his line's left.[69]

As Parke's soldiers cut through the undergrowth, a most incongruous sight greeted many on the battlefield. Newsboys roamed the lines looking to sell their papers. Amid the deadly chaos, these children canvassed the field on horseback seeking readership among the ranks. Even as bullets zipped through the air, one reporter heard these aggressive salesmen shouting, "New York Herald," at the top of their lungs.[70]

"the leaden messengers, and iron too"

Warren's Fifth Corps also arrived on the Duncan Road around 9 A.M., pouring out from the newly cut wood road. The troops had completed their circuitous journey and emerged near the Clements house, the same location Parke's Ninth Corps had gained simply by marching west along Hawks' Road. Griffin's division, still in the lead, passed south of the Clements place and ventured west on the Creek Road through the woods. Colonel Edgar Gregory's four-regiment brigade pushed ahead, forming two lines south of the road, with the 188th New York and the 91st Pennsylvania regiments at the head, supported by the 187th New York and the 155th Pennsylvania. In front, his skirmishers soon encountered slashed trees, strong abatis, and "quite a lively fire."[71]

For Henry Didcock, a member of the inexperienced 187th New York the morning's activities brought the first taste of combat. Beyond the Clements house, his unit, which had only arrived at Petersburg a few days before, paused in the woods about thirty yards behind a veteran regiment.[72] Brigade commander Edgar Gregory arrived at the battle line encouraging his troops and assuring them that only "about 20 minutes work" would win the day. Didcock's unit surged forward with strict orders not to fire until directed.[73] "Getting within 300 yards of the rebel works, we formed in line of battle," wrote Captain Daniel Loeb of the 187th New York. A "charge was ordered, and our boys moved forward in good style, in spite of a dense thicket of undergrowth and heavy timber."[74] Back at the 187th New York, Didcock found himself "in front of a big Tree top and in turning out to pass it, the Balls come from the enemy flying around us all the time."[75] The Confederate trenches stretched across their path one hundred or two hundred yards ahead. When the rebel line began to fire, all forward movement stopped.[76] As the infantrymen halted, Fifth Corps artillery commander, Colonel Charles Wainwright, like his comrades in the Ninth Corps, searched for firing positions, but "a dense wood covered nine-tenths of the country, and the openings were all small." He finally gave up.[77]

Soon General Warren and his staff arrived to direct operations. Robert Tilney, who had been riding to join Warren's entourage much of the morning, caught up with the general just as things were heating up. Tilney found Warren under the trees near the firing line, "very busy, very energetic, and very mad." Lead and iron filled the air. As rebel sharpshooters placed him in their sights, Warren, his staff around him, remained calm. But after several bullets nearly hit him and a shell exploded in the middle of the group, the general considered "it prudent to alter his position."[78]

Warren and his aides withdrew from the danger but soon faced another, unexpected threat. The enemy's withering fire had demoralized some of the raw recruits of Gregory's 187th and 188th New York regiments.[79] The 187th was so new that "three-fourths of the men had never loaded or fired a musket until the morning we went into the fight," wrote one member immediately after the battle.[80] Tossing away their guns, knapsacks, and other encumbrances, they raced back through portions of the 155th Pennsylvania. While the Keystone State men resupplied themselves with the New Yorkers' detritus, the panicked men flew past General Warren and his staff, leaving the officers to face "a severe shower of bullets." [81] Surprisingly, no one in Warren's party fell from the deadly spray as they struggled to rally the greenhorns.[82] For his part, Henry Didcock remained at the front, firing his weapon and peering out at the glow of enemy rifle fire bursting from the trenches beyond. After surviving the ordeal, he concluded, "There is more men hit by Skulking that by being in there proper place."[83]

Although most reports, official and not so, suggested that Warren's men did not get within one hundred yards of the enemy trenches, at least one account indicates otherwise. A few adventurous members of the 155th Pennsylvania from Gregory's brigade apparently squeezed through the slashing and abatis to reach the Confederate works. Corporal George Clever of Company K and several of his comrades climbed the parapet. On the other side, a shocked Confederate officer shouted, "Look at the damned Yankee! Shoot him! Shoot him!" Realizing his predicament, Clever reversed his course and navigated his way back through the obstructions unharmed.[84]

With the advance completely stalled, the Fifth Corps had little to cheer. A *Philadelphia Inquirer* reporter summed up Warren's morning: "The opposition met by the Fifth seemed more determined than that encountered by the Ninth. At any rate there was more firing, and, so as far as I could see, more losses."[85] The Fifth Corps troops found too many obstructions, too many Confederates, and too much enemy fire. With no chance to gain ground, Warren's lead units began to entrench.[86] Their losses proved high, given the paucity of their gains. Gregory's brigade, at the front, suffered 202 in casualties, mostly wounded men. The inexperienced New York units lost disproportionately, accounting for well over half of the brigade's casualties.[87]

"Our line of breastworks must be held"

To the Union attackers, the Confederate line appeared well manned. In reality, however, the rebels had conducted a frantic scramble all morning to defend their position. For the cavalry and infantry under Henry Heth's command, uncertainty and anxiety filled the first hours of the assault. The federal attacks threatened a mile of the trench line. Along this stretch, only James Dearing's cavalry brigade, with several hundred dismounted men on the Boydton Plank Road, furnished the initial Confederate resistance. Dearing's men woke that morning to firing and rushed to preassigned positions.[88] They managed to beat back Union probes just long enough for Heth's infantry to arrive. Heth rushed several brigades from the north, including Cooke's North Carolinians, Joseph Davis's Mississippi brigade, and Robert Mayo's command, which contained both Archer's Tennessee brigade and remnants of Walker's Virginia brigade.[89] Heth directed these troops, along with William MacRae and his North Carolina regiments, to "close in on Cooke" along the trenches.[90] The orders brought a wholesale shift of the Confederate right wing, freeing thousands of infantrymen to confront the Union attack. Heth also had several brigades from Cadmus Wilcox's division in his charge, and directed Samuel McGowan's South Carolinians and James Lane's North Carolinians to fill those gaps left by his own brigades closer to Petersburg.[91] Wilcox's brigades also prepared for the enemy, but the true danger lay to the southwest.[92]

Heth's infantrymen had endured a hectic morning. A member of Joseph Davis's Mississippi brigade recalled hearing the sound of rifle fire before dawn. Within a half hour, his brigade began "double-quicking" south along the trench line. Deploying to counter the federal threat from the east, his unit spread along the breastworks, "two paces apart," in a single rank. "We had never yet fought behind breastworks," a member of the brigade recalled, "although we had constructed miles, but we felt that our line was impregnable."[93]

The Mississippians found Dearing's cavalrymen in the trenches, where the horsemen had fended off Union probes for nearly an hour.[94] On the heels of Davis's brigade, Heth ordered Cooke's North Carolinians down the trench line to relieve the cavalry. "About 9 A.M., we moved to the right about ½ mile, then deployed in single rank," wrote Joseph Mullen Jr., a member of Cooke's brigade from the 27th North Carolina. The Tar Heels continued to shift slowly right. After traveling about half a mile, they received fire from enemy sharpshooters. Mullen and his comrades ducked below the new parapet but continued to hurry south another half a mile.[95] The newly arrived foot soldiers went straight to work strengthening the defenses.[96]

The advance of Edward Ferrero's black troops from the Ninth Corps east of the Dawson house brought the morning's second series of federal attacks. Ferrero's effort stretched the federal assault several hundred yards northward. Near the Dabney house, the rebel line bent eastward, allowing artillery to enfilade both Parke's and Warren's positions.[97] When Ferrero's men began their probe around 10 A.M., Joseph Davis's brigade was there to greet them. Charles R. Jones of the 55th North Carolina regiment, brigaded with Davis's Mississippians at the time, witnessed Ferrero's probe and recalled that a "long line of negro troops did come in sight of our position—a few well-directed shots from our line, and a certain knowledge that this was but a foretaste of what would succeed if they came on, soon induced them to change their tactics and scamper off in the opposite direction." Once the probe ended, Davis's brigade shifted a half mile to the south to bolster the dismounted cavalrymen in their efforts to hold back Warren's Fifth Corps.[98]

As the infantry shuffled madly to fill the ditches, Hampton's troopers remained in the federal crosshairs farther down the line, near Hatcher's Run. For them, the day brought some rough work. J. M. Hough and his detachment of eighty men, since sunrise, had covered several hundred yards of works just north of the run. For three hours, his men stood firm. In Hough's estimation, the Yankees out in the woods outnumbered his small band twenty to one. These were probably the Fifth Corps troops of Griffin's division. During this trial, Hough encountered no Confederate officers, nor did he receive any orders. Though he understood the importance his position held for Petersburg and the Confederates, prospects for a successful defense looked bleak.

But help arrived eventually. "At last, when I had almost despaired," Hough later recalled, "I looked up towards Petersburg and saw an old Confederate flag floating in the breeze and beneath it a thousand true and tried Tar Heels, Cook[e]'s brigade, then next Barksdale's [Davis's Mississippi] brigade. We received the compliments of these troops."[99] Their arrival secured Heth's trenches. According to Charles Jones from Davis's command, his brigade reached the works near Hatcher's Run to find the dismounted cavalrymen thinly spread and almost out of ammunition. In some locations, the enemy was "within ten paces of the breastworks." Jones recalled, "Our boys went into line with their accustomed cheer, and the yankees seeing our line reinforced, withdrew in considerable confusion, leaving many of their dead and wounded behind them."[100] Though sharpshooting continued across the works, the danger for the Confederates had passed.

"this trenching has come to be a science"

The Union soldiers pushed no farther. There would be no grand assault, for Meade had given neither Parke nor Warren such orders, and the pair had no reason to act on their own initiative. In hindsight, the two corps may have possessed the strength to overwhelm the Confederate defenses, but the commanders had no way of knowing that at the time. Successful attacks against entrenched positions were a rarity in the Civil War. In May, the Second Corps had overrun the "Mule Shoe" at Spotsylvania, and, in late September, the Eighteenth Corps had stormed Fort Harrison. But for every such success in Virginia, several cautionary tales arose from other battlefields, such as Fredericksburg, Ox Ford, Cold Harbor, the Hare House, and the Crater. These disasters lurked in the minds of the Union high command. At the Clements house on that Thursday, Meade's subordinates had no appetite for such risks.

Parke and Warren and many under their command knew of the Confederate fondness for hitting back. Thus, all along the Fifth and Ninth Corps front, soldiers resorted to a common practice on the battlefields of 1864. They dug in where they stood.[101] John Parke also sought to consolidate his position and cover his flanks. Orlando Willcox's troops entrenched within three hundred yards of the Confederate works and stretched to connect with Griffin's division from the Fifth Corps on their left. At the Watkins house near Parke's center, Colonel John Curtin's brigade crossed the cornfield and began to construct breastworks. They demolished the Watkins outbuildings, using shingles as makeshift shovels and heavy boards as backing for the parapet.[102] In "a very short season a strong breastwork, composed of logs covered with earth, was thrown up along the whole front of our brigade," chronicled a Wisconsin soldier in Hartranft's brigade of Willcox's division.[103] On the Ninth Corps' right, Edward Ferrero's USCTs bent their flank back to the northeast.[104] In nearly every location, the men hurried to turn over the Virginia soil. In describing these efforts, the Wisconsin soldier noted, "By the way, this trenching has come to be a science in the Army of the Potomac, and we have learned it partly from the rebels and partly by the peculiar 'quailing of the flesh' which a fellow feels when a rebel gun is pointed at him. You will remember that when the war first broke out skirmishers were as often thrown forward into an open field as under cover, and the man who hadn't nerve enough to stand it was marked as a coward. Now, skirmishers have small shovels strung to their belts by which they can *dig their way into safety* in a few minutes."[105]

Robert Potter's division, in reserve, joined with Ferrero's right and extended the Ninth Corps' line north and east, all the way back to the fortified camp at Fort Welch.[106] Potter also established a picket line, a half mile northwest of Fort Welch, and positioned the 19th New York Battery near the Hawks house.[107] Thus arrayed, Parke's divisions completely covered the Union right.

On the left along the Fifth Corps' front, John Griffin's division stretched from the Clements house south to Hatcher's Run. Like their Ninth Corps counterparts, these men, after falling back, began throwing up dirt "while exposed to a galling fire from the rebel sharpshooters."[108] With Griffin in front, Samuel Crawford's division provided support, and Warren stationed his other division, under Romeyn Ayres, in reserve. Ayres, an aggressive combat leader, established his headquarters at the Armstrong house, next to the Duncan Road, a few hundred yards north of Hatcher's Run.[109] For more than a month, the opposing lines had framed the Armstrong place. That morning, the owner greeted the Union troops with exclamations of loyalty to the U.S. government. But his admiration for government property apparently surpassed his attachment to the government itself. Union soldiers inspecting his buildings found "500 horse-shoes, a number of carbines, and 25 United States sabres." A reporter with the *New York Times* quipped that this was "the way the citizens hide their sentiments."[110]

"from some unexplained reason"

The Ninth and Fifth Corps advanced no farther. Meade and his planners had hoped for weak and ill-formed enemy defenses, a shallow ditch perhaps but little else. But Parke's and Warren's men collided with something much more substantial. The slashing and abatis set down by slaves, free blacks, and rebel soldiers formed a prodigious obstacle. The Union battle lines simply could not penetrate the mass of twisted branches and piled limbs.

Parke executed his role as well as could be expected, or so it seemed. He supervised actions at the front in person and received high marks for handling his divisions from a *Philadelphia Inquirer* reporter on the scene.[111] But while the shape and depth of his attack impressed, the pace raised questions. Of all the units involved in the offensive, the Ninth Corps had the shortest, most direct route to the Confederate defenses. The operation presented little complication. Parke marched his command out of the works at Fort Cummings due west on Hawks' Road and headed straight for the rebel earthworks. But he halted outside Fort Cummings for more than an hour that morning.[112] The reasons for this delay are unclear. The orders directed the Ninth Corps to leave early enough to "attack the right of the enemy's infantry, between Hatcher's Run and their new works at Hawk's and Dabney's, at the dawn of day."[113] The plan also instructed Parke to "*move* and *attack* vigorously at the time named, not later than 5.30."[114] Meade clearly expected the Ninth Corps to reach the enemy works at or before 5:30 A.M. But at dawn, Parke's men had only just encountered the outer pickets. Parke apparently interpreted his orders to mean that he was to begin his "move" at 5:30 A.M. Thus, it was not until 9:00 A.M., more than three full hours later, that his lead units actually began to "attack" the main Confederate trenches. The Ninth Corps took nearly five hours to leave camp and move two miles along a well-known road against light resistance.

The incongruity between Meade's orders and Parke's actions received no attention in official reports after the battle.[115] The day's subsequent events may have overshadowed these details. In his postwar account, Andrew Humphreys, Meade's chief of staff, suggested that the movement was delayed "necessarily" because it was a "dark, rainy morning."[116] Not everyone saw it that way. A *New York Times* correspondent noted, "From some unexplained reason, the Ninth Corps did not get out on the enemy's line at daylight, as anticipated, and the Second Corps had already become engaged when they did so get out—thus revealing the extent of our scheme of operations."[117] According to the *Army and Navy Journal*, rebel prisoners later confirmed that the attack on the new trenches "was detected by them in abundant season to ward against it, and that there was no surprise."[118]

The lost time damaged the chances for Union success. By failing to reach the teeth of the rebel defenses before 9 A.M., Parke provided even the most lethargic of Hampton's dismounted units ample time to fill the trenches. The delay also furnished crucial moments for Heth's infantry brigades to occupy the line. The slow advance diluted the value of Parke's demonstrations in aiding Hancock. By 9 A.M., Hancock had been marching around the Confederate right flank for several hours. The rebels, with Heth and Hampton at the helm, scrambled to block his way. An earlier Ninth Corps start might have drawn more of these rebel troops north of Hatcher's Run, depleting the forces available to challenge Hancock.

Though Parke may have slipped, Warren's performance did not aid matters. His carping about timing certainly did not improve his reputation with Meade and Grant. In addition, he assigned his least experienced division to lead the advance. Later, he took pains to note that over half of Griffin's 4,700-man division "had never fired off a musket." Yet he chose to put these green troops at the head of his column and tuck his other divisions behind the van.[119] Other factors, outside of his control, also conspired to blunt his success. The inaccuracy of the Union maps proved a significant handicap. Given the presence of Union cavalry on those roads over the previous two months and the area's relative proximity to the Union picket line,

Meade's staff should have had access to better maps. In the face of that burden, Warren demonstrated resourcefulness in cutting a road through the second-growth timber to reach the Confederate line. However, he did not let matters rest there. In his official report, he complained about the poor information he had been provided about the local geography, going so far as to append a detailed map comparing the Hatcher's Run region, as it had been depicted before the operation, to the actual ground he had encountered during his movements.[120]

Despite their mistakes, Parke and Warren did not deserve full blame for this initial failure. Indeed, inaccurate intelligence probably doomed the operation. When the troops reached the full Confederate line west of the Clements house, they could see that the trenches were not the half-formed, ill-prepared works envisioned in Meade's plans. Union planners mistook the strength of the Confederate trenches. Instead of weakness, Union troops found strength.

Union commanders did not realize the real progress Confederates had made in constructing their defenses. They supposed that the enemy trenches terminated at Burgess Mill. In reality, the line ended more than a mile downstream from the mill, closer to the Union advance than thought. Accordingly, the Confederate works formed a wedge between the advancing Union columns on either side of Hatcher's Run. As the morning progressed, the Union offensive split on either side of the run, with Hancock to the south and Parke and Warren on the north. While Parke's and Warren's advance sputtered to a halt, Hancock and his Second Corps proceeded on the left, stretching farther and farther from support and safety. Poor Union intelligence and clever rebel engineering had combined to create this divide. The cramped forests and the tangled banks around Hatcher's Run stood between the two Union wings, severely complicating matters. For many federal soldiers, this impenetrable portion of Dinwiddie County would become all too familiar before the day ended.

The first stage of Grant's offensive at Petersburg had failed to break the line. Though the Ninth and Fifth Corps troops pinned down some Confederate forces along the Boydton Plank trench line, such a task hardly required two army corps. The Union high command had committed much of its strength to a mere demonstration. Had Meade and Humphreys clearly understood the location and strength of Heth's trench line, they might have committed only one corps to this task, leaving the remaining two for the flanking column stretching out toward the South Side Railroad.

"I fear there is no chance"

Ulysses S. Grant began his morning on October 27 at City Point. At 7 A.M., under overcast skies, he climbed aboard a train headed for the front. The day held much promise. He arrived at Fort Cummings around 8:30 A.M. and joined Meade in observing the Fifth Corps troops file through the parapet. Earlier, Meade had written Parke to express concern over the slow progress of the Ninth Corps. As Warren and Parke pushed west, a quick, decisive breakthrough seemed less and less of a possibility. In all likelihood, Meade and Grant discussed Parke's progress, or lack thereof, when they met that morning. At 9 A.M., Meade wrote Hancock, "Parke has confronted the enemy on the Hawks Road and is pushing them back to their works. I fear there is no chance of his getting into them." Meade also noted, "Warren is working his way to cross Hatcher's Run on Parke's left—slow work, having to make a road. It would be well for you to keep up a communication with Warren, to ascertain his progress. I will direct him to communicate with you."[121]

Andrew Humphreys joined Warren around 9 A.M. and became convinced of the rebel position's overwhelming strength. He understood the need to change course and advised Warren to prepare to cross Hatcher's Run.[122] Warren dispatched Captain W. T. Gentry to open communications with Hancock's corps and asked his aide de camp, Washington Roebling, to examine the terrain along Hatcher's Run. Armed with the hard lessons of earlier battles, Warren wanted to avoid stumbling into any unwelcome surprises. With Gentry and Roebling probing southward, Warren rode to Griffin's front, looking to revive the advance.[123]

Roebling trotted down the Duncan Road on his reconnaissance. At Armstrong's Mill, he examined the rebel works lining a portion of the south bank. Farther upstream, on the north bank, he tangled with enemy videttes but eventually arrived back at the Union position in a field near Hatcher's Run. During much of his ride, he had encountered only thick woods on the stream's south bank above Armstrong's Mill. He returned to Warren's field headquarters near the Clements house around 10:15 A.M.[124]

Several minutes later, Grant and Meade arrived at the Clements house. It was clear to all that the effort was not going well. According to Adam Badeau, a member of Grant's staff, "Warren . . . was still groping his way in the woods, feeling out to the left for the end of the enemy's line."[125] After the generals listened to Roebling describe the conditions along Hatcher's Run,[126] Grant affirmed the need for a connection with Hancock across the run. Under the new plan, Warren would detach one of his divisions for the job.[127] As Warren commenced the operation,[128] Meade and Grant trotted south, riding down to Armstrong's Mill toward Hancock's Second Corps.[129] Parke's and Warren's initial advance had failed to bear fruit. It was time to see if Hancock could do better with his column.[130]

As the attack against the Boydton Plank Road line slowed to a crawl and Union commanders adjusted their plans, the signal stations dotting the Union works searched for rebel activity around Petersburg. At 8:30 A.M., Sergeant A. K. Carothers at the Jerusalem Plank Road station reported, "Enemy's force in works on our front and left remains unchanged. Camps west of Weldon railroad apparently the same. Enemy is drilling in small squads in vicinity of railroad."[131] The stations caught no sign of Confederate movement, at least not yet.

CHAPTER 11

Second Corps Moves Out

∼

"A Sour Mood for Marching"

Earlier that Thursday morning, the soldiers of the Second Corps rose for the day's work. John Haley of the 17th Maine took note of the "dark and drizzly" conditions and recorded that the men "were in a sour mood for marching."[1] The schedule afforded little time for breakfast. One New York recruit found the time too short by far. Unacquainted with his regiment's "short order meal system," the unlucky soul had only begun to gather firewood when his comrades fell in. In response to his sergeant's barking, the recruit exclaimed, "I can't go this time! I haven't had a bit of breakfast yet!" The vain plea triggered a hearty laugh from his new comrades.[2]

Once roused, the Second Corps wound south along the Halifax Road, then veered west on the Lower Church Road. The corps, led by Winfield Hancock, formed the operation's vital flanking column. It passed the Conway house and turned onto the Wyatt Road.[3] The soldiers wore the trefoil on their caps. This symbol also marked the few wagons that joined the column. Brigadier General Thomas Egan's division took the lead, with Brigadier General Thomas Smyth's brigade at the head. A colonel from the Topographical Engineers guided the troops on their route.[4] A squadron of the 6th Ohio Cavalry forged well ahead, protecting the pioneers who cleared trees and other obstructions left by the rebels.[5]

After a mile or so, the lead units passed the Wyatt plantation, "a fine, large mansion, surrounded by a colony of outbuildings and slave huts."[6] The property, which had served as a recent haunt for Union cavalry pickets, marked the outer reaches of Union-controlled territory. A Pennsylvania horseman stationed at the plantation during October described Colonel Wyatt, the owner, as "a fine man & tired of the war," who "blames the conflict on Southern 'fire eaters' & Northern Abolitionists" and "sees no hope for their confederacy."[7] In cavalry fighting at the end of September, two shells, probably from rebel cannon, had pierced the walls of the mansion as the family huddled inside.[8] Now, with thousands of Union infantrymen tramping past the mansion, the unpleasantness threatened to return. As the marching column approached the place, the 4th Ohio Battalion and

7th West Virginia Volunteers, under Lieutenant Colonel Frank Spalter, deployed ahead as skirmishers. Thankfully for Wyatt and his family, the troops marched by without firing or halting. Several hundred yards beyond the mansion, the column crossed a stream called Arthur's Swamp, ascended the opposite bank, and emptied onto the Vaughan Road near the Davis house.[9] Hancock's first obstacle, Hatcher's Run, meandered across the countryside a mile and a half away.

As the head of the Second Corps entered the Vaughan Road at about 6 A.M., enemy cavalry, posted ahead near the Cummings house, fired on the federal skirmishers.[10] The skirmishers replied.[11] Soldiers marching with the column soon encountered the day's first victims limping rearward or lying lifeless beside the road.[12] The 12th New Jersey, a regiment in Smyth's brigade, "moved out through the woods, pressing back the quarrelsome Johnnies, who resisted stoutly."[13] The troops also found more felled trees blocking the Vaughan Road, but they cleared the obstructions to allow the gun batteries to cross.[14] The barriers did not delay the march.[15]

Beyond the Cummings house, the Vaughan Road plunged downhill under a thick canopy of trees on its way to the Cummings Ford at Hatcher's Run.[16] Thomas Egan's division rolled forward, while Hancock held Brevet Major General Gershom Mott's third division at the Cummings house.[17] Egan's first units approached the ford shortly after daylight.[18] Near the run, they found more rebel pickets and more clumps of felled trees in their path.[19] At the stream, earthworks crowned the opposite bank.[20] To Union eyes, the works appeared "well defended by a slashing, and a deep ditch of water into which brush, &c., had been tangled."[21] The obstacles lined both banks of Hatcher's Run "for some distance,"[22] and funneled the advancing column to the ford itself and into the face of the rebel trenches.[23]

For Winfield Hancock, the morning's first challenge had arrived. There was much to like in this imposing Pennsylvanian. The ever-observant Colonel Theodore Lyman described him as "a tall soldierly man, with light-brown hair and military heavy jaw . . . [and] the massive features and the heavy folds round the eye that often mark a man of ability."[24] Intelligent and popular, Hancock was also a "vehement talker" who usually had something to say worth hearing.[25] According to one of his staffers, the general was "very winning in his ways and the embodiment of courtesy when calm." "He was a man of the most perfect bravery," the staffer continued, "and in battle . . . he would sit up erect in his saddle and give orders, launch out his oaths, and fight his corps without apparently perceiving that he was in danger."[26] The Virginia campaign had been particularly taxing for Hancock. He spent much of the year suffering from a groin wound received at Gettysburg. The injury slowed him, sometimes to incapacity. He also gained considerable weight. In late June, nearly a year after the epic battle, the festering wound discharged a large bone shard and then appeared to improve.[27] Though it still bothered him into the autumn, he was well enough to command from the saddle.[28]

Hancock's command had also suffered over the past few months. Indeed, the 1864 campaigns bled the Second Corps dry. During the fighting in Virginia, Grant and Meade had tapped the unit to perform the most crucial movements and attacks. This thrust Hancock's men into many of the Overland campaign's fiercest assaults in the Wilderness, at the Mule Shoe in Spotsylvania, and on the dusty fields at Cold Harbor. By the time the army reached Petersburg in June, thousands of Second Corps men lay in Northern hospital beds or slept under Virginia's soil. In their places, greenhorns from Washington's garrisons, draftees, and new recruits filled the ranks. At Petersburg and outside Richmond, Grant and Meade continued to call upon Hancock's men. But the command failed to shine. On June 18, during the initial assaults against Petersburg defenses, some units in the Second Corps simply refused to obey orders to attack. The tremendous casualties of the previous month and fatigue from constant campaigning had sapped the troops fighting edge and aggressiveness.[29] On June 22, the corps, temporarily led by David Birney in place of the ailing Hancock, collapsed under a rebel flank attack at the Jerusalem Plank Road southeast of Petersburg. Hundreds became prisoners. The mediocre performance continued during unsuccessful excursions to Deep Bottom.

Hancock's problems peaked at Reams Station in late August, when the Second Corps marched down the Weldon Railroad to destroy miles of track and cripple Confederate supply efforts. In response, a strike force under A. P. Hill scrambled from the Petersburg trenches. In the face of this threat, Hancock's men curled into ill-contrived defenses dug by a previous Union expedition. Hill's infantry, joined by Wade Hampton's cavalry, drove home a determined attack and broke the Second Corps. Though Hancock and his officers prevented complete disaster, Reams Station stood out as a particularly embarrassing defeat. Over the next two months, Meade spared the Second Corps from active operations. However, for the October 27 effort, he assigned Hancock the crucial task of seizing and holding the South Side Railroad.

At dawn, many miles remained between Hancock's men and their objective. As the column approached Hatcher's Run, Frank Spalter's skirmish line, drawn from the 7th West Virginia and the 4th Ohio entered the creek and tested the enemy position. However, this initial attempt failed, frustrated by the ford's depth, the tangled slashing, and a sharp enemy fire.[30] Spalter himself died when a bullet drilled into his head.[31] Stymied, the skirmishers fell back, but soon more men arrived.[32] Brigadier General Thomas Smyth then deployed his entire brigade across the road in line at battle and prepared to rush the ford and storm the works.[33] A second line formed in support, with Colonel James Willett's brigade on the right and Lieutenant Colonel Horace Rugg's on the left.[34]

In the works across the run, sixty unlucky members of Pierce Young's cavalry brigade waited to again welcome the federal infantry. One of the many squads Wade Hampton had scattered at bridges and fords in Hancock's path, the detachment of Georgians at Cummings Ford guarded two dams. More men had

occupied this spot earlier in the month, but many had recently shifted upstream
closer to the infantry. The small force remaining knew they could do little to stop
Hancock's advance. Nevertheless, they stuck to their post as an entire Union division deployed before their eyes.[35]

Thomas Smyth's regiments, including men from New Jersey, Delaware, Pennsylvania, and New York, gathered to renew the attack.[36] Smyth's officers shouted
the command "Forward." The men leaned into the fire spraying from the opposite
bank and splashed across at the double-quick.[37] The new advance swept away the
Confederates, sending them in "a right oblique direction."[38] Smyth's men scaled

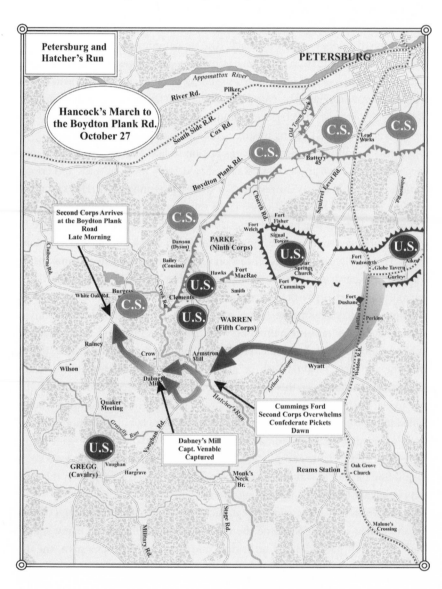

SECOND CORPS MOVES OUT 201

the works, and, led by a sergeant from the 69th Pennsylvania, pursued the enemy troops scampering into the woods beyond.[39]

Though the assault was quick and decisive, it was not easy. The commander of the 69th New York wrote that the "sharp dash" afforded no "time to pick a crossing place." "We jump in," he said, "some places knee deep, often up to the armpits, while some of the lucky ones (writer included), strike a hole and are 'out of sight.'" The regiment's color bearer, Elwood Griscom, balanced on a fallen log and gained the far side well before his soaked comrades. He stood atop the earthworks "proudly waving the flag, shouting defiance at the fleeing rebels."[40] The attackers netted about twenty prisoners, including a major.[41] Beyond the south bank, Sergeant Albert De-Forest of the 14th Connecticut, leading the flankers on the right, encountered telegraph lines stretching off in "almost every direction" and promptly cut them.[42]

The Second Corps had passed the day's first test and breached the ditch guarding the Confederate rear. Ahead, the network of narrow roads, coursing through fields and dense woods, eventually led to the South Side Railroad. With their work completed at the Hatcher's Run crossing, Smyth's men emptied the water out of their shoes and prepared to resume the march.[43] They also buried the body of Lieutenant Colonel Spalter at the roadside, not far from where he fell.[44] Amid the debris scattered about the rebel works, a Union soldier found a letter that read, "I understand every man in Petersburg is put in trenches, and the old soldiers sent to where they are mostly needed."[45]

As the captured note suggested, Wade Hampton could not post his troops everywhere. Hoping to strike the flanks of Union attacking columns north of Hatcher's Run, he had placed a token force at Cummings Ford. However, Hancock had swept these men aside. "I have forced the crossing after a little brisk firing," he informed Meade's headquarters at 7:30 A.M. "It was held by Young's brigade of cavalry. Firing has been heard in the direction of Gregg, but nothing from Parke. I am a little anxious about this last matter."[46]

"the bugle sounded to saddle up"

Early Thursday, Major General David M. Gregg's horsemen gathered their equipment, climbed onto their mounts, and left their temporary camp near the Weldon Railroad with Colonel Charles H. Smith's newly formed third brigade in the lead. Gregg planned to keep pace and maintain communications with the Second Corps column.[47] The column headed for Monk's Neck Bridge, which spanned Rowanty Creek almost three miles downstream from Hancock's crossing at Cummings Ford, then trotted down the railroad, and turned west at a country post office. At the Hargrave house, not more than a mile from the Rowanty, the lead units stirred up rebel pickets and pushed on.[48]

The cavalry reached Monk's Neck Bridge shortly after daybreak. Gregg tapped the 6th Ohio and a battalion of the 1st Maine to brush aside enemy troopers crouched in breastworks on the far bank. The Maine battalion, led by Captain John Freese, deployed along a bend in the stream and poured "an enfilading fire along the enemy's line with their sixteen shooters."[49] Meanwhile, the 6th Ohio waded across the stream above and below the bridge.[50] As General Gregg and his staff observed the action, a bullet cracked the elbow of Captain John Harper, acting provost marshal, making him one of the morning's first casualties.[51] According to a *New York Herald* reporter, the works formed a "strong line" and the rebels "could have given us considerable trouble in taking the position" if properly manned.[52] Fortunately for Gregg, only a thin force covered the trench, and the Ohio and Maine troopers easily flushed the rebels back into their camps. The brief attack netted about half a dozen wagons loaded with commissary stores and tobacco, along with several prisoners.[53]

As Gregg advanced, Wade Hampton received news of the approaching Union columns and hastened to action. He surmised Meade's target, predicting that the enemy "were certainly bound for the Southside road."[54] Though Hampton had predicted an attack, the Union offensive was not following his script. Hancock's movement thwarted his plans to hit the enemy's flank north of Hatcher's Run. With his original scheme now obsolete, Hampton realized that the federals hoped to bypass Heth's position and drive through his cavalry. He understood the need to check the Union columns until more men could be brought up to meet the attackers.[55]

Hampton's two divisions, led by Matthew Butler and Rooney Lee, covered a front stretching from Burgess Mill several miles south to Malone's bridge. With the rebel camps sited away from the key fords and bridge crossings, Hampton had posted picket forces of about thirty men each at Armstrong's Mill, on the Vaughan road, and at "an old mill below there."[56] Though too small to offer determined resistance, these groups could sound the alarm. By daybreak, Gregg's and Hancock's blue columns had brushed aside these obstacles.

As Union troops flooded deep into Dinwiddie County, Hampton struggled to consolidate his widely spread units and orchestrate a response. Much of Matthew Butler's division occupied camps on the Quaker Road near Burgess Mill.[57] Hampton ordered Butler to reinforce his pickets along Hatcher's Run and the Rowanty. Artillery batteries, parked close by at the Wilson Farm on the Boydton Plank Road, also rolled forward. However, Rooney Lee's command lay farther south. Hampton directed Lee to advance north and press against the left flank of Gregg's column.[58]

In the cavalry bivouacs, news of the federal operation spurred a flurry of activity. In Rooney Lee's sector, the 9th Virginia Cavalry had spent the previous days lounging in camp, "drilling and doing picket duty" near Malone's Crossing, a spot on the Weldon Railroad two miles south of Reams Station. However, at 7 A.M., a courier galloped into camp and reported enemy columns to the north. "In a moment the bugle sounded to saddle up and then to march," recalled Virginian Byrd Willis. "Tearing down our fly tents and strapping these up hastily, [we] mounted, fell into line and moved off at a brisk trot in the direction of Reams Station." The regiment dismounted in a field near the railroad and formed in line, holding their horses' reins, as the sound of distant combat met their ears.[59]

Similar scenes played out in Butler's cavalry division to the north. One South Carolinian chronicler wrote, "On Thursday morning about sunrise the late sleepers in the camp of Butler's brigade were awakened by the news that our pickets on the Vaughan road had been driven in, and we were ordered to saddle up and get ready to meet the enemy."[60] Along the Quaker Road, the men first assumed that the commotion merely signaled an enemy demonstration at Armstrong's Mill and other points along the run.[61] At daybreak, Matthew Butler ordered his aide, U. R. Brooks, to head to the front and determine the cause of all the gunfire.[62] Brooks's reconnaissance revealed an enemy "advancing in full force."[63] Butler, in turn, ordered his units to meet the oncoming tide at all points. The South Carolinians emerged from their camps at a trot.[64] To the rear, at the Wilson house on the Plank Road, the teams of Captain James Hart's battery, one of Hampton's horse artillery units, drove east. When "firing was heard at daylight that morning in the direction of Armstrong's Mill, 'Boots and Saddles' sounded at once," Hart recalled, "and my Battery was put in motion for the firing." While racing to the front, he encountered one of Hampton's couriers, who urged him to drive his guns to Armstrong's Mill immediately.[65] The Confederates scrambling into action had precious little time, for the heavy Union columns would arrive soon.

CHAPTER 12

Dabney's Mill and the Quaker Meeting House

~

"pressing forward"

With Gregg covering the left flank to the south, Hancock's Second Corps resumed its westward march from Cummings Ford. Thomas Egan's division crossed first, with Thomas Smyth's brigade in the lead.[1] Smyth, in turn, deployed a Pennsylvania regiment to pursue the retreating Confederates and then followed with his entire brigade southwest along the Vaughan Road for a short distance, scattering aside pockets of resistance.[2] Soon, however, the brigade retraced its steps to the ford. Egan's entire division then resumed the march, turning north onto the Duncan Road and proceeding along the south bank of Hatcher's Run toward Armstrong's Mill, with Lieutenant Colonel Horace Rugg's brigade at the head, followed by James Willett's brigade, then Smyth's.[3]

As Egan tramped north on the Duncan Road, Brevet Major General Gershom Mott's division filled the Vaughan Road in place of Egan's division and ventured southwest toward Gravelly Run. Brigadier General Regis de Trobriand's brigade fanned out with the 2nd U.S. Sharpshooters and the 73rd New York at the point, driving Confederates away from hastily dug rifles pits.[4] A mile down the road, Mott's column left the Vaughan Road and took a narrow path in the direction of the Dabney Mill, a working sawmill at a remote crossroads a mile north. Flankers spread out in advance of the column, a difficult task given the terrain. "[To] us the march was particularly severe," reported Lieutenant Colonel Casper Tyler of the 141st Pennsylvania, "the woods and bushes being so dense as at times to be almost impenetrable."[5]

The Confederate cavalry struggled to delay Hancock's progress. To the southwest, members of the Jeff Davis Legion from Young's brigade saddled up and probed along the Vaughan Road, where they encountered comrades retreating from Cummings Ford smarting from Hancock's blow. As the legion neared Hatcher's Run, they dismounted, left their horses in the care of a few comrades, and formed a weak line along the Vaughan Road in Mott's path. When shots rang

out, their commander, Lieutenant Colonel Fred Waring, discovered Union cavalry threatening his rear, probably elements of Gregg's division heading west from
Monk's Neck Bridge. Waring was in a tight spot, and, in the confusion, his men
failed to reach their horses and fled on foot west toward the Quaker Road.[6]

To the north, Egan's division continued its trek on the Duncan Road, which
"led mostly through a thick forest of princely pines."[7] At 8:30 A.M., the formation
reached Armstrong's Mill. Egan's column approached the rebel works there from
the rear. His men soon found that rebel pickets had already abandoned the position.[8] In seizing Armstrong's Mill, the Second Corps formed a direct connection
to the Fifth and Ninth Corps north at the Clements house and a solid line of communication to the rest of the army. With Armstrong's Mill secured, Egan pressed
westward toward Dabney's Mill along a narrow tree-lined road, deploying two
of Rugg's regiments as a rear guard.[9] Thus, both of Hancock's prongs, Mott's and
Egan's divisions, headed for Dabney's Mill on separate routes. Shortly after 9 A.M.,
Egan reached the crossroads and skirmishers of the 36th Wisconsin, led by Captain George A. Fisk, overwhelmed enemy pickets, seizing rifle pits at the sawmill
and capturing about forty men from Young's and Butler's cavalry brigades.[10]

More rebels were not far away. Members of the 6th South Carolina regiment
reined up within six hundred yards of the Dabney Mill crossroads to find Egan's
skirmishers a short distance ahead. The rebels dismounted and stepped forward
to fight. But as they fired their weapons at the blue forms ahead, news arrived of
another enemy column approaching from the south. The cavalrymen postponed
the bloodshed and, as one soldier explained, "fell back a mile and a half . . . put
two pieces of Hart's battery in position and awaited the approach of the enemy."[11]
The horsemen simply could not stop the heavy infantry columns.

Mott's infantry division approached the mill from the south to join Egan. The
march had not been peaceful. A member of the 124th New York recalled, "Every
few moments a wounded man would be carried past toward the rear. Some of
these wounded men looked very pale and others presented blood-stained faces
or garments, suggesting unpleasant thoughts to those who were pressing forward,
for all believed we would soon find our advance disputed by a battle line instead
of skirmishers."[12] Along the way, Mott's men drove the rebel skirmishers through
forests and an open field. The vanguard eventually reached Dabney's Mill and
joined Egan. Hancock, who had accompanied Mott's division, guided his horse
into the crossroads, where he received news that Gregg's cavalry column had
crossed the Rowanty. Given Gregg's progress, Hancock had no reason to tarry at
Dabney's. The cramped intersection left little room to deploy two infantry divisions. Once Mott reached the spot, Hancock prepared to forge westward toward
the Boydton Plank Road.[13]

"My person is at your disposal, but my tongue is not"

Hancock's progress bred new troubles for Confederate General Henry Heth. The federal attacks at the Boydton Plank line tied up his forces, preventing efforts to aid the cavalry to the south of Hatcher's Run. James Dearing's unit, still supporting Heth's efforts, offered an obvious choice to bolster Hampton. Unlike some of the cavalrymen protecting Heth's trench line, Dearing's men had horses and could shift south rapidly. But when Hampton called Dearing south, Heth countermanded the instruction, concerned with the immediate threat in his front.[14] Accordingly, Dearing remained in the works north of the run until reinforcements could relieve him.

Heth's decision to detain Dearing highlighted a crucial challenge for the Confederate commanders. North of Hatcher's Run, Heth threw everything into trenches to block the most direct route to the Confederate rear and the South Side Railroad. At the same time, Hampton's scattered squads to the south lacked the strength to contest Hancock's juggernaut. In the face of these competing priorities, Heth's need won out. This decision, however, created two problems. First, with Dearing's brigade north of Hatcher's Run, the approaches to the Burgess Farm and the South Side Railroad remained largely unprotected. Second, not knowing of Heth's decision to countermand his directive to Dearing, Hampton assumed Dearing's brigade was on its way to help.

To warn Hampton that Dearing was not coming, Heth dispatched Major Andrew Reid Venable, Hampton's inspector general. Venable galloped across Hatcher's Run, most likely by way of Burgess Mill, and headed east toward Dabney's Mill. In his haste, however, he stumbled "headlong" into pickets of the 19th Maine from Egan's division and thus into captivity, his task unfulfilled.[15] According to a *New York Herald* reporter, Venable "was very much surprised, not to say chagrined, to find himself so suddenly a prisoner on a spot where he said he had expected to find his own skirmish line deployed."[16] His captors, understandably curious about his mission, prodded the major for information. According to a postwar account from one of Venable's comrades, a Union officer on picket "very improperly, threatened [Venable] with direful bodily harm" after he refused to answer any of their questions. As the interview progressed, the officer became "more irate" at Venable's reluctance to reveal Confederate troop strength and positions. Venable likewise became angered at this treatment and "blazed out upon the Federal commander with such scathing words as the latter probably never forgot."[17] Winfield Hancock soon came forward, and, in response to the general's inquiries, Venable remained tight lipped. When asked about his unit, he simply replied, "I am a major in the Confederate army . . . I am on the side of the South; I have the cause of my country very much at heart; and I think I can best promote her interest, under the present circumstance, by declining to answer any further questions until later in the day. My person is at your disposal, but my tongue is not."

Venable's answer surprised Hancock, who may have not been privy to Venable's earlier exchange. Hancock then said, "Perhaps you have about you some papers which it would be no harm for us to see."[18] Indeed, Venable's papers betrayed his identity and perhaps other details of the morning. But one of Hancock's staffers assured Venable that they knew Hampton's cavalry stood in their front. Venable soon retrieved his papers, and Hancock's provost marshal led him to the rear. According to a reporter, one Unionist offered eight thousand Confederate dollars for Venable's "handsome blooded mare." But in Venable's opinion, "She was too good an animal, to be ridden by a Yankee officer." Nevertheless, the horse joined Hancock's staff on the march, a "contraband of war."[19]

Hancock resolved to proceed west toward the Burgess Farm. Before doing so, he directed some cavalrymen with him to cover the rear and fan "well out on all by-roads." With the arrival of Mott's force at the crossroads, Egan's division struck out along the Dabney Mill Road, "a mere path, barely passable for guns," through very thick woods.[20] As the infantry resumed the march, the "sound of Gregg's guns became more distinct" to Hancock, and, he later reported, he "hoped that we might strike the plank road in time to inflict some damage to the enemy."[21] At 10:45 A.M., he wrote to Humphreys that the second division (Egan's) had passed Dabney's Mill, followed by the third (Mott's). He acknowledged that heavy skirmishing had delayed his advance.[22] But despite this annoyance, Hancock's prospects remained bright. He was well over Hatcher's Run. Once across the Boydton Plank Road, he could drive his column deep behind the rebel defenses and swing north onto the South Side Railroad. But in the face of Hancock's advance, the Confederate cavalrymen drew back to the Boydton Plank Road. One rebel squad "built stockades" there. As a trooper recalled, "We had been maneuvered out of our positions. But this flanking process was at an end."[23]

"with a bound and yell"

Gregg's cavalry to the south proved more than a mere nuisance for Hampton, who quickly directed his forces to meet the danger. Rebel gunner Captain James Hart, with orders to take his battery toward Armstrong's Mill, hurried his crews from the Wilson Farm to the Quaker Road. There he received reports of "a heavy force of cavalry" approaching from the south, which threatened the underbelly of Hampton's position, not to mention the Confederate cavalry trains parked at a schoolhouse adjacent to the Quaker Road. In response to these alarming reports, Hart split his battery, sending one section of guns south on the Quaker Road under the temporary command of Lieutenant William T. Adams and the other eastward under the care of Major T. G. Barker. Hart urged Barker to round up every man he could find. Hart himself managed to scrape together about sixty men from the wagon trains parked around the schoolhouse and then rushed south toward Gravelly Run.[24]

Over the past several months, Gregg's blue-clad cavalrymen had probed the roads and farm paths south of Petersburg but only rarely ventured so deep into enemy territory and in such force. Once across Monk's Neck Bridge, the column had trotted west under thick woods and, after more than a mile, reached the Vaughan Road intersection, where a wide field stretched out to the west. At the junction, the Union horsemen stumbled upon several unlucky Confederate wagons containing commissary stores and tobacco.[25]

At the Vaughan Road, some of the Union cavalry received a volley from their friends in the Second Corps, members of Gershom Mott's division then probing from the northeast. Though the fire did not harm any of Gregg's men, it managed to kill a few horses.[26] With this unfortunate incident behind them, Gregg's procession turned left on the Vaughan Road, plunged into more forest, and soon crossed Little Cattail Run, with Smith's third brigade in front, followed by Colonel Michael Kerwin's men, and Brigadier General Henry Davies's unit at the rear.[27]

The horse soldiers passed the Hargrave house and then rode through recently abandoned Confederate camps where "considerable quantities of grain and hay were left, and any amount of small articles pertaining to camp life."[28] Gray skirmishers tumbled back before the column, resisting stubbornly at points but failing to halt Gregg's progress.[29] Nevertheless, Confederates threatened the Union formation at both ends, and the skirmishing soon became constant. "Taken as a whole, it was a very uncomfortable place," recalled a journalist with Gregg's column.[30] As his men pressed on, Gregg learned from captured rebel couriers of the presence of Rooney Lee's division near Stony Creek to the south. But Gregg's command was not headed there. He planned to turn north onto the Quaker Road, cross over Gravelly Run, and push on to the Boydton Plank Road and the Burgess Farm.[31]

With Gregg headed north, Wade Hampton sought to do more than blunt the Union effort. He looked to land a devastating blow by trapping Gregg between two forces. First, in front of Gregg's advance, Captain James Hart raced to block the way at the Quaker Meeting House on a steep hill overlooking Gravelly Run. Second, as Hart's guns moved to bar the way at the front, Hampton relayed orders for Rooney Lee to hit the flank and rear of the Union force at the intersection of the Quaker and Vaughan roads. Hampton's simple plan promised tremendous results. However, at the Burgess Farm, Hampton, without the benefit of Venable's message, expected Dearing's brigade to establish a blocking position to buy vital time. But Dearing remained north of Hatcher's Run in accordance with Henry Heth's instructions. Thus, Hampton hatched his plan with imperfect information.[32]

To the south, Rooney Lee's division prepared to pounce on Gregg's column. His command included North Carolinians under Rufus Barringer and Virginians

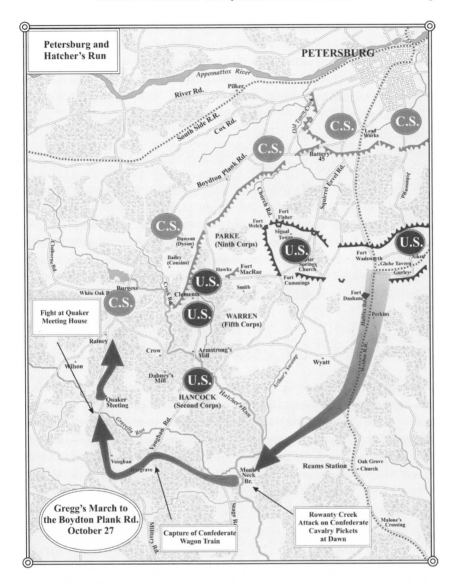

Petersburg and Hatcher's Run

PETERSBURG

Appomattox River

River Rd.

Pilker

South Side R.R.

Cox Rd.

Boydton Plank Rd.

C.S.

C.S.

C.S.

Lead Works

Battery 45

Old Town Creek

Church Rd.

Squirrel Level Rd.

Pegram

Fort Fisher

Fort Welch

Signal Tower

PARKE (Ninth Corps)

Poplar Springs Church

Fort Wadsworth

U.S.

Globe Tavern

Gurley

Aiken

U.S.

C.S.

Dawson (Dyson)

Bailey (Cousins)

Claiborne Rd.

Hawks

Fort MacRae

Creek Rd.

White Oak P.

Burgess

Clements

Smith

Fort Cummings

Fort Dushane

Perkins

U.S.

Halifax Rd.

Weldon R.R.

Fight at Quaker Meeting House

C.S.

U.S.

WARREN (Fifth Corps)

Rainey

Crow

Armstrong's Mill

Wyatt

Wilson

Dabney's Mill

U.S.

Arthur's Swamp

Quaker Meeting

HANCOCK (Second Corps)

Hatcher's Run

Gravelly Run

Vaughan Rd.

Vaughan

Pegrave

Monks Neck Br.

Reams Station

Oak Grove Church

Gregg's March to the Boydton Plank Rd. October 27

Stage Rd.

Military Rd.

Capture of Confederate Wagon Train

Rowanty Creek Attack on Confederate Cavalry Pickets at Dawn

Malone's Crossing

led by Richard Beale, a unit referred to as "Chambliss's Brigade" after its former commander, John R. Chambliss. For members of the 9th Virginia, waiting near Malone's Crossing since early morning, the new orders triggered a burst of activity. "At 10 o'clock we are ordered to mount and moved off towards Burgess Mill on the Military Road," wrote Byrd Willis. "Gen. Wm. [Rooney] Lee has just moved to the head of the command loading his pistol as he passed. It would seem as if he was expecting to have use for it."[33]

Ahead of Gregg's column, the Confederates set their trap. To the east, Beale's

Virginians and the 4th North Carolina skirmished with the rear of Gregg's column.[34] To the west, Barringer's North Carolinians, eager to attack, approached the Vaughan Road intersection from the south via a military road. They concealed themselves several hundred yards from the road junction and waited patiently as Gregg's column filed past. [35] However, the jaws formed by Hampton's plan did not shut. According to one account, "Only a few shots were fired by each party" in Barringer's front.[36] One North Carolinian recalled that Rooney Lee received "express orders from Army Headquarters not to interfere with the enemy's movements."[37]

Despite the tempting target offered by Gregg's force, Hampton bowed to his priority. He simply could not allow Hancock's column to punch through the Burgess Farm and reach the South Side Railroad. He later explained "I have no doubt but that this combined attack would have defeated them entirely, but just before Lee got into position the enemy were found to be advancing rapidly from Armstrong's Mill to the plank road in my rear."[38] The threat from Hancock's infantry loomed too large. Hampton needed Rooney Lee and Butler's divisions with him on the Boydton Plank Road.

Though Rooney Lee did not fall on Gregg's cavalry as Hampton originally envisioned, some fighting occurred at the Vaughan and Quaker roads. According to Confederate artillery commander Major Preston Chew, one of his horse batteries kept up "quite a brisk fire for a quarter of an hour."[39] Byrd Willis from the Virginia brigade also recalled that his regiment "had a brisk fight for about a half hour when the enemy retired." The Virginians wrapped their fallen comrades in their blankets and left them on the road side.[40] According to Henry Davies, commander of the Union brigade at the tail of the column, the rebels launched "a spirited attack" at the Quaker Road, even while the leading units approached Gravelly Run, but the 10th New York Cavalry "readily" drove off this effort. Davies assigned the 1st Pennsylvania to cover the rear from further rebel harassment.[41]

David Gregg had wriggled through a tight spot deep in enemy territory, with his men strung out over a road covered with trees. His column had slid between two Confederate cavalry divisions, avoiding a disastrous trap. He continued on the Quaker Road north toward Gravelly Run and a junction with Hancock on the Plank Road. A short distance from the run, the road veered right, descended between thick bushes, and crossed Gravelly Run over a narrow bridge.[42] As Gregg's column eased through the defile, the Union troopers met an unpleasant surprise.

Near the Quaker Meeting House, James Hart had unlimbered his horse battery in a blocking position on a knoll overlooking Gravelly Run. Well suited for defense, the hillock frowned down upon the bridge, which promised to create a perfect bottleneck. Difficult, swampy ground bracketed the otherwise unimposing stream. Hart's supports, including a company from the 6th South Carolina Cavalry, arrived and spread along the flanks. As this small band dug in its heels, the Confederate cavalry trains parked at a schoolhouse along the Quaker Road clattered rearward to safety.[43]

Just minutes after Hart unlimbered his guns and trained them at the bridge below, the head of Gregg's column appeared, with the 1st Maine in front, led by Colonel Jonathan Cilley. From the knoll, the rebel crews opened fire, transforming the narrow space into a killing ground. As the cavalrymen trotted along the exposed road bed, two shells whistled past Colonel Cilley, the second one missing his head by inches.[44] He quickly halted and pulled out his field glasses as projectiles crashed through nearby pines. Hart's guns brought the Union cavalry to a dead halt. The "enemy's position was one of great natural strength," sited upon a "commanding eminence," recalled General Gregg.[45] Charles Smith, whose brigade arrived first, recalled that the Confederates had "formed for a determined resistance."[46]

At Hart's position, a courier galloped up to the booming cannon, bearing a message from General Hampton: "Hold the bridge at all hazards until I can support you."[47] Hart's force, probably not much more than 100 men, stymied Gregg's entire division.[48] The federals countered with musket fire from 150 yards and a steady spray of canister from guns unlimbered near the bridge. One defender recalled, "Pouring in upon us a heavy fire from front, right and left, it seemed that our little band of cannoneers must soon be demolished. Several had already fallen at their pieces, but the guns were still rapidly served and committed fearful execution in the enemy's columns across the run."[49]

After a few failed attempts to storm the hill with skirmishers, Gregg eventually dismounted the 6th Ohio and 1st Maine as skirmishers, placing the 21st Pennsylvania, in support, mounted. Thus deployed, the Northerners waded across the swampy creek, pushing back a few Confederate skirmishers. The 1st Maine reformed under the steep north bank, with one half to the right of the road commanded by Colonel Cilley and the other to the left led by Captain Paul Chadbourne. The 6th Ohio formed farther on the right, and the 21st Pennsylvania split on either side of the road in support.[50]

Smith gave the order to charge. Beyond the streambed, his men faced a climb of two hundred yards. "With a bound and yell," they emerged into the open, "in full range" of the Confederate guns. Captain Chadbourne's line stepped ahead in single rank and open file. As the bullets sang, his men wavered, but, holding his left hand high, he shouted, "Forward on the left!" At that moment, the Confederate rifles "poured a most deadly fire," and a bullet hit Chadbourne's hand, severing his index finger and "completely demolishing his pistol."[51] Undaunted, he picked up his shattered weapon and urged his men on.[52]

Though the Confederate gunners had delayed Gregg admirably, it was time for them to leave. As Hart prepared to withdraw, he received a terrible leg wound, one that would require amputation. His officers and men limbered their guns and raced north to join the rest of Hampton's command at the Burgess Farm.[53] As the federals seized Hart's position, several hogs broke from nearby woods and scampered through the Union battle line, receiving scattered shots from Maine troopers.[54] Back at Gravelly Run, soldiers buried comrades killed in the fighting on the north bank near the bridge.[55] General Gregg ordered his men to burn the bridge behind his column.[56] With that, the cavalry continued its march on the Quaker Road toward the Boydton Plank Road.

Hart's blocking force had provided a great service to Wade Hampton. With the defenses along Hatcher's Run crumbling at all points and the Union Second Corps sweeping around Heth's entrenched line, an unimpeded federal cavalry division marching up the Boydton Plank Road could have seized the Burgess Farm before the arrival of Confederate reinforcements. Hart's stand at the Quaker Meeting House, aided by additional men rushed to the scene by Hampton, helped to ease the pressure. His fight aptly demonstrated the impact that good terrain, bold decision making, and luck could have on the battlefield. Though more challenges lay ahead for the Confederate cavalry, the fight at the Quaker Meeting House stood as a bright spot in an otherwise bleak morning.

With the Union advance pressing from several sides, Hampton understood the need to consolidate his forces and find somewhere to block further enemy progress. In response, he ordered Rooney Lee to swing northwest onto the Plank Road and Butler to pull his men back to the Burgess Farm. With these movements, Hampton gathered his men at the Plank Road for a determined defense. He also looked north for James Dearing's brigade.

"a mere atom of flesh"

As Hampton and Heth handled the tactical details at the Boydton Plank Road, A. P. Hill sought to grasp the broader picture at Petersburg and divine Union intentions. Often plagued by uneven health, Hill probably followed the developments from his headquarters tent in the front yard of the Knight family estate, called Indiana, on Petersburg's western fringe.[57] Perhaps due to his chronic illness, Hill did not rush to the point of danger on Thursday morning. However, he understood the threat posed by the Union offensive.

To aid Heth and Hampton, Hill looked to strip units from the trenches east of Petersburg. To do so, he turned to Major General William Mahone, the intense, diminutive Virginian who had emerged over the past year as one of army's best division commanders. Mahone enjoyed the deep admiration of his soldiers, particularly fellow Petersburg men who had served under him in the 12th Virginia Infantry. George S. Bernard, a member of that unit and a political ally of the general's after the war, explained, "Mahone, cool, courageous, and able, was by nature fitted for generalship as few men are, and none knew this better than the men of his command. Wherever he led or placed them, they always felt a moral certainty that they were being properly led or placed, either to inflict the most damage on the enemy or to have the enemy inflict the least damage on them."[58]

Mahone was not one for convention. His dress was unusual, sometimes composed of a "plaited brown linen jacket, buttoned to trousers, of same material, like a boy's; topped off by a large Panama straw hat." He could also be "strictly uniformed when he chose."[59] At thirty-eight years of age, he was short and slight, "a mere atom of flesh." When his wife learned of a "flesh wound" he had received, her retort was, "Now I know it is serious, for William has no flesh whatever."[60] In camp, he kept his own cows and hens, which furnished a diet to ease a troubled stomach. During the Petersburg campaign, he rarely left his camp and, according to one observer, was "quiet, uncommunicative, absorbed in his own thoughts, taking care of his men."[61]

As a combat leader, he often displayed a confident, quick mind. Long after the war, one of the general's contemporaries recalled, "Mahone was a man absolutely devoid of fear. He did the right thing as he saw it under all circumstances without regard to consequences."[62] Early in life, he explained to a friend, "Wherever there is something to be fought for—there I wish to be."[63] Tough and persistent, he usually refused to compromise with his opponents. "The only way Mahone will bury the hatchet is in the heads of every one who opposes him," wrote a postwar admirer.[64]

Mahone could be arrogant, brusque, and tactless in dealing with others. As one of his friends diplomatically put it, Mahone, while "obedient to the commands of his superiors, . . . exercise[d] a most liberal right of private judgment when he was sure of his facts."[65] Another acquaintance described him as "a tyrant and presumptuous dictator."[66] Though popular with many of his soldiers, some did not share this adoration. For example, an Alabama infantryman, whose brigade was in the thick of many attacks led by Mahone, recalled bitterly, "Billey Mahone was always volunteering to charge. Some place or other he wanted to git his name up for promotion. But he didant think of us poor fellows lives so he came out all right we didant like him any how."[67]

During the Petersburg campaign, the Confederate high command often looked to Mahone to deliver stinging counterattacks to blunt Union advances. Where Union columns sought to gain ground, Mahone was usually there. He achieved significant tactical success at the Jerusalem Plank Road in June, the Crater in July, and the Weldon Railroad in August. Ultimately, his efforts failed to reverse the Union progress, but his attacks captured thousands of U.S. soldiers and demonstrated that, even against immense odds, the Confederate infantry could punish its enemy severely.

During October, Mahone's division occupied about a mile of the Confederate trenches southeast of Petersburg stretching from the Jerusalem Plank Road, a segment known as Rives Salient, west past the Branch house, due south of Petersburg.[68] On Thursday morning, A. P. Hill tapped Mahone to aid Heth's efforts along the Boydton Plank Road. Hill's messenger arrived near the Branch house and directed Mahone to send troops west along the city's Dimmock line to Battery 45.[69] In response,

Mahone ordered three of his brigades to move, including the Virginians of Brigadier General David Weisiger's brigade, Brigadier General Nathaniel Harris's Mississippians, and Alabamians under Colonel Horace King. The 12th Virginia Regiment,
in the Virginia brigade, had spent the past week in a pine grove near the Branch
house.[70] Because Harris's troops occupied works flush against the enemy lines, his
brigade withdrew gradually to avoid creating a sudden gap in the defenses.[71] The
Virginia and Alabama brigades, however, set out quickly.

John Walters, a gunner in the trenches nearby, could hear the faint thunder of
artillery from Dinwiddie County, which began early and grew heavier as the day
progressed.[72] Observing the departure of Mahone's brigades, he wrote, "All this
gave evidence of heavy work, as these are choice troops who always make their
mark when engaged, representing three states of the Confederacy, the troops
which have always been first among the foremost."[73] Major General Bushrod
Johnson's troops spread themselves out to occupy the vacant space left by the
departing units.[74] Arriving at Battery 45 ahead of his troops, Mahone encountered artillery captain Hampden Chamberlayne returning from Heth's front, who
reported that the enemy had appeared in force to the south. Mahone did not wait
to hear more and rushed toward Burgess Mill.[75]

Mahone's exodus did not escape the watchful eyes of Union signal officers. Atop
their trees and towers, they trained telescopes on any enemy activity they could
find. At the Jerusalem Plank Road signal station, A. K. Carothers could see the
rebel lines stretching from Rives Salient west to the Lead Works, where the Weldon Railroad bisected the Confederate trench line. By 9 A.M., Carothers began to
observe Confederates breaking camp. He estimated that two brigades were heading
southwest. His comrade, a sergeant at the Church Road Station tower farther west,
spied the same thing and viewed rebels breaking camp all along his front. Though
hills, houses, and trees obscured much, the Union signal officers often judged the
size of enemy commands by gauging the time it took a column to pass a specific
point within view. Observers at the Church Road station that morning noted that
one rebel column took eight minutes to pass a reference point in the distance. The
sergeant soon concluded that there "are apparently but very few men left in their
works north from this station." By 10 A.M., the officer at the Jerusalem Plank Road
observed approximately three thousand enemy troops moving west.[76] These observations probably surprised few. Throughout the campaign, the Confederates had
reacted quickly to blunt Union advances south of the city. Today was no different.
The signal station reports revealed that the rebels were on their way.

Civil War Richmond. (Library of Congress)

Civil War Petersburg. (Library of Congress)

Typical scene on the Petersburg Lines. Several bombproofs dot the foreground. The parapet is topped with sandbags and supported by a revetment of cut tree trunks. Rows of abatis stand outside the walls. (Library of Congress)

Benjamin F. Butler. (Library of Congress)

Top left: August V. Kautz. (Library of Congress)

Top right: Charles W. Field. From Francis Trevelyan Miller and Robert S. Lanier, *The Photographic History of the Civil War in Ten Volumes,* Vol. X (New York: The Review of Reviews Co., 1910). (Photo courtesy of The House Divided Project at Dickinson College)

Above left: David B. Birney. (Library of Congress)

Above right: Mary Curtis Burgess. From Burgess, Mary C., *A True Story,* n.p.: 1907. (Photo courtesy of Robert Diehl)

Top left: Godfrey Weitzel. (Library of Congress)
Top right: Winfield S. Hancock. (Library of Congress)
Above left: Henry Heth. (Library of Congress)
Above right: William Mahone. (National Archives)

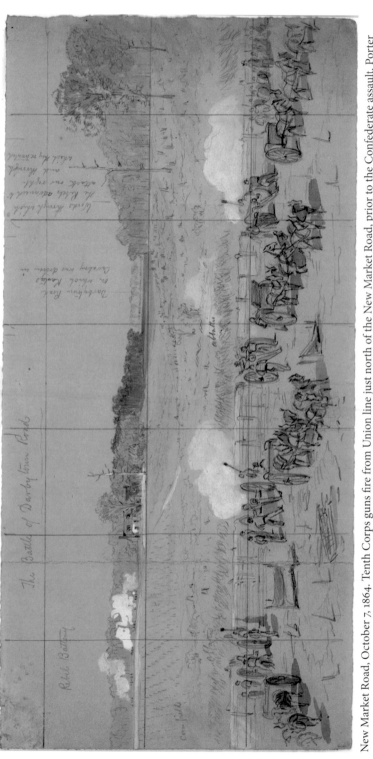

New Market Road, October 7, 1864. Tenth Corps guns fire from Union line just north of the New Market Road, prior to the Confederate assault. Porter Alexander's Confederate batteries reply from the Kell House in the distance. William Waud. (Library of Congress)

New Market Road, October 7, 1864. Union Tenth Corps troops engage Field's division. The inscription on the back of the sketch reads: "Friday [7th] attempt of the Rebels to turn our right flank / The fighting was done in thick woods. Our men shewn [*sic*] in this sketch are armed with the Spencer Rifle, a short—Breech loading seven shooter." William Waud. (Library of Congress)

Captain Babcock's October 24, 1864, map of Boydton Plank Road trench line. The Confederate line did not, in fact, end at the intersection of the Plank Road and Hatcher's Run as depicted on the map. Instead, it terminated about a mile east and downstream from that point. *The War of the Rebellion: a Compilation of the Official Records of the Union and Confederate Armies.* (Image courtesy of Cornell University Library, Making of America Digital Collection)

Darbytown Road, October 27, 1864. "Gen. Butler and Staff watching the Battle from Johnson House. . . ." William Waud. (Library of Congress)

Hatcher's Run, October 27, 1864. "A rebel prisoner explaining to General Warren the Position and movements of the rebel forces on Thurs the 27th // Sketched on the evening of the 27th on the field of battle." Joseph Becker (Title: "A Rebel Prisoner Explaining to General Warren the Position and Movement of Rebel Forces [Battle of Hatcher Creek]"). (Courtesy of the Becker Collection, Boston, MA)

Darbytown Road, October 27, 1864. William Waud's sketch from the Johnson House. The inscription on the back reads: "View of the action on Thursday 27th from the Johnson House looking across the Darby town road on the 10th Corps front. Gen Butler Staff & Body Guard riding to the House. Raining Hard." (Library of Congress)

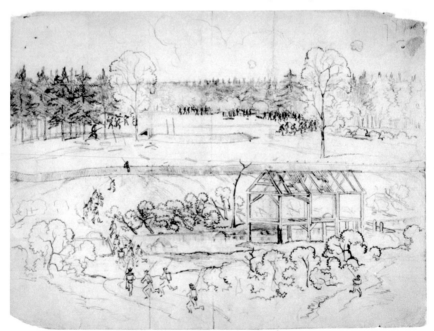

Armstrong's Mill on Hatcher's Run, October 27, 1864. "Hancocks 2nd Corps flanking the rebel works at Armstrong's Mill. . . ." Joseph Becker (Title: "The Battle of Hatcher Creek: The Fight on Thurs 27 64"). (Courtesy of the Becker Collection, Boston, MA)

Fifth and Ninth Corps Advance, October 27, 1864. "The Battle in the Woods // Our line of battle composed of the 5th and 9th Corps pressing the rebels on the afternoon of the 27th . . . The road in the foreground crowded with stragglers and wounded men." Joseph Becker (Title: "The Battle in the Woods at Vaughn [*sic*] Road [Hatcher Creek]"). The sketch probably depicts the Creek Road, not the Vaughan Road as the artist indicates. (Courtesy of the Becker Collection, Boston, MA)

Near Hatcher's Run, October 27, 1864. "Hospital attendants—collecting the wounded after the engagement—within our lines. . . ." William Waud. (Library of Congress)

CHAPTER 13

Reaching the Boydton Plank Road

∼

"beautiful place, falling off around"

At 10:40 A.M. on October 27, Hancock received a message from Meade reporting the dim prospects for success on Parke's Ninth Corps front. The dispatch urged Hancock to open communications with Warren's Fifth Corps and noted that one of Warren's divisions was headed his way.[1] But Hancock's mission to seize the South Side Railroad remained unchanged. The Second Corps continued west through heavy timber lining the Dabney Mill Road, with Thomas Egan's division in the lead. Despite the chilly, damp air and cloudy skies, the autumn leaves yielded an "unusual beauty and brilliancy" in the eyes of a *New York Herald* reporter.[2] In the midst of these pleasant surroundings, rebel cavalry and sharpshooters "annoyed and delayed" Hancock's march. In one house, the Northerners found seven loaded muskets.[3] A Maine soldier from Mott's division later remarked, "Rebels continued to fall back, and if it was a trap they were setting, it was a deep one."[4]

Around 11 A.M., Lieutenant Colonel Horace P. Rugg's brigade, at the tip of the column, emerged from the pine trees and onto a long open field approximately a mile and a half wide.[5] In the distance, the soldiers could see the Boydton Plank Road running roughly north to south and bordered by a rail fence.[6] A cornfield stood on their immediate right; it descended to a narrow stream that meandered through a wooded belt of swampy ground. Farther north beyond this soggy thicket, the ground rose to a hill which held the houses and outbuildings of the Burgess Farm. Beyond the farm and the soldiers' view, the Plank Road sloped down to a narrow bridge at Hatcher's Run. Just upstream, a dam formed the Burgess Mill pond. On the far bank rose a prominent hill, partially covered with pine trees. According to one Union officer, the Burgess Farm was a "beautiful place, falling off around and with small springs, runs and streams all around it."[7] Near the Burgess house, the Plank and the White Oak roads met at a three-pronged intersection, where an unpainted wooden building known as the Burgess Tavern stood. The barns of the Burgess property lay just east across the road. The White Oak Road, stretching to the west, formed the next leg of Hancock's appointed route. It led toward the Claiborne Road, which, in turn, pointed to the South Side Railroad, the ultimate target.[8] Before Hancock could proceed to those roads, he had to seize and control the Burgess Farm.

As Hancock's second division left the wooded confines of the Dabney Mill Road, Horace Rugg's skirmishers spied distant rebel cavalry forming on the grassy hill at the Burgess Farm.[9] Beyond the cavalrymen, a Confederate wagon train hurried over the bridge at Hatcher's Run, escaping unharmed.[10] Hancock later complained that a "small party of good cavalry might perhaps have captured a part of the train . . . but nothing could be accomplished with the cavalry I had in my advance."[11] Back on the Dabney Mill Road, General Egan deployed skirmishers from the 19th and 20th Massachusetts, led by Henry Embler, Egan's assistant adjutant general that day.[12]

Oddly, one of the first Union captures at the Burgess Farm proved to be William Burgess Sr., Mary Burgess's father-in-law. The elder Burgess had driven his wagon to the cornfield at the east side of the Plank Road, in clear view of Hancock's column. The Union soldiers seized his horse team and wagon, corn and all. His own detainment was brief, however, for, as the Union skirmish line surged north, he slipped away and hid between two logs. By his own account, thousands of soldiers passed over and around him throughout the day, but he remained safe in his hiding place.[13] An historian for the 152nd New York later provided a slightly different version of events, however. He claimed that Burgess, a native New Yorker, sought protection at headquarters, while slaves from the Burgess Farm rapidly made their way to freedom behind the federal lines.[14]

For Hampton's Confederates, the enemy's appearance at the Boydton Plank Road threatened to tear their defense line apart. Hancock's troops had pushed a wedge between Heth's infantry north of Burgess Mill and much of Hampton's cavalry to the south. Hampton witnessed Egan's deployment from a spot near the Bevill house, which lay just five hundred yards north of where the Quaker Road emptied into the Plank Road. He quickly threw a few skirmishers up the Plank Road and directed Butler to abandon his fight against Gregg to the south.[15]

But as the threat grew, Hampton received some welcome support. James Dearing finally arrived at Burgess Mill after a morning protecting the trenches north of Hatcher's Run. Upon handing over the works there to Cooke's North Carolina infantry brigade, Dearing's men had mounted their horses and headed south. Colonel V. H. Taliaferro's 7th Confederate Cavalry took the lead and crossed the bridge at Burgess Mill. Colonel Dennis Ferebee's 4th North Carolina posted on the north bank of the run just downstream from the bridge.[16] The 8th Georgia, under Colonel Joel Griffin, also remained north of the Run. From the Burgess Farm, Dearing could see the Union Second Corps fanning out from the Dabney Mill Road and filling Mr. Burgess's broad cornfield.

"The Yankees are coming"

At the Burgess house, the gloomy October morning quickly turned darker for Mary Burgess and her family. With her husband away and her father-in-law tending to his cornfield, she found herself alone with her children and mother-in-law as the sound of combat drifted from the east.[17] Late in the morning, she stepped out of her front door to shake out a tablecloth and met "an unusual silence; no booming of cannon, no fusillade of small arms, all seemed hushed—which was oppressive." When she asked for news from some nearby Confederate cavalrymen, the simple reply was: "The Yankees are coming." She raced back inside and urged her mother-in-law to hide the family valuables, including $400 in gold pieces, a photo of a family member killed at Bull Run, and "pictures of departed friends." When she peered out again, a new sight greeted her. Dearing's dismounted troopers paced south across the Burgess field toward the Union skirmishers in the distance. She recalled years later that it "was a beautiful sight, the awfulness was lost in admiration for the discipline of the brave fellows; forward march, tramp, tramp, tramp."[18] The orderly vision soon vanished as both sides opened with artillery and small arms. Mary Burgess's home became a death trap: "Our house was a target for both sides. Shells burst about us and minie balls peppered the house like hail. Mother and I took the little ones down into the cellar, where we cuddled together in as retired a place as possible, for the cellar was shallow. The young horses from the field came neighing with fright, the dogs howled and yelped with fear, and the little canaries sang at the top of their voices (as is an unusual noise). Such a medley I never could describe, for it was so terrible."[19]

The battle of Burgess Mill, along the Boydton Plank Road, had begun. Two Massachusetts regiments from Rugg's brigade advanced toward Dearing's force, which contained "three regiments of dismounted cavalry with a battery of five guns," by one Unionist's estimate.[20] According to one soldier correspondent, a howitzer from Dearing's command, under the guidance of Lieutenant Billy Mathews, alone faced "withering" fire from federal guns. "Left with only one man, Billy sponged, rammed, pricked the cartridge and sighted the gun himself; afterward one of General Hampton's aides served the vent for him, using the thumb of his gauntlets for a thumb stall."[21] While Mathews operated his howitzer, Dearing's regiments stepped forward, formed their battle line in Hancock's path, and offered the first heavy resistance Hancock had seen all morning.

The Union skirmish line, led by Captain Henry Embler, ventured forward about two hundred yards before the air became alive with rebel bullets. Blue-clad soldiers began to collapse on the cornfield.[22] All of Embler's men, whether wounded or not, hit the ground. Gustave Magnitzky, leading the 20th Massachusetts, urged his men forward but soon halted in the face of the Confederate fire and bent his regiment's flanks rearward. Egan approved of the caution and directed Magnitzky to hold his position. He realized that a mere skirmish line would not clear the Burgess Farm.[23]

As Embler's skirmishers hugged the earth, General Hancock arrived on the field and aided Egan in deploying the rest of the division. The balance of Rugg's brigade shifted left of the skirmish line, and Colonel James Willett's brigade came up in support. As these units deployed, rebel batteries appeared on several sides and began firing from the high ground across Hatcher's Run, from the small hill at the Burgess Farm, from nearby at the White Oak Road intersection, and, most alarmingly, from near the Rainey house south on the Plank Road, practically in Egan's rear.[24] Some rebel projectiles crossed paths over the heads of the Unionists.[25] Egan ordered his third brigade, under Brigadier General Thomas Smyth, to form on his left and rear facing southwest.[26]

The rebel artillery fire drew an immediate Union response. Lieutenant Butler Beck, commanding a battery of the 5th U.S. Artillery, rushed to the junction of the Dabney Mill and Plank roads, unlimbered his guns, and opened a "furious cannonade."[27] The gunners' outstanding execution rapidly silenced the enemy cannons on all sides.[28] The Confederate crews near the Rainey house quickly limbered up after hurling a few shots at the Second Corps and scurried out of Beck's range.[29] The appearance of Gregg's cavalry to the south may have hastened the rebels.[30] At Dearing's position, the shells passed over the 7th Confederate in front and fell among the 8th Georgia on the north bank of Hatcher's Run.[31]

Confederate small arms also added to the threat. A member of Hancock's staff later recalled that the artillery shelling was "accompanied by some unpleasantly accurate practice by some of their sharp-shooters on Gen. H. and staff."[32] The rebel riflemen also targeted the Union infantrymen and gunners, killing and wounding several, including Lieutenant Thomas Burnes of Beck's battery.[33] Hancock had seen enough. He prepared to end the harassment and sweep the Confederates off the Burgess Farm. Around this time, Gregg's cavalry column arrived on the Quaker Road, thus uniting Meade's two flanking columns.[34] The White Oak Road and the South Side Railroad lay only a few miles away.

"near enough to be uncomfortable"

As the federals brushed back the Confederate gunners, Wade Hampton funneled his cavalrymen forward to resist further Union progress. The White Oak Road provided the passageway to the South Side Railroad. To protect this vital route, Hampton dispatched Aiken's South Carolinians, along with other men in Matthew Butler's division.[35] The Palmetto staters pursued "a circuitous route" across the fields west of the Burgess Farm.[36] They eventually gained the White Oak Road, dismounted, and threw up "some easily constructed stockades within sight of the

Plank Road."[37] They also began to construct temporary breastworks with dirt and nearby fence logs.[38] The cavalry formed athwart the White Oak Road, their left resting on the Burgess Mill pond and their right stretching south.[39]

James Hart's gun crews, fresh from their fight at the Quaker Meeting House, joined Butler's men at the White Oak Road. Commanding the battery in place of the wounded Hart, Lieutenant Frank Bamberg unlimbered the guns in the midst of Matthew Butler's brigades.[40] The gunners trained their pieces at the Burgess Farm, searching for targets. From behind their new barricades, they spied over a dozen riders galloping toward them. According to Butler, the day "was cold, disagreeable, drizzly, and therefore objects at a distance were not easily discernable." The artillery men went quickly to work, ramming home shells and opening a vigorous fire on the mounted squad. But Butler, squinting through his field glasses, discovered an alarming fact. Instead of reckless Unionists probing his position, the horsemen in front proved to be Confederate staff couriers joined by their commanding officer, James Dearing. The youthful general "came gayly dashing up" and remarked to Matthew Butler that the "shells landed near enough to be uncomfortable."[41] In all likelihood, Dearing's ride opened communications between Heth to the north at Hatcher's Run, and Hampton.

Hampton's other division, under Rooney Lee, soon arrived from the southwest along the Plank Road. Lee placed the 1st and 2nd North Carolina regiments of Brigadier General Rufus Barringer's brigade on the west side of the road and the 9th and 13th Virginia regiments of Lieutenant Richard L. T. Beale's command on the other.[42] One of Major Preston Chew's rebel batteries also rushed forward and found the enemy "in strong force near Wilson's House." Chew deployed four guns and drove the Unionists back.[43] In response, Gregg's cavalry forming a semicircle southwest near the Quaker Road's intersection with the Plank Road.[44] The third brigade, under Charles Smith, probed south and began trading shots with Rooney Lee's men.

"Virginia highway regulations were not observed"

At the Burgess cornfield, Thomas Egan sought to regain his division's momentum. Earlier, his skirmish line, soldiers from the 19th and 20th Massachusetts, had ground to a halt short of the swampy ravine rimming the Burgess plateau. Egan now ordered Willett's brigade, posted behind the skirmishers, "to advance and carry the enemy's position on the hill crest near the Burgess house." He also brought his two other brigades, Smyth's and Rugg's, up into support.[45] The attacking force stepped forward to their task.

Mary Burgess's house stood in Egan's path. Outside her home, the din from the initial clash had subsided. She climbed out of the cellar and opened the front door. There she caught the attention of General Dearing across the Plank Road behind the cover of the family's barn. He admonished her to leave and head north to Petersburg. Burgess gathered her three young children and fled from the house, "bareheaded and empty handed, with no thought but safety for" her children. Her mother-in-law remained behind for a moment to gather valuables. On the road, her daughter fell when a minie ball appeared to graze her arm. Mary Burgess cried out, fearing the worst, but the little girl picked herself up, saying, "No, mamma, I only hurt my knee." The party reached Hatcher's Run just as a shell killed a large artillery horse nearby. General Dearing caught up with them and, seeing the young mother "flushed by excitement and frightened into a frenzy," told her, "do not hurry fast, as you may be overcome" and urged her to rest beyond the first knoll before continuing to Petersburg. Several minutes later, her mother-in-law caught up, "laboring for breath and with a face as white as marble" but carrying a loaf of bread and a box of gold pieces.[46]

Shortly after the women began their perilous journey, Egan unleashed his multi-tiered attack on the Burgess Farm. The first wave came from the original skirmish line, led by Captain Andrew Henry Embler on horseback with help from Charles McAnally of the 69th New York. Embler, Egan's acting assistant adjutant general,[47] spurred his horse and urged his men over the swamp and up the hill. His gallantry would earn him the Medal of Honor nearly thirty years later.[48] Charles McAnally, on the left of the skirmish line, met Embler and observed the Confederates piling fence rails for cover. With only a handful of volunteers from the 20th Massachusetts, McAnally pushed ahead and scattered the rebels back to the barns on the hill crest.[49]

Willett's brigade of about eight hundred New Yorkers followed closely behind.[50] "I advanced my whole command as a skirmish line," Willett wrote. "Without deploying, [my brigade] crossed the open field and charged through a belt of timber in a ravine, reformed the line upon the opposite side, and charged and carried the elevated ground." His men drove James Dearing's line away from the barns toward Hatcher's Run.[51] Egan had gained the crest near the Burgess house. In the process, his men swept through a tollgate on the Plank Road and a Confederate barricade. Egan joked in his report that the "Virginia highway regulations were not observed."[52] The way to the White Oak Road was now open. Willett reformed his brigade just beyond the Burgess house, with his left resting across the Plank Road.[53] But Dearing's men, from the 7th Confederate and 8th Georgia, stubbornly clung to the run's south bank, huddling in shallow earthworks built to protect Confederate camps at the Burgess Farm. Unfortunately, these works faced north and thus provided them imperfect cover.[54]

At noon, Hancock received word of the Fifth and Ninth Corps operations north of Hatcher's Run had failed to pierce Confederate positions. The dispatch also revealed that the high command had initiated the backup plan. Warren had crossed a division at Armstrong's Mill to connect with the Seconds Corps. The note, written by Andrew Humphreys, advised Hancock to look out "for your right flank and see that there is no enemy between you and Hatcher's Run."[55]

At 12:30 P.M., the second half of Hancock's force, Gershom Mott's division, emerged from the Dabney Mill Road, increasing the number of Union infantry brigades on the field to six. Mott's force gathered to protect the heart of Hancock's position. His first brigade, led by the outspoken Frenchman, Brigadier General Regis de Trobriand, formed near the Plank Road facing south and west. Skirmishers also pushed north and linked with Horace Rugg's line just near the Burgess house. Mott's second brigade, with Brigadier General Byron Pierce at the helm, massed in the cornfield near the Dabney Mill Road. Colonel Robert McAllister's brigade arrived last.[56] The appearance of Mott's division freed Egan to consolidate north at the Burgess Farm. There Egan formed his three brigades in a semicircle facing north and west. With his position secure, Winfield Hancock prepared to strike out for the South Side Railroad using the White Oak Road. If Egan could seal off the rebels at Burgess Mill, perhaps Mott's column could roll west to the target. "I am at the Burgess house, on Boydton plank," Hancock reported to Meade. "General Gregg has just come up. Part of the enemy's cavalry retired by Burgess' across Hatcher's Run. General Gregg captured a few wagons. I am about moving out on White Oak road."[57] Shortly after writing this, at 1 P.M., Hancock received orders from Meade to halt.[58]

"no one would have taken him for the commander"

Soon, Meade and Grant arrived at Hancock's field headquarters followed by an entourage of armed escorts, officers, orderlies, and servants. Throughout the day, Grant had personally visited key points along the front, including the Clements house, where Warren tested the Confederate works. This mobility ensured that he could observe conditions in person, and make well-informed command decisions. Grant and Meade found Hancock under an immense oak tree near the intersection of the Dabney Mill and Plank roads. Meade explained that Samuel Crawford's division was "feeling its way up along the south bank" of Hatcher's Run. Repeating Humphrey's earlier written instructions, he urged Hancock to forge a link with Crawford. Hancock immediately assigned the mission to one of his aides, Henry H. Bingham. Bolstered by a ten-man escort, Bingham pointed his horse east and entered a narrow farm road leading from the Burgess fields. After traveling about a mile, he found Crawford with little difficulty and reported the conditions at the Burgess Farm. Returning west, he informed Hancock that Crawford was "a short three-quarters of a mile from the right of the Second Corps line."[59]

Following Grant and Meade's arrival, another officer tramped onto the field. The curious Washington Roebling, Warren's staff officer, had guided his horse along the Dabney Mill Road in the wake of Grant and Meade's party. Nearing the Burgess cornfield, he passed one of Mott's brigades, most likely McAllister's, resting along the wooded road, and emerged into a space he described as "very large, three-fourths mile wide by two and a half long, running north and south." Across this expanse, he spied Grant, Meade, and Hancock off to the left. He continued north, passing General Egan with his division, and observed a section of Beck's battery about two hundred yards in front near Burgess Tavern: "The enemy fired all his shots at this section, and was knocking it pretty badly. The right flank of this section was protected by about 100 cavalry drawn up in line beyond, though farther north; I could see no troops of ours. While I was standing there another rebel battery opened from some point on the north side of Hatcher's Run, taking this advanced section of ours somewhat on the right and rear. The first shot fortunately burst about 100 yards from me, else it would have knocked me over. I left then."[60] Concluding his observations, Roebling, like Bingham, departed the field on one of the narrow paths leading east. He wandered about two hundred yards, saw nothing of interest, and chose another route to return to the Fifth Corps.[61]

Back at the Burgess Farm, the arrival of the Union high command at the massive oak tree caused a stir among the rank and file. Members of the 57th Pennsylvania from Pierce's brigade nearby craned their necks to glimpse the luminaries. One soldier described Grant as "quite plainly dressed, and no one would have taken him for the commander of all the armies of the United States." Meade wore plain clothes, too, and glasses that gave him the appearance of "an old college professor."[62] Grant and Meade's arrival at the Boydton Plank Road brought with it a drizzling rain.[63] The gathering of officers, numbering upward of one hundred, crowded around the oak. To the north, past the Burgess Farm and across Hatcher's Run, they could discern an unlimbered rebel battery on the distant bank. Unfortunately, the rebel gunners enjoyed a reciprocal view. Before long, their cannon opened fire on the conspicuous gathering. One shell "almost took off several heads," recalled Thomas Livermore of Hancock's staff, "including that of General John Rawlins [one of Grant's aides] and myself, for we all sat on a fence flank to the enemy, and the shot whistled so close to us as to make the others cry out a caution to us."[64] In the wake of that close call, Livermore received an order to ride to Egan and direct him to silence the annoying battery. With much of the army's high command watching, Livermore mounted his horse and galloped along the Plank Road in clear view of the distant gunners. Framed by the road's rail fences, the solitary horseman offered a tempting target, and the Confederate rounds soon "flew along the road as if it was their natural path,"[65] but Livermore managed to avoid injury. As he delivered the order to Egan, a shell passed directly under his horse and ricocheted harmlessly away. Unscathed, Livermore rode swiftly back to the oak tree.

"cheering the men"

At the Burgess Farm, Egan's three brigades formed a crescent, with Rugg's brigade on the left (west of the Plank Road), Willett's unit at the center near the Burgess house, and Thomas Smyth's command on the right. Butler Beck's twelve-pound guns offered support, with one section, under Richard Metcalf, deployed back in the cornfield south of the narrow swamp, another on the Burgess Farm plateau near a large barn, and the third back near the oak tree at Hancock's headquarters.[66] The rebel artillery across Hatcher's Run (most likely Edward Graham's battery) and west in the woods along the White Oak Road (Hart's guns) shelled Egan's position and sparred with Beck's gunners.[67]

Oddly, James Dearing's cavalry continued to hug the works on the northern rim of the Burgess Farm, with their backs to Hatcher's Run. Hoping to regain the Burgess property and with it the White Oak Road intersection, Dearing conducted an early afternoon attack with the 7th Confederate Cavalry Regiment in the lead. Discarding the cover of the slope, the rebels gave a yell and charged up the hill with "a perfect rush."[68] In the process, the regiment's colonel, Valentine H. Taliaferro, received a "painful though, not serious, contused wound." Dearing's charge swept bluecoats through the Burgess orchard and flushed others from Burgess Tavern, though some Federals remained on the second floor.[69] Many federals rushed "pell mell" in full retreat, exposing Beck's battery on the hillcrest near the barn. A soldier from the 14th Connecticut in Smyth's brigade, who was nearly captured, recalled that a "rifle ball cut the strap of my knapsack clean off my shoulder and went through my rubber blanket. The knapsack, lurching over to one side, nearly threw me down."[70]

A squad of cavalry supported Beck's gun section behind the barn. According to a Union infantryman nearby, the horsemen held little interest in tangling with Dearing's attack. When their commander cajoled them into emerging from behind the barn, the squad refused to form a skirmish line and eventually crowded together "like a flock of scared sheep with wolves on all sides." The officer in charge, who seemed just as reluctant to stand there as his men, ordered them to "hold the line firm" and then promptly galloped to the rear. When one man received "a slight wound," the entire group broke off to escort him to safety, "and the cavalrymen appeared no more at the front."[71]

Seeing the federal artillery thus exposed, Dearing ordered his entire brigade to advance.[72] But Butler Beck's guns sprayed canister into the oncoming wave, and Egan's men stepped forward to meet the charging Confederates.[73] Thomas Smyth led the infantry effort. An Irish native and Wilmington, Delaware, resident, Smyth's mind was well stored "with history, philosophy, and poetry."[74] He also possessed fighting qualities. Leading from the front with the help of his staff, he rushed the 1st Delaware and the 108th New York forward while holding the 12th New Jersey and the 69th New York in reserve. "We were moved at double-quick for a little way,"

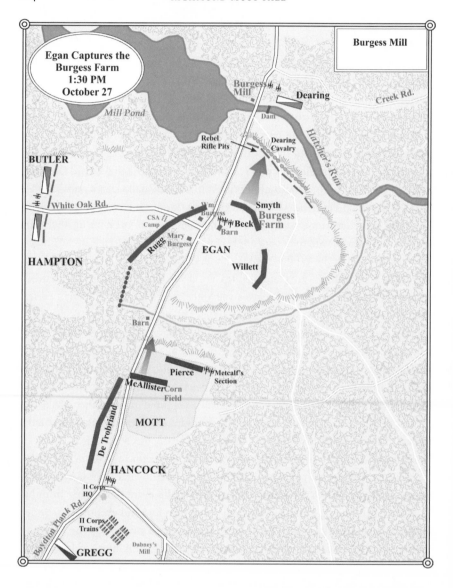

a member of the brigade recalled, "when we saw the Johnnies forming behind a house and barn pretty close to our battery."[75] Smyth also took charge of some of Willett's regiments and ordered the better part of the two brigades forward.[76]

Smyth's men rolled forward in two heavy lines, overlapping Dearing's relatively meager force. Overwhelmed, the Confederates withdrew "sullenly and slowly," firing as they went.[77] Smyth drove on and scattered the rebels over Hatcher's Run and onto the wooded hill beyond.[78] According to one cavalryman in the 8th Georgia, most of his regiment's casualties for the entire day were incurred during the retreat across the bridge.[79] General Smyth himself "dashed into the creek, waving his hat in his hand, and cheering the men on by his example."[80] The Unionists seized the rifle pits on the brow of the hill on the south bank.[81] Some enthusiastic members of the 1st Delaware and 108th New York even ventured across the run but soon found the position untenable. In addition, aggressive souls from the 108th New York reportedly "captured a gun, limber, and caisson from a battery near the bridge on Hatcher's Run" and, lacking hauling ropes, destroyed the weapon and limber and brought back the caisson.[82] Dearing's men had fought hard all morning, but their plucky counterattack had folded under the sheer weight of Egan's division. Dearing's efforts won "golden opinions" from Heth's infantry, who arrived just as the charge was made.[83] But the Confederates could only watch from the north bank as Egan consolidated his force and improved his hold on the Burgess Farm.

"I suppose I ought not to have gone down there"

Back at the oak tree, Grant and Meade considered the next steps. To gain a better view of conditions at the front, the two generals, with some staff officers, ventured into the open, drawing the attention of enemy artillery once again. Soon "the whistling of projectiles and the explosion of shells made the position rather uncomfortable." The barrage killed an orderly and severely wounded others.[84] One missile nearly killed General Meade, and "a little speck of blood appeared on Hancock's cheek after the bursting of a shell."[85] Meade sugar-coated the episode for his wife later, saying, perhaps incorrectly, "Both Grant and myself were under a heavy artillery fire, but luckily neither of our large corteges were touched."[86] As the entourage endured the artillery shells, several of Grant's staffers inched toward the run to gather information, and Hancock himself reported what he had seen there.

Concerned that a strong Confederate force would threaten any advance on the White Oak Road toward the South Side Railroad, Grant desired more than secondhand reports and sought to examine the ground at Burgess Mill personally. He requested the company of his aide-de-camp, Orville E. Babcock, and directed the rest of the party to stay behind. The two galloped on the Plank Road, past Egan, and to within several yards of the bridge at Hatcher's Run, exposed to sharpshooter and artillery fire from the opposite bank.[87] Severed telegraph wires littered the road in a tangled mass. Grant's horse, distressed by the shells and balls zipping through the air, became ensnared, and strained to pull away, only tightening the coil. With their commander in a tight spot, Union officers to the rear watched with increasing anxiety. But Babcock coolly dismounted and untangled the horse, while Grant sat calmly in the saddle admonishing his aide to avoid hurting the animal's leg. The two pushed even closer to the bridge, where Grant noted the dense brush on the banks, the trees slashed by the rebels, and the dams blocking the run.[88] He then turned "slowly back as unperturbed as a man could be." When he reached his fretful staff, he responded to their protests with a smile, saying, "Well, I suppose I ought not to have gone down there."[89] Thomas Livermore, the Hancock aide who ran the gauntlet earlier, noted that Grant had "exposed his own life . . . to find out with his own eyes whether our men were being killed to no purpose."[90]

Grant's personal reconnaissance provided information that helped him determine the fate of the entire offensive. First, it showed that the Confederates maintained a strong force north of Hatcher's Run that would threaten Hancock's communication should the Second Corps continue its march west. Second, it revealed that, contrary to previous assumptions, the new Confederate line terminated well downstream and southeast of Burgess Mill, a configuration that would hamper a successful connection between Hancock and Warren.[91] The position of the line also allowed Confederates to fend off the Fifth and Ninth Corps and concentrate on Hancock's column. According to a Hancock staffer nearby, Grant seemed "rather disgusted to find what a stubborn resistance we were meeting."[92] His military secretary, Adam Badeau, later described the general's thinking:

> The rebel position could perhaps be carried, but only with extreme difficulty and loss of life; a loss which the advantage to be gained would not compensate; while in the event of repulse, disaster might be grave, stretched out as the army was, with its flanks six miles apart, and the creek dividing Warren's corps. Any serious rebuff or loss was especially to be deprecated at this crisis; the Presidential elections was only ten days off, and the enemies of the nation at the North were certain to exaggerate every mishap. Success at the polls was just now even more important than victory in the field, and it would have been most unwise to risk greatly on this occasion.[93]

Grant abandoned hope of reaching the South Side Railroad and ordered Hancock to halt the advance. With this decision, the Union offensive ended for all practical purposes. By 2:30 P.M., the generals and staff returned to the oak tree to discuss matters further.[94] Grant chose to keep the Second Corps in its position until the next morning and prepared to return to Armstrong's Mill, while Hancock's men remained at the Burgess Farm.[95] Hancock hoped to seize the bridge at Burgess Mill to secure the north bank and protect his position on the Boydton Plank Road. But he made no plans for further major operations.[96] Still, for reasons unknown, the Second Corps did not begin to throw up works systematically along its position.

While the generals gathered and discussed, curious Second Corps soldiers observed the deliberations. A Michigan color sergeant noted that the commanders "are having gay times, and talk and laugh as though nothing was going to happen."[97] But another observer strolled over and noted that there "was high tension easily to be seen." General Grant sat on a rock near the oak, smoking his ubiquitous cigar, deliberately raising it "to his lips, taking a puff or several, then lowering it while he said something." As he returned the cigar to his mouth, a shell screamed through the sky, exploding in the tree top overhead. The trooper noted that the "General's hand never faltered, but reached his face and he took his puff leisurely." Grant then delivered an inaudible word to his officers, mounted his horse, and trotted east with this staff toward Armstrong's Mill. Soon after their departure, another artillery shell landed on the spot occupied by the group only a minute before.[98]

It was about 3 P.M.[99] With unconfirmed reports that the Second and Fifth Corps had forged a connection south of Hatcher's Run, Grant's party picked a wood road on the field's east side for their return; it was probably the path Roebling and Bingham had used earlier to reach Crawford's division. But Grant's group soon discovered a problem. The road, which held no U.S. troops, led into a perfect wilderness. To avoid unnecessary risks, the group wisely reversed its course, much to Grant's annoyance. The officers searched for a direct path to the Dabney Mill Road, but none was found. So they doubled back to Hancock's field and headed back using the more familiar Dabney Mill Road. Hancock's force remained at the Burgess Farm to rest, consolidate, and prepare for withdrawal in the morning.[100]

CHAPTER 14

Crawford at Hatcher's Run

∼

"heavy galling volley"

Several miles east of the Burgess Farm, the afternoon near the Clements house had settled into a wet, uncomfortable calm. Parke and Warren arranged their two corps in a continuous line to guard against Confederate counterattacks. In the Ninth Corps sector to the north, Potter's division anchored the right flank, with Ferrero's USCTs in the center, and Orlando Willcox's brigades dug in north of the Clements house. The men felled timber for several dozen yards in their front with the tree tops pointed toward the enemy and, as one Wisconsin soldier described, "the boughs 'so intimately connected' as to form 'a slashing,' the most adventurous Johnny would hardly care to endeavor to penetrate, at least with hostile intention."[1] On Willcox's left, the Fifth Corps held the line, with Griffin's men entrenched along the front south to Hatcher's Run. Romeyn Ayres's division, also from the Fifth Corps, remained in reserve behind Griffin.

For the green New York regiments in Griffin's division, the day had been unpleasantly eventful. Undrilled and untested, the rookies faltered in the initial morning attack and tumbled backward, leaving wounded comrades in their wake. However, the regiments regrouped and began constructing temporary works from old logs and dirt in a dense strip of timber. As the units girded their line, the wounded suffered in the woods to the front, directing their cries of help back to their comrades. When an officer in the 187th New York solicited volunteers to rescue the stricken men, about thirty soldiers stepped forward. John Haskin, whose son Monroe lay somewhere in the woods, sought to join the party. However, as he climbed over the new breastworks, his regiment's commander, Lieutenant Colonel Daniel Myers, ordered him back, explaining that the mission required younger men. Haskin, desperate to find his son, tried a second time, but Myers repeated his instruction. The relief squad crept forward without Myers and soon met a "heavy galling volley of musketry." Most of these New Yorkers scrambled back to safety. But four of them, Lieutenant Richard Shannon of Company G, the diminutive Charles A. Orr, the large John Williams, and another man, remained in the timber

228

searching for their wounded friends. Orr and Williams sifted through the woods in front, picking through the brush and downed trees. Each time the group bore back an injured comrade, John Haskin asked for any news of his son. Each time the answer was no. The party kept at their task for an hour or two, rescuing several New Yorkers as well as members of the 155th Pennsylvania. The brave effort would later earn the Medal of Honor for Charles Orr.[2] Eventually, John Haskin's missing son was found alive; he continued to serve in the regiment.[3] Except for the sporadic firing and scattered heroics, little occurred along the Boydton Plank Road line the rest of the day. With the federal units earnestly entrenching, there would be no more attempts to pierce the abatis and gain the rebel earthworks.

"almost impossible to proceed"

With Hancock's force halted to the southwest at Burgess Mill, most of the Ninth and Fifth Corps remained north of Hatcher's Run doing next to nothing. To form a connection, Meade and Grant had dispatched a single division, led by Brigadier General Samuel Crawford into the space between the two formations. Crawford's command had joined the Fifth Corps procession earlier that morning. But around 11 A.M., one of Warren's aides directed Crawford onto the Duncan Road and south toward Hatcher's Run. Shortly afterward, Washington Roebling escorted him across the stream at Armstrong's Mill.[4] To augment Crawford's two brigades (a third brigade of his remained in the trenches on October 27), Warren ordered the Maryland brigade, led by Colonel Andrew W. Denison, from General Ayres's division, and an artillery battery to join the movement.

Crawford's mission was complicated. As he recalled, Roebling directed him to "advance up [the] right bank, my right resting upon it, and guided by it. My orders were to advance and connect with the left of First [Griffin's] Division."[5] If possible, Crawford was expected to ascend the right bank of Hatcher's Run, bypass the rebel earthworks on the north side, cross over to the left bank, and attack the enemy position there from the rear. By prying the defenders from Griffin's front, Crawford would clear the way for the Fifth and Ninth Corps and compromise the Confederate position at Burgess Mill. If successful, Crawford's action would free Hancock to march toward the South Side Railroad, a possibility that was still open when Crawford began his move.

The scheme tasked Crawford with two goals, to support Hancock and to threaten the enemy's flank. The Union high command seemed to believe that he could accomplish both at the same time. Unfortunately, no one, including Roebling, seemed to have actually reconnoitered the stream's south bank for any significant distance. And no one seemed to realize that the terrain gave life to a deciduous jungle, crowded with tree branches, choked with dense undergrowth,

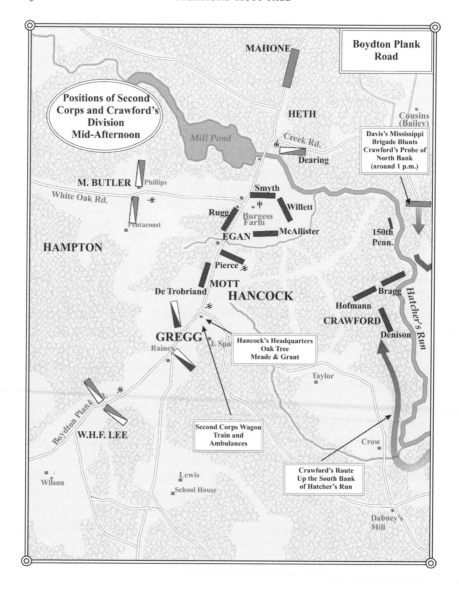

and checkered by swampy ground. It was the kind of region that could swallow whole commands. Crawford's column crossed Hatcher's Run at Armstrong's Mill shortly before noon and shunted off into the thick woods on the right.

Samuel Crawford had experienced much of the war and this seasoning generally served his men well. One soldier described him as a "chesty, glowering man, with heavy eyes, a big nose, and bushy whiskers; and he wore habitually a turn-out-the-guard expression, which was . . . fairly indicative of his military character."[6] He was no army luminary though. Some Fifth Corps officers took a dim view of his martial qualities. Joshua Chamberlain, one of the heroes of Gettysburg, described him as "not of the iron fiber, nor spring of steel" but a conscientious officer who obeyed orders in a literal fashion to avoid criticism.[7]

With preliminary instructions in hand, he prepared to shepherd his division through the tangled confines south of Hatcher's Run. Washington Roebling recommended a two-brigade front to ensure a connection with Hancock.[8] Rejecting this advice, Crawford formed his three brigades one behind the other, with Brigadier General Edward Bragg's "Iron Brigade" in front, Colonel William Hofmann's brigade second, and the Maryland brigade in the rear.[9] The formation proceeded with a double skirmish line in the head of Bragg's brigade.[10] Hofman deployed the 147th New York as flankers off to the left. As Crawford prepared to embark, Warren arrived and reiterated the directive to turn the rebel works facing Griffin.[11] Because no one knew what lay in Crawford's path, it was an occasion for careful, calculated movement; it was no time to march blindly into trouble.

But Crawford's men did blunder ahead. There was no helping it. As the division stepped off the road, it entered a bewildering mass of vegetation on the stream's south bank, an impossible array of briars, saplings, scrub pines, and weeds. With leaves crunching and twigs crackling underfoot, the men struggled to maintain contact with nearby comrades unseen in the undergrowth. Though Crawford and his superiors had expected steady, rapid progress, Hatcher's Run had a surprise for them. Less than a mile from Armstrong's Mill, the stream swerved sharply north, nearly bending back on itself for a few hundred yards. Crawford's formation, its right flank touching the stream bank, headed directly toward this severe twist. Though such topographical challenges were commonplace in Virginia's unfamiliar, densely wooded, and poorly mapped regions, the stream's crooked shape would cause more than routine mischief for Crawford's mission.[12]

Along Hatcher's Run, Crawford's division struggled through the undergrowth. Grasping his difficult task, Warren ordered Charles Griffin to open fire at 1 P.M. from his skirmish line to guide movements south of the run.[13] No audible signal could help Crawford, though. As he later explained, "The advance was attended with great difficulty. So thick were the woods and so tangled the undergrowth, that it was almost impossible to proceed, and it was only practicable by using the compass."[14] O. B. Curtis, a historian of the 24th Michigan, recalled that Bragg's Iron Brigade "marched about three miles up hill and down hill, by the right flank and by the left flank, but actually advanced only about half that distance."[15]

It did not take long for the large bend in the run to complicate matters. As Crawford's division stumbled west, the severe turn caused confusion for the officers. To make matters worse, a small branch, flowing west to east, emptied into the run at the great bend. In the dark, wet undergrowth, the men guiding Bragg's right flank mistook this tributary for Hatcher's Run. The deception was complete. The entire brigade missed the northward turn and sailed due west guided by the minor rivulet.[16] Bragg's formation drifted along on this tack for quite some time until a staffer found the column, halted it, wheeled the line, and guided it north over the small branch. Another officer rode up and expressed astonishment that the men had "taken a little Spring ditch for Hatcher's Run."[17]

Not everyone lost his way. Most of the regiments in Hofmann's brigade, coming up behind Bragg, avoided the mistake and wheeled at the bend, proceeding north along Hatcher's Run. However, the 147th New York, deployed as Hofmann's flankers on the left, lost touch with its sister regiments and continued west through the forest, finding itself thoroughly lost and out of action for the balance of the day.[18] The rest of Hofmann's brigade stayed on course and soon found the ground north along Hatcher's Run even more difficult. Hofmann, ignorant of Bragg's whereabouts, obtained permission from Crawford to move "by the right flank" along the bank in a narrow column instead of a wide battle line. After pushing along for almost a mile, he began to entertain "serious doubts" as to whether Bragg's men were still in his front.[19] His concerns were well founded. His scouts found no sign of the Iron Brigade out ahead. Indeed, it was well behind, floundering along the branch its officers had mistaken for Hatcher's Run.

Hofmann found himself at the point of Crawford's advance, stumbling blindly in column with few men out ahead. Sensing the danger, he deployed skirmishers and brought his brigade out of its vulnerable column formation. After advancing in this fashion for about two hundred yards, he encountered rebel skirmishers. The Confederates opened fire but quickly scampered across Hatcher's Run. As Hofmann tangled with Confederate pickets, Bragg's brigade recovered the ground lost by the faulty navigation. Facing north, the regiments traversed the cultivated fields of the Crow Farm and reentered the woods. There, Bragg encountered the rear of Hofmann's line. One of his aides directed Hofmann to pull back five hundred yards and fall in line with the Iron Brigade.[20]

Crawford's line soon reached a point opposite Griffin's flank across the run. Not far ahead on the north bank loomed the fresh Confederate works. Crawford "detached a regiment to examine the right bank of the creek . . . and to feel the enemy's works."[21] This regiment, unnamed in Crawford's battle report, attacked the end of the rebel defenses on the north side of the run, driving the enemy away. The Confederates manning the works, however, "immediately re-enforced it by a line of battle."[22] Apparently, the rebel reinforcements brought a halt to the Union regiment's attack. Hofmann's brigade, which had withdrawn behind Bragg earlier, now stepped back and began to dig in.[23]

Crawford's report offers a surprisingly brief account of this important event. For a short time, the Union forces had pushed the Confederates out of the extreme end of the Boydton Plank line, perhaps the key to the entire Confederate position. Though Crawford did not dwell on this event, the Confederate defenders recalled it as a time of extreme danger. In particular, Joseph Davis's Mississippians fended off

this Union attack on Heth's earthworks. By afternoon, Heth had successfully reinforced Hampton's dismounted cavalry and filled the trenches east of the Plank Road
with veteran infantry brigades. Brigadier General John R. Cooke's North Carolinians and Davis's Mississippians manned the lower end of the trenches.[24] Davis, a
nephew of the Confederate president and "a very pleasant and unpretending gentleman,"[25] had led his Mississippians at Gettysburg and throughout the brutal Virginia
campaigns of 1864. That fall, his force contained four Mississippi regiments, the 1st
Confederate battalion, and the 55th North Carolina. An inspection at the end of
September identified 988 men and 84 officers present for duty.[26]

By early afternoon, Davis's brigade manned the tip of Heth's line, the spot where
the works touched the north bank of Hatcher's Run. At 1 P.M., men in Davis's brigade heard gunfire to the right. Some of this racket may have come from Griffin's rifles giving the signal directed earlier by Warren. But there was more to the
commotion. A Union force, most likely the regiment dispatched by Crawford, had
crossed the run and made its way behind the trenches. A lieutenant in the 2nd
Mississippi, commanding the skirmishers, reported to Davis, "General they have
broken our line and my command has been forced to retreat."[27] The "enemy had
pierced our lines," confirmed Charles Jones, a North Carolinian in Davis's brigade,
"forcing back the men they did not kill, wound or capture, and were thus enabled
to get completely in the rear of the line we were holding, and enfilading it at plea-
sure." "Now ensued a scene," wrote Jones, "when stout hearts almost faltered."[28]

With Unionists free in the rear of the trenches, General Davis directed Colonel
John M. Stone to lead three regiments of the brigade and repel the attackers by
wheeling his command "perpendicular to the trench line" and driving the enemy
back across the run. The column filed off to the right and rear and, after advancing
about two hundred yards, halted and formed a single rank. Some of the men, taking
advantage of a slight delay, stacked tree limbs to form a meager cover. The unseen
attacking force sent bullets zipping through the air.[29] The two hundred or so Tar
Heels in the 55th North Carolina took their places on the left of this formation.[30]

Pacing along his battle line, Colonel Stone reportedly murmured, "We are going to advance and I expect will be cut to pieces"[31] His men navigated fifty yards
of dense undergrowth and soon halted to reform. After resuming their advance,
they overtook their own skirmishers and then unleashed a volley into the trees
ahead. As Charles Jones led his two North Carolina companies forward, a Union
sharpshooter, secreted behind a pine tree sixty-five yards away, aimed and fired
at him. The deadly messenger missed his ear by three inches and penetrated the
forehead of his friend, Private B. G. Mason.[32] But Stone's temporary command,
fighting with resolve, drove the Unionists back across Hatcher's Run "in great
disorder and confusion," ending the federal threat to Heth's works.[33]

"The lower end of it was vacated"

On the south bank of the run, Crawford continued to advance his units. In the midst of this effort, General Warren arrived to discuss matters. "I was just where he wanted me," recalled Crawford, "I should not make any further attack or advance until I received further orders."[34] Warren found Crawford's line "just then on the right flank of the enemy's position fronting Griffin" and the firing "quite lively." Warren chose not to order any strong push forward. He explained in his report, "The crossing of the run was here very difficult naturally, and made more so by the trees cut into it, and by the opposition of the enemy. As Crawford's line of march had now led him to quite a different position from what had been expected, and as he was in a dense forest of great extent, where it was difficult to find him, and as his men were getting lost in great numbers, in fact, whole regiments losing all idea of where to find the rest of the division, I ordered him to halt his line and get it in good order and press the enemy with his skirmishers."[35]

The decision reflected Warren's sound thinking. The situation before him presented many uncertainties. It was growing late. Men were getting lost. The terrain was impossibly difficult. It was not the time to take chances. Certainly, he made a reasonable choice given the facts available, one that many would have reached under the circumstances. But, in doing so, he may have missed an opportunity.

After 3 P.M., Washington Roebling, back from his visit to the Burgess Farm, examined Crawford's position. His day of rambling touched many key locations: the Clements house, Armstrong's Mill, Dabney's Mill, and the Burgess Farm. Apparently, Roebling, who would survive the war to oversee construction of the Brooklyn Bridge, frequently conducted such treks. According to Colonel Lyman, Roebling, with his light hair and blue eyes, had a "countenance as if all the world were an empty show" and a proclivity for "poking about in the most dangerous places."[36] In a letter home that month, Lyman had noted that Roebling, "stoops a good deal, when riding has the stirrups so long that the tips of his toes can just touch them, and, as he wears no boots, the bottoms of his pantaloons are always torn and ragged."[37]

Roebling ventured forward to Bragg's skirmishers and found them anchored on Hatcher's Run directly across from the rebel trenches. He saw no rebel troops there. "The lower end of the line was vacated," as he later reported. But, as he observed the scene, a small squad of Confederates appeared and fired from across the stream, killing his orderly and forcing Roebling himself to hurry downstream to safety. There, he located the end of Griffin's skirmish line on the opposite bank, thus confirming that Crawford's division had formed the necessary connection. On his side of the run, he discovered a wayward group from Griffin's division and urged them to inform their commander about the rebel works ripe for the taking. He then located Crawford and asked why the general "had halted at the very moment when he had victory in his grasp."[38] Crawford replied that he had "positive orders from General Warren not to advance another step." Soon after, a Captain Dailey joined the discussion,[39] and he "begged hard to be allowed to cross the creek with fifty men and clear out the line of breast-works."[40]

Despite the earlier combat in the vicinity, the Confederates had left this key position unmanned or at least thinly guarded. Its capture would expose the entire rebel line and open a direct path for Griffin's division toward Burgess Mill. Though evening approached, even a partial Union lodgment might create opportunities for the following day. On the other hand, the rebels had resisted the earlier probes here, and the opportunity sensed by Roebling might have already slipped away. It was rainy. The terrain was confusing. The enemy line could be bristling with muskets. Though he might have weighed these competing factors, in the end, he believed his duty was clear. He had firm orders from his commander to cease further attacks, and saw no need for equivocation. He refused Dailey's request. No attack would occur.

Roebling departed to locate General Warren.[41] Eventually, he found the general at Dabney's Mill and explained the situation on Crawford's front. Warren agreed with Roebling and sent him back to Crawford with orders to "take possession of the breast-works if he could cross the creek." However, when Roebling returned to Crawford at about 4:45 P.M., a new development dampened his ardor for an attack. Rebel stragglers had appeared to the left and rear of Crawford's position. Some of them reported that an entire Confederate division lurked in the woods to the southwest. Crawford changed Holman's front to protect against this contingency. Roebling and Crawford "concluded it would not be advisable to make the attack under the circumstances."[42]

"So many different moves I cant recollect"

As Warren, Crawford, and Roebling wrestled with these decisions, many of Crawford's men endured a bewildering afternoon. "We marched all the time, first by the flank, then in line &c.," recorded William Ray of the 7th Wisconsin in his diary. "So many different moves I cant recollect, with skirmishing first to our right, then front, then to the left & sometimes in our rear &c."[43] As the afternoon wore on, the federals found the woods teeming with Confederates. Soldiers from both sides lost their way in the heavy timber and became prisoners, but, within minutes, many would duck away from their captors and stumble back to their own units.

Sergeant Robert Gibbons, from the 24th Michigan, ventured out beyond Bragg's battle line and encountered a small Confederate squad. With no weapon save his wits and words, he captured the rebels, convincing them to go "where their safety and good feeding were assured." The squad's leader protested at first and threatened to blow the loquacious Yankee's head off, but Gibbons eventually convinced the demoralized rebels to give up. The mixed group remained lost in the forest, however.

Eventually, Gibbons heard a loud "Baw-baw-baw" in the distance and recognized the call of Native American soldiers from one of the Iron Brigade's Wisconsin regiments. He led his prisoners into the skirmish line of the 7th Wisconsin.[44]

The 7th Wisconsin had wandered up the run with the rest of the Iron Brigade and, in the middle of the afternoon, had stopped to rest in the wet underbrush. "We were allowed to sit down, ly down &c.," William Ray wrote. "Some took off their knapsacks but few would venture so much. Some go to sleep some eat a hard tack &c."[45] As Ray and his comrades lounged uncomfortably in the damp, General Crawford walked by with two prisoners asking the rebels about the location of their units out in front. When pressed for an answer, one southerner replied, "Well Gen I don't know & if I did I wouldn't like to tell."[46] Shortly afterward, orders sent Ray's regiment forward into the woods to protect the brigade's flank.

The vexing terrain ultimately produced vague and contradictory accounts of the day's operations in Crawford's sector, making the time and location of troop movements difficult to decipher. At some point, Bragg deployed the 150th Pennsylvania, led by Major George W. Jones, in front as skirmishers. The Pennsylvanians drifted well ahead of the entire division where they met rebel pickets and came under "quite a heavy fire."[47] Eventually, the unit moved farther upstream and halted for more than an hour waiting for support. As it turned out, the 150th lost contact with Crawford's division entirely and took a position well upstream from the main battle line. So far upstream, in fact, that the regiment's members could see Confederate artillery parked in plain view on the opposite side of Hatcher's Run, well behind the rebel trenches. Near these guns, Confederate commissary officers stood beside tobacco wagons issuing rations. According to one account, the Confederates appeared oblivious to the presence of the Pennsylvanians.[48]

With no orders to withdraw, Major Jones stood his ground. Later, Bragg would boast that his skirmish line, presumably the 150th Pennsylvania, "advanced half a mile up the creek toward the plank road and in full view of the Confederate hospital."[49] During the afternoon, however, Bragg may not have known the regiment's location. In fact, Thomas Chamberlin, an officer with the 150th, recalled, "It was not known either at brigade or division headquarters whether the major and his Bucktails—when their absence was finally remarked—had not been 'gobbled up' bodily by the enemy, and much anxiety was felt for their safety."[50] The regiment formed a remote outpost, well beyond Bragg's control and well beyond the terminus of the Confederate works on the opposite bank. Jones, recognizing his regiment's vulnerability, remained in position but cautioned his men not to fire unless attacked.[51]

Jones dispatched Adjutant William Wright rearward to inform Bragg of the regiment's predicament.[52] Wright picked his way through a large swamp "full of tussocks" and interspersed with pools of deep water. After navigating this bog, his mission abruptly ended in the face of a pair of Confederate rifles. His captors led him around the swamp and to a road that crossed the run just upstream of his regiment's position. While on this track, the small party stumbled upon Colonel Henry Peyton, of Robert E. Lee's staff.[53] It was then that Wright learned that his captors were stragglers from a North Carolina regiment. Peyton questioned Wright in earnest, expressing surprise that a Fifth Corps officer was lurking so deep behind Confederate lines. Realizing that the Pennsylvanians were nearby, Peyton left the three and rode off to learn more about the Union regiment now lining the south bank of the run. A bemused Wright gazed on as Peyton "went directly to its rear, not very far from the line, and rode the full length of it. He was mounted on as pretty a bay horse as I ever saw, and was handsomely uniformed in gray, buttoned up to the neck, the buttons nearly as large as blacking-boxes. I expected him to be shot, every instant, but no doubt our men were so intently viewing the park of artillery, the tobacco train (it was 'Tobacco Day' with the 'rebs'), and the troops marching to the left on the other side of the run, that they did not look to the rear at all."[54] Peyton returned and handed Wright over to a Sergeant Pollard of Lee's headquarters guard. Wright's battle was over. As he trudged off into captivity, his regiment remained in its isolated position.

At Crawford's main battle line, Bragg's and Hofmann's brigades settled in. Whatever opportunities had existed to turn the Confederates trenches had faded away in the dense terrain. Crawford's efforts during the afternoon had amounted to little. In failing to either connect with Hancock or turn Heth out of his earthworks, he had become bogged down in the forests north of the Crow house. As his men remained in their dark, uncomfortable position, Fifth Corps staffers encountered troubles navigating the wilderness south of Hatcher's Run.

"Tenth Alabama"

George Dresser, Warren's artillery inspector, visited Crawford's front around 4 P.M. were he found plenty of soldiers resting in line but no suitable place for artillery. He turned back south toward the Crow house and Dabney's Mill. On his way, he crossed a trail recently churned up by a column of troops moving northwest to southeast. After traversing a small field, he encountered the "tail of a rebel column resting in the road, sitting down, arms in their hands and in good order." Assuming he had stumbled upon rebel prisoners, he asked, "To what regiment do you belong?" The men answered, "Tenth Alabama." Dresser then asked, "Where is your provost guard?" The Confederates replied, "None here; we are a brigade; Wilcox's old brigade." The group constituted at least two companies. The discovery must have been alarming for Dresser, for this rebel regiment belonged to the Alabama brigade of William Mahone's division. Dresser had found it just off the flank of Crawford's command south of Hatcher's Run.[55] He abruptly ended the interview and swerved his mount east toward the run and headed back upstream to Crawford to report his findings.[56]

CHAPTER 15

The Bull Pen

~

"As Soon as You Hear Our Guns"

Mary Burgess, safely removed from her battle-wrecked farm, resolved to reach
Petersburg, nearly seven miles away. With the children in tow, she and her
mother-in-law carried nothing save the bread and gold pieces salvaged from their
home. The bewildered party found the Boydton Plank Road filled with Confederate soldiers from Heth's and Mahone's commands rushing south toward the fight.
Despite their urgent mission, the Confederate infantrymen yielded the road to
the refugees. Some Mississippians, Alabamians, and Virginians broke ranks and
carried the baby to the rear of their column, allowing Burgess to rest her weary
arms. In one instance, an officer ordered an ambulance to convey the family to
the end of his column. Despite this aid, the journey soon exhausted the children.
The route passed few homes and, when the women found their way to the Venable house, they paused to rest. According to Mary Burgess, the dwelling was "at
one time a beautiful home . . . but . . . was now surrounded by soldiers, in and out
everywhere, more like a hive of bees than the abode of human beings."[1] As the
children lunched on bread, rain began to fall. Determined to reach Petersburg,
she called an end to the respite and resumed their journey.

While Mary Burgess headed for safety, William Mahone hurried his brigades
to the battle. Riding ahead of his troops, Mahone reached Battery 45 on the cor-
don of trenches ringing Petersburg. From there, he could hear gunfire to the
southwest. Leaving a courier at the fortifications with instructions for his command, he galloped down the Plank Road. Along the way to Burgess Mill, Mahone
encountered wagons from Dearing's cavalry heading away from the battlefield
and learned that Union troops had reached the Burgess Farm. After traveling a
few miles, he met Henry Heth and his staff resting by the side of the Plank Road.
Mahone reined his mare in and asked Heth what was happening. Heth said, "Dismount. Let's talk over the matter." But, by his own recollection, Mahone replied,
"No, we will ride and talk."[2]

Heth had survived a challenging morning, ably juggling his limited troops, shuttling infantry brigades here, and shifting dismounted cavalry squads there. He had managed to patch together a sound defense. The Boydton Plank trench line, first manned by Dearing's cavalry and then by infantrymen, had held against all comers. About 2 P.M., Heth received a message from A. P. Hill that Mahone was on his way with three infantry brigades.[3] Though Hampton's men formed only a thin screen against the federal offensive, Heth's force, gathering at Burgess Mill, blocked further progress by Hancock. In fact, the Confederates confronted Hancock on three sides at the Burgess Farm, with Heth's artillery and Dearing's cavalry at Burgess Mill, Butler's cavalry division west on the White Oak Road, and, finally, Rooney Lee's cavalry southwest on the Boydton Plank Road near the Wilson Farm.[4] As a result, the Confederates nearly surrounded the Union Second Corps, wedging Hancock's force into a vise, albeit a weak one.

True to form, the Confederate commanders did not sit and watch the Union attackers operate unmolested; as was their custom, they arranged counterstrike.[5] "About a quarter of a mile from the point where the right of our works rested on Hatcher's Run and in the direction of Burgess' Mill," wrote Heth, "Maj. Gen. Hampton had constructed a dam across the stream. Leading from the dam a blind path, or abandoned road, ran diagonally through dense woods, intersecting the Boydton Plank Road about ½ a mile west of Burgess Mill."[6] During the fall, Heth had traversed this path on several occasions, examining the ground south of Hatcher's Run. The remote trail continued southwest and emptied into the Burgess cornfield just north of the Dabney Mill Road. On its way, it passed through the woods between Hancock's and Crawford's positions. A Confederate column pushing along this road would strike deep into the heart of Hancock's position.

A plan emerged. However, the architects later disagreed on its author. Wade Hampton, in his official report, wrote that he "advised General Heth to attack by throwing a force across the dam at my works, and he sent me word that he would do so."[7] William Mahone, writing decades later, remembered things a little differently. Upon meeting Heth on the Plank Road, he recalled riding to Burgess Mill, where the two found James Dearing on the run's north bank. An impromptu conference followed. Mahone listened to his fellow commanders and then interrupted to ask Dearing about conditions in front. Mahone then asked if the Burgess millpond could be crossed. It could, Dearing explained, but such a move would consume two miles of marching to the west. Mahone recalled, "I then desired to know if there was any way to cross the mill-race, which had been dammed up, and quickly came the reply from both General Heth and himself that we could cross it on Hampton's dam against which General Heth's right abutted. I then said, 'General Dearing, we will cross on General Hampton's dam and get shortly behind whatever force there is in your front, and as soon as you hear our guns, press the enemy in your front and force a crossing.'"[8]

Mahone's official report is not extant, but an excerpt quoted by Heth in his own report, states, "A hasty survey of the situation led me [Mahone] to seek [the enemy's] rear from the concave side of his line, the most expedient means of disorganizing his plans."[9] So there it was. In Mahone's memory, he took charge that afternoon, making order out of chaos, providing much needed direction to fellow commanders who did not share his affinity for decisive action. One of his staffers shared this view of the events. In 1889, his former ordnance officer, Edward N. Thurston, recalled that Heth and Mahone held a roadside conference. Arriving after the discussion had ended, Thurston heard Mahone ask whether Hatcher's Run could be crossed for a strike against the enemy's flank.[10]

Mahone's account angered Heth. In his own official report, Heth explained that Mahone received orders to report to him with three brigades. In accordance with Heth's directive, Mahone had arrived on the field about 3 P.M. with two brigades just behind him and another, Harris's, delayed by its careful withdrawal from the trenches at Petersburg. In an unusually sharp tone, Heth directly challenged Mahone's statements: "General Mahone did not seek the enemy's rear from the concave side of his line as the most expedient mode of disorganizing his (the enemy's) plans, for the concave, or convexity of the enemy's lines were unknown to him, myself, or any one else at this time, the nature of the ground precluding the possibility of a reconnaissance. He sought the enemy in the way and manner he did by my order, passing over a road unknown to him until pointed out by myself."[11]

To Heth, the facts were clear. He was the Confederate commander in charge. He had identified the threat. And he made the decisive choice to attack the enemy and identified the route to be used.[12] As Heth's report suggests, Mahone, no stranger to bombast, probably exaggerated his role in the planning. However, considering all the accounts, some collaboration certainly enriched the decision making. As Heth recalled in his report, "A plan of attack [was] agreed upon."[13] And with it, the Confederates concentrated north of Burgess Mill and prepared to hurl Mahone's force at the Second Corps.

The plan sent the attacking column into the heart of an entire Union corps. Although bold, perhaps even reckless, it was utterly predictable for it matched a firm pattern followed by rebel commanders from the campaign's outset. Repeatedly at Petersburg, A. P. Hill's generals had thrown their men into the flank of Union columns that ventured out of the federal fortifications. Thus, Heth, Mahone, and Hampton showed little reluctance to detach three brigades and send them off on a path deep into enemy-infested ground. In fact, Heth concluded that the enemy (Parke) confronting the Boydton Plank Road line would "make no serious assault" and that the force downstream on Hatcher's Run (Crawford) was "quiet."[14] The plan also demonstrated that Heth and Mahone enjoyed the freedom to take tremendous risks even in the absence of their corps and army commanders. With Hill's chronic

illness and Lee's unending burdens north of the James, these officers had grown accustomed to coordinating operations on their own. Hill's generals had developed a
talent for finding the vulnerable seams, cutting into the flanks of advancing enemy
forces, and unleashing ferocious assaults. The Confederates stuck to this script at
the Jerusalem Plank Road in June, the Weldon Railroad in August, and the Squirrel
Level Road in September. This rainy Thursday in October was no different. Heth,
Hampton, and Mahone prepared to take the fight to the enemy.

"guard against any surprise"

As the Confederate leaders schemed, Winfield Hancock settled his command into
the fields south of Burgess Mill. His staff lounged near the massive oak on the
Plank Road, some reading or dozing on the wet grass. With Grant gone, Hancock
prepared to hold the position until morning. His corps, along with Gregg's cavalry, now filled the long tree-lined corridor stretching along the Plank Road from
Burgess Mill south to the Quaker Road. Apparently, the Second Corps soldiers
received no orders to entrench, an unusual omission at this stage of the war. Perhaps Hancock did not expect to remain at the Burgess Farm for long. Given the
condition of matters, such an expectation seemed reasonable. His corps' position
resembled an oblong box, with Gregg's cavalry at the south end, Mott's division
(with de Trobriand's and Pierce's brigades) in the middle, and Egan's division at
the north end.[15] Just southeast of the oak tree and off the Dabney Mill Road, a
mass of ambulances, held horses, and reserve artillery stood parked in a small
field.[16] Enemy troops threatened him on nearly all sides.

To the north, Thomas Egan kept his three brigades in a crescent hugging the
Burgess property. Horace Rugg's brigade covered the left, facing west toward the
White Oak Road. Thomas Smyth commanded the center, pointing north toward
Burgess Mill, and James Willett's brigade controlled the right. Smyth's men filled
the captured rebel rifle pits on the slope overlooking the stream.[17] These shallow
trenches, not more than three feet high, by one account, provided some cover
from rebel fire.[18] In addition to his own division, Egan enjoyed the services of
Robert McAllister's brigade, detached from Mott for the afternoon. On the Burgess Farm, McAllister formed his regiments to the rear and to the right of Thomas
Smyth's line.[19]

During the afternoon, members of Egan's division explored the Burgess Farm.
One young recruit from the 152nd New York of Rugg's brigade found himself on
his grandparents' property. The private, most likely Andrew W. Burgess of Water-
town, New York, wandered over to the house and "secured the family record, photographs, and a small powder horn of his own make."[20] Yet another member of

the extended Burgess family, Daniel Maynard Burgess, a surgeon on Grant's staff and a nephew of William Burgess, arrived on the field with the Union forces that afternoon. "I was under severe fire at this occurrence," he wrote, "and candidly admit that I did not relish the reception of my comrades and myself upon my visit to my uncle's home." He observed that his uncle's house lay directly between the two lines and became "riddled by gun fire."[21]

By three o'clock, Egan's artillery support was wearing out. The two sections of Lieutenant Butler Beck's battery stationed next to the Plank Road had dueled with Confederate gunners for several hours and exhausted all their ammunition, except for their canister rounds.[22] In Beck's estimation, his crews had bested their rebel counterparts. Such an observation was not unusual. Faulty fuses, bad powder, and limited equipment often reduced the effectiveness of the Confederate guns.[23] Lieutenant Beck could see the rebels' shots flying high and shells bursting well short. He attributed this poor performance to his own constant "vigorous fire." "I have the satisfaction of knowing that the enemy ceased firing first," he wrote in his report.[24]

Beck's crews did not pass through the combat unscathed, though. By mid-afternoon, they had lost three killed and seven wounded. To relieve Beck, Major John Hazard, commanding the Second Corps artillery, ordered up the six rifled Parrott guns of Lieutenant Henry Granger's 10th Massachusetts Battery.[25] Leaving their caissons behind near the Dabney Mill Road, the Bay Staters drove their teams along the Plank Road at a "lively trot." The guns and limbers soon became the target of rebel cannon, and shells crashed "through the trees and fence by the roadside."[26] Granger wheeled off the road and unlimbered his sections near the Burgess barn. The crews sprang to work, loading rounds, aiming the pieces over Hatcher's Run, and hurling three-inch shells toward the enemy. In a short time, the rebel guns across the stream fell silent, and Granger's rifles turned their attention to Hart's rebel battery eight hundred yards to the west along the White Oak Road.[27] With his infantrymen now well supported, Egan relieved Beck, sending the weary gunners and their smoothbore "Napoleon" guns trotting back down the Plank Road to replenish their limber chests.

Though Hancock's dispositions countered the visible enemy threats, to the east the fields of the Burgess Farm gave way to a vast expanse of forest spreading toward downstream sections of Hatcher's Run. Somewhere through those trees, Crawford's division struggled up the stream. The distance was not great. But through the woods, Crawford might as well have been miles away.

By all indications, Hancock's unsuccessful mission to the South Side Railroad had run its course. He had little to do but wait, hold the Boydton Plank Road until morning, and look after the safety of his command. A "handsome striking-looking man," Hancock possessed the qualities of a natural leader. He did not shrink from the responsibility of command. By one description, "authority was in his open face, which, when times were storming became the mirror of his bold heart."[28] On an open battlefield, he had presence unsurpassed in the army. According to his wartime aide and postwar biographer, Francis Walker, Hancock could lift his troops "to the level of his impetuous valor when his men could see him in open battle."[29] But where woods enveloped the fight and shrouded the enemy, he "was restless and shorn of much of his effectiveness" in Walker's view.[30] He was not a master tactician, and "topographic insight was not one of [his] strong points." According to Walker, the general possessed little of the "peculiar form of genius which enables some men, even in a strange country, to know intuitively the direction of roads, 'the lay of the land,' the course of streams, the trend of ranges."[31]

Although Hancock may have lacked a keen eye for terrain, he recognized the vulnerability of his position that afternoon. As long as he lacked a connection to Crawford, the woods to the east presented a source of danger. By mid-afternoon, only the two twelve-pound guns of Richard Metcalf's section stood in the Burgess cornfield.[32] Hancock realized the need for more protection at that tree line and ordered Gershom Mott to bolster the sector. In response, about 2:30 P.M., Mott released two regiments from Brigadier General Byron Pierce's brigade to Metcalf's support,[33] admonishing Pierce "to throw out pickets well into the woods to guard against any surprise in the quarter."[34] In turn, Pierce sent the 5th Michigan and the 93rd New York, both under the command of the battle-scarred veteran Colonel John Pulford, into the trees east of the cornfield. Pulford fanned the two regiments out, forming a thin screen.

As Pulford's skirmish line took shape, Mott dispatched the rest of Pierce's brigade in support. These regiments gathered in the cornfield and stood "ready for any emergency," soon attracting artillery fire from the enemy guns north of Hatcher's Run.[35] "It was curious to see the black projectiles evolving out of the murky sky," recalled a member of the 84th Pennsylvania who reclined in the cornfield, "and funny, too, to see the boys dance about in the mud to avoid them when they struck the ground in our midst."[36] Though the force contained many new recruits and few officers, the men in the cornfield "behaved most gallantly and acted like veterans" under the artillery fire, according to Mott.[37]

Along Hatcher's Run, the Confederates kept Egan's division busy. The rebel battery fire continued, hurling shells southward. Heth and Dearing also conducted several demonstrations against Egan's battle line throughout the afternoon—as many as four, according to a New Yorker from Willett's brigade. As the rain fell, the sounds of trains floated in from the South Side Railroad.[38] To ease the pressure on Egan, Hancock wanted to clear the annoying rebel cannon from the high ground north of the run.[39] In turn, Egan directed Thomas Smyth's brigade to lead an assault against that position, ordering Robert McAllister's brigade to join.

Granger's Massachusetts gunners, directed to furnish close support, rolled two of
their Parrott rifles down the hill in the face of heavy musketry and reached within
150 yards of the bridge.[40]

As he sought to bolster his position, Hancock also looked to connect with the
Fifth Corps. He dispatched First Lieutenant M. H. Stacey to inform Crawford of
the plans to take the north bank of Hatcher's Run.[41] Also concerned about a link
with Crawford, Egan instructed Smyth to stretch two regiments, the 10th New
York and 12th New Jersey, to the east.[42] The 10th New York extended well into the
trees, each man standing ten steps apart, but found no sign of Crawford's pickets
from the Fifth Corps.

"the glimmer of steel"

To the north, Henry Heth and William Mahone discussed the details of their
strike. In the midst of their scheming, however, troubling news arrived. Union
troops had appeared downstream on the right bank of Hatcher's Run. It was Crawford's division, clawing its way through the brambles and dense undergrowth.[43]
The unwelcome development complicated the Confederate plan because an
enemy force approaching from that direction could wreak havoc on Mahone's
flanking column. But the concern melted away as additional reports revealed that
Brigadier General Joseph Davis had fixed the problem. Davis "had anticipated the
orders necessary to be given," Heth wrote and checked the enemy "causing him to
commence fortifying."[44]

With Crawford halted, Heth and Mahone assigned three brigades to their
strike force: Brigadier General David Weisiger's Virginians and Colonel Horace
King's Alabamians (i.e., "Sanders's" brigade), both from Mahone's division, as well
as Brigadier General William MacRae's North Carolinians from Heth's division.
Alfred Scales's North Carolinians and Nathaniel Harris's Mississippians were also
expected, but neither command had arrived yet. Weisiger's and MacRae's men
briefly rested north of Burgess Mill, but after a few minutes, the two brigades
filed east onto the Creek Road, passing several pieces of artillery. They entered a
stand of pines and marched toward Hampton's dam downstream about a quarter
of a mile.[45] At the head of the column, Heth rode with Mahone, explaining that
the attack would occur from three sides: Mahone's infantry assault from the east,
Hampton's cavalrymen from the southwest and west, and James Dearing's horsemen and any available infantry from the north at Burgess Mill.[46]

Mahone's column turned off the Creek Road and reached Hampton's dam,
where the crossing "would admit only about two men going abreast." The three
brigades clambered over the run and up the south bank. To avoid unpleasant
surprises, Mahone planned to push out a strong skirmish line. Before barking

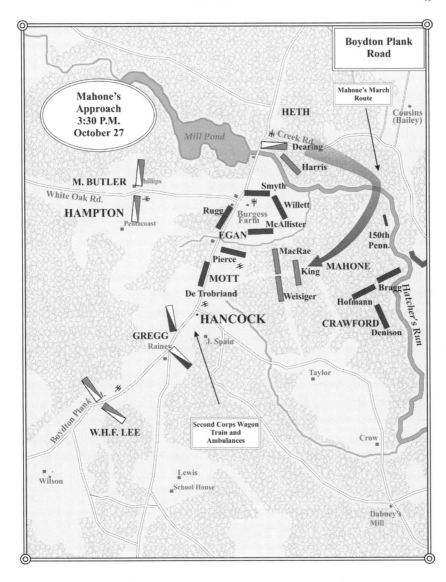

out orders, though, he checked with Heth to confirm who would lead the attack. As Mahone recalled, Heth replied, "I turn the command over to you," and then returned to Burgess Mill.[47]

According to Heth, though, an urgent message from James Dearing spurred his return. Dearing reported that "the enemy had driven him from the bridge" and "that all roads leading to the rear of [the] lines were open to his advance."[48] This was disturbing news, indeed. A Union lodgment on the north bank of Hatcher's Run would open the way to the South Side Railroad and bypass the trench line along the Plank Road. Though these thoughts must have clouded Heth's mind as he rushed back to the Burgess Mill, the concerns disappeared when he found that "the enemy had not, as yet, possession of the bridge and apparently was making no effort to cross Hatcher's Run in force."[49]

Though Heth found no enemy troops at Burgess Mill, he did not find many Confederates, either. For some reason, Dearing's battle line, along with Nathaniel Harris's recently-arrived Mississippi brigade, lay a "third or a half a mile" north of Hatcher's Run, leaving the lonely guns deployed at Burgess Mill. To remedy the problem, Heth immediately ordered the troops back. At around 3 P.M., he also directed Harris and his brigade to form on the bank with Dearing's brigade and attack when General Mahone became engaged.[50]

South of Hampton's dam, Mahone took charge, as his column tramped along the narrow wood path.[51] The Virginian ordered his skirmishers to fan out through the trees and, upon contact, engage the enemy in only "conversation" to give the full column time to prepare.[52] These skirmishers included the sharpshooters of William MacRae's brigade, joined perhaps by some of Weisiger's Virginians.[53] MacRae, an able leader, had created the sharpshooter battalion himself. Such detachments had become common in the Army of Northern Virginia by 1864. MacRae's sharpshooters, eighty picked men under Captain Thomas Lilly, wore gold crosses on their sleeves as they waded through the wet leaves and bushes searching for signs of the enemy.[54]

As Mahone's column moved forward, Thomas Smyth's brigade initiated the Union attack at Burgess Mill with the 14th Connecticut in the lead and the 164th New York from Willett's brigade close behind.[55] Sam Porter on Smyth's staff observed, "Genl Smyth and staff seemed liable to lose a few horses at least."[56] But just as these gears began to turn, curious developments transpired in the trees to Egan's right. The 10th New York and 12th New Jersey, both tasked with forging a connection to Crawford's Fifth Corps division, had found more than trees in the forest. East of the Burgess plateau, a company of New Yorkers, cautiously advancing through the boggy woods, "suddenly discovered the glimmer of steel ahead."[57] The men halted, and the company commander, Major Anthony Woods,[58] along with Adjutant Charles Cowtan, "advanced some rods with a squad of men, and discovered a strong column of the enemy marching quickly along a wood road directly towards the rear" of the Union position.[59] Alarmed, Cowtan hurried back and reported his findings to Egan and Smyth on the Burgess property.[60]

Egan ordered Cowtan to the woods to obtain a closer look. Cowtan plunged back into the forest, accompanied by Dugald Gilkson, a fellow New Yorker from Company D. The two crossed the road where the enemy had been seen and began to examine "the locality." They soon turned tail when a Confederate squad approached, but their flight was impeded by bulky overcoats, equipment, and heavy clothes still wet from their Cummings Ford crossing earlier that day. Their path collided with another group of rebels "busily engaged in rifling the knapsacks" of captured men. The Confederates raised their weapons, and bullets nipped the air. Cowtan and Gilkson swerved away and eventually returned to Egan to confirm the presence of a heavy enemy column between the Second Corps and Crawford's division.[61] Instead of finding Crawford, Egan's flankers had stumbled onto Mahone's attacking column. According to Sam Porter, the brigade commander reported these developments to headquarters.[62] But Egan's discovery would do little good, for events would soon overtake this news.

Mahone's three-brigade column crept quietly along the tree-covered track for a third of a mile before reaching a stand of large oaks.[63] There Mahone's aide Edward Thurston encountered members of Hampton's staff cut off in these woods earlier in the day.[64] At the head of the column, the Tar Heel sharpshooters caught glimpses of their Union counterparts in the thickets ahead.[65] Word of the contact passed to Mahone who ordered the men to form battle lines on both sides of the path. Officers deployed Weisiger's brigade in silence, using only hand signals to direct troops through the twisted young trees and bushes that crowded the ground ahead.[66] Officers warned that "the enemy were in the woods immediately in front . . . in close proximity."[67]

"deadly volley into our ranks"

Mahone's force headed straight for Byron Pierce's Union brigade posted in the Burgess cornfield. Pierce's regiments, guarding the two twelve-pound guns of Metcalf's 5th U.S. artillery section, stretched across the field, which was framed by the Plank Road on the west and a rail fence to the east.[68] At one point along this fence, a narrow path emerged from the gloom. Deep in the forest beyond, John Pulford pushed out three companies of the 5th Michigan to search for trouble.[69] Within minutes, they spied Mahone's sharpshooters darting through the trees. Bullets began to fly.[70] The sound of this skirmishing reached Pierce's ears at the cornfield,[71] but he dismissed it as "a few stragglers that General Crawford's pickets were driving."[72] Gershom Mott, Pierce's division commander, also heard the firing and ordered the picket line strengthened, a task assigned to the 1st U.S. Sharpshooters. As the sharpshooters hurried into position, the cadence of gunfire increased and Pierce augmented Pulford's screening force with the 105th Pennsylvania. Pierce had now piled four regiments into the woods. With his concern growing, he called on the balance of his brigade lying in the cornfield to turn east toward the escalating combat.[73] On Pulford's skirmish line in the woods, a Michigan veteran recalled that the pickets laughed and talked, not suspecting any danger lay ahead in trees. When a shot sounded from the woods, they assumed someone in front had discharged his gun "to reload again with a fresh cartridge." But they heard "pop, pop, pop" again and soon the pickets tumbled back toward

them followed by heavy rebel lines.[74] Men from the 93rd New York, aligned with
the 5th Michigan, soon found the Confederates advancing toward them "with a
quick but steady tread."[75]

Mahone's assault had arrived. He formed a two-brigade front with the fourteen
hundred men of MacRae's North Carolinians on the right and the Virginia brigade, about a thousand men, on the left. Deployed two rows deep, this battle line
probably stretched more than 2,000 feet wide. Mahone also massed the Alabama
brigade, an additional thousand rifles, in column of regiments behind the front.[76]
He spread a skirmish line on his left flank,[77] using sharpshooters who positioned
themselves at twenty-foot intervals.[78] As the Virginians and North Carolinians
fixed bayonets and dressed to the colors, Mahone rode along the ranks encouraging his men, urging them to hold their fire and rely on the bayonet. "In a minute
or two we were ordered forward," recalled George Bernard in the 12th Virginia,
"and came immediately upon the enemy's line of skirmishers, who were in the
woods not a hundred feet in front of us." The Virginians began to fire, and the
blue skirmishers retreated rapidly.[79] As the rebels stepped forward, Mahone's
ranks received a "fusillade from the enemy's repeating rifles," weapons carried by
members of the 5th Michigan and the 105th Pennsylvania.[80] The rebels pushed
the federals back, driving them to Pulford's main line. Some members of the 12th
Virginia retrieved Spencer repeating rifles discarded by the fallen and the frightened.[81] Others became scattered negotiating the thick undergrowth and lost sight
of comrades through the branches and leaves.[82] When the Confederates reached
Pulford's full line, the Federals greeted them with a volley.[83] The Virginians and
Carolinians returned the favor, though they could hardly see their targets in the
thick woods. But the rebels pressed on, stepping past wounded men in blue.

The full weight of Mahone's attack now hit Pulford's line near the edge of the
Burgess cornfield. In Mahone's way stood the 93th New York, 5th Michigan, and
105th Pennsylvania, along with the 1st U.S. Sharpshooters posted on the right
flank, its line bending back into the field.[84] The sharpshooters joined the other
units at the wood road, the axis of Mahone's attack. More of a light screen than a
heavy battle line, Pulford's force did not budge at first. It poured a volley into the
Confederates, forcing the rebels to halt and return fire. But the stand lasted only
about ten minutes by Pulford's estimate,[85] consuming five volleys, by one Union
officer's count.[86] Mahone's wide formation soon wrapped around Pulford's flanks.
MacRae's Carolinians swirled beyond the Union left, and Weisiger's Virginians
piled through the woods on the right, where the 1st U.S. Sharpshooters had formed
a weak hinge with its sister regiments. The Virginians burst through this seam,
reaching the flanks of the 5th Michigan and the 105th Pennsylvania and exposing
the Union ranks to a destructive enfilade fire.[87] "For a while we hold them," wrote
Daniel Crotty, a color bearer in the 5th Michigan, "but they are too many for us,
and charge right into our midst."[88] Crotty glanced back at the cornfield and saw no

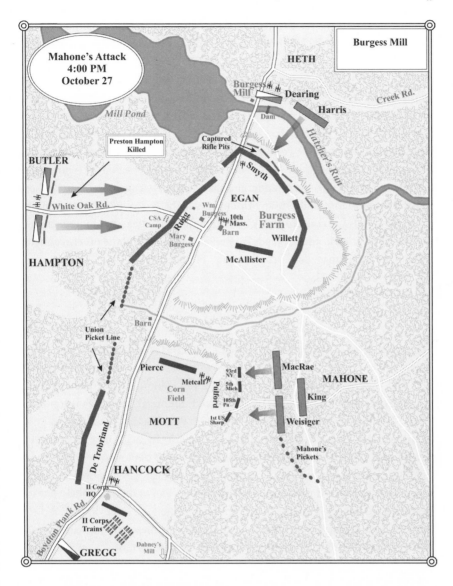

Mahone's Attack
4:00 PM
October 27

Burgess Mill

HETH

Burgess Mill

Dearing

Creek Rd.

Harris

Mill Pond

Dam

Preston Hampton
Killed

Captured
Rifle Pits

BUTLER

Smyth

White Oak Rd.

EGAN

Hatcher's Run

CSA
Camp

Wm
Burgess

10th
Mass.

Burgess
Farm

Ridge

Barn

Willett

Mary
Burgess

McAllister

HAMPTON

Barn

Union
Picket Line

Pierce

Corn
Field

Metcalf

93rd
NY

MacRae

MAHONE

5th
Mich

King

Pulford

105th
Pa

MOTT

1st US
Sharp

Weisiger

De Trobriand

HANCOCK

Mahone's
Pickets

II Corps
HQ

II Corps
Trains

Boydton Plank Rd.

GREGG

Dabney's
Mill

choice but to run. Though some stood their ground, most of the men in Pulford's line joined him, and a mass of Unionists sped toward the Boydton Plank Road.

The brief clash sparked desperate hand-to-hand fighting.[89] Sergeant H. H. Drinkard, of the 12th Virginia, ordered a Union soldier "to throw down his arms and go to the rear." Unobliging, the man thrust out his bayonet, but Drinkard parried the blade with his bare hand just before a fellow Virginian stepped in to help end the contest.[90] During the melee, the 105th Pennsylvania lost their flags, one of them taken by Orderly Sergeant Thomas Richardson of the 12th Virginia. Richardson had eyed the "beautiful stand of state colors" as he neared the federal line and nearly lost his life struggling for the banner. A large red-haired Unionist aimed his musket at the Virginian, but, at the last moment, Confederate Robert Atkinson knocked the assailant down and Richardson seized his prize.[91]

The 105th Pennsylvania lost more than its flags. Captain John Conser fell dead on the spot.[92] Though he had survived multiple wounds early in the war, Mahone's assault proved fatal for him.[93] As the rebel troops overwhelmed his line near the Boydton Plank Road, Conser had pleaded, "Men, we are surrounded. Will you surrender? Won't you fight it out?" Three rebels lunged at him, and, as Conser fought them off with sword and pistol, a fourth appeared and shot him at close range.[94] Captain Oliver Reddic and several others struggled to drag Conser's body back to the cornfield.[95] Many Unionists sought to cut their way out, spilling out of the woods into the cornfield.[96] Though the casualties were high, members of the 93rd New York, 5th Michigan, 105th Pennsylvania, and the other regiments in Pulford's line managed to escape the jaws of the assault.[97]

"swept across the field"

As a matter of size, Mahone's force posed little threat. The two divisions of Hancock's Second Corps, augmented by Gregg's cavalry, numbered upwards of twenty thousand, dwarfing the few thousand in Mahone's column. Even Gershom Mott's two brigades near the Burgess cornfield outnumbered Mahone's Virginians, North Carolinians, and Alabamians combined. But, whether by chance or good planning, Mahone had achieved numerical superiority at Hancock's most vulnerable spot. On the battlefield, superior position and deployment could trump force size. During combat, units usually formed in neat, yet cumbersome battle lines of two ranks. To unleash firepower, regiments had to maintain these lines as they marched, wheeled, and changed position, sometimes over difficult terrain. Once pointed in the proper direction, the fire from these compact lines could have a devastating effect. But efforts to direct these formations proved difficult, especially when time was short. A regiment or brigade assailed on its flank, where most of its muskets held no field of fire, could easily collapse. Under such conditions, men often turned and fled through their comrades, spreading panic and confusion and blocking lines of fire. At the Burgess cornfield, Mahone had delivered such a blow. His line enveloped Pulford's force, eventually routing whole regiments. The blue-clad refugees raced through the field and punched through the balance of Pierce's brigade, placing Hancock's entire command in jeopardy.

In the cornfield itself, Pierce struggled to turn his force into the oncoming secessionists. But "different officers gave conflicting orders," recalled one Pennsylvanian.[98] Some units received word to "change front forward," a slow, intricate maneuver that required the regiment to perform a wide pivot, rotating on its end and requiring each company to travel a different distance to accomplish the movement. Under conditions of duress, an attempt to change front forward could scatter companies and dissolve cohesion. Many of Pierce's regiments failed to conduct the maneuver and quickly devolved into an ineffective mass.[99] To make matters worse, the jumbled remnants of Pulford's force flooded through the rest of the brigade.[100]

One regiment, however, managed to avoid the confusion. Lieutenant Colonel C. W. Tyler's 141st Pennsylvania occupied the far side of Pierce's line, its left touching the Plank Road.[101] When the noise of gunfire poured from the forest, Tyler, unwilling to wait for instructions, ordered his men to hasten toward the danger. He simply ordered his command, some two hundred men, to face right and march forward toward the threat. Commenting on his decision, he wrote in his official report, "It seems to me that this was the only movement that could be made in time to offer any resistance to the swiftly advancing line of the enemy. I was surprised that instead the line commenced changing front forward, a long and somewhat intricate movement, and hazardous under fire. I had expected to unite with the right of the line as it moved to the right; instead, I found my command isolated and the line to the left in confusion and rapidly falling back."[102]

As the Confederates streamed out of the woods, Pierce rode among his regiments shouting, "Men, for God's sake, follow me and form on the woods!"[103] He looked back and saw Tyler's Pennsylvanians rushing to meet the onslaught and urged them to bolster the right flank of his flagging line. But despite Tyler's quick thinking, his regiment failed to arrive in time and became separated from the rest of the brigade. Weisiger's Virginians simply pushed past the Pennsylvanians.[104] Tyler managed to organize several companies at the woods' edge. This little band exchanged over a dozen rounds with the Confederates, firing into Weisiger's flank and slowing the pace of the attack there.[105] But Pierce's command soon fell apart completely. "Efforts were made to reform the regiment on a line facing the enemy," reported Captain John Ross of the 84th Pennsylvania, "but owing to the different orders given, the regiment could not be formed until the brigade commenced falling back in confusion."[106]

The Confederates pressed on. As Mahone recalled, the "left of the Virginia brigade became at once involved with the forces on its left, while the right of the brigade swept across the field in its front."[107] On the right, there was little to hinder their progress. MacRae's North Carolinians, along with some of the Virginians, drove deep into Pierce's force, hitting federal units as they changed position, obliterating cohesion, and dooming any attempts to rally them.[108] Virginian George Bernard recalled, "A hundred yards through the oak woods and undergrowth brought us to the edge of the woods, with an open field between the woods and the plank road immediately [south] of the little branch to the [south] of the Burgess house. In this field were numbers of the enemy in full retreat, at whom we have parting shots. Our brigade was now out in the open field, in fine feather."[109]

Some of the Virginians formed along the fence bordering the cornfield and began unloading their rifles into the retreating federals. At the field's edge, the Virginians divided. One section wheeled left toward the Dabney Mill Road, and the other continued through the rows of corn heading for the Plank Road. A member of the 12th Virginia, Captain Thomas Pollard, dressed in captured blue pants and wearing a blue cap, surged ahead with the Virginians and came face to face with a Union infantryman. Ignoring Pollard's demands to surrender, the federal soldier lunged forward with his bayonet. "Catching his gun between the first and second . . . bands," Pollard wrote, "I shoved him off, drew my pistol (all of the barrels of which, save one, had been discharged) placed it at his temple, and pulled the trigger." But only the cap in Pollard's pistol ignited, leaving the bullet safely in its chamber. Pollard then wrenched the rifle away, and his new prisoner "moved toward the fence muttering something in a foreign language." Soon after this struggle played out, Pollard spied another enemy soldier standing ten yards away loading his gun, his eyes fixed on the Virginian. "Will no one shoot this man?" Pollard thought. As the Yankee adjusted his firing cap, one of Pollard's comrades finally fired, knocking the soldier down with an audible thud.[110] The unorganized federals massed in the field, providing easy targets for the rebels. "Had there been any wagon to carry artillery in with us, many hundred more would have been shot," recalled one Virginian.[111] In fact, young William Pegram, commanding thirty guns north of Hatcher's Run, had been anxious to lend close support to Mahone's attack, but, he said, the terrain prevented the deployment of artillery.[112]

For the Union gunners manning Lieutenant Richard Metcalf's two cannon in the cornfield, the Confederate attack brought disaster. As Mahone's line broke through Pierce's brigade, Metcalf's crews had barely wheeled their pieces into position and hurled a few shots before the rebels swallowed them.[113] In short order, rebel fire killed most of Metcalf's horses and then wounded Metcalf. However, most of the gunners escaped and managed to save one limber, leaving the two guns and at least one caisson to MacRae's Tar Heels. The unattended cannon stood silently as Mahone's force flooded into the cornfield. Two members of the 11th North Carolina mounted the horse team attached to the caisson and drove back east through the woods, "landing" back on the north bank of Hatcher's Run.[114]

Pierce's men struggled to escape the closing gray cloud and gain the safety of the Plank Road. A nurse with the 5th Michigan, Anna Etheridge, found herself caught in the attack. A true heroine to the regiment, she had served with the Michigan men since early in the war. As the bullets flew "thick and fast," the regiment's surgeon urged her to find a safer place, but she remained in the action, hoping to aid her comrades. While some men passed to the rear, a drummer boy paused beside her but soon fell against her and slumped dead to the ground, the victim of a rebel ball. Shaken, Etheridge hurried to where she supposed the regiment's line stood but found only rebels in her front. According to an account of the event, "she did not pause, however, but dashed through their line unhurt, though several of the chivalry fired at her."[115]

Mahone had achieved a complete rout of the Union brigade. North on the cornfield, MacRae's five regiments rolled west and lapped over the Plank Road. To the south, near the Dabney Mill Road, some of Weisiger's Virginia brigade also gained the Plank Road. Some Virginians remained at the fence or on the cornfield facing south toward Union troops gathering along the Dabney Mill Road. The bulk of the Alabama brigade remained in reserve back in the trees, though some may have participated in the attack.[116] But out on the cornfield and the Plank Road, the Virginians and North Carolinians had, in essence, split Hancock's position in two.

Amid the chaos, Oliver Reddic and his comrades from the 105th Pennsylvania struggled through the woods with their precious burden, the body of their regimental commander, John Conser. Reaching the field's eastern edge, they found it "in full possession of the rebels." Capture seemed imminent. But the men lay Conser's body on the ground, crouched at the edge of the woods, and fired their Spencer rifles into the Confederates barring their path. The rebels, not expecting such danger from the rear, scattered and opened a corridor for Reddic's team. The Union men sprang forward, but the enemy, realizing the true size of the party, demanded them to halt. Reddic refused. He sprinted across the field. Balls pierced his coat and haversack. Another whacked his scabbard. Finally, he reached the far side of the Plank Road and rested behind a tree.[117]

In routing Pierce's brigade, William Mahone had blown a hole through the heart of Hancock's entire position and deranged the shape of the Union Second Corps. To the north around Burgess Tavern, Egan's division became isolated, facing Dearing's cavalry and several rebel guns looming across the run at Burgess Mill. To the west, Butler's cavalry division and more Confederate artillery barred the White Oak Road. Horace Rugg's thin blue skirmish line, sprinkled along the west side of the Plank Road, offered Egan's only connection back to Hancock. The rebels also increased pressure on the balance of the Union command. To the south, Gregg's Union cavalry continued to tangle with Rooney Lee's horsemen pressing up the Plank Road. And, with Robert McAllister's brigade joined to Egan, Hancock only mustered two infantry brigades of Mott's division at the point of Mahone's attack. One of these, Pierce's brigade, was already in tatters. The other, Brigadier General Regis de Trobriand's brigade, remained ready for combat, though de Trobriand had divided his command, with some regiments on the west side of the Plank Road and others to the east below the Dabney Mill Road.

Some Union veterans referred to this battle as the "Bull Pen."[118] There was little reason to question the moniker for the Confederates had certainly corralled Hancock's and Gregg's men into the Burgess fields. As Sam Porter noted immediately after the fight, "Our line of battle was almost a complete circle."[119] Though Hancock maintained his line of communication along the Dabney Mill Road, rebel bullets and shells crossed the fields from all directions, some passing clear through the Union troops and landing at Confederates' feet on the other side. The rebels threatened more than the Union combat units. Just south of the Dabney Mill Road lay the Second Corps ambulances and supply wagons, along with the held horses and equipage of Gregg's cavalry. These prizes sat a few hundred yards to Mahone's left, in the clear view of the Virginians and North Carolinians filling the cornfield.

In the wake of his initial success, William Mahone rode forward to survey matters. Not far from the cornfield, an artillery shell screamed through the trees, wounding his horse. Borrowing the mount of his courier, J. H. Blakemore, he reached the field and examined the panorama before him. Peering to the right, he observed Egan's force on the hill of the Burgess Farm. To his front lay Mott's men, and, off to the left, stood the artillery ordnance wagons and ambulances of Hancock's command. "The whole Federal force, save Egan's troops on my right," wrote Mahone, "were in great disorder and confusion." Mahone could hear the sounds of Hampton's troops pressing from the west and southwest.[120] He understood that attacks from Hampton's cavalry and Heth's infantrymen could further threaten Hancock's safety. If all the pieces fell into place, perhaps the Confederates would smash the Union offensive and, with it, the Union Second Corps.

"my force was too weak"

As Mahone drove his assault home, Confederates north of Hatcher's Run also attacked. Under Henry Heth's direction, James Dearing's cavalrymen and the Mississippi infantry in Nathaniel Harris's brigade lurched across Hatcher's Run at the mill to press Egan's division. The effort failed. According to Harris, his "force was too weak to press the enemy to advantage."[121] Heth offered a more direct assessment. "The attack was feeble and without result," he wrote. "General Dearing behaved with conspicuous gallantry, leading a portion of his command on the west side of Hatcher's Run, but the rest of the force failed to assist him."[122] The failure stemmed mostly from the condition and size of the units at hand. Dearing's brigade, numbering about 1,300 men, had been fighting all day.[123] Likewise, Harris's small Mississippi brigade had only 539 men and officers present for duty at its October inspection.[124] In fact, Harris later recalled that, after deploying his skirmishers, he had only 150 men remaining to form his main battle line.[125] In hindsight, Heth doubted whether Harris's and Dearing's small force could have held the Burgess Farm even if it had gained the crest.[126] To the federals, the attack made little impression. Thomas Smyth, in Egan's front, reported that the "enemy advanced in my front and were gallantly repulsed" by the 8th New York Heavy

Artillery and the 164th New York.[127] The effort from which Mahone had sought much had yielded nothing.

"charged forward with a yell"

Wade Hampton's two divisions also pressed from the west as Mahone attacked at the cornfield and Heth sought to cross Hatcher's Run. Hampton's cavalry formed a broad arc stretching from the Burgess Mill pond south across Dinwiddie farms and woods toward the Boydton Plank Road. Throughout much of the day, they had fought on their heels, rolled back by Hancock's heavy columns. Now the mounted arm prepared to the turn the tables.

A prominent figure in the slaveholding aristocracy, General Hampton possessed immense wealth before the war, owning several plantations and many slaves. With much to lose, he invested substantially in the Confederate war effort. At the start of the war, he raised and equipped a legion of troops with his own funds. As he rose in rank and responsibility through the conflict, he risked his life repeatedly in battle, receiving a severe wound at Gettysburg. But he had staked more than his own wealth and safety on the war. Two of his sons served with him, Wade Jr. and the young Preston Hampton, his aide-de-camp.

Hampton fought in nearly every major campaign in Virginia. Though lacking formal military training, he proved to be a superb tactician and combat leader. Following J. E. B. Stuart's death in May, he rose to command Lee's mounted arm. He demonstrated great skill in conducting traditional cavalry operations: screening the army's movements, conducting raids, and performing vital reconnaissance. However, he also adapted to evolving tactics by fighting his men dismounted as infantry where necessary. In doing so, he kept pace with an enemy that, by 1864, was amply equipped, battle seasoned, and well led. After the war, a South Carolina veteran concluded that "Hampton succeeded in making his men good, hard-fighting infantry on occasion, capable of practically doubling or quadrupling, their strength by celerity of movement, and at the same time preserved intact all their good qualities as cavalry."[128]

Hampton excelled in getting his troops to vital positions, fighting them on foot, and forming strong battle lines. His record in the 1864 campaign confirmed his tactical acumen. At Haw's Shop, Trevilian Station, and Sappony Church, his command fought well on the ground against the Union cavalry. He had also teamed successfully with A. P. Hill throughout the Petersburg campaign, perhaps most notably at Reams Station in August.

On October 27, Hampton had continued his outstanding performance. Though overwhelmed by the scale of the Union offensive and hampered by imperfect information, his fighting withdrawal pestered Hancock throughout the morning. Now, in the afternoon, his collaboration with Heth and Mahone had borne fruit. As Mahone's assault hammered Hancock's weak eastern flank, Hampton unleashed Butler's division from the west. Matthew Butler's two brigades stood athwart the White Oak Road behind makeshift breastworks, facing east toward the Burgess Farm. In this line, Pierce Young's Georgians anchored the left on the Burgess Mill pond. On the right, the South Carolina brigade, led by Colonel Hugh Aiken, stretched southwest toward Rooney Lee's division. Butler posted his field headquarters at the corner of the Burgess garden and orchard, just south of the White Oak Road. James Hart's battery, commanded now by Lieutenant Bamberg in the absence of its wounded commander, lent its weight to Butler's line.

As the roar of Mahone's rifles reached Hampton, the South Carolinian ordered Butler's force to attack. The directive reached commanders along the line including Lieutenant Colonel Robert J. Jeffords of 5th South Carolina, the "idol of his regiment." The whole line immediately surged forward toward the Plank Road. After scrambling over their breastworks, the dismounted men advanced, firing their weapons as Hart's guns hurled shells over them.[129] The men "charged forward with a yell," reported one cavalryman immediately after the battle.[130] As the air filled with bullets from friend and foe, one hit Jeffords, knocking him off his mount and killing him on the spot.[131]

Matthew Butler observed the charge from Hart's position near the orchard. Among the throng of gray and butternut, he identified several mounted staffers including Major T. G. Barker, his brother Captain Nat Butler, and Wade Hampton's son Preston.[132] The youthful trio waved their hats and cheered on the men in front.[133] Not far from the federals, these young officers offered conspicuous targets. "Of course, they had no business in such a perilous position, especially on horseback," General Butler recalled much later, "but there they were, resolutely and fearlessly, taking the chances of life under such hazardous circumstances."[134] Arms waving, Butler called on the young men to withdraw, but the musketry and cheers drowned his words. Nat Butler finally turned and noticed his brother's gestures. Steering his horse rearward, he galloped around the garden as a shot pierced his mount's neck. Preston Hampton followed, shouting, "Hurrah, Nat!" He wheeled toward his father's headquarters "a hundred yards to the right and rear." But as he turned, a Union bullet pierced his groin, bringing him to the ground.[135]

Preston Hampton had witnessed the war's opening at Fort Sumter. Four years later, he now lay on the wet Virginia ground, his life ebbing away. A crowd of mounted officers rushed to the scene. Dr. B. W. Taylor, the chief cavalry surgeon, knelt by Preston's side, but the great loss of blood revealed that the young man would die.[136] Soon General Hampton reined up, dismounted, and cradled his son. He whispered something in the young man's ear and kissed him.[137] With a tear on his face, he remounted and issued some orders.[138] The grieving collection of officers and aides, many holding their horses, drew the attention of the enemy riflemen, and soon a volley sprayed through the small crowd wounding the general's other son, Wade Hampton Jr., and three other men.[139] Zimmerman Davis, an aide to General Butler, helped Wade Jr. onto his horse and back to the division's field headquarters. Davis then rode to the rear to find a surgeon.

When Matthew Butler arrived at the scene, General Hampton cried, "Poor Preston has been wounded." Hampton then asked Butler to retrieve a small farm wagon from one of the Burgess sheds and carry his son out of range of the enemy fire.[140] Davis returned with another surgeon to find officers and couriers pulling the wagon rearward and General Hampton riding alongside. Dr. Taylor, in the wagon, supported "the head of Preston Hampton upon his shoulders, but the gallant youth had ceased to breathe."[141] The general sighed, "Too late, doctor," and rode over to two guns of Hart's battery. No doubt immersed in his grief, he stationed himself next to the cannon and personally commanded the pieces for a time. He gave particular attention to the timing of the fuses "and the elevation of each gun at each discharge."[142]

At the front, Butler's cavalry continued to push forward. According to Southern accounts, the assault marked a glorious success and drove back the federals.[143] The "gallant boys dashed forward," wrote General Butler years later, "firing as they advanced, in a heavy, galling fire from the enemy."[144] The cavalrymen "drove the enemy back to the cover of a dense pine thicket on the Boydton plank-road," recalled another Confederate veteran, "where their entire infantry was massed, while they had placed several batteries of artillery in position on the brow of a hill just beyond the thicket, and out of view of the battlefield."[145]

These rebel war stories, however, conflicted with the reports and eyewitness accounts of their counterparts in blue. Indeed, the Confederate cavalry attacks did not impress Union commanders and soldiers. In his official report, Thomas Egan noted the probes against his position but indicated that Rugg's regiments held the enemy "completely in check by a heavy skirmish line."[146] Charles McAnally, commanding a portion of the 69th Pennsylvania from Smyth's brigade, thought the charge deserved little attention and that the Confederates only sought to seize some rebel stores assembled in his front. "They came in a mob. They cheered and rushed up," he recounted several days later. "They were not skirmishers—they appeared like a storming party [headed] for the point where the stores were." He also saw Confederates across the field "continually moving down towards our left" through the trees like "flankers for a line of march." McAnally estimated about fourteen hundred Confederates either in the field or in the woods.[147] But the attack, as witnessed by him, accomplished little.

Butler's men, however, managed to advance past their own breastworks, push back the federal picket line, and stake a new position within 150 yards of Rugg's skirmish line.[148] "Our line of battle was halted at the crest of a small hill and along a rail fence," recalled Zimmerman Davis, "only a hundred yards or so from the enemy's line of battle, and heavy and continuous fire was kept up until long after dark."[149] "Our men fell by scores," wrote a South Carolinian immediately afterward, "but, with undaunted hearts, the remainder held their ground and returned the Yankee fire."[150] The fire was "terrible," recalled another Confederate, as the men "fought like devils" faced off against Egan's men "stationed in the woods, and in the old field in our front."[151]

Fierce or not, Hampton's operations failed to exploit the advantage gained by Mahone's attack. In the end, the cavalry did not affect Egan's position at the Burgess Farm. In fact, Confederate cavalry commanders may not have realized the success Mahone had achieved on the Burgess cornfield. Much continued to separate Hampton and Heth from Mahone's force—the high ground at the Burgess Farm, the Union battle line, thick timber in places, and a distance of nearly half a mile. With Harris and Dearing failing at Burgess Mill and Butler gaining little along the White Oak Road, Confederate prospects rested with Mahone's force, now isolated at the Burgess cornfield.

CHAPTER 16

The Second Corps Redeemed

~

"at the post of danger"

Only three months after the Reams Station debacle, Winfield Hancock's command faced another crisis at the Boydton Plank Road. In the wake of Mahone's attack, conditions had turned grim. The assault had nearly stranded Egan's division at the Burgess Farm. Gershom Mott's command, at the Dabney Mill Road, operated with only one functioning brigade. To the southwest, General Gregg's cavalry continued to tangle with Rooney's Lee's horsemen. The Confederates threatened to sever Hancock from the rest of the Union army.

Hancock and his officers strained to regain control and bring "order out of chaos."[1] "General Hancock was at all times at the post of danger," a Maine veteran recalled, "and gave his personal attention to affairs."[2] "At times there was firing on all sides, every road being closed by the enemy," wrote a member of the Second Corps staff.[3] At the height of the attack, another staffer found Hancock positioning reserves and, in a clear and distinct voice, ordering batteries to fire on the rebels.[4] At one point, according to a post-war recollection, the general ordered a group of soldiers to throw up breastworks. One man turned to his corps commander and exclaimed, "We have no shovels!" "Use tin plates, canteens, sticks—anything, but throw up works!" came Hancock's reply. "General, will you kindly tell us which side of the breastwork to get on after it is made?" Hancock simply smiled and rode off.[5]

But Hancock recognized an opportunity to reverse Mahone's success. The rebel brigades had swept through the middle of his position, and some enemy troops had even crossed the cornfield, piled over the Plank Road and penetrated the woods beyond. The audacious attack deformed Mahone's solid battle lines into scattered pockets and squads. Hancock prepared his command to smash the rebels.

"give them a shell!"

Hancock and his officers coordinated a swift and comprehensive response to Mahone's attack by landing blows in two sectors. From the north at Egan's position, Colonel Robert McAllister's brigade turned away from Hatcher's Run to lunge south against the North Carolinians. From the south, Mott regrouped his splintered division and formed against the Virginians. These two counterpunches occurred almost simultaneously and ensured that the debacle of Reams Station would not be repeated.

At the first signs of Mahone's attack, Hancock dispatched Major W. G. Mitchell to cancel Egan's strike at Burgess Mill and order that division to turn rearward and repulse the rebel breakthrough. As Mitchell galloped along the Plank Road, he witnessed Mahone's force cresting the cornfield off to his right. Reaching the Burgess house, he found Egan already scrambling to blunt Mahone's assault.[6] One brigade, led by Robert McAllister, a "Puritanical man, not brilliant of intellect, but an indomitable fighter," waited in reserve at Egan's position. McAllister's unit, part of Mott's division but assigned that afternoon to help Egan, numbered nearly as many muskets as Egan's entire force. However, many of McAllister's men were green—they had "never fired a gun and had had but very little drill."[7]

In response to Mahone's attack, McAllister simply turned his line around and charged, forgoing a more conventional but intricate maneuver that would surely have left his raw troops in disarray.[8] The advancing line, which included the 120th New York, 8th New Jersey, and 11th Massachusetts aimed for MacRae's North Carolinians. As McAllister kept two of his regiments, the 5th and 7th New Jersey, in reserve. He also ordered part of the 11th New Jersey to protect his left flank.[9] His men rushed down the hill, over the swampy ground, through the hazel brush, and up toward the cornfield. The 11th New Jersey outdistanced its sister regiments, reached a portion of the cornfield, and recaptured Metcalf's abandoned guns. However, the Confederate veterans poured a withering fire into McAllister's ranks.[10]

At the edge of the woods, Mahone watched as MacRae's men faltered under a "heavy fire." He immediately ordered the Alabama brigade from its reserve position to bolster MacRae's flank.[11] Horace King's Alabamians ratcheted up the pressure on McAllister, and, according to several Union reports, a rebel squad strained to roll a battery out from the tree line.[12] The rebel response overwhelmed McAllister's men. His brigade wilted, and, as McAllister recalled, the "line faltered and broke as we rose up the hill on the opposite side."[13] The regiments fled back over the marshy ravine to the Burgess Farm. McAllister and his staff struggled to rally them, but it was no use.[14] Despite this failure, McAllister could take solace in the fact that he had blunted Mahone's progress.

On the hill at the Burgess Farm, Major Mitchell, after relaying orders to General Egan, steered his horse along the Boydton Plank Road to locate Hancock and report his findings. But upon reaching the shallow ravine separating the Burgess houses and the cornfield, he could see Confederates covering the Plank Road and working their way into the woods. He wheeled his horse about and encountered the 36th Wisconsin, a regiment reprimanded after the Reams Station debacle.[15] Mitchell immediately ordered the regiment's commanding officer to head for the ravine. Members of the unit, which numbered only sixty-five muskets and three officers, turned about to "see the faded end of Mott's Division coming out of the woods into a cornfield" with many Confederates in pursuit.[16] But following Mitchell's directive, the regiment lunged forward.

With the Wisconsin men on their way, Mitchell resumed his efforts to return to Hancock. But before riding far he encountered Lieutenant Colonel Horace P. Rugg, the commander of Egan's first brigade. "I told him that Genl Hancock wished him to advance his brigade and attack the enemy who held possession of the Boydton plank-road," recalled Mitchell. The major left Rugg with those instructions and returned to Hancock by creeping along the thin Union picket line hidden in the trees west of the Plank Road.[17]

Rugg began his army career with the 59th New York in 1861 at the age of twenty. He had suffered an uneven tenure with the Army of the Potomac. In July 1863, he failed to report for picket duty near Markham Station, Virginia. However, he managed to weather the subsequent charges.[18] Weeks after rising to brigade command in August 1864, the young man led his unit at Reams Station.[19] There, his career began to unravel. As Confederates broke through a gap in Hancock's line, Rugg's command failed to engage the enemy. The brigade "could neither be made to go forward nor fire," reported Hancock.[20] A nearby battery commander pleaded with Rugg to advance his unit in support, but Rugg replied that he had no orders to do so. "To h-ll with orders!" shouted the gunner. "March your men in there and cut off the enemy from getting back." Rugg did nothing. One veteran later recalled, "Never in the history of the Second Corps had such an exhibition of incapacity and cowardice been given."[21]

The engagement at the Boydton Plank Road offered Rugg's next opportunity to lead in combat. With the Confederates splitting the Second Corps in half, decisive action was imperative. But once again, Rugg did not budge, even in the face of Major Mitchell's directive. Later, Rugg offered a string of excuses: Egan had ordered him to hold his position "at all hazards." The enemy cavalry threatened his front from the west. The rebel force on the Plank Road was, in his view, "but a disorganized body." "I considered that one good-sized regiment, charging down the road in line, would be as effectual as the whole brigade," he explained.[22] His subsequent explanations did not convince his superiors, however. They concluded he simply had failed to follow orders. His inaction led to formal charges, a court martial proceeding, and his dismissal from the army just days later. During his trial, held at the Globe Tavern on the Weldon Railroad, Mitchell's directions to Rugg were analyzed in detail, along with Rugg's state of mind, various instructions from Egan's staff, and the conditions on the battlefield.[23] Decades later, John Billings, from Granger's Massachusetts battery, recalled that Rugg, at the time of crisis, simply "lay cowering and immovable in his tracks."[24] Billings explained, "Major Mitchell told me since the war that Rugg's excuse was that Mitchell had no authority to order him but while that was literally true, the circumstances so fully justified it that Hancock stood loyally by his Aide. I well remember this brigade as I saw them that day lying low behind a hastily improvised barricade of boards and fence rails which they had collected early in the fight."[25] Though subsequent proceedings would nullify Rugg's dismissal months later, in the chaos of combat at the Plank Road, he clearly faltered.[26]

As McAllister's infantry counterattacked and Horace Rugg's men stood still, the Union artillery in Egan's sector pitched in. Next to the Burgess barn, the gunners of Granger's 10th Massachusetts Battery were "anxious for the order to fire to the rear" as the enemy spread out in the cornfield behind them.[27] Much to their relief, Sergeant George Townsend directed the men to wheel the Parrott rifled guns toward Mahone's attack force. At short range, Townsend and his comrades lobbed Hotchkiss percussion shells, deadly rounds designed to explode on impact, into the woods. While Granger's guns concentrated on Mahone, the rebel cannon north of Hatcher's Run resumed their fire at the back of the Bay Staters. In the midst of the duel, some of Robert McAllister's men came streaming through the battery's position, retreating from their bout with the North Carolinians in the cornfield. The gunners chided the panicked foot soldiers, and one of McAllister's officers sought in vain to stop their withdrawal. One gunner, recognizing some of the members of the 11th Massachusetts, shouted, "Shame on you boys! Will you leave the old Tenth Battery to fight it out alone?" Lieutenant Granger seized one of the infantry regiment's flags and sought to rally McAllister's men himself. But nothing worked, and the 10th Massachusetts Battery faced the advancing Tar Heels.[28]

"Give them a shell!" commanded Lieutenant Granger. "We can whip them alone." While Granger's crews rammed home their charges and sent them screaming at the rebels, Sergeant George Townsend glanced back at the Confederate cannon across Hatcher's Run. Each time the rebels fired from the far bank, he yelled, "Down!" and the men hugged the ground until the danger passed. The rebel crews failed to find the range, and the shells passed harmlessly overhead. Granger's guns soon used their last shell, and the men dipped into their limber chests for the canister rounds. But in a few minutes these were gone, too. Lieutenant Asa Smith, who commanded the center section, rode to General Egan to report that his guns were out of action and waiting near the barn. Seconds later, Smith tumbled "from his horse, shot through the bowels—a mortal wound." Completely out of ammunition, the other gun crews returned to the Burgess barn along with the wounded Smith.[29] Though Granger's men withdrew, Egan's division remained in control of the Burgess Farm. McAllister's brigade reformed and warded off the rebels as musketry and shell rained from all sides.[30]

"a fat, jolly Frenchman"

As the Unionists at the Burgess Farm turned on Mahone's force, Mott's division to the south coiled to land a punch of its own. Mahone's men still covered the cornfield and portions of the Plank Road. But with the cavalry furnishing support,[31] Mott scraped his troops together for a counterattack. After the collapse of Pierce's position, Mott and his staff galloped out to rally the demoralized men. Brigadier General Regis de Trobriand's brigade, the only cohesive, unengaged infantry unit available, shifted to face the onslaught and shield the Second Corps wagon trains.

Lawyer, poet, master swordsman, and the son of French nobility, Regis de Trobriand immigrated to the United States in 1841 at the age of twenty-five. Settling in New York City, he spent much of his time working for French literary publications, soon gaining a reputation as a "brilliant writer and amateur artist" with a "fluent and brilliant power of description."[32] When the Civil War broke out, he gained his U.S. citizenship and, along with it, the command of the 55th New York, a unit predominantly populated by fellow French émigrés. De Trobriand became somewhat of a character in the army. One veteran wrote, "What a fat, jolly Frenchman Trobriand was! What a funny figure he cut on horseback! His short, stubby legs projecting stiffly at right angles with his body, rigidly perpendicular with his body. . . . Yet he was a good soldier withal, and popular with his command."[33] Many of the men adored him. "I always enjoyed his company immensely," wrote one Maine soldier, "and feel honored in being under command of such a distinguished personage."[34]

As the crisis mounted at the Burgess cornfield, Mott directed de Trobriand to secure the Dabney Mill Road with a regiment. The 17th Maine, stationed nearby, received the call and marched at the double quick to protect the vital line of communication. Earlier, most of de Trobriand's regiments had formed on the far side of the Plank Road facing west. Leaving his skirmishers there, de Trobriand turned several of his regiments north toward the cornfield and Mahone's force.[35]

De Trobriand formed the 1st Maine Heavy Artillery on the left at the Boydton Plank Road and his other regiments, the 40th New York, 20th Indiana, 99th Pennsylvania, and part of the 110th Pennsylvania, shoulder to shoulder along the Dabney Mill Road. With this arrangement scarcely complete, one of Hancock's staffers shouted, "Charge!" The four regiments pressed forward, with de Trobriand at their front. He later recalled "my men opened fire while marching. The balls went faster than they did. A part of the rebels turned promptly against us,

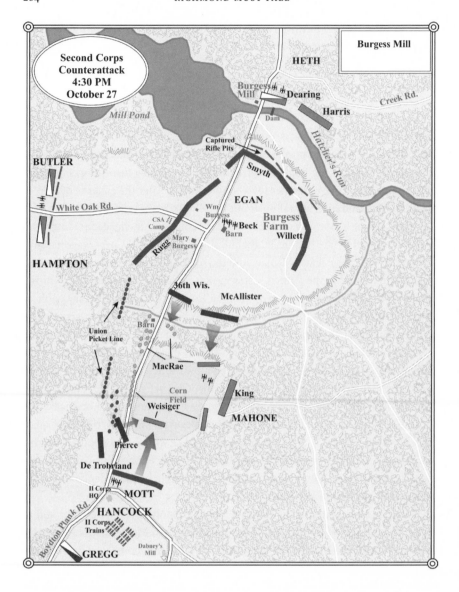

and the fire became very brisk." Three of de Trobriand's staff officers received wounds—one shot in the leg, another in the lungs, and the third in the foot.[36] De Trobriand's units did not step forward alone. To the left, Mott and Pierce managed to rally some units broken by Mahone's attack. In particular, John Pulford of the 5th Michigan, Major Shatswell of the 1st Massachusetts, and Benjamin C. Butler of 93rd New York reformed their men on the Plank Road and charged toward Metcalf's captured guns.[37]

To aid de Trobriand, Lieutenant John Roder of Battery K (5th U.S.) unlimbered his four Napoleons near the junction of Plank and Dabney Mill roads. Butler Beck, recently returned from the Burgess barn, also deployed his four guns to Roder's left. The eight twelve-pounder guns unleashed solid shot and spherical case into the Confederates.[38] Even Granger's Massachusetts guns, now with replenished ammunition chests, joined in, though Granger himself received a wound.[39] Unfortunately, several rifled pieces from Gregg's horse artillery stood unused nearby with the ambulances, apparently unnoticed by those who needed them.[40]

"It was like one man getting in between four"

The blue wave broke across the field with irresistible force, as Hancock and other officers led the way.[41] The tenacity, organization, and resolve of his Second Corps became manifest. For MacRae and Weisiger's men, the two-fisted Union counterpunch brought a stunning reversal and erased their momentary success. Confederates milling about the cornfield quickly found themselves crushed on nearly all sides, with McAllister's effort threatening from the north and de Trobriand and Pierce pushing from the Dabney Mill Road. "It was like one man getting in between four," observed Confederate artilleryman William Pegram.[42] Confederate Captain Thomas Pollard of the 12th Virginia, having occupied the Plank Road with other comrades, looked back to see a door closing behind him. At first, Virginian David Weisiger sought to repel the attack. He ordered Pollard to sprint across the field and inform Mahone of the threat. But before Pollard had traveled fifty yards, Weisiger realized the crisis had accelerated and called him back. Weisiger knew it was time to withdraw and directed his men near the Plank Road. The Virginians milled about "in much confusion," recalled Pollard, "hardly half a dozen of a company together." He climbed atop an embankment at the side of the road and "called on the men to follow [him] into the field in fours regardless of companies." Once in the field, Weisiger formed the remnants of his command and rushed back toward the safety of the trees, reaching the far side just before the jaws of the federal lines shut.[43]

Not far away, MacRae's North Carolinians faced the same threat. Like the Virginians, many Tar Heels reached the Plank Road, while others pressed against McAllister on the Burgess Farm hill to the north. J. S. Bartlett, a member of the 11th North Carolina, recalled, "After reaching the opposite side of the field from where we first struck the Yankees, we discovered that we had only knocked a gap out of the Yankee line, and that the two ends were closing together behind us."[44] From the north bank of Hatcher's Run, a cavalryman in Dearing's brigade could hear MacRae's men yelling during the fight, but, as he explained shortly after, the rise near the Burgess dwellings "hid them from our view, and we were most eagerly awaiting their appearance on the hill, in rear of those who were fighting us, but were disappointed."[45] General William MacRae had entered the field on foot, and, as the federal forces pressed from all sides, he gathered his command together.[46] He expected reinforcements, perhaps from the Alabama brigade, but there was no sign of fresh troops. With their next course unclear, some officers urged surrender, while others vowed to fight to the last man. But MacRae ended all discussion and ordered his men to cut their way out. To "escape Point Lookout or some other place of torment," J. S. Bartlett and his comrades turned about and raced to avoid the trap.[47] While helping a wounded comrade back, Bartlett passed by the abandoned Union twelve-pound cannons of Metcalf's section. Pausing, he stooped down, pulled a sassafras sprout from the ground, and wedged it into the vent of one of the guns, preventing its immediate use.[48]

In a matter of minutes, the Union vise tightened. The rebel attack, which began with such promise, became an unmitigated rout. Virginians and North Carolinians fled for their lives back into the woods. Not all of them reached safety. Some fell wounded or killed. Many others became prisoners. As MacRae and Weisiger hurried their men off the field, various pockets of Confederates remained behind, trapped in the Union battle lines.

The roar of the fight subsided. Charles Mills, from Hancock's staff, headed north on the Plank Road to check on Egan, guiding his horse along the western edge of the cornfield, the scene of such excitement only minutes before. Rebel skirmishers still at the tree line to the east kept firing at Union soldiers. To avoid the threat, Mills galloped across the field of fire and reached the shallow ravine where a small barn stood, just west of the Plank Road.[49] There a surprising sight greeted his eyes. Off to the left, not twenty yards away, two hundred Confederates stood quietly tucked away in the trees, completely cut off from their comrades. Captured Union soldiers, about fifty of them, mingled with the secessionists, and several of these blue-clad prisoners called out to Mills, pleading for rescue. "Seeing that they were in a tight place," he wrote, the Federals "had apparently about made up their minds to surrender."[50] "As I did not propose to attempt this feat single-handed," Mills explained later, "I turned my horse rather quickly and dug my spurs in farther than I ever remember."[51] He sped back down the road, expecting a shower of lead to follow him. The Confederates, though, perhaps apprehending their own dire straits, held their fire. As Mills raced toward Hancock's headquarters, he encountered Major W. G. Mitchell, who had returned from Egan's front. The two discussed the enemy soldiers clustered at the barn.

As Mills and Mitchell pondered the situation, a group of federal soldiers across the cornfield sought to haul Metcalf's guns back to safety. Lieutenant Colonel Joseph Smith, Hancock's chief commissary, had asked Major R. S. Littlefield from the 1st Massachusetts Heavy Artillery to retrieve the guns. Littlefield, whose left hand was still numb from a previous wound, reached the first gun, and with the help of about fifty others, he pushed and rolled the guns back by hand "amid cheers from the line."[52] Though accounts conflict, this group probably included members of the 1st Maine Heavy Artillery, the 110th Pennsylvania, and the 5th Michigan.[53]

With the artillery pieces secure, elements of Egan's division and Pierce's brigade converged on the small barn near the ravine. The federals scooped up pockets of rebels hidden in the woods near the Plank Road. As Mills resumed his mission to check on Egan's command, Major Mitchell rode out and gathered about fifty Union men.[54] He then descended with this force on the rebel group. One of the men captured by the Confederates, Lieutenant Benjamin Conlin from the 155th New York, rushed out of the group and shouted to Mitchell, "Major, I'm a prisoner. You can capture all of them."[55] Mitchell's party succeeded in gathering about two hundred en masse and freeing the prisoners Mills had seen in the woods minutes before.[56] Mitchell may have proceeded simultaneously with the 36th Wisconsin of Egan's command charging from the opposite side of the ravine. The tiny Wisconsin regiment claimed one hundred prisoners and a stand of colors.[57] Lieutenant Edward Schoff of the 19th Massachusetts joined members of the 7th Michigan to capture "a major and several line officers, and over 40 men." Sergeant Daniel J. Murphy of the 19th Massachusetts took the colors of the 47th North Carolina Regiment, earning the Medal of Honor through his bravery.[58]

Though the swirl of accounts complicates the task of assigning credit, the result was clear. The Confederates in the woods became prisoners, and the captured Union men were set free. Lieutenant Conlin, his face bloodied from a rebel blow, walked back on the Plank Road with "a bundle of rebel swords under his arm."[59] Mills, obliged to follow his earlier orders from Hancock, had continued up the Plank Road to Egan's post at the Burgess Farm and, much to his regret, missed the opportunity to share in the credit of the capture, most of which went to Mitchell.[60]

Hancock's men gobbled up other groups of Confederates in the field. As with the incident at the barn and the recapture of Metcalf's guns, subsequent accounts offer murky and confusing details. According to Regis de Trobriand, who attempted to sort out the conflicting reports, a group of Union soldiers from the 110th Pennsylvania captured about one hundred rebels near a "clump of pine trees," independent of the captures at the barn.[61] De Trobriand also estimated that his brigade alone had captured two hundred prisoners.[62] More rebels were taken elsewhere. Gershom Mott estimated that his division captured between four and five hundred Confederates. General Meade later reported that Hancock had captured seven hundred and several stands of colors (one news report identified three).[63]

Individual unit accolades aside, the Second Corps, as a whole, performed well. In the midst of extreme peril, its commanders and men rose to the occasion and rapidly shut down Mahone's attack. At the Burgess Farm, Egan and McAllister conducted their commands effectively, pushing against MacRae's flank with McAllister's green brigade performing just well enough to make a crucial difference. At

the cornfield, de Trobriand, whose regiments offered the last line of defense, coun-
termarched his men and brought them into position on the Dabney Mill Road in
a manner of minutes. While there is no doubting McAllister's crucial contribution,
de Trobriand's regiments delivered the crushing blow, sweeping the rebels from
the cornfield. The energetic Hancock and Mott supervised these movements on
the spot. Even Pierce, whose brigade had folded at the outset, quickly rallied his
broken command and added its punch to the counterattack. In all, there was no
dysfunction, no hesitation, and no lack of will. The Second Corps recovered and
won the day.

"cut to pieces"

The engagement devastated Mahone's command. Though Weisiger's brigade managed to escape the field with three stands of federal colors,[64] the Virginians likely
would have traded the flags to regain the comrades lost on the Burgess cornfield.
According to one estimate, the brigade suffered as many as 328 casualties in all,
277 reported as missing. For MacRae's North Carolinians, the results were worse.
The Tarheels lost 12 killed, 73 wounded, and 431 missing, for a total of 516 total
casualties. Almost half its entire strength had evaporated in the course of an hour
or two.[65] The 26th North Carolina lost its flag in the struggle.[66] The day's events
filled MacRae with rancor. His brigade was part of Heth's division, but during
the attack at the Burgess Farm, it fell under Mahone's immediate charge. MacRae
reportedly "complained bitterly about his superiors in command allowing him to
be cut to pieces when it could have been prevented."[67] After the war, North Carolina veterans noted his disappointment in their regimental histories. According
to them, MacRae had expected support in the attack, but none was given.[68] One
Carolina veteran wrote, "Awaiting reinforcements, which long since ought to have
been with him, he [MacRae] held his vantage ground at all hazards, and against
enormous odds. No help came whilst his men toiled, bled and died."[69] The historian of the 44th North Carolina also claimed that the affair had "been marred by
the misunderstanding of his orders by an officer of high rank, by which he failed
to reinforce General MacRae, as instructed."[70] MacRae's concern about the lack of
support from Mahone appeared in print after the war. When the matter reached
Mahone's attention, he wrote several letters to former officers and aides seeking
their version of the story.[71]

MacRae may have had some cause for his bitterness. As the Virginians and
North Carolinians drove deep into Hancock's position and became virtually surrounded, the Alabama brigade, did not fully enter the fray. According to Mahone's
account, he deployed Colonel Horace King's Alabama soldiers in reserve and, at

one point, ordered them to support MacRae's right flank.[72] A Georgian, writing to the *Macon Telegraph* on November 1, perhaps delivering a veiled criticism of the Alabama brigade, remarked that, if Mahone "had one more brigade, or even a better one in place of the one he had, we would have captured the whole party."[73] In any event, the "stout and polite" King was probably only following Mahone's orders.[74] The few accounts of the brigade's actions that afternoon shed little light on events. One veteran of the 8th Alabama remembered that his regiment "was only slightly engaged and lost seven men, wounded."[75] Heth's report indicates that King's brigade was "for some time" under William MacRae's command.[76] Another member of the same regiment recalled, "We got into the fight late in the evening, and drove the Yankees over a mile until dark."[77] One estimate puts the Alabamian casualties at about forty to fifty men.[78]

But amid these vague descriptions lies another possible explanation for the Alabamians' whereabouts. Earlier in the afternoon, Union Lieutenant George Dresser, the Fifth Corps' artillery inspector, had stumbled onto a column from the 10th Alabama behind Samuel Crawford's lines north of the Crow Farm, well to the east of Mahone's position.[79] If Dresser's report is accurate, large portions of the Alabama brigade may have simply lost their way south of Hatcher's Run and lost their own opportunity to participate in the fight. There is no indication that they were heavily engaged in the battle. Mahone later gave no clear explanation for holding back his reserve after the resounding initial success at the cornfield. Long after the war, he would write, "I had made my attack, but was powerless to do more." He sought to hit Egan's flank, but an "impassable quag-mire, along the bed of the little branch that runs between" the Burgess Farm and the corn field prevented the effort.[80]

Mahone probably chose to hold back this last brigade from the cornfield and instead limited the Alabamians to a supporting role. In any case, he believed he had exhausted his options. He considered a direct attack against Egan's force. But an impassable creek stood in his way, the downstream portion of the same boggy stream that ran through the Burgess Farm.[81] Support for the attack would have had to come from Heth's assault at Burgess Mill or from Hampton's cavalry across the Plank Road. However, these attempts failed to yield significant results. Years later, Mahone recalled the strange beauty of the scene as he peered out "in the dimness of the mist and the thickening darkness through which the blaze of the musketry shone like lightning against a black cloud."[82] At the time, however, he could not have been pleased. He expected more from the forces under Heth at Burgess Mill. His attack was over, and he had little to show for it. Henry Heth directed his fellow Virginian back to the north bank to join Dearing's and Harris's brigades on the north bank near Burgess Mill.[83]

"There was something deadly going on"

Though Mahone's assault was spent, more fighting occurred along the Boydton Plank Road. Following Mahone's operation, Rooney Lee and his cavalry attacked from the southwest toward Hancock's position.[84] Lee deployed the 1st and 2nd North Carolina Cavalry regiments of Rufus Barringer's brigade on the west side of the Plank Road and the 9th and 13th Virginia on the east. As some of the Virginians trotted between the tall rail fences lining the road, they encountered a nasty surprise. "When about 2 miles from the Mills and about sun set we are suddenly startled . . . and in a moment a column of Yankee cavalry come charging down upon us from a body of woods just in our front," wrote a member of the 9th Virginia.[85] The Virginians offered little resistance. Lee, riding at the head of the Virginia regiment, ordered the men to dismount. But then realizing there was no time for a stand, he ordered them back in the saddle. Hemmed in by the rails and near panic, Luther Jerrell "drew a saber, sprang from his horse, climbed the high fence and, carbine in hand, shouted 'Rally here 9th and we will drive them back in a moment!'"[86] The men gathered around Jerrell and poured a "murderous volley" into the Union riders, scattering them back up the road. With the rout in check, the Virginians resumed on foot. Barringer's Tar Heels advanced on the left and outpaced the Virginians.[87] McGregor's battery provided support.[88]

For much of the afternoon, Union cavalry commander David Gregg had aligned his three brigades to protect Hancock's left flank and rear. Henry Davies's brigade faced south down Quaker Road; Charles Smith's regiments stood across the Plank Road; and portions of Michael Kerwin's unit, the division's second brigade, remained on Gregg's right joined to de Trobriand's infantry picket line.[89] During Hancock's attack, Gregg shifted many of his regiments north to aid Hancock but left the 21st Pennsylvania to guard the Plank Road. When the Confederates pressed from all sides, Hancock rode up to Gregg and remarked, "General, we seem to be getting in a tight place." "Humph," Gregg replied, "I have a few sabers strapped to my saddles yet."[90] Gregg heard heavy firing south on the Plank Road. After a quick ride, he found "the enemy's cavalry dismounted, attacking strongly, aided by the fire of four rifled guns."[91] There the Pennsylvanians, though severely outnumbered, "stoutly" resisted.[92] But Rufus Barringer's North Carolina regiments overlapped the short Union line.[93] As the Confederates pressed, Gregg called for all available regiments. Soon the 1st Maine Cavalry arrived at a dead run and formed to the right of the Pennsylvanians, and the 6th Ohio added its strength to the line.[94] Hancock, heeding Gregg's call, also sent the 2nd, 4th, and 13th Pennsylvania Cavalry regiments from Kerwin's brigade.[95] A section of Beck's battery unlimbered in support.[96] Gregg's horsemen settled down for a "pretty sharp" fight.[97]

The Spencer and Henry repeating rifles of the 1st Maine Cavalry belched fire into the approaching rebels. A near-sighted Maine colonel, Jonathan Cilley, failed to make out the enemy in his front and wondered what all the fuss was about. "You are acting like a fool with your ammunition," he shouted to one of his men. A Corporal from Company B, suggested that Cilley kneel down and take a closer look at the ground ahead. Cilley did so and then "said no more of wasting ammunition, but remained on his knees and commenced firing with his revolver."[98] He was not alone in his bewilderment. The nature of the ground confused men on both sides. As one Virginia horseman confided to his cousin several days later, "We fought mostly in woods and . . . I was [as] afraid of the Rebs as the Yanks."[99] At one point, the Maine troopers wavered but soon snapped back as Colonel Cilley rallied them with his "inspiring voice."[100] According to one account, some hand-to-hand fighting occurred.[101] At dusk, more Confederate cavalrymen tested the Union picket line near the Plank Road. The 16th Pennsylvania Cavalry, armed with revolvers and repeating rifles, hugged the ground, listening to the enemy gather across a meadow. Second Lieutenant Samuel Cormany paced along the line, urging his men to fire their carbines first and then empty their revolvers in the enemy's direction. The Confederates soon emerged from the trees, and the command "Fire" rang along the Union ranks. "There was something deadly going on," one trooper wrote, "and it was kept up til some of the enemy were within 40–50 yards of our fence, when the boys did such awful execution that the enemy broke & ran back—our boys yelling like Hyenas and kept 'shooting at will,' and cries of the enemy wounded, fairly vent the air."[102] The rebels believed they had achieved much. One North Carolinian concluded, "The enemy were driven back and pressed rapidly before us for nearly a mile. Our victory was complete."[103] Rooney Lee's men, who began their afternoon at the Wilson Farm managed to advance a substantial distance, perhaps as much as a mile, up the Plank Road. But, in the end, Gregg's dismounted men, fighting well past dark, halted the rebels and left them with ground of little consequence.

Near the Dabney Mill Road, Hancock had no infantry to spare.[104] He also had problems of his own to address. Near nightfall, the Confederate cavalry, perhaps men from Barringer's brigade, hit de Trobriand's troop, threatening Hancock's position.[105] Hampton's men rolled out several cannon astride a farm path in front of the 124th New York and artillery shells soon "tore through the trees in a most unpleasant manner." Some projectiles reached the Second Corps ambulance park. The New Yorkers "threw themselves on the ground, and all kept up as rapid a fire as they possibly could."[106] In the end, members of the 124th New York and the 2nd U.S Sharpshooters blunted the rebel advance. The attack may have caused confusion along de Trobriand's line, but the men rallied and repulsed the enemy advances.[107] Wade Hampton reported, "Lee struck the enemy on the plank road and drove him handsomely." With night approaching, however, he called a halt to the attack and directed his commanders to hold their positions.[108] The battle of Burgess Mill ended and, with it, Grant's offensive toward the South Side Railroad.

Part III

The Beginning of the End

On the evening of the 27th, Grant and his commanders withdrew their men from the field, ending the sixth offensive. In the wake of the operation's failure, ample discussion appeared in the press, and plenty of finger pointing occurred within the army. While many wondered whether the battles at Burgess Mill and the Williamsburg Road would affect the election, Grant began to consider what lessons the operation held for unlocking the door to Richmond and Petersburg.

CHAPTER 17

Retreat

~

"withdraw rather than take the responsibility of disaster"

Colonel Charles Weygant, of the 124th New York, struggled to the rear with his third wound of the war. Leaving his command near the Plank Road, he staggered to a small house beyond the park of wagons and ambulances.[1] After having his wound examined by a surgeon, he stepped out into the dusk and headed for a row of ambulances. Weak from loss of blood, he crawled into a wagon and lay down. Outside, the rain increased noticeably as the sound of gunfire faded. Raising himself, he gazed forward toward the horse team hitched to his wagon. His daze ended abruptly when several enemy artillery shells thundered past, one tearing a horse's head off. "I became convinced that I had taken the wrong conveyance and forthwith crawled out at the rear end," he wrote later.[2] In the momentary glare, Weygant spied his aide leading his horse away from the front line. He hobbled to his mount, climbed into the stirrups, and headed for what he "supposed" to be the Union rear.[3]

At dusk, General Hancock weighed his options. He considered remaining at the Burgess Farm but despaired, as he later reported, that "unless the Fifth Corps moved up and connected with me, I could not answer for the result."[4] With the offensive over, his position served little purpose. The prospect of remaining isolated for the night south of Hatcher's Run could not have been inviting. However, without specific orders to withdraw, he sought more guidance from his superiors. At 5 P.M., he sent Major H. H. Bingham to find General Crawford and provide a status report. Bingham steered his horse along a cart path east but soon stumbled into a thicket of enemy troops. Reversing his course, he chose the Dabney Mill Road instead. After several hundred yards on this route, he jogged left toward the Crow house. In a mile or so, he abruptly encountered two hundred members of a North Carolina regiment. The Tar Heels, fresh from the repulse at the Burgess cornfield were making their way back toward Hatcher's Run, albeit in a roundabout way. Upon surrendering to the Carolinians, Bingham told the officer in charge that he did so "because I considered resistance as useless, but that I was of the opinion he was my prisoner instead of my being his." The Carolinians had captured three ambulances, twenty or so horses, and about twenty prisoners. Bingham remained with his captors into the early evening. But around 8 P.M., he managed to convince his guard that the Carolinians had drifted into the Union lines. The frightened rebels plunged into the bushes, and Bingham escaped into the darkness.[5]

Around five o'clock, shortly after Bingham set out on his fruitless mission, a messenger arrived at Hancock's field headquarters bearing some obsolete news from Meade's chief of staff, Andrew Humphreys. Throughout the afternoon, federal signal stations had observed Confederate troops streaming west from Petersburg and southwest along the Boydton Plank Road. From the high tower at the Church Road station, lookouts spotted six rebel regiments headed for Hancock at 2:30 P.M.[6] Humphreys's note warned Hancock, "Signal officers report the movement of the enemy's troops down the Boydton plank road. No doubt they are concentrating toward you." Though the warning was late, the note also directed the Second Corps chief to hold his position until morning and coordinate his actions with Crawford, whose command still remained along Hatcher's Run. Humphreys cautioned that the Dabney Mill Road, Hancock's lifeline, was "still infested by small parties of the enemy's cavalry or guerillas," a fact that had become steadily apparent all afternoon as couriers and staff officers sought to navigate the wilderness.[7]

Hancock was in a bind. The Confederates nearly encircled the "bull pen" that held his troops. The safety of the Union entrenchments were six miles to the east over cramped roads. His tired units had little ammunition. The men had been marching and fighting most of the day and, as a result, were in considerable disorder.[8] The artillery batteries were worse off. One had no shells left, another had very little, and the third had lost too many officers and men to operate its pieces effectively. Gregg's cavalry also lacked cartridges and remained disorganized from the late afternoon fight.[9] The frail line of communication between Hancock's position and Meade's headquarters at Armstrong's Mill exacerbated matters. In a sign of his desperation, Hancock directed his men to construct breastworks along the Dabney Mill Road that could be used from either side. The unusual order was "anything but a cheering aspect of things to us," recalled a Maine veteran.[10]

In the early evening, Hancock dispatched a string of messengers to Meade. A confusing batch of written messages and oral reports followed. Some notes took as long as an hour and a half to make their way through the murky woods.[11] As Hancock's couriers arrived at Meade's headquarters, a better understanding of his situation began to emerge. North of Hatcher's Run, both Warren's Fifth Corps and Parke's Ninth Corps formed a strong, continuous line. But south of Hatcher's Run, the picture held little promise. Hancock remained isolated, and most of Crawford's Fifth Corps division floundered in the wet, impenetrable thickets north of the Crow house.[12] Meade and Humphreys discussed whether to bolster Hancock further by sending Romeyn Ayres's Fifth Corps division. Meade still held hope that Hancock would connect with the Fifth Corps.

Beginning at 5:15 P.M., several dispatches arrived at the Boydton Plank Road asking Hancock to consider further attacks using Crawford's and Ayres's troops. However, at the same time, Humphreys granted Hancock what the Second Corps commander really needed, the discretion to withdraw that evening.[13] Meade sent his staffer Thomas Livermore to ensure that Hancock understood that he could leave the confines of the Burgess Farm if necessary.[14] In addition, a dispatch from Humphreys informed Hancock, "[The] commanding general directs me to say that you can withdraw at once if you deem it most judicious, or at any time during the night."[15]

With permission in hand, Hancock chose to take his corps from the field. Too many uncertainties existed to act otherwise. He did not know whether the two Fifth Corps divisions would be available for an attack in the morning. In fact, he had not communicated with Crawford since 4 P.M. In addition, he could not be certain that reserve ammunition would arrive in time to refill empty cartridge boxes.[16] Without more rounds for his own troops, Hancock understood Ayres and Crawford would provide only a marginal benefit. Considering these factors, Hancock explained to Humphreys that withdrawal was the proper course under the circumstances. "I have a frail hold on the roads between me and the Fifth Corps, and if any accident should prevent my receiving the ammunition and troops at an early hour, the result would be a disaster, as the enemy have hemmed me in and pressed me closely."[17]

Hancock directed his troops to fall back along the Dabney Mill Road to the Gurley house, within the Union trenches west of the Weldon Railroad. To maintain a connection with the Fifth Corps, he ordered Egan's division to halt for the evening at the Dabney's Mill.[18] He later explained, "Reluctant as I was to leave the field, and by so doing lose some of the fruits of my victory, I felt compelled to order a withdrawal rather than risk disaster by awaiting an attack in the morning only partly prepared."[19] He set departure for 10 P.M.

From Armstrong's Mill, Meade wired the news to Grant. Later that evening, the Lieutenant General regretted the need to withdraw "now that the enemy have taken to attacking." For Grant, Mahone's aggressiveness signaled opportunity. He sensed that the enemy was off balance and hoped they would now launch costly attacks against Union positions and create conditions to resume the offensive. "If ammunition could have been taken up on pack animals, it might have enabled us after all to have gained the end we started out for," he wrote.[20] But this was only wishful thinking. Though Grant's note gently conveyed disappointment, he knew his forces could not hold the lodgment on the Boydton Plank Road. With Weitzel withdrawing from the Williamsburg Road north of the James, the entire offensive ended.

"dismal and comfortless"

South of Petersburg, a heavy rain began around seven o'clock and turned the night into "an inky blackness."[21] The men, fully exposed in the fields and forests, soaked up the misery that only a chilly, autumn storm could bring. The evening was "dismal and comfortless," recorded a Maine infantryman.[22] The rain fell continuously and soon drenched the shivering men. "We spread our tarpaulins," recalled a Massachusetts gunner, "and lying down, doubled them over us for shelter and warmth, while we attempted to catch a little sleep in anticipation of the next move."[23]

At the Boydton Plank Road, the withdrawal of the Second Corps raised a host of logistical challenges. Hancock and his officers faced the tasks of removing his wounded, pulling back the artillery batteries, funneling thousands of men through the Dabney Mill Road, and maintaining a strong picket line to ward off opportunistic rebels. A successful Confederate assault during the withdrawal would be disastrous, catching the Union columns in transit, unable to defend themselves. Dead and wounded littered the length and breadth of the Burgess Farm. The wails of the injured penetrated the night.[24] Two houses near the Plank Road served as shelters for many wounded men. Elias Marsh, the army's surgeon-in-chief, scrounged for wagons to convey the injured off the field.[25] "We went to work & got all the wounded we could," recalled Sergeant John Uban of the ambulance corps. "We loaded 11 ambulances & captured wagons & five ammunitions wagons with them & left the field of battle at midnight."[26] Unfortunately, many more remained. A Pennsylvania cavalryman found the carnage almost too much to bear. "If you would see one you woulden want to see another. Its not that I am fraid that I haint . . . but it is the grones and cries ove the wounded and the dying the cutting to peases ove men it seams like the sinfullness work that men can do."[27] There was little Hancock and his officers could do. Additional ambulances from the rear could not fit through the crowded, narrow Dabney Mill Road without bottling up the troops gathered at the Burgess Farm. As the rain poured, the men collected the remaining wounded and placed them in nearby houses under the care of Second Corps surgeons.[28]

Robert McAllister, whose green New Jersey regiments had helped blunt Mahone's attack, wandered through dimly lit houses and barns early in the evening. At one dwelling, he found fifty men from his brigade, a dozen in another. The soldiers were in bad shape. Some grabbed his hand and asked, "Colonel, did I do my duty?" McAllister could only reply to them, "Yes! Yes! You did nobly." He grieved for these men so far away from home and "soon to be left in the hands of the enemy." Only one surgeon tended to the men in both houses visited by McAllister. "There were no nurses, no chaplains, no consolation, no relief." During the visit, he came across David A. Granger, a Bostonian who led the 11th Massachusetts, lying on the floor in intense agony. Granger pleaded to be taken from the field. McAllister ordered some members of the regiment to carry their captain and many of the other wounded to the ambulances. Despite the efforts of McAllister and others, Granger died on the field.[29]

Some of the injured, however, managed to escape through the shear exertion of their comrades. For example, members of the 8th New York Heavy Artillery bore Lieutenant George Rector of Company F on a stretcher for many miles, saving him from captivity. But their extraordinary efforts did not spare him from death, which came two days later.[30] Other casualties remained in the woods surrounding the Burgess Farm or at the edge of the road. Many begged to be carried away. Departing soldiers sought to comfort the wounded with encouraging words they knew were not true: "Do not trouble yourselves; be a little patient. The ambulances are going to return; we are here to wait for them."[31]

Other problems vexed Hancock. He still needed to pull his entire command from under the enemy's nose. To accomplish this, he planned to withdraw his two divisions one at a time beginning at 10 P.M. A strong picket line would remain until 1 A.M. Given the operation's delicate nature, he needed someone to manage the picket line and oversee their departure. He chose Regis de Trobriand, the Frenchman who had performed so well during Mahone's attack. In a short interview conducted from a covered wagon "fitted up like an office," Hancock charged de Trobriand with protecting the rearguard and bringing the pickets off the field. Dabney's Mill would serve as the rallying point should any disaster befall the operation. De Trobriand thanked Hancock for his confidence and headed back out into the night.[32]

De Trobriand, joined by an orderly, rode out to find the picket line, leaving behind the campfires dotting the Burgess Farm. When he plunged into the pines west of the Plank Road, a suffocating darkness greeted him, "doubly opaque under the green canopy." He could see nothing. The tree branches whipped his face, as his horse brushed past the young tree trunks. Speech offered the only contact with his orderly. The pair soon lost all sense of direction but eventually stumbled toward a "reddish glimmer of light" and soon found Colonel Michael Burns of the 73rd New York who relayed the order to withdraw to others on the picket line. De Trobriand returned to Hancock, now "sitting on a log, before a campfire."[33]

At 10 o'clock, Gershom Mott's column led the way off the field and onto the Dabney Mill Road. The men "defiled in silence, with bayonets in the scabbard, the muskets under the arm, and the blankets rolled over the shoulders."[34] Near the road, a wounded young soldier lying under a cart asked the passing men, "Are not the ambulances coming?" The men assured him help was on the way but then "hurried on in order not to hear any more."[35] Egan's division followed, stopping at Dabney's Mill, and David Gregg's cavalry slipped away at 10:30 P.M., heading south on the Quaker Road, retracing their route to the battlefield.[36] The last ambulances departed at midnight.[37] They encountered difficulty crossing Hatcher's Run but eventually reached the Halifax Road along the Weldon Railroad.[38]

The departure from the Boydton Plank Road produced much hardship. "The night was one of the darkest in history," wrote one hyperbolic veteran. "Nothing could be seen on our road through the forest, not a star in the heavens nor an opening in the clouds above us."[39] The march overwhelmed many tired and hungry men, who simply crumpled asleep beside the road.[40] The hard rain soon turned the roads to mud, ankle and sometimes knee-deep, along the route to Dabney's Mill and Hatcher's Run. Brush and fallen trees also littered the path.[41] Hancock's prisoners, a column of several hundred Confederates led by their captors, trudged past Dabney's Mill and soon lost their way. "After marching and counter-marching for an hour or two," the group returned to the sawmill. "It was so very dark and the woods so dense," recalled one observer from Hancock's staff, "that all the prisoners who wished could and did probably escape during our peregrinations."[42]

The narrow, wooded roads, the persistent rain, and darkness baffled others.[43] The woods filled with small bands of blue and gray picking their way through the shrouded maze. Men lost contact even when walking or riding next to each other. In many cases, only the accents of strangers distinguished friend from foe. Soldiers were captured and recaptured. Wounded New Yorker Colonel Charles Weygant stumbled through the woods, often finding groups of rebel horsemen. At one point, he encountered the house of a frightened, elderly woman who provided directions back to the Union lines. He then wandered in the rain for several hours but eventually discovered the federal picket line at Dabney's Mill. "Little fires with squads of men gathered around them were burning all about this mill," wrote Weygant. With the help of an acquaintance, he dressed his wound and curled up in the sawdust to watch the ambulances and army wagons roll past toward the safety of the Union lines. In the wake of the trains, small groups of infantry appeared, followed by three or four light batteries, and then several squadrons of cavalry. The last elements of Hancock's command had withdrawn from the Burgess Farm.[44]

In Crawford's sector, more troops lost their way. On the right bank of Hatcher's Run, the 7th Wisconsin became completely isolated in the woods on the division's left flank. William F. Ray of Company F wrote in his journal, "Well, after eating lay down on the leaves, sticks &c and put my oilcloth over me & try to catch a little sleep. But to no use. The rain pours down. I feel the water soaking through my clothes and underneath but too tired to move."[45] Around 11 P.M., word spread that the enemy had appeared in the rear of the regiment. Though this proved untrue, the men decided to return to their lines anyway. This decision led to a confusing, fruitless trek. We "wandered & wandered & still wandered & and found no brigade," wrote Ray. By 2 A.M., they gave up and bivouacked where they stood, forming a small web in the woods, which managed to snare several lost rebels.[46]

One such Confederate was William Harrison. A member of the 12th Virginia's sharpshooter screen on Mahone's left flank, he had become completely lost after the Burgess Mill engagement. After the war, he shared his story of that night.

To his recollection, after wandering on horseback with a companion for several hours, he spied a light in the distance, which he hoped was the Dinwiddie courthouse. As he approached, the call "Who comes there?" caught his ears. Trying his hand at a bluff, Harrison called out, "Mahone's brigade." The voice in the dark shouted back, "7th Wisconsin," and offered to surrender. Unhesitating, Harrison turned in his saddle and sang out into the empty woods behind him, "Boys, come up and take charge of these prisoners." The ruse could not last long, though, and soon the federal officer ordered Harrison to dismount and blurted, "Why this is a real Yankee trick causing a full fledged regiment to surrender to two unarmed rebels." According to Harrison, he joined his foe at the campfire and fell asleep on the Union officer's rubber air bed.[47]

The evening's discomfort was shared by nearly everyone. Along the Ninth Corps front, the newly entrenched troops also endured the cold, soaking ran. An infantryman in Hartranft's brigade described the conditions to his friends back home in Appleton, Wisconsin: "The next time you have a rainy night, just imagine you belong to the Army of the Potomac, go out in the Park, let the pile of cord wood that generally adorns the southwest angle of the capitol represent the breastwork, wrap yourself in a cavalry overcoat, and take a seat on the bare ground, your back against the end of the sticks of wood, and if before morning you are not picked up by the patrol as a lunatic or inebriate, you will know how the night of October 27th was passed by a large portion of the Army of the Potomac."[48]

At the Boydton Plank Road, the last Union units slipped into the darkness smothering the Dabney Mill Road. Regis de Trobriand later reported that he "remained alone by the fire with my staff officers and my orderlies."[49] He kept the wood burning all along the line. The Confederates showed no sign of activity along the front. Finally, at one o'clock, de Trobriand ordered the picket line to withdraw. The men emerged from the woods and prepared to march back on the road.[50] De Trobriand left the field an hour later and rode along the Dabney Mill Road sweeping up stragglers. He passed the sawmill surrounded by Egan's men and crossed Hatcher's Run.

One Confederate correspondent from Matthew Butler's division described the Union withdrawal as a "perfect stampede."[51] But instead, Hancock, as he had done all day, managed his corps with skill and disengaged his two divisions right under the nose of the enemy. However, the failure to remove all the Union wounded from the Boydton Plank Road weighed on all involved, including Meade, who expressed regret about the event in his report.[52] By 3 A.M., the rain finally stopped, and the stars appeared over Dinwiddie County.[53] For those weary men still alive and awake at that hour, the sight of the twinkling heavens may have provided some solace after the trials of the previous day.

"pouring down upon me"

Hungry, soaked, and exhausted, the Confederates suffered just as much as their foes across the picket lines. Their thin blankets and oilcloth covers did little to buffer the uncomfortable conditions. "When I lay down that night in the pine woods with the rain pouring down upon me and the water six inches deep all around me I thought to never enjoy the luxuery of a sleep in bed again at home," recalled one rebel cavalryman.[54] Wounded men wandered along the dark farm paths searching for more substantial shelter than the pine branches overhead.

Captain A. B. Mulligan of the 5th South Carolina Cavalry, injured in his right hand, rode through the downpour with a companion, seeking a resting place. He found a large house near the battlefield owned by a man named Stone. Injured soldiers attended by busy surgeons packed the dwelling and its yard. The house had little room for two more men. Perhaps too weary to be polite, Mulligan entered a room reserved for the ladies of house and sat by the fire, apologizing for his intrusion. Mr. Stone later gently asked him to leave, but after the latter gave the Masonic distress sign, he found himself the sole occupant of a vacant adjoining room. He sent word to the surgeons to usher any wounded men from his regiment into this newly found space. As the night wore on, the room filled with the injured, several slipping into death before sunrise.[55] Mulligan survived the ordeal.

For Wade Hampton, the night brought particular agony. Thomas Taylor, from the general's staff, drew the task of attending to Preston Hampton's lifeless body. Taylor brought the young lieutenant's remains to the cavalry headquarters, now on the north side of Hatcher's Run near Burgess Mill. "Upon reaching there I took him into a tent which had been put up, changed his clothes which were saturated with his blood, and dressed him."[56] Later General Hampton returned from the field, having left his command in charge of Rooney Lee.[57] Taylor led the commander to his son's tent. Hampton entered and remained with his son's body for some time. That night, the deceased was taken to William R. Johnson's house in Petersburg, where Taylor and his staff prepared the body for burial.[58] Taylor later boarded a train at the Old Street Depot in Petersburg, along with his precious burden. After a long journey on the dilapidated rails of the Confederacy, he arrived with Preston's body in Columbia.[59]

In the midst of his grieving, Hampton still had work to do. He kept his men in line for the night, anticipating further action in the morning. According to William Mahone, word arrived during the evening from A. P. Hill in Petersburg, urging a new attack the next morning. Mahone, Heth, and Hampton met at Hampton's camp and planned a combined operation for daybreak. Under the scheme, Mahone, with fresh brigades from Heth's and Wilcox's divisions, would swing west of the Burgess Mill pond and join with Hampton's men south of Hatcher's

Run.[60] New troops arrived at Burgess Mill to participate in the morning assault. Cooke's North Carolina brigade marched out of its position at the Boydton Plank trench line and formed on the north bank of Hatcher's Run, just downstream from Burgess Mill. The Carolinians understood the dangerous work slated at the bridge the next morning and feared Unionist sharpshooters and artillery posted on the hills of Burgess Farm would enjoy a clear field of fire at the crossing. With "this pleasant prospect before us," wrote one veteran, "you may imagine we passed a comfortable night in anticipation."[61]

"attempt to break through the enemy's lines"

While Hancock's men quietly withdrew from the Burgess Farm, combat flared miles away in the trenches close to Petersburg. Earlier in the day, Brigadier General Nelson Miles had received a note from Meade's aide Seth Williams recommending an "attempt to break through the enemy's lines" should the opportunity arise.[62] Based on reports from pickets and signal stations, Miles ordered two probes that evening, one from Fort Morton near the Crater and another from Fort Sedgwick near the Jerusalem Plank Road.

At Fort Morton, one hundred men from the 148th Pennsylvania climbed over the Union works, hacked through the chevaux-de-frise, and crept toward the Confederate line near Davidson's battery. Armed with Spencers, the party advanced silently in the rain, forgoing shouts and calls. The appearance of the Union men coincided with a scheduled rotation of the rebel pickets, and, in the dreary darkness, many of the Confederates mistook the attackers for their own men while others guessed the blue-clad soldiers were deserters.[63] In the confusion, the Pennsylvanians snatched several prisoners, including some officers from the 46th Virginia regiment of Brigadier General Henry Wise's brigade. General Wise's nephew counted among the captured.[64] However, Confederate reinforcements quickly responded and repulsed the Pennsylvanians before more Unionists could arrive.[65] The brief moment of glory cost the attackers nearly four times as many casualties as the Confederates, including Lieutenant Henry Price, who led the storming party and went down with a bullet in his head as his men entered the battery. During the second probe, near Fort Sedgwick, members of the 88th New York seized a two-hundred-yard section of the rebel trench line near Fort Sedgwick.[66] However, in the face on a counterattack from South Carolina units, they withdrew to their own fortifications, losing more than a dozen men according to Confederate reports.[67]

"Hordes sank to their knees"

In Henrico County, Benjamin Butler's columns had begun their withdrawal from the day's fighting. Like the soldiers south of Petersburg, they faced the mud, rain, and darkness. The Eighteenth Corps, fresh from its repulse along the Williamsburg Road, commenced a night march south "with the grim cheerfulness that only veteran soldiers know." Everything, the wagons, ambulances, artillery batteries, horses, mounted officers, and troops, passed in a single column along a narrow wood road "scarcely wide enough for two wagons to pass each other." "Hordes sank to their knees almost every step," wrote one journalist. "Wagons went down to their axles, and among these the troops waded and swore, and cracked grim jokes."[68] A heavy rain fell continuously for seven hours.[69] The night march did not bring the soldiers to warmth or shelter, however. Most men in the Tenth and Eighteenth Corps spent the evening hiding from the cold rain.

The Eighteenth Corps halted and took positions at the Charles City Road, connecting with the right of the Tenth Corps. Both corps remained in these positions well into the afternoon of the 28th.[70] By keeping these units on the field, Grant sought to bait Lee, hoping to lure the Confederates into a costly counterattack. Grant may have sought to generate another unsuccessful rebel assault like the recent attacks on Fort Harrison and at the New Market Road.[71]

CHAPTER 18

Aftermath

~

Testimony of Captain James C. Farwell, 1st Minnesota Volunteers

Question by the Judge Advocate: What did you do at 9:30 o'clock in the morning of the 28th of October 1864 with your command?

Answer: I called in what men I had posted in my front during the night and also the 19th Regt Mass Vol. which I knew were posted in the edge of the timber. I sent out men from 7 until 8:30 AM, in different parties to see if our troops were occupying the same position they did on the night before or had left. They failed to report back. I then sent a commissioned officer up to the house where the Battery was stationed in the afternoon on the 27th. He went to the house; came back on the run and reported that we had no forces there but that the enemy's cavalry were advancing. I satisfied myself that our troops had left and started out of the timber. Ninety-three enlisted men and five commissioned officers was the command I had. As soon as we commenced marching out the enemy followed in our rear and struck the timber and commenced firing. We crossed the plank road and the enemy's cavalry came down on a charge from the plank road at the same time we were crossing. I about faced the command and ordered them to fire. We broke the cavalry—they scattered and went back to the rear. I then marched into the timber, after we had gone some quarter of a mile in the timber the enemy charged in where we were, with a yell. I did not halt the command. I kept marching, and marched about a mile and a half and halted the command to rest them, then formed them in two ranks and took the course by the sun; struck the Weldon Rail-road about 1½ miles north of Reams Station about four or half past four o'clock in the afternoon of the 28th. I then followed the Rail-road up until I came to our cavalry pickets. On the morning of the 29th I reported to Division and Brigade headquarters.[1]

As revealed by Captain Farwell's testimony, the imperfect withdrawal of the Union Second Corps had stranded a significant portion of Egan's picket line. Farwell's command, men from the 1st Minnesota and the 7th Michigan,[2] awoke

Friday morning to an empty battlefield. During their cross-country trek to the Union lines, Farwell tore the Minnesota flag from its staff and handed it to the color sergeant, who wrapped it around his body under his clothing. Farwell also ripped the national colors into pieces and handed each man a star or other portion of the cloth, "so that the enemy would have failed to capture them, except after the death of the whole command, and the search of their bodies."[3] After escaping the rebel videttes, Farwell and his band tramped through the wet, tangled Dinwiddie countryside, forded over Hatcher's Run, and gained the Weldon Railroad. They returned to camp as heroes, garnering praise for their courage and perseverance.[4] Hancock made sure to mention the feat in his battle report.[5]

Farwell's exploits would not have been necessary without the gross negligence of someone in command. That distinction fell to Lieutenant Colonel Horace Rugg, the unfortunate brigade commander who had frozen during Mahone's attack. The Farwell incident added a second stain to Rugg's performance. In the rainy night following the battle, Rugg had tried to remove his picket line. Early in the evening, he dispatched an orderly to locate Farwell, but the messenger had no luck in the heavy timber. Around midnight, Lieutenant William Sawyer of the 19th Maine then unsuccessfully searched the fields and forests for forty-five minutes.[6] These efforts received little credit during Rugg's court-martial hearing at Yellow Tavern just days after the battle. In the end, the result spoke for itself, and Rugg was found guilty in the matter.

"a lively run to prevent being captured"

South of Hatcher's Run at 1 A.M. Friday, Samuel Crawford received orders to withdraw his Fifth Corps division. He threw out a strong skirmish line in front and ushered his command across Hatcher's Run at 3 A.M. on a bridge built the previous evening.[7] With his force safe and his skirmishers gathered in, he sent the 24th Michigan back across the run as a rear guard. Picking their way through the bushes, the Michigan men soon stumbled headlong into the enemy and "had a lively run to prevent being captured."[8] Crawford's column clawed its way downstream through the undergrowth and eventually emerged into the open near the Armstrong house.[9] At 5:30 A.M., Crawford informed Warren that his men had all reached the north bank.[10] But Crawford was mistaken, for more men remained in the woods.

During the withdrawal, Washington Roebling, from General Warren's staff, rode toward the Dabney Mill at dawn, searching for stragglers. After encountering General Egan from the Second Corps at the sawmill, Roebling traveled northwest to the Crow Farm and found an officer and two men searching for the wayward 7th Wisconsin. Joining the hunt, Roebling rode through the woods and stumbled into the lost regiment, which had sixty rebel prisoners in tow. Roebling pointed the Wisconsin men toward the Union lines.[11] At 7:20 A.M., Crawford reported the regiment's return.[12]

Ten minutes later, Roebling returned to the sawmill and "found everything but stragglers gone."[13] Instead of heading back east to Warren's headquarters, the curious major rode toward the Plank Road and Hancock's battlefield from the day before. He found many stragglers, including some of Gregg's cavalry returning from the Burgess Farm. Near the Rainey house, he observed more Union men. However, Confederate troops began to appear on the edge of the woods beyond the Plank Road. "When I turned to come back, say 8.30," he reported, "there were still some wounded men limping along. There was plenty of time to have taken them safely that morning."[14]

Despite the abundance of stragglers, the Confederates pulled the drawstrings of a mostly empty net. If sprung earlier, the trap would have yielded more, including Farwell's command, but rebels advanced Friday morning cautiously. West of the Burgess Farm, Mahone marched several brigades beyond the head of the mill pond. Just as he crossed Hatcher's Run and turned east toward the Burgess Farm, he met Wade Hampton. "Gen. Hampton and I had gone but a short distance before we met [Pierce] Young . . . who informed us that the enemy had retreated."[15] At Burgess Mill, rebel sharpshooters clambered across the millrace to find the works empty on the hill above.[16] Nathaniel Harris pushed ahead two companies of his Mississippi brigade and captured eighty stragglers.[17] The Confederates continued to press east and eventually encountered Union cavalry led by Lieutenant Colonel James Walsh protecting the Dabney Mill Road. Walsh's men blunted the rebel probe with "two well-directed volleys" but soon pulled back across Hatcher's Run and warned Warren about the approaching foe.[18]

By 11 A.M., Meade reported that all his forces had recrossed Hatcher's Run.[19] Weary from the night march back from the Boydton Plank Road, Mott's Second Corps division spread out along the Vaughan Road near the Wyatt house, and Egan's division rested at the Armstrong house, just north of Armstrong's Mill. By 10 A.M., both divisions had stumbled back toward the Union trenches, headed for their old camps east of Petersburg.[20] As Hancock rode past a Pennsylvania regiment, one soldier noted that he showed a "clouded, angry brow and hatless head."[21]

Along Parke and Warren's front, the Ninth and Fifth troops remained in their makeshift works through much of the morning inviting the kind of hopeless Confederate attacks Grant desired.[22] At daybreak near the Clements house, Confederates tested the Union lines, but rifles from Griffin's division sent the attackers tumbling back with well-directed fire.[23] On the Union right to the north, Parke's Ninth Corps began to withdraw about 1 P.M., with Orlando Willcox's division shoving back first amid only "slight interference" from the enemy.[24] On the left, in Robert Potter's front, Confederate cavalry sought to cut off the retreat, but an intervening swamp mired their attempt.[25] Potter's division then formed in battle line and opened to allow the other divisions to pass into the Union fortifications. As the Ninth Corps soldiers withdrew, a loud cheer rose from portions of the rebel line.[26] By 6 P.M. on the 28th, the corps had safely ensconced itself in the forts and trenches around the Peebles Farm, and the men had time to reflect on the fight many would soon call the "Boydton Plank Road," "Hatcher's Run," or "Burgess Mill."[27] Back at camp, Colonel Lyman wrote home to say, "To-day we marched back scientifically (we are hard to beat on a retreat I can tell you)."[28]

"suffered quite severely"

With the Union forces huddled in the safety of their fortifications, it was time to count heads and assess damage. Their losses seemed unremarkable in comparison to those ginned out by other battles. But the human damage was not trivial. Southwest of Petersburg, Meade's forces suffered nearly 1,800 casualties. Much of this number came from Hancock's Second Corps, which totaled 1,058 losses, including nearly 100 killed and more than 400 captured or missing.[29] Byron Pierce's brigade, which had been swept up by Mahone's attack, contributed the most to the count, with Regis de Trobriand's unit running a close second.[30] Gregg's cavalry, also along the Boydton Plank Road, lost 171 men, more than two-thirds from the 1st Maine and 21st Pennsylvania of Colonel Charles Smith's brigade. After the battle, A. P. Hill claimed that a total of 700 Union soldiers had fallen into his hands.[31] At least one participant expressed surprise at the low tallies. "It was truly astonishing that under such an artillery fire as that concentrated upon that field filled with troops, ambulances, caissons, horses, and pack mules, so few were injured by the shrieking missiles," recalled a Massachusetts veteran. "The losses from infantry fire were quite small, when we call to mind the volleys poured into our ranks."[32]

To the north of Hatcher's Run, Warren and Parke lost fewer men, suffering more than 400 casualties in all. In Warren's command, the green regiments of Colonel Edgar Gregory's brigade had the greatest loss. These units broke during the early morning combat and flooded rearward over General Warren and his staff.[33] Remarkably, Samuel Crawford's division, enveloped by the Hatcher's Run wilderness for much of the operation, reported only 47 casualties. In Parke's corps, Hartranft's and Cutcheon's brigades from Willcox's division counted 30 casualties apiece, and the USCTs of Edward Ferrero's first brigade lost 75.[34]

The Confederate losses at the Boydton Plank Road spoke of the battle's ferocity. Not surprisingly, Mahone's task force took the brunt of the blow. The astounding casualties in William MacRae's North Carolina brigade and in the Virginia brigade rendered the battle at Burgess Mill one of the war's costliest engagements for both veteran brigades. According to Heth's official return, the Tar Heel brigade suffered

516 casualties, 431 of which were captured after the failed assault. David Weisiger's Virginians, Mahone's old brigade, lost 328 to combat, 277 of whom were missing. Only 25 men from both brigades died in the fight.[35] Union reports confirmed Mahone's losses. On Friday morning, John Babcock informed Meade's headquarters that Union forces had captured 689 Confederates near Burgess Mill. Though more than 500 of these were taken by the Second Corps, the Fifth Corps managed to scoop up 148 Confederates, mostly from Weisiger's Virginia brigade.[36] Heth's and Hampton's commands lost fewer. Casualties from Davis's Mississippi brigade, Cooke's North Carolinians, and Harris's Mississippians were comparatively light.[37] Hampton's official returns are not extant, either, but newspaper reports place losses in Dearing's brigade at 88 and Butler's South Carolina brigade at 69.[38] One study estimates total Confederate casualties along the Boydton Plank Road at 956 infantrymen and 318 cavalry, for a total loss of 1,274.[39]

The fight at Burgess Mill produced as least one false casualty report. Following the battle, rumors of the death of Confederate cavalry commander James Dearing circulated widely. On the 28th, Grant's dispatch to Washington contained the news about Dearing's demise, which echoed reports from rebels captured at the battle.[40] The *New York Herald* ran an obituary of sorts for the "brave and dashing" Virginian, describing him as a promising young officer.[41] Union soldiers reported Dearing's death to his mother in Campbell County, showing her his sword and explaining that her son had been buried near Burgess Mill.[42] Fortunately for Dearing and his family, the story was untrue. Catching wind of the rumors, Dearing rushed a telegraph message to his wife on Friday, assuring her he was very much alive. The next day, he managed to provide more detail in a letter, explaining that his brigade had "suffered quite severely in killed and wounded." He had lost "twelve or fifteen officers" but successfully navigated the fight unscathed. In the midst of battle, however, a bullet passed through his horse, "going in just behind my left leg & carrying out at the shoulder on the other side."[43] This incident may have fueled the stories about his death.

North of the James, the Union losses belied the mistakes committed by Butler and his generals. At the Williamsburg Road, Weitzel's Eighteenth Corps lost 1,064 men (63 killed, 330 wounded, and 671 captured) mostly from the two brigades that conducted the ill-fated assault there. Harrison Fairchild's command had 366 casualties (263 of which were captured), and Edgar Cullen's brigade suffered 344 (258 captured).[44] Confederate General James Longstreet reported 600 prisoners and 11 stands of colors at Williamsburg Road in his official report.[45] At the Darbytown Road, the Union Tenth Corps lost 526 men, according to the official returns. Most of these casualties came from Colonel Martin Curtis's brigade, which had launched the useless advance in the late afternoon.[46] The Confederates of Charles Field's division, manning the trenches in front, claimed nearly 400 prisoners and 7 stands of colors.[47] The Confederate losses were predictably light. Field's entire division lost only 64, of which 42 were listed as wounded in his casualty return.[48] There is no official record of the losses in Robert Hoke's command, but it is likely they were very small.

"strewn all through the woods and fields"

The neat, printed numbers on the official casualty returns yield an abstract, sanitized picture of the day's results. Only those who walked the ground at the Williamsburg Road and the Burgess Farm could appreciate the real damage. On these fields, the detritus of battle generated gut-wrenching scenes. In correspondence with the Confederate War Department, Robert E. Lee reported 250 Union dead found in the fields near the Boydton Plank Road.[49] A South Carolina cavalryman ventured out on the Burgess Farm Friday morning to find Union dead left unburied: "Hundreds of their wounded were abandoned, guns, cartridge boxes, ammunition . . . strewed the ground." The horseman also observed three charred ambulances sitting in the fields unattended. "The scenes of Manassas were in a manner reenacted," he remarked.[50] Another South Carolinian spied a new red flannel shirt on the body of a Union soldier. With his comrades looking on, he dismounted and sought to tug the shirt off the corpse. "As he turned him over on his face he found very little of the Yankee or the shirt either, as his whole back had been torn off by a shell." He rode off in silence, trailed by his friends' laughter.[51]

There were other grim scenes. A North Carolinian discovered Union bodies "partially eaten up by hogs."[52] "The enemy's dead were found thickly strewn through the woods and fields," reported a North Carolina paper. At one spot in the woods west of the Plank Road, Confederates found and buried fifty-three bodies. Corpses were crowded around the Burgess house "by the score."[53] Members of the 12th Virginia Infantry in Weisiger's brigade arrived at the Burgess property to help bury the dead.[54] To the north of Hatcher's Run, the Confederates found the dead of the Union Fifth Corps in front of the new trenches. Wade Hampton visited the lines at one point and found fifteen blue-clad corpses in one location.[55]

The fields along the Boydton Plank Road contained more than bodies. Edward Wells, a cavalryman from Charleston, managed to find canteens, coats, blankets, hats, and "a countless number" of enemy rifles. He also picked up a knapsack packed with crackers, which he used to break his long fast.[56] A Richmond paper reported that the plunder from Burgess Mill was "quite plentiful and varied. Blankets, overcoats, pistols, oil clothes, haversacks, etc., were strewn all through the woods and fields, and were gathered up in large quantities by our soldiers."[57]

At the Williamsburg Road, the fields before the Confederates held the results of Weitzel's folly. After the battle on the 27th, a detail retrieved the corpses of the unlucky men from Fairchild's and Cullen's brigades. The rebels promptly filled a few nearby water wells with the bodies. To the north on the Nine Mile Road, the remains of black soldiers killed during or after the engagement were left to rot on the ground. One Confederate cavalryman, riding along the road three months later, encountered the bodies lying where they fell on October 27, "skin intact minus the eye ball." "It was a horrid, gruesome sight to behold," recalled the horseman. "I've seen dogs preying upon some of the dead."[58]

Away from the fields, wounded soldiers clad in blue continued to trickle into the Confederate hospitals. John H. Claiborne, in charge of the medical facilities at Petersburg, wrote home that the rebels had buried more than three hundred federals. The captured federal wounded were hungry and tired. Many died.[59] Conditions were better for the hundred or so Union wounded taken off the field by Union ambulances on Thursday night. The wagons crossed Hatcher's Run in the darkness and by morning had reached the Halifax Road. Near the Perkins house, Union medical staff dressed wounds and fed the men in a temporary hospital. By dark, military trains were carrying the wounded from Warren's Station, a stop on the military road, to City Point.[60] The Union hospitals filled with wounded. "I am very busy at present," wrote a surgeon in the Second Corps. "My hospital is overcrowded—so full indeed that I was compelled to send some fifty or sixty of my wounded to the 1st Division Hospital. Yesterday and today I have had a great deal of operating."[61]

"torn to pieces"

As disturbing as the battlefield may have been for hardened veterans, the carnage profoundly unsettled the people who called the place home. Mary Burgess and her children remained in Petersburg after the fight, hearing little from the family's farm "save the passing of the soldiers." Soon, however, Mrs. Burgess and her children traveled home on the floorboards of an empty army wagon. As they neared the house, her father-in-law greeted them with tears in his eyes. He explained that he had survived Thursday's combat hidden under a log. Following the battle, he had heard nothing about his family except for the vague reports that the women had last been seen headed north over the bridge. The elder Burgess gathered up one of his grandchildren in his arms and rejoiced.

Nearly every inch of the Burgess Farm bore the battle's impact. As Mary Burgess entered the property, she witnessed the dead spread about, some curled up beside the road. The Burgess dwellings had served as a combat zone during the battle and as a field hospital after the fight. She entered anyway. In her father-in-law's home, as she recalled years later, blood covered the parlor, and the couch bore a legless soldier from Maine, who cried out, "My poor wife and children." In the dining room, twelve wounded Union men lay about the floor; many could not speak English. The kitchen table had held patients after the battle, and the family's dish tub "was a receptacle for amputated members—toes, fingers, in fact, anything coming from under the surgeon's knife."[62]

Mary Burgess's house had been "nearly demolished, riddled by shells and finally torn to pieces, the remnants being burned." Though men had sought refuge there, sixteen lost their lives in her sitting room. She recalled that "one poor soldier seated himself to rest on the floor, gun by his side, with his back to the wall, when a shell struck him in the small of the back, tearing his body to shreds all over the room, his entrails dangling from the walls." In clearing the carnage, the Confederates threw the bodies into a shallow pit "not sufficient to prevent the hogs from rooting them up and devouring them."[63]

Nothing of value remained in the Burgess houses. Soldiers had blown open the family safe, pried open locked bookcases with their bayonets, taken all Mary Burgess's clothes, and pilfered every morsel of food. Shortly after the battle, one Union infantryman, rifling through her clothes trunk, was overheard to say, "Here goes a handsome silk dress for the prettiest girl in Herkimer County," not knowing that the dress's real owner actually hailed from that very New York locale. Later, Burgess located her watch in the possession of a liveryman in Herkimer, but failed to regain it, for "it was looked upon as a relic of the war."[64]

The evening of their return, a "renegade" free black woman brought the family a dinner of chicken, biscuits, corn bread, and coffee. According to Mary Burgess, the woman "purloined her living by raiding chicken coops, working by day in the field and foraging when she could." She provided the food to the Burgess family and then left, asking for nothing in return. Afterward, the Confederate soldiers camped at the farm furnished the family with what they could. "Biscuit and coffee were our main diet," recalled Mary Burgess. Eventually, conditions became unbearable. With the help of General Wade Hampton, she arranged to travel through the lines near the Cummings house. There, Petersburg native Roger Pryor piloted her and the children through a ravine to the Union picket line. After many interviews with Union officials, Mary Burgess left Petersburg and headed for Washington to rejoin her husband.[65]

Grant's Sixth Offensive Considered

~

"reconnaissance in force"

Grant's sixth offensive at Petersburg ended a failure in many respects. Union troops did not reach the South Side Railroad, seize the Boydton Plank Road, or break rebel trench lines in Henrico County. In fact, compared to the successes of the fifth offensive in September, the sixth was underwhelming. It gained no significant ground and merely added to the long list of Union casualties already generated by the Virginia campaign.

Faced with these discouraging results, Union leaders downplayed the operation's significance. Instead of the determined effort to seize the South Side Railroad, originally envisioned by Union planners, the movement became a "reconnaissance." Reporting the day's events to the secretary of war, Grant described the operation as a "reconnaissance, which I had intended for more."[1] In Washington, Secretary of War Edwin Stanton embellished the spin, announcing in an official dispatch that "an advance in force, for the purpose of reconnaissance, was made yesterday."[2] After the fact, the operation was transformed into a modest undertaking with a limited scope and inconsequential results, a mere information-gathering exercise. In a sense, these post hoc characterizations accurately described the operation as it played out. Although the Union high command may not have intended a reconnaissance, the operation certainly resembled one at the end of the day. Cautious probes and careful positioning marked the activity at the Clements house and the Burgess Farm. None of Meade's forces launched a determined attack against rebel positions. And, with the exception of the response to Mahone's attack, Union forces did little fighting during the day. Oddly enough, the only serious attack had occurred in Butler's sector, the very place Grant did not want such combat.

Lincoln's opponents, north and south, pounced on the explanations offered by the Union generals and the administration. The indignation of the *New York Daily News* was typical: "The effort to mislead the public by representing Gen. Grant's late movement as a complete success, turns out to be a complete failure. The absurdity of calling the movement a reconnaissance in force, is so palpable, that none will be deceived by it. It was a real advance, long prepared for, carefully planned. . . . The statement that a movement in which two large armies were engaged was nothing more than a reconnaissance is simply preposterous, and may be looked upon as a gratuitous insult to the common intelligence of the people."[3]

The *New York World,* which was quick to pronounce Grant's campaign as a failure, correctly noted that the term "reconnaissance" had become attached to the operation as a "convenient afterthought."[4] The same newspaper also printed a soldier's letter about the move "on Thursday that will be called a reconnaissance," saying, "In fact, we started for Richmond and failed badly."[5] In the south, the *Charleston Mercury* argued that the statements from Washington and the Northern press simply verified its prediction "that a 'reconnaissance in force' would be" the report stemming from the "bloody defeat" on Thursday.[6] The *Richmond Whig* scoffed that, if the affair was in fact a reconnaissance, "then it was certainly the biggest reconnaissance, we ever heard of."[7] Years later, a Confederate veteran echoed the sentiment: "If it was a victory for the blue coats, all I have to say is that about three more just like it would have demolished Grant's army."[8]

The skepticism was not limited to Copperheads and secessionists. Many in the army also found the story troublesome. Charles Mills, a member of Hancock's staff, warned his family not to believe "what you see in the papers that the movement of the 27th October was merely a reconnaissance."[9] According to Charles Wainwright, the Fifth Corps artillery chief, the semantic game as amplified by the newspapers afforded "a vast deal of amusement in the army."[10] Robert McAllister, one of the heroes at Burgess Mill, wryly observed that the force employed was quite large for a mere reconnaissance.[11] Colonel Lyman, at Meade's headquarters, placed matters in context: "As the Mine was to be termed an ill-conducted fizzle," he wrote, "so this attempt may be called a well-conducted fizzle."[12] One Second Corps sharpshooter, a McClellan supporter, took a more severe, albeit unreasonable view, describing the event as the "most disastrous defeat" suffered by Grant yet.[13]

Whatever they called it, few Unionists cheered the operation's results. In the wake of Friday's withdrawal, soldiers and officers dissected the ill-fated offensive, seeking to pin down the reasons for failure. The finger pointing began almost immediately. William C. Church, editor of the *Army and Navy Journal,* canvassed the camps at Petersburg on Saturday, gathering information on the recent movement.[14] First, Samuel Crawford's division, which had floundered in the thickets along Hatcher's Run, fell under his scrutiny. Church's paper declared, "The failure of Crawford's . . . division of the Fifth to connect with the Second corps on the left . . . was calamitous."[15] However, the article also acknowledged that Crawford's men would have "gladly performed their part" but struggled, "completely astray," in the impenetrable woods.[16] Confederate General Henry Heth agreed that Crawford's movement held the key. In a postwar letter to his friend Winfield Hancock, Heth wrote that the

"grave error of the day committed on your side, in my opinion . . . was that, after crossing Hatcher's Run and starting to march up, Crawford permitted himself
to be stopped in certainly half a mile or less, of my right flank." A more vigorous
movement by Crawford, in Heth's view, would have turned the Confederate works
completely and forced them out of their prepared positions.[17] Even Grant expressed
concern with Crawford's effort, asking Meade immediately after the battle, "Where
was Crawford . . . by boldly pushing up, he could have annihilated all of the enemy
south of the run."[18] In a lengthy reply, Meade explained that Crawford's inability to
advance along Hatcher's Run and connect with Hancock rested on the nature of the
ground and the presence of the enemy in his sector.[19]

Crawford was not the sole target of criticism. John G. Parke and his Ninth
Corps also drew fire. Charles Wainwright, the Fifth Corps artillery chief, believed
the operation's failure stemmed from the Ninth Corps' late start. Everyone held
this opinion, at least according to Wainwright. Parke's assigned route covered less
than a mile beyond Fort Cummings through country easily reconnoitered before
the operation. But when the morning of the offensive arrived, Parke's columns
crawled forward.[20] The *Army and Navy Journal* noted this "want of prompt-
ness."[21] The charge held merit. Parke's vanguard waited more than an hour before
sweeping toward the rebel pickets at Fort MacRae. This inexplicable delay granted
the Confederates all the time necessary to rush men into the new works and block
the heaviest portion of the Union offensive.

"a stronger flanking column"

While Crawford's misadventures and Parke's sluggishness certainly contributed to
the unsatisfactory result, the root cause of failure stemmed from the operation's
design, not its execution. Meade, the chief architect, offered a candid assessment:
"This project was based upon information which led to the belief that the enemy's
line only extended to the crossing of Hatcher's Run by the Boydton plank road,
and that it was not completed this far and was weakly manned. The movement
was promptly made as directed, but, instead of finding the enemy's line as expected, it was found to extend over the run nearly to Armstrong's Mill, was fully
completed, and very strongly fortified by slashings and abatis."[22]

In other words, Union intelligence got it wrong. The general plan had been
a decent one. The Confederates could not stretch their right flank indefinitely.
Indeed, the nascent rebel Boydton Plank line offered the Unionists an opportunity. But because the planners assumed that the new Confederate earthworks
were weak and vulnerable, they flung their strength directly at the fresh rebel line.
Parke's Ninth Corps found the enemy works formidable, manned, and covered
with obstacles. Instead of sweeping over them, his men spent the day digging in

and extending their line back to the Union fortifications. Warren's Fifth Corps also failed to make progress against the same trenches. In fact, the instructions to Warren mischaracterized the ground in his sector. The plans assumed that the Confederate line terminated at Burgess Mill. It did not. The plan assumed that Warren could easily cross Hatcher's Run and join Hancock. He could not. The concentration of so many troops north of the run deprived Hancock's flanking column of the strength it desperately needed. As Meade's chief of staff Andrew Humphreys explained years later, "It kept two-thirds of our force at the right of Lee's intrenchments substantially doing nothing, when the two-thirds should have been at the movable end of the column."[23] Charles Mills, at Hancock's headquarters, also noted this concern. "Why the 5th and 9th didn't do more, I can't say, but that was what spoiled it. Unless it was intended that they should really fight, and not skirmish, we ought to have had a stronger flanking column."[24]

Why didn't Parke and Warren do more? Why did Union intelligence misjudge the nature of the rebel line? Why did Crawford not push harder through the wilderness south of Hatcher's Run? These were the questions no doubt discussed in camp after Grant's sixth offensive. Such ex post facto analysis had become common with the Army of the Potomac. Time and again in Virginia, the army set out to end the war but inevitably fell short or came reeling back. Some problem always arose. The performance of Confederate commanders often aided the failure. During the Second Manassas campaign and at Chancellorsville, for example, Robert E. Lee's operational and tactical acumen made the difference. In other cases, the failure rested with the Union leaders. At Fredericksburg, Cold Harbor, and the Crater, poor intelligence, weak planning, ineffective battlefield leadership, or just plain bad luck brought disaster. Soldiers in Meade's army grew accustomed to disappointment, and so did the Northern public.

Grant's sixth offensive would not rank among these other disasters. There had been no crushing loss, no backward movement, and no mortal blow. Nevertheless, the barren gains fueled despondency. New Yorker Robert Tilney, a clerk at the Fifth Corps headquarters, confessed to his diary, "This is a gloriously unlucky army. I begin to think it never will do anything."[25] One Union officer in the western theater observed shortly afterward, "Three different times had Richmond and Petersburg been virtually in his hands and by some unexcusable neglect or slowness each time his plans were ruined and the opportunity. How Grant stands it I do not see."[26]

"I did more than I was ordered to do"

Events north of the James did not improve anyone's assessment. Butler's operation achieved its objective, namely to occupy the Confederates east of Richmond and prevent their redeployment to the fighting at Petersburg. But Butler had gone too far. The attacks at the Darbytown Road, at Oak Grove on the Williamsburg Road, and at the Nine Mile Road had yielded the fruitless bloodletting Grant had sought to avoid. Butler and his generals believed their plan held promise. After the operation, Godfrey Weitzel concluded that a faster march would have gained the Confederate flank and turned Longstreet out of his position.[27] He also delivered an accurate self-appraisal in his official report: "I regret that six colors were lost by the two brigades which attacked on the Williamsburg road, but under the circumstances I attach no blame to these brigades for this loss—they got in too hot a place, for which I and the rapid movement of the enemy's troops are responsible. I did more than I was ordered to do. I knew that my orders were simply to make a demonstration. I probably made a more lively demonstration than was intended, but at the same time I did not wish to march sixteen miles and then come back without finding out exactly what the enemy had there."[28]

The young general understood the depth of his failure. Apparently, weighed down by the burdens of command, he had sought to honor the spirit of Butler's orders. His doubt and anxiety may have clouded his judgment, causing him to focus more on Butler's ambitions than the well-being of his troops. Though his actions may have appeared bold and decisive, the grim results spoke for themselves.

While some blame certainly stuck to Weitzel, most of it lay at Benjamin Butler's feet. Butler's vision for the day outpaced Grant's expectations. Success at Fort Harrison in September may have fueled an unrealistic optimism. On October 27, casting aside his role as an integral part of the high command, he acted for his own glory. His orders demonstrated neglect for Grant's directive and put unnecessary pressure on Weitzel to launch an attack, even under uncertain conditions. Butler's poor leadership led to more than a thousand casualties.

Butler's overreaching did not escape the attention of Cyrus Comstock, a member of Grant's staff, who spent the day along the Henrico front. Comstock clearly understood that Grant had instructed his corps commanders to avoid attacking entrenchments.[29] He also knew the limited nature of Butler's assigned role as he observed the action outside Richmond. He took notice as General Terry, "under pressure" from Butler, threw his line at the Darbytown Road and as Weitzel launched his disastrous assault at the Williamsburg Road. Comstock worked "hard to prevent both," but Butler's determination, applied either directly or indirectly to his subordinates, controlled the day and led to the unfortunate attacks. Butler had his eyes on Richmond and, in Comstock's estimation, was willing to risk up to three thousand men to gain the capital.[30] After a long day with him, Comstock had developed a marked disdain for the Massachusetts lawyer. That evening "Butler told many stories," wrote Comstock "mostly about himself—if they are not colored he is most unscrupulous & would stop at nothing to carry out his ends/ at no means fair or foul to punish one who crossed his path."[31] At Grant's headquarters, John Rawlins noted in his diary that Butler had lost many men and

failed to cause damage to the enemy despite "positive orders not to attack" fortifications. "I am free to say I fear the continuance of General Butler in command
will some day work disaster of a serious character to our arms," he wrote.[32]

Soon after the operation, Butler's tenure outside Richmond came to an abrupt
end. The administration called for his services in New York City to maintain peace
there on election day. The general threw himself into that job, a mission well-suited
for his intelligence and organizational skills. By December, he was directing operations against Fort Fisher in North Carolina, where his scheme to breach the fort
by igniting a power-laden ship resulted in a loud noise, but nothing more. Grant,
weary of Butler's military ineffectiveness and no longer burdened by his political
connections in the election's wake, relieved him.

"the success of the operation"

For all the concern and despair, the events of October 27 held a silver lining for
the Union army. Winfield Hancock's beleaguered Second Corps had fought its
way out of a tight spot and reversed a long string of setbacks. When William
Mahone launched his attack shortly after 4 P.M., the day had the markings of another Reams Station debacle. But Hancock and his generals rallied their men and
crushed the Confederates. "I am induced to believe the success of the operation,
which was most decided," wrote Meade, "was mainly due to the personal exer-
tions of Major-General Hancock and the conspicuous gallantry of Brigadier-General Egan."[33] Grant's sentiments echoed Meade's report.[34]

Hancock generously praised his men. He thanked both his division commanders, Egan and Mott, but heaped particular attention on the former and, two days
after the battle, personally complimented Robert McAllister.[35] On November 4,
Hancock issued congratulatory orders to the entire corps, also acknowledging
General Gregg's contributions. "Newspaper correspondents who were not on the
field have misrepresented the affair," he explained, "speaking of it as a disaster,
giving those troops less credit than is accorded them by our enemies."[36] The next
day, Hancock held a formal review of his entire command.[37] On the 7th, General
Meade augmented the accolades by allowing several regiments that had lost their
colors during previous battles to carry them once again.[38]

Not everyone was so thrilled. Some viewed the attention lavished upon Egan's
division as an intentional slight to Gershom Mott's command, which contained
remnants of the old Third Corps, broken up before the commencement of the
1864 campaigning. Some former Third Corps members believed their old formation never received the respect it deserved. Brigade commander Regis de Trobri-
and was one of them. To him, Hancock's report reeked with a deep-seated bias:
"When a landscape-painter finds his subject for a painting in nature, on transfer-

ring it to his canvas, he puts in the lights and shades as pleases him." De Trobriand complained that the report bestowed prominence to Egan's troops but shoved Mott's command, especially de Trobriand's brigade, into the background. De Trobriand respected Hancock and understood that the general yearned to restore his corps' reputation following Reams Station. But, in the Frenchman's eyes, he had done so "while giving a lesson in modesty to those of the old Third Corps."[39]

Though Hancock may have expressed public satisfaction with the results of the offensive, his private correspondence betrayed unhappiness. In a November 3, 1864, letter to Francis Barlow, one of his division commanders who was convalescing in Boston, Hancock confessed, "I am tired of serving here. We do not get our share of credit considering the fighting we do."[40] He predicted that Sheridan would soon command the Army of the Potomac in reward for his recent successes in the Valley. For his part, Hancock had no interest in commanding the army but, instead, preferred a separate assignment. He was simply tired of serving under "ungenerous people."[41] Burgess Mill would prove to be Winfield Hancock's last battlefield command. Several weeks into November, he left the Army of the Potomac to organize a new corps, composed entirely of veterans. In his place, Andrew A. Humphreys, Meade's intelligent chief of staff, assumed charge of the Second Corps and ably led the men for the war's duration.[42]

Hancock found little success in organizing the new corps and finished the war with no further campaigning. After the conflict's end, he supervised the execution of the Lincoln conspirators and, during Reconstruction, headed the Fifth Military District, which covered Texas and Louisiana; he eventually became the army's most senior Major General. In 1880, he won the Democratic nomination for president but lost the general election to James Garfield.

"a great calamity will befall us"

The Confederates celebrated the results of October 27. "It now seems that our success beyond Petersburg was quite as complete as it was below Richmond," announced a Charleston paper.[43] Two days after the fight, James Longstreet suggested the effort had damaged "the prospects of the present Yankee administration." He even expected further operations to bring additional success before the election.[44] However, some in the ranks did not agree. A trooper in the 9th Virginia Cavalry wrote home several days after the fighting, explaining that the Union troops "are in their old position they started from on that morning, I think it will be some time before they can make another fight."[45]

Southern eyes viewed Mahone's attack on the Burgess Farm as a smashing victory, the kind of daring, clever assault that yielded good newspaper copy and boosted morale. At the same time, Confederate accounts, beginning with that of

Robert E. Lee, downplayed the effort's tremendous costs, focusing little attention on the havoc wrought on two reliable veteran brigades. In addition, few noted or perhaps even realized that Mahone's attack had been unnecessary given Grant's decision earlier that afternoon to cancel the offensive.

Henry Heth, who orchestrated the Confederate defense along the Boydton Plank Road, praised those under his command. In his report, he singled out gunner Lieutenant Colonel William Pegram for "gallant and efficient" service and also commended MacRae's, Cooke's, and Davis's brigades. "Brigades less resolute might have been shaken," he wrote, "receiving fire, as they did, from the front, flank and rear during the greater portion of this day."[46] Heth did not thank everyone, though. He severely criticized William Mahone for alleged inaccuracies and exaggerations in the latter's own battle report. To Heth, Mahone falsely claimed credit for the attack plan and slighted Wade Hampton's contributions. Heth also objected to Mahone's accusation that the forces at Burgess Mill—Harris's and Dearing's units under Heth's immediate control—failed to support the assault.[47] Finally, Heth did not appreciate Mahone's refusal to acknowledge that he had topped the chain of command that day. "He was not ordered, as he states, to my support by Lt. Gen. Hill," complained Heth, "but ordered to report to me with three brigades of his division." Heth apologized to Hill for complaining about a "brother officer" in an official report but insisted that a "sense of duty to others, as well as to myself, has alone compelled me to do so as the only means left me to correct misapprehension, that must be entertained by all, if I had permitted his report to go unanswered."[48]

Despite his lack of diplomacy, few could doubt Mahone's tenacity. Even Heth concluded that he had handled the operation well and accomplished "all and even more" than Heth had expected.[49] The initial success of Mahone's attack had suggested that a great rebel victory was in the making. Isolated on the Boydton Plank Road, Hancock's corps was in a vulnerable position. The Virginian's attack hit the weakest possible spot of the Union line, slicing through the federal position. Though he generally did well with what he had, his attack may have ultimately played into Union hands, allowing Grant's men to hit back hard and bleed more from Lee's army. In the end, the quality and resolve of the Union Second Corps shone through, transforming Mahone's victory into a costly defeat.

Following Grant's late October offensive, Mahone continued to lead his men throughout the Petersburg campaign. Three days after the Burgess Mill fight, his forces carried out an audacious maneuver against the Union trench line east of the city. Learning of a gap in the enemy picket line from deserters, Mahone sent three of Joseph Finegan's Florida regiments through the void. Finegan's men, some dressed in blue, filed behind the Union pickets and swept up nearly the entire line, capturing over two hundred Union soldiers.[50] The Confederates returned hefting tents, blankets, raincoats, and overcoats.[51] Most of the men captured were members of the 69th New York Infantry. The incident caused quite a stir among Union commanders, generating multiple reports and leading to court-martial proceedings for officers on the picket line, which included new recruits confused about the identity of the attackers.[52]

Throughout the balance of the war, Mahone's reputation swelled. He continued to perform well, commanding his troops during the fighting in 1865 and eventually ending the struggle with his men at Appomattox.[53] In postwar Virginia, Mahone returned to the railroad business and entered politics. During the 1870s and 1880s, he forged a new political coalition of blacks and whites that took shape in the Readjuster Party. He served in political posts, including service in the U.S. Senate. His reformist policies and brusque personal style alienated many of his former Confederate comrades and nudged him out of the pantheon of generals admired by adherents of the Lost Cause movement. Mahone did not count himself among the rebel veterans who helped plunge the South into the Jim Crow era. He chose a different route. "I have thought it wise to live for the future," he wrote in 1882, "and not the dead past . . . while cherishing honorable memories of its glories."[54]

For Wade Hampton, the fighting along the Boydton Plank Road brought bitter personal tragedy. In the midst of his grief, however, he continued to discharge his duties at the front. Two days after the battle, he explained to Lee that the Union offensive demonstrated "the importance of completing the defenses on Hatcher's Run. . . . I hope that we will take prompt measures to strengthen it."[55] Hampton appreciated the vital role his men had played in the new trenches on the Boydton Plank Road line to the north. For a brief time on the morning of the 27th, his dismounted men held back the Union advance near the Clements house. The thin screen prevented a coup de main and may have saved the South Side Railroad. Hampton would not remain at Petersburg to oversee future operations. He soon departed south to aid efforts to impede Sherman's drive up the coast from Savannah.

Despite Mahone's actions and Wade Hampton's leadership at Burgess Mill, Robert E. Lee had little reason for cheer in early November. The simultaneous movement of two Union armies underscored Confederate vulnerability and demonstrated that the length of the Confederate defensive works had become untenable. The Richmond-Petersburg front simply occupied more ground than the Confederates could effectively cover. Several days after the fighting on the 27th, Lee warned President Davis, "Unless we can obtain a reasonable approximation to his [the enemy's] force I fear a great calamity will befall us. On last Thursday at Burgess' Mill we had three brigades to oppose six divisions. On our left two divisions to oppose two corps. The inequality is too great."[56] Nevertheless, Lee appreciated the service provided by his commanders at Petersburg. "I am much grateful at the results obtained and pleased with the good conduct and courage displayed by officers and men," he wrote A. P. Hill the following Monday. He acknowledged Hampton's role in the operation and emphasized the cavalry commander's excellent performance, efficiency, and bravery.[57] "Our cavalry at Burgess' Mill I think saved the day," Lee wrote to Davis.[58] The Virginian also had personal words for Hampton himself. "I grieve with you at the death of your gallant son, so young, so brave, so true."[59]

A week after the Boydton Plank Road battle, Lee managed to travel to Burgess Mill. During his inspection south of Hatcher's Run, he visited General Hampton, as well as his own sons, Rooney and Rob.[60] Camped south of Hatcher's Run on November 6, he toured the area the next day. "I visited the battlefield in that quarter," he reported to his daughter, "and General Hampton in describing it said there had not been during the war a more spirited charge than [Rooney's] division made that day up the Boydton plank road, driving cavalry and infantry before him."[61] The visit may have buoyed Lee's spirits, but the future was grim for the Virginian, his army, and his cause.

"Double Victory"

As October yielded to November, the presidential election resumed its leading role in camp discourse. For the first time in the country's history, soldiers would cast their ballots from the field. However, the voting procedures for men under arms varied from state to state. Some soldiers could cast their ballots in camp; others received furloughs to go home; and still others voted by proxy or through commissioners. In many cases, they voted well before election day. On Thursday, November 3, Colonel Lyman's diary reported, "Flocks of election commissioners, scurvy looking fellows, are coming down here to look after the presidential election."[62] Many soldiers sealed their ballots into envelopes and handed them over to the commissioners.

In the weeks before the election, *New York Times* journalist and Lincoln partisan George F. Williams passed through the camps interviewing soldiers and officers to conduct an informal survey. Among Pennsylvania units, "the leaven of Unionism permeated throughout the entire force, and it was not an unusual thing to hear, upon asking how a regiment had gone in balloting, that it was unanimous for 'Abe and Andy.'"[63] At the New York camps, he found whole regiments voting for Lincoln. But in one unit, he discovered that the colonel stood alone in his support for the president. The commander joked that "his 'eagles' only saved him from being tossed in a blanket."[64] Almost everywhere the reporter ventured, however, support for the administration dominated. Throughout the army "the Union element grew stronger with each day's sun."[65] In Williams's view, the reason was simple. Like anyone else, the soldiers yearned for an end to the war, but they also viewed compromise with the Confederates as disgraceful. Williams observed a calm confidence, resilience, and optimism among the rank and file. "If any of your readers could have seen on that day the readiness of even new troops to resume the offensive, and could have realized at the moment the jeopardized situation of the entire corps," he wrote, "they would have gained new hope and greater confidence in the final result."[66]

A wet and gloomy election day arrived in the District of Columbia. Lincoln began his evening in the telegraph office, reviewing early reports. They were promising. News from Baltimore, Philadelphia, and Boston hinted at an early lead. The president drifted over to Edwin Stanton's office, where the secretary of war and other officials had gathered to review the returns. In front of the small captive audience, Lincoln pulled out a thin, yellow book from his pocket and recited favorite selections from humorist David Ross Locke, author of the *Nasby Letters*, a satirical slap at Copperheads. A somber Stanton, suffering from chills and a fever, did not appreciate Lincoln's frivolity. To Stanton's relief, no doubt, Lincoln would pause periodically to review fresh telegrams as they arrived.[67]

To the south, at City Point, Grant gathered outside headquarters with his staff. The lieutenant general had been a strong advocate of soldier access to the ballot in the field, arguing that the men had more right than any other to vote and "should not be deprived of a most precious privilege."[68] For his own part, Grant did not cast a vote. But his support for Lincoln was no secret. As election night wore on, he controlled access to the fresh telegrams. When a new dispatch appeared, he would shake his head in disappointment but keep the details to himself. His staff began to lose heart, and some even retreated to an early bed, shattered by Grant's grim news. But the general was having another laugh, just as he had done with the tidings from Cedar Creek less than three weeks earlier.

The news was clear. Lincoln was well on his way to a resounding victory.[69] The president's supporters turned out in force at Republican strongholds across the North. In Philadelphia, one banner paraded through the streets proclaimed, "We are coming, Father Abraham, with an overwhelming majority."[70] The sign spoke the truth. In the armies, the soldiers voted in droves for the Union ticket, confirming the results of George Williams's informal canvass. In the Army of the Potomac, Lincoln garnered about 70 percent of the vote. In armed camps across the country, he outpolled McClellan more than three to one.[71]

Grant would later characterize Lincoln's achievement on November 8 as a "double victory," because the electoral success had "passed off quietly" with "no bloodshed or riot throughout the land."[72] In Washington, Lincoln knew by midnight that the results favored him, and, around 2 A.M., he made his way back to the White House. There he greeted well wishers, saying, "I give thanks to Almighty for this evidence of the people's resolution to stand by free government and the rights of humanity."[73] The president then retired for the evening, victorious.

"To Cut Loose From Its Base"

The election's results extinguished any serious hope for a Confederate victory. With
the ballots cast, Lincoln and his generals would continue their tenacious drive to
defeat the rebellion. Nevertheless, Lee continued his search for offensive opportunities, always looking to free a column for a strike against Grant. He sought every
reasonable opportunity to achieve some tangible gain, even at significant risks to
his command. Confederate operations on October 7 at the Darbytown Road and on
October 27 at Burgess Mill seemed to provide such opportunities. But like similar
efforts earlier that year, the attempts failed. Time had run out for Lee. The Lincoln
victory doomed Lee's army and sealed the fate of his cause. Grant, with unfettered
political support and ample time, would prosecute the war vigorously to the end.
Nevertheless, despite the hopelessness of his plight, Lee fought on.

Following the election, on November 21, Lee wrote to Wade Hampton about the
"practicability of striking Grant a blow, either this side or the north side of James
River," and asking the cavalry commander to find a vulnerable point in the Union
lines.[74] No such movement occurred. In fact, the Confederate attack at the Darbytown Road on October 7 would stand as one of Lee's last offensive efforts of the war.
Though he tried to free a mobile column to strike against Grant, the length of his
lines, the loss of men to desertion and casualties, and outstanding Union leadership
conspired to make this nearly impossible. Grant retained the initiative and dictated
the terms of the campaign. In addition, the nature of the campaign often prevented
Lee from taking command at key locations and at the crucial moments. Tied down
by operations north of the James on the 27th, he missed the fight at Burgess Mill and
had to rely on the judgment of his commanders at Petersburg.

Lee had few choices. He could remain in the lines until Grant breached them
or surrounded his army. Alternatively, he could launch desperate assaults against
Union positions. John Bell Hood had followed a similar approach at Atlanta over
the summer, with disastrous results. Lee could also abandon Richmond and draw
Grant into the interior, away from the Union water-borne supply lines. However,
such a move would severely damage Confederate morale and eliminate any chance
of using the Valley further to spread Union forces and threaten Northern territory.
As George Williams of the *New York Times* explained on November 10, "Lee, with
the flower of the Southern army, cooped up within the environs of Richmond, paw-
ing and raving furiously, but futilely, against the unyielding bars of his cage, vainly
endeavoring to inflict a sly scratch now and then upon his captors."[75]

William Stokes, a South Carolina cavalryman, accurately described Confederate prospects when he wrote home saying, "I don't think there is anything for us to
gain" by further campaigning.[76] But, despite the bleak outlook, Lee pushed ahead.
Though he may have harbored his own doubts, his subsequent actions demonstrated a clear commitment to the fight for the Confederacy. His deep sense of pro-

fessional duty and intense loyalty to the Confederate cause drove him to continue. In February, he explained to his wife that he would "endeavor to do my duty & fight to the last."[77] He and other Confederate leaders continued to defend the rebellion beyond all reasonable hope. Several days after Lincoln's victory, the *Richmond Examiner* captured the unrealistic expectations nurtured by many Confederates: "The Yankee nation has committed itself to the game of all or nothing; and so must we. The only question for us now is, whether we shall call forth all the energies and resources of our country, all the courage and manhood of our race, to drive back the foul invaders."[78]

For Grant, the election cemented his unfettered control over military strategy. In launching the October 27 offensive, he had demonstrated a willingness to push matters where others might have held back. While his gambit did not pay off, it did not bring disaster, either. By November, many of the pieces of his 1864 campaign had fallen into place. Sherman had taken Atlanta. Mobile Bay had fallen into Union hands. Sheridan had defanged Early in the Valley. While Grant, Meade, and Butler had achieved limited success at Richmond, their efforts did not yield the type of gains that secured newspaper headlines. Nevertheless, Grant, always patient and focused, remained at City Point, content to allow Sherman and Sheridan to bask in the glory achieved elsewhere. Their success did not appear to perturb him.

Grant focused on Virginia. As his aide Adam Badeau would explain later, "Now that Confederate threats had been tamed elsewhere, Grant sought success at Richmond. He was like a chess-player, looking forward to . . . a finishing move, and clearing the board in advance of the pieces of his adversary which might obstruct his plan."[79] Such a successful move would also nudge the Army of the Potomac back into the limelight. Toiling under uneven leadership throughout the war, the army had suffered through heavy combat, especially during the bloody Overland campaign in the spring. It deserved some accolades.

During the fall, the spotlight had turned to Richmond and Petersburg, but the forces under Meade and Butler failed to achieve victory there. The modest gains of the September offensive raised hopes, but the problems encountered by the Union operation on October 27 must have disappointed Grant. He had taken a calculated risk in launching a major operation shortly before the election, a decision that underscored his willingness to gamble despite the risk of disastrous results. Overwhelming success would have cut the last Southern supply lines to Petersburg and Richmond, forcing Lee to either break out of his position there or hunker down for a true siege. In either case, the Confederacy would not have lasted long. In the October offensive, Grant, as with earlier operations, had sought to hit both ends of the extensive Confederate front. However, on the left, Union planners, burdened by imperfect information, sent the bulk of their attacking column against completed earthworks. Hancock's force successfully skirted the rebel line and threatened to drive deep behind Lee's position. But with its small size and little in the way of reserve ammunition, the command could not operate independently for an extended time in this location. On the afternoon of the 27th, Grant prudently ordered Hancock to halt. Throughout the day, Grant had exercised his direct, hands-on command style. In the Petersburg sector, he rode directly to the key locations and consulted with the commanders and his staff officers. He also took personal risks to examine conditions on the front firsthand. This method of command helped him make reasonable choices throughout the day and avoid unnecessary casualties for his men.

As the lieutenant general rode with his staff away from the Burgess Farm and boarded a rail car for City Point that rainy afternoon, he discussed the offensive's failure. The weakness of Hancock's turning column, a mere two divisions, had furnished a lesson. Throughout the campaign, Grant had sought various combinations to penetrate or circumvent Lee's lines. In doing so, he had kept his columns firmly tethered to existing fortifications and to the Union supply base at City Point. The October 27 operation had been no different. As his aide, John Rawlins, noted the next day, "Being so far separated from our base of supplies, and not having what we conceived to be a sufficient force to warrant cutting loose from it altogether, we determined to return to our entrenchments."[80] On the ride back from the Burgess Farm, Grant proposed a new approach. "It will be necessary for the Army of the Potomac to cut loose from its base, leaving only a small force at City Point and in front of Petersburg to hold those positions," he remarked. "The whole army can then swing completely round to the left and make Lee's present position untenable."[81] He had a new plan, grounded in the raiding strategy he and Sherman had pursued elsewhere. He wrote to Stanton, explaining that the day's operation "points out to me what is to be done."[82] In early April, he would unleash Union forces to operate on Lee's flank, resulting in the crushing defeat of Confederate forces at a remote crossroads named Five Forks southwest of Petersburg. Soon afterward, Grant's operation would bring Petersburg's collapse and Richmond's fall.

"lost to our rememberance"

Richmond Dispatch, July 11, 1866

The fortifications which formerly swept around the greater portion of this city are now gradually disappearing, and before many years have passed over us not a vestige of them may be expected to remain. Those formidable bastions and redoubts, lunettes and salients, star forts and enclosed works, from which the cannon frowned defiance, are now dismantled and falling to decay! The gabions have rotted, the revetments have fallen or been carried away; and on the parapet, where the sentry paced his round, the lock and the thistle now grow in wild and riotous luxuriance. The rifle-pits, where Lee's "barefooted boys" so often lay in silence, have been filled in and levelled; the sharp crack of the rifle has given place to the golden-eared wheat and sprouting corn; and where schrapnel and cannister, shot and shell, mowed down long files of men, the husbandman peacefully wields his glistening scythe. Still of the war many sad traces are left besides those that sorrow has given upon our hearts! The spot in the old field where a soldier fell is marked by a brighter green, and the rank grass shows only too plainly where one of the "unknown and unrecorded dead" lies buried. No mound or head-board marks the grave, and the plough of the farmer must soon obliterate all traces of the place which had been made sacred forever by its baptism in a hero's blood. The remains of many of the fallen soldiers have been disinterred and placed, by the hand of care and affection, in the cemeteries, where they can be honored and cared for by succeeding generations; but many, too many, must be lost to our rememberance and respect.

As the massive earthen forts and miles of ditches disintegrated around Richmond and Petersburg, a new struggle began for control of the war's memory. Though the firing had ceased, the bitterness remained sharp. Many Northern veterans harbored disdain for men who fought against the U.S. flag and viewed them as nothing more than traitors. Most white Southerners, devastated by the Confederate defeat, rankled under Reconstruction. But the years brought change. White Southerners regained control of their state governments. Union and Confederate veterans began to meet, not in anger, but in fellowship to share their memories of the war. Former Confederates and their partisans launched a successful campaign to blur and twist the fundamental causes of the conflict in the country's collective memory. Slavery and emancipation gradually faded from the public discourse and were replaced by vague, less provocative, notions of honor and duty. Collectively, many whites shunted aside memories of black Union veterans and their accomplishments to facilitate the reunion of the white veterans, blue and gray.

Amid these transformations, veterans and historians sought to recount the war's military campaigns. There was much to cover—hundreds of engagements, dozens of campaigns, each with its own impact on the course of events. The battles of October 1864 folded into what would be called the Petersburg campaign, the connected series of attempts by Grant to take Richmond and Petersburg during 1864 and 1865. The October operations would receive scant coverage in many histories of the war. There was no decisive Union breakthrough and no stunning Confederate victory. Lee's offensive operations on the Darbytown Road on October 7 constituted the little noticed last gasp of Confederate forces in Virginia. Grant's October offensive, the sixth in the series, though grand in scale and expectations, received little attention. For the veterans of those fights, however, the operations had their own importance. Names such as Darbytown Road, Johnson's Farm, New Market Road, Burgess Mill, Hatcher's Run, Boydton Plank Road, Bull Pen, Second Fair Oaks, Williamsburg Road, and Nine Mile Road would retain special meaning for the veterans who suffered through those battles.

"solemnity reigned supreme"

On a pleasant morning in 1888, a pair of high-stepping grays pulled a carriage south along the Boydton Plank Road toward Hatcher's Run. The passenger, a middle-aged visitor from Massachusetts, stared intently out at the Dinwiddie countryside. He searched for landmarks in the growing light, features that lay deep in his memory—a stream, a mill, a pond, a slight rise, an intersection, several barns, and a pair of houses. But the traveler recognized little. When the carriage halted beside a barn, he was surprised to learn that he had reached his destination. The carriage wheels rolled over the same ground his artillery battery had occupied on October 27, 1864. John D. Billings, Union veteran of the 10th Massachusetts Artillery, climbed out onto the Burgess Farm. A young man emerged from the barn, greeted him, and gave his name as Burgess. Soon the youngster's father, Clark Burgess, strolled up. Billings joked that he had not seen the Burgess family for nearly twenty-five years. The farmer "retorted quickly that unless [Billings] was more friendly than when here last he did not care to see" him.[83] The elder Burgess explained that his father, William (Mary Burgess's father-in-law) had survived the battle that day but had since passed away.

As the men spoke, Clark Burgess pointed west down the White Oak Road to a large tree half a mile away and identified the spot as Wade Hampton's headquarters during the fight. He recounted how a family member, most likely Mary Burgess, had returned the day after the battle to find the hogs running about with amputated human limbs in their mouths. He also told how family members found William Burgess "perfectly demented" by the ordeal, for he had "engaged in collecting in one vast, unassorted pile, knapsacks, blankets, overcoats, muskets, shelter tents."[84]

Billings continued to listen and gaze around the property as memories of the battle returned. He identified the spot where Major W. G. Mitchell, on his errand from General Hancock, had ordered Rugg's brigade to move into action. He recognized his battery's position, where many comrades, including Lieutenant Asa Smith, had fallen under enemy fire. He learned that the large barn had replaced the one torn down by Union troops during the battle. Across the Plank Road, a cotton field stretched along the White Oak Road. Billings "plucked a few bolls as mementos" and then climbed back into the carriage. As they exchanged farewells, Clark Burgess handed over a twelve-pound cannonball, a relic from the sixties. Billing's conveyance wheeled farther down the Boydton Plank Road to the intersection of the Dabney Mill Road. There he viewed the scene of Mahone's charge and the spot where Regis de Trobriand had formed his Union brigade for the counterattack. The oak tree that sheltered Grant, Meade, and Hancock still adorned the road junction. Billings mused that the massive oak should "be marked for the information of tourists" but then reconsidered, concluding that such attention would "ensure its destruction."[85] With his visit complete, the carriage rolled toward the Dinwiddie court house.

Over the years, others drew notice to the old battlefield. In 1896, George Bernard, a member of the 12th Virginia and a prominent Petersburg attorney, wrote an account of the Burgess Mill fight, complete with a letter from William Mahone prepared shortly before the general's death. During his lifetime, Bernard served in political office, allied himself with the reform-minded Mahone, and also later became active in the Petersburg chapter of the United Confederate Veterans, where he organized occasional "war talks" at camp meetings and collected the stories of veterans, blue and gray, for publication. He frequently rode along the Plank Road over Hatcher's Run and through the Burgess Farm on his way to conduct legal work at the Dinwiddie courthouse. During these trips, he gazed off the road at the tremendous oak that had served as Hancock's headquarters during the battle. Over the decades, the majestic hardwood furnished a reminder of those distant events. By 1895, the ancient oak had disappeared, and new pines trees covered the Burgess cornfield. The young timber adorned the edge of the Plank Road south to the Quaker Road. Nevertheless, Bernard wrote that he had "rarely ridden over that part of the road within a mile of Hatcher's Run bridge, on either side, without recalling the battle of Burgess's Mill."[86]

More than twenty years after Billings's visit to Hatcher's Run and more than a decade after Bernard prepared his article, a South Carolina veteran traveled through the countryside south of Petersburg. By 1910, the rise of reconciliation between the blue and the gray, celebrated at grand reunions in the North and South, had crested and begun to recede, but only due to the age of old foes. Memories of the war, particularly its causes, continued to transform. Many white Southerners, through the Lost Cause movement, successfully shaped popular memory by emphasizing Confederate military accomplishments, deifying rebel generals, and largely ignoring the issue of slavery. The emancipationist view of the war, which firmly acknowledged slavery's central role in the conflict, enjoyed fewer and fewer adherents in the south and north.[87]

It was in this era that Confederate veteran J. M. Hough returned to the fields of Dinwiddie County. On October 27, 1864, Hough had led a squad of Wade Hampton's dismounted cavalry along the Boydton Plank line. In 1910, he returned to the battlefields alone. He found that this section of the country had "never recovered from the shock of war." The land was "dotted and streaked by huge earthworks" that had not succumbed to the farmer's plow. These were the same works his command had defended nearly fifty years before.[88] East of the Plank Road, he walked the entire length of the old trenches, finding sections where his men had deployed that morning in 1864. To his surprise, the country was deserted. Even the Creek Road, which had passed through the works south of the Clements house, was no longer in use. For Hough, the desolation was remarkable. He wrote, "Not a house, not a field, not a human voice to break the silent spell, and as I looked and wandered I could not locate a single one of my boys—solemnity reigned supreme."[89]

The Battlefields Today

~

Today, the sites of the October 1864 battles go largely unnoticed by people in their daily lives around Richmond and Petersburg. North of the James, Johnson's Farm, the focal point of the initial Confederate attack on October 7, 1864, at the Darbytown Road, is now the site of Henrico County's Dorey Park, a recreation area complete with ball fields and a fitness center. A stone "Freeman" marker, named after historian Douglas Southall Freeman, sits beside the Darbytown Road, where the old exterior works crossed the Johnson fields. At the entrance to the park, a historical marker provides some details of the October 7 battle for those willing to pull their cars off the road. North of Dorey Park and the Darbytown Road, much of the land remains undeveloped. At this writing, opportunities still exist to preserve significant portions of the October 7, 1864, battlefield as well as the ground where Pond's brigade launched its disastrous attack on October 13, 1864. South of Dorey Park, Alfred Terry's line on the New Market Road sits in a quiet suburban neighborhood; the Union line itself is traced by the Lammrich Road. If one looks carefully, remnants of the Union works are noticeable on the northern side of the street in some locations. Several miles to the north, the fields over which Weitzel's men charged at the Williamsburg Road on October 27 are now part of the Richmond International Airport. Some of the Confederate earthworks remain, lining the east side of the airport's entrance road. Modern ditches and culverts in front of these remnants appear to mark the low ground where Union soldiers huddled after their disastrous charge on the afternoon of the 27th. The site of the USCT attack on the Nine Mile Road is now a residential neighborhood in Highland Springs. The portion of the Confederate line attacked by the black troops stands in the vicinity of the modern intersection of Nine Mile Road and North Battery Street.

South at Petersburg, the area around the Ninth and Fifth Corps' advance along Smith Grove Road ("Hawks' Road") on October 27 remains largely undeveloped. Some of the same fields and house sites exist today. The Confederate trenches north of Hatcher's Run (the Boydton Plank Road line) still snake along the ground through largely undeveloped and inaccessible private land. The former Burgess

Farm holds several houses but retains much of its wartime geographic character. Recently, however, a new development has appeared, which surrounds the pond with new homes. The pond itself is part of a private park, known as Lake Jordan, which is used for boating and fishing. The road that connected the Boydton Plank Road to Dabney Mill is no longer used and has been replaced by another, which intersects the Boydton Plank Road several hundred yards north of the former route.

Orders of Battle

~

Union Forces

For the most part, this table reflects unit organization as of October 31, 1864, for the principal combat units featured in this book, as reflected in the Official Records. However, some changes have been made to identify commanders or units present during the battles of October 7, 13, and 27. In addition, this table does not include miscellaneous units such as the Naval Brigade, the "Separate" Brigade, engineers, siege artillery, signal corps, and various unattached units. For a complete table of the Army of the Potomac, see O.R. 42(3): 457–64. For a complete table of the organization of the Department of Virginia and North Carolina (Butler's entire command) as of October 31, 1864, see O.R. 42(3): 464–70.

ARMY OF THE POTOMAC
Maj. Gen. George G. Meade

General Headquarters

Second Army Corps
Maj. Gen. Winfield S. Hancock

First Division
Brig. Gen. Nelson A. Miles

Consolidated Brigade
Col. Clinton D. MacDougall
7th New York (seven companies)
39th New York (seven companies)
52nd New York (six companies)
57th New York (two companies)

63rd New York (seven companies)
69th New York
88th New York (five companies)
111th New York
125th New York
126th New York

First Brigade
Col. William Wilson
28th Massachusetts
26th Michigan
5th New Hampshire
61st New York
81st Pennsylvania
140th Pennsylvania
183rd Pennsylvania
2nd New York Heavy Artillery
4th New York Heavy Artillery

Fourth Brigade
Col. St. Clair A. Mulholland
64th New York
66th New York
53rd Pennsylvania
116th Pennsylvania
145th Pennsylvania
148th Pennsylvania
7th New York Heavy Artillery

Second Division
Brig. Gen. Thomas W. Egan

First Brigade
Lieut. Col. Horace P. Rugg
19th Maine
19th Massachusetts
20th Massachusetts
7th Michigan
1st Minnesota (Companies A and B)
59th New York
152nd New York

184th Pennsylvania
36th Wisconsin

Second Brigade
Col. James M. Willett
155th New York
164th New York
170th New York
182nd New York (69th New York National Guard Artillery)
8th New York Heavy Artillery

Third Brigade
Brig. Gen. Thomas A. Smyth
14th Connecticut
1st Delaware
12th New Jersey
10th New York (six companies)
108th New York
4th Ohio (four companies)
69th Pennsylvania
106th Pennsylvania (three companies)
7th West Virginia (five companies)

Third Division
Bvt. Maj. Gen. Gershom Mott

First Brigade
Brig. Gen. P. Regis de Trobriand
20th Indiana
17th Maine
40th New York
73rd New York (seven companies)
86th New York
124th New York
99th Pennsylvania
110th Pennsylvania
2nd U.S. Sharpshooters
1st Maine Heavy Artillery

Second Brigade
Brig. Gen. Byron R. Pierce

5th Michigan
93rd New York
57th Pennsylvania
84th Pennsylvania
105th Pennsylvania
141st Pennsylvania
1st U.S. Sharpshooters (three companies)
1st Massachusetts Heavy Artillery

Third Brigade
Col. Robert McAllister
11th Massachusetts (seven companies)
5th New Jersey (five companies)
7th New Jersey (four companies)
8th New Jersey
11th New Jersey
72nd New York (one company)
120th New York

Artillery Brigade
Maj. John G. Hazard
Maine Light, 6th Battery (F)
Massachusetts Light, 10th Battery (at Boydton Plank Road)
New Hampshire Light, 1st Battery
1st New Jersey Light, Battery B
New Jersey Light, 3rd Battery
1st New York Light, Battery G
4th New York Heavy, Battery C
4th New York Heavy, Battery L
New York Light, 11th Battery
New York Light, 12th Battery
1st Pennsylvania Light, Battery F
1st Rhode Island Light, Battery B
4th United States, Battery K (at Boydton Plank Road)
5th United States, Batteries C and I

Fifth Army Corps
Maj. Gen. Gouverneur K. Warren

First Division
Brig. Gen. Charles Griffin

First Brigade
Col. Horatio G. Sickel
185th New York
198th Pennsylvania

Second Brigade
Bvt. Brig. Gen. Edgar M. Gregory
187th New York (six companies)
188th New York
91st Pennsylvania
155th Pennsylvania

Third Brigade
Brig. Gen. Joseph J. Bartlett
20th Maine
32nd Massachusetts
1st Michigan
16th Michigan
83rd Pennsylvania (six companies)
118th Pennsylvania

Second Division
Brig. Gen. Romeyn B. Ayres

First Brigade
Bvt. Brig. Gen. Frederick Winthrop
5th New York
140th New York
146th New York
8th United States
11th United States
12th United States
14th United States
15th New York Heavy Artillery

Second Brigade
Col. Andrew W. Denison
1st Maryland
4th Maryland
7th Maryland
8th Maryland

Third Brigade
Col. Arthur H. Grimshaw
3rd Delaware
4th Delaware
157th Pennsylvania (four companies)
190th Pennsylvania
191st Pennsylvania
210th Pennsylvania

Third Division
Brig. Gen. Samuel W. Crawford

First Brigade
Brig. Gen. Edward S. Bragg
24th Michigan
143rd Pennsylvania
149th Pennsylvania
150th Pennsylvania
6th Wisconsin
7th Wisconsin
Independent Wisconsin (two companies)
1st Battalion New York Sharpshooters

Second Brigade (remained in trenches on Oct. 27)
Brig. Gen. Henry Baxter
16th Maine
39th Massachusetts
94th New York
97th New York
104th New York
11th Pennsylvania
88th Pennsylvania
90th Pennsylvania
107th Pennsylvania

Third Brigade
Col. J. William Hofmann
76th New York (six companies)
95th New York
147th New York

56th Pennsylvania
121st Pennsylvania
142nd Pennsylvania

Artillery Brigade
Col. Charles S. Wainwright
Massachusetts Light, 5th Battery (E)
Massachusetts Light, 9th Battery
1st New York Light, Battery B
1st New York Light, Battery C
1st New York Light, Battery D
1st New York Light, Battery E
1st New York Light, Battery H
1st New York Light, Battery L
New York Light, 15th Battery
1st Pennsylvania Light, Battery B
4th United States, Battery B
5th United States, Battery D

Ninth Army Corps
Maj. Gen. John G. Parke

First Division
Brig. Gen. Orlando B. Willcox

First Brigade
Brig. Gen. John F. Hartranft
8th Michigan
27th Michigan
109th New York
51st Pennsylvania
37th Wisconsin
38th Wisconsin
13th Ohio Cavalry (dismounted)

Second Brigade
Lieut. Col. Byron M. Cutcheon
1st Michigan Sharpshooters
2nd Michigan
20th Michigan
46th New York

60th Ohio
50th Pennsylvania

Third Brigade
Col. Napoleon B. Mclaughlen
3rd Maryland (four companies)
29th Massachusetts
57th Massachusetts
59th Massachusetts
100th Pennsylvania
14th New York Heavy Artillery

Second Division
Brig. Gen. Robert B. Potter

First Brigade
Bvt. Brig. Gen. John I. Curtin
21st Massachusetts
35th Massachusetts
36th Massachusetts
58th Massachusetts
39th New Jersey
51st New York
45th Pennsylvania
48th Pennsylvania
4th Rhode Island
7th Rhode Island

Second Brigade
Brig. Gen. Simon G. Griffin
31st Maine
32nd Maine
2nd Maryland
56th Massachusetts
6th New Hampshire
9th New Hampshire
11th New Hampshire
179th New York
186th New York

17th Vermont
2nd New York Mounted Rifles (dismounted)

Third Division
Brig. Gen. Edward Ferrero

First Brigade
Col. Ozora P. Stearns
27th U.S. Colored Troops
30th U.S. Colored Troops
39th U.S. Colored Troops
43rd U.S. Colored Troops

Second Brigade
Col. Henry G. Thomas
19th U.S. Colored Troops
23rd U.S. Colored Troops
28th U.S. Colored Troops
29th U.S. Colored Troops (seven companies)
31st U.S. Colored Troops

Artillery Brigade
Col. John C. Tidball
Maine Light, 7th Battery (G)
Massachusetts Light, 11th Battery
New York Light, 19th Battery
New York Light, 27th Battery
New York Light, 34th Battery
Pennsylvania Light, Battery D

Cavalry

Second Division
Brig. Gen. David McM. Gregg

First Brigade
Brig. Gen. Henry E. Davies, Jr.
1st Massachusetts
1st New Jersey

10th New York
24th New York
1st Pennsylvania (four companies)

2nd Brigade
Col. Michael Kerwin
2nd Pennsylvania
4th Pennsylvania
8th Pennsylvania
13th Pennsylvania
16th Pennsylvania

Third Brigade
Col. Charles H. Smith
1st Maine
6th Ohio
21st Pennsylvania

Artillery
1st United States, Battery I
2nd United States, Battery A

Army of the James

Maj. Gen. Benjamin F. Butler

Tenth Army Corps
Maj. Gen. David B. Birney (October 7)
Bvt. Maj. Gen. Alfred H. Terry (October 13 and 27)

First Division
Bvt. Maj. Gen. Alfred H. Terry (October 7)
Brig. Gen. Adelbert Ames (October 13 and 27)

First Brigade
Col. Francis B. Pond (October 7 and 13)
Col. Alvin C. Voris (October 27)
39th Illinois

62nd Ohio
67th Ohio
85th Pennsylvania (detachment)
(199th Pennsylvania—did not participate in October battles)

Second Brigade
Col. Joseph C. Abbott (October 7 and 27)
Brig. Gen. Joseph R. Hawley (October 13)
6th Connecticut
7th Connecticut
3rd New Hampshire
7th New Hampshire
16th New York Heavy Artillery

Third Brigade
Col. Harris M. Plaisted
10th Connecticut
11th Maine
24th Massachusetts
100th New York (term of service expired after October 7)

Second Division
Brig. Gen. Robert S. Foster

First Brigade
Col. N. Martin Curtis (October 27)
3rd New York
112th New York
117th New York
142nd New York

Second Brigade
Col. Galusha Pennypacker
47th New York
48th New York
76th Pennsylvania
97th Pennsylvania
203rd Pennsylvania

Third Brigade
Col. Louis Bell
13th Indiana (three companies)
9th Maine
4th New Hampshire
115th New York
169th New York

Third Division
Brig. Gen. William Birney (October 13)
Brig. Gen. Joseph R. Hawley (October 27)

First Brigade
Col. Alvin C. Voris (October 13)
Col. James Shaw Jr. (October 27)
7th U.S. Colored Troops
9th U.S. Colored Troops
41st U.S. Colored Troops
127th U.S. Colored Troops (not present October 13 and 27)

Second Brigade
Col. Ulysses Doubleday
29th Connecticut Colored Troops
8th U.S. Colored Troops
45th U.S. Colored Troops

Artillery Brigade
Lieut. Col. Richard H. Jackson
Connecticut Light, 1st Battery
New Jersey Light, 4th Battery
New Jersey Light, 5th Battery
16th New York Heavy (detachment)
1st Pennsylvania Light, Battery E
3rd Rhode Island Heavy, Battery C
1st United States, Battery D
1st United States, Battery M
3rd United States, Battery E
4th United States, Battery D

Eighteenth Army Corps (October 27)
Bvt. Maj. Gen. Godfrey Weitzel

> First Division
> Brig. Gen. Gilman Marston

>> First Brigade
>> Lieut. Col. John B. Raulston
>> 13th New Hampshire
>> 81st New York
>> 98th New York
>> 139th New York

>> Second Brigade
>> Col. Edgar M. Cullen
>> 5th Maryland
>> 10th New Hampshire
>> 93rd New York
>> 96th New York
>> 118th New York

>> Third Brigade
>> Lieut. Col. Joab N. Patterson
>> 21st Connecticut
>> 40th Massachusetts
>> 2nd New Hampshire
>> 58th Pennsylvania
>> 188th Pennsylvania

> Second Division
> Brig. Gen. Charles A. Heckman

>> First Brigade (not engaged October 27)
>> Lieut. Col. William H. McNary
>> 148th New York
>> 158th New York
>> 55th Pennsylvania

Second Brigade
Col. Edward H. Ripley
8th Maine
9th Vermont

Third Brigade
Col. Harrison S. Fairchild
89th New York
19th Wisconsin
2nd Pennsylvania Heavy Artillery

Third Division
Col. John H. Holman

First Brigade
Col. John H. Holman (though division commander, Holman
commanded only first brigade on October 27)
Lieut. Col. Abial G. Chamberlain
1st U.S. Colored Troops
22nd U.S. Colored Troops
37th U.S. Colored Troops

Second Brigade
Col. Alonzo G. Draper
5th U.S. Colored Troops
36th U.S. Colored Troops
38th U.S. Colored Troops

Third Brigade (not engaged October 27)
Col. John W. Ames
4th U.S. Colored Troops
6th U.S. Colored Troops
10th U.S. Colored Troops

Provisional Brigade
107th U.S. Colored Troops
117th U.S. Colored Troops
118th U.S. Colored Troops

Artillery Brigade
Col. Alexander Piper

3rd New York Light, Battery E
3rd New York Light, Battery H
3rd New York Light, Battery K
3rd New York Light, Battery M
New York Light, 7th Battery
New York Light, 16th Battery
New York Light, 17th Battery
1st Pennsylvania Light, Battery A
1st Rhode Island Light, Battery F
4th United States, Battery L
5th United States, Battery A
5th United States. Battery F

Cavalry Division
Brig. Gen. August V. Kautz (October 7 and 13)
Col. Robert M. West (October 27)

 First Brigade
 Col. Robert M. West (October 7 and 13)
 Col. George W. Lewis (October 27)
 3rd New York, Capt. George F. Dem
 5th Pennsylvania, Lieut. Col. Christopher Kleinz

 Second Brigade
 Col. Samuel P. Spear
 1st District of Columbia
 11th Pennsylvania

 Third Brigade
 Col. Andrew W. Evans
 1st Maryland
 1st New York Mounted Rifles

 Artillery
 1st United States, Battery B
 Wisconsin Light, 4th Battery

Confederate Forces

The following table presents the principal combat units under Robert E. Lee's command at Richmond and Petersburg. For the most part, it reflects organization as of October 31, 1864, for the principal combat units featured in this book, as dcoumented in the Official Records. However, some changes have been made to identify commanders or units present during the battles on October 7, 13, and 27. It omits several units not directly involved in the events discussed in this book, such as those in the First and Third Military Districts and those serving in the Shenandoah Valley. For a complete table listing the organization of the Army of Northern Virginia and the Department of Richmond as of October 31, 1864, see OR 42(3): 1187–97.

First Army Corps
Lieut. Gen. James Longstreet

    Pickett's Division
    Maj. Gen. George E. Pickett

        Steuart's Brigade
        Brig. Gen. George H. Steuart
        9th Virginia
        14th Virginia
        38th Virginia
        53rd Virginia
        57th Virginia

        Corse's Brigade
        Brig. Gen. Montgomery D. Corse
        15th Virginia
        17th Virginia
        29th Virginia
        30th Virginia
        32nd Virginia

        Hunton's Brigade
        Brig. Gen. Eppa Hunton
        8th Virginia
        18th Virginia

19th Virginia
18th Virginia
56th Virginia

Terry's Brigade
Brig. Gen. William R. Terry
1st Virginia
3rd Virginia
7th Virginia
11th Virginia
24th Virginia

Field's Division
Maj. Gen. Charles W. Field

Law's Brigade
Brig. Gen. Evander M. Law
4th Alabama
15th Alabama
44th Alabama
47th Alabama
48th Alabama

Anderson's Brigade
Brig. Gen. George T. Anderson
7th Georgia
8th Georgia
9th Georgia
11th Georgia
59th Georgia

Benning's Brigade
Col. Dudley DuBose
2nd Georgia
15th Georgia
17th Georgia
20th Georgia

Gregg's Brigade
Brig. Gen. John Gregg (killed in action October 7, 1864)
Col. Clinton Winkler
3rd Arkansas
1st Texas
4th Texas
5th Texas

Bratton's Brigade
Brig. Gen. John Bratton (wounded in action October 7, 1864)
1st South Carolina
2nd South Carolina
5th South Carolina
6th South Carolina
Palmetto Sharpshooters

Hoke's Division (serving with First Corps)
Maj. Gen. Robert F. Hoke

Colquitt's Brigade
Brig. Gen. Alfred H. Colquitt
6th Georgia
19th Georgia
23rd Georgia
27th Georgia
28th Georgia

Clingman's Brigade
Brig. Gen. Thomas L. Clingman
8th North Carolina
31st North Carolina
51st North Carolina
61st North Carolina

Kirkland's Brigade
Brig. Gen. William W. Kirkland
17th North Carolina
42nd North Carolina
66th North Carolina

Hagood's Brigade
Brig. Gen. Johnson Hagood
11th South Carolina
21st South Carolina
20th South Carolina
27th South Carolina
7th South Carolina Battalion

Third Army Corps
Lieut. Gen. Ambrose P. Hill

Heth's Division
Maj. Gen. Henry Heth

Davis's Brigade
Brig. Gen. Joseph R. Davis
2nd Mississippi
11th Mississippi
26th Mississippi
42nd Mississippi
1st Confederate Battalion

MacRae's Brigade
Brig. Gen. William MacRae
11th North Carolina
26th North Carolina
44th North Carolina
47th North Carolina
52nd North Carolina

Cooke's Brigade
Brig. Gen. John R. Cooke
15th North Carolina
27th North Carolina
46th North Carolina
48th North Carolina

Archer's Brigade
Col. Robert M. Mayo
13th Alabama
1st Tennessee
7th Tennessee
14th Tennessee

Walker's Brigade
40th Virginia
47th Virginia
55th Virginia
2nd Maryland Battalion

Wilcox's Division
Maj. Gen. Cadmus M. Wilcox

Thomas's Brigade
Brig. Gen. Edward L. Thomas
14th Georgia
35th Georgia
45th Georgia
49th Georgia

McGowan's Brigade
Brig. Gen. Samuel McGowan
1st South Carolina (Provisional Army)
12th South Carolina
13th South Carolina
14th South Carolina
Orr's (First South Carolina) Rifles

Lane's Brigade
Brig. Gen. James H. Lane
7th North Carolina
18th North Carolina
28th North Carolina
33rd North Carolina
37th North Carolina

Scales's Brigade
Brig. Gen. Alfred M. Scales

13th North Carolina
16th North Carolina
22nd North Carolina
34th North Carolina
38th North Carolina

Mahone's Division
Maj. Gen. William Mahone

Sander's Brigade
Col. J. Horace King
8th Alabama
9th Alabama
10th Alabama
11th Alabama
14th Alabama

Harris's Brigade
Brig. Gen. Nathaniel H. Harris
12th Mississippi
16th Mississippi
19th Mississippi
48th Mississippi

Weisiger's Brigade
Brig. Gen. David A. Weisiger
6th Virginia
12th Virginia
16th Virginia
41st Virginia
61st Virginia

Wright's Brigade
Col. William Gibson
3nd Georgia
22nd Georgia
48th Georgia
64th Georgia
2nd Georgia Battalion
10th Georgia Battalion

Finegan's Brigade
Brig. Gen. Joseph Finegan
2nd Florida
5th Florida
8th Florida
9th Florida
10th Florida
11th Florida

Anderson's Corps
Lieut. Gen. Richard H. Anderson

Johnson's Division
Maj. Gen. Bushrod R. Johnson

Elliot's Brigade
Brig. Gen. William H. Wallace
17th South Carolina
18th South Carolina
22nd South Carolina
23rd South Carolina
Holcombe Legion

Wise's Brigade
Col. John T. Goode
26th Virginia
18th Virginia
46th Virginia
59th Virginia

Ransom's Brigade
Brig. Gen. Matthew W. Ransom
24th North Carolina
25th North Carolina
35th North Carolina
49th North Carolina
56th North Carolina

Gracie's Brigade
Brig. Gen. Archibald Gracie Jr.
41st Alabama

43rd Alabama
59th Alabama
60th Alabama
23rd Battalion Alabama Sharpshooters

Cavalry Corps
Maj. Gen. Wade Hampton

Hampton's (old) Division
Brig. Gen. Matthew C. Butler

Butler's Brigade
Col. Hugh K. Aiken
4th South Carolina
5th South Carolina
6th South Carolina

Young's Brigade
Brig. Gen. Pierce M. B. Young
7th Georgia
Cobb's (Georgia) Legion
Phillips (Georgia) Legion
Jefferson Davis Legion

Lee's Division
Maj. Gen. William ("Rooney") H. F. Lee

Chambliss's Brigade
Col. Richard L. T. Beale
9th Virginia
10th Virginia
13th Virginia

Barringer's Brigade
Brig. Gen. Rufus Barringer
1st North Carolina
2nd North Carolina
3rd North Carolina
5th North Carolina

Dearing's Brigade (unassigned)
Brig. Gen. James Dearing
7th Confederate
8th Georgia
4th North Carolina
Graham's (Virginia) Battery

Horse Artillery
Graham's Battery
Hart's Battery
McGregor's Battery

Artillery Reserve
Brig. Gen. William N. Pendleton

First Corps Artillery
Brig. Gen. E. Porter Alexander
Cabell's Battalion
Haskell's Battalion
Johnson's Battalion
Huger's Battalion
Stark's Battalion
Hardaway's Battalion

Third Corps Artillery
Col. R. Lindsay Walker
McIntosh's Battalion
Poague's Battalion
Lane's Battalion
Pegram's Battalion
Richardson's Battalion
Eshleman's Battalion
Gibbe's Battalion

Artillery Anderson's Corps
Col. Hilary P. Jones
Read's Battalion
Coit's Battalion
Boggs's Battalion
Moseley's Battalion

Department of Richmond
Lieut. Gen. Richard S. Ewell

  Johnson's Brigade
  Col. John M. Hughs
  17th and 23d Tennessee (consolidated)
  44th and 28th Tennessee (consolidated)
  63rd Tennessee

  Cavalry Brigade
  Brig. Gen. Martin W. Gary
  Hampton Legion
  7th South Carolina
  24th Virginia

  Not Brigaded
  25th Virginia Battalion
  Local Defense Troops
  Virginia Reserves
  Irregular troops and 18th Georgia Battalion

Artillery Defenses
Lieut. Col. John C. Pemberton

  First Division (Inner Line)
  Lieut. Col. John W. Atkinson
  10th Virginia Battalion Heavy Artillery
  19th Virginia Battalion Heavy Artillery

  Second Division (Inner Line)
  Lieut. Col. James Howard
  18th Virginia Battalion Heavy Artillery
  20th Virginia Battalion Heavy Artillery

  Light Artillery
  Lieut. Col. Charles E. Lightfoot
  Caroline (Virginia) Artillery
  Second Nelson (Virginia) Artillery
  Surry (Virginia) Artillery

Notes

∽

Introduction

1. Billings, *History of the Tenth Massachusetts,* 322; Walker, *General Hancock,* 275.

2. Long, *Jewel of Liberty,* 188–94; McPherson, *Battle Cry of Freedom,* 768–73.

3. Long, *Jewel of Liberty,* 192; Harris, *Lincoln's Last Months,* 16–17.

4. Lincoln, *Collected Works,* 507.

5. See, e.g., Nevins, *Diary of Battle,* 477. Colonel Charles S. Wainwright, an artillery officer in the Fifth Corps, heard rumors that McClellan planned to crush the South.

6. McClellan's opposition to emancipation and conscription would have made it very difficult, if not impossible, for him to fill the army's ranks. By 1864, approximately 100,000 African Americans served under the U.S. flag. The loss of these troops would have severely complicated the war effort. McPherson, *Negro's Civil War,* 223; Long, *Jewel of Liberty,* 265–66.

7. Long, *Jewel of Liberty,* 191–95.

8. Nelson, *Bullets, Ballots, and Rhetoric,* 114.

9. Thompson, *Thirteenth Regiment,* 493.

10. Nelson, *Bullets, Ballots, and Rhetoric,* 123–25.

11. Ibid., 123–30, 132.

12. Chamberlaine, *Memoirs of the Civil War,* 109.

13. Brinton, *Personal Memoirs,* 239.

14. U.S. War Department, *The War of the Rebellion: A Compilation of the Official Records of the Union and Confederate Armies* (hereafter "O.R."), Series 1, Vol. 33, Part I, 394–95 (hereafter "O.R. 33(1): 394–95"). All O.R. citations refer to Series 1 unless otherwise stated.

15. Ibid., 395. For further analysis of Grant's raiding strategy, see Beringer et al., *Why the South Lost,* 309–17; Hattaway and Jones, *How the North Won,* 501–15; Archer Jones, *Civil War Command and Strategy,* 181–86.

16. O.R. 33(1): 394–95.

17. For a discussion of Grant's strategy of simultaneous advances, see Hattaway and Jones, *How the North Won,* 492.

18. See, e.g., Rafuse, *Robert E. Lee,* 253–54.

19. R. E. Lee to G. W. C. Lee, Feb. 28, 1863, in Lee, *Wartime Papers,* 411.

20. R.E. Lee to his wife, Apr. 19, 1863, Ibid., 438.

21. Nelson, *Bullets, Ballots, and Rhetoric,* 117 (quoting the *Richmond Examiner,* Aug. 31, 1864).

22. O.R. 38(5): 777.

23. *New York Times,* Sept. 3, 1864.

24. *Richmond Examiner,* Sept. 5, 1864.

25. Woodward, *Mary Chesnut's Civil War,* 645.

26. See the *New York World,* Oct. 28 and Nov. 1, 1864.

27. Porter, *Campaigning with Grant,* 70.

28. Grant, *Personal Memoirs,* vol. 2, 489.

29. Simon, *Papers of Ulysses S. Grant,* vol. 28, 409–10.

30. W. T. Sherman to his brother, Oct. 1, 1862, in Sherman and Thorndike, *Sherman Letters,* 166.

31. Robert S. West, *Lincoln's Scapegoat General,* 229–30.

32. Rev. J. William Jones, *Personal Reminiscences,* 40.

33. U. S. Grant to H. W. Halleck, June 5, 1864, in Simon, *Papers of Ulysses S. Grant,* vol. 11, 19.

34. See Hattaway and and Jones, *How the North Won,* 587.

35. Historian Earl J. Hess has described Grant's approach of continuous contact as "the only major innovation in grand tactics during the Civil War" other than the extensive use of temporary fieldworks (Hess, *In the Trenches,* 282–83).

36. Lee to Davis, Sept. 2, 1864, O.R. 42(3): 1228.

37. Wert, *From Winchester to Cedar Creek,* 142.

38. Grant, *Personal Memoirs,* vol. 2, 337.

39. Lee to Mitchell, Oct. 24, 1864, O.R. 42(3): 1175–76.

40. Badeau, *Military History,* vol. 3, 115. Porter recalled that bridging equipment was collected in late May "in order to be prepared to cross the James River, if deemed best, and attack Richmond and Petersburg from the south side, and carry out the views expressed by Grant in the beginning of the Wilderness campaign as to his movements in certain contingencies." See Porter, *Campaigning with Grant,* 161.

41. Excerpt from the *New York World,* Oct. 19, 1864, reprinted in the *Charleston Mercury,* Nov. 2, 1864. The article suggested that unless Grant could flush Lee out of Richmond through the capture of Lynchburg, the campaign would end in failure.

42. On a late summer day in 1864, several dozen ragged soldiers rested near a farmhouse in the Virginia countryside west of Richmond. The aroma of fresh bread filled the air. A Confederate cavalryman approached the group and asked for the commanding officer. A man named Fuller stepped forward. In reply to the cavalryman's queries, Fuller claimed he and his men were conducting a reconnaissance up the James River. He even produced a paper authorizing the mission. The cavalryman was suspicious, though, and directed the squad to march toward a nearby railroad station. He wanted to telegraph Richmond and verify Fuller's story. The men consented and followed the officer. When they reached the main road, however, the cavalryman turned right and his new acquaintances marched off to the left. Galloping back to the squad, the horseman attempted to arrest Fuller, but a member of the squad raised a rifle to his shoulder. The trooper's suspicions were confirmed. This was no reconnaissance party. With the odds against him, the cavalryman wheeled his horse around and raced away at "lightning speed." Lieutenant Fuller and the other former members of the 9th Alabama infantry regiment turned west and resumed their journey away from the Petersburg trenches and toward their far-away homes (Mason, "Three Years in the Army").

43. Lee to Seddon, Aug. 14, 1864, O.R. 42(2): 1175.

44. Haley, *Rebel Yell,* 197.

45. Thompson, *Thirteenth Regiment,* 494. The same writer noted, "Next to bridegrooms in their honeymoons, the happiest men the writer ever set eyes upon (and he had seen many hundreds of them in all), have been the men captured from the Confederate army by the Union army in this war."

46. Abstract of Monthly Return from Army of Northern Virginia, Oct. 31, 1864, O.R. 42(3): 1186–87; see also O.R. 42(2): 1213 (monthly return, Aug. 31, 1864).

47. O.R. 42(3): 1186–97 (numbers reflect men and officers "present for duty").

48. Taylor, *General Lee,* 275.

49. Lee to his wife, Sept. 18, 1864, in Lee, *Wartime Papers,* 855.

50. Lee to Davis, Sept. 2, 1864, O.R. 42(2): 1228.

51. Lee to Bragg, Sept. 26, 1864, O.R. 42(2): 1292–93.

52. Lee to secretary of war, Oct. 4, 1864, O.R. 42(3): 1134.

53. Lee to Governor Vance, Oct. 8, 1864, O.R. 42(3): 1141–42.

54. See, e.g., *Philadelphia Inquirer,* Oct. 10, 1864.

55. See, e.g., O.R. 42(1): 944–45 (Hampton report).

56. Lee to Hampton, Oct. 4, 1864, O.R. 42(3): 1133.

1. Johnson's Farm

1. See Andrew A. Humphreys, *Virginia Campaign,* 242.

2. O.R. 42(1): 39–41; see also O.R. 42(3): 457. By the end of Oct., the effective strength of the Army of the Potomac had risen to fifty-seven thousand. See O.R. 42(1): 40.

3. See, e.g., Andrew A. Humphreys, *Virginia Campaign,* 282 ("[Hancock] attributed the bad conduct of some of his troops to their great fatigue and to their heavy losses during the campaign, especially in officers"). See also W. S. Hancock to Francis Barlow, Nov. 3, 1864, Massachusetts Historical Society ("our men as a mass are a *little* shaky for want of officers").

4. O.R. 42(1): 39.

5. Longacre, *Army of Amateurs,* 46–47.

6. Ibid., 47–48.

7. Grant to Butler, Sept. 27, 1864, in Simon, *Papers of Ulysses S. Grant,* vol. 12, 219–21.

8. Sommers, *Richmond Redeemed,* 4.

9. The outer layer of Confederate defenses ran along Bailey's Creek facing southwest, while another strung along the base of New Market Heights. Both of these curtains covered the Union bridgehead at Deep Bottom, a landing on the north bank of the James.

10. The so-called exterior line is also referred to as the "outer" line in at least one study. See Manarin, *Henrico County,* vol. 2, 664; but cf. Sommers, *Richmond Redeemed,* 14–15 (referring to the works as the "exterior line").

11. U. S. Grant to Major General Meade, 8:15 A.M., Sept. 30, 1864, O.R. 42(2): 1118.

12. Hess, *In the Trenches,* 160.

13. See Meade to Hancock, 11:45 a.m,, Oct. 2, 1864, O.R. 42(3): 39.

14. Meade, *Life and Letters,* 231.

15. Gallagher, *Fighting for the Confederacy,* 475.

16. Grant to Butler, Oct. 1, 1864, O.R. 42(3): 31–32; Butler to Grant, Oct. 2, 1864, O.R. 42(3): 48.

17. On Oct. 3, Butler reported that engineer Peter Michie was at work on these new

trenches with a detail of a thousand black troops (Butler to Grant, 11:30 A.M., Oct. 3, 1864, O.R. 42(3): 65).

18. Ibid.

19. Sommers, *Richmond Redeemed*, 119. Union correspondence identifies this location as the "Clyne" house, but the property is identified at "T. Lines" on at least two contemporary maps. See "Map of the vicinity of Richmond and part of the Peninsula" (Confederate engineering map from 1864), *Civil War Maps*, 626 (G3884.R5 1864 .C3); and "Copy of section of photograph map captured from the enemy showing country adjacent to Richmond and lines of defensive works surrounding the city" (Confederate map captured in Aug. 1864), *Civil War Maps*, 642.5 (G3884.R5S5 1864 .U51).

20. Butler to Birney, 1:10 P.M., Oct. 2, 1864, O.R. 42(3): 49.

21. Twain, *Mark Twain's Notebooks & Journals, Volume I*, 494.

22. West, *Lincoln's Scapegoat General*, 42.

23. Longacre, *Army of Amateurs*, 160–61.

24. Lowe, *Meade's Army*, 300.

25. Ibid.

26. Kreutzer, *Notes and Observations*, 238.

27. Butler to Stanton, 7:45 P.M., Oct. 3, 1864, O.R. 42(3): 65.

28. Grant to Halleck, July 1, 1864, O.R. 45(2): 558–59.

29. Kreutzer, *Notes and Observations*, 238.

30. Butler posted the "Provisional Brigade," led by Colonel Joseph Potter and numbering about three thousand men, in the trenches along the narrow neck of Bermuda Hundred. According to one account, Union soldiers considered the Howlett line as a choice assignment, for "more peaceful relations seemed to exist between the lines than anywhere" else along the Richmond-Petersburg front (Bartlett, *History of the Twelfth Regiment*, 242).

31. For detailed accounts of the engagement at Roper's Farm, see Sommers, *Richmond Redeemed*, 158–77; and Manarin, *Henrico County*, vol. 2, 696–707.

32. Taylor, "Reports of Operations."

33. Butler to Grant, 9:45 A.M., Oct. 2, 1864, O.R. 42(3): 48. See also Briscoe, "A Visit to General Butler," 442.

34. Grant to Butler, Oct. 3, 1864, O.R. 42(3): 66–67.

35. Grant to Meade, Oct. 4, 1864, O.R. 42(3): 69.

36. Eisenschiml, *Vermont General*, 244.

37. *New York Herald*, Oct. 9, 1864.

38. *Richmond Dispatch*, Oct. 8, 1864.

39. Ibid.; Eisenschiml, *Vermont General*, 245.

40. Thompson, *Thirteenth Regiment*, 490.

41. Ibid., 491.

42. *Richmond Whig*, Oct. 7, 1864.

43. *Richmond Whig*, Oct. 6, 1864.

44. Eisenschiml, *Vermont General*, 245.

45. Thompson, *Thirteenth Regiment*, 493.

46. *Richmond Dispatch*, Oct. 4, 1864. The article erroneously identified the location as "Enterprise," which was another house owned by Atlee farther west (closer to Richmond) on the Darbytown Road. The property's correct name was "Plainfield." For the purposes of this study, the property is referred to as "Johnson's Farm."

47. Manarin, *Henrico County,* vol. 2, 715.

48. Alexander to his wife, Oct. 3, 1864, Porter Alexander Papers, UNC.

49. McGuire, *Diary of a Southern Refugee,* 310.

50. Tower, *Lee's Adjutant,* 195.

51. Alexander to his wife, Oct. 3, 1864, Porter Alexander Papers, UNC.

52. Ibid.

53. Organization of Army of Northern Virginia, Oct. 31, 1864, O.R. 42(3): 1188.

54. Organization of Army in the Department of Richmond, Oct. 31, 1864, O.R. 42(3): 1197.

55. Pfanz, *Richard S. Ewell,* 417–18.

56. Tower, *Lee's Adjutant,* 194.

57. Brooks, *Stories of the Confederacy,* 370; *Biography of General Martin Witherspoon Gary,* VHS. See also Manarin, *Henrico County,* vol. 2, 842. The meeting did not escape the attention of the press; see *Charleston Mercury,* Oct. 14, 1864.

58. Field, "Campaign of 1864 and 1865," 557–58.

59. Davis, *Jefferson Davis: The Essential Writings,* 345.

60. Tower, *Lee's Adjutant,* 195.

61. Field, "Campaign of 1864 and 1865," 557–58; *Richmond Enquirer,* Nov. 22, 1864.

62. Taylor, "Reports of Operations."

63. Daly, *Alexander Cheves Haskell,* 144–155. According to a post war account, each cavalryman in the 7th South Carolina received a saber before the operation. By this point in the war, combat rarely involved the use of sabers, because cavalrymen usually fought dismounted with rifles and carbines. Accordingly, this story seems unlikely. Daly, *Alexander Cheves Haskell,* 144. A Nov. 1, 1864, inspection report for Rooney Lee's division states, "Sabres have become an obsolete arm as none can even be found" (Daughtry, *Gray Cavalier,* 228).

64. At the beginning of the conflict, he served as chief of cavalry in the Army of the Ohio's 23rd Corps for a time.

65. Briscoe, "A Visit to General Butler," 438.

66. Kautz, "How I Won My First Brevet," 375.

67. Ibid.

68. See O.R. 42(1): 823 (Kautz report); see also Kautz, "How I Won My First Brevet," 375.

69. O.R. 42(1): 848 (Noggle report).

70. O.R. 42(1): 845–47 (Hall report).

71. Eyland, *Evolution of a Life,* 245.

72. Ibid. David Edward Cronin, an artist and writer after the war, wrote under the pen name "Seth Eyland."

73. Kautz to Birney, Oct. 6, 1864, O.R. 42(3): 98–99; Roper, Archibald, and Coles, *History of the Eleventh,* 142. An account in the *Richmond Enquirer* indicated that eight members of the Virginia reserves deserted and disclosed news of the Confederate offensive (*Richmond Enquirer,* Nov. 22, 1864). See also *Edgefield Advertiser,* Oct. 20, 1864 ("Unfortunately for the complete success of the movement, a number of the Richmond local troops had deserted the night before, and warned the enemy of the purpose of the Confederates").

74. Accounts differ on the location and description of this road. One suggests that the road was not cut until Oct. 6, while another indicates that the path was in fact a preexisting road connecting the Darbytown and New Market roads. See Eyland, *Evolution of a Life,* 245 (road was already in existence); Davis, *Life of David Bell Birney,* 265 (road was cut the previous day); Roper, Archibald, and Coles, *History of the Eleventh,* 142.

75. Shreve to Generals Terry, Foster, and Birney, Oct. 6, 1864, O.R. 42(3): 99.

76. *New York Herald*, Oct. 9, 1864.

77. Daly, *Alexander Cheves Haskell*, 155 (Hinson account).

78. Ibid., 144.

79. Gallagher, *Fighting for the Confederacy*, 479–82.

80. Pryor, *Reading the Man*, 407.

81. Taylor to Bettie, Aug. 15, 1864, Tower, *Lee's Adjutant*, 182.

82. Taylor to Bettie, Mar. 8, 1864, Tower, *Lee's Adjutant*, 134.

83. Glatthaar, *General Lee's Army*, 339 (quoting Charles Venable to his wife, June 21, 1863).

84. Alexander to his wife, Oct. 25, 1864, Porter Alexander Papers, UNC.

85. Gallagher, *Fighting for the Confederacy*, 479–482.

86. Ibid., 479–82.

87. *Biography of General Martin Witherspoon Gary*, VHS.

88. Harold Simpson, *Hood's Texas Brigade*, 438.

89. *Army and Navy Journal*, Nov. 5, 1864.

90. Ibid.

91. O.R. 42(1): 823–24 (Kautz report).

92. Sources mention that Spear's line lay behind the "Gerhardt" house, while others refer to the "McKensy" house. ; see O.R. 42(1): 826 (West report); Roper, Archibald, and Coles, *History of the Eleventh*, 143–44. Some period maps contain two McKensy properties in the area between the Darbytown and Charles City roads; see, e.g., *Civil War Maps*, H41. One house ("J. McKensy") stood just north of the Darbytown Road in front of Kautz's line. The other ("R. McKensy") was much closer to the Charles City Road, near a portion of the exterior line. Given the general location of Kautz's position, it is likely Spear's brigade deployed behind the "J. McKensy" property, as marked on these maps. One period sketch of the ground north of the Johnson house, drawn later that month, clearly shows the Gerhardt house north of the Darbytown house and outside the federal line. See Waud, "Battle of Darby Town Rd." DRWG/US—Waud, no. 689, Prints and Photographs Division, LOC.

93. An anonymous account in the *Army and Navy Journal* described Spear's line as "nearly parallel and coincident with the Darbytown Road" (*Army and Navy Journal*, Nov. 5, 1864). It does not appear that Spear's position was a mere northward continuation of West's line. Rather, Spear's detached work sat on the far right flank of Kautz's position.

94. *Army and Navy Journal*, Nov. 5, 1864.

95. Roper, Archibald, and Coles, *History of the Eleventh*, 143–44.

96. O.R. 42(1): 848 (Noggle report).

97. O.R. 42(1): 845 (Hall report); Roper, Archibald, and Coles, *History of the Eleventh*, 556 (Union battery 400 yards in rear of main line).

98. Stahler, *Enoch Stahler*, 2.

99. Ibid., 3.

100. O.R. 42(1): 826 (West report).

101. Daly, *Alexander Cheves Haskell*, 144–45.

102. Ibid., 145. These trenches may have been the portion of the exterior line that ran west, north of Kautz's position.

103. Daly, *Alexander Cheves Haskell*, 146.

104. Ibid.

105. O.R. 42(1): 826–27 (West report). See also Manarin, *Henrico County*, vol. 2, 718.

344 NOTES TO PAGES 38–41

106. *Richmond Enquirer,* Nov. 22, 1864.

107. Stahler, *Enoch Stahler,* 3.

108. O.R. 42(1): 826 (West report).

109. Stahler, *Enoch Stahler,* 3.

110. *Richmond Enquirer,* Nov. 22, 1864 (anonymous letter from soldier in Field's division).

111. Ibid.

112. O.R. 42(1): 845–46 (Hall report); *Richmond Enquirer,* Nov. 22, 1864.

113. Roper, Archibald, and Coles, *History of the Eleventh,* 143.

114. Daly, *Alexander Cheves Haskell,* 156.

115. Ibid., 146.

116. O.R. 42(1): 824–25 (Kautz report).

117. Roper, Archibald, and Coles, *History of the Eleventh,* 143.

118. O.R. 42(1): 831–32 (Kleinz report).

119. O.R. 42(1): 824–25 (Kautz report).

120. Daly, *Alexander Cheves Haskell,* 146:

121. Bratton, "Report of Operations," 556.

122. James R. Hagood, "Memoirs of the First S.C. Regiment."

123. *Richmond Enquirer,* Nov. 22, 1864.

124. Roper, Archibald, and Coles, *History of the Eleventh,* 143. The Alabama brigade, under Gary's direct command during the operation, appears to have participated in the main attack against Kautz's front.

125. James R. Hagood, "Report of Colonel J. R. Hagood," 437–38.

126. O.R. 42(1): 824–25 (Kautz report).

127. James R. Hagood, "Memoirs of the First S.C. Regiment."

128. Roper, Archibald, and Coles, *History of the Eleventh,* 143.

129. O.R. 42(1): 845–46 (Hall report).

130. O.R. 42(1): 829–30 (Jacobs report).

131. Stahler, *Enoch Stahler,* 3.

132. O.R. 42(1): 827 (West report)

133. Ibid.

134. Stahler, *Enoch Stahler,* 4.

135. O.R. 42(1): 826–28 (West report).

136. Bratton,"Report of Operations."

137. O.R. 42(1): 826–28 (West report).

138. *Philadelphia Inquirer,* Oct. 10, 1864.

139. O.R. 42(1): 826–28 (West report); O.R. 42(1): 829–30 (Jacobs report).

140. O.R. 42(1): 830–31 (Jacobs report).

141. *Appleton Motor,* Oct. 27, 1864.

142. O.R. 42(1): 845–46 (Hall report).

143. O.R. 42(1): 830–31 (Jacobs report). Brigade commander Robert West's report confirmed the desertion incident described in Lieutenant Colonel Jacobs's report. "Lieutenant-Colonel Jacobs refers to the incident of a portion of the enemy's line throwing down their arms and shouting 'deserters.' This is substantiated by other officers of the Third New York, who saw and heard it. They chose a most unfortunate season for throwing themselves upon our protection, since we had more than we could do to protect ourselves just then" (O.R. 42(1): 827 [West report]). Kautz indicated in his own report that the claims of desertion by

the Confederates may have been a ruse. This seems unlikely, however, given Jacobs's report that other enemy units fired into the men attempting to desert. (O.R. 42(1): 824).

144. O.R. 42(1): 830–31 (Jacobs report). The identity of these "deserters" is unclear. They were most likely from either Anderson's Georgians, Bratton's South Carolinians, or Bowles's Alabamians, as those were the units most involved in the attack on Kautz. See James R. Hagood, "Memoirs of the First S.C. Regiment"; James R. Hagood, "Report of Colonel J. R. Hagood," 438; Bratton, "Report of Operations," 556–57. The precise location of the Alabama brigade during the attack is unclear.

145. O.R. 42(1): 830–31 (Jacobs report).

146. O.R. 42(1): 938 (Hagood report).

147. James R. Hagood, "Report of Colonel J. R. Hagood," 437–38.

148. James R. Hagood, "Memoirs of the First S.C. Regiment."

149. Ibid.

150. O.R. 42(1): 830–31 (Jacobs report).

151. O.R. 42(1): 826–28 (West report).

152. James R. Hagood, "Memoirs of the First S.C. Regiment."

153. Stocker, *From Huntsville to Appomattox* 186.

154. James R. Hagood, "Memoirs of the First S.C. Regiment."

155. O.R. 42(1): 845–47 (Hall report).

156. Ibid.

157. Bratton, "Report of Operations," 557.

158. Hagood, "Report of Colonel J. R. Hagood," 438.

159. O.R. 42(1): 847 (Hall report).

160. O.R. 42(1): 845–46 (Hall report); James R. Hagood, "Report of Colonel J. R. Hagood," 438.

161. O.R. 42(1): 847 (Hall report).

162. Davis, *Life of David Bell Birney,* 266.

163. Eyland, *Evolution of a Life,* 246.

164. Ibid.

165. O.R. 42(1): 848 (Noggle report).

166. Kautz's full description the road's location is as follows: "The Johnson House was located in the forks of Four Mile Creek, both branches of which were swamps on my right and left, and there was but one narrow country road that crossed the north branch and the main stream near their junction" (Kautz, "How I Won My First Brevet," 375). Lieutenant Hall's report indicates that the swampy crossing was at least three hundred yards into the woods south of the Johnson Farm (O.R. 42(1): 845–46 [Hall report]).

167. O.R. 42(1): 848 (Noggle report).

168. O.R. 42(1): 831–32 (Kleinz report).

169. O.R. 42(1): 846 (Hall report).

170. Daly, *Alexander Cheves Haskell,* 147.

171. O.R. 42(1): 824–25 (Kautz report).

172. O.R. 42(1): 848 (Noggle report).

173. O.R. 42(1): 831–32 (Kleinz report).

174. O.R. 42(1): 845–46 (Hall report).

175. Ibid. The enemy force referred to by Hall could have been either Haskell's group or Hagood's South Carolina infantry regiment (see James R. Hagood, "Report of Colonel J. R.

Hagood," 437–38). It is possible that Haskell had already charged through the Wisconsin battery and pushed along the wood road before Hall's arrival at the swamp crossing. However, this is unclear from the accounts. Because Hall mentions his escape in the face of approaching Confederates, it is more likely that he arrived at the stream before Haskell's charge.

176. Daly, *Alexander Cheves Haskell,* 147.

177. See A. V. Kautz Memoirs, USAMHI (after the battle, Kautz estimated the rebel cavalry strength at two thousand men, a far cry from the hundred or so claimed by Southern accounts); Waring, "Diary of William G. Hinson," 112.

178. Daly, *Alexander Cheves Haskell,* 147.

179. Ibid., 148.

180. Waring, "Diary of William G. Hinson," 112.

181. Haskell's account, written long after the war, suggests that the charging column emerged from the forest at a spot on the "Darbytown Road." This is doubtful, however, for Kautz's men began their retreat from the Johnson Farm, itself along the Darbytown Road, and Haskell charged through the withdrawing Union column for "probably a half mile." It is more likely that Haskell emerged into the fields of the Cox Farm between the New Market Road and the Four Mile Creek. Two points support this conclusion. First, Kautz indicates in his report that Haskell's men had formed a line of battle near the Cox Farm (O.R. 42(1): 824–25 [Kautz report]). Second, Haskell personally captured the wagon of the 1st New York Mounted Rifles, a unit that was stationed near the Cox and Kell houses just north of the New Market line (and not with Kautz's force at the Johnson Farm).

182. Daly, *Alexander Cheves Haskell,* 156–57.

183. Ibid., 148–49.

184. Ibid., 149.

185. Eyland, *Evolution of a Life,* 247. Cronin ("Eyland") describes the road from which the Confederate cavalry emerged as the "Charles City Road." Throughout his narrative, he misidentifies the local road names. From the context of his account and the description he gives, it is clear that the road he describes is the small path through the swamp used by Kautz in his retreat and by Haskell in his pursuit.

186. Daly, *Alexander Cheves Haskell,* 149–50.

187. Ibid., 150, 157 (accounts of Haskell and Welch).

188. Kautz, "How I Won My First Brevet," 382.

189. Haskell's postwar account indicates that the man in the middle of the Union group was Kautz himself (Daly, *Alexander Cheves Haskell,* 150). Kautz's account suggests that one of the other Union men in the party took credit for wounding Haskell (Kautz, "How I Won My First Brevet," 383).

190. Daly, *Alexander Cheves Haskell,* 150.

191. Ibid., 157.

192. Kautz, "How I Won My First Brevet," 383.

193. Daly, *Alexander Cheves Haskell,* 151–152.

194. Kautz, "How I Won My First Brevet," 383.

195. The attack extracted a heavy toll on the officers of Anderson's brigade. The casualties included Captain Robert R. Fudge, commanding the 11th Georgia, who died scaling the works in Kautz's front, and Lieutenant Colonel M. T. Allman of the 7th Georgia (*Richmond Enquirer,* Nov. 22, 1864).

196. Eyland, *Evolution of a Life,* 247.

197. Ibid.

198. Aug. V. Kautz Collection, LOC; Kautz, "How I Won My First Brevet," 375–76.

2. The New Market Road

1. Trumbull, *Knightly Soldier,* 292.

2. Roe, *Twenty-Fourth Massachusetts Volunteers,* 362.

3. Ferdinand Davis Memoirs, Bentley Historical Library.

4. O.R. 42(1): 663 (Michie report).

5. Agassiz, *Meade's Headquarters,* 266; Warner, *Generals in Blue,* 34.

6. Kreiser, *Defeating Lee,* 157.

7. Agassiz, *Meade's Headquarters,* 266.

8. *New York Herald,* Oct. 10, 1864.

9. Butler to Birney (various dispatches), Oct. 7, 1864, O.R. 42(3): 109.

10. Ibid.

11. Butler to Birney, Oct. 2, 1864, O.R. 42(3): 49.

12. *New York Herald,* Oct. 10, 1864.

13. Wood, *Reminiscences of the War,* 169.

14. *New York Times,* Dec. 17, 1890; Warner, *Generals in Blue,* 497–98.

15. *New York Times,* Sept. 23, 1864; see also Longacre, *Army of Amateurs,* 61.

16. O.R. 42(1): 703 (Abbott report).

17. *New York Herald,* Oct. 10, 1864.

18. *New York Times,* Oct. 11, 1864.

19. Ibid.

20. O.R. 42(1): 703 (Abbott report).

21. Roe, *Twenty-Fourth Massachusetts Volunteers,* 362.

22. *New York Herald,* Oct. 10, 1864.

23. O.R. 42(1): 731 (Plaisted report).

24. *New York Herald,* Oct. 10, 1864.

25. Ferdinand Davis Memoirs, Bentley Historical Library.

26. Stowits, *History of the One Hundredth,* 308.

27. Mowris, *History of the One Hundred and Seventeenth,* 139.

28. *Philadelphia Inquirer,* Oct. 10, 1864.

29. *New York Herald,* Oct. 10, 1864.

30. *Philadelphia Inquirer,* Oct. 10, 1864.

31. O.R. 42(1): 845 (Sumner report).

32. Ibid.

33. Eyland, *Evolution of a Life,* 248.

34. Taylor, "Reports of Operations."

35. James R. Hagood, "Memoirs of the First S.C. Regiment."

36. *Daily Richmond Enquirer,* Nov. 22, 1865.

37. James R. Hagood, "Memoirs of the First S.C. Regiment."

38. *Daily Richmond Enquirer,* Nov. 22, 1865. Though the cause of the Confederate delay in advancing against the New Market Road is not entirely clear, the time lag does not appear to have stemmed from disorganization of troops after the attack or the failure to

gather the men into formation. Two separate sources, written within a short time after the battle, note that Field's division quickly came into position following the victory on the Johnson Farm. See Taylor, "Reports of Operations" ("Field's and Hoke's divisions were quickly moved up and formed in line of battle at right angles to the exterior of works, the former on the east and the latter on the west side of the works"); and *Daily Richmond Enquirer,* Nov. 22, 1865 ("Immediately Field's division was deployed in battle order"). But James Hagood, who commanded the 1st South Carolina, recalled that General Field had expected Hoke to lead the attack after Johnson's Farm had been captured. According to Hagood, Field's command waited "hour after hour," and, when no news arrived from Hoke, Field chose to advance his own division (Hagood, James R., "Memoirs of the First S.C. Regiment").

39. Field, "Campaign of 1864 and 1865," 558.

40. James R. Hagood, "Memoirs of the First S.C. Regiment."

41. O.R. 42(1): 784 (Jackson report).

42. Eyland, *Evolution of a Life,* 248.

43. Ibid.

44. Ibid.

45. In his report, Randlett indicated, "My left connected with a detachment of General Kautz's cavalry" (O.R. 42(1): 721 [Randlett report]). Though Randlett does not name this force, it probably was the 1st New York Mounted Rifles. Neither Kautz nor his subordinates mention involvement in Terry's picket line.

46. Ibid.; Maxfield, *Company D,* 52; Maxfield, *Story of One Regiment,* 275.

47. O.R. 42(1): 721 (Randlett report).

48. *New York Herald,* Oct. 10, 1865.

49. Gallagher, *Fighting for the Confederacy,* 483.

50. Trumbull, *Knightly Soldier,* 293.

51. Ferdinand Davis Memoirs, Bentley Historical Library.

52. Ibid.; Davis, *Life of David Bell Birney,* 266.

53. Gallagher, *Fighting for the Confederacy,* 483.

54. O.R. 42(1): 783 (Jackson report).

55. Ibid.

56. See Lord, *Civil War Collector's Encyclopedia,* 160; Coggins, *Arms and Equipment of the Civil War,* 44. Union records indicate that Requa guns were present during operations at Fort Wagner in South Carolina in 1863; see O.R. 28(1): 291.

57. O.R. 42(1): 784 (Jackson report).

58. Gallagher, *Fighting for the Confederacy,* 483; Eyland, *Evolution of a Life,* 249.

59. O.R. 42(1): 789 (Tully report).

60. Waud, "Battle of Darbytown Rd."

61. Gallagher, *Fighting for the Confederacy,* 483.

62. O.R. 42(1): 791–92 (Myrick report).

63. *New York Times,* Oct. 11, 1864.

64. *New York Herald,* Oct. 10, 1864.

65. Ibid.

66. O.R. 42(1): 784 (Jackson report).

67. Gallagher, *Fighting for the Confederacy,* 483.

68. Warner, *Generals in Gray,* 87–88.

69. Barefoot, *General Robert F. Hoke,* 212. The source of blame for the setbacks at Cold Harbor (June 1), Petersburg (June 24), and Fort Harrison (Sept. 20) is unclear. Historian Douglas Southall Freeman faulted Hoke. However, Hoke biographer Daniel Barefoot argues that "Hoke's actions were either proper or at least defensible under the circumstances existing at the time." See Freeman, *Lee's Lieutenants,* vol. 3, 592–93; Sommers, *Richmond Redeemed,* 116–17; and Barefoot, *General Robert F. Hoke,* 230.

70. Field, "Campaign of 1864 and 1865," 557–58.

71. *Daily Richmond Enquirer,* Nov. 22, 1864.

72. Ibid.

73. *New York Herald,* Oct. 10, 1864; Roe, *Twenty-Fourth Massachusetts Volunteers,* 362.

74. O.R. 42(1): 704 (Abbott report).

75. *New York Times,* Oct. 11, 1864.

76. Maxfield, *Company D,* 52.

77. O.R. 42(1): 703–4 (Abbott Report); *New York Times,* Oct. 11, 1864 (says Confederates omitted skirmishers).

78. *New York Times,* Oct. 11, 1864.

79. O.R. 42(1): 703–4 (Abbott report).

80. O.R. 42(1): 716 (Prince report says he faced South Carolinians).

81. Styple, *Writing and Fighting,* 300.

82. *Daily Richmond Enquirer,* Nov. 22, 1865.

83. O.R. 42(1): 881 (Bratton report).

84. Joskins, "Sketch of Hood's Texas Brigade," 440.

85. The tabulation of effective strengths and casualties presented a difficult task. The size of units constantly changed with the loss of men from battle wounds and other causes and the addition of those returning from leave or arriving as new recruits or conscripts. An examination of period inspection reports provides a rough idea of the ebb and flow from various units during this period. Aug. 1864 inspection reports for Field's division show the following "present for duty" numbers (men and officers): Anderson (939), Bratton (1,373), Law (804), Texas (597), and Benning (671), for a total of 4,391. The Oct. 31, 1864, inspection report for Field's division shows the following numbers present for duty (men and officers): Anderson's brigade (1,056), Law's Alabama brigade (878), the Texas brigade (549), Dubose brigade (640), and Bratton's brigade (1,258), for a total of more than 4,300. The Sept. 20, 1864, inspection reports show Bratton's brigade (1,459), and the Texas brigade (609) (Confederate Inspection Reports, Record Group 109 (M935), NARA).

86. Terry to Butler, 2:30 P.M., Oct. 12, 1864, O.R. 42(3): 187–88.

87. O.R. 42(1): 721 (Randlett report).

88. *New York Herald,* Oct. 10, 1864.

89. Cleveland, *Hints to Riflemen,* 165–166.

90. Lord, *Civil War Collector's Encyclopedia,* 253.

91. *New York Times,* Oct. 11, 1864. The men of the 7th Connecticut had received their repeaters almost a year before. Armed with these weapons, the regiment made a decisive impact during fighting at Olustee, Florida, in Feb. 1864 (Bilby, "Repeating Rifles," 51–52).

92. Bratton aligned his brigade with the regiments "from right to left—Walker's [Palmetto Sharpshooters] on the right; Steedman's [6th S.C.], Hagood's [1st S.C.], Bowen's [2nd S.C.], and Coward's [5th S.C.] on the left" (O.R. 42(1): 881 [Bratton Report]).

93. Maxfield, *Story of One Regiment,* 275.

94. Eyland, *Evolution of a Life*, 249.

95. Inspection Report of the Texas Brigade, Oct. 31, 1864, Confederate Inspection Reports, Record Group 109 (M935), NARA.

96. Polley, *Hood's Texas Brigade*, 258.

97. Harold Simpson, *Hood's Texas Brigade*, 118–19.

98. Eyland, *Evolution of a Life*, 249.

99. At Fort Donelson, Gregg surrendered the 7th Texas, a unit he had recruited himself in 1861. Following his exchange, he rose to brigadier general and served in Mississippi. Later, he led a brigade of mostly Tennessee regiments at Chickamauga, where he received a serious neck wound after stumbling into the enemy skirmish line. Tumbling to the ground, he managed to hold on to his horse's reins, but the animal dragged him between the opposing forces, where he lost his sword and other personal possessions to Union soldiers. Fortuitously, men of the Texas brigade observed his condition and rushed forward, driving away the blue-clad soldiers and recovering Gregg (Harold Simpson, *Hood's Texas Brigade*, 320).

100. Brewer, *Alabama*, 312.

101. Polley, *Hood's Texas Brigade*, 258.

102. Harold Simpson, *Hood's Texas Brigade*, 441. "The brave and chivalrous Gregg had fallen, pierced through the neck by one of those enfilading balls. The command of his brigade devolved upon Col. Boss; he, also, was wounded and had to retire" (*Daily Richmond Enquirer*, Nov. 22, 1864). Another obituary suggests that Gregg was wounded in the chest (*Richmond Daily Examiner*, Oct. 10, 1864).

103. Winkler, *Confederate Capital*, 195.

104. Cutrer, *Longstreet's Aide*, 222.

105. Winkler, *Confederate Capital*, 195; Harold Simpson, *Hood's Texas Brigade*, 442.

106. O.R. 42(1): 704 (Abbott report).

107. Styple, *Writing and Fighting*, 300.

108. O.R. 42(1): 704 (Abbott report).

109. Styple, *Writing and Fighting*, 300.

110. O.R. 42(1): 881 (Bratton report).

111. Ferdinand Davis Memoirs, Bentley Historical Library.

112. Heyman, "The Gay Letters," 410.

113. Maxfield, *Story of One Regiment*, 275; O.R. 42(1): 731.

114. O.R. 42(1): 731 (Plaisted report).

115. Trumbull, *Knightly Soldier*, 304.

116. Ferdinand Davis Memoirs, Bentley Historical Library.

117. *New York Times*, Oct. 11, 1864.

118. O.R. 42(1): 704 (Abbott report).

119. Thomas L. McCarty Diary (Oct. 7, 1864, entry), Eugene C. Barker Texas History Center.

120. Bratton, "Report of Operations," 556–57.

121. O.R. 42(1): 731 (Plaisted report). See also Laine and Penny, *Law's Alabama Brigade*, 307–8.

122. O.R. 42(1): 731 (Plaisted report).

123. Trumbull, *Knightly Soldier*, 294–95.

124. Ibid.

125. Maxfield, *Company D*, 52.

126. Maxfield, *Story of One Regiment*, 276.

127. Stowits, *History of the One Hundredth,* 309; O.R. 42(1): 759.

128. O.R. 42(1): 759 (Brunck report); Stowits, *History of the One Hundredth,* 309.

129. *Supplement to the Official Records of the Union and Confederate Armies,* vol. 7, 443 (report of Colonel John Lord Otis, 10th Connecticut, of engagement near Four-Mile Creek, Virginia, Oct. 7, 1864).

130. Trumbull, *Knightly Soldier,* 295.

131. O.R. 42(1): 731 (Plaisted report).

132. Trumbull, *Knightly Soldier,* 296.

133. *New York Times,* Oct. 11, 1864.

134. Field, "Campaign of 1864 and 1865," 558.

135. *Richmond Enquirer,* Nov. 22, 1864.

136. Ibid.

137. Dawson, *Reminiscences of Confederate Service,* 127.

138. O.R. 42(1): 721 (Randlett report).

139. O.R. 42(1): 704 (Abbott report).

140. O.R. 42(1): 731 (Plaisted report).

141. Maxfield, *Company D,* 52.

142. Trumbull, who had enlisted in Sept. 1862, had been captured at Morris Island, South Carolina, in 1863 (American Civil War Research Database).

143. O.R. 42(1): 731 (Plaisted report).

144. Ibid., 732.

145. O.R. 42(1): 716 (Prince report).

146. O.R. 42(1): 704 (Abbott report); O.R. 42(1): 716 (Prince report); O.R. 42(1): 145 (general return of casualties). The 16th New York Heavy Artillery had sixty-five casualties including eleven dead.

147. O.R. 42(1): 732 (Plaisted report); O.R. 42(1): 144 (general return of casualties).

148. Laine and Penny, *Law's Alabama Brigade,* 307–8. One of the casualties was Captain John D. Adrian, commanding Company K, 44th Alabama. Five Alabama soldiers lay next to the twenty-one-year-old lawyer.

149. See Bratton, "Report of Operations," and Inspection Report for Bratton's Brigade, Sept. 20, 1864, Confederate Inspection Reports, Record Group 109 (M935), NARA.

150. *Richmond Examiner,* Nov. 1, 1864. Major Frederick Prince, commander of the 16th New York Heavy Artillery, reported that the South Carolinians had "lost heavily" in his front, including a captain and two lieutenants left dead on the field (O.R. 42(1): 716 [Prince report] and 42(1): 145 [Union casualty returns]). Another source recorded the loss from Anderson's Georgia brigade at 71. *Daily Constitutionalist,* October 14, 1864.

151. *Daily Constitutionalist,* October 14, 1864.

152. Harold Simpson, *Hood's Texas Brigade,* 441.

153. Inspection Report for Gregg's Brigade, Sept. and Oct., 1864, Confederate Inspection Reports, Record Group 109 (M935), NARA.

154. *Richmond Enquirer,* Oct. 10, 1864.

155. *Richmond Daily Enquirer,* Nov. 22, 1864.

156. Butler to Meade, 7:45 P.M., Oct. 8, 1864, O.R. 42(3): 119. A reporter wrote, "The rebel loss is quite one thousand in killed, wounded and missing. This latter estimate is based upon the statement of prisoners" (*New York Herald,* Oct. 10, 1864).

157. Trumbull, *Knightly Soldier,* 296.

158. Birney to Butler, 11:15 A.M., Oct. 7, 1864, O.R. 42(3): 110.

159. O. R. 42(3): 115–16 (several dispatches between Butler and Birney).

160. Butler to Birney, 11:15 A.M., Oct. 7, 1864, O.R. 42(3): 110.

161. Birney to Butler, 12:50 P.M., Oct. 7, 1864, O.R. 42(3): 110–11.

162. Jackson and O'Donnell, *Back Home in Oneida,* 169.

163. Birney to Smith, Oct. 7, 1864, O.R. 42(3): 112.

164. Taylor, "Reports of Operations."

165. Eyland, *Evolution of a Life,* 251.

166. Grant to Meade, Oct. 7, 1864, O.R. 42(3): 102.

167. Sauers, *Civil War Journal,* 233; see also Sommers, "Battle No One Wanted"; *Army and Navy Journal,* Oct. 22, 1864; *Petersburg Express,* Oct. 11, 1864.

168. Grant to Meade, Oct. 9, 1864, O.R. 42(3): 143.

169. "Army Life in the Twenty-Fourth Regiment, Massachusetts Volunteer Infantry," John M. Spear Papers, Massachusetts Historical Society.

170. Maxfield, *Company D,* 52. The news of Butler's victory also made its way to the Petersburg front. "The report is here," wrote a member of the 17th Vermont, "that [Butler] is up past fort Darling and if that is the case I think that Richmond must fall soon" (Charles Manson to his mother, Oct. 9, 1864, Charles Manson Letters, University of Vermont Library).

171. Eyland, *Evolution of a Life,* 250.

172. Laine and Penny, *Law's Alabama Brigade,* 308.

173. Keyes, *Lewis Atterbury Stimson,* 41–42.

174. Davis, *Life of David Bell Birney,* 270.

175. *New York Herald,* Nov. 10, 1864.

176. Davis, *Life of David Bell Birney,* 275.

177. Birney to Smith, Oct. 9, 1864, O.R. 42(3): 150.

178. General Orders #124 (Army of the James), Oct. 10, 1864, O.R. 42(3): 157; Davis, *Life of David Bell Birney,* 276.

179. Davis, *Life of David Bell Birney,* 275.

180. C.W. Graves to Butler, Oct. 15, 1864, Benjamin F. Butler Papers, LOC.

181. *Philadelphia Inquirer,* Oct. 22, 1864.

182. Ibid.

183. *New York Herald,* Oct. 10, 1864.

184. *Army and Navy Journal,* Oct. 15, 1864.

185. Kautz, "How I Won My First Brevet," 378.

186. *Army and Navy Journal,* Nov. 5, 1864 (T., "The Cavalry on the Darbytown Road").

187. A letter from "S." appeared in the *Army and Navy Journal* on Oct. 22, 1864, providing details of the performance of Hall's battery during the battle, no doubt in an effort to explain the circumstances surrounding the loss of the battery's guns (S., "Hall's Battery at Johnson's Farm," *Army and Navy Journal,* Oct. 22, 1864).

188. *New York Times,* Oct. 11, 1864.

189. Kautz, "How I Won My First Brevet," 380.

190. Ibid.

191. In fact, Kautz titled an article covering his reminiscences of this period "How I Won My First Brevet."

192. Butler to Grant, Oct. 6, 1864, O.R. 42(3): 98.

193. Lee to Seddon, Oct. 8, 1864, O.R. 42(1): 852.

194. *Richmond Enquirer,* Oct. 10, 1864.

195. *Columbia Daily,* Oct. 23, 1864.

196. For criticisms of Hoke's performances, see Freeman, *R. E. Lee,* vol. 3, 509–10, and *Lee's Lieutenants,* vol. 3, 592–93. For a defense of Hoke's actions, see Barefoot, *General Robert F. Hoke,* 229–31, and Weymouth T. Jordan Jr., *North Carolina Troops,* vol. 14, 648–50; see also Manarin, *Henrico County,* vol. 2, 741, 844, n.345.

197. Johnson Hagood, *Memoirs of the War,* 309.

198. See Johnson Hagood, *Memoirs of the War,* 309 (referring to James R. Hagood's account).

199. Field, "Campaign of 1864 and 1865," 558.

200. *Raleigh Confederate,* Oct. 21, 1864 (quoting the *Conservative*).

201. *Raleigh Confederate,* Oct. 25, 1864.

202. Dunlop, *Lee's Sharpshooters,* 216. The reliability of Dunlop's account is unclear. His description of the events that day is muddled. For example, his account indicates that Hoke did in fact attack and was repulsed. It also suggests that the attack on the Union cavalry occurred simultaneously with that launched against the infantry.

203. Gallagher, *Fighting for the Confederacy,* 483.

204. O.R. 42(1): 783–84 (Jackson report).

205. O.R. 42(1): 876 (Diary of First Corps, Army of Northern Virginia).

206. Taylor, "Reports of Operations."

207. Johnson Hagood, *Memoirs of the War,* 309.

208. Ibid., 308–9.

209. Porter Alexander wrote that "Scarcely any of our generals had half of what they needed to keep a constant & close supervision on the execution of important orders" (Gallagher, *Fighting for the Confederacy,* 236). Alexander also emphasized "how important in a big army is the detail, which only a large & well trained staff can supply" (ibid., 273). General Lafayette McLaws identified staff organization and practice as the greatest defect in Lee's army. (Lafeyette McLaws, quoted in Krick, "The Great Tycoon Forges a Staff System," 101.

210. See, e.g., Piston, "Longstreet, Lee, and Attack Plans," 42–43. See also, Palmer, *Lee Moves North,* 121–36.

211. Krick, "The Great Tycoon Forges a Staff System," 97.

212. Gallagher, *Fighting for the Confederacy,* 483.

213. *Richmond Enquirer,* Nov. 22, 1864.

214. Johnson Hagood, *Memoirs of the War,* 309.

215. Gorgas and Wiggins, *Journals of Josiah Gorgas,* 136.

216. The Mar. 1865 attack at Fort Stedman offers the only other example of Lee's late-war efforts to take the offensive. With the operation at the Johnson's Farm and New Market Road on Oct. 7, however, Lee arguably sought even greater gains than he did at Fort Stedman.

217. *Richmond Examiner,* Oct. 10, 1864.

218. Ibid.

219. Ibid.

220. Harold Simpson, *Hood's Texas Brigade,* 442.

3. Union Reconnaissance on the Darbytown Road (Oct. 13)

1. Trumbull, *Knightly Soldier,* 308.

2. O.R. 42(1): 666 (Michie report); Hess, *In the Trenches,* 173.

3. On Oct. 10, Grant, Meade, and Butler, along with Admiral David Farragut, visited the fort and viewed the Confederate works to the west (Thompson, *Thirteenth Regiment,* 493).

4. Gallagher, *Fighting for the Confederacy,* 486.

5. Johnson Hagood, *Memoirs of the War,* 309; Taylor, "Reports of Operations."

6. Gallagher, *Fighting for the Confederacy,* 486; see also Edward R. Crockett Diary, Eugene C. Barker Texas History Center.

7. Field, "Campaign of 1864 and 1865," 557–59.

8. Hess, *In the Trenches,* 179.

9. John B. Jones, *Rebel War Clerk's Diary,* vol. 2 (Oct. 12, 1864), 304.

10. Thomas, *Confederate Nation,* 196.

11. Lee to secretary of war, Oct. 4, 1864, O.R. 42(3): 1134; Sommers, "Dutch Gap Affair," 52.

12. Sommers, "Dutch Gap Affair," 52; John B. Jones, *Rebel War Clerk's Diary,* vol. 2 (Oct. 12, 1864), 303.

13. Benj. F. Butler to Robert Ould, Oct. 12, 1864, O.R. Series 2, 7: 967–68 (Inclosure 1, Deposition of Sam. Miller).

14. O.R. Series 2, 7: 968–69.

15. Seddon to Beauregard, Nov. 30, 1864, O.R. Series 2, 4: 954.

16. See Berlin, *Freedom,* 567–70; Manning, *What This Cruel War Was Over,* 160–62 (Confederate policy); Bernard, *War Talks,* 159 (Southern accounts of atrocities at the Crater).

17. R. E. Lee to Grant, Oct. 3, 1864, O.R. Series II, 7: 914.

18. See Berlin, *Freedom,* 567–70; Dobak, *Freedom by the Sword,* 186.

19. Butler to Ould, Oct. 12, 1864, O.R. Series II, 7: 967.

20. O.R. 42(3): 185.

21. Grant to Butler, Oct. 12, 1864, O.R. Series II, 7: 967.

22. Butler to Ould, Oct. 12, 1864, O.R. Series II, 7: 967.

23. See O.R. 42(3): 183–86.

24. O.R. 42(3): 182. In closing his note, Kautz mentioned that the swamp road connecting his position on the Darbytown Road with the infantry at the New Market Road was almost complete.

25. Grant to Butler, Oct. 12, 1864, O.R. 42(3): 182.

26. Butler to Terry, 2:30 P.M., Oct. 12, 1864, O.R. 42(3): 186.

27. Terry to Butler, Oct. 12, 1864, O.R. 42(3): 187–188. Terry planned to leave out the 199th Pennsylvania because it was simply too green for such an operation.

28. Kautz Diary, Oct. 12, 1864, Kautz Papers, LOC.

29. Trumbull, *Knightly Soldier,* 298–99.

30. O.R. 42(3): 183–84.

31. Dickey, *History of the Eighty-Fifth,* 399.

32. Styple, *Writing and Fighting,* 301 (letter from "Jackson").

33. Terry to Butler, Oct. 12, 1864, O.R. 42(3): 189.

34. O.R. 42(3): 190 (Tenth Corps orders).

35. O.R. 42(3): 190–91.

36. O.R. 42(3): 190.

37. Putnam, *Major General Joseph R. Hawley,* 61.

38. Trumbull, *Knightly Soldier,* 300.

39. "Army Life in the Twenty-Fourth Regiment, Massachusetts Volunteer Infantry," John M. Spear Papers, Massachusetts Historical Society.

40. Trumbull, *Knightly Soldier*, 300.

41. O.R. 42(1): 681 (Terry report).

42. Field, "Campaign of 1864 and 1865," 558–59. Gary's cavalry picketed the countryside in this area but was spread all over the road network east of Richmond. Haskell's 7th South Carolina, for instance, was camped north of the Williamsburg Road, more than a mile away.

43. Field, "Campaign of 1864 and 1865," 558–59.

44. Edward R. Crockett Diary, Eugene C. Barker Texas History Center.

45. Terry to Butler, 1 A.M., Oct. 13, 1864, O.R. 42(3): 218.

46. Trumbull, *Knightly Soldier*, 300.

47. O.R. 42(1): 681 (Terry report).

48. Aug. V. Kautz Collection, LOC. Perhaps Kautz's effort to escort the artillery to the field delayed him. His assigned route took him past the Four Mile Church far to the east and then along the Darbytown Road (O.R. 42(1): 681 [Terry report]).

49. Terry to Butler, Oct. 13, 1864, O.R. 42(3): 218.

50. O.R. 42(1): 685 (Ames report).

51. O.R. 42(1): 707 (Hawley report).

52. O.R. 42(1): 733 (Plaisted report).

53. O.R. 42(1): 690 (Pond report). Plaisted's report indicates that "the division advanced across an open field at Gerhardt's house and entered a thick growth of scrub oaks" (O.R. 42(1): 733).

54. O.R. 42(1): 706 (Hawley report); O.R. 42(1): 712–13 (Atwell report).

55. Longacre, *Army of Amateurs*, 198.

56. *Richmond Enquirer*, Nov. 22, 1864.

57. O.R. 42(1): 777 (Doubleday report).

58. O.R. 42(1): 681 (Terry report).

59. O.R. 42(1): 732–34 (Plaisted report).

60. Ibid.

61. O.R. 42(1): 717 (Prince report).

62. Trumbull, *Knightly Soldier*, 301–2.

63. Terry to Butler, 10:30 A.M., Oct. 13, 1864, O.R. 42(3): 218–19.

64. Terry to Kautz, Oct. 13, 1864, O.R. 42(3): 224.

65. O.R. 42(1): 782 (Bates report).

66. Grant to Butler, Oct. 13, 1864, O.R. 42(3): 213.

67. O.R. 42(1): 682 (Terry report).

68. Ibid.

69. Terry to Butler, 2 P.M., Oct. 13, 1864, O.R. 42(3): 219.

70. Butler to Terry, 1:30 P.M., Oct. 13, 1864, O.R. 42(3): 219.

71. Terry to Butler, 2 P.M., Oct. 13, 1864, O.R. 42(3): 219.

72. In Henry B. Flanner's battery, Union fire ignited some ammunition lying about. The ensuing explosion wounded six men. One of them discarded any notion of personal safety and "caught up several shells with burning fuses and extinguished them in a pool of water near by" as other shells burst around him" (O.R. 42(1): 860 [Pendleton report]). Though the source of this incident, Brigadier General William N. Pendleton's official report, does not mention the full name of this corporal, it was mostly likely Wallace Fulsher of North Carolina.

73. Field, "Campaign of 1864 and 1865," 558.

74. *Columbia Daily*, Oct. 23, 1864.

75. Field, "Campaign of 1864 and 1865," 558.

76. As the Alabama infantrymen dug in, a lone Confederate cavalryman tore past in the direction of oncoming Unionists. Soon the same trooper galloped back with a Union horseman in close pursuit. The Union horseman had picked the wrong time and place for this duel. As he raced into the Southern infantrymen, some dropped their shovels, lifted their rifles, and knocked him off his mount with a well-directed volley (McClendon, *Recollections of War Times,* 222). See also, *Richmond Enquirer,* Nov. 22, 1864.

77. O.R. 42(1): 690–91 (Pond report); O.R. 42(1): 681–82 (Terry report).

78. Dickey, *History of the Eighty-Fifth,* 404.

79. O.R. 42(1): 690–91 (Pond report).

80. Trumbull, *Knightly Soldier,* 302.

81. Ibid., 303.

82. Hawley to his wife, Oct. 18, 1864, Joseph Hawley Papers, LOC.

83. Charles M. Clark, *History of the Thirty-Ninth,* 226.

84. McClendon, *Recollections of War Times,* 222.

85. *Richmond Enquirer,* Nov. 22, 1864.

86. O.R 42(1): 741 (Otis report).

87. Trumbull, *Knightly Soldier,* 305.

88. Charles M. Clark, *History of the Thirty-Ninth,* 228; American Civil War Research Database.

89. Charles M. Clark, *History of the Thirty-Ninth,* 229.

90. O.R. 42(1): 682 (Terry report).

91. Ibid.

92. Trumbull, *Knightly Soldier,* 305.

93. Silas Mead to Tillie, Oct. 15, 1864, Silas Mead Letters, Greenwich Historical Society.

94. Ibid., 307.

95. Charles M. Clark, *History of the Thirty-Ninth,* 226.

96. Trumbull, *Knightly Soldier,* 307.

97. Yates was captured, then paroled, and died of his wounds in Annapolis, Maryland, on Oct. 26 (Charles M. Clark, *History of the Thirty-Ninth,* 226).

98. Ibid., 226.

99. A few accounts suggest that the Confederate counterattack was a substantial one and met with a severe repulse, leaving dead and wounded Southerners lying in the slashing in front of their works ("Army Life in the Twenty-Fourth Regiment, Massachusetts Volunteer Infantry," John M. Spear Papers, Massachusetts Historical Society; and *Army and Navy Journal,* Oct. 22, 1864).

100. *Richmond Enquirer,* Nov. 22, 1864.

101. Charles M. Clark, *History of the Thirty-Ninth,* 229–30.

102. O.R. 42(1): 682 (Terry report).

103. O.R. 42(1): 146–47 (casualty returns for Darbytown Road, Oct. 13, 1864).

104. *Richmond Enquirer,* Nov. 22, 1864.

105. O.R. 42(1): 691 (Pond report).

106. *Richmond Enquirer,* Nov. 22, 1864. The dead included Lieutenant Colonel Terrill of the 47th Alabama.

107. *Richmond Dispatch,* Oct. 21, 1864. Elsewhere along the line, General Field's chief of staff, Major W. F. Jones, received a bullet to his head while shuttling an order along the front (*Richmond Enquirer,* Nov. 22, 1864).

108. *Army and Navy Journal,* Oct. 22, 1864.

109. O.R. 42(1): 853 (Lee report).

110. Venable to Anderson, Oct. 13, 1864, 5:15 P.M., Porter Alexander Papers, UNC.

111. *Richmond Dispatch,* Oct. 21, 1864.

112. *Columbia Daily,* Oct. 23, 1864.

113. "Army Life in the Twenty-Fourth Regiment, Massachusetts Volunteer Infantry," John M. Spear Papers, Massachusetts Historical Society.

114. *Richmond Examiner,* Oct. 20, 1864 (quoting the *New York Herald*).

115. O.R. 42(1): 722 (Randlett report).

116. O.R. 42(1): 741 (Otis report).

117. *Hartford Daily Courant,* Oct. 22, 1864 (the letter is signed "H.C.T.").

118. Hawley to his wife, Oct. 18, 1864, Joseph Hawley Papers, LOC.

119. Charles M. Clark, *History of the Thirty-Ninth,* 226.

120. Silas Mead to Tillie, Oct. 15, 1864, Silas Mead Letters, Greenwich Historical Society.

121. Dickey, *History of the Eighty-Fifth,* 403.

122. O.R. 42(1): 686 (Ames report).

123. Dickey, *History of the Eighty-Fifth Regiment,* 404.

124. Smith to Terry, Oct. 19, 1864, O.R. 42(3): 279.

125. Butler, *Autobiography and Personal Reminiscences,* 717–773. Butler did not devote any ink to the Oct. 7 fight, either.

126. Trumbull, *Knightly Soldier,* 303.

127. *New York Tribune,* Oct. 13, 1864.

128. Butler, *Private and Official Correspondence,* vol. 5, 256–57.

129. *New York Times,* Oct. 17, 1864. An account in a Richmond paper identified one of the two Confederate civil servants as "Henley" (not "Henly") (*Richmond Daily Examiner,* Oct. 20, 1864).

130. Upon reaching the canal, McCrae allegedly "addressed his fellow-captives, stating that the retaliation was just, as of his own knowledge, he could say that negro soldiers had been used by the Confederate authorities in the manner complained of" (*New York Times,* Oct. 18, 1864). However, in a letter to a Richmond paper several days later, McCrae vehemently denied the account, claiming, "I never saw any such prisoners at work any where, and never made any such speech—The whole story is an unmitigated falsehood" (*Richmond Daily Examiner,* Oct. 26, 1864).

131. John B. Jones, *Rebel War Clerk's Diary,* vol. 2 (Oct. 22, 1864), 312–13.

132. Ibid., 438.

133. Sommers, "Dutch Gap Affair," 54–61. After the war, Confederate artillerist William Poague recalled, "I was also directed to have a corral built around my mortars sufficient for 400 men and was told that when it was completed General Lee would send down from Richmond that number of Yankee prisoners to be confined therein under an adequate number of guards—this in retaliation. On the 22nd of Oct., we were ordered to suspend work on the corral, inasmuch as Grant had taken our men out of the canal" (Cockrell, *Gunner with Stonewall,* 107).

134. Porter Alexander to his wife, Oct. 25, 1864, Porter Alexander Papers, UNC.

135. Butler to Patrick, 9 P.M., Oct. 18, 1864, O.R. 42(3): 268.

136. O.R. Series 2, 7: 1010–12. Lee's letter to Grant appears to have been based in part on an even longer note that James Seddon had prepared for Lee on the 15th (O.R. Series 2, 7: 990–93). See also Berlin, *Freedom,* 567–69.

137. O.R. Series 2, 7: 1010–12.

138. Turner to Hatch, Oct. 14, 1864, O.R. Series 2, 7: 988.

139. Ibid.

140. John B. Jones, *Rebel War Clerk's Diary*, vol. 2, 311.

141. Grant to Lee, Oct. 20, 1864, O.R. Series 2, 7: 1018–19.

142. Ibid.

143. Over the years, much mythology has developed about Lee's views on slavery. Though his positions have been often obscured by popular history, recent scholarship indicates that Lee's slavery views were typical of many white Southern leaders—complicated, nuanced, but ultimately supportive. Lee was an active participant in the institution before the war and used the services of slaves throughout the conflict. He may have found slave ownership and management distasteful, inefficient, and simply aggravating, but he did not seriously challenge the underpinnings of the system. As a public figure before and during most of the war, he made no significant effort to oppose the Confederacy's defining institution. See Pryor, *Reading the Man*, 141–54 (Pryor provides a detailed discussion of Lee's views on slavery based on an examination of recently discovered personal correspondence); see also Nolan, *Lee Considered*, 9–10. In an 1856 letter to his wife, Lee described human bondage as a "moral and political evil." However, in the same letter, he went on to say that blacks were better off under slavery than they were in Africa and that only "a wise Merciful Providence" could tell how long "their subjugation may be necessary" (Freeman, *R. E. Lee*, vol. 1, 372). In Feb. 1865, with the Confederacy and slavery on the brink of disintegration, Lee recommended arming slaves for use in the military and instituting a program of gradual emancipation to ensure the "fidelity of this auxiliary force." However, in prefacing his recommendation, Lee wrote that "Considering the relation of master and slave, controlled by humane laws and influenced by Christianity and an enlightened public sentiment, as the best that can exist between the white and black races while intermingled as at present in this country, I would deprecate any disturbance of that relation unless it be necessary to avert a calamity to both" (O.R. Series 4, 3: 1012–13).

144. *New York Tribune*, Oct. 21, 1864.

145. Blackett, *Thomas Morris Chester*, 147.

146. For instance, Confederate troops under John Bell Hood captured the 44th USCT at Dalton, Georgia, en masse. The Confederates stripped the prisoners of much of their clothing and immediately forced them into labor tearing up railroad tracks; see Bailey, *Chessboard of War*, 35–37.

147. *Philadelphia Inquirer*, Oct. 18, 1864.

148. Ibid. Subsequently, the same editors wrote of Butler's Dutch Gap, "There is no love lost on either side, and the hatred which Butler holds toward the Rebellion and everything connected with it, fully equals that which the Southern traitors cherish against him. Again he has triumphed over the barbarism of an enemy who has, through the entire war, presumed on the forbearance of the national Government. In Butler they find a man of Jacksonian stamp, a man not afraid to take the responsibility of acting, promptly, energetically and decisively. Although they may style him 'the beast,' they have learned by this time that he is not to be trifled with" (*Philadelphia Inquirer*, Oct. 22, 1864).

149. Silas Mead to William Edward, Oct. 20, 1864, Silas Mead Papers, Greenwich Historical Society.

150. *New York Tribune*, Oct. 27, 1864.

151. Weitzel to Terry, 9:18 P.M., Oct. 16, 1864, O.R. 42(3): 252.

152. Terry to Smith, Oct. 17, 1864, O.R. 42(3): 261.

153. *Richmond Whig,* Oct. 25, 1864. During her visit, Sarah Butler reportedly toured the Union lines and observed the activities at the Dutch Gap canal close at hand. Thomas to Butler, Oct. 18, 1864, O.R. 42(3): 267.

154. O.R. 42(3): 268–69 (Special Orders No. 297). On the 24th, the 118th USCT joined Butler, about one thousand strong (Rand to Seally, Oct. 24, 1864, O.R. 42(3): 336).

155. Butler, *Private and Official Correspondence,* vol. 5, 274–75.

156. Kautz Diary, Oct. 8, 1864, Kautz Papers, LOC.

157. *Philadelphia Inquirer,* Oct. 24, 1864.

4. The Petersburg Front

1. *New York Times,* Oct. 30, 1864.

2. Ibid.

3. Horn, *Destruction of the Weldon Railroad,* 171–72.

4. Porter, *Campaigning with Grant,* 212.

5. *New York Times,* Oct. 30, 1864.

6. Pomfret, "Letters of Fred Lockley," 96.

7. Cowtan, *Services of the Tenth New York,* 318–19.

8. Pomfret, "Letters of Fred Lockley," 96–97.

9. Haley, *Rebel Yell,* 207.

10. Cowtan, *Services of the Tenth New York,* 319.

11. Pomfret, "Letters of Fred Lockley," 69.

12. Cowtan, *Services of the Tenth New York,* 319–20.

13. Ibid., 320.

14. Hyndman, *History of a Cavalry Company,* 236–37.

15. Thompson to Sister Fanny, Oct. 30, 1864, Alfred B. Thompson Letters, University of Vermont Library.

16. "Dear Mother," Oct. 4, 1864, Isaac Williams Papers, USAMHI.

17. O.R. 42(1): 944–47 (Hampton report).

18. Gregg to Williams, Oct. 12, 1864, O.R. 42(3): 182.

19. Hyndman, *History of a Cavalry Company,* 236–37.

20. Bibber to Davies, Oct. 15, 1864, O.R. 42(3): 241–42.

21. Axford, *To Locaber Na Mair,* 130 (diary of William Eppa Fielding, Sept. 29, 1864).

22. A. Wilson Greene, *Civil War Petersburg,* 190–219.

23. Mary C. Burgess, *True Story,* 29–31.

24. Ibid., 38.

25. Ibid. According to one account, Hampton grazed his captured cattle on the Burgess Farm in late Sept. Mary Burgess does not mention such an occurrence in her memoir, however. See Billings, *History of the Tenth Massachusetts,* 464.

26. Mary C. Burgess, *True Story,* 34.

27. Lee to his wife, Oct. 25, 1864, in Lee, *Wartime Papers,* 865.

28. See Freeman, *R. E. Lee,* vol. 4, 71.

29. Grant later explained, "My anxiety for some time before Richmond fell was lest Lee should abandon it. My pursuit of Lee was hazardous. I was in a position of extreme difficulty.

You see I was marching away from my supplies, while Lee was falling back on his supplies. If Lee had continued his flight another day, I should have had to abandon the pursuit, fall back to Danville, build the railroad, and feed my army. So far as supplies were concerned, I was almost at my last gasp when the surrender took place" (Young, *Around the World,* vol. 2, 460).

30. For a discussion of the importance of the Petersburg campaign, see Power, *Lee's Miserables,* 317–19.

31. Near the war's close, Lee supposedly claimed that he "was determined to die rather than yield" and that with his "army in the mountains of Virginia, I could carry on this war for twenty years longer" (Rev. J. William Jones, *Personal Reminiscences,* 295).

32. Lee to A. P. Hill, June—, 1864, O.R. 40(2): 702–3.

33. Lee to secretary of war, Aug. 23, 1864, O.R. 42(2): 1199–1200.

34. Lee to Kemper, Sept. 3, 1864, O.R. 42(2): 1230.

35. O.R. 42(1): 898–907 (Johnson's reports).

36. McClure, *Annals of War,* 703.

37. Wiatt, *Confederate Chaplain William Edward Wiatt,* 203.

38. Ibid., 299, 306.

39. Lee to Hampton, Oct. 4, 1864, O.R. 42(3): 1133.

40. Lee to Seddon, Oct. 7, 1864, in Lee, *Wartime Papers,* 862–83.

41. In the middle of Sept., Lee had recalled Kershaw's infantry division from Early to support an attack against Grant outside Richmond and Petersburg. After Sheridan's attack at Winchester, however, Kershaw's men shuttled back to the Valley before they even arrived in Richmond. Sommers, *Richmond Redeemed,* 4.

42. Lee to Early, Sept. 27, 1864, O.R. 43(2): 881.

43. O.R. 43(1): 559; O.R. 43(1): 61.

44. Lee to Early, Oct. 12, 1864, O.R. 43(2): 892.

45. Lee to Governor Vance, Aug. 29, 1864, O.R. 42(2): 1206–7.

46. Porter, *Campaigning with Grant,* 288; Stanton to Grant, Sept. 1, 1864, O.R. 42(2): 624; O.R. 39(2): 364, 412 (Grant and Sherman correspondence). See also Fonvielle, *Wilmington Campaign,* 59–72.

47. Seddon to Lee, Oct. 5, 1864, O.R. 42(3): 1135–36.

48. Ibid.

49. See general orders from the adjutant and inspector general's office, C.S.A., 107–8 (Order No. 76); see also *Richmond Examiner,* Oct. 7, 1864; Lee to Cooper, Oct. 10, 1864, O.R. 2(3): 1144.

50. R. E. Lee to Gen. A. P. Hill, Oct. 10, 1864, O.R. 42(3): 1145.

51. Claiborne to his wife, Oct. 17, 1864, J. H. Claiborne Papers, Small Special Collections Library, University of Virginia Library.

52. Welch, *Confederate Surgeon's Letters,* 108.

53. Wiley, *Norfolk Blues,* 163.

54. Mackintosh, *Dear Martha,* 148.

55. Hess, *Lee's Tar Heels* (quoting letter of Lemuel J. Hoyle), 270.

56. Hancock to Williams, Oct. 26, 1864, O.R. 42(3): 357.

57. Meade to Grant, 12 m., Oct. 20, 1864, O.R. 42(3): 280–81.

58. *Richmond Examiner,* Nov. 22, 1864.

59. *Columbia Daily,* Oct. 23, 1864.

60. Baldwin, *Struck Eagle,* 334.

61. Alexander to his wife, Oct. 19, 1864, Porter Alexander Papers, UNC.

62. *New York Tribune*, Oct. 13, 1864.

63. See *Richmond Whig*, Oct. 13, 1864; *Columbia Daily*, Oct. 23, 1864.

64. *Daily Confederate*, Oct. 23, 1864.

65. *Richmond Dispatch*, Oct. 20, 1864 (quoting from *Philadelphia Inquirer*).

66. Peyton to S. Cooper, Nov. 29, 1864 (cover letter transmitting inspection reports), Record Group 109, Entry 65 (Microfilm Reel M935), NARA.

67. Hampton to Lee, Oct. 24, 1864, O.R. 42(3): 1161–62.

68. For a discussion of Confederate manpower and military policy in 1864, see Newton, *Lost for the Cause.*

69. Cutrer, *Longstreet's Aide,* 137.

70. *Richmond Enquirer,* Oct. 6, 1864 (quoted in Levine, *Confederate Emancipation,* 32).

71. *Richmond Sentinel,* Nov. 2, 1864. The Confederate discussions about arming slaves also received coverage in the Northern press. The *New York Times* reprinted a story out of Georgia predicting that 300,000 slaves would be under rebel arms by the spring (*New York Times,* Nov. 1, 1864); see also *Philadelphia Inquirer,* Oct. 14, 1864.

72. Levine, *Confederate Emancipation,* 36.

73. The proposed policy to create regiments from slaves raised questions that have fueled debate for years since the war, such as whether such a policy would bring into question slavery's importance to the rebellion and whether slaves would have enlisted in great numbers to fight for a government that sanctioned their bondage. As historian William Marvel observed, such a policy appeared to contradict "the anthropological pretense behind the nation's defining institution" (Marvel, *Lee's Last Retreat,* 5). In a recent study of Confederate efforts to enlist slaves, Bruce Levine suggests that the policy simply reflected an effort to boost Southern muster rolls, while allowing white Southerners to continue their subjugation of blacks on their own terms. In Levine's view, the proposal did not reflect any serious intention to change black social and political status. The debate about arming slaves simply foreshadowed the subtle and not so subtle efforts to suppress African American political rights in the nineteenth- and twentieth-century South (Levine, *Confederate Emancipation,* 139–64).

74. Longstreet to W. H. Taylor, Oct. 7, 1864, 42(3): 1140. Two days later, he wrote Lee offering his thoughts on Sheridan's next moves. Longstreet to Lee, Oct. 9, 1864, 42(3): 1142–43.

75. Wert, *General James Longstreet,* 392–93.

76. Ibid., 394–95.

77. *Charleston Daily Courier,* Oct. 18, 1864.

78. Waring, "Diary of William G. Hinson," 112.

79. Cutrer, *Longstreet's Aide,* 137; *Columbia Daily,* Oct. 23, 1864 (says Longstreet rode the lines on the 15th).

80. *Richmond Daily Enquirer,* Nov. 22, 1864.

5. Petersburg Becomes the Key

1. Nevins, *Diary of Battle,* 472.

2. Chamberlain, *Passing of the Armies,* 12.

3. The soldier "decidedly objects to vote for the party that insults him by saying that 'all he has done since the commencement of the war is a miserable failure,'" wrote one Lincoln supporter (Tilney, *My Life in the Army,* 142). Theodore Lyman, from Meade's staff,

estimated in mid-Oct. that the soldiers would support Lincoln five to one because they identified the administration with "the support of the war" and the troops "make thrashing the rebs a matter of pride, as well as patriotism" (Agassiz, *Meade's Headquarters*, 245). "I think if [Lincoln] is elected the fighting will stop," wrote a Vermont infantryman, "and if the other one [McClellan] 4 more years of fighting" (Charles Manson to his mother, Oct. 9, 1864, Charles Manson Letters, University of Vermont Library). A Pennsylvania cavalryman with the Army of the Potomac wrote that the soldiers were learning who "their true friends" were and would support Lincoln. He predicted that the "rebellion will crumble, Union peace & universal liberty prevail" following a Republican victory (Romig, *Porter Phipps' Letters*, 74).

4. Longacre, *From Antietam to Fort Fisher*, 212.

5. *New York Tribune*, Oct. 12, 1864.

6. *Appleton Motor*, Nov. 17, 1864.

7. Marbaker, *History of the Eleventh*, 228.

8. Ibid.

9. Robertson, *Civil War Letters*, 524.

10. Sparks, *Inside Lincoln's Army*, 433.

11. Hastings, *Letters from a Sharpshooter*, Letter #111.

12. Long, *Jewel of Liberty*, 220.

13. *Philadelphia Inquirer*, Oct. 12, 1864, and Oct. 14, 1864.

14. *Richmond Dispatch*, Oct. 18, 1864.

15. Petersburg Express, Oct. 15, 1864.

16. Tilney, *My Life in the Army*, 142.

17. Long, *Jewel of Liberty*, 248.

18. See Agassiz, *Meade's Headquarters* (Lyman's letters home); Lowe, *Meade's Army* (Lyman's journals).

19. See, e.g., Meade to Parke, 10 A.M., Oct. 17, 1864, O.R. 42(3): 259.

20. Agassiz, *Meade's Headquarters*, 248–49; Meade to his wife, Oct. 18, 1864, Geo. G. Meade Papers, Historical Society of Pennsylvania.

21. Nevins *Diary of Battle*, 474.

22. Porter, *Campaigning with Grant*, 305.

23. Ibid.

24. Ibid.

25. Ibid., 306.

26. Ibid.

27. Wert, *From Winchester to Cedar Creek*, 173.

28. Grant to Halleck, Oct. 18, 1864, O.R. 43(3): 402.

29. In his landmark study of the late Sept. 1864 battles, published in 1981, Richard J. Sommers classified Grant's military operations at Petersburg and Richmond into a series of nine offensives; see Sommers, *Richmond Redeemed*, xii–xiii; and Horn, *Petersburg Campaign* (following Sommers's classification). In a more recent work, Earl Hess has slightly modified Sommers's approach by identifying three Confederate offensives separate from Grant's operations. The second Confederate offensive designated by Hess includes the Darbytown Road battles of Oct. 1 and Oct. 7. Sommers included those battles as part of Grant's fifth offensive. See Hess, *In the Trenches*, xx.

30. Nevins, *Diary of Battle*, 477.

31. Lyman also described General J. G. Barnard as "deaf as a post, extremely ill bred; vastly book learned; and thoroughly unreliable" (Lowe, *Meade's Army,* 195). See also Briscoe, "A Visit to General Butler," 441 ("General Barnard . . . attracts especial attention, as he is almost the only grey-headed officer in the army").

32. In response to Grant's request, Barnard considered whether a Union attack could pierce the Howlett line, the Confederate works stretching across Bermuda Hundred. He concluded that success in that sector was very doubtful and observed that the rebels could rapidly deploy reinforcements to Bermuda Hundred, and "hence, unless we can carry the lines at once, we cannot do it at all" (J. G. Barnard Memorandum, Oct. 15, 1864, O.R. 42(3): 233–34).

33. Union engineering officers had examined the Appomattox River north of Petersburg to seek a viable crossing but found none (Hess, *In the Trenches,* 189).

34. J. G. Barnard Memorandum, Oct. 15, 1864, O.R. 42(3): 233–34.

35. Porter's accounts, though not always reliable, appear to hit the mark here: "Even before the completion of Sheridan's victory in the Valley, Grant was planning another movement for the purpose of threatening Lee's position, keeping him occupied, and attacking his communications" (Porter, *Campaigning with Grant,* 309).

36. Wert, *From Winchester to Cedar Creek,* 173.

37. Porter, *Campaigning with Grant,* 307.

38. Welch, *Confederate Surgeon's Letters,* 110.

39. Wiggins, *Journals of Josiah Gorgas,* 137.

40. Cutrer, *Longstreet's Aide,* 138.

41. Nevins, *Diary of Battle,* 473–75.

42. Grant to Meade, Oct. 21, 1864, O.R. 42(3): 290.

43. Agassiz, *Meade's Headquarters,* 238.

44. Sauers, *Civil War Journal,* 233.

45. William P. Hopkins, *Seventh Regiment,* 222.

46. A rumor making the rounds at City Point suggested that Secretary Stanton had planned the movement during his visit. *New Hampshire Patriot,* Nov. 9, 1864. However, nothing in Grant's dispatches suggests this.

47. Grant, *Personal Memoirs,* vol. 2, 243.

48. James C. Biddle Letter, Oct. 21, 1864, Civil War Letters, Historical Society of Pennsylvania.

49. Lowe, *Meade's Army,* 283.

50. Charles Manson to his mother, Oct. 22, 1864, Charles Manson Letters, University of Vermont Library.

51. Grant to Sheridan, 3 P.M., Oct. 21, 1864, O.R. 43(2): 436.

52. Some of these stations were more useful than others. For example, one of the towers in Butler's sector, which soared 125 feet over the ground, generated a particularly large number of reports (Fishel, *Secret War,* 550).

53. Longacre, *Army of Amateurs,* 27.

54. Briscoe, "Visit to General Butler," 446, 447.

55. Varon, *Southern Lady,* 110–13.

56. Ibid., 148; Van Lew, Yankee Spy in Richmond, 72 ("precious dust").

57. McEntee to Humphreys, Oct. 14, 1864, O.R. 42(3): 226. The Oct. 14 dispatch was written by John McEntee, an assistant to Grant's chief intelligence officer, General George Henry Sharpe, who reported information received from agents in Richmond.

58. McEntee to Bowers, Oct. 20, 1864, O.R. 42(3): 282.

59. McEntee to Humphreys, Oct. 21, 1864, O.R. 42(3): 290–91.

60. O.R. 42(1): 39 (trimonthly returns).

61. O.R. 42(1): 40 (Oct. returns).

62. An Oct. 20 communication to Meade's assistant adjutant general demonstrates the confusion that sometimes arose regarding the size of the army: "Your report of the 30th of Sept. gives aggregate present for duty at 55,012; that of Oct. 10, at 54,525; loss in ten days, from Sept. 30 to Oct. 10, 487. During these ten days the provost-marshal-general sent forward recruits amounting to 5,594. Adding these accessions to the loss above reported would make a loss of 6,081. Will you please inform me what has occasioned this serious diminution. Does sickness prevail to a large extent, or are many old regiments going out? Any information you can furnish on this subject will much oblige" (Bowers to Williams, Oct. 20, 1864, O.R. 42(3): 281).

63. Meade to Hancock, Oct. 21, 1864, O.R. 42(3): 294.

64. Meade, *Life and Letters*, 236.

65. Meade to Warren, Oct. 22, 1864, O.R. 42(3): 305.

66. Hancock to Humphreys, Oct. 24, 1864, O.R. 42(3): 322.

67. Hancock to Meade, Oct. 22, 1864, O.R. 42(3): 303–4.

68. See O.R. 42(3): 457 (casualty returns).

69. The correspondence in the *Official Records* contains no reply from Warren to Meade on this subject. Warren's report, however, filed after the operation, details the strength of his first and second divisions and specifies that Baxter's brigade remained in the lines with 2,500 men. The figure of 13,000 is an estimate based on returns in the *Official Records* for Warren's corps at the end of the month, which indicates 16,102 men and 707 officers for duty (O.R. 42(1): 434 [Warren report]).

70. Parke to Meade, Oct. 23, 1864, O.R. 42(3): 313.

71. Badeau, *Military History*, vol. 3, 115–16.

72. Letter from George G. Meade to his wife, May 19, 1864, Historical Society of Pennsylvania, (quoted in Rhea, *Cold Harbor*, 9).

73. In response to criticism after Gettysburg, Meade offered his resignation. It was not accepted. Meade did not resume active campaigning until Oct., and then only because Lee initiated matters by flushing the Army of the Potomac from its position and forcing Meade to cover his line of communications. The Oct. maneuvering culminated in a short, sharp fight at Bristoe Station, where fortune and reckless Confederate decision making combined to win the day for the national army. The Union victory at Bristoe Station did not satisfy officials in Washington, though. Several days after this action, Meade entered a testy exchange with his superior in Washington, Henry Halleck, who had been prodding him to find and pursue Lee. Meade angrily replied, "I take this occasion to repeat what I have before stated, that if my course, based on my own judgment, does not meet with approval, I ought to be, and I desire to be, relieved from command" (Meade to Halleck, 8:30 P.M., Oct. 18, 1863, O.R. 29(2): 346).

74. O.R. 29(1): 18 (Meade report).

75. Some historians have suggested that the unsuccessful assault at Cold Harbor in early June 1864 was due, in part, to Meade's disinterest in managing the attack because Grant had planned, dictated, and orchestrated much of the affair (Rhea, *Cold Harbor*, 318–19; Ferguson, *Not War But Murder*, 239 ("Grant left the details to Meade, and Meade left the details to Grant").

76. Coco, *Through Blood and Fire*, 184.

77. Meade, *Life and Letters*, 234.

78. Meade to his wife, Oct. 16, 1864, George C. Meade Papers, Historical Society of Pennsylvania. Indeed, Meade's decision making power had shrunk considerably. His correspondence suggests he may not have been privy to even basic decisions, such as the likely replacements for his own corps commanders or whether his Army would go into winter quarters. Meade to his sister, Nov. 11, 1864, George G. Meade Papers, Historical Society of Pennsylvania ("Hancock is to go away, and they say Humphreys is to take his place." "We are not yet in Winter Quarters and no one knows whether we will go in at all").

79. Meade to Grant, Oct. 24, 1864, O.R. 42(3): 316–17.

80. Meade, *Life and Letters*, 236.

81. Grant to Meade, Oct. 24, 1864, O.R. 42(3): 318.

82. Meade, *Life and Letters*, 238.

83. Lowe, *Meade's Army*, 284.

84. Cauthen, *Family Letters*, 110.

85. Longstreet to Lee, Oct. 20, 1864, O.R. 42(3): 1155.

86. Mims to his wife, Oct. 7, 1864, "Letters of Maj. W. J. Mims," 225.

87. H. Hammond to his wife, Oct. 8, 1864, Hammond, Bryan, and Cummings Family Papers.

88. Dobbins, *Grandfather's Journal*, 218. On the 20th, a member of the 17th South Carolina Infantry, wrote home that the men expected to hear of new fighting every day but did not expect the center of the line to be attacked (Mackintosh, *"Dear Martha,"* 149).

89. Claiborne to his wife, Oct. 23, 1864, J. H. Claiborne Papers, Small Special Collections Library, University of Virginia.

90. *Daily Confederate*, Oct. 28, 1864.

91. *Richmond Dispatch*, Oct. 17, 1864.

92. *Richmond Dispatch*, Oct. 26, 1864. Both the *Richmond Whig* and a Northern paper, the *Springfield Republican*, also concluded that Grant would not move before the election. See the *Daily Confederate*, Oct. 28, 1864 (containing excerpts from other papers).

6. Plans for the Sixth Offensive

1. Lowe, *Meade's Army*, 284.

2. Grant to Meade, Oct. 24, 1864, O.R. 42(3): 317–18.

3. Grant to Butler, Oct. 24, 1864, O.R. 42(3): 331–32. A copy of Grant's dispatch in Benjamin Butler's papers at the Library of Congress bears an Oct. 20 date. As cited above, the version in the *Official Records* gives the date as Oct. 24. In the author's opinion, the Oct. 24 date is correct. It seems implausible that Grant would have issued such detailed instructions to Butler on the 20th in light of the other corresponding events detailed in this chapter. [Butler Papers, LOC; and Simon, *The Papers of Ulysses S. Grant*, Vol. 12, 331–332 (notes this inconsistency between the Butler Papers and *Official Records* and suggests that Oct. 24 may be the correct date).] Several years after the war, Hancock would recall that Butler was slated to send troops to Petersburg, but contemporary documents give no indication of this (Winfield S. Hancock Report to Adjutant General, Aug. 19, 1872, Record Group 94, M-098, Roll #3, NARA).

4. Humphreys wrote, "The labor and responsibility of arranging the plan and carrying it out was for General Meade, the Chief of Staff, and the Corps Commanders. It was no slight undertaking and has occupied us fully for not less than five days." (Henry H. Humphreys, *Andrew Atkinson Humphreys*, 255).

5. Sommers, *Richmond Redeemed*, 180.

6. The author thanks historian David Lowe for sharing these observations on the Confederate and Union fortifications at Petersburg.

7. O.R. 42(3): 1191–92 (organization of the Army of Northern Virginia).

8. Hampton to Mary Fisher Hampton, Oct. 16, 1864, in Cauthen, *Family Letters*, 110.

9. Hampton to Lee, Oct. 11, 1864, O.R. 42(3): 1146.

10. Ibid.

11. Hampton to Hill, Oct. 22, 1864, O.R. 42(3): 1159–60.

12. Wiley, *Norfolk Blues*, 163; Hutchinson, *My Dear Mother*, 163 (Mulligan).

13. Major Harry Hammon of McGowan's staff to his wife, Oct. 8, 1864, Hammond, Bryan, and Cummings Family Papers, University of South Carolina.).

14. Locke to Humphreys, Oct. 7, 1864, O.R. 42(3): 106.

15. See, e.g., Fisher to Humphreys, Oct. 10, 1864, O.R. 42(3): 153.

16. Sleeper to Davis, 6 P.M., Oct. 13, 1864, O.R. 42(3): 202.

17. Humphreys to Babcock, Oct. 18, 1864, Babcock Papers, LOC.

18. Babcock to Humphreys, Oct. 24, 1864, O.R. 42(3): 318–19. The mill at the Burgess Farm is referred to in various accounts as "Burgess Mill," "Burgess' Mill," and "Burgess's Mill." For consistency, this study refers to the location simply as "Burgess Mill," which follows the spelling used by Burgess family members in a 1907 autobiography by Mary Curtis Burgess. See Burgess, *A True Story*, 6 and 67.

19. The most direct route from the Union positions passed along modern route 673 (referred to as Hawks' Road in this book), a road that apparently bore no formal name in 1864. The Clements house is identified on Union engineering maps as the "Clemens" house, but it is consistently referred to in Union reports as "Clements." Petersburg and Five Forks [1864–65], from surveys under the direction of Bvt. Brig. General N. Michler, major of engineers, *Civil War Maps*, 607.8, 607.9.

20. S. Williams circular, Oct. 25, 1864, O.R. 42(3): 340–43. Upon reviewing Meade's orders on the 26th, Grant reminded him that if Parke found the enemy's fortifications in manned and good defensible condition, "he should only confront them until the movement of the other two corps had its effect" (Grant to Meade, Oct. 26, 1864, O.R. 42(3): 355). Adam Badeau, Grant's wartime aide and postwar biographer, noted that this incident demonstrated the perils of passing orders through different layers of command (Badeau, *Military History*, vol. 3, 116–17).

21. S. Williams circular, Oct. 25, 1864, O.R. 42(3): 340–42.

22. Ibid.

23. Petersburg and Five Forks (1864–65), from surveys under the direction of Bvt. Brig. General N. Michler, major of engineers, *Civil War Maps*, 607.8, 607.9.

24. Ibid.

25. Sherman to Grant, Oct. 9, 1864, 7:30 P.M., O.R. 39(3): 162; Porter, *Campaigning with Grant*, 292–93.

26. Grant to Sherman, Apr. 4, 1864, O.R. 32(3): 246.

27. O.R. 42(3): 340 (circular, Army of the Potomac Headquarters).

28. Williams, *Mississippi Brigade*, 178–79.

29. Hutchinson, *My Dear Mother*, 163.

30. Hampton to A. P. Hill, Oct. 22, 1864, O.R. 42(3): 1159.

31. Hampton to Lee, Oct. 24, 1864, O.R. 42(3): 1162.

32. A subsequent analysis of the operation in the *Army and Navy Journal* stated, "Scouts on the extreme left, and deserters, had reported the enemy to be constructing a new series of works along Hatcher's Run, which were still unfinished" (*Army and Navy Journal*, Nov. 5, 1864).

33. A mile and a half west of the Union trenches, the new rebel line faced the Dabney house and outbuildings. To the south of this spot, a small stream ran through the works, flowing east into Arthur's swamp. To the west a few hundred yards, the house marked "Dawson" on Union maps sat behind the new rebel earthworks. Four or five hundred yards farther south, the rebel works crossed another small creek and then stretched on about half a mile past the Cousins or "Bailey" house. Over the final mile, the works faced the Clements house off to the east, crossed the Creek Road, and terminated at Hatcher's Run, where the trenches turned back against the bank, forming a small hook.

34. Agassiz, *Meade's Headquarters*, 252.

35. Babcock to Humphreys, Oct. 25, 1864, O.R. 42(3): 338

36. Grant to Butler, Oct. 24, 1864, O.R. 42(3): 331–32. Grant also dropped a note about Butler's cavalry: "Your cavalry, I believe, is not now well commanded. If it was, and the opportunity occurred, I would favor sending that to the Central road, to destroy as much track as possible, and return to the James River, in rear of your army."

37. O.R. 42(3): 354 (circular).

38. Butler to Terry, Oct. 26, 1864, O.R. 42(3): 366–68.

39. Ibid. For Confederate returns, see O.R. 42(3): 1186, 1197.

40. Ibid.

41. Grant to Butler, 2:10 p.m., Oct. 26, 1864, Benjamin Butler Papers, LOC.

42. Wheeler to Marston, Oct. 26, 1864, O.R. 42(3): 371.

43. *New York Herald*, Oct. 31, 1864.

44. Sheridan to Grant, Oct. 25, 1864 (received 26th), O.R. 43(2): 464–65.

45. Hampton to Mary Fisher Hampton, Oct. 16, 1864, in Cauthen, *Family Letters*, 110.

46. Welch also stated that the men had eaten almost all of the beef captured by Hampton in Sept. (Welch, *Confederate Surgeon's Letters*, 110–11).

47. Henry Heth Report, Museum of the Confederacy.

48. Hampton to A. P. Hill, Oct. 22, 1864, O.R. 42(3): 1159–60.

49. Ibid.

50. Hampton to Lee, Oct. 24, 1864, O.R. 42(3): 1161–62.

51. Byrd Willis Diary, Byrd C. Willis Papers, Library of Virginia.

52. Halliburton, *Saddle Soldiers*, 176.

53. Brooks, *Butler and His Cavalry*, 357.

7. The Union Army Prepares for Battle

1. Tilney, *My Life in the Army*, 144.

2. Chamberlin, *History of the One Hundred and Fiftieth*, 281–82.

3. O.R. 42(3): 323–24 (Carncross circular, Oct. 24, 1864).

4. Carncross to Egan, Oct. 25, 1864, O.R. 42(3): 347.

5. Billings, *History of the Tenth Massachusetts,* 353.

6. The Southall property appears on some Union engineering maps as "Southwell."

7. Robertson, *Civil War Letters,* 525.

8. Haley, *Rebel Yell,* 213.

9. O.R. 42(3): 345 (Carncross circular, Second Army Headquarters, Oct. 25, 1864).

10. Ibid.

11. O.R. 42(3):c359 (Carncross circular, Second Corps Headquarters, Oct. 26, 1864); Humphreys to Gregg, Oct. 24, 1864, O.R. 42(3): 330–31.

12. Robertson, *Civil War Letters,* 526.

13. Armstrong, *Nuggets of Experience,* 65.

14. William B. Jordan Jr., *Red Diamond Regiment,* 207.

15. Sommers, *Richmond Redeemed,* 193.

16. Davies's regiments hailed mostly from a mix of northeastern states. Smith's brigade contained five Pennsylvania regiments, along with the 1st Maine. On Oct. 18, Gregg reshuffled his units and created a third brigade. He tapped Smith to lead the new command, which consisted of the 1st Maine, 6th Ohio, and 21st Pennsylvania. Colonel Michael Kerwin of the 13th Pennsylvania assumed command of the second brigade in Smith's stead. On the 23rd, the new brigade rode before Gregg at a dress parade led by a band from the 1st Maine (O.R. 42(3): 267 [Special Orders No. 177]); Tobie, *History of the First Maine,* 361–62.

17. See, e.g., Romig, *Porter Phipps' Letters,* 72: "Our Division is doing picket in the rear of our army & for some time all has passed off quiet with us."

18. Tobie, *History of the First Maine,* 361.

19. Mohr, *Cormany Diaries,* 483.

20. O.R. 42(3): 366 (circular, headquarters, 2nd Cavalry Division).

21. O.R. 42(3): 349 (Fifth Corps Circular, Oct. 25, 1864).

22. O.R. 42(3): 362–63 (General Orders No. 53, headquarters, Fifth Army Corps).

23. O.R. 42(1): 434 (Warren's report).

24. O.R. 42(1): 495 (Crawford report).

25. Phillips, *Richard and Rhoda,* 51.

26. Parke to Meade, Oct. 26, 1864, 8 p.m., O.R. 42(3): 364.

27. Warren would "take a road through the woods which leads out to the Duncan road, or at least to a house on that road (Westmoreland house, marked Miss Pegram's originally) . . . from that you will probably be able to find a route to Hatcher's Run" (Humphreys to Warren, 6:15 p.m., Oct. 26, 1864, O.R. 42(3): 361).

28. Locke to Humphreys, Oct. 26, 1864, O.R. 42(3): 361.

29. O.R. 42(1): 434 (Warren's report).

30. Sauers, *Civil War Journal,* 234.

31. Humphreys to Parke, Oct. 24, 1864, O.R. 42(3): 328.

32. Ibid.; Humphreys to Parke, 7:30 p.m., Oct. 26, 1864, O.R. 42(3): 364; O.R. 42(1): 599 (Tidball report). Only Rogers's and Roemer's batteries went with the Ninth Corps.

33. Hancock's column had failed to reach the Vaughan house, which actually lay to the west of his new camp. In a dispatch to army headquarters, he explained that he would take the Church Road the next morning and then switch to the Vaughan Road well south of the federal lines. Recognizing that this program conflicted with the route assigned to him by orders, Hancock offered to start earlier to reach the correct route. Andrew Humphreys assured him that the shortest road would suffice. Humphreys also reported that a small cavalry picket would join the march to aid the Second Corps (Humphreys to Hancock, 7 p.m., Oct. 26, 1864, O.R. 42(3): 358).

34. O.R. 42(1): 346 (Mott report).

35. Haley, *Rebel Yell*, 213.

36. O.R. 42(3): 359–60 (Second Corps orders).

37. Hancock to Humphreys, Oct. 26, 1864, O.R. 42(3): 358.

38. Humphreys to Hancock, Oct. 26, 1864, O.R. 42(3): 359.

39. *Army and Navy Journal*, Nov. 5, 1864.

40. Ibid.; *Philadelphia Inquirer*, Oct. 31, 1864.

41. Benham to Bowers, Oct. 25, 1864, O.R. 42(3): 342–44.

42. *Richmond Whig*, Oct. 24, 1864, U.S. Navy Department, *Official Records* ("O.R. Navies") Series 1, vol. 10: 585–92 (various reports from action); Blackett, *Thomas Morris Chester*, 166.

43. Hawley to his wife, Oct. 26, 1864, Hawley Papers, LOC.

44. This was not the same Cox plantation north of New Market Road, which was the site of fighting on Oct. 7 (Thompson, *Thirteenth Regiment*, 498).

45. Thompson, *Thirteenth Regiment*, 499.

46. During this operation, Colonel Alonzo Draper's second brigade of the third division was attached to Heckman's second division. John Holman commanded the first brigade (1st, 22nd, and 37th USCT; O.R. 42(1): 814–15 [Draper's report]).

47. O.R. 42(1): 813 (Tremain report); see also Thompson, *Thirteenth Regiment*, 499.

48. O.R. 42(3): 354 (Eighteenth Corps circular).

49. Blackett, *Thomas Morris Chester*, 177.

50. Eisenschiml, *Vermont General*, 260.

51. Blackett, *Thomas Morris Chester*, 177.

52. Thompson, *Thirteenth Regiment*, 499.

53. U. S. Grant to Julia Dent Grant, Oct. 26, 186[4], in Simon, *Papers of Ulysses S. Grant*, vol. 12, 350–51.

54. Wilson, *The Life of John A. Rawlins*, 269.

55. Sparks, *Inside Lincoln's Army*, 433.

56. O.R. 42(1): 871 (Longstreet report).

57. Longstreet, *From Manassas to Appomattox*, 575.

58. William P. Hopkins, *Seventh Regiment*, 223.

59. O.R. 42(1): 905 (Johnson report, Oct. 26, 1864).

8. *The Williamsburg Road*

1. Longacre, *Army of Amateurs*, 228.

2. *New York Herald*, Oct. 31, 1864.

3. O.R. 42(1): 767–68 (Pennypacker report) and 763–64 (Foster report).

4. O.R. 42(1): 762 (Foster report).

5. *New York Herald*, Oct. 31, 1864.

6. O.R. 42(1): 767–68 (Pennypacker report) and 763–64 (Foster report).

7. O.R. 42(1): 771 (Shaw report).

8. Burkhardt, *Double Duty*, 130–31.

9. Ibid., 131–32.

10. O.R. 42(1): 771–72 (Shaw report).

11. Mowris, *History of the One Hundred and Seventeenth*, 143.

12. See Ames to Shreve, 12:30 P.M., Oct. 27, 1864, O.R. 42(3): 395 (Ames's right ended 250 yards short of the Charles City Road); O.R. 42(1): 705 (Abbott report).

13. O.R. 42(1): 697 (Hunt report).

14. Ferdinand Davis Memoirs, Bentley Historical Library.

15. Ames to Shreve, Oct. 27, 1864, O.R. 42(3): 395.

16. Stowits, *History of the One Hundredth*, 316.

17. Wagner, *Civil War Desk Reference*, 826.

18. *New York Herald*, Oct. 31, 1864; O.R. 42(2): 541. See also Ray, *Our Special Artist.*

19. *New York Times*, Oct. 31, 1864.

20. Mowris, *History of the One Hundred and Seventeenth*, 142.

21. Butler to Grant, 9:30 A.M., Oct. 27, 1864, O.R. 42(3): 390.

22. *Orphan's Friend and Masonic Journal*, Mar. 7, 1919.

23. John Kennedy Coleman Diary, Oct. 8, 1864, South Caroliniana Library.

24. Tower, *Lee's Adjutant*, 200.

25. Ibid., 200–1.

26. *Orphan's Friend and Masonic Journal*, Mar. 7, 1919. Because Hoke described these events in a rare interview several decades after the war, it is reasonable to assume that time clouded his recollections. He did not specify the date on which this event occurred. In fact, there are some elements of his story that do not fit the facts and events of the 27th. On balance, however, it appears more likely than not that he is referring to events that occurred on the 26th and 27th. This is also the conclusion of his modern biographer. See Barefoot, *General Robert F. Hoke*, 233–34.

27. Longstreet, *From Manassas to Appomattox*, 579.

28. Tower, *Lee's Adjutant*, 200–1.

29. *Richmond Enquirer*, Nov. 22, 1864.

30. Field, "Campaign of 1864 and 1865," 559.

31. *Richmond Enquirer*, Nov. 22, 1864.

32. Longstreet, *From Manassas to Appomattox*, 577–79. One source, however, suggests that Gary's pickets had discovered the Union movement and raised the alarm. Perhaps this news arrived after Longstreet had reached his conclusions about the Union attack. See James R. Hagood, "Memoirs of the First S.C. Regiment" ("The vigilance of General Gary, however, discovered the movement in time to warn Lieutenant General Anderson, commanding our troops on the north side, and a portion of Field's Division was at once started for that point").

33. Longstreet, *From Manassas to Appomattox*, 577; see also, O.R. 42(1): 872 (Longstreet report).

34. Longstreet, *From Manassas to Appomattox*, 577–79. See also *Richmond Enquirer*, Nov. 22, 1864 ("Gen. Longstreet at once ordered Gen. Field to take position on the Nine Mile Road"); and O.R. 42(1): 872 (Longstreet report) .

35. Ames to Shreve, 2:48 P.M., Oct. 27, 1864, O.R. 42(3): 395–96.

36. Johnson Hagood, *Memoirs of the War*, 309.

37. Weitzel to Smith, 8 A.M., Oct. 27, 1864, O.R. 42(3): 397; *Appleton Motor*, Nov. 17, 1864.

38. Blackett, *Thomas Morris Chester*, 180.

39. *Philadelphia Inquirer*, Oct. 31, 1864.

40. Blackett, *Thomas Morris Chester*, 180.

41. Weitzel to Smith, 8 A.M., Oct. 27, 1864, O.R. 42(3): 397.

42. Weitzel to Smith, 9:50 A.M., Oct. 27, 1864, O.R. 42(3): 397.

43. Weitzel's parents brought him to the United States as an infant in the 1830s. Con-

cerned about immigrant prejudice, they held out young Godfrey as a U.S. native, a fiction that he maintained until late in his life (Mowery, "Major-General Godfrey Weitzel"). On the Richmond front, one observer described him as a "tall and powerful man" who "speaks with a marked German accent" (Briscoe, "Visit to General Butler," 440).

44. Mowery, "Major-General Godfrey Weitzel."

45. Butler, *Private and Official Correspondence*, vol. 5, 298–99.

46. Butler to Terry (and Weitzel), Oct. 26, 1864, O.R. 42(3): 368.

47. Weitzel to Smith, 9:50 A.M., Oct. 27, 1864, O.R. 42(3): 397.

48. Ibid.

49. *Daily Confederate*, Oct. 31, 1864 ("Owing to the small quantity of rain that has fallen during the summer and fall, the Eighteenth corps were able to cross the head of White Oak Swamp and reach the Williamsburg road").

50. O.R. 42(1): 871–2 (Longstreet report).

51. Haynes, *History of the Second Regiment*, 255.

52. *New York World*, Nov. 1, 1864.

53. *Philadelphia Inquirer*, Oct. 31, 1864.

54. Trumbull, *War Memories*, 227 (remarks from a visit to the field in 1865).

55. Blackett, *Thomas Morris Chester*, 172.

56. *New York World*, Nov. 1, 1864.

57. Blackett, *Thomas Morris Chester*, 173.

58. O.R. 42(1): 802 (Marston report).

59. Weitzel to Smith, Oct. 27, 1864, O.R. 42(3): 398.

60. Blackett, *Thomas Morris Chester*, 174.

61. Tabulated Union casualty returns from the fighting on Oct. 27, 1864, referred to the engagement as "Fair Oaks" (O.R. 42(1): 149 [return of casualties]). Some Union veterans remembered the engagement as "Second Fair Oaks." In reality, the rebel line across the Williamsburg Road, where much of the fighting on the 27th occurred, was closer to Oak Grove than to Fair Oaks. Because "Fair Oaks" and "Oak Grove" are often associated with 1862 battles, this book uses "Williamsburg Road" in descriptions of the Oct. 27, 1864, fighting.

62. The 118th New York had 205 total in the regiment (Watson, *Military and Civil History*, 288).

63. Watson, *Military and Civil History*, 254.

64. Thompson, *Thirteenth Regiment*, 500.

65. Watson, *Military and Civil History*, 289.

66. Ibid., 289; see also American Civil War Research Database.

67. Thompson, *Thirteenth Regiment*, 500.

68. *Philadelphia Inquirer*, Oct. 31, 1864.

69. O.R. 42(1): 802 (Marston report).

70. Kreutzer, *Notes and Observations*, 185.

71. O.R. 42(1): 808 (Heckman report).

72. Joseph Scroggs Diary, Oct. 27, 1864, USAMHI.

73. Butler to Terry (and Weitzel), Oct. 26, 1864, O.R. 42(3): 368.

74. *Philadelphia Inquirer*, Oct. 31, 1864.

75. O.R. 42(1): 802 (Marston report).

76. O.R. 42(1): 796 (Weitzel report).

77. *New York World*, Nov. 1, 1864.

78. Butler, *Private and Official Correspondence*, vol. 5, 298–99.

79. Many years later, a cavalryman attached to General Marston's staff during the battle recalled that Weitzel sent an orderly to Butler seeking guidance. According to his story, Butler replied with an order "to charge the works" (*National Tribune*, Sept. 9, 1909 [letter of S. P. Ridly]). However, Weitzel's report and contemporary dispatches clearly suggest that the decision to attack was Weitzel's (O.R. 42(1): 795–96 [Weitzel report]; O.R. 42(3): 397–400 [various Weitzel dispatches]).

80. Haynes, *History of the Second Regiment*, 256.

81. *National Tribune*, Sept. 9, 1909.

82. The son of a Brooklyn doctor, Cullen graduated from Columbia College in 1860. After the war, he led a long, distinguished career as a lawyer and jurist, serving as chief judge of the New York Court of Appeals after the turn of the century (Chester and Williams, *Courts and Lawyers*, 947–48). At Petersburg, on June 24, Cullen "fainted away" during a Confederate attack near the banks of the Appomattox and reached the rear on a stretcher. But, as a fellow New Yorker later explained, Cullen "was not a coward; the fault was in his nervous constitution" (Kreutzer, *Notes and Observations*, 199, 217).

83. Ibid., 199.

84. Sommers, *Richmond Redeemed*, 143–44; O.R. 42(1): 801 (Stannard report).

85. O.R. 42(1): 813 (Fairchild report) and 151. Fairchild was cited for gallantry at Fort Gregg, in Apr. 1865, and elsewhere; see O.R. 46(1): 1184.

86. *New York World*, Nov. 1, 1864.

87. Butler, *Private and Official Correspondence*, vol. 5, 298–99.

88. Wagner, *Civil War Desk Reference*, 494; Wilcox, *Rifles and Rifle Practice*, 212.

89. Trowbridge, "Conspicuous Feats of Valor," 25–26.

90. W. H. Stevens, "Map of the Confederate Lines from Fort Gregg to Mrs. Price's," *Civil War Maps*, 630. It is unclear whether the Confederates referred to the work on the Charles City Road as Battery Longstreet at this time. Another account labels the work "Fort Lee" (Thompson, *Thirteenth Regiment*, 504).

91. W. H. Stevens, "Map of the Confederate Lines from Fort Gregg to Mrs. Price's," *Civil War Maps*, 630.

92. Robert Jerald L. West, *Found Among the Privates*, 91–93.

93. Trowbridge, "Conspicuous Feats of Valor," 25–26. Another report indicated that members of the 24th Virginia Cavalry, led by Colonel Robins, also manned the works at the Williamsburg Road (*Daily South Carolinian*, Oct. 22, 1864).

94. *National Tribune*, Aug. 5, 1909 (James Estes, 118th New York).

95. Trowbridge, "Conspicuous Feats of Valor," 25–26; Longstreet, *From Manassas to Appomattox*, 577.

96. O.R. 42(1): 810 (Murray report); *Appleton Motor*, Nov. 17, 1864.

97. Longstreet, *From Manassas to Appomattox*, 577.

98. O.R. 42(1): 810 (Murray report); *Appleton Motor*, Nov. 17, 1864.

99. O.R. 42(1): 803 (Marston report).

100. Trowbridge, "Conspicuous Feats of Valor," 25–26.

101. Ibid.

102. Polley, *Hood's Texas Brigade*, 259.

103. O.R. 42(1): 810 (Murray report).

104. Ibid.

105. *New York World,* Nov. 1, 1864.

106. *Philadelphia Inquirer,* Oct. 31, 1864.

107. Eisenschiml, *Vermont General,* 265.

108. Robert Jerald L. West, *Found Among the Privates,* 91–93.

109. Eisenschiml, *Vermont General,* 266.

110. Longstreet, *From Manassas to Appomattox,* 577.

111. John Kennedy Coleman Diary, Oct. 27, 1864, South Caroliniana Library.

112. O.R. 42(1): 810 (Murray report).

113. O.R. 42(1): 812 (Fairchild report).

114. *Appleton Motor,* Nov. 17, 1864.

115. American Civil War Research Database.

116. *Appleton Motor,* Nov. 17, 1864.

117. Ibid.

118. Ibid.

119. Ibid.; *New York World,* Nov. 1, 1864.

120. O.R. 42(1): 810–11 (Murray report).

121. James R. Hagood, "Memoirs of the First S.C. Regiment."

122. Watson, *Military and Civil History,* 254.

123. *National Tribune,* Sept. 9, 1909.

124. O.R. 42(1): 803 (Marston report).

125. Ibid.

126. *National Tribune,* Sept. 9, 1909. Though the author of the account did not identify Cullen by name, he referred to the colonel commanding the charging brigade as one who had been "under a cloud on account of cowardice."

127. *Appleton Motor,* Nov. 17, 1864.

128. Blackett, *Thomas Morris Chester,* 181.

129. O.R. 42(1): 813 (Fairchild report). In the 19th Wisconsin, Sergeant Henry R. Howard of Company I received four bullet wounds. His son, a private in the same company, pulled him from the field and carried him to the field hospital despite receiving a head wound that covered his own face with blood (*Appleton Motor,* Nov. 17, 1864; American Civil War Research Database).

130. Polley, *Hood's Texas Brigade,* 260.

131. *Philadelphia Inquirer,* Oct. 31, 1864; *Army and Navy Journal,* Nov. 5, 1864.

132. One of the men who escaped to the rear was Major S. K. Vaughan of the 19th Wisconsin, who "showed great pluck, and . . . came off unhurt amid a shower of bullets, only a single ball passing through his coat" (*Appleton Motor,* Nov. 17, 1864 [Chandler letter]).

133. *Richmond Enquirer,* Nov. 22, 1864.

134. A minister's son born in 1829, Lyle had attended the College of South Carolina, where he earned the nickname "General." After college, he established an academy for boys. At the beginning of the war, he organized his students into a unit named the Southern Rights Guards. He was unable to obtain weapons from the governor, however, and joined the 5th South Carolina (Parker, "Captain Lyle," 165–72; Trowbridge, "Conspicuous Feats of Valor," 25–26).

135. Lyle Service Record, Record Group 109, M-267, NARA.

136. Trowbridge, "Conspicuous Feats of Valor," 25–26.

137. Parker, "Captain Lyle," 165–72.

138. James R. Hagood, "Memoirs of the First S.C. Regiment."

139. Trowbridge, "Conspicuous Feats of Valor," 25–26.

140. See *Richmond Enquirer,* Nov. 22, 1864; *Daily Confederate,* Oct. 31, 1864; Field, "Campaign of 1864 and 1865," 560; Bond and Coward, *South Carolinians,* 163; O.R. 42(1): 872 (Longstreet report).

141. Parker, "Captain Lyle," 165–72. Lyle's diary is inconsistent with General Bratton's account published in Trowbridge's article in the *Confederate Veteran* ("Conspicuous Feats of Valor"). Bratton, who based his account on a report provided to him a few days later, suggests that several skirmishers joined Lyle shortly after he left the trench line. According to Bratton, two men called out, "Hold on, Captain, you shan't go by yourself," and joined him (Trowbridge, "Conspicuous Feats of Valor," 25–26). However, Lyle's diary account is consistent with a letter from Bratton dated Feb. 12, 1865, which states, "Capt. Lyle advanced alone several hundred paces in front of our line and captured over three hundred prisoners, his arms full of swords and several stands of colors—others went to his assistance and succeeded in capturing 6 hundred prisoners in all" (Lyle Service Record, Record Group 109, M-267, NARA).

142. James R. Hagood, "Memoirs of the First S.C. Regiment."

143. Trowbridge, "Conspicuous Feats of Valor," 25–26.

144. Parker, "Captain Lyle," 165–72. Longstreets report estimated 11 stand of colors and about 600 prisoners (O.R. 42(1): 872 [Longstreet report]).

145. Trowbridge, "Conspicuous Feats of Valor," 25–26. In addition to Lyle's spectacular feat, there is evidence of at least one other similar act of bravery. According to one Texas veteran, W. A. Traylor of the 5th Texas leapt over the works alone and proceeded to gather Union prisoners (Polley, *Hood's Texas Brigade,* 260, referring to a letter from Captain W. T. Hill of the 5th Texas).

146. Priest, *Stephen Elliott Welch,* 66; *Appleton Motor,* Nov. 17, 1864.

147. American Civil War Research Database.

148. O.R. 42(1): 150 (Return of Casualties).

149. O.R. 42(1): 151 (Return of Casualties). *Appleton Motor,* Nov. 17, 1864 (letter from S. K. Vaughan). Vaughan placed the regiment's initial strength in the battle at 180, though a reporter for the *Philadelphia Inquirer* believed it was 225 (*Philadelphia Inquirer,* Oct. 31, 1864). Because Vaughan commanded the units, his estimate appears to be more reliable.

150. Blackett, *Thomas Morris Chester,* 181.

151. O.R. 42(1): 877 (Return of Casualties).

9. Nine Mile Road

1. O.R. 42(1): 796 (Weitzel report).

2. O.R. 42(1): 814–15 (Draper report).

3. Longacre, *Army of Amateurs,* 50–55.

4. See, e.g., O.R. 42(3): 464–70.

5. New York Times, Dec. 9, 1863.

6. Longacre, *Army of Amateurs,* 51.

7. See "White House to Harrisons Landing," *Civil War Maps,* 594 (junction of New Bridge and Nine-Mile roads is labeled "Old Tavern Chimney").

8. "Mrs. Price's" property is marked "E. Baker" on Union engineering maps. See, e.g., N. Michler, "Richmond [1862–1865] From surveys under the direction of Bvt. Brig. Gen. N., Michler, Maj. of Engineers and Bvt. Lieut. Col. P. S. Mitchie, Capt. of Engineers," *Civil War Maps,* 632.7.

9. See Sears, *To The Gates of Richmond*, 159.

10. Blackett, *Thomas Morris Chester*, 176.

11. J. Paul Hoffman, "Map of the Confederate Lines from Fort Gregg to Mrs. Price's," *Civil War Maps*, 630. (Though undated, this map would have been prepared sometime after the second week of Oct. 1864, because it depicts the Alexander line joining Fort Gilmer to the exterior line. The map identifies the work in question as "Battery Ewell.")

12. Trudeau, *Like Men of War*, 215; Stein, *History of the Thirty-Seventh*.

13. American Civil War Research Database.

14. Oct. returns for Gary's brigade indicate 1,227 men and officers "effective total present" (O.R. 42(3): 1197).

15. Waring, "Diary of William G. Hinson," 113.

16. Priest, *Stephen Elliott Welch*, 64–65.

17. Ibid.

18. *Richmond Daily Examiner*, Nov. 7, 1864.

19. O.R. 42(1): 814–15 (Draper report); Waring, "Diary of William G. Hinson," 113.

20. Blackett, *Thomas Morris Chester*, 179.

21. American Civil War Research Database.

22. O.R. 42(1): 819 (Terry report).

23. O.R. 42(1): 815–16 (Draper report).

24. Priest, *Stephen Elliott Welch*, 65.

25. Blackett, *Thomas Morris Chester*, 179.

26. O.R. 42(1): 816 (Draper report).

27. Three days after the engagement on the Nine Mile Road, seven officers of the 22nd USCT petitioned for Colonel Joseph Kiddoo's removal, seeking to lift the veil, "which enshrouds our disgraceful rout on the 27th instant." The officers complained that they were forced "to carry out the sublime views and plans of a whisky-crazed brain" (Morey et al. to Sealy, Oct. 30, 1864, O.R. 42(3): 442–43). The solicitation made its way up the 18th Corps chain of command. Alonzo Draper, commander of the third division, wrote that the officers might have had some cause for complaint regarding the handling of their regiment during the battle. But Godfrey Weitzel, apparently putting an end to the matter, wrote, "I have had as much opportunity for judging of Colonel Kiddoo's conduct on this occasion and others as anybody else. I think all this unwarranted and prompted by malice somewhere. I consider Colonel Kiddoo the finest gentleman and officer in my Third Division" (ibid., 443; Weitzel's remark appears as the fourth endorsement on the communication). However, other accounts suggest that Kiddoo suffered from a serious drinking problem, which caught the attention of his superiors after the war (Carpenter, *Sword and Olive Branch*, 98). Nevertheless, Kiddoo maintained his position, eventually becoming a major general and serving the Freedman's Bureau after the war; see Crouch, *The Freedmen's Bureau*, 21–22.

28. O.R. 42(1): 816 (Draper report); American Civil War Research Database.

29. O.R. 42(1): 819 (Terry report). Many of the new recruits, however, discharged their rifles, adding to the confusion.

30. Blackett, *Thomas Morris Chester*, 179.

31. O.R. 42(1): 818 (Terry report).

32. O.R. 42(1): 816 (Draper report); Blackett, *Thomas Morris Chester*, 179. Corporal Nathan Stanton of the regiment, "who carried the colors, was also wounded, but would not give up the colors until the regiment retired" (O.R. 42(1): 817 [Draper report]).

33. Blackett, *Thomas Morris Chester*, 180.

34. Ibid.

35. O.R. 42(1): 815 (Draper report); Blackett, *Thomas Morris Chester,* 176.

36. Blackett, *Thomas Morris Chester,* 176–77.

37. O.R. 42(1): 816 (Draper report).

38. *Richmond Daily Examiner,* Nov. 7, 1864.

39. Ibid.

40. Priest, *Stephen Elliott Welch,* 65.

41. Blackett, *Thomas Morris Chester,* 177.

42. Longstreet, *From Manassas to Appomattox,* 578. Colonel Asbury Coward of the 5th South Carolina Regiment proposed a sweep around the federal right to Fair Oaks Station in Weitzel's rear, but, according to Coward, General Bratton deemed such a move too risky, because it would leave the front line too thin (Bond and Coward, *South Carolinians,* 163).

43. Robert Jerald L. West, *Found Among the Privates,* 91–93.

44. O.R. 42(1): 815 (Draper report).

45. According to one account, the 4th Alabama from Field's division also joined the Southern horsemen as they hurried toward the Nine Mile Road (Laine and Penny, *Law's Alabama Brigade,* 313).

46. Robert Jerald L. West, *Found Among the Privates,* 91–93. Another South Carolina veteran recalled that the black soldiers had been killed in retaliation for the murder of a South Carolina cavalryman captured by the USCTs early in the attack. Crosland, *Reminiscences of the Sixties,* 34–35.

47. Priest, *Stephen Elliott Welch,* 65.

48. Waring, "Diary of William G. Hinson," 113; see also *Daily South Carolinian,* Nov. 4, 1864.

49. O.R. 42(1): 816 (Draper report).

50. Robert Jerald L. West, *Found Among the Privates,* 91–93.

51. *Daily South Carolinian,* Nov. 4, 1864.

52. Blackett, *Thomas Morris Chester,* 177.

53. O.R. 42(1): 816.

54. *New York World,* Nov. 1, 1864.

55. Weitzel to Smith, Oct. 27, 1864, O.R. 42(3): 398–99.

56. Ibid.

57. O.R. 42(1): 816 (Draper report).

58. Colonel Robins, the commander of the 24th Virginia Cavalry, received a foot wound (*Richmond Daily Examiner,* Nov. 7, 1864).

59. O.R. 42(1): 877 (casualty returns). Three days later, Stephen Welch reported home that the brigade had lost only one killed and one wounded (Priest, *Stephen Elliot Welch,* 65).

60. Longstreet, *From Manassas to Appomattox,* 578.

61. Butler to Grant, Oct. 27, 1864, O.R. 42(3): 390.

62. Ames to Shreve, 2:48 P.M., Oct. 27, 1864, O.R. 42(3): 395.

63. Hawley to Terry, Oct. 27, 1864, O.R. 42(3): 396.

64. Shreve to Hawley, Oct. 27, 1864, O.R. 42(3): 396.

65. O.R. 42(1): 705 (Abbott report).

66. O.R. 42(1): 692–93 (Hannum report). On Randlett's left, Lieutenant James Hannum of the 39th Illinois in the first brigade reported that his skirmishers advanced within 150 yards of the Confederate line and found a single line of battle in the works. Hannum's advance went unseen by Randlett off to the left.

67. O.R. 42(1): 723 (Randlett report).

68. Longacre, *From Antietam to Fort Fisher,* 213.

69. *Philadelphia Inquirer,* Oct. 31, 1864.

70. Charles M. Clark, *History of the Thirty-Ninth,* 235; *Philadelphia Inquirer,* Oct. 31, 1864.

71. Mowris, *History of the One Hundred and Seventeenth,* 143.

72. O.R. 42(1): 860 (Pendleton report).

73. O.R. 42(1): 763 (Foster report).

74. Jackson and O'Donnell, *Back Home in Oneida,* 174.

75. O.R. 42(1): 935 (itinerary of Hardaway's battalion).

76. Longacre, *From Antietam to Fort Fisher,* 213.

77. *Philadelphia Inquirer,* Oct. 31, 1864.

78. Ibid.

79. Jackson and O'Donnell, *Back Home in Oneida,* 174.

80. Some of Pennypacker's men deployed as skirmishers on Foster's right. Here, Sergeant John A. Porter of the 76th Pennsylvania received instructions to take three companies forward. His men "started with a yell," but the Confederates opened on the Pennsylvanians. Porter sensed a "stinging sensation" in his leg, "the blood running down" into his shoes. He wrote later that the wound "forever put an end to all ambition I had for military glory" (Chrisman, *76th Regiment,* 65).

81. O.R. 42(1): 763 (Foster report).

82. O.R. 42(1): 149 (Return of Casualties).

83. Mowris, *History of the One Hundred and Seventeenth,* 144.

84. James H. Clark, *Iron Hearted Regiment,* 161.

85. Charles M. Clark, *History of the Thirty-Ninth,* 231.

86. Ibid., 232.

87. Mowris, *History of the One Hundred and Seventeenth,* 144.

88. Beginning in the summer, Clara Barton worked at the "flying hospital" of the Tenth Corps. "She was placed in charge of the 'light diet department,' and furnished with untiring zeal delicacies and appetizing dishes for the many sick" (Charles M. Clark, *History of the Thirty-Ninth,* 231–32; see also Pryor, *Clara Barton;* and John J. Craven to his wife, Oct. 19,1864, Craven Papers, LOC).

89. The story of the family caught between the lines at the Darbytown Road appears in four separate sources: *New York Herald,* Nov. 4, 1864 (James Wardell dispatch); Charles M. Clark, *History of the Thirty-Ninth,* 231; Mowris, *History of the One Hundred and Seventeenth,* 144; and James H. Clark, *Iron Hearted Regiment,* 161. There are various inconsistencies among them. Most notably, Charles Clark's account, which is the only one that mentions the family name ("Gerault," according to Clark), indicates that the incident occurred during the fighting on Oct. 13. However, the other sources, particularly Wardell's newspaper dispatch several days after the battle, identify Oct. 27 as the date. Notably, after the battle Wardell spoke to the mother, who "expressed more sorrow at the loss of her feather bed than anxiety about herself or child."

90. Grant to Butler, Oct. 27, 1864, O.R. 42(3): 390–91.

91. Ibid.

92. Califf, *Record of the Services,* 48.

93. Lemuel Newcomb to father, Oct. 29, 1864, Lemuel E. Newcomb Papers, Stanford University.

94. *New York World,* Nov. 1, 1864.

95. Weitzel to Smith, Oct. 27, 1864, O.R. 42(3): 399.

96. Blackett, *Thomas Morris Chester*, 175.

97. The next morning, the black troops discovered their predicament and picked their way through the dense woods, making it back to the Williamsburg Road and then south to White Horse Tavern (ibid.).

10. The Fifth and Ninth Corps Advance

1. *Appleton Motor*, Nov. 17, 1864 (letter from "R.C.E." of the 37th Wisconsin).

2. Agassiz, *Meade's Headquarters*, 213.

3. Lowe, *Meade's Army*, 292.

4. Modern maps identify the column's path as Route 673 or the "Smith Grove Road," but in 1864 General Meade referred to it as the "Hawks' Road" after a nearby house of that name (Meade to Hancock, 9 A.M., Oct. 27, 1864, O.R. 42(3): 379). For the purposes of this study, Route 673 is referred to by General Meade's designation, "Hawks' Road" or "the Hawks Road."

5. Allen, *Forty-Six Months*, 313.

6. See O.R. 42(1): 560–61 (Hartranft report; indicates the column halted outside Fort Cummings until daybreak); see also O.R. 42(1): 437 (Warren's report; indicates that it was light enough to see at 5:30 A.M.).

7. O.R. 42(1): 556 (Willcox report).

8. O.R. 42(1): 576 (McLaughlen report).

9. Ibid.

10. *New York Times*, Nov. 3, 1864.

11. O.R. 42(1): 556 (Willcox report).

12. Humphreys to Warren, 7 A.M., Oct. 27, 1864, O.R. 42(3): 384, 389 (Willcox to Lydig).

13. O.R. 42(1): 568 (Cutcheon report).

14. O.R. 42(1): 576 (McLaughlen report).

15. Humphreys to Parke, 7:30 A.M., Oct. 27, 1864, O.R. 42(3): 388.

16. O.R. 42(1): 568 (Cutcheon report).

17. Herek, *These Men*, 263.

18. O.R. 42(1): 556 (Willcox report); O.R. 42(1): 560–61 (Hartranft report).

19. *New York Herald*, Oct. 30, 1864.

20. O.R. 42(1): 568 (Cutcheon report).

21. At the beginning of June, Warren looked "care-worn," which was understandable given the weeks of constant combat. At one point, Theodore Lyman overheard him say, "For thirty days now, it has been one funeral procession, past me; and it is too much! To-day I saw a man burying a comrade, and, within half an hour, he himself was brought in and buried beside him. The men need rest" (Agassiz, *Meade's Headquarters*, 147).

22. Ibid., 110.

23. Hennessy, "I Dread the Spring," in Gallagher, *Wilderness Campaign*, 90.

24. Grant, *Personal Memoirs*, Vol. II, 214–15.

25. Ibid., 445.

26. Agassiz, *Meade's Headquarters*, 110.

27. O.R. 42(1): 437 (Warren report).

28. Burgess F. Ingersoll Diary, Oct. 27, 1864, USAMHI.

29. Curtis, *History of the Twenty-Fourth*, 278.

30. *Army and Navy Journal*, Nov. 5, 1864 (says only an old map of Dinwiddie County was available).

31. Chamberlin, *History of the One Hundred and Fiftieth*, 282.

32. H. D. Didcock to father, mother, & brother, Nov. 21, 1864, Gowanda Area Historical Society.

33. O.R. 42(1): 437 (Warren report).

34. Tilney, *My Life in the Army*, 146.

35. O.R. 42(1): 434–39 (Warren report).

36. Brooks, *Butler and His Cavalry*, 382.

37. Henry Heth Report, Feb. 1, 1865, Museum of the Confederacy.

38. See, e.g., Sears, *Gettysburg*, 165.

39. See Benjamin, "Gray Forces Defeated," 24–35; Brown, *Retreat from Gettysburg*, 337–52.

40. Morrison, *Memoirs of Henry Heth*, lvii.

41. See Sommers, *Richmond Redeemed*, 217.

42. Morrison, *Memoirs of Henry Heth*, 192.

43. Henry Heth Report, Feb. 1, 1865, Museum of the Confederacy.

44. *New York Herald*, Oct. 30, 1864; O.R. 42(1): 568–69 (Cutcheon report).

45. O.R. 42(1): 568–69 (Cutcheon report).

46. O.R. 42(1): 560 (Hartranft report).

47. O.R. 42(1): 561 (Hartranft report).

48. O.R. 42(1): 556 (Willcox report).

49. O.R. 42(1): 157–58 (casualty return). A member of the 100th Pennsylvania, from McLaughlen's brigade, recalled that the regiment lost one killed and four wounded (a few more than reported in the *Official Records*) (Gavin, *Campaigning with the Roundheads*, 584).

50. Gavin, *Campaigning with the Roundheads*, 584.

51. O.R. 42(1): 548–49 (Parke report).

52. Ibid.

53. O.R. 42(1): 568–70 (Cutcheon report).

54. Ibid.

55. O.R. 42(1): 556 (Willcox report).

56. O.R. 42(1): 549 (Parke report).

57. Blair and Pencak, *Making and Remaking*, 302–3.

58. Trudeau, *Like Men of War*, 303

59. *New York Herald*, Oct. 30, 1864.

60. O.R. 42(1): 592 (Ferrero report).

61. Ibid.

62. Trudeau, *Like Men of War*, 304.

63. O.R. 42(1): 159 (casualty returns).

64. Blair and Pencak, *Making and Remaking*, 161.

65. *New York Herald*, Oct. 30, 1864; see also *Philadelphia Inquirer*, Oct. 31, 1864.

66. Potter's troops had met with misfortune a month before, at Jones Farm, near Poplar Spring Church, where an enemy counterattack swept them back. Perhaps mindful of these recent setbacks, Parke set Potter's division well away from the firing line. Potter's second brigade, led by Simon Griffin, settled around Fort MacRae (O.R. 42(1): 580 [Potter report]). "It seemed to me, as I rode by the veteran brigades of Curtis and Griffin," remarked a reporter, "that [Potter's] men chafed at the restraint imposed upon them; that they longed

to advance into the woods beyond, where the imagination located an enemy behind every tree, and where they would have an opportunity of retrieving the mishap, not the disgrace, of Poplar Spring. But 'strategy' assigned them, for the time, the responsibility of holding the flank" (*New York Herald,* Oct. 30, 1864).

67. O.R. 42(1): 599 (Tidball report).

68. *New York Herald,* Oct. 30, 1864.

69. Ibid.

70. Ibid.

71. O.R. 42(1): 459 (Griffin report); John L. Smith, *History of the Corn Exchange Regiment,* 528.

72. H. D. Didcock to father, mother, & brother, Nov. 21, 1864, Gowanda Area Historical Society. Didcock wrote that the regiment in front was the 85th Pennsylvania. However, that unit was not in his division. The regiment may have been the 91st Pennsylvania, which was in his brigade.

73. Ibid.

74. *Dunkirk Union,* Nov. 9, 1864.

75. H. D. Didcock to father, mother, & brother, Nov. 21, 1864, Gowanda Area Historical Society.

76. O.R. 42(1): 459 (Griffin report); John L. Smith, *History of the Corn Exchange Regiment,* 528.

77. O.R. 42(1): 543 (Wainwright report).

78. Tilney, *My Life in the Army,* 146.

79. *Dunkirk Union,* Nov. 9, 1864.

80. *Daily Courier* (Buffalo), Oct. 29, 1864.

81. One Hundred and Forty-Fifth Pennsylvania Association, *Under the Maltese Cross,* 325.

82. Tilney, *My Life in the Army,* 146.

83. H. D. Didcock to father, mother, & brother, Nov. 21, 1864, Gowanda Area Historical Society.

84. One Hundred and Forty-Fifth Pennsylvania Association, *Under the Maltese Cross,* 325.

85. *Philadelphia Inquirer,* Oct. 31, 1864.

86. O.R. 42(1): 459 (Griffin report).

87. O.R. 42(1): 155 (casualty returns); *Philadelphia Inquirer,* Oct. 31, 1864.

88. *Macon Telegraph,* Nov. 7, 1864.

89. Joseph Davis's brigade contained mostly Mississippi regiments but also the 55th North Carolina at the time.

90. Henry Heth Report, Feb. 1, 1865, Museum of the Confederacy.

91. Ibid.

92. Welch, *Confederate Surgeon's Letters,* 112. A member of McGowan's South Carolina brigade recalled that his unit "was not in action, but only moved up and down the works, prepared to defend them from an attack in front. Some shelling occurred, but there were no casualties among us" (Caldwell, *History of a Brigade,* 187).

93. Charles R. Jones, "Historical Sketch."

94. Ibid.; *Macon Telegraph,* Nov. 7, 1864.

95. Diary of Joseph Mullen Jr., Oct. 27, 1864, Museum of the Confederacy.

96. Buford, *Lamar Rifles,* 30.

97. See O.R. 42(1): 435 (Warren report).

98. Charles R. Jones, "Historical Sketch."

99. Brooks, *Butler and His Cavalry*, 382.

100. Charles R. Jones, "Historical Sketch."

101. See, e.g., H. D. Didcock to father, mother, & brother, Nov. 21, 1864, Gowanda Area Historical Society; One Hundred and Forty-Fifth Pennsylvania Association, *Under the Maltese Cross*, 325.

102. William P. Hopkins, *Seventh Regiment*, 222; Allen, *Forty-Six Months*, 314.

103. *Appleton Motor*, Nov. 17, 1864.

104. O.R. 42(1): 556 (Willcox report).

105. *Appleton Motor*, Nov. 17, 1864 (letter from "L" of the 38th Wisconsin).

106. O.R. 42(1): 580 (Potter report).

107. Ibid.

108. O.R. 42(1): 459 (Griffin report); *Dunkirk Union*, Nov. 9, 1864.

109. O.R. 42(1): 496 (Crawford report).

110. *New York Times*, Nov. 3, 1864.

111. *Philadelphia Inquirer*, Oct. 31, 1864.

112. See O.R. 42(1): 560 (Hartranft report). Hartranft wrote that his unit followed "the Second Brigade, commanded by Lieut. Col. B. M. Cutcheon, who after passing outside of the fortifications on the road leading westwardly from Fort Cummings, halted until daylight. At daybreak he moved forward as rapidly as his skirmishers could advance through the woods." See also O.R. 42(1): 568 (Cutcheon report; "at 4 A.M. halted at our outer vedettes"); and O.R. 42(1): 599 (Tidball report; "moved with the Corps at daylight").

113. O.R. 42(3): 340–41 (circular signed by S. Williams, Oct. 25, 1864).

114. Ibid. Emphasis added.

115. In addition, Parke did not acknowledge in his report that such a halt occurred: "This [Willcox's] division advanced at the appointed time, but failed to effect the capture of the rebel vedette post, owing to the premature discharge of a piece" (O.R. 42(1): 548 [Parke report]).

116. Andrew A. Humphreys, *Virginia Campaign*, 296.

117. *New York Times*, Nov. 3, 1864.

118. *Army and Navy Journal*, Nov. 5, 1864.

119. O.R. 42(1): 434 (Warren report). Though all three of Warren's divisions contained large numbers of inexperienced troops, Griffin's division had the largest percentage of green soldiers by far.

120. O.R. 42(1):435 (Warren report).

121. Meade to Hancock, 9 A.M., Oct. 27, 1864, O.R. 42(3): 379.

122. O.R. 42(1): 437 (Warren report); Andrew A. Humphreys, *Virginia Campaign*, 296.

123. O.R. 42(1): 437 (Warren report).

124. O.R. 42(1): 440–42 (Roebling addendum in Warren report).

125. Badeau, *Military History*, vol. 3, 119.

126. O.R. 42(1): 437 (Warren report).

127. O.R. 42(1): 440 (Roebling addendum in Warren report).

128. According to one of Warren's staff, Grant then told Warren, "If there is an enemy's line there, I want to know it at once." Warren and his staff mounted and galloped down the Duncan Road to the left "at a tremendous pace, a most exhilarating exercise; the General ahead, then his staff, Corps flag and flag guard, then myself, then the signal party, mounted orderlies and a squadron of cavalry escort; dashing full speed along the road or across the fields" (Tilney, *My Life in the Army*, 147).

129. Lowe, *Meade's Army*, 286.

130. O.R. 42(1): 35–37 (Meade report).

131. Carothers to Fisher, 7:30 A.M., Oct. 27, 1864, O.R. 42(3): 375.

11. Second Corps Moves Out

1. *Philadelphia Enquirer*, Oct. 31, 1864; Haley, *Rebel Yell*, 213 ("sour mood").

2. Armstrong, *Nuggets of Experience*, 65.

3. *New York Times*, Nov. 3, 1864 (Second Corps' route).

4. *Army and Navy Journal*, Nov. 5, 1864 (Topographical Engineers).

5. O.R. 42(1): 295 (Egan report); *Army and Navy Journal*, Nov. 5, 1864 (obstructions); and O.R. 42(1): 325 (Smyth report).

6. Houghton, *Campaigns of the Seventeenth Maine*, 240 (Wyatt plantation).

7. Romig, *Porter Phipps' Letters*, 74.

8. Ibid.

9. Haines, *Men of Company F*, 85; *New York Times*, Nov. 3, 1864.

10. O.R. 42(1): 295 (Egan report).

11. Sam Porter to Mary, Oct. 30, 1864, Porter Family Papers, University of Rochester Libraries.

12. Haines, *Men of Company F*, 85.

13. Ibid.

14. Ibid.

15. *New York Herald*, Nov. 2, 1864.

16. Though the name "Cummings' ford" does not appear in Union reports from the 27th, a subsequent report refers to the ford as such (O.R. 46(1): 164 [Hess report]).

17. Martin, *History of the Fifty-Seventh*, 131.

18. O.R. 42(1): 231 (Hancock report).

19. O.R. 42(1): 332–33 (Chew report).

20. *New York Herald*, Nov. 2, 1864; O.R. 42(1): 336–37 (McAnally report).

21. O.R. 42(1): 332–33 (Chew report).

22. *New York Herald*, Nov. 2, 1864.

23. Ibid., Oct. 30, 1864.

24. Agassiz, *Meade's Headquarters*, 82.

25. Ibid., 189.

26. Livermore, *Days and Events*, 411.

27. Meade, *Life and Letters*, 208–9.

28. Forney, *Life and Military Career*, 321.

29. Kreiser, *Defeating Lee*, 190–200; Hess, *In the Trenches*, 33.

30. O.R. 42(1): 339 (Fordyce report).

31. *New York Herald*, Oct. 30, 1864.

32. O.R. 42(1): 338–39 (Fordyce report).

33. O.R. 42(1): 325 (Smyth report).

34. O.R. 42(1): 295 (Egan report).

35. *New York Herald*, Nov. 2, 1864.

36. At Cummings Ford, the 12th New Jersey formed a battle line with its right resting on the road. The 1st Delaware formed just across the way. The 106th Pennsylvania came up

on the left side, along with elements of the 4th Ohio. The 10th New York led at the front. O.R. 42(1): 332–33 (Chew report), 336 (McAnally report).

37. O.R. 42(1): 332–33 (Chew report).

38. O.R. 42(1): 336 (McAnally report).

39. Ibid.

40. Haines, *Men of Company F*, 86.

41. *New York Herald*, Oct. 30, 1864; *Army and Navy Journal*, Nov. 5, 1864. According to one of the captured cavalrymen, Major Henry Farley commanded the detachment at the ford and was erroneously reported as mortally wounded (O.R. 42(1): 295 [Egan report]). Though Farley commanded a number of Hampton's dismounted troops, it is not clear whether he was present at the ford on the morning of Oct. 27. He survived the war to try his hand at a myriad of professions, including law, teaching, mining, and journalism. He even appeared in silent movies. He died in 1927 (Krick, *Staff Officers*, 125).

42. O.R. 42(1): 330.

43. Haines, *Men of Company F*, 86.

44. *New York Herald*, Nov. 2, 1864. Lieutenant Colonel Spalter's body was later exhumed and reburied at Poplar Grove cemetery. American Civil War Research Database.

45. *New York Herald*, Nov. 2, 1864.

46. Hancock to Humphreys, 7:30 A.M., Oct. 27, 1864, O.R. 42(3): 379.

47. *New York Herald*, Oct. 31, 1864.

48. O.R. 42(1): 608–10 (Gregg report).

49. Tobie, *First Maine Cavalry*, 363.

50. *New York Herald*, Oct. 31, 1864.

51. Ibid.

52. Ibid. (dispatch by L. A. Hendricks).

53. *New York Herald*, Oct. 31, 1864; O.R. 42(1): 608 (Gregg report); Holmes, *Horse Soldiers*, 186. The precise number of captured wagons is unclear.

54. Cooke, *Mohun*, 310. Mohun is a fictionalized account of the war prepared by Cooke in 1869. Certain elements of the book, however, contain events as he remembered them, and this quote from Hampton is marked with the annotation "his words."

55. Wade Hampton "Narrative," 95, South Caroliniana Library.

56. O.R. 42(1): 953 (Hampton report).

57. Halliburton, *Saddle Soldiers*, 177.

58. O.R. 42(1): 949 (Hampton report).

59. Byrd Willis Diary, Byrd C. Willis Papers, Library of Virginia.

60. *Charleston Daily Courier*, Nov. 4, 1864 (letter from "Delta").

61. Ibid.

62. Brooks, *Butler and His Cavalry*, 357.

63. Ibid. "General Butler never ordered a soldier to go where he would not go himself. He loved his brave men and they loved him. He is one of the coolest men in danger that was ever seen in battle. On the morning of the 27th October, 1864, he got very angry with a man named Hunter, who, among others was leading some horses too fast to the rear belonging to some dismounted men on picket who were stubbornly contesting every inch of ground with Hancock's advancing columns. After the riot act was so thoroughly read to Hunter by the General he (Hunter) behaved well during the rest of the day" (Brooks, *Butler and His Cavalry*, 54).

64. *Charleston Daily Courier*, Nov. 4, 1864.

65. Brooks, *Butler and His Cavalry*, 367.

12. Dabney's Mill and the Quaker Meeting House

1. O.R. 42(1): 295 (Egan report).

2. O.R. 42(1): 336 (McAnally report).

3. O.R. 42(1): 295 (Egan report); *New York Times*, Nov. 3, 1864.

4. *New York Herald*, Nov. 2, 1864; O.R. 42(1): 345–49 (Mott report).

5. O.R. 42(1): 386 (Tyler report).

6. Donald A. Hopkins, *Little Jeff*, 239–40.

7. *New York Herald*, Nov. 2, 1864.

8. O.R. 42(1): 295 (Egan report).

9. *New York Herald*, Nov. 2, 1864.

10. *New York Times*, Nov. 3, 1864; O.R. 42(1): 316 (Fisk report).

11. *Charleston Daily Courier*, Nov. 4, 1864 ("Letter from Va.," signed by "Delta").

12. Weygant, *History of the One Hundred and Twenty-Fourth*, 381.

13. *New York Herald*, Nov. 2, 1864; Weygant, *History of the One Hundred and Twenty-Fourth*, 381–82; O.R. 42(1): 231 (Hancock report).

14. Henry Heth Report, Feb. 1, 1865, Museum of the Confederacy.

15. See O.R. 42(1): 306 (Starbird report): "We afterward marched by the flank to [Burgess'] Mill, where a portion of the regiment was sent on picket, capturing a major belonging to the Confederate army." The nineteenth-century editors of the *Official Records* inserted the word "Burgess'" here, but it probably should read "Dabney's," based on the context of events described in the report.

16. *New York Herald*, Nov. 2, 1864.

17. After the war, Gordon McCabe recounted Venable's ordeal. In addition to the story of his capture, McCabe described extraordinary details of Venable's subsequent experience as a prisoner of war. After confinement in the Old Capitol Prison in Washington, he escaped captivity by leaping out of the window of a train car near Philadelphia during his transfer to Fort Delaware. With the help of Southern sympathizers, he held himself out as an "oil-land promoter" and made his way south, where he finally returned home by swimming across the Potomac at an unguarded point (McCabe, "Major Andrew Reid Venable, Jr.").

18. *New York Herald*, Nov. 2, 1864.

19. Ibid.

20. Coco, *Through Blood and Fire*, 208.

21. O.R. 42(1): 231 (Hancock report).

22. Hancock to Humphreys, 10:45 A.M., Oct. 27, 1864, O.R. 42(3): 380.

23. *Charleston Daily Courier*, Nov. 4, 1864.

24. Brooks, *Stories of the Confederacy*, 270; Trout, *Galloping Thunder*, 574; Brooks, *Butler and His Cavalry*, 367.

25. Woodward, "Civil War of a Pennsylvania Trooper," 57; *New York Herald*, Oct. 31, 1864. One North Carolina newspaper explained that the captured stock consisted of "four teams belonging to the Southern railroad company, en route to Stony Creek, and loaded with coal and two thousand pounds of bacon. The coal and bacon were thrown out on the roadside, and wounded Yankees crowded in to the wagons and hurried off to the rear" (*Daily Confederate*, Nov. 4, 1864).

26. *New York Herald,* Oct. 31, 1864. The friendly fire incident on the Vaughan Road near Gravelly Run is corroborated by one of Mott's men who did the firing. See Matthews, *Soldiers in Green,* 261 ("Drove the enemy some three miles then pitched into our own Cavalry through mistake giving them a volley or two. The mistake was soon discovered and we were recalled").

27. Mohr, *Cormany Diaries,* 485.

28. *New York Herald,* Oct. 31, 1864.

29. Mohr, *Cormany Diaries,* 485.

30. *New York Herald,* Oct. 31, 1864.

31. O.R. 42(1): 608–11 (Gregg report).

32. O.R. 42(1): 949 (Hampton report).

33. Byrd Willis Diary, Byrd C. Willis Papers, Library of Virginia.

34. *Daily Confederate,* Feb. 22, 1864.

35. Fred C. Foard Reminiscences, Fred C. Foard Papers, Department of Archives and History, Raleigh, NC.

36. Ibid.

37. Fred C. Foard Reminiscences, Fred C. Foard Papers, Department of Archives and History, Raleigh, NC.

38. O.R. 42(1): 953 (Hampton report).

39. "Excerpt of report of Major Roger Preston Chew, C.S. Army, of operations in the Richmond, Virginia, Campaign, July 1–Dec. 7, 1864," in Hewett, *Supplement to the Official Records,* vol. 7, 320–23.

40. Byrd Willis Diary, Byrd C. Willis Papers, Library of Virginia.

41. O.R. 42(1): 629 (Davies report).

42. Gray, "Echoes," 281–82.

43. Calhoun, *Liberty Dethroned,* 165.

44. Gray, "Echoes," 281–82.

45. O.R. 42(1): 608 (Gregg report).

46. O.R. 42(1): 648 (Smith report).

47. Trout, *Galloping Thunder,* 574–75.

48. Calhoun, *Liberty Dethroned,* 165.

49. Brooks, *Stories of the Confederacy,* 270.

50. Tobie, *History of the First Maine Cavalry,* 363; American Civil War Research Database.

51. Tobie, *History of the First Maine Cavalry,* 363–64.

52. Ibid.

53. According to Smith, "Maj. S. W. Thaxter, First Maine Cavalry, was very conspicuous in this charge" even though his term of "service had expired and he had received the order for his muster-out" (O.R. 42(1): 648 [Smith report]).

54. Gray, "Echoes," 281–82.

55. Ibid.

56. O.R. 42(1): 608–9 (Gregg report).

57. Robertson, *General A. P. Hill,* 303. Beginning in Sept., Hill's wife and children took residence just across the street from the Knight property in a cottage on the Venable estate.

58. Bernard, *War Talks,* 178.

59. Sorrel, *Recollections,* 277.

60. Ibid., 276.

61. Claiborne, *Seventy-Five Years,* 248.

62. Blake, *William Mahone,* xv.

63. Ibid., 22.

64. Ibid., 266.

65. Claiborne, *Seventy-Five Years,* 248.

66. Blake, *William Mahone,* 266.

67. Mason, "Three Years in the Army," 24. The same soldier also recalled, "We didant want a virginian over us. For when we done the fighting he would give the prase to his old Va brigade that couldant show a good fight. But they were ready to be praised for what other brigades done."

68. *Petersburg Index Appeal,* June 14, 1896; George S. Bernard War Diary, Bernard Papers, University of Virginia Library.

69. After the war, Mahone recalled that Hill asked for only one brigade, but a portion of Mahone's official report quoted by General Heth clearly stated that Mahone was asked to send three brigades (*Petersburg Index Appeal,* June 14, 1896; Henry Heth Report, Feb. 1, 1865, Museum of the Confederacy; an excerpt from Mahone's report is quoted in Heth's report).

70. *Petersburg Index Appeal,* June 14, 1896; George S. Bernard War Diary, Bernard Papers, University of Virginia Library.

71. Dobbins, *Grandfather's Journal,* 218; *Petersburg Index Appeal,* June 14, 1896.

72. Wiley, *Norfolk Blues,* 168.

73. Ibid.

74. Mackintosh, "*Dear Martha,*" 103. A member of Wise's Virginia brigade wrote, "Today we had orders to move immediately, we packed up & was ready in a few minutes, soon we had orders to move in the trenches, at the Crater, at the same time [there] was heavy cannonading heard distinctly" off to the right (William Russell Diary, Oct. 27, 1864, Petersburg National Battlefield).

75. *Petersburg Index Appeal,* June 14, 1896.

76. Sleeper to Fisher, 9:05 A.M., Oct. 27, 1864, O.R. 42(3): 375.

13. Reaching the Boydton Plank Road

1. Meade to Hancock, 9 A.M., Oct. 27, 1864, O.R. 42(3): 379.

2. *New York Herald,* Nov. 2, 1864.

3. *New York Herald,* Oct. 30, 1864.

4. Haley, *Rebel Yell,* 213.

5. Sources differ on the exact time that Hancock's corps reached the Boydton Plank Road. Egan's report (O.R. 42(1): 296) says 10:30 A.M., but cf. the *New York Herald* (Oct. 30, 1864), which says 11:15 A.M.

6. Armstrong, *Nuggets of Experience,* 67.

7. Robertson, *Civil War Letters,* 527.

8. Marbaker, *History of the Eleventh New Jersey,* 231; Robertson, *Civil War Letters,* 527.

9. O.R. 42(1): 295–300 (Egan report).

10. Coco, *Through Blood and Fire,* 211.

11. O.R. 42(1): 231 (Hancock report).

12. O.R. 42(1): 296 (Egan report).

13. Mary C. Burgess, *True Story,* 47.

14. Roback, *Veteran Volunteers,* 128. The regimental history accurately identifies Burgess as "a former resident of Winfield, N.Y., a brother to the late Dean Burgess."

15. O.R. 42(1): 953 (Hampton report).

16. *Macon Telegraph,* Nov. 7, 1864; Inspection Report of Dearing's Brigade, Confederate Inspection reports, Record Group 109 (M935), NARA.

17. Mary Burgess's husband had escaped across the lines in late Sept. to avoid Confederate conscription (Burgess, *True Story,* 43).

18. Mary C. Burgess, *True Story,* 47–48.

19. Ibid., 48–49.

20. O.R. 42(1): 310 (Magnitzky report); *Army and Navy Journal,* Nov. 5, 1864.

21. *Columbus Sun,* Nov. 8, 1864. A recent inspection report for Dearing's command had tallied four guns commanded by Edward Graham: one twelve-pound howitzer and three three-inch ordnance rifles. Inspection Report of Dearing's Brigade, Sept. 30, 1864, Confederate Inspection reports, Record Group 109 (M935), NARA.

22. O.R. 42(1): 310 (Magnitzky report).

23. Ibid.

24. O.R. 42(1): 295–300 (Egan report).

25. Tobie, *History of the First Maine Cavalry,* 64. At first, Egan feared that the shots from the Rainey house came from Gregg's cavalry, but he soon realized otherwise (*New York Herald,* Oct. 30, 1864).

26. O.R. 42(1): 295–300 (Egan report).

27. *New York Herald,* Nov. 2, 1864.

28. O.R. 42(1): 295–300 (Egan report).

29. *New York Herald,* Oct. 30, 1864.

30. Tobie, *History of the First Maine Cavalry,* 364.

31. *Macon Telegraph,* Nov. 7, 1864.

32. Coco, *Through Blood and Fire,* 211.

33. *New York Herald,* Oct. 30, 1864.

34. O.R. 42(1): 231 (Hancock report).

35. Brooks, *Butler and His Cavalry,* 357.

36. On their way to the area west of the Burgess Farm, the South Carolinians most likely crossed open country between the Rainey plantation on the Plank Road and the Pentacoast property near the White Oak Road (*Charleston Daily Courier,* Nov. 4, 1864; Letter from Va.). Some sources suggest that Butler used a new military road but this is unclear; see *New York Herald,* Oct. 30, 1864.

37. *Charleston Daily Courier,* Nov. 4, 1864 (letter from Virginia).

38. Calhoun, *Liberty Dethroned,* 152.

39. Ibid.

40. *Charleston Daily Courier,* Nov. 4, 1864.

41. Wilcox, "Gen. James Dearing," *Confederate Veteran,* vol. 9, 216.

42. O.R. 42(1): 949 (Hampton report); *Daily Confederate,* Feb. 22, 1865.

43. "Excerpt of report of Major Roger Preston Chew, C.S. Army, of operations in the Richmond, Virginia, Campaign, July 1–Dec. 7, 1864," in Hewett, *Supplement to the Official Records,* vol. 7, 320–23.

44. O.R. 42(1): 609 (Gregg report).

45. O.R. 42(1): 296 (Egan report).

46. Mary C. Burgess, *True Story,* 49–50.

47. Embler had a "commanding physique and engaging presence." He was also a "strict disciplinarian" yet kind and courteous and would correct mistakes by his subordinates

"in a quiet and friendly [manner] that . . . endeared him to all." Embler had enlisted in the New York militia in 1854 and served as a captain in the 82nd New York Regiment earlier in the war. He received a gunshot wound in the neck and shoulder at Antietam (letter from record and pension officer to Hon. J. H. Hawley, U.S. Senate, June 10, 1901, typewritten clipping in Andrew H. Embler's Pension File, Record Group 94 [R&P 374260], NARA). He was the senior aide to Major General John Gibbon, the commander of Hancock's second division, who was absent on leave on Oct. 27.

48. Record Group 94 (R&P 374260) (Embler pension file), NARA.

49. O.R. 42(1): 337 (McNally report).

50. O.R. 42(1): 296 (Egan report).

51. O.R. 42(1): 319 (Willett report).

52. O.R. 42(1): 296 (Egan report).

53. O.R. 42(1): 296 (Egan report). Gustave Magnitzky, of the 20th Massachusetts, wrote, "General Egan ordering me to remain where I was until further orders I did not advance when the Second Brigade charged beyond us and drove the enemy from his position, which we had failed to take" (O.R. 42(1): 310 [Magnitzky report]).

54. O.R. 42(1): 230–37 (Egan and Hancock reports); Horace Rugg Court Martial Transcript, Record Group 153 (LL-649), NARA (map appended to transcript); *Macon Telegraph*, Nov. 7, 1864.

55. Humphreys to Hancock, 10:45 A.M., Oct. 27, 1864, O.R. 42(3): 379.

56. O.R. 42(1): 346 (Mott report).

57. Hancock to Humphreys, 12:30 P.M., Oct. 27, 1864, O.R. 42(3): 380.

58. O.R. 42(1): 231 (Hancock report).

59. O.R. 42(1): 239–40 (Bingham addendum to Hancock report).

60. O.R. 42(1): 440–41 (Roebling addendum in Warren report).

61. Period maps show three roads heading east from the fields bordering the Plank Road near the Second Corps' location. The first, the Dabney Mill Road, was the route Hancock had followed to reach the field. The second, an offshoot of the Dabney Mill Road, branched due east and headed to the Taylor house and Crow Farm along Hatcher's Run. The third path exited the field several hundred yards north of the Dabney Road intersection and headed northeast, crossing Hatcher's Run downstream from the Burgess Mill. Given his description, it is likely Roebling first rode down this third path when leaving the Burgess Farm. See "Petersburg and Five Forks. [1864–1865] from surveys under the direction of Bvt. Grig. Gen. N. Michler, Maj. of Engineers . . . 1867," *Civil War Maps*, 607.8, 607.9.

62. Martin, *History of the Fifty-Seventh Regiment*, 129.

63. Coco, *Through Blood and Fire*, 21; Martin, *History of the Fifty-Seventh Regiment*, 129.

64. Livermore, *Days and Events*, 402.

65. Ibid., 403.

66. O.R. 42(1): 297–98 (Egan report); O.R. 42(1): 426 (Beck report).

67. O.R. 42(1): 297–98 (Egan report).

68. *Macon Telegraph*, Nov. 7, 1864.

69. *Columbus Sun*, Nov. 8, 1864.

70. Page, *History of the Fourteenth Regiment*, 317.

71. Armstrong, *Nuggets of Experience*, 67–69.

72. *Macon Telegraph*, Nov. 7, 1864.

73. O.R. 42(1): 426 (Beck report).

74. Beaudot, *Irish Brigade,* 541; Derek Smith, *Gallant Dead,* 345. In honor of Smyth's promotion, the men of his old regiment purchased a horse, and members of his brigade bought him a saddle, sash, belt, shoulder straps, and other accoutrements of his new rank. The men presented their gifts to the much admired Smyth on Oct. 22 (Maull, *Life and Military Services,* 37–38); and Smyth Diary (Oct. 22, 1864), Delaware Public Archives.

75. Page, *History of the Fourteenth Regiment,* 317.

76. It is unclear why Smyth, not Willett, directed Willett's regiments forward (O.R. 42(1): 32 [Smyth report]); Armstrong, *Nuggets of Experience,* 67–68; O.R. 42(1): 335 (Tinen report).

77. *Columbus Sun,* Nov. 8, 1864.

78. Members of the 152nd New York of Rugg's brigade also helped in this effort (Roback, *Veteran Volunteers,* 129).

79. *Macon Telegraph,* Nov. 7, 1864. According to this account, the 8th Georgia lost thirty-one killed, wounded, and missing crossing Hatcher's Run during the retreat from Burgess Farm.

80. Maull, *Life and Military Services,* 39.

81. The 69th and 170th New York regiments filed into the positions west of the Plank Road, and the 8th New York Heavy Artillery and 164th New York formed to the east (O.R. 42(1): 326 [Smyth report]). Some members of the 8th New York Heavy Artillery from Willett's brigade "crossed over from the right to the left of the road and occupied the works at the left of the bridge crossing the Run. The remainder of the regiment occupied the defenseless line at the right of the road" (Armstrong, *Nuggets of Experience,* 67–68).

82. O.R. 42(1): 297 (Egan report). The artillery piece captured by the New Yorkers may have been one of the four guns in Graham's battery, which was attached to James Dearing's cavalry brigade. The Sept. inspection reports for that unit list four guns, while the late Oct. report (prepared after the battle) lists only three (Inspection Report of Graham's Battery, Sept. 1864, Confederate Inspection reports, Record Group 109 [M935], NARA). According to a dispatch from Hancock, Oct. 29, 1864 (O.R. 42(3): 423), the 164th New York captured a gun at Burgess Mill and threw it in the mill pond.

83. Subsequent reports put Dearing's total casualties for the day at eighty-eight, including sixteen killed, losses that most likely occurred near Burgess Mill during the combat with Egan's division (Suderow, "Casualties at Burgess Mill," citing the *Daily Express,* Nov. 8, 1864). Various sources offer confusing, often contradictory, accounts of Egan's advance that afternoon. In the author's judgment, the events described here occurred around 1 P.M., when Smyth's and Willett's brigades pushed Dearing's men off the south bank of Hatcher's Run. However, because Dearing's men apparently attempted several less successful efforts to regain the ground at the Burgess Farm, this conclusion cannot be made with absolute certainty. The 7th Confederate Cavalry, one of Dearing's units, suffered heavy casualties among its officers. "Col. Taliaferro was wounded. Poor little Ben Edwards fell a corpse near by. Here Lieut. Bryant was severely wounded in both legs. Lt. Johnson fell to rise no more; and Capt. Clements, Adj. Haden and Lieut. Welsh, were stricken down wounded beside their comrades" (*Columbus Sun,* Nov. 8, 1864).

84. Porter, *Campaigning with Grant,* 310; Badeau, *Military History,* vol. 3, 120.

85. Porter, *Campaigning with Grant,* 310.

86. Meade, *Life and Letters,* 237.

87. Badeau, *Military History,* vol. 3, 120–21; Porter, *Campaigning with Grant,* 310.

88. Porter, *Campaigning with Grant*, 311; Badeau, *Military History*, vol. 3, 121. The accounts of Grant's reconnaissance have the air of myth. However, several different sources corroborate the event, including a contemporaneous news report from the *New York Herald* (Oct. 30, 1864) ("General Grant, unattended by any members of his staff, made a personal reconnaissance down the road near where the enemy was posted in works across another stream"); see also John D. Smith, *History of the Nineteenth Regiment*, 251; Livermore, *Days and Events*, 403; *New York Times*, Nov. 3, 1864.

89. Livermore, *Days and Events*, 403.

90. Ibid.

91. Badeau, *Military History*, vol. 3, 121.

92. Coco, *Through Blood and Fire*, 212.

93. Badeau, *Military History*, vol. 3, 121.

94. O.R. 42(1): 239–40 (Bingham addendum to Hancock report); see also O.R. 42(1): 232 (Hancock report): "As soon as Major Bingham returned to General Crawford and reported his (General Crawford's) whereabouts, Lieutenant-General Grant and General Meade left the field."

95. Badeau, *Military History*, vol. 3, 121.

96. O.R. 42(3): 35–37 (Meade report); O.R. 42(1): 232 (Hancock report).

97. Crotty, *Four Years Campaigning*, 159.

98. Mohr, *Cormany Diaries*, 486.

99. Coco, *Through Blood and Fire*, 213.

100. Badeau, *Military History*, vol. 3, 121–22.

14. Crawford at Hatcher's Run

1. *Appleton Motor*, Nov. 17, 1864 (letter from "R.C.E.," 37th Wisconsin).

2. Charles A. Orr Pension File, Record Group 94 (R&P 654675) (affidavits of John Haskins and Richard E. Shannon), NARA.

3. John Haskins and Monroe Haskins both mustered out of the 187th New York at Arlington, Virginia, on July 1, 1865. American Civil War Research Database.

4. O.R. 42(1): 496 (Crawford report).

5. Ibid. As Warren explained in his report, "I then was directed to send a division across Hatcher's Run, place its right flank on the run, and then move up, supporting General Hancock, and upon arriving at the enemy's right of the line in front of General Griffin to attack it in flank, and endeavor to cause him to abandon the line, and thus open the way for the rest of my corps and the Ninth Corps." (O.R. 42(1):437 [Warren report]). Meade's report says essentially the same thing with an additional statement explaining, "This, it was hoped, would enable Warren to cross near the Boydton plank road and secure the connection between the Second and Ninth Corps" (O.R. 42(1): 36 [Meade report]).

6. Small, *Road to Richmond*, 149.

7. Trulock, *In the Hands of Providence*, 261.

8. O.R. 42(1): 496 (Crawford report).

9. Ibid.

10. O.R. 42(1): 440 (Roebling addendum to Warren report).

11. O.R. 42(1): 496 (Crawford report).

12. O.R. 42(1): 440–43 (Roebling addendum to Warren report).

13. O.R. 42(1): 438 (Warren report).

14. O.R. 42(1): 496–97 (Crawford report).

15. Curtis, *History of the Twenty-Fourth Michigan,* 278.

16. O.R. 42(1): 496 (Crawford report).

17. Chamberlin, *History of the One Hundred and Fiftieth,* 283.

18. O.R. 42(1): 529–30 (McKinlock report).

19. O.R. 42(1): 525–26 (Hofmann report).

20. Ibid.

21. O.R. 42(1): 496 (Crawford report).

22. Ibid.

23. O.R. 42(1): 525–26 (Hofmann report).

24. William MacRae's Carolinians were also on hand. Robert Mayo (commanding two brigades) and Lane and McGowan, from Wilcox's division, took positions farther north. See Henry Heth Report, Feb. 1, 1865, Museum of the Confederacy.

25. Tagg, *Generals of Gettysburg,* 352.

26. Davis's Brigade Inspection Report, Sept. 1864, Confederate Inspection reports, Record Group 109 (M935), NARA.

27. Jones's account appears to identify this lieutenant as "G. W. Coonehes," but this author has been unable to find any record of such an individual (Charles R. Jones, "Historical Sketch," May 13, 1874).

28. Charles R. Jones, "Historical Sketch," May 13, 1874. Charles Mather Cooke, an adjutant in the 55th North Carolina, recalled that the enemy had "broken through our lines on the south side of Hatcher's Run and the first we knew of it they had crossed the run and were firing into our rear" (Williams, *Mississippi Brigade,* 181).

29. Charles R. Jones, "Historical Sketch," May 13, 1874.

30. The Sept. 30 inspection report for the 55th North Carolina regiment lists 218 men and 12 officers present for duty. Brigade Inspection Report, Sept. 1864, Confederate Inspection reports, Record Group 109 (M935), NARA. Williams, *Mississippi Brigade,* 181 (quoting Adjutant Cooke of the 55th North Carolina of Davis's Mississippi brigade).

31. Charles R. Jones, "Historical Sketch," May 13, 1874.

32. Ibid.

33. Williams, *Mississippi Brigade,* 181 (quoting Adjutant Cooke of the 55th North Carolina of Davis's Mississippi brigade); see, e.g., O.R. 42(1): 496 (Crawford report); Henry Heth Report, Feb. 1, 1865, Museum of the Confederacy. By the end of the day, Davis's brigade had lost ten killed and thirty wounded. These casualties rivaled the losses in Crawford's entire division, which were reported as two killed, seven wounded, and thirty-four missing. The identity of the Union regiment that crossed the run and threatened the Confederate flank is unclear. It is possible that it was the 150th Pennsylvania, but nothing in accounts from that regiment suggests that this unit crossed over to the north side of the run. No regiment with Crawford had significantly greater casualties that day than the others (O.R. 42(1): 157 [Return of Casualties]).

34. O.R. 42(1): 496 (Crawford report).

35. O.R. 42(1): 438 (Warren report).

36. Agassiz, *Meade's Headquarters,* 240.

37. Ibid.

38. O.R. 42(1): 442 (Roebling statement).

39. The "Captain Dailey" referred to here was probably Dennis B. Dailey of the 6th Wisconsin, who later commanded the 147th New York; see O.R. 46(3): 977.

40. O.R. 42(1): 441–42 (Roebling addendum in Warren report).

41. Ibid.

42. Ibid., 442.

43. Herdegen and Murphy, *Four Years*, 331.

44. Curtis, *History of the Twenty-Fourth Michigan*, 279.

45. Herdegen and Murphy, *Four Years*, 331.

46. Ibid., 331–33.

47. O.R. 42(1): 496 (Crawford report). This combat could have been against Davis's Mississippi brigade, as discussed earlier, but this is unclear.

48. Chamberlin, *History of the One Hundred and Fiftieth*, 283.

49. O.R. 42(1): 507 (Bragg report).

50. Chamberlin, *History of the One Hundred and Fiftieth*, 285.

51. Ibid., 284.

52. Major Jones directed another officer, Sergeant Major Benjamin Topping, to check on the extreme left of the Pennsylvanian's line. Topping complied but just as he reached the flankers, the regiment's entire skirmish line for some reason swung toward Hatcher's Run, isolating him and several pickets in the thick woods. A Confederate soldier wearing a Union cavalry overcoat stepped forward, thrust a pistol in Topping's face, and captured him on the spot (Chamberlin, *History of the One Hundred and Fiftieth*, 282–84).

53. Though Wright's account identified the Confederate officer only as "Peyton," the individual was most probably Henry E. Peyton, the inspector general of Lee's army, the same Colonel Peyton who had reported increases in the army to Lee earlier that month. Peyton conducted many brigade inspections that fall and may have been on the Boydton Plank front on Oct. 27 to conduct the end-of-the-month brigade inspections of Heth's division. After the war, he lived in a variety of locations, including Texas and Maryland. He fell on hard times and in 1900 moved to St. Louis, where, broke and homeless, he died on the street (Chamberlin, *History of the One Hundred and Fiftieth*, 282–84). See also Williams, *Mississippi Brigade*, 177–78; Krick, *Staff Officers*, 242; Bernard, *War Talks*, 256.

54. Chamberlin, *History of the One Hundred and Fiftieth*, 288.

55. O.R. 42(1): 456–57 (Dresser report). A slightly different version of Dresser's story also appeared in the *New York Herald*: "Lieutenant Dresser, of Col. Wainwright's staff, Chief of Artillery, came very near being taken prisoner. He rode in the enemy lines, and coming upon a rebel regiment asked what regiment it was. 'Ninth Alabama,' was the answer. 'All right. Stay where you are . . .'" said Dresser, and he rode in the direction of the Union lines (*New York Herald*, Nov. 1, 1864).

56. The day generated many similar stories. L. A. Hendrick, a reporter for the *New York Herald* who accompanied the Fifth Corps, at one point inadvertently encountered a squad of rebel cavalry and was "astonished by the whizzing of Minie balls about his person." In his account of the day's operations, he wrote: "Captain Chester, of General Crawford's staff, in trying to work his way through the dense thicket occupied by our forces also found himself temporarily a prisoner. He escaped by the strategy of a pistol, having first effectually emptied the contents of a barrel into the body of his captor. Lieut. Woolsey, of Gen. Meade's

staff had a similar adventure, and by a like bold use of his revolver effected a like escape" (*New York Herald,* Nov. 1, 1864).

15. The Bull Pen

1. Mary C. Burgess, *True Story,* 52.
2. *Petersburg Daily Index-Appeal,* June 14, 1896.
3. Henry Heth Report, Feb. 1, 1865, Museum of the Confederacy.
4. Ibid.
5. Hampton, separated from Heth for much of the morning, established communication with him by the afternoon. Some of Hampton's couriers had even slipped through the woods between Hancock's and Crawford's forces east of the Burgess Farm (E. N. Thurston to W. Mahone, Sept. 26, 1889, Mahone Papers, Library of Virginia).
6. Henry Heth Report, Feb. 1, 1865, Museum of the Confederacy.
7. O.R. 42(1): 953 (Hampton report).
8. *Petersburg Daily Index-Appeal,* June 14, 1896.
9. Henry Heth Report, Feb. 1, 1865, Museum of the Confederacy.
10. E. N. Thurston to Mahone, Sept. 26, 1889, Mahone Papers, Library of Virginia. Thurston, a South Carolina native, worked as a rice broker in Charleston after the war (Krick, *Staff Officers,* 287).
11. Henry Heth Report, Feb. 1, 1865, Museum of the Confederacy.
12. Ibid.
13. Ibid.
14. Walker, *History of the Second Army Corps,* 637.
15. O.R. 42(1): 359 (de Trobriand report).
16. O.R. 42(1): 425 (Roder report) and 42(1): 23 (map in Hancock's report).
17. O.R. 42(1): 297–98 (Egan report); *Macon Telegraph,* Nov. 7, 1864. Egan shifted the positions of his brigades several times during the day.
18. Armstrong, *Nuggets of Experience,* 73 (three-foot earthworks).
19. O.R. 42(1): 297 (Egan report); O.R. 42(1): 396 (McAllister report); Robertson, *Civil War Letters,* 529–31.
20. Roback, *Veteran Volunteers,* 129; American Civil War Research Database.
21. Daniel M. Burgess, *Personal and Professional Recollections,* 52.
22. O.R. 42(1): 412 (Hazard report).
23. See, e.g., Gallagher, *Fighting for the Confederacy,* 260. According to Alexander, the Union army "had superiority in number, & calibre of guns, &, of even greater importance, in quality and quantity of ammunition. Their policy should have been always to fight us to exhaustion if we would give them the chance."
24. O.R. 42(1): 426–27 (Beck report).
25. O.R. 42(1): 411–12 (Hazard report).
26. Billings, *History of the Tenth Massachusetts,* 354.
27. Ibid., 357.
28. Schaff, *Battle of the Wilderness,* 42.
29. Ibid (quote from Francis Walker).
30. Ibid.
31. Walker, *General Hancock,* 236–37.

32. See Bush, "Fifth Regiment of Artillery," 393.

33. O.R. 42(1): 346 (Mott report).

34. Ibid. and O.R. 42(1): 367 (Pierce report).

35. Ibid.

36. *National Tribune,* Jan. 14, 1886.

37. O.R. 42(1): 346–47 (Mott report).

38. Armstrong, *Nuggets of Experience,* 70.

39. O.R. 42(1): 232 (Hancock report).

40. O.R. 42(1): 416 (Smith report).

41. Stacey to Carncross, Oct. 31, 1864, O.R. 42(3): 450–51.

42. O.R. 42(1): 326 (Smyth report).

43. It is unclear when Heth heard of Crawford's movement along Hatcher's Run. Heth's after-action report suggests that the news arrived after Mahone's strike force had begun its movement. However, his postwar correspondence with Hancock indicates that the report reached him before he decided to send Mahone on his mission (Henry Heth Report, Feb. 1, 1865, Museum of the Confederacy; Walker, *History of the Second Army Corps,* 637).

44. Henry Heth Report, Feb. 1, 1865, Museum of the Confederacy. Years later, in correspondence with his friend Winfield Hancock, Heth claimed to have blocked Crawford's movement by deploying fifty to seventy-five sharpshooters across the run "to find out definitely what this force consisted of, and to delay it as much as possible." "Crawford, not knowing the smallness of the force opposed to him," wrote Heth, "formed line of battle, and, as I was informed, commenced to entrench" (Walker, *History of the Second Army Corps,* 637). No such account appeared in Heth's official report, written in Feb. 1865. Indeed, as described in chapter 14, accounts from Davis's brigade suggest that several regiments, more than the few dozen sharpshooters recalled by Heth, blunted Crawford's efforts; see, e.g., Williams, *Mississippi Brigade,* 181.

45. *Petersburg Daily Index-Appeal,* June 14, 1896; *Progress-Index,* Apr. 30, 1961. Mahone and Heth probably crossed Hatcher's Run approximately three-quarters of a mile downstream from Burgess Mill and about a half mile upstream from the spot where the Confederate trench line terminated on the north bank of Hatcher's Run. Both Heth's report and a letter from a member of Dearing's brigade located the crossing point three-quarters of a mile from the Burgess Mill. Heth's report identifies the point as being upstream from the Confederate trenches (Henry Heth Report, Feb. 1, 1865, Museum of the Confederacy; *Macon Telegraph,* Nov. 7, 1864). Hampton's own reports indicate that his men had built multiple dams along the run (Hampton to Lee, Oct. 24, 1864, O.R. 42(3):1162).

46. Henry Heth Report, Feb. 1, 1865, 4, Museum of the Confederacy. Not surprisingly, Mahone remembered the conversation differently. Years later, he recalled that he had called the shots and asked Heth to ensure that Dearing and Harris crossed the run at Burgess Mill to attack the enemy position (*Petersburg Daily Index-Appeal,* June 14, 1896).

47. *Petersburg Daily Index-Appeal,* June 14, 1896.

48. Henry Heth Report, Feb. 1, 1865, Museum of the Confederacy.

49. Ibid.

50. Ibid.; Hewett, *Supplement to the Official Records,* vol. 7, serial no. 87, 471–72 ("Postwar account of Brigadier-General Nathaniel Harrison Harris, C.S. Army, of the Battle of Burgess' Mill, Virginia, Oct. 27, 1864").

51. *Petersburg Daily Index-Appeal,* June 14, 1896.

52. Ibid.

53. Clark, *Histories of the Several Regiments,* vol. 3, 250 (52nd Regiment sketch by John H. Robinson).

54. Hess, *Lee's Tar Heels,* 237; see also Ray, *Shock Troops;* Henry Heth Report, Feb. 1, 1865, Museum of the Confederacy (mentions that MacRae's report praises Lilly's performance).

55. O.R. 42(1): 326 (Smyth report).

56. Sam Porter to Mary, Oct. 30, 1864, Porter Family Papers, University of Rochester Libraries.

57. Cowtan, *Services of the Tenth,* 325.

58. American Civil War Research Database.

59. Cowtan, *Services of the Tenth,* 325.

60. Ibid.

61. Ibid.

62. Sam Porter to Mary, Oct. 30, 1864, Porter Family Papers, University of Rochester Libraries.

63. *Petersburg Daily Index-Appeal,* June 14, 1896 (Bernard account).

64. E. N. Thurston to Mahone, Sept. 26, 1889, Mahone Papers, Virginia State Library.

65. Clark, *Histories of the Several Regiments,* vol. 3, 250.

66. James Eldridge Phillips Papers, VHS.

67. *Petersburg Daily Index-Appeal,* June 14, 1896 (Bernard account).

68. O.R. 42(1): 386 (Tyler report).

69. O.R. 42(1): 374 (Pulford report).

70. Ibid.

71. O.R. 42(1): 368 (Pierce report); O.R. 42(1): 375 (Butler report).

72. O.R. 42(1): 347 (Mott report).

73. O.R. 42(1): 386 (Tyler report); O.R. 42(1): 368 (Pierce report).

74. Crotty, *Four Years Campaigning,* 160.

75. King, *History of the Ninety-Third Regiment,* 567.

76. Confederate inspections conducted in late Sept. indicated that MacRae's brigade had 1,394 officers and men present for duty; Weisiger's brigade had 1,040. The Oct. inspection report for the Alabama brigade, commanded by Horace King on the 27th, lists 1,054 present for duty (Confederate Inspection reports, Record Group 109 [M935], NARA).

77. *Petersburg Daily Index-Appeal,* June 14, 1896 (Mahone account).

78. To bolster the sharpshooters, Lieutenant "Dug" Chappell of the 12th Virginia volunteered to bring twenty additional men. Several Petersburg natives, including William H. Harrison, answered Chappell's call and found themselves temporary sharpshooters (*Progress-Index,* Apr. 30, 1961).

79. *Petersburg Daily Index-Appeal,* June 14, 1896 (Mahone account).

80. *Petersburg Daily Index-Appeal,* June 14, 1896; Crotty, *Four Years Campaigning,* 160; Scott, *History of the One Hundred and Fifth,* 122.

81. James E. Phillips Papers, VHS.

82. Stewart, *Pair of Blankets,* 184.

83. O.R. 42(1): 374 (Pulford report).

84. The precise alignment of these regiments is unclear, but, in this author's estimation, the 93rd New York held the left, the 5th Michigan the center, and the 105th Penn the right flank, with the 1st U.S. Sharpshooters off to the right and rear. The report of Benjamin

Peck, commanding the 1st U.S. Sharpshooters, suggests that his unit connected with the right flank of the 5th Michigan, but this may be incorrect, as Pierce had previously sent the 105th Pennsylvania into that position. See O.R. 42(1): 368 (Pierce report), and O.R. 42(1): 388 (Peck report).

85. O.R. 42(1): 374 (Pulford report).

86. O.R. 42(1): 375 (Butler report).

87. O.R. 42(1): 388 (Peck report); O.R. 42(1): 383 (Miller report).

88. Crotty, *Four Years Campaigning,* 160.

89. Scott, *History of the One-Hundred and Fifth,* 173.

90. *Petersburg Daily Index-Appeal,* June 14, 1896.

91. Ibid. Hancock would later excuse the loss of the colors from the Pennsylvania regiment. The unit "is a gallant regiment and lost its colors without disgrace," he wrote (O.R. 42(3): 450).

92. O.R. 42(1): 383 (Miller report).

93. Scott, *History of the One-Hundred and Fifth,* 173.

94. Ibid., 174.

95. Ibid., 122.

96. Some of the trapped federals broke through the Virginians. Weisiger's men did not have time to load and knocked down some of the fleeing soldiers with their rifle butts (James Eldridge Phillips Papers, VHS).

97. O.R. 42(1): 155 (Return of Casualties).

98. *National Tribune,* Jan. 14, 1886.

99. O.R. 42(1): 386 (Tyler report).

100. Roe, *History of the First Regiment,* 194.

101. Sept. 30 returns for the 141st Pennsylvania showed 188 officers and men present for duty (with another 57 men on "extra duty" and not present at the inspection; Craft, *History of the One Hundred Forty-First,* 228).

102. O.R. 42(1): 386 (Tyler report).

103. *National Tribune,* Jan. 14, 1886.

104. O.R. 42(1): 368 (Pierce report).

105. O.R. 42(1): 368 (Tyler report); O.R. 42(1): 380 (Ross report).

106. O.R. 42(1): 380 (Ross report).

107. *Petersburg Daily Index-Appeal,* June 14, 1896 (Mahone account).

108. O.R. 42(1): 378 (Bumpus report).

109. *Petersburg Daily Index-Appeal,* June 14, 1896.

110. Ibid.

111. James E. Phillips Papers, VHS.

112. See ibid. and Robertson, "Boy Artillerist," 253.

113. O.R. 42(1): 412 (Hazard report).

114. James Bartlett Diary, Bartlett Papers, Southern Historical Collection.

115. Brockett, *Woman's Work,* 747–53.

116. *Petersburg Daily Index-Appeal,* June 14, 1896.

117. Scott, *History of the One Hundred and Fifth,* 122.

118. See, e.g., *National Tribune,* Jan. 14, 1886.

119. Sam Porter to Mary, Oct. 30, 1864, Porter Family Papers, University of Rochester Libraries.

120. *Petersburg Daily Index-Appeal,* June 14, 1896.

121. Hewett, *Supplement to the Official Records,* vol. 7, 472; see also Dobbins, *Grandfather's Journal,* 218 ("We [Harris' brigade] deployed skirmishers, leaving only 150 in line. We drew heavy fire.").

122. Henry Heth Report, Feb. 1, 1865, Museum of the Confederacy.

123. Dearing's Sept. inspection report listed 1,374 present for duty, and the Oct. report, conducted after the battle, tallied 1,290 present for duty (Inspection Report for Dearing's Brigade, Sept. and Oct. 1864, Confederate Inspection reports, Record Group 109 [M935], NARA).

124. Harris's Oct. inspection report, conducted after the battle, showed 644 present for duty (Inspection Report for Harris's Brigade, Oct. 1864, Confederate Inspection reports, Record Group 109 [M935], NARA).

125. Hewett, *Supplement to the Official Records,* vol. 7, 472; see also Dobbins, *Grandfather's Journal,* 218.

126. Henry Heth Report, Feb. 1, 1865, Museum of the Confederacy.

127. O.R. 42(1): 326–27 (Smyth report).

128. Wells, *Hampton and His Cavalry,* 150–51.

129. Brooks, *Butler and His Cavalry,* 358.

130. *Charleston Daily Courier,* Nov. 4, 1864.

131. Brooks, *Butler and His Cavalry,* 358, 372; Halliburton, *Saddle Soldiers,* 178. A letter, written by "Delta," says, "Col. Jeffords' death has cast a deep gloom over our Regiment. He was a dashing, fearless officer, and possessed the confidence of all" (*Charleston Daily Courier,* Nov. 4, 1864).

132. Brooks, *Butler and His Cavalry,* 358.

133. Ibid.

134. Ibid., 568–69 (speech of Matthew Butler).

135. Ibid., 358.

136. Ibid., 354, 358.

137. Ibid., 358; Wells, *Hampton and His Cavalry,* 344.

138. In an unpublished memoir, Hampton later wrote, "His comrades in arms . . . will testify to that almost womanly tenderness which marked his intercourse with his friends, & to that courage which even among men when the possession of that quality was the rule & not the exception made him conspicuous on the battlefield" (Wade Hampton, "Narrative," 103–4, South Caroliniana Library).

139. Brooks, *Butler and His Cavalry,* 352 (account of Zimmerman Davis).

140. Ibid., 569 (speech of Butler).

141. Ibid., 354.

142. Ibid. (account of Zimmerman Davis).

143. Several Confederate sources suggest that the attack achieved substantial results; see, e.g., Wells, *Hampton and His Cavalry,* 334 ("drove the enemy rapidly towards the Boydton road"); *Charleston Daily Courier,* Nov. 4, 1864 ("drove the enemy from their position"); O.R. 42(1): 949 (Hampton report; "Butler's men charged gallantly across an open field & drove the enemy rapidly towards the Plank Road"). One South Carolina veteran argued that the success of Hampton's cavalry charge "convinced Hancock of his inability to place himself in rear of the Confederate lines, or to make and maintain connection with the Federal corps operating on his right" (Wells, *Hampton and His Cavalry,* 339).

144. Brooks, *Butler and His Cavalry*, 568.

145. Ibid., 352.

146. O.R. 42(1): 297–98 (Egan report). Confederate veteran Edward Wells claimed, "The long Enfields of Butler's command frequently misled the enemy as to the character of the troops" (Wells, *Hampton and His Cavalry*, 338; see also O.R. 42(1): 306 [Starbird report; "and at one time almost completely surrounded by infantry"]).

147. Testimony of Charles McAnally, 69th Pennsylvania, Horace Rugg Court-Martial Transcript, 95–100, Record Group 153 (LL-649), NARA. Lieutenant Colonel J. W. Starbird of the 19th Maine, also on Rugg's front line, explained that his line "was not driven in but was at one time forced back a short distance" (ibid., 80).

148. See Wells, *Sketch of Charleston Light Dragoons*, 77; see also Horace Rugg Court-Martial Transcript, 96 (McAnally testimony), Record Group 153 (LL-649), NARA.

149. Brooks, *Butler and His Cavalry*, 352.

150. *Charleston Daily Courier*, Nov. 4, 1864.

151. Brooks, *Butler and His Cavalry*, 358.

16. The Second Corps Redeemed

1. Crotty, *Four Years Campaigning*, 161.

2. Houghton, *Campaigns of the Seventeenth Maine*, 242.

3. Luther Rose Diary, Oct. 27, 1864, Petersburg National Battlefield.

4. Ibid.

5. *National Tribune*, Jan. 14, 1886.

6. O.R. 42(1): 234 (Hancock report); Horace Rugg Court-Martial Transcript, Record Group 153 (LL-649), NARA.

7. Robertson, *Civil War Letters*, 528.

8. Marbaker, *History of the Eleventh New Jersey*, 232.

9. O.R. 42(1): 396 (McAllister report).

10. Marbaker, *History of the Eleventh New Jersey*, 232.

11. *Petersburg Daily Index-Appeal*, June 14, 1896.

12. Several Union sources mention the presence of a rebel battery with Mahone's force. See O.R. 42(1): 396 (McAllister report; "As our charge was made the enemy tried to get a battery into position in front of our left center, but seeing us charging upon them, they limbered up and moved off (One hundred and twentieth New York Volunteers) swung around onto them."); O.R. 42(1): 297 (Egan report; "rebel battery narrowly escaped"); O.R. 42(3): 448 (Hancock correspondence; "A battery they brought out unlimbered, but before opening fire limbered up and retired"). Also, a map drafted only a few days after the battle places a Confederate battery at that location (Horace Rugg Court-Martial Transcript, Record Group 153 (LL-649), NARA). Confederate sources do not mention the presence of this battery. In fact, a letter from William Pegram specifically states that he was unable to bring along any guns with Mahone. Perhaps the guns belonged to Graham's battery attached to Dearing's cavalry brigade. See Carmichael, *Lee's Young Artillerist*, 150.

13. Robertson, *Civil War Letters*, 528.

14. Ibid.

15. General Orders No. 41, Nov. 7, 1864, O.R. 42(3): 544. The 36th Wisconsin was one of three regiments (including the 8th New York Heavy Artillery and the 164th New York) to lose the right to carry their colors in Aug., following poor conduct in battle.

16. *National Tribune,* Nov. 3, 1892.

17. Horace Rugg Court-Martial Transcript (Mitchell testimony), Record Group 153 (LL-649), NARA.

18. At his court-martial proceeding, Rugg explained that he had detailed an officer in his place while he was off washing. He was found "guilty" and received a reprimand but continued his service (Horace Rugg Court-Martial Transcript, Record Group 153 [LL-649], NARA).

19. Rugg took command of the brigade after Colonel George N. Macy became disabled in Aug. 1864 (O.R. 42(1): 117 [Return of Casualties]).

20. O.R. 42(1): 226 (Hancock report).

21. Aldrich, *History of Battery A,* 378–79. A similar account appeared in Francis Walker's biography of Hancock: "The brigade from the Second Division commanded by Lieutenant-Colonel Rugg, though called upon by General Miles in person to go forward and drive back the enemy, cowered in the railroad cut and were captured, nearly entire, without resistance. " (Walker, *General Hancock,* 271–72).

22. O.R. 42(1): 303 (Rugg report).

23. The handwritten transcript of Rugg's court-martial proceeding is housed at the National Archives. It contains testimony by several officers in the Second Corps, along with a map drafted by Rugg and entered as evidence. Horace Rugg Court-Martial Transcript, Record Group 153 (LL-649), NARA.

24. Billings, *History of the Tenth Massachusetts,* 465.

25. Ibid., 465–66.

26. A footnote in Winfield Hancock's battle report states, "Rugg was found guilty of neglect of duty and disobedience of orders, and by Gen. Court-Martial Orders. No. 45, headquarters Army of the Potomac, Nov. 17, 1864, was dismissed from the service. The disability arising from this dismissal was removed by letter from the Adjutant-Gen.'s Office Jan. 26, 1865, on report of the Judge-Advocate-Gen., and the Governor of New York was authorized to re-commission the officer." See O.R. 42(1): 234 (Hancock report).

27. Billings, *History of the Tenth Massachusetts,* 359.

28. Ibid.

29. Ibid., 360.

30. O.R. 42(1): 396 (McAllister report).

31. Cavalry commander David Gregg ordered several regiments to Hancock's aid. Charles Smith, commanding the Third Brigade, brought two regiments up through the wagon park, forming a line just south of the Dabney Mill Road (O.R. 42(1): 609 [Gregg report] and O.R. 42(1): 233 [map accompanying Hancock's report]). Three more regiments from Colonel Michael Kerwin's Second Brigade advanced along the west side of the Plank Road to help repel the assault there (O.R. 42(1): 609 [Gregg report]).

32. Styple, *Our Noble Blood,* xii (quoting the *Home Journal*).

33. Billings, *History of the Tenth Massachusetts,* 467.

34. Haley, *Rebel Yell,* 220. De Trobriand performed well at Gettysburg, where he led a brigade in the Third Corps. His commander there, David Birney, recommended his promotion to brigadier general following the action. His promotion did not occur, however, until Jan. 1864, and he did not receive a brigade to command until July (Tagg, *Generals of Gettysburg,* 72).

35. De Trobriand, *Four Years,* 662.

36. Ibid.

37. O.R. 42(1): 368 (Pierce report).

38. O.R. 42(1): 416 (Smith report); O.R. 42(1): 424 (Roder report); O.R. 42(1): 427 (Beck report).

39. O.R. 42(1): 416 (Smith report).

40. See O.R. 42(1): 647 (Garvin report; "I stood under fire doing nothing for 6 hours [I could find no staff officer to direct me], and was there with the led horses, which were in confusion, and the ambulance also").

41. Roe and Nutt, History of the First Regiment, 193.

42. Carmichael, Lee's Young Artillerist, 149.

43. Petersburg Daily Index-Appeal, June 14, 1896 (account of Thomas Pollard).

44. J. S. Bartlett Diary, Bartlett Papers, Southern Historical Society.

45. Macon Telegraph, Nov. 7, 1864 (Sgt. Major W.G. White, 8th Ga. Cav.).

46. Clark, Histories of the Several Regiments, vol. 3, 32.

47. J. S. Bartlett Diary, Bartlett Papers, Southern Historical Society.

48. Ibid.

49. O.R. 42(1): 367–69 (Pierce report); O.R. 42(1): 374 (Pulford report); Horace Rugg Court-Martial Transcript, Record Group 153 (LL-649), NARA.

50. Coco, Through Blood and Fire, 215.

51. Ibid., 214.

52. Roe and Nutt, History of the First Regiment, 195–96, 469; New York Herald, Nov. 2, 1864.

53. See O.R. 42(1): 360 (de Trobriand report); O.R. 42(1): 367–69 (Pierce report); O.R. 42(1): 372 (Shatswell report); New York Herald, Nov. 2, 1864. Another source mentions that members of the 1st Minnesota may have joined in retrieving the guns (Billings, History of the Tenth Massachusetts, 363).

54. Several accounts suggest that Mitchell personally led the 36th Wisconsin in this effort (see, e.g., New York Herald, Nov. 2, 1864; Walker, History of the Second Army Corps, 629; John D. Smith, History of the Nineteenth Regiment, 247). However, Mott's report indicates that Mitchell led men from the 1st Maine Heavy Artillery and the 110th Pennsylvania (O.R. 42(1): 347 [Pulford report]). Pulford's report and Mills's personal account clearly indicate that Union units from both sides of the ravine charged, and that Mitchell led men from the cornfield, not from Egan's front. Mitchell's testimony at Rugg's court-martial also suggests that Mitchell only ordered the Wisconsin men forward and did not accompany them (Horace Rugg Court-Martial Transcript, Record Group 153 [LL-649], NARA).

55. New York Herald, Nov. 2, 1864; American Civil War Research Database.

56. Various recollections offer conflicting accounts of the discovery and subsequent capture of the force of Confederates in the woods near the barn. A reporter for the New York Herald indicated that Mitchell discovered the force as he was riding toward Egan (New York Herald, Nov. 2, 1864). Livermore (Days and Events, 404–5) states that Mitchell discovered these men while returning from General Egan. For his part, Mitchell stated at Rugg's court-martial hearing that "quite a number of prisoners were captured at this point on the left hand side of the road at from a quarter to half an hour" after he had spoken to Lieutenant Colonel Rugg and returned to Hancock. Charles Mills's account helps to put the pieces together. From his description, it appears that the following occurred: (1) Mitchell rode to Egan as ordered by Hancock; (2) Mills was then directed to ride to Egan; (3) en route to Egan, Mills discovered the Confederates in the woods west of the Plank Road;

(4) Mills immediately reversed course and encountered Mitchell, who had returned from Egan and had finished reporting to Hancock; (5) Mills resumed his effort to contact Egan; and (6) Mitchell effected the capture of the isolated Confederates (Coco, *Through Blood and Fire*, 210–16 [Mills's diary]).

57. O.R. 42(1): 316 (Fisk report). See also *New York Herald*, Nov. 2, 1864 (capture of the 26th North Carolina flag). One Wisconsin veteran recalled that the regiment "charged into the enemy's flank, poured in a volley, captured a stand of colors and many prisoners" (*National Tribune*, Nov. 3, 1892).

58. O.R. 42(1): 309 (Boyd report); O.R. 42(1): 849 (Medal of Honor awarded to Murphy).

59. *New York Herald*, Nov. 2, 1864.

60. See O.R. 42(1): 235–37 (Hancock report); Coco, *Through Blood and Fire*, 210–16.

61. O.R. 42(1): 360 (de Trobriand report).

62. Styple, *Our Noble Blood*, 165.

63. O.R. 42(1): 36 (Meade report); *New York Herald*, Nov. 2, 1864. Credit for the captured flags was also a matter of some disagreement. Sergeant Alonzo Smith from the 7th Michigan received the Congressional Medal of Honor for capturing the flag of the 26th North Carolina (O.R. 42(1): 850). Smith's own account of the incident appears in J. W. Jones, *Story of American Heroism*, 562–63. De Trobriand complained in his official report that a sergeant in the 7th Michigan (presumably Smith) incorrectly claimed one of the captured enemy flags. In addition, Mott explained that Private W. W. Scott, Company A, 1st Maine Heavy Artillery, had earned the prize but it had been "taken from him by a sergeant of the Seventh Michigan, who was himself a prisoner of the rebels in the barn" (O.R. 42(1): 348 [Mott report]).

64. *Richmond Dispatch*, Oct. 31, 1864. The men credited with capturing the three Union flags included a member of "Company E, Twelfth Virginia regiment; . . . Sergeant Emmit Richardson, Company K, of the same command, and . . . a member of the sixty first Virginia regiment."

65. Suderow, Bryce, "Oct. 27, 1864: Burgess Mill," (unpublished analysis of casualties at Burgess Mill).

66. Hess, *Lee's Tar Heels*, 274.

67. Clark, *Histories of the Several Regiments*, vol. 3, 98. One officer from another brigade remarked after the battle that mismanagement had caused much suffering in MacRae's brigade. (Hess, *Lee's Tar Heels*, 276).

68. Clark, *Histories of the Several Regiments*, vol. 3, 250 (52nd North Carolina).

69. Ibid., 32 (44th North Carolina).

70. Ibid.

71. See, e.g., E. N. Thurston to Mahone, Sept. 26, 1889, Mahone Papers, Library of Virginia. Thurston stated in his letter, "I never heard of any dissatisfaction as to the conduct of this battle, or if Genl McRae [*sic*] was aggrieved, & so expressed himself at the time or shortly after. I never heard of it, or it has entirely escaped my memory." Mahone's letter (Sept. 16, 1889) to Thurston, requesting the latter's account of the battle, mentions a newspaper article questioning Mahone's performance but does not provide the publication's name or date.

72. *Petersburg Daily Index-Appeal*, June 14, 1896.

73. *Macon Telegraph*, Nov. 7, 1864.

74. Lowe, *Meade's Army*, 216 (Colonel Lyman met King during a truce).

75. Herbert, "History of the Eighth Alabama," 147. According to a postwar account, the 14th Alabama suffered more than a dozen casualties during the fight. *Confederate Veteran,* vol. xxxvi (1928), 426 (obituary of T. J. Thomason).

76. Henry Heth Report, Feb. 1, 1865, Museum of the Confederacy.

77. Axford, *To Locaber Na Mair,* 131 (diary of William Eppa Fielding). The member of the 8th Alabama also recalled, "We held our positions in front 'till a late hour, it raining steadily all the time. About 9 o'clock we moved back a mile or two, and kindled fires to dry ourselves in the thick woods."

78. Suderow, "Oct. 27, 1864: Burgess Mill" (unpublished analysis of casualties at Burgess Mill), cites a casualty report for the 8th Alabama in the *Mobile Evening News* (Nov. 21, 1864). Union reports indicate that prisoners taken on Oct. 27 included members of the Alabama brigade (Babcock to Humphreys, Oct. 29, 1864, O.R. 42(3): 424; see also Griffin, *11th Alabama,* 214–15 [stating that the 11th Alabama suffered fourteen casualties, including three killed]).

79. O.R. 42(1): 457 (Dresser report).

80. *Petersburg Daily Index-Appeal,* June 14, 1896.

81. Ibid.

82. DePeyster, "Military Memoir," 406.

83. Henry Heth Report, Feb. 1, 1865, Museum of the Confederacy.

84. One Confederate account suggests that Rooney Lee's attack occurred an hour after Butler's attack along the White Oak Road. "An hour of carnage passed here [at the White Oak Road], and the sun went down to rise no more for many a gallant Southron. Soon a heavy and prolonged volley on our right and front shook the air. W. H. F. Lee had attacked the enemy's left flank, and the approach of the firing told us he was driving them" (*Charleston Daily Courier,* Nov. 4, 1864).

85. Byrd Willis Diary, Byrd C. Willis Papers, Library of Virginia.

86. Ibid.

87. *Daily Confederate,* Feb. 22, 1865.

88. Hewett, *Supplement to the Official Records,* vol. 7, 525.

89. O.R. 42(1): 609 (Gregg report).

90. *National Tribune,* Mar. 4, 1886.

91. O.R. 42(1): 609 (Gregg report).

92. O.R. 42(1): 647–48 (Smith report); O.R. 42(1): 609 (Gregg report).

93. *Daily Confederate,* Feb. 22, 1865.

94. O.R. 42(1): 647–48 (Smith report); O.R. 42(1): 609 (Gregg report).

95. O.R. 42(1): 609 (Gregg report). Gregg also wrote, "These regiments, coming up successively as fast as their legs could carry them, entered the fight, and at dark the enemy retired repulsed without having accomplished other than his own punishment, which was severe, much of which was inflicted by a section of Battery I, First U.S. Artillery, under command of Lieutenant Reynolds."

96. Ibid.

97. Byrd Willis Diary, Byrd C. Willis Papers, Library of Virginia.

98. Tobie, *History of the First Maine,* 365.

99. Edgar A. Jackson, *Three Rebels Write Home,* 67.

100. Tobie, *History of the First Maine,* 364.

101. "We were gradually forced back to the fence, over which we had a hand-to-hand con-

test," recalled a member of the 21st Pennsylvania, "our boys using their carbines and revolvers against the bayonets, but were finally forced back" (*National Tribune,* June 10, 1886).

102. Mohr, *Cormany Diaries,* 487.

103. *Daily Confederate,* Feb. 22, 1865.

104. O.R. 42(1): 235 (Hancock report).

105. Styple, *Our Noble Blood,* 165.

106. Weygant, *History of the One Hundred and Twenty-Fourth,* 383; de Trobriand, *Four Years,* 664–65.

107. O.R. 42(1): 360 (de Trobriand report).

108. O.R. 42(1): 950 (Hampton report).

17. Retreat

1. The house Weygant found may have been the "J. Spain" dwelling marked on maps drafted by Union topographic engineers after the battle. See "Map of Dinwiddie and parts of Prince George and Sussex counties, Virginia / Engineer Dept. Hd. Qrs. Army of the Potomac; official N. Michler," Nov. 2, 1864, *Civil War Maps,* 533.5.

2. Weygant, *History of the One Hundred and Twenty-Fourth,* 385.

3. Ibid., 386.

4. O.R. 42(1): 235 (Hancock report).

5. O.R. 42(1): 239 (Bingham addendum to Hancock report); Agassiz, *Meade's Headquarters,* 253. In his report of the incident, Bingham identified the enemy regiment as the 39th North Carolina. This could not have been the case, as that unit did not serve in Virginia at the time. The unit may have been the 47th North Carolina, and the Confederate officer, identified by Bingham only as "Colonel Hunter," may have been William K. Hunter of Wake County (American Civil War Research Database).

6. Sleeper to Fisher, 2:30 P.M., Oct. 27, 1864, O.R. 42(3): 377.

7. Humphreys to Hancock, 4:15 P.M., Oct. 27, 1864, O.R. 42(3): 380.

8. O.R. 42(1): 235 (Hancock report).

9. Hancock to Humphreys, Oct. 27, 1864, O.R. 42(3): 382–83.

10. Houghton, *Campaigns of the Seventeenth Maine,* 242.

11. O.R. 42(3): 381 (various dispatches from Hancock to headquarters). For example, Humphreys's order fixing Hancock in place for the night had been drafted at 4:15 P.M., well before any news had arrived regarding Mahone's attack or the condition of Hancock's corps.

12. Herdegen and Murphy, *Four Years,* 332.

13. Humphreys to Hancock, 5:15 P.M., Oct. 27, 1864, O.R. 42(3): 381.

14. Livermore, *Days and Events,* 406.

15. Humphreys to Hancock, 6:20 P.M., Oct. 27, 1864, O.R. 42(3): 381–82.

16. W. S. Hancock to Francis C. Barlow, Nov. 3, 1864, Francis Channing Barlow Papers, Massachusetts Historical Society.

17. Hancock to Humphreys, Oct. 27, 1864, O.R. 42(3): 382–83.

18. Hancock to Humphreys, 9 P.M., Oct. 27, 1864, O.R. 42(3): 382.

19. O.R. 42(1): 236 (Hancock report).

20. Grant to Meade, 12 P.M., Oct. 27, 1864, O.R. 42(3): 374.

21. De Trobriand, *Four Years,* 664.

22. Haley, *Rebel Yell,* 214.

23. Billings, *History of the Tenth Massachusetts*, 288.

24. Ibid.

25. O.R. 42(1): 622 (Marsh report).

26. Hand, *One Good Regiment*, 171.

27. Boag, "Dear Friends," 196.

28. O.R. 42(1): 236 (Hancock report).

29. Robertson, *Civil War Letters*, 529; American Civil War Research Database.

30. Armstrong, *Nuggets of Experience*, 75; American Civil War Research Database.

31. De Trobriand, *Four Years*, 667.

32. Ibid., 664–65.

33. Ibid.

34. Ibid.

35. Ibid.

36. O.R. 42(1): 236 (Hancock report). Gregg's retreat across Gravelly Run was delayed because he had burned the bridge there behind him earlier in the day.

37. Hand, *One Good Regiment*, 169.

38. O.R. 42(1): 622 (Marsh report).

39. Armstrong, *Nuggets of Experience*, 74.

40. Haley, *Rebel Yell*, 214.

41. Cowtan, *Services of the Tenth*, 328.

42. Luther Rose Diary, Oct. 27, 1864, Petersburg National Battlefield.

43. See, e.g., Weygant, *History of the One Hundred and Twenty-Fourth*, 386.

44. Ibid., 389.

45. Herdegen and Murphy, *Four Years*, 310–12. The passage appears in an undated section of William R. Ray's journals. In this author's estimation, the entries refer to events on Oct. 27 and 28, because they track experiences of the 7th Wisconsin during that operation.

46. Ibid.

47. *Progress-Index*, Apr. 30, 1961.

48. *Appleton Motor*, Nov. 17, 1864.

49. De Trobriand, *Four Years*, 667–68.

50. Ibid., 668.

51. *Charleston Daily Courier*, Nov. 4, 1864.

52. O.R. 42(1): 37 (Meade report).

53. Wiley, *Norfolk Blues*, 169.

54. Diary of Henry A. Garrett, Oct. 27, 1865, in J. H. Claiborne Papers, University of Virginia Library.

55. Hutchinson, *My Dear Mother*, 189.

56. United Daughters of the Confederacy, *Recollections and Reminiscences*, 116.

57. Fred C. Foard Reminiscences, Fred C. Foard Papers, Department of Archives and History, Raleigh, North Carolina.

58. *Petersburg Daily Index-Appeal*, June 2, 1877. Johnson was an uncle of General John Pegram, who was killed during fighting along Hatcher's Run in Feb. 1865.

59. United Daughters of the Confederacy, *Recollections and Reminiscences*, 116.

60. *Petersburg Daily Index-Appeal*, June 14, 1896. Not surprisingly, Mahone's recollections of the battle, recorded over thirty years later, placed him at the helm of the planned attack next day. No doubt he was slated for a substantial role, but it is notable that neither Hampton nor Heth mentioned his part in the planning in their battle reports prepared

after the operation. See Henry Heth Report, Feb. 1, 1865, Museum of the Confederacy. Hampton did report, however, "The plan of attack had been agreed on between General Heth and myself, but at 3.30 A.M. he informed me that he would not be able to get the troops he expected to operate with" (O.R. 42(1): 950 [Hampton report]). Heth mentions this in his report, as well.

61. Sloan, *Reminiscences,* 107–8.

62. Williams to Miles, Oct. 27, 1864, O.R. 42(3): 383.

63. O.R. 42(1): 906 (Johnson report).

64. Mulholland, *Story of the 116th Regiment,* 325–26; Muffly, *Story of Our Regiment,* 49–56.

65. O.R. 42(1): 254–55 (Miles report).

66. The Union forces suffered a total of four officers, sixty-three men casualties in the Oct. 27 trench raids (O.R. 42(1): 254–55 [Miles report]).

67. O.R. 42(1): 933 (Wallace report).

68. *Philadelphia Inquirer,* Oct. 31, 1864.

69. Edward Powers, *War and Weather,* 57.

70. O.R. 42(1): 796 (Weitzel report).

71. O.R.(1): 22–23 (Grant report).

18. Aftermath

1. Horace Rugg Court-Martial Transcript (Farwell testimony), Record Group 153 (LL-649), NARA.

2. O.R. 42(1): 299 (Egan report).

3. Ibid. See also J. W. Jones, *Story of American Heroism,* 563–64.

4. Coco, *Through Blood and Fire,* 217.

5. O.R. 42(1): 236 (Hancock report).

6. Horace Rugg Court-Martial Transcript (Farwell Testimony), Record Group 153 (LL-649), NARA.

7. O.R. 42(1): 497 (Crawford report).

8. Curtis, *History of the Twenty-Fourth Michigan,* 280.

9. O.R. 42(1): 496 (Crawford report).

10. Crawford to Warren, 5:30 A.M., Oct. 28, 1864, O.R. 42(3): 414.

11. O.R. 42(1): 442 (Roebling addendum to Warren report).

12. Crawford to Warren, 7:20 A.M., Oct. 28, 1864, O.R. 42(3): 413.

13. O.R. 42(1): 443 (Roebling addendum to Warren report).

14. Ibid.

15. *Petersburg Daily Index-Appeal,* June 14, 1896.

16. Sloan, *Reminiscences,* 107–8.

17. James Eldridge Phillips Papers, VHS; Hewett, *Supplement to the Official Records,* vol. 42, serial no. 87, 471–72 ("Postwar account of Brigadier-General Nathaniel Harrison Harris, C.S. Army, of the Battle of Burgess' Mill, Virginia, Oct. 27, 1864").

18. Warren to Egan, 10 A.M., Oct. 28, 1864, O.R. 42(3): 413; O.R. 42(1): 205 (Walsh dispatch in Patrick report).

19. Meade to Grant, 11 A.M., Oct. 28, 1864, O.R. 42(3): 404.

20. O.R. 42(1): 236 (Hancock report).

21. John L. Smith, *History of the Corn Exchange Regiment,* 529.

22. O.R. 42(1): 570 (Cutcheon report).

23. O.R. 42(1): 459 (Griffin report).

24. O.R. 42(1): 549 (Parke report).

25. Allen, *Forty-Six Months*, 315.

26. Gavin, *Campaigning with the Roundheads*, 583.

27. O.R. 42(1): 549 (Parke report); Enos Bennage Diary, Emory University Library.

28. Agassiz, *Meade's Headquarters*, 252. Some reports indicated that the federals extended the lines to Hatcher's Run after the operation; see *Boston Evening Transcript*, Oct. 31, 1864; see also Becker Collection, Boston College (Becker) CW-JB-VA-10/27/64c. However, Union commanders were content to withdraw into their existing fortifications. In the wake of more fighting at Hatcher's Run in Feb., Union engineers would sketch out a line from Fort Sampson to Hatcher's Run near Armstrong's Mill (Hess, *In the Trenches*, 232–33).

29. The *Official Records* include detailed casualty returns for the engagement, down to the regimental level. Returns for the Army of the Potomac can be found at O.R. 42(1): 153–61. Returns for the Army of the James (Butler's command) are at O.R. 42(1): 148–53. Many Union casualties appeared by name in the *New York Herald* (Nov. 2 and 8, 1864).

30. Pierce's brigade suffered 270 casualties (24 killed, 112 wounded, and 134 missing or captured), while de Trobriand listed 182 causalities (18 killed, 112 wounded, and 52 missing) (O.R. 42(1): 154).

31. O.R. 42(1): 853–54 (Lee to Seddon, Oct. 31, 1864). Lee reported that Mahone captured four hundred Federals during his attack.

32. Roe and Nutt, *History of the First Regiment*, 194.

33. The casualties from Colonel Edgar Gregory's brigade accounted for 202 of the 279 men lost from the entire Fifth Corps (O.R. 42(1): 153–55).

34. O.R. 42(1): 157–59 (Return of Casualties).

35. Suderow, "Oct. 27, 1864, Burgess Mill" (MS). No official returns for the entire Alabama brigade have been found. An Alabama newspaper reported that the 8th Alabama lost nine wounded (*Mobile Evening News*, Nov. 21, 1864).

36. Babcock reported to Humphreys on Friday morning, "There are at this point 530 prisoners of war, sent in from Second Corps, fully representing Mahone's, Cooke's, and MacRae's brigades. There are about twenty cavalry from Young's, Dearing's, Dunovant's, and Davis' brigades. These all were taken by the Second Corps. There are also at this point 148 prisoners of war, sent in by the Fifth Army Corps, taken last night; all from Mahone's old brigade, save a very few stragglers from Cooke's brigade. No prisoners taken from any other brigade than the above" (Babcock to Humphreys, 11:20 A.M., Oct. 28, 1864, O.R. 42(3): 406). See also McEntee to Hancock, Oct. 31, 1864, O.R. 42(3): 449 ("Prisoners captured on the 27th are from Weisiger's, Harris', and Sanders' [King's] brigades, of Mahone's division; Kirkland's [MacRae's] brigade, of Heth's division, and Butler's, Young's, Barringer's, Dearing's, and Chambliss' [Beale's] (old) brigades of cavalry").

37. Heth reported a loss in Davis's Mississippi brigade of forty-two and eight casualties in Cooke's North Carolina brigade. Losses for Harris's Mississippi brigade can only be estimated, but were probably not significant. See Suderow, "Oct. 27, 1864 Burgess Mill" (MS) (quoting Heth's official returns).

38. See the *Daily Express* (Petersburg), Nov. 8, 1864 (Dearing's cavalry; also contains a list of casualties for the 16th Virginia Infantry and the 4th North Carolina Cavalry). Casualty returns, by name, for Butler's South Carolina brigade were printed in the *Charleston Daily Courier* (Nov. 3, 1864).

39. Suderow, "Oct. 27, 1864 Burgess Mill" (MS) (quoting Heth's official returns).

40. O.R. 42(1): 23 (Grant dispatch); Meade to Grant, 11 A.M., Oct. 28, 1864, O.R. 42(3): 404.

41. *New York Herald*, Oct. 31, 1864.

42. James Dearing to his wife, Nov. 1, 1864, James Dearing Papers, VHS.

43. James Dearing to his wife, Oct. 19 and Nov. 1, 1864, James Dearing Papers, VHS.

44. O.R. 42(1): 151 (Return of Casualties).

45. O.R. 42(1): 872 (Longstreet report).

46. O.R. 42(1): 150 (Return of Casualties).

47. O.R. 42(1): 854 (Lee dispatch, Oct. 28, 1864).

48. O.R. 42(1): 877 (partial Return of Casualties).

49. O.R. 42(1): 853 (Lee report).

50. *Charleston Daily Courier*, Nov. 4, 1864.

51. Calhoun, *Liberty Dethroned*, 149.

52. Daughtry, *Gray Cavalier*, 227.

53. *Daily Confederate*, Nov. 2, 1864.

54. James Phillips Diary, James Eldridge Phillips Papers, VHS.

55. Brooks, *Butler and His Cavalry*, 382.

56. Emerson, *Sons of Privilege*, 97.

57. *Richmond Sentinel*, Nov. 2, 1864.

58. Robert Jerald L. West, *Found Among the Privates*, 91–93. For those USCTs who survived the fight but could not rejoin their command, the usual Confederate mistreatment and disdain awaited them. For example, several days after the battle, the *Richmond Examiner* reported, "In the fighting on the north side on Thursday a negro soldier, belonging to one of the Yankee regiments was shot in the head and left upon the field for dead. But after all were gone, and the battle over and done, Sambo got up and made a reconnaissance in the direction of Dr. Garnett's residence, hard by, where his wound was looked into. Subsequently, the negro was recognised as Albert, a slave of Mrs. Octavia Taylor of Williamsburg, who ran away from liberty into bondage. He was placed hors du combat through fright more than by the bullet, which glanced from his skull like shot from an iron-clad, and left him worth a thousand dead niggers yet" (*Richmond Examiner*, Nov. 3, 1864).

59. A wounded New Jersey soldier remarked, "I was told that men from the grave & babies from the cradle was all that kept us out of Petersburg, but I think that sight looks more like babies trying to get in" (Claiborne to his wife, Oct. 30, 1864, J. H. Claiborne Papers, University of Virginia Library).

60. O.R. 42(1): 622 (Marsh report). Some Confederates traded stories about the demoralization of the Union men on the field. A soldier's letter to a Charleston paper explained that a "citizen, whose house was surrounded by them, says even their officers displayed great anxiety and alarm. He tells a fine story of a Colonel riding up to General Davis [most likely Henry E. Davies Jr., commander of Gregg's first cavalry brigade]—a Yankee Brigadier—and delivering himself thus: 'General, I hold the Plank Road, but my right is turned; I don't know where my left is and my men are scattered. Give me men that won't run and I'll hold the road'" (*Charleston Daily Courier*, Nov. 4, 1864).

61. Fatout, *Letters of a Civil War Surgeon*, 137.

62. Mary C. Burgess, *True Story*, 54.

63. Ibid., 57.

64. Ibid.

65. Ibid., 59–75.

19. Grant's Sixth Offensive Considered

1. Grant to Stanton, 9 P.M., Oct. 27, 1864, O.R. 42(3): 373.

2. *Army and Navy Journal*, Nov. 5, 1864 (Stanton's dispatches).

3. *Richmond Whig*, Nov. 9, 1864 (quoting an article in the *New York Daily News*); see also *New York World*, Nov. 1, 1864.

4. *New York World*, Nov. 1, 1864.

5. A New York soldier's letter to the *New York World* added, "One of our men got lost, and meeting General Warren, told him so. General Warren answered that by the looks he guessed we are all lost" (*New York World*, Nov. 4, 1864).

6. *Charleston Mercury*, Nov. 7, 1864.

7. *Richmond Whig*, Nov. 1, 1864. The *Richmond Sentinel* similarly concluded that Grant had been severely punished at Burgess Mill (*Richmond Sentinel*, Nov. 2, 1864).

8. Brooks, *Butler and His Cavalry*, 356.

9. Coco, *Through Blood and Fire*, 219.

10. Nevins, *Diary of Battle*, 478.

11. Robertson, *Civil War Letters*, 532.

12. Agassiz, *Meade's Headquarters*, 251.

13. Hastings, *Letters from a Sharpshooter*, 266.

14. Lowe, *Meade's Army*, 289.

15. *Army and Navy Journal*, Nov. 12, 1864.

16. Charles Wainwright also noted that the "impenetrable and immense stretch of wood south of the Run" contributed to the problems with the offensive (Nevins, *Diary of Battle*, 479).

17. Walker, *History of the Second Army Corps*, 637.

18. Grant to Meade, Oct. 28, 1864, O.R. 42(3): 402–3.

19. Ibid.

20. Nevins, *Diary of Battle*, 479.

21. *Army and Navy Journal*, Nov. 12, 1864.

22. Meade to Bowers, Oct. 28, 1864, O.R. 42(3): 405.

23. Andrew A. Humphreys, *Virginia Campaign*, 300.

24. Coco, *Through Blood and Fire*, 217.

25. Tilney, *My Life in the Army*, 146.

26. Brooks Simpson, *Ulysses S. Grant*, 387 (quoting Grenville Dodge to Richard Oglesby, Oct. 29, 1964).

27. Weitzel to Smith, 9:15 P.M., Oct. 27, 1864, O.R. 42(3): 399.

28. O.R. 42(1): 796–97 (Weitzel report).

29. Sumner, *Diary of Cyrus B. Comstock*, 292–93.

30. Ibid.

31. Ibid.

32. Wilson, *The Life of John H. Rawlins*, 270.

33. O.R. 42(1): 23 (Meade, quoted in Grant report).

34. O.R. 42(1): 37 (Meade report). Egan, in turn, thanked Robert McAllister for his performance at the Boydton Plank Road (O.R. 42(2): 297 [Egan report]).

35. Robertson, *Civil War Letters*, 531.

36. O.R. 42(1): 240 (Carncross, General Orders No. 40). Hancock was not alone in his criticism of the press. One soldier reported home that the correspondents of the New York

papers wrote nothing about performance of the Second Corps at Burgess Mill because most of them remained in the rear with the Fifth and Ninth Corps during the day (Dunn, *Full Measure of Devotion*, 455).

37. Menge and Shimrak, *Civil War Notebook*, 47.

38. The regiments that had lost their colors included the 36th Wisconsin, the 8th New York Heavy Artillery, and the 164th New York (O.R. 42(3): 544 [S. Williams, General Orders No. 241]).

39. De Trobriand, *Four Years*, 668–69. Not everyone in Mott's division was as perturbed as de Trobriand. Robert McAllister, one of Mott's brigade commanders, wrote his wife that she "will find Genl. Egan gets greate credit. Well, he deserves it, and he seems to do me full justice" (Robertson, *Civil War Letters*, 531).

40. W. S. Hancock to Francis C. Barlow, Nov. 3, 1864, Francis Channing Barlow Letters, Massachusetts Historical Society.

41. Ibid.

42. Walker, *History of the Second Army Corps*, 640–41.

43. *Charleston Daily Courier*, Nov. 4, 1864.

44. Longstreet to Lee, Oct. 29, 1864, O.R. 42(3): 1182.

45. J. Nathaniel Peed to Nancy Owen Peed, Oct. 30, 2011, Peed Family Letters, University of Notre Dame.

46. Heth also indicates that William MacRae singled out Adjutant Martin of the 11th North Carolina Regiment, Major Steadman of the 44th North Carolina, Capt. Lilly of the sharpshooters, and Colonel Horace King of the Alabama brigade for their contributions (Henry Heth Report, Feb. 1, 1865, Museum of the Confederacy).

47. In Heth's view, Mahone incorrectly asserted that Scales's brigade had joined the forces at Burgess Mill.

48. Henry Heth Report, Feb. 1, 1865, Museum of the Confederacy.

49. Ibid.

50. Hancock to Humphreys, 10:30 P.M., Oct. 30, 1864, O.R. 42(3): 437; Horn, *Petersburg Campaign*, 196; Wiley, *Norfolk Blues*, 170. The dash snagged 387 men by one account (*New York Tribune*, Nov. 2, 1864); see also *Richmond Dispatch*, Nov. 2, 1864.

51. Dobbins, *Grandfather's Journal*, 218.

52. Union reports indicate that the 69th New York lost 164, and the 111th New York lost 82 (O.R. 42(1): 255–66 [MacDougall enclosure in Miles report]).

53. Blake, *William Mahone*, 68. According to one story told after the war, Lee explained that he would have preferred Mahone to command of the Army of Northern Virginia in the event of his own demise. Lee supposedly made the statement to Wade Hampton and J. Horace Lacy at a dinner party after the war. Lacy claims to have recorded the words spoken by Lee immediately after the dinner. A facsimile of Lacy's handwritten letter to Mahone explaining the incident can be found in Butler, *Autobiography and Personal Reminiscences*, 881–87. See also Wise, *Military History*, 181–82.

54. Blight, *Race and Reunion*, 293.

55. O.R. 42(1): 953–54 (Lee to Hampton).

56. R. E. Lee to Jefferson Davis, Nov. 2, 1864, in Dowdey and Manarin, *Wartime Papers*, 868.

57. R. E. Lee to A. P. Hill, Oct. 31, 1864, Lee's Headquarters Papers, VHS.

58. R. E. Lee to Jefferson Davis, Nov. 2, 1864, in Dowdey and Manarin, *Wartime Papers*, 868.

59. Wellman, *Giant in Gray,* 162.

60. Daughtry, *Gray Cavalier,* 228.

61. Long, *Memoirs of Robert E. Lee,* 398–99.

62. Lowe, *Meade's Army,* 292.

63. *New York Times,* Nov. 10, 1864.

64. Ibid.

65. Ibid.

66. Ibid.

67. Waugh, *Reelecting Lincoln,* 343–52.

68. Horace Porter, *Campaigning with Grant,* 321–22.

69. Simpson, *Ulysses S. Grant,* 388.

70. Waugh, *Reelecting Lincoln,* 354.

71. Ibid.

72. Grant to Stanton, 10:30 P.M., Nov. 10, 1864, O.R. 42(3): 581.

73. Waugh, *Reelecting Lincoln,* 351–55.

74. Longstreet to Lee, Nov. 21, 1864, O.R. 42(3): 1223.

75. *New York Times,* Nov. 10, 1864.

76. Halliburton, *Saddle Soldiers,* 181.

77. R. E. Lee to his wife, Feb. 21, 1865, in Dowdey and Manarin, *Wartime Papers,* 907. For a critical assessment of Lee's decision to continue fighting into 1865, see Nolan, *Lee Considered,* 112–33.

78. *New York Tribune,* Nov. 17, 1864 (quoting the *Richmond Examiner,* Nov. 11, 1864).

79. Badeau, *Military History,* vol. 3, 133.

80. Wilson, *The Life of John A. Rawlins,* 269.

81. Porter, *Campaigning with Grant,* 312; see also Badeau, *Military History,* vol. 3, 128–34 (Porter's recollection is corroborated by Adam Badeau. The latter quoted Grant).

82. Grant to Stanton, 9 P.M., Oct. 27, 1864, O.R. 42(1): 23.

83. Billings, *History of the Tenth Massachusetts,* 464.

84. Ibid.

85. Ibid., 466–67.

86. *Petersburg Daily Index-Appeal,* June 14, 1896 (Bernard account). Another landmark, the Rainey house at the intersection of the Plank and Rainey roads, burned down during the 1890s, according to Bernard's 1896 article.

87. See Blight, *Race and Reunion.*

88. Brooks, *Stories of the Confederacy,* 53–54.

89. Ibid., 54.

Bibliography

∾

Abbreviations

LOC	Library of Congress
NARA	National Archives and Records Administration
MOC	Museum of the Confederacy
O.R.	*The War of the Rebellion: A Compilation of the Official Records of the Union and Confederate Armies*
SHSP	Southern Historical Society Papers
USAMHI	The U.S. Army Military History Institute
VHS	Virginia Historical Society

Newspapers

Appleton Motor (WI)
Army and Navy Journal (NY)
Boston Evening Transcript (MA)
Charleston Daily Courier (SC)
Charleston Mercury (SC)
Columbia Daily (SC)
Columbus Sun (GA)
Daily Confederate (Raleigh, NC)
Daily Constitutionalist (SC)
Daily Courier (Buffalo, NY)
Daily Express (Petersburg, VA)
Daily Richmond Enquirer (VA)
Daily South Carolinian (Columbia)
Dunkirk Union (NY)
Edgefield Advertiser (SC)
Hartford Daily Courant (CT)
National Tribune (DC)
New Hampshire Patriot (Concord, NH)
New York Herald (NY)
New York Times (NY)
New York Tribune (NY)

New York World (NY)
Orphan's Friend and Masonic Journal (NC)
Petersburg Daily Index-Appeal (VA)
Petersburg Express (VA)
Philadelphia Inquirer (PA)
Progress-Index (Petersburg, VA)
Raleigh Confederate (NC)
Richmond Dispatch (VA)
Richmond Enquirer (VA)
Richmond Examiner (VA)
Richmond Sentinel (VA)
Richmond Whig (VA)

Diaries, Letters, Memoirs, and Official Records

Agassiz, George R., ed. *Meade's Headquarters, 1863–1865: Letters of Colonel Theodore Lyman from the Wilderness to Appomattox.* Boston: The Atlantic Monthly Press, 1922. Reprint, Lincoln: University of Nebraska Press, 1994.

Allen, George, H. *Forty-Six Months with the Fourth R.I. Volunteers in the War of 1861 to 1865: Comprising a History of the Marches, Battles, and Camp Life.* Providence, RI: J.A. & R.A. Reid, 1887.

Alexander, Edward Porter, Papers, Southern Historical Collection, University of North Carolina.

Annual Report of Adjutant-General of the State Connecticut, April 1, 1865, New Haven, CT: Carrington, Hotchkiss, & Co., 1865.

Armstrong, Dr. Nelson. *Nuggets of Experience: Narratives of the Sixties and Other Days, With Graphic Descriptions of Thrilling Personal Adventures.* N.p.: Times Mirror P. and B. House, 1906.

Axford, Faye Acton. *To Locaber Na Mair: Southerners View the Civil War.* Athens, GA: Athens Publishing, 1986.

Babcock, John C., Papers, Library of Congress.

Badeau, Adam. *Military History of Ulysses S. Grant.* 3 vols. New York: D. Appleton and Co., 1881.

Barlow, Francis Channing Papers, Massachusetts Historical Society, Boston.

James Bartlett Papers, Southern Historical Collection, University of North Carolina, Chapel Hill.

Basler, Ray P., ed. *Collected Works of Abraham Lincoln.* Vol. 7. New Brunswick, NJ: Rutgers University Press, 1953.

Becker Collection: Drawings of the American Civil War Era, Boston College Fine Arts Department, Boston, MA.

Bennage, Enos, Diary, Special Collections Department, Emory University Library, Atlanta.

Bernard, George S., Papers, Small Special Collections Library, University of Virginia Library.
———. Papers, Southern Historical Collection, University of North Carolina, Chapel Hill.
———. *War Talks of Confederate Veterans.* Petersburg, VA: Fenn and Owen, 1892.

Biddle, James C., Civil War Letters, Historical Society of Pennsylvania, Philadelphia.

Blackett, R. J. M., ed. *Thomas Morris Chester, Black Civil War Correspondent, His Dispatches from the Virginia Front.* Baton Rouge: Louisiana State University Press, 1989.

Boag, Peter C., ed. "Dear Friends: The Civil War Letters of Francis Marion Elliot, a Pennsylvania Country Boy." *Pittsburgh History* 72 (1989): 193–8.

Bond, Natalie Jenks, and Osmond Latrobe Coward, eds. *The South Carolinians: Colonel Asbury Coward's Memoirs.* New York: NeVantage Press, 1968.

Bratton, John. "Report of Operations of Bratton's Brigade from May 7th, 1864 to January 1865." *Southern Historical Society Papers* 8 (January–December 1880): 547–559.

Brinton, John H. *Personal Memoirs of John H. Brinton.* New York: Neale Publishing, 1914.

Briscoe, E. "A Visit to General Butler and the Army of the James." *Fraser's Magazine of Town and Country* 71 (April 1865): 434–48.

Burgess, Daniel M. *Personal and Professional Recollections.* New York: Privately printed, 1911.

Burgess, Mary C. *A True Story.* Lincoln, NE: n.p.1907.

Burkhardt, George, ed. *Double Duty in the Civil War: The Letters of Sailor and Soldier Edward W. Bacon.* Carbondale: Southern Illinois University Press, 2009.

Butler, Benjamin F. *Autobiography and Personal Reminiscences of Major-General Benj. F. Butler: Butler's Book.* Boston: A.M. Thayer, 1892.

———. Papers, Library of Congress.

———. *Private and Official Correspondence of General Benjamin F. Butler.* 5 vols. Norwood, MA: Plimpton Press, 1917.

Calhoun, C. M. *Liberty Dethroned: A Concise History of Some of the Most Startling Events before, during, and since the Civil War.* Greenwood, SC: 1903.

Cauthen, Charles E., ed. *Family Letters of the Three Wade Hamptons, 1782–1901.* Columbia: University of South Carolina Press, 1953.

Cavaness, I. F., Diary, 1860–1865, Center for American History, University of Texas at Austin.

Chamberlain, Joshua. *The Passing of the Armies: An Account of the Final Campaign of the Army of the Potomac.* Lincoln: University of Nebraska Press, 1998.

Chamberlaine, W.W. *Memoirs of the Civil War Between the Northern and Southern Sections of America 1861 and 1865.* Washington, DC: Press of Byron S. Adams, 1912.

Civil War Maps, 2nd ed. Library of Congress Geography and Map Division. Prints and Photographs Division, Washington, DC.

Claiborne, J. H., Papers, Small Special Collections Library, University of Virginia Library.

Claiborne, John Herbert. *Seventy-Five Years in Old Virginia.* New York: Neale Publishing, 1904.

Cockrell, Monroe F., ed. *Gunner with Stonewall: Reminiscences of William Thomas Poague.* Jackson, TN: McCowat-Mercer Press, 1957.

Coco, Gregory A., ed. *Through Blood and Fire: The Civil War Letters of Major Charles J. Mills, 1862–1865.* Gettysburg, PA: Gregory A. Coco, 1982.

Coleman, John Kennedy, Diary, South Caroliniana Library, University of South Carolina, Columbia, SC.

Cooke, John E. *Mohun, or, The Last Days of Lee and His Paladins: Final Memoirs of a Staff Officer Serving in Virginia. From the Mss. of Colonel Surry, of Eagle's Nest.* New York: F.J. Huntington Co., 1869.

Craven, John Joseph, Papers, Library of Congress.

Crockett, Edward R., Diary, Eugene C. Barker Texas History Center, University of Texas at Austin.

Crosland, Charles, *Reminiscences of the Sixties,* Columbia, SC: The State Company, 1910.

Crotty, D. G. *Four Years Campaigning in the Army of the Potomac.* Grand Rapids, MI: Dygert Bros., 1874.

Cutrer, Thomas W., ed. *Longstreet's Aide: The Civil War Letters of Major Thomas J. Goree.* Charlottesville: University Press of Virginia, 1995.

Davis, Ferdinand, Memoirs, Bentley Historical Library, University of Michigan, Ann Arbor.

Davis, Jefferson and William J. Cooper, ed. *Jefferson Davis: The Essential Writings.* New York: Random House, 2004.

Dawson, Francis W. *Reminiscences of Confederate Service, 1861–1865.* Edited by Bell I. Wiley. Baton Rouge: Louisiana State University Press, 1980.

De Trobriand, Regis. *Four Years with the Army of the Potomac.* Boston: Ticknor and Co., 1889.

Dearing, James, Papers, Virginia Historical Society.

Didcock, Henry D., Letters, Gowanda Area Historical Society, Gowanda, NY.

Dobbins, Austin C. *Grandfather's Journal, Company B, Sixteenth Mississippi.* Dayton, OH: Morningside Press, 1998.

Dowdey, Clifford, and Louis H. Manarin, eds. *The Wartime Papers of R. E. Lee.* Boston: Little, Brown, 1961.

Eisenschiml, Otto, ed. *Vermont General: The Unusual War Experiences of Edward Hastings Ripley 1862–1865.* New York: Devin-Adair, 1960.

Eyland, Seth [David Edward Cronin]. *The Evolution of a Life Described in the Memoirs of Major Seth Eyland.* New York: Green's Sons, 1884.

Fatout, Paul. *Letters of a Civil War Surgeon.* West Lafayette, IN: Purdue University Press, 1996.

Field, C. W. "Campaign of 1864 and 1865. Narrative of Major-General C.W. Field." *Southern Historical Society Papers* 14 (January–December 1886): 542–563.

Foard, Fred C., Reminiscences, Fred C. Foard Papers, Department of Archives and History, Raleigh, North Carolina.

Gallagher, Gary, ed. *Fighting for the Confederacy: The Personal Recollections of General Edward Porter Alexander.* Chapel Hill: University of North Carolina Press, 1987.

Hennessey, John, "I Dread the Spring: The Army of the Potomac Prepares for the Overland Campaign." In *The Wilderness Campaign.* 66–105. Edited by Gary G. Gallagher. Chapel Hill: University of North Carolina Press, 2006.

Garrett, Henry, A., Diary of, Papers of John F. H. Claiborne, Library of Congress, Washington, DC.

Gary, Louella Pauline, *Biography of General Martin Witherspoon Gary,* Virginia Historical Society, Richmond.

General Orders from the Adjutant and Inspector-General's Office, CSA. Columbia, SC: Evans and Cogswell, 1865.

Grant, U. S. *Personal Memoirs of U. S. Grant.* 2 vols. New York: Charles L. Webster, 1886.

Gray, Stephen. "Echoes." *Maine Bugle,* Campaign 3, Call 1 (January 1896), 281–282.

Hagood, James R., "Memoirs of the First S.C. Regiment of Volunteer Infantry in the Confederate War for Independence from 12 April to 10 April 1865," South Caroliniana Library, University of South Carolina.

———. "Report of Colonel J. R. Hagood, First S.C. Volunteers of Campaign of 1884." *Southern Historical Society Papers* 8 (January–December 1885): 437–438.

Hagood, Johnson. *Memoirs of the War of Secession from the Original Manuscripts of Johnson Hagood.* Columbia, SC: State Co., 1910.

Haley, John W. *The Rebel Yell and the Yankee Hurrah: The Civil War Journal of a Maine Volunteer.* Edited by Ruth Silliker. Camden, ME: Down East Books, 1985.

Halliburton, Lloyd, ed. *Saddle Soldiers: The Civil War Correspondence of General William Stokes of the 4th South Carolina Cavalry.* Orangeburg, SC: Sandlapper Publishing, 1993.

Hammond, Bryan, and Cummings Family Papers, South Caroliniana Library, University of South Carolina.

Hampton, Wade, "Narrative," South Caroliniana Library, University of South Carolina.

Hastings, William, ed. *Letters from a Sharpshooter: The Civil War Letters of William B. Greene, Co. G 2nd United States Sharpshooters (Berdan's) Army of the Potomac 1861–1865.* Belleville, WI: Historic Publications, 1993.

Hawley, Joseph, Papers, Library of Congress.

Herdegen, Lance, and Sherry Murphy, eds. *Four Years with the Iron Brigade: The Civil War Journals of William R. Ray.* Cambridge, MA: Da Capo Press, 2002.

Heth, Henry, Papers, Report, February 1, 1865, Eleanor S. Brockenbrough Library, Museum of the Confederacy, Richmond, VA.

Heyman, Max L. "The Gay Letters: A Civil War Correspondence." *Journal of the West* 9 (July 1970): 377–412.

Humphreys, Andrew A. *The Virginia Campaign of '64 and '65: The Army of the Potomac and the Army of the James.* New York: Charles Scribner's Sons, 1883.

Humphreys, Henry H. *Andrew Atkinson Humphreys: A Biography.* Philadelphia: John C. Winston, 1924.

Hutchinson, Olin F., ed. *My Dear Mother and Sisters: Civil War Letters of Captain A. B. Mulligan.* Spartanburg, SC: Reprint Company, 1992.

Ingersoll, Burgess F., Diary, U.S. Army Military History Institute, Carlisle, PA.

Jackson, Edgar A. *Three Rebels Write Home.* Franklin, VA: News Publishing, 1955.

Jackson, Harry F., and Thomas F. O'Donnell. *Back Home in Oneida: Hermon Clarke and His Letters.* Syracuse, NY: Syracuse University Press, 1965.

Jones, Charles R. "Historical Sketch." *Our Living and Our Dead,* no. 45 (May 13, 1874).

Jones, J. W., ed. *The Story of American Heroism: Thrilling Narratives of Personal Adventures during the Great Civil War as told by the Medal Winners and Roll of Honor Men.* Springfield, OH: J.W. Jones, 1897.

Jones, John B. *A Rebel War Clerk's Diary at the Confederate States Capital.* 2 vols. Philadelphia: J.B. Lippincott, 1866.

Joskins, Joe, "A Sketch of Hood's Texas Brigade in the Virginia Army," General Manuscripts Collection, University of Texas of San Antonio.

Kautz, August V. "How I Won My First Brevet." In *Sketches of War History 1861–1865: Papers Read Before the Ohio Commandery of the Military Order of the Loyal Legion of the United States.* Vol. 4: 363–87. Edited by W. H. Chamberlin. Cincinnati: Robert Clarke, 1896.

———. Memoirs, U.S. Army Military History Institute, Carlisle, PA.

———. Papers, Library of Congress, Washington, DC.

Keyes, Edward Lawrence. *Lewis Atterbury Stimson.* New York: Knickerbocker Press, 1918.

Kreutzer, William. *Notes and Observations Made During Four Years of Service with the Ninety-Eighth N.Y. Volunteers in the War of 1861.* Philadelphia: Grant, Faires & Rodger, 1878.

Lee's Headquarters Papers, Virginia Historical Society, Richmond.

Livermore, Thomas L. *Days and Events 1860–1866.* Boston: Houghton Mifflin, 1920.

Long, Lindsay L., *Memoirs of Robert E. Lee: His Military and Personal History*, London: Sampson Low, Marston, Searle, and Rivington, 1886.

Longacre, Edward G., ed. *From Antietam to Fort Fisher: The Civil War Letters of Edward King Wightman, 1862–1865*. Madison, NJ: Fairleigh Dickinson University Press, 1995.

Longstreet, James. *From Manassas to Appomattox: Memoirs of the Civil War in America*. Philadelphia: J.B. Lippincott, 1896.

Lowe, David W., ed. *Meade's Army: The Private Notebooks of Lt. Col. Theodore Lyman*. Kent, OH: Kent State University Press, 2007.

Mackintosh, Robert Harley, Jr., ed. "Dear Martha," the Confederate War Letters of a South Carolina Soldier [Alexander Faulkner Fewell]. Columbia, SC: R.L. Bryan, 1976.

Mahone Papers, Library of Virginia, Richmond.

Manson, Charles, Letters, University of Vermont Library, Burlington.

Mason, John. *Three Years in the Army or the Life and Adventures of a Rebel Soldier*. John M. Mason Jr.; n.p. 1950.

Matthews, James M. *Soldiers in Green: The Civil War Diaries of James Mero Matthews 2nd U.S. Sharpshooters*. Sandy Pointe, ME: Civil War Round Table, 2002.Maxfield, Albert. *Company D of the Eleventh Maine Infantry Volunteers in the War of the Rebellion*. New York: Press of Thomas Humphreys, 1890.

McCabe, Gordon W. "Major Andrew Reid Venable, Jr." *Southern Historical Society Paper*, 37: 61–73 (January–December 1909).

McCarty, Thomas L., Diary, Eugene C. Barker Texas History Center, University of Texas at Austin.

McClendon, W. *Recollections of War Times by an Old Veteran While Under Stonewall Jackson and Lieutenant General James Longstreet*. Montgomery, AL: Paragon Press, 1909.

McClure, Alexander K. *The Annals of War Written by Leading Participants North and South Originally Published in the Philadelphia Weekly Times*. Philadelphia: Times Publishing, 1879.

McGuire, Judith. *Diary of a Southern Refugee during the War*. New York: EJ Hale & Son, 1867.

Mead, Silas Edward, Papers, William E. Finch, Jr. Archives, Greenwich Historical Society.

Meade, George. *The Life and Letters of George Gordon Meade*. New York: Charles Scribner's Sons, 1913.

———. George G., Papers, Historical Society of Pennsylvania.

Menge, W. Springer, and J. August Shimrak, eds. *The Civil War Notebook of Daniel Chisholm: A Chronicle of Daily Life in the Union Army 1864–1865*. Westminster, MD: Ballantine Books, 1990.

Mims, W. J. "Letters of Maj. W. J. Mims." *Alabama Historical Quarterly* 3, no. 2 (Summer 1941), 203–31.

Mohr, James, ed. *The Cormany Diaries: A Northern Family in the Civil War*. Pittsburgh, PA: University of Pittsburgh Press, 1982.

Morrison, James L., ed. *The Memoirs of Henry Heth*. Westport, CT: Greenwood, 1974.

Mullen, Joseph, Jr., Corporal, Co. F, Diary of (entry of October 27, 1864), Eleanor S. Brockenbrough Library, Museum of the Confederacy, Richmond, VA.

Nevins, Allan, ed. *A Diary of Battle: The Personal Journals of Colonel Charles S. Wainwright, 1861–1865*. Cambridge, MA: Da Capo Press, 1998.

Newcomb, Lemuel E., Papers, Department of Special Collections and University Archives, Stanford University, Palo Alto, CA.

Peed Family Letters, Rare Books and Special Collections, University of Notre Dame, Notre Dame, IN.

Phillips, James Eldridge, Papers, Virginia Historical Society, Richmond.

Phillips, Marion G. *Richard and Rhoda: Letters from the Civil War.* Rhinebeck, N.Y.: Open Studio Printshop, 1981.

Pomfret, John E., ed. "Letters of Fred Lockley, Union Soldier of 1864–1865." *Huntington Library Quarterly* 16 (1952–53), 75–112.

Porter Family Papers, Department of Rare Books and Special Collections, University of Rochester Libraries, Rochester, NY.

Porter, Horace. *Campaigning with Grant.* New York: Century, 1907.

Priest, John. *Stephen Elliott Welch of the Hampton Legion.* Shippensburg, PA: White Mane Publishing, 1994.

Records of the Adjutant General's Office, 1780's–1917. Record Group 94. Washington, DC: National Archives and Records Administration.

Records of the Office of The Judge Advocate General. Record Group 153. Washington, DC: National Archives and Records Administration.

Robertson, James I., Jr., ed. "The Boy Artillerist: Letters of Colonel William Pegram, CSA." *Virginia Magazine of History and Biography* 98, no. 2 (April 1990), 221–60.

———, ed. *The Civil War Letters of General Robert McAllister.* Piscataway, NJ: Rutgers University Press, 1965.

Romig, Nancy Byers, ed. *Porter Phipps' Letters Home from the Civil War.* Export, PA: N.B. Romig, 1994.

Rose, Luther, Diary, Petersburg National Battlefield, Petersburg, VA.

Russell, William, Diary of, Petersburg National Battlefield, Petersburg, VA.

Sauers, Richard A., ed. *The Civil War Journal of Colonel William J. Bolton.* Conshohocken, PA: Combined Publishing, 2000.

Scroggs, Joseph, Diary, U.S. Army Military History Institute.

Sherman, John, and Rachel Sherman Thorndike, eds. *The Sherman Letters: Correspondence between General and Senator Sherman from 1837 to 1891.* New York: Scribner & Sons, 1894.

Simon, John, Y., ed. *The Papers of Ulysses S. Grant.* 31 vols. Carbondale: Southern Illinois University Press, 1967–2008.

Small, Harold Adams, ed. *The Road to Richmond: The Civil War Memoirs of Major Abner R. Small of the Sixteenth Maine Volunteers.* Berkeley: University of California Press, 1939.

Smyth, Thomas A., Diary, Delaware Public Archives.

Sorrel, Moxley. *Recollections of a Confederate Officer.* New York: Neale Publishing, 1905.

Sparks, David S. *Inside Lincoln's Army: The Diary of Marsena Rudolph Patrick Provost Marshal General, Army of the Potomac.* New York: Thomas Yoseloff, 1965.

Spear, John M., Papers, Massachusetts Historical Society, Boston.

Stahler, Enoch. *Enoch Stahler: Miller and Soldier.* Washington, DC: n.p. 1909.

Stewart, William. *A Pair of Blankets: War-Time History in Letters to the Young People of the South.* Wilmington, NC: Broadfoot Publishing, 1992.

Styple, William B., ed. *Our Noble Blood: The Civil War Letters of Regis de Trobriand, Major-General U.S.V.* Kearny, NJ: Belle Grove Publishing, 1997.

———, ed. *Writing and Fighting the Civil War: Soldier Correspondence to the New York Sunday Mercury.* Kearny, NJ: Belle Grove Publishing, 2000.

Sumner, Merlin E., ed. *The Diary of Cyrus B. Comstock.* Dayton, OH: Morningside Press, 1987.

Supplement to the Official Records of the Union and Confederate Armies. Vol. 7, serial no. 7. Wilmington, NC: Broadfoot, 1997.

Taylor, W. H. "Reports of Operations of Longstreet's Corps from 7 May 1864–19 October 1864 by W. H. Taylor," 1865, Lee's Headquarters Papers, Virginia Historical Society, Richmond.

Taylor, Walter H. *General Lee: His Campaigns in Virginia, 1861–1865.* Dayton, OH: Morningside Press, 1975.

Thompson, Alfred B., Letters, University of Vermont Library, Burlington, VT.

Thompson, Gilbert, Papers, Library of Congress.

Tilney, Robert. *My Life in the Army: Three Years and a Half with the Fifth Army Corps, Army of the Potomac 1862–1865.* Philadelphia: Ferris and Leach, 1912.

Tower, Lockwood, ed. *Lee's Adjutant: The Wartime Letters of Colonel Walter Herron Taylor, 1862–1865.* Columbia: University of South Carolina, 1995.

Trowbridge, J. W. "Conspicuous Feats of Valor." *Confederate Veteran,* 24 (1916): 25.

Trumbull, H. Clay. *The Knightly Soldier: A Biography of Major Henry Ward Camp.* Philadelphia: JD Wattles, 1892.

———. *War Memories of an Army Chaplain.* New York: Charles Scribner, 1898.

Twain, Mark, *Mark Twain's Notebooks & Journals, Volume I: (1855–1873),* Berkeley, CA: University of California Press, 1975.

The Union Army: A History of Military Affairs in the Loyal States, 1861–1865. Vol. 8. Madison, WI: Federal Publishing, 1908.

United Daughters of the Confederacy. *Recollections and Reminiscences: 1861–1865 through World War I.* Vol. 6. n.p.: South Carolina Division, 1995.

U.S. Navy Department. *Official Records of the Union and Confederate Navies in the War of the Rebellion.* 30 vols. Washington, DC: Government Printing Office, 1894–1922.

U.S. War Department. *War of the Rebellion: A Compilation of the Official Records of the Union and Confederate Armies.* 129 vols. Washington, DC: Government Printing Office, 1881–1901.

Van Lew, Elizabeth, *A Yankee Spy in Richmond, The Civil Diary of "Crazy Bet" Van Lew,* David D. Ryan, ed., Mechanicsburg, PA: Stackpole Books, 1996.

War Department Collection of Confederate Records. Record Group 109. Washington, DC: National Archives and Records Administration.

Waring, Joseph Ioor, ed. "The Diary of William G. Hinson During the War of Secession." *South Carolina Historical Magazine* 75, no. 2 (April 1974), 14–23.

Waud, Alfred, "Battle of Darby Town Rd. Gen'l Butler & his staff," DRWG/US——Waud, no. 689, Prints and Photographs Division, Library of Congress, Washington, DC.

Waud, William, "The battle of Darbytown Road," DRWG/US-Waud (W.), No. 8, William Waud Drawings, Prints and Photographs Division, Library of Congress, Washington, DC.

Welch, Spencer Glasgow. *A Confederate Surgeon's Letters to His Wife.* New York: Neale Publishing, 1911.

Wells, Edward L. *A Sketch of the Charleston Light Dragoons: From the Earliest Formation of the Corps.* Charleston, SC: Lucas, Richardson, 1888.

West, Robert Jerald L., ed. *Found Among the Privates: Recollections of Holcomb's Legion 1861–1864, by James L. Strain and Adolphus E. Fant, Correspondents to the Union County News, Union County, S.C.* Sharon, SC: Privately printed, 1997.

Wiatt, Edward W. *Confederate Chaplain William Edward Wiatt, An Annotated Diary.* Lynchburg, VA: H.E. Howard, 1994.

Wiggins, Sarah Woolfolk, ed. *The Journals of Josiah Gorgas 1857–1878.* Tuscaloosa: University of Alabama Press, 1995.

Wilcox, Cadmus. *Rifles and Rifle Practice: An Elementary Treatise upon the Theory of Rifle Firing, Explaining the Causes of Inaccuracy of Fire, and the Manner of Correcting It.* New York: Van Rostrand, 1859.

Wilcox, J.W., "Gen. James Dearing," *Confederate Veteran,* vol. 9, 216 (1901).

Wiley, Ken, ed. *Norfolk Blues: The Civil War Diary of the Norfolk Light Artillery Blues.* Shippensburg, PA: Burd Street Press, 1997.

Wilson, James H, *The Life of John A. Rawlins: Lawyer, Assistant Adjutant-General, Chief of Staff, Major General of Volunteers and Secretary of War,* New York: Neale Publishing, 1916.

Williams, Isaac, Papers, U.S. Army Military History Institute, Carlisle, PA.

Williams, T. P. *The Mississippi Brigade of Brig. Gen. Joseph R. Davis.* Dayton, OH: Morningside, 1999.

Willis, Byrd, Diary, Byrd C. Willis Papers, Library of Virginia, Richmond.

Wise, Jennings C. *The Military History of the Virginia Military Institute from 1839 to 1865.* Lynchburg, VA: J.P. Bell, 1915.

Wood, C. J., *Reminiscences of the War: Biography and personal sketches of all the commanding officers of the Union Army,* n.p.: 1880.

Woodward, C. Vann, ed. *Mary Chesnut's Civil War.* New Haven, CT: Yale University Press, 1981.

Woodward, Daniel H. "The Civil War of a Pennsylvania Trooper." Pennsylvania Magazine of History and Biography 87, no. 1 (January 1963): 39–62.

Young, John Russell. *Around the World with General Grant: A Narrative of the Visit of General U.S. Grant, Ex-President of the United States, to Various Countries in Europe, Asia, and Africa, in 1877, 1878, 1879.* Vol. 2. New York: American News Company, 1879.

Regimental and Unit Histories

Aldrich, Thomas A. *The History of Battery A, First Regiment Rhode Island Light Artillery.* Providence, RI: Snow Farnham, 1904.

Bartlett, A. W. *History of the Twelfth Regiment New Hampshire Volunteers in the War of the Rebellion.* Concord, NH: I.C. Evans, 1897.

Beaudot, William J. *The Irish Brigade: And Its Campaigns.* New York: Fordham University Press, 1994.

Beecher, Herbert W. *History of the First Light Battery Connecticut Volunteers, 1861–1865.* New York: A.T. De La Mare, 1901.

Billings, John D. *The History of the Tenth Massachusetts Battery of Light Artillery in the War of the Rebellion.* Boston: Hall & Whiting, 1881.

Brooks, U. R. *Butler and His Cavalry in the War of Secession, 1861–1865.* Columbia, SC: State Co., 1909.

———. *Stories of the Confederacy.* Camden, SC: J.J. Fox, 1991.

Buford, T. P. *Lamar Rifles: A History of Company G Eleventh Mississippi Regiment, C. S.A.* Stone Printing, 1902.

Bush, James. "Fifth Regiment of Artillery." In *The Army of the United States Historical Sketches of Staff and Line with Portraits of Generals-in-Chief.* Edited by T. R. Rodenbough. 376–398. New York: Mayard, Merrill, 1896.

Caldwell, J. F. J. *The History of a Brigade of South Carolinians.* Philadelphia: King & Baird, 1866.

Califf, Joseph M. *Record of the Services of the Seventh Regiment U.S. Colored Troops.* Providence, RI: Freeman, 1878.

Chamberlin, Thomas. *History of the One Hundred and Fiftieth Regiment, Pennsylvania Volunteers, Second Regiment, Bucktail Brigade Penn. Vols.* Philadelphia: F. McManus, Jr., 1905.

Chrisman, James A., ed. *76th Regiment Pennsylvania Volunteer Infantry, Keystone Zouaves: The Personal Recollections 1861–1865 of Sergeant John A. Porter Company "B."* Wilmington, NC: Broadfoot, 1988.

Clark, Charles M. *The History of the Thirty-Ninth Regiment Illinois Volunteer Veteran Infantry.* Chicago: Veteran Association of the Regiment, 1889.

Clark, James H. *The Iron Hearted Regiment: An Account of the Battles, Marches and Gallant Deeds Performed by the 115th Regiment N.Y. Vols.* Albany, NY: J. Munsell, 1865.

Clark, Walter. *Histories of the Several Regiments and Battalions from North Carolina in the Great War 1861–5.* 5 vols. Goldsboro, NC: Nash Brothers, 1901.

Cowtan, Charles. *Services of the Tenth New York Volunteers (National Zouaves) in the War of the Rebellion.* New York: Ludwig, 1882.

Craft, David. *History of the One Hundred Forty-First Regiment: Pennsylvania Volunteers.* Towanda, PA: Reporter-Journal, 1885.

Curtis, O. B. *History of the Twenty-Fourth Michigan of the Iron Brigade.* Detroit, MI: Wynn & Hammond, 1891.

Dickey, Luther S. *History of the Eighty-Fifth Regiment Pennsylvania Volunteer Infantry, 1861–1865: Comprising an Authentic Narrative of Casey's Division at the Battle of Seven Pines.* New York: Powers, 1915.

Dunn, Wilbur Russell. *Full Measure of Devotion: The Eighth New York Volunteer Heavy Artillery.* Kearney, NE: Wilbur Russell Dunn Morris, 1997.

Emerson, W. Eric. *Sons of Privilege: Charleston Light Dragoons in the Civil War.* Columbia: University of South Carolina Press, 2005.

Gavin, William G. *Campaigning with the Roundheads: The History of the Hundredth Pennsylvania Veteran Volunteer Infantry Regiment in the American Civil War: The Roundhead Regiment.* Dayton, OH: Morningside Press 1989.

Griffin, Ronald G. *The 11th Alabama Volunteer Regiment in the Civil War.* Jefferson, NC: McFarland & Company, 2008.

Haines, William P. *History of the Men of Company F, with Description of Marches and Battles of the Twelfth New Jersey Volunteers.* Mickleton, NJ: 1897.

Hand, Harold. *One Good Regiment: The Thirteenth Pennsylvania Cavalry.* Victoria, BC: Trafford, 2000.

Haynes, Martin A. *A History of the Second Regiment, New Hampshire Volunteer Infantry, in the War of Rebellion.* Lakeport, NH: 1896.

Herbert, Colonel Hilary A. "History of the Eighth Alabama Volunteer Regiment, CSA." *Alabama Historical Quarterly* 39 (1977): 5–321.

Herek, Raymond J. *These Men Have Seen Hard Service: The First Michigan Sharpshooters in the Civil War.* Detroit, MI: Wayne State University, 1998.

Holmes, Torlief S. *Horse Soldiers in Blue: The First Maine Cavalry.* Gaithersburg, MD: Butternut Press, 1985.

Hopkins, Donald A. *The Little Jeff: The Jeff Davis Legion, Cavalry, Army of Northern Virginia.* Shippensburg, PA: White Mane, 2000.

Hopkins, William P. *The Seventh Regiment of Rhode Island Volunteers in the Civil War, 1862–1865.* Providence, RI: Snow & Farnham, 1903.

Houghton, Edwin B. *The Campaigns of the Seventeenth Maine*. Portland, ME: Short and Loring, 1866.

Hyndman, William. *History of a Cavalry Company: A Complete Record of Company A, 4th Penn'a Cavalry*. Philadelphia: Jas. B. Rodgers, 1870.

Jordan, William B., Jr. *Red Diamond Regiment: The 17th Maine Infantry, 1862–1865*. Shippensburg, PA: White Mane, 1996.

King, David H., et al. *History of the Ninety-Third Regiment, New York Volunteer Infantry*. Milwaukee, WI: Swain and Tate, 1896.

Maxfield, Albert. *The Story of One Regiment in the War of the Rebellion: The Eleventh Maine Infantry Volunteers in the War of the Rebellion*. New York: Regimental Association, 1896.

Marbaker, Thos. D. *History of the Eleventh New Jersey Volunteers from Its Organization to Appomattox*. Trenton, NJ: McCrellish & Quigley, 1898.

Martin, James M., et al. *History of the Fifty-Seventh Regiment Pennsylvania Veteran Volunteer Infantry*. Meadeville, PA: McCoy and Calvin, 1906.

Mowris, James, A. *A History of the One Hundred and Seventeenth Regiment, N.Y. Volunteers*. Hartford, CT: Case, Lockwood, 1866.

Muffly, Joseph W., *The Story of Our Regiment: A History of the 148th Pennsylvania Vols.,* Des Moines, IA: Kenyon Printing, 1904.

Mulholland, St. Clair, *The Story of the 116th Regiment Pennsylvania Volunteers in the War of the Rebellion,* Philadelphia, PA: McManus & Co., 1903.

One Hundred and Forty-Fifth Pennsylvania Association. *Under the Maltese Cross, Antietam to Appomattox, the Loyal Uprising in Western Pennsylvania, Campaigns of the 155th Pennsylvania Regiment, Narrated by the Rank and File*. Pittsburgh, PA: 155th Regimental Association, 1910.

Page, Charles Davis. *History of the Fourteenth Regiment, Connecticut Vol. Infantry*. Meriden, CT: Horton Printing, 1906.

Roback, Henry, ed. *The Veteran Volunteers of Herkimer and Otsego Counties in the War of the Rebellion; Being a History of the 152d N.Y.V. with Scenes, Incidents, Etc., which Occurred in the Ranks, of the 34th N.Y., 97th N.Y., 121st N.Y., 2d N.Y. Heavy Artillery, and 1st and 2d N.Y. Mounted Rifles*. Utica, NY: Press of L.C. Childs & Son, 1888.

Roe, Alfred S. *The Twenty-Fourth Massachusetts Volunteers 1861–1865*. "New England Guard Regiment." Worcester, MA: Twenty-Fourth Veteran Association, 1907.

Roe, Alfred Seelye, and Charles Nutt. *History of the First Regiment of Heavy Artillery, Massachusetts Volunteers 1861–1865*. Boston: Commonwealth Press & Regimental Association, 1917.

Roper, John L., Henry C. Archibald, and George W. Coles. *History of the Eleventh Pennsylvania Volunteer Cavalry, Together with a Complete Roster of the Regiment and Regimental Officers*. Philadelphia: Franklin Printing, 1902.

Scott, Kate. *History of the One Hundred and Fifth Pennsylvania*. Philadelphia: New World, 1877.

Sloan, John. *Reminiscences of the Guilford Grays, Co. B., 27th N.C. Regiment*. Washington, DC: Polkinhorn, 1883.

Smith, John D. *The History of the Nineteenth Regiment of Maine Volunteer Infantry 1864–1865*. Minneapolis: Great Western Printing, 1909.

Smith, John L. *History of the Corn Exchange Regiment, 118th Pennsylvania Volunteers*. Philadelphia: John L. Smith, 1905.

Stein, A. H. *History of the Thirty-Seventh Regt. U.S.C. Infantry*. Philadelphia: King & Baird Printers, 1866.

Stowits, George. *History of the One Hundredth Regiment of New York State Volunteers*. Buffalo, NY: Matthews & Warner, 1870.

Thompson, S. Millett. *Thirteenth Regiment of New Hampshire Volunteer Infantry in the War of the Rebellion 1861–1865, A Diary Covering Three Years and a Day*. Boston: Houghton, Mifflin, 1888.

Tobie, Edward Parsons. *History of the First Maine Cavalry, 1861–1865*. Boston: Press of Emery & Hughes, 1887.

Trout, Robert J. *Galloping Thunder: The Stuart Horse Artillery Battalion*. Allentown, PA: Stackpole Books, 2002.

Walker, Francis A. *History of the Second Army Corps in the Army of the Potomac*. New York: C. Scribner's Sons, 1886.

Watson, Winslow Cossoul. *The Military and Civil History of the County of Essex, New York*. Albany, NY: J. Munsell, 1869.

Weygant, Charles H. *History of the One Hundred and Twenty-Fourth Regiment, New York State Volunteers 124th New York*. Newburgh, NY: Journal Printing House, 1877.

Campaign Studies, Biographies, and Other Secondary Sources

American Civil War Research Database. Historical Data Systems. www.civilwardata.com.

Bailey, Anne. *Chessboard of War: Sherman and Hood and the Autumn Campaigns of 1864*. Lincoln: University of Nebraska Press, 2000.

Baldwin, James J. III. *The Struck Eagle: A Biography of Brigadier General Micah Jenkins, and a History of the Fifth South Carolina Volunteers and the Palmetto Sharpshooters*. Shippensburg, PA: Burd Street Press, 1996.

Barefoot, Daniel W. *General Robert F. Hoke: Lee's Modest Warrior*. Winston-Salem, NC: John F. Blair, 1996.

Benjamin, J. W. "Gray Forces Defeated in Battle of Lewisburg." *West Virginia History* 20, no. 1 (October 1958), 24–35.

Beringer, Richard E., Herman Hattaway, Archer Jones, and William N. Still Jr. *Why the South Lost the Civil War*. Athens: University of Georgia Press, 1986.

Berlin, Ira. *Freedom, The Black Military Experience, A Documentary History of Emancipation 1861–1867*, Series 2. New York: Cambridge University Press, 1982.

Bilby, Joseph. "Repeating Rifles: A Weapons System Seeking a Tactical Role." *North & South* 9(5) (October 2006): 51–52.

Blair, William, and William Pencak, eds. *Making and Remaking Pennsylvania's Civil War*. University Park: Pennsylvania State University Press, 2001.

Blake, Nelson. *William Mahone of Virginia: Soldier and Political Insurgent*. Richmond, VA: Garrett & Massie, 1935.

Blight, David. *Race and Reunion: The Civil War in American Memory*. Cambridge, MA: Harvard University Press, 2001.

Brewer, Willis. *Alabama, Her History, Resources, War Record, and Public Men: From 1540 to 1872*. Montgomery, AL: Barrett & Brown, 1872.

Brockett, L. P. *Woman's Work in the Civil War: A Record of Heroism, Patriotism and Patience*. Boston: Zeigler, McCurdy, 1867.

Brown, Kent Masterson. *Retreat from Gettysburg: Lee, Logistics, and the Pennsylvania Campaign*. Chapel Hill: University of North Carolina Press, 2005.

Carmichael, Peter S. *Audacity Personified: The Generalship of Robert E. Lee.* Baton Rouge: Louisiana State University Press, 2004.

———. Carmichael, Peter S., *Lee's Young Artillerist: William R.J. Pegram,* Charlottesville, VA: University Press of Virginia, 1995.

Carpenter, John A. *Sword and Olive Branch: Oliver Otis Howard.* New York: Fordham University Press, 1999.

Chester, Alden, and Edwin Williams. *Courts and Lawyers of New York: A History, 1609–1925.* Clark, NJ: Lawbook Exchange, 2004.

Cleveland, H.W.S., *Hints to Riflemen,* New York: D. Appleton and Company, 1864.

Coggins, Jack. *Arms and Equipment of the Civil War.* Mineola, NY: Courier Dover, 2004.

Crouch, Barry A. *The Freedmen's Bureau and Black Texans.* Austin: University of Texas Press, 1992.

Daly, Louise Haskell. *Alexander Cheves Haskell: The Portrait of a Man.* Wilmington, NC: Broadfoot, 1989.

Daughtry, Mary Bandy. *Gray Cavalier: The Life and Wars of General W. H. F. "Rooney" Lee.* Cambridge, MA: Da Capo Press, 2002.

Davis, Oliver W. *Life of David Bell Birney, Major-General United States Volunteers.* Philadelphia: King & Baird, 1867.

DePeyster, John W. "A Military Memoir of William Mahone, Major-General in the Confederate Army." *History Magazine* 7 (1870).

Dobak, William A. *Freedom by the Sword: The U.S. Colored Troops, 1862–1867.* Washington, DC: Government Printing Office, 2011.

Dunlop, William S. *Lee's Sharpshooters: Or, The Forefront of Battle.* Little Rock, AR: Tunnah & Pittard, 1899.

Ferguson, Ernest B. *Not War But Murder: Cold Harbor 1864.* New York: Knopf, 2000.

Finan, William J. *Major General Alfred Howe Terry (1827–1890): Hero of Fort Fisher.* Connecticut Civil War Centennial Commission, 1965.

Fishel, Edwin D. *The Secret War for the Union: The Untold Story of Military Intelligence in the Civil War.* Boston: Houghton Mifflin, 1996.

Fonvielle, Chris E., Jr. *The Wilmington Campaign: Last Rays of Departing Hope.* Mechanicsburg, PA: Stackpole Books, 1997.

Forney, John Wein. *Life and Military Career of Winfield Scott Hancock.* Philadelphia: Hubbard Bros., 1880.

Freeman, Douglas Southall. *Lee's Lieutenants.* 3 vols. New York: Charles Scribner's Sons, 1945.

———. *R. E. Lee: A Biography.* 4 vols. New York: Charles Scribner's Sons, 1934.

Glatthaar, Joseph T., *General Lee's Army: From Victory to Collapse,* New York: Free Press, 2008.

Greene, A. Wilson. *Civil War Petersburg: Confederate City in the Crucible of War.* Charlottesville: University of Virginia Press, 2007.

———. *Breaking the Backbone of the Rebellion: The Final Battles of the Petersburg Campaign.* Savas, 2000.

Putnam, Albert D., ed. *Major General Joseph R. Hawley, Soldier and Editor (1826–1905).* Connecticut Civil War Centennial Commission, 1964.

Harris, William G. *Lincoln's Last Months.* New York: Belknap Press, 2004.

Hattaway, Herman, and Archer Jones. *How the North Won: A Military History of the Civil War.* Champaign: University of Illinois Press, 1991.

Hess, Earl J. *Field Armies and Fortifications in the Civil War.* Chapel Hill: University of North Carolina Press, 2005.

———. *In the Trenches at Petersburg: Field Fortifications & Confederate Defeat.* Chapel Hill: University of North Carolina Press, 2009.

———. *Lee's Tar Heels: The Pettigrew-Kirkland-MacRae Brigade.* Chapel Hill: University of North Carolina Press, 2002.

Hewett, Janet B., et al. *Supplement to the Official Records of the Union and Confederate Armies.* 51 vols. Wilmington, NC: Broadfoot, 1994–97.

Horn, John E. *Destruction of the Weldon Railroad Deep Bottom Globe Tavern and Reams Station August 14–25, 1864,* Lynchburg, VA: H.E. Howard, 1991.

———. *The Petersburg Campaign, June 1864–April 1865.* Conshocken, PA: Combined, 1993.

Jones, Archer. *Civil War Command and Strategy: The Process of Victory and Defeat.* New York: Free Press, 1992.

Jones, Rev. J. William. *Personal Reminiscences, Anecdotes, and Letters of Gen. Robert E. Lee.* New York: D Appleton, 1875.

Jordan, Weymouth T., Jr. *North Carolina Troops 1861–1865 A Roster.* Vol. 14. Raleigh, NC: Division of Archives and History, 1998.

Jordan, David M. *Happiness Is Not My Companion: The Life of General G. K. Warren.* Bloomington: Indiana University Press, 2001.

———. *Winfield Scott Hancock: A Soldier's Life.* Bloomington: Indiana University Press, 1988.

Kreiser, Lawrence A., Jr. *Defeating Lee: A History of the Second Corps, Army of the Potomac.* Bloomington: Indiana University Press, 2011.

Krick, Robert E. L. *Staff Officers in Gray: A Biographical Register of the Staff Officers in the Army of Northern Virginia.* Chapel Hill: University of North Carolina Press, 2003.

———. "The Great Tycoon Forges a Staff System." In *Audacity Personified: The Generalship of Robert E. Lee.* Edited by Peter S. Carmichael. Baton Rouge: Louisiana State University Press, 2004.

Laine, J. Gary, and Morris M. Penny. *Law's Alabama Brigade in the War Between the Union and the Confederacy.* Shippensburg, PA: White Mane, 1996.

Levine, Bruce. *Confederate Emancipation: Southern Plans to Free and Arm Slaves During the Civil War.* New York: Oxford University Press, 2006.

Long, David E. *The Jewel of Liberty: Abraham Lincoln's Re-Election and the End of Slavery.* Cambridge, MA: Da Capo Press, 1997.

Longacre, Edward G. *Army of Amateurs: General Benjamin F. Butler and the Army of the James, 1863–1865.* Mechanicsburg, PA: Stackpole Books, 1997.

Lord, Francis. *Civil War Collector's Encyclopedia: Arms, Uniforms, and Equipment of the Union and Confederacy.* New York: Castle Books, 1963.

McPherson, James. *Battle Cry of Freedom: The Civil War Era.* New York: Oxford University Press, 1988.

———. *The Negro's Civil War: How American Blacks Felt and Acted During the War for the Union.* New York: Vintage, 2003.

Manarin, Louis H. *Henrico County: Field of Honor.* 2 vols. Henrico County, Va.: Henrico County, 2005.

Manning, Chandra. *What This Cruel War Was Over: Soldiers, Slavery, and the Civil War.* New York: Random House, 2008.

Marvel, William. *Lee's Last Retreat: The Flight to Appomattox*. Chapel Hill: University of North Carolina Press, 2002.

Maull, D. W. *The Life and Military Services of the Late Brigadier General Thomas A. Smyth*. Wilmington, DE: H. & E.F. James, 1870.

Miller, Francis Trevelyan. *The Photographic History of the Civil War in Ten Volumes*. New York: Review of Reviews, 1911.

Mowery, David. "Major-General Godfrey Weitzel, Delivered at Spring Grove Cemetery, Cincinnati, Ohio, June 15, 2002." Spring Grove Cemetery Collection, Cincinnati Civil War Round Table, 2002. http://www.cincinnaticwrt.org/data/ohio in the war/bios/mowery_weitzel.html.

Newton, Steven H. *Lost for the Cause: The Confederate Army in 1864*. Cambridge, MA: Da Capo Press, 2000.

Nelson, Larry E. *Bullets, Ballots, and Rhetoric: Confederate Policy for the United States Presidential Contest of 1864*. Tuscaloosa: University of Alabama Press, 1980.

Nolan, Alan T. *Lee Considered: General Robert E. Lee and Civil War History*. Chapel Hill: University of North Carolina Press, 1991.

Palmer, Michael. *Lee Moves North: Robert E. Lee on the Offensive*. New York: Wiley, 1998.

Parker, Elmer Oris. "Captain Lyle: Forgotten Hero of the Confederacy." *Prologue* 4(3) (Fall 1972): 165–172.

Pfanz, Donald C. *Richard S. Ewell: A Soldier's Life*. Chapel Hill: University of North Carolina Press, 1988.

Piston, William G., "Longstreet, Lee, and Attack Plans." In *The Third Day at Gettysburg and Beyond*. 31–55. Edited by Gary G. Gallagher. Chapel Hill: University of North Carolina Press, 1998.

The Third Day at Gettysburg and Beyond, 42–43 (essay by William G. Piston, "Longstreet, Lee, and Attack Plans")

Polley, J. B. *Hood's Texas Brigade, Its Marches, Its Battles, Its Achievements*. New York: Neale, 1910.

Power, J. Tracy. *Lee's Miserables: Life in the Army of Northern Virginia from the Wilderness to Appomattox*. Chapel Hill: University of North Carolina Press, 1998.

Powers, Edward. *War and Weather*. Chicago: S.C. Griggs, 1871.

Powers, Ron. *Mark Twain: A Life*. New York: Simon & Schuster, 2005.

Pryor, Elizabeth Brown. *Clara Barton: Professional Angel*. Philadelphia: University of Pennsylvania Press, 1998.

———. *Reading the Man: A Portrait of Robert E. Lee Through His Private Letters*. New York: Viking Press, 2007.

Rafuse, Ethan. *Robert E. Lee and the Fall of the Confederacy, 1863–1865*. Lanham, MD: Rowman & Littlefield, 2008.

Ray, Frederick. *Our Special Artist: Alfred R. Waud's Civil War*. Mechanicsburg, PA: Stackpole Books, 1994.

Ray, Fred L. *Shock Troops of the Confederacy: The Sharpshooter Battalions of the Army of Northern Virginia*. Asheville, NC: CFS Press, 2006.

Rhea, Gordon C. *Cold Harbor: Grant and Lee, May 26–June 3, 1864*. Baton Rouge: Louisiana State University Press, 2000.

———. *The Battle of the Wilderness, May 5–6, 1864*. Baton Rouge: Louisiana State University Press, 1994.

———. *To the North Anna River: Grant and Lee, May 13–25, 1864*. Baton Rouge: Louisiana State University Press, 2000.

Robertson, James I., Jr. *General A. P. Hill: The Story of a Confederate Warrior*. New York: Vintage Books, 1987.

Rodenbough, T. R. *The Army of the United States Historical Sketches of Staff and Line with Portraits of Generals-in-Chief*. New York: Mayard, Merrill, 1896.

Schaff, Morris. *The Battle of the Wilderness*. Boston: Houghton Mifflin, 1910.

Sears, Stephen W. *To the Gates of Richmond: The Peninsula Campaign*. New York: Ticknor & Fields, 1992.

———. *Gettysburg*. Boston: Houghton Mifflin, 2003.

Simpson, Brooks. *Ulysses S. Grant: Triumph over Adversity 1822–1865*. Boston: Houghton Mifflin, 2000.

Simpson, Harold. *Hood's Texas Brigade: Lee's Grenadier Guard*. Fort Worth, TX: Landmark Press, 1970.

Smith, Derek. *The Gallant Dead: Union and Confederate Generals Killed in the Civil War*. Mechanicsburg, PA: Stackpole Books, 2005.

Sommers, Richard J. "The Battle No One Wanted." *Civil War Times Illustrated* 14 (August 1975) 10–18.

———. "Dutch Gap Affair: Military Atrocities and the Rights of Negro Soldiers." *Civil War History* (March 1975): 51–64.

———. *Richmond Redeemed: The Siege at Petersburg*. Garden City, NY: Doubleday, 1981.

Stocker, Jeffrey D., ed. *From Huntsville to Appomattox: R. T. Cole's History of the 4th Regiment, Alabama Volunteer Infantry, C.S.A., Army of Northern Virginia*. Knoxville: University of Tennessee Press, 1996.

Suderow, Bryce. "Casualties at Burgess Mill." Suderow Private Collection, Washington, DC.

———. Suderow, Bryce, "October 27, 1864: Burgess Mill." Suderow Private Collection, Washington, DC.

Tagg, Larry. *The Generals of Gettysburg: The Leaders of America's Greatest Battle*. Campbell, CA: Savas, 1998.

Thomas, Emory. *The Confederate Nation: 1861–1865*. New York: Harper & Row, 1979.

Trulock, Alice Rains. *In the Hands of Providence: Joshua L. Chamberlain and the American Civil War*. Chapel Hill: University of North Carolina Press, 1992.

Trudeau, Noah Andre. *The Last Citadel: Petersburg, Virginia, June 1864–April 1865*. Boston: Little, Brown, 1991.

———. *Like Men of War: Black Troops in the Civil War, 1862–1865*. Boston: Little, Brown, 1998.

Tuchman, Barbara W. *Stilwell and the American Experience in China, 1911–45*. New York: Grove Press, 2001.

The Union Army: A History of Military Affairs in the Loyal States, 1861–1865. 8 vols. Madison, WI: Federal Publishing Company, 1908.

Varon, Elizabeth R. *Southern Lady, Yankee Spy: The True Story of Elizabeth Van Lew, a Union Agent in the Heart of the Confederacy*. New York: Oxford University Press, 2003.

Wagner, Margaret E. *The Library of Congress Civil War Desk Reference*. New York: Simon & Schuster, 2002.

Walker, Francis A. *General Hancock*. New York: D. Appleton, 1894.

Warner, Ezra J. *Generals in Blue: Lives of the Union Commanders*. Baton Rouge: Louisiana State University Press, 1964.

————. *Generals in Gray: Lives of Confederate Commanders*. Baton Rouge: Louisiana State University Press, 1959.

Waugh, Jack. *Reelecting Lincoln: The Battle for the 1864 Election*. New York: Crown, 1988.

Wellman, Manly Wade. *Giant in Gray: A Biography of Wade Hampton of South Carolina*. New York: Charles Scribner's Sons, 1949.

Wells, Edward L. *Hampton and His Cavalry in '64*. Richmond, VA: B.F. Johnson, 1899.

Wert, Jeffrey. *From Winchester to Cedar Creek: The Shenandoah Campaign of 1864*. Mechanicsburg, PA: Stackpole Books, 1987.

————. *General James Longstreet: The Confederacy's Most Controversial Soldier*. New York: Simon & Schuster, 1993.

West, Robert S. *Lincoln's Scapegoat General: A Life of Benjamin Butler 1818–1893*. Boston: Houghton Mifflin, 1965.

Williams, T. P. *The Mississippi Brigade of Brig. Gen. Joseph R. Davis*. Dayton, OH: Morningside, 1999.

Winkler, A.V. *The Confederate Capital and Hood's Texans*. Austin, TX: Eugene Von Blockmann, 1894.

Index

Dabney house, 130–33, 180, 190, 193; Hampton predicts Union will attack Boydton Plank Road here, 139

Dabney Mill Road, 207; in 1888, 309; de Trobriand sweeps stragglers along, 281; Second Corps falls back along, 277; Second Corps withdraws on, 278–79; small units of

Dabney Mill Road (cont.)
Confederate cavalry on, 276; Union gathering on, 253–54; Union picket line on, 280

Dabney's Mill, 140, 204; Union discovers end of Mahone's Alabama brigade, 237; Union takes mill and prisoners, 205

Dahlgren, Uric (Col.), 122–23

Daily (Capt.), 235

Daily Confederate, 111, 128–29

Dance's (Powhatan) battery, 175

Danville Railroad, 11

Darbytown, VA: Butler orders depopulation of, 95–96

Darbytown Road, Oct. 1, 26, 28

Darbytown Road, fighting on, Oct. 7: attack one of Lee's last offensives, 304

Darbytown Road, fighting on, Oct. 13: battery discovered by Union, 78; casualties, 88; improved entrenchments planned by Confederates, 74–75; Pond's assault, *84*, 85–87; Union advance, 82; USCT prisoners as military laborers, 75–77

Darbytown road, fighting on, Oct. 27: analysis of, 297; battery sketched by Waud brothers, 152; Butler tests enemy works, afternoon, 173–74; casualties, 150–51, 289; little historical memory of operation, 307–8; Longstreet suspects Union action is a feint, 154; Union artillery along, 174–75; Union operations, morning, 148–49, *151*, 153; Union operations find no opening in Confederate line, 150–51

Davidson's battery, 283

Davie's, Henry E. (Brig. Gen.), Cavalry Brigade, 270; fighting near Quaker Meeting House, 208–10; preparations for Oct. 27 attack, 142, 146

Davis, Ferdinand, 62, 150

Davis, Jefferson, 1, 2, 10; at Chaffin's Farm, 30–31; concern about troop strength, 15–16; speech in Montgomery, 30–31

Davis, W. W., farm, 67

Davis, Zimmerman (M. Butler's aide), 257–58

Davis house, 198

Davis's, Joseph R. (Brig. Gen.), Mississippi Brigade, 136, 189–91; casualties, 289; fighting along Hatcher's Run, 232–33; praised by Heth, 300; reinforces trenches near Boydton Plank Road, 185; stops Crawford's division at Hatcher's Run, 244

Dawson house, 190

Dearing, James (Lt. Col.), 136; advises Burgess family in fleeing their farm, 219–20; joins Hampton's cavalry at Burgess Farm, 219; ordered back to Burgess Mill by Heth, 245–46; reports bridge at Burgess Mill taken by Union, 246–47; reports of the death of, 289

Dearing's, James, cavalry brigade: Battle of Burgess Mill, 216–18; casualties, 289; collapse of, at Egan's attack, 225; counterattack against, by Hancock, 265; demonstrations against Egan's battle line, 243–44; detained by Heth, 206, 208, 212; dismounted men protect Heth's trenches, 189–90, 239; fighting at Burgess Farm, 220, 223–24; joins Hampton's cavalry, 216, 219; troop strength against Egan, 254–55, 258; withdraws from, 238–39

Deep Bottom, 10, 30, 50, 54; Eighteenth Corps passes, 155; 115th USCT arrives, Oct. 1864, 95

Deep Bottom, Battle of, 20, 21

DeForest, Albert (Sgt.), 201

Delaware infantry: 1st, 223–25

Democratic Party, 1–2

Denison, Andrew W. (Col.), 229, 231

Dern, George F. (Capt.), 38, 40, 42

deserters, Confederate: 22–23; reports regarding use of prisoner labor, 75–77, 93; and slave labor, 110; as source of Union intelligence, 122–23; 131, 145

De Trobriand, P. Regis (Brig. Gen.): biographical, 263; disappointment at Hancock's failure to praise his troops, 298–99; oversees picket line and withdrawal of troops, 279–80

De Trobriand's, P. Regis, Brigade: attacked by M. Butler's division, 271; brigade's position during attack as seen in 1888, 309; casualties, 288; fighting at Burgess Farm, 221; marches along Vaughan Road, 204; ordered to secure the Dabney Mill Road, Oct. 27, 4:30 P.M., 263–65, *264*, 268; picket line ordered to withdraw, 281; position after Mahone's initial attack, 253; positioned in middle of Burgess property, 241; prisoners, 267

Didcock, Henry (U.S.), 183, 187–88

Dimmock line, 129–30, 213

District of Columbia infantry: 1st, 36

Doherty, James (Maj.), 179

Dominy, Levi (Maj.), 158

Doubleday's, Ulysses (Col.), USCT Brigade, 83

draft, 1; northern opposition to, 4

Draper, Alonzo (Col.): division marches west, 155

Dresser, George (Lt.), 237, 269

Drill Room, 155

Drinkard, H. H. (Sgt.), 249–50

DuBose, Dudley (Col.), 53. *See also* Benning's Brigade